D1230179

# The Electron
# and the Bit

# The Electron
# and the Bit

ELECTRICAL ENGINEERING
AND COMPUTER SCIENCE AT THE
MASSACHUSETTS INSTITUTE OF TECHNOLOGY,
1902-2002

*John V. Guttag, Editor*

Copyright © 2005 Electrical Engineering and Computer Science Department, Massachusetts Institute of Technology
ISBN 0-9764731-0-0

All rights reserved. No part of this book may be reproduced in any form or by any electronic or mechanical means, including information storage and retrieval systems, without permission in writing from the publisher, except by a reviewer who may quote brief passages in a review.

Designed by Marc Harpin, Rhumba, Chestnut Hill, Massachusetts
Edited and produced by Vern Associates, Inc., Newburyport, Massachusetts
Composition by Folio Publishing Services, Newburyport, Massachusetts
Printed and bound in Hong Kong by C&C Offset Printing Co., Ltd.

Department of Electrical Engineering and Computer Science
Massachusetts Institute of Technology
77 Massachusetts Avenue — Building 38
Cambridge, Massachusetts 02139-4307

Arthur Edwin Kennelly, *Impedance* © 2004 Institute of Electrical and Electronics Engineers. Reprinted with permission from American Institute of Electrical Engineers, *Seventy-sixth Meeting of the AIEE* (New York, April 18, 1893): 175–232.

Dugald Caleb Jackson, "The Typical College Courses Dealing with the Professional and Theoretical Phases of Electrical Engineering." Reprinted with permission from American Association for the Advancement of Science, *Science* (New Series) XVIII no. 466 (Dec. 4, 1903): 710–716.

Vannevar Bush, "The Differential Analyzer: A New Machine for Solving Differential Equations." Reprinted from *Journal of the Franklin Institute* 212 no. 4 (Oct. 1931): 447–488. Reprinted with permission from Elsevier.

Harold L. Hazen, "Theory of Servo-Mechanisms." Reprinted from *Journal of the Franklin Institute* 218 no. 3 (Sept. 1934): 279–331. Reprinted with permission from Elsevier.

Wilmer L. Barrow, "Transmission of Electromagnetic Waves in Hollow Tubes of Metal." © 2004 Institute of Electrical and Electronics Engineers. Reprinted with permission from Institute of Radio Engineers, *IRE Proceedings* 24 no. 10 (Oct. 1936): 1298–1328.

William H. Radford, "Technology's Radar School." Reprinted with permission from *Technology Review* (Feb. 1946): 227–250.

Robert G. Gallager, "Claude E. Shannon: His Life, Work, and Impact." ©2004 Institute of Electrical and Electronics Engineers, IEEE Reprinted with permission from *IEEE Transactions on Information Theory* 47 no. 7 (Nov. 2001): 2681–2695.

Lan Jen Chu, abstract for "Physical Limitations of Omni-Directional Antennas." Reprinted with permission from *Journal of Applied Physics* 19 (1948): 1163–1175.

Peter Elias, "Coding for Noisy Channels." © 2004 Institute of Electrical and Electronics Engineers. Reprinted with permission from *IRE Convention Record,* part 4 (1955): 37–46.

Gordon Stanley Brown, "Educating Electrical Engineers to Exploit Science." Reprinted with permission from *The Journal of Engineering Education* 43 no. 4 (Dec. 1952): 274–281.

Walter A. Rosenblith, "The Quantification of Neuroelectric Activity." Reprinted with permission from Research Lab of Electronics, Massachusetts Institute of Technology.

Arthur von Hippel, "Molecular Designing of Materials." ©2004 The American Association for the Advancement of Science. Reprinted with permission from *Science* 138 (1962): 91–108.

Louis D. Smullin, excerpts of memoir of Jerome Bert Wiesner. Reprinted with permission from *Biographical Memoirs* by the National Academy of Sciences, courtesy of the National Academies Press, Washington, D.C.

Robert M. Fano, excerpts of memoir of Joseph Carl Robnett Licklider. ©1998 by the National Academy of Science. Reprinted with permission from *Biographical Memoirs* 75 by the National Academy of Sciences, courtesy of the National Academies Press, Washington, D.C.

Fernando J. Corbató, "An Experimental Time-Sharing System." © 2004 Institute of Electrical and Electronics Engineers. Reprinted with permission from Spring Joint Computer Conference, May 3, 1962.

Paul Penfield, Jr., William M. Siebert, John V. Guttag, and Campbell L. Searle, "MIT EECS Master of Engineering: A Status Report." © 2004 Institute of Electrical and Electronics Engineers. Reprinted with permission from Frontiers in Education Conference (Nov. 2–6, 1994): 228–232.

**Picture credits**
AI Archives, 251 (bottom)
AI Archives: Sam Ogden, 252 (middle)
from Edward Tatnall Canby, *A History of Electricity,* vol. 6. New York: Hawthorn Books, 1963, 3 (p. 44), 4 (bottom; p. 58), 5 (bottom, 3rd from left; p. 63), 5 (bottom left; p. 68), 5 (bottom, 2nd from left; p. 84)
Chandrakasan Archive, 275 (bottom)
Photo courtesy Dresselhaus Photo Archives, 229
Photo courtesy Dresselhaus Photo Archives: Georgia Litwack, 226 (top), 228
Photo © Harold & Esther Edgerton Foundation, 2004; courtesy of Palm Press, 242
EECS Photo Archives, ix (top left & right; middle left), xi, 4 (top), 8, 24, 35, 63 (top), 64 (bottom), 67, 68 (bottom), 76, 77, 167 (all), 217, 220, 226 (bottom), 234–237, 240 (top left & 2nd from top)
EECS Photo Archives: Elizabeth Cooper, 211 (bottom)

EECS Photo Archives: Barry Hetherington, ix (bottom), 225, 240 (bottom), 247
EECS Photo Archives: Patricia Sampson, 1 (all), 5 (bottom right), 17 (bottom), 59, 130, 209
EECS Photo Archives: John Tucker, 58
Photo courtesy Robert Fano Archives, 215
Photo © Felice Frankel, 276 (bottom)
Photo courtesy Dennis Freeman Archives, 243
Ivan Massar/Black Star, 17 (2nd from top),159, 256 (top), 268 (top)
LCS Photo Archives, 232, 256 (all), 257 (all), 258 (bottom)
LCS Photo Archives: Peter Szolovits, 233
LCS Photo Archives: Sam Ogden, 258 (top)
LEES Photo Archives, 249 (2nd from left), 260 (bottom), 261, 262 (all), 263 (all), 264
LIDS Photo Archives, 104, 249 (2nd from right), 265–268 (all), 269 (top)
LIDS Photo Archives: David Dugail, 270 (bottom)
LIDS Photo Archives: Michael Lewy, 269 (bottom), 270 (top)
Liskov Photo Archives: Nathan Liskov, 237
Melgar Photographers, Inc., 274 (all)
Menzel Studio, 252 (bottom), 253 (top)
Photo courtesy MIT Museum, ix (middle right), 5 (top), 7, 10 (bottom), 16 (top & bottom), 17 (top, 2nd & 3rd from top), 21, 25, 32, 33 (top), 36, 44, 45, 50, 53, 55, 62, 63 (bottom), 64 (top), 65, 68 (top), 75, 79, 83, 88, 90, 93, 107, 117, 118, 133 (all), 135 (all), 139, 159, 160, 163, 164, 172 (bottom), 178, 181, 211 (top right), 241, 249 (center & right), 250 (all), 251 (top), 254 (all), 255 (top & middle), 260 (top)
Photo courtesy of the MIT News Office, 16 (middle), 49, 180
Photo courtesy of the MIT News Office: Donna Coveney, 211 (middle), 231, 240 (3rd from top), 255 (bottom)
Photo courtesy MIT Museum: MIT News Office, Calvin Campbel, 240 (top right)
Photo courtesy MIT Museum; © Black Star, 259
MTL Photo Archives, 207, 249 (left), 272–274 (all), 275 (top left & right; middle), 276 (top left, 2nd from left, 2nd from right, & right; middle)
Sam Ogden, 252 (top)
Photo © Sam Ogden, 253 (bottom)
RLE Photo Archives, xv, 9, 10 (top), 211 (top left), 277–282 (all)
Photo © John Soares, 251 (middle)
Laura Wulf, 2002, 238
Linda Zahn, 138, 140
Victor Zue, 172 (top)

# Contents

# Preface

Facing page:

Top left: EE staff, 1920

Top right: EE Department in 1929. Top row
(left to right): C.E. Tucker, C.L. Dawes, Mul-
ligan, Morash, Sullivan, Frazier, Lane, Coleman, Bowles, Quinlan, Moon - Second row
from top: Stratton, Fay, Hentz, J.B. Russell,
Bangratz, Van Pelt, A.L. Russell, M.L. Porter,
Jr., M. Dixon, Entwistle, Wildes, Lansil - Second row from bottom: Hudson, Timbie, R.R.
Lawrence, Laws, Jackson, Bush, Dwight,
Barker, Woodruff, Dahl, Guillemin - Bottom
row: M.F. Gardner, Kingsley, Caldwell,
Peterson, Hazen, Barrow, Edgerton, Bing-
ham, Horcross, Gager

Middle left: EE faculty meeting at Endicott
House, on 24 May 1956, under the leadership of Gordon S. Brown (standing at right)

Middle right: EE faculty on the eve of World
War II

Academic year 2002–2003 marks the 100th anniversary of MIT's Department of Electrical Engineering and Computer Science, née Electrical Engineering. That isn't to say that electrical engineering at MIT is a mere one hundred years old. Electrical engineering at MIT was first recognized in 1882 with the establishment in the physics department of Course VIII-B: "an alternative course in physics for the benefit of students wishing to enter upon any of the branches of electrical engineering." The MIT catalog of 1884–85 marked the debut of Course VI as a course of study within the physics department. By 1892, over a quarter of MIT's graduates were showing the good sense to major in Course VI. In 1902, electrical engineering split off from physics, perhaps the most successful spinout in history.

The department's recipe for success is simple: adhere to a set of core values, attract the best people, provide an excellent working environment, and encourage people to pursue their dreams.

Superficially, there is little resemblance between the EE department of 1902 and the EECS department of 2003, but the core values of the department have remained remarkably consistent. Our primary mission has always been to provide our undergraduate and graduate students with an education that combines rigorous academics with the excitement of discovery. Dugald C. Jackson, who served as department head from 1907–35, enunciated early in his tenure a philosophy of engineering education: *"principles, principles, principles,* and rational methods of reasoning." Jackson's dictum is the root of the department's current educational philosophy. We focus on helping students acquire knowledge, skills, and attitudes that will serve them well throughout their careers. The specifics of the knowledge and skills that we think important are ever changing, but we have consistently believed that engineering education and research require a deep understanding of underlying sciences and mathematics and the ability to extend science or mathematics when necessary.

EECS faculty, February 2003: Front row (left to right): Bers, Peake, Reif, Guttag, Liskov, Kaelbling, Sarpeshkar, Kolodziejski; Second row: Ezekiel, Devadas, Leiserson, Arvind, Winston, Mitter, Sudan, Teller, Balarishnan, Morris; Third row: Meyer, Perrott, Weiss, Staelin, Dennis, Shapiro, Popovic, Aggarwal, Ward, Amarasinge; Fourth row: Braida, Zahn, Daniel, Freeman, Han, Gifford, Corbató, Penfield, Grimson, Brooks, Schindall, Bertsekas; Fifth row: Tsitkllis, Hennie, Frishkopf, Stevens, Reinjtes, Chan, A. Smith, Gallager, Fujimoto, Karger, Medard, Ozdaglar, Zheng, Dresselhaus, Fonstad; Sixth row: Parker, Hagelstein, Abelson, Zue, Oppenheim, Kong, Indyk, Forney, Akinwande, Senturia, Baldo, Boning, Bulovic, Schmidt, Hoyt, Orlando; Seventh row: P. Gray, Kassakian, Antonidias, Wilson, Perreault, Rivest, Troxel, Knight, H. Smith, Darrell, Massaquoi, Verghese, W. Freeman, Sussman, Lynch; Eighth row: Berwick, Haus, Kaertner, Terman, Voldman, Wyatt, Dahleh, Davis, Del Alamo, Lozano-Perez, Tidor, Ward, Roberge, Jaakola, Collins; Ninth row: Durand, Asanovic, Lee, Chandrakasan, Micali, Sodini, Magnanti, Larson, Wornell, Jackson, Szolovitz; Back row: Lang, Lampson, Rinard, Saltzer, Leeb, Kirtley, Horn, Ippen, Moses, Kaashoek. Faculty not pictured: Bruce, Demaine, Goldwasser, M. Gray, Grodzinsky, Hu, Lim, Megretski, Ram, White, Willsky.

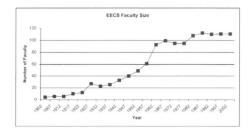

EECS faculty size from 1902 to 2002

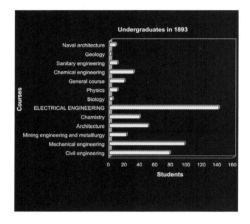

Even before electrical engineering was a department, students were interested in the major.

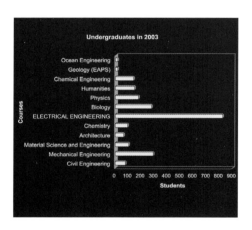

Although student choices have expanded since 1893, interest in EECS has remained strong. Courses listed on this graph correspond to those in 1893. (No course comparable to sanitary engineering could be found in the current course catalog.) Students today have many more choices than those listed here.

Perhaps the hardest, and most important, thing to teach is attitude. But attitude is of enduring value. When I meet with successful alumni, I often ask them, "What is the most important thing you learned at MIT?" To a first approximation, the answer is invariant across both occupation and graduation date. I don't recall anyone ever answering "Weiner filtering," "Laplace's equations," or even "data abstraction." The answers are "to work hard," "not to be afraid of tackling hard problems," "to tackle problems in a logical manner," and other answers along the same lines.

One hundred years ago, the members of the department could hardly be described as a diverse group. The faculty was composed entirely of white, Anglo-Saxon Protestant men from east of the Mississippi. Today, the situation is quite different. The men and women of our current faculty were born in over thirty different nations. In a recent faculty search season, we hired extraordinary young men and women hailing from China, England, France, Israel, Italy, Syria, Turkey, and even the United States. Our students are even more diverse.

Providing an excellent working environment is always a challenge. Fortunately, we have almost always been well supported by MIT and by our loyal friends and alumni. The soon to be completed Ray and Maria Stata Center, comprised of the Alexander W. Dreyfoos and William H. Gates Buildings, is tangible evidence of that support.

The most important dreams to pursue are those that take us places we never expected to go; it is those dreams that have kept the Department healthy over its long history. These dreams have led us to continuously reshape the boundaries of first EE and then EECS. Almost every day almost every one of us uses a piece of technology that owes its existence to work carried out within EECS or by our alumni. Seven faculty winners of the National Medal of Science (and numerous alumni winners) have prowled the halls of the department. Many successful corporations have their roots in EECS. Members of the MIT EECS family are honored every year for their contributions to engineering, science, business, and society.

Several years ago, we started thinking about pulling together a book in honor of the department's centennial. We quickly dismissed the idea of producing a comprehensive history; it would entail far more work than we could manage. Instead, we decided to try to capture the flavor of the department's evolution with an eclectic collection of materials.

John Guttag with Ph.D. graduates, 2002

A committee comprised of Fernando J. Corbató, Robert M. Fano, Paul E. Gray, John Guttag, Hermann A. Haus, Paul L. Penfield, Jr., and J. Francis Reintjes selected classic research papers written by members of the department. This was a daunting task, but it was simplified by deciding to eliminate papers written by still-active researchers. (And what department head would be fool enough to join in the business of deciding which of his colleagues had written the most important papers?) The same committee selected a few departmental pioneers to be profiled in the book. Again, prudence suggested that we not include people still actively involved in the department.

When this process was complete, we noticed two glaring problems: computer science and women were largely unrepresented. The explanation was simple—the department's pioneering computer scientists and women are, for the most part, still active. This left us with three alternatives: (1) find a way to deactivate a few people, (2) settle for a book that gave an inaccurate impression of the department, or (3) make exceptions to our self-imposed rule. After some debate (the details of which I leave to your imagination), we chose the third alternative. This allowed us to include Fernando Corbató's pioneering research paper on time sharing and to profile two pioneering women faculty members, Millie Dresselhaus and Barbara Liskov.

Another major part of the book is a collection of abstracts. Each member of the department's faculty (both current and emeritus) was asked to choose one abstract as representative of the most important work that he or she had done. This was a bit like asking

William Shakespeare to choose the one item that best represents his oeuvre. But I think that readers will find the selections and the reasons for choosing them quite interesting.

I suspect that very few readers will find themselves in complete agreement with our decisions about what and whom to include in this book. If this were not the case, I would be worried. The staggering number of notable accomplishments and people that we have omitted is indicative of the enormous accomplishments of those who have populated this department over the years. I feel enormously privileged to be part of the chain of people that is MIT EECS.

John Guttag

EECS Department Head

Cambridge, March 2003

## POSTSCRIPT

The alert reader may have noticed a discrepancy between the March 2003 date of the above preface and the 2005 copyright for this volume. Most of the material for this book was, in fact, prepared in time for the official celebration of the EECS centenary in May 2003. However, editorial difficulties led to our postponing publication.

Typesetting the classic papers in a way that was both legible and preserved the look and feel of the original was a challenge that our publisher was willing to undertake. But in the process of doing this, we may have inadvertently introduced some errors. If you read something that doesn't seem to make sense, you might want to consult the original source material. Similarly, we may have made errors in reproducing the abstracts, etc. We hope that the spirit of the undertaking will more than compensate for any errors we may have introduced.

A lot happened in the interval between the preparation and our finally sending the book to the printer: the Artificial Intelligence Laboratory and the Laboratory for Computer Science merged to form the Computer Science and Artificial Intelligence Laboratory (CSAIL), the Ray and Maria Stata Center opened, Millie Dresselhaus and Barbara Liskov won major IEEE awards, many faculty members wrote new favorite papers, etc. We thought about updating the content of this book, but good sense prevailed and we did not.

John Guttag

June 2004

# Acknowledgments

*by John V. Guttag*

This book could not have been assembled without the help of many individuals and groups. While it is not possible to thank everybody, we do want to thank those who dedicated a significant amount of time and effort to the project.

Paul Penfield wrote the text that ties the book together. If the book has an author (as opposed to editor) it is Paul. But the book could not have been assembled without the contributions of the other book committee members: Fernando Corbató, Robert Fano, Paul Gray, Hermann Haus, and Frank Reintjes. Initially they worked with editor Ellen Williams, '67. With her help, the structure and content of the book took shape. Patsy Sampson took over this task after Ellen's departure, providing follow up editorial and administrative oversight. Patsy has done a truly heroic job getting the book into print — attending to all the photographs, editorial changes, and last-minute details necessary to complete the project. She was significantly aided in this effort by Elizabeth Cooper.

We appreciate the contributions of our colleagues in EECS who provided appreciations, introductions to classic papers, and laboratory profiles: Duane Boning, Rodney Brooks, Vincent Chan, Robert Gallager, Eric Grimson, Judy Hoyt, John Kassakian, Barbara Liskov, Sanjoy Mitter, Martin Schmidt, Jeffrey Shapiro, David Staelin, Gerald Wilson, Markus Zahn, and Victor Zue. We are also grateful for the contributions of Abigail Mieko Vargus '97, who wrote several of the appreciations and of Lauren Clark who worked on the profile of LIDS.

Jenny O'Neill, collections assistant at the MIT Museum, was a huge help. She not only scanned numerous historic photos for possible use, but patiently answered questions about images and documents. Mary Anne Hansen from the MIT News Office also responded to countless requests for information and guidance on photos and news articles.

Marilyn Pierce, graduate administrator in EECS, took personal interest in reviewing the lists of nearly 2,500 Ph.D. and Sc.D. recipients — often recalling details that led to corrections in database errors. When database questions arose, Helen Schwartz also provided important feedback.

Annika Pfluger, Raina Duran, John Kassakian, Michael Lewy, Jason Decker, Samuel Crooks, William Smith, and Krista Van Guilder were instrumental in obtaining pictures and related materials for the laboratory profiles.

Finally, we are grateful to our publisher Vern Associates, specifically Peter Blaiwas, creative director, and Brian Hotchkiss, executive director, for patiently solving many technical difficulties such as typesetting the classic papers.

# Dedication

We proudly dedicate this book to the memory of Professor Hermann Anton Haus.

Hermann, who played a key role in pulling this volume together, died unexpectedly the very week that we celebrated our 100th anniversary. He was greatly missed at the celebration and subsequently.

Hermann arrived at MIT in 1951. For over half a century, he excelled as a researcher, classroom teacher, mentor, and friend. He was a giant, comparable to the best in our department's history. A man such as Hermann Haus can never be replaced, but he will long be remembered with admiration, respect, and fondness.

# The Electron
# and the Bit

*by Paul L. Penfield, Jr.*

During the last one hundred years our department has attracted people with a passion for the electron or the bit—for things electrical or things computational. It has been an exciting time, and those of us who lived through part of it are lucky to have had the opportunity. We were in the right place, at the right time, to pursue our passion. This story of the department's first century is *our* story.

But what about those born too late for our experience? A hundred years from now *their* story will be told, and it is sure to be just as exciting as *our* story. The future of the department will be in their hands, and this history is dedicated to them.

My focus here—our educational activities—matches the department's priorities. MIT started the first electrical engineering program and has emphasized its undergraduate mission ever since. Because an engineering discipline is determined by its degree programs, this department has, arguably, done nothing less than define what it means to be an electrical engineer and, more recently, a computer scientist.

Paul Penfield explains the electron-and-bit cane to the audience at the start of the EECS one-hundredth-anniversary symposium on 23 May 2003.

In 1974, at the time the department added computer science to its name, the electron-and-bit cane was built by Michael Dertouzos, then the director of the Laboratory for Computer Science (LCS), and presented to Department Head Wilbur B. Davenport, Jr. The bottom of the cane is made of a piece of amber and half a quarter. The Greek word for amber is *electra*, while a quarter (two bits) halved is a bit. Thus the cane symbolizes the two components of the department. It is traditionally passed from one department head to the next at the time the new Head takes office.

# 1 The Dawn of the Electrical Age

*by Paul L. Penfield, Jr.*

When should the story of MIT's Department of Electrical Engineering and Computer Science begin? In 1902 when it was formed? In 1882 when the electrical engineering degree program was started? Even earlier, I think, when the American electrical enterprise started to emerge.

Scientists, industrialists, and inventors all played a part. The scientist was curious about natural phenomena. The industrialist wanted to make money. The inventor liked to create useful innovations. The electrical engineer did not yet exist, but would, eventually, have all these motivations.

The leading electrical scientist in America in 1830 was Joseph Henry, teaching at Albany Academy in New York. He made the most powerful magnets available and carried out many scientific studies. His machines cleverly illustrated scientific ideas, but were not designed for practical applications.

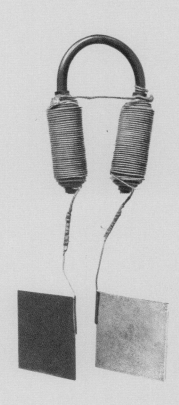

One of the first successful electromagnets, which was made in 1828 by Joseph Henry

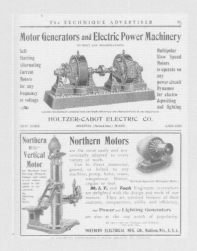

By 1912, electrical motors were common enough to be advertised in *The Technique*.

Samuel F. B. Morse, c. 1845

The first industrial use of electricity was in mining. In 1831 Allen Penfield, who owned an iron mine in Crown Point, New York, used a magnet purchased from Henry to magnetize parts of an ore separation drum, to get higher iron density.

Thomas Davenport, a Vermont blacksmith, had heard about magnets, at that time a scientific novelty. He visited Crown Point and was so impressed that he bought one from Penfield (trading his horse in order to raise the money, so the story goes). By 1833 he had made a motor with continuous rotary motion and in the process invented the commutator, an essential part of every DC motor. (William Sturgeon in England had independently made the same invention a few months earlier.)

Henry held Davenport's motor in disdain. His scientific arguments would not be considered convincing today, but his practical concern was that the motor could not compete with steam engines because the batteries then available were so cumbersome and expensive. He was right—this motor was ahead of its time. Although Davenport got a U.S. patent (no. 132) in 1837, the first issued for any electrical machine, he could not interest anyone in using motors. He went to his grave in 1851 a defeated man.

Electricity needed what would be known today as a killer app—an application so compelling that an underlying technology would be acquired just to run it. Henry concluded, correctly, that the killer app for electricity was the telegraph. As early as 1816 an electric telegraph line had been built in Europe, but it took advances in technology—the hand key and Morse code—by the American painter and inventor Samuel F.B. Morse, a native of Charlestown, Massachusetts, to make it practical. Henry gave Morse strong encouragement and sound scientific advice, so much so that they tangled later about who had really invented what.

Morse sent the famous message, "WHAT HATH GOD WROUGHT" from Washington, D.C., to Baltimore, Maryland, in 1844. The telegraph spread like wildfire. Electricity caught the fancy of the public. The mood was not unlike the Internet euphoria 150 years later.

Finally there was a bona fide electrical industry. Universities, including MIT, took note. MIT admitted its first students in 1865 and provided instruction in physics right from the start. Two MIT physicists recognized the importance of electricity. Edward C. Pickering, a member of the National Academy of Sciences, was extraordinarily energetic and eclectic, judging from the range of his projects. At MIT from

1867 to 1877, he beefed up laboratory instruction and, perhaps most importantly, persuaded one of his students, Charles R. Cross, to join the physics faculty and continue the electrical work.

It was Cross who in 1874 invited Alexander Graham Bell, then teaching at Boston University, to use MIT's acoustics and electrical laboratory. Bell did so, since the facilities were superior to what he had at Boston University, and demonstrated a working telephone in 1876. Three years later Thomas Edison invented the electric light bulb and in 1882 commissioned the first electric power plant. Had Davenport still been alive, he would have seen that his 1833 invention of the DC motor made this power plant possible: the generator was simply a motor running backwards.

By 1882 five major electrical devices and systems were of growing national importance: telegraph, telephone, rotating machines, illumination, and the power grid. These were the products of scientists, industrialists, and inventors. It was now time to define electrical engineering, and the way to do that was to design an educational program.

Charles Cross understood. He was the right person, in the right place, at the right time. He started, at MIT, the nation's first electrical engineering degree program.

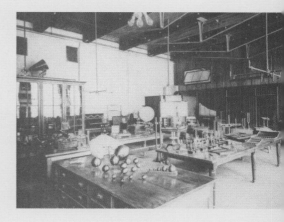

The Acoustics and Electrical Laboratory in the physics department, where Alexander Graham Bell worked at the invitation of Charles Cross

   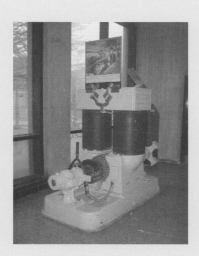

(left to right): Examples of late-19th-century telephone, light bulb, and electron tube

This Edison Company DC dynamo (above), installed in Boston in 1886, is now located in the lobby of Building 36.

# Electrical Engineering Is Born

*by Paul L. Penfield, Jr.*

In 1882, Charles R. Cross, head of the MIT physics department, decided the nation needed a degree program in electrical engineering and he started Course VIII-B. Two years later, even before the first students graduated, it was redesignated Course VI. Between 1882 and 1902 the electrical engineering program was run by Cross, out of the physics department.

Then, as now, students could sniff out fields with a bright future. By 1892, 27 percent of all MIT undergraduates were in electrical engineering. Early graduates included Charles A. Stone '88 and Edwin S. Webster '88, who founded Stone and Webster, the firm that built MIT's new Cambridge campus in 1916; another was Alfred P. Sloan '95, who became president of General Motors and a major MIT benefactor.

Electrical engineering programs were also springing up at other universities. Of those that grew out of physics or mathematics departments, some were very scientific or theoretical. Others, designed to train people for the rapidly growing electrical industry, taught contemporary techniques but not the underlying science. MIT, whose programs had always maintained a balance between practice and theory,

Professor Charles R. Cross, who founded the first course in electrical engineering in 1882

7

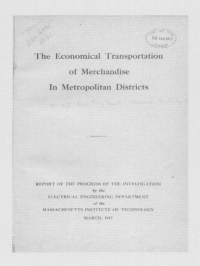

The Economical Transportation
of Merchandise
In Metropolitan Districts


REPORT OF THE PROGRESS OF THE INVESTIGATION
by the
ELECTRICAL ENGINEERING DEPARTMENT
of the
MASSACHUSETTS INSTITUTE OF TECHNOLOGY
MARCH, 1912

"The Economical Transportation of Merchandise in Metropolitan Districts," a report completed by the EE department at MIT in 1912

avoided both extremes. Cross himself fit the pattern, working in a science department but with a definite industrial and engineering bent.

In 1900 Cross began to press for a new Department of Electrical Engineering, but when it was established in 1902 he did not join. He assisted with the teaching, but stayed in the physics department, where he served as department head for another fifteen years.

To lead the new department, MIT looked outside and recruited Louis Duncan. This selection did not work out too well; Duncan's real interests were with industry, and he left before long. But the next department head from outside, Dugald C. Jackson, was a spectacular success.

# Impedance

ARTHUR EDWIN KENNELLY

17 DECEMBER 1861–18 JUNE 1939

PAPER PRESENTED AT THE SEVENTY-
SIXTH MEETING OF THE AMERICAN
INSTITUTE OF ELECTRICAL ENGINEERS
IN NEW YORK ON 18 APRIL 1893

*Introduced and edited by Hermann A. Haus*

In modern times, the concept of impedance is taken in stride. But it was not always that way. During the latter part of the nineteenth century, when the country was shifting from direct-current to alternating-current power, a need arose for a way to analyze a-c circuits that contain inductance and capacitance as well as resistance. Scholars of the time freely exchanged their ideas in an effort to find an acceptable concept that would yield a clear understanding of circuits with alternating voltage as a driving force. Among them was Arthur Edwin Kennelly. He advocated adoption of the concept of impedance.

An extensive biography written by Vannevar Bush, his former student, was published in the *Biographical Memoirs of the National Academy of Sciences*, 1943. From Bush we learn that Kennelly was born in Bombay, India, in 1861. His father was harbor master at Bombay. His mother died when he was three. He was sent to England, where he received his elementary education. He did not attend school beyond the age of fourteen, when he started work as a telegraph engineer. Later he was promoted to chief electrician on cable ships. In 1887 he joined Thomas A. Edison's lab, where he became Edison's assistant. He was appointed professor of electrical engineering at Harvard in 1902, and from 1913 to 1925 he was professor of electrical communications at MIT. He served as chairman of the MIT faculty from 1917 to 1919. Among

Professor Hermann A. Haus teaching in the 1960s

Dr. Hermann Haus (left), associate professor of electrical engineering, discusses power flow in a microwave tube, in 1954, with Abraham Bers, an electrical engineering graduate student at the time.

Professor A. E. Kennelly

his many honors were the gold medal of honor of the IRE in 1932 and four honorary doctorates. Before his death in 1939, Kennelly published over 380 articles and authored or coauthored 29 books. He is best known for proposing the existence of a layer of the ionosphere, which explained the success of Marconi's wireless transmission from Europe to North America and which was subsequently named the Kennelly–Heaviside layer.

Kennelly's paper on impedance, which is forty-one pages long, is a good illustration of the efforts of the professional community to provide a theoretical basis for the voltage-current laws in circuits carrying alternating currents. He begins his paper with a definition of impedance, a discussion of sinusoidal-wave generation, and his vectorial approach to impedance calculations. (Noteworthy are the electrical symbols and terms that were in vogue at the time.) Kennelly writes:

> The impedance of a conductor is its apparent resistance, and is expressible in ohms. More strictly, it has been defined as the ratio of the effective E.M.F. between the terminals of the conductor, to the effective current strength it carries. By voltage or current in the sequel, effective voltage and effective current, unless otherwise specified, will be intended,—such as would be indicated by properly calibrated alternating current voltmeters and ammeters.
>
> With steady continuous currents, the impedance of a conductor is its simple resistance. With periodically fluctuating currents, the impedance will in general differ from the resistance, and will be greater or less, but in common practice greater. With such voltages and currents, Ohm's law becomes
>
> $$C = \frac{E}{I}$$
>
> where the impedance is represented by $I$.
>
> We may first consider periodic currents and voltages of the simple harmonic type, following waves in time such as could be traced upon a band of paper, moving steadily lengthwise, by the vertical shadow of the crank-pin on a fly-wheel revolving uniformly in a vertical plane perpendicular to the band. [Fig. 1] The ratio of the velocity between wheel and paper would control the spacing and steepness of the waves, but would not alter their sinusoidal type, while the motion of the shadow would be simply harmonic.
>
> If the fly-wheel makes $n$ complete periods or revolutions per second, and the distance of the crank-pin from the shaft axis—its crank radius—is unity, then the circumference of the circle it traces will be $2\pi$, and the total distance it will run through in one second will be $2\pi n$ or $6.283\,n$ linear units, which we may call its speed, and denote by $p = 2\pi n$. If then the pin is shifted outwards upon the wheel until its crank radius or distance from the axis is $l$ units, where $l$ is the number of henrys in any particular inductance, then the corresponding travel of the pin will be $2\pi l n$ linear units per second, and this speed $pl$ we may call the inductance-speed for the particular frequency and inductance $l$ considered.

Non-ferric inductances (if the term be permitted), or inductances without iron may be first assumed, leaving ferric inductances and conductors embracing iron, for later examination.

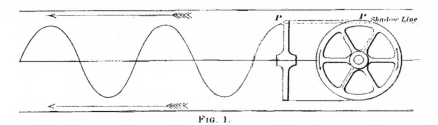

FIG. 1.

In order to find the impedance of any conductor whose resistance is $r$ ohms, and inductance $l$ henrys, we construct the triangle having as base the length $r$, the perpendicular of $pl$ units, and draw the hypothenuse, which will have the length $\sqrt{r^2+(pl)^2}$, between their free extremities. [See Fig. 1.] This length will be the impedance in ohms. The impedance is therefore the geometrical or vector[1] sum of the resistance and inductance speed, when these are plotted on two rectangular axes. Calling this impedance $i$, Ohm's law gives

$$c = \frac{e}{i} \qquad e = ic \qquad i = \frac{e}{c}$$

corresponding to the usual formulas for continuous currents. In Fig. 2 a resistance of 75 $\omega$ having an inductance of 0.06 henry with a consequent inductance speed at 100 $\sim$, of $6.283 \times 100 \times 0.06 = 37.7$

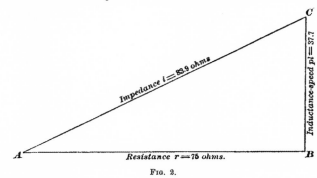

FIG. 2.

is shown to possess an impedance $i$ of

$$\sqrt{(75)^2+(37.7)^2} = 83.9 \text{ ohms.}$$

If two such impedances, $i_1$ and $i_2$, be connected in series, their total impedance [Fig. 3] will be the vector sum A C of $i_1$ and $i_2$ corresponding to the arithmetical sum for unvarying currents. This vector sum is most conveniently constructed geometrically by summing separately the component resistances $r_1$, $r_2$, A G, and then the component inductance-speeds, G C, as shown. Calling the vector sum $I$,

1 The vector sum of the two lines A B and B C is the line A C, since a transference from A to B followed by a transference from B to C is geometrically equivalent to a transference from A to C.

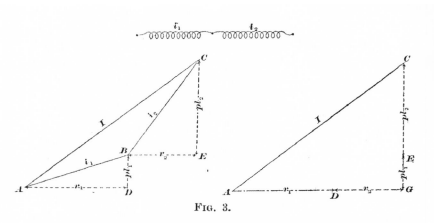

FIG. 3.

the voltage on $I$ for a current of $c$ amperes will be $c\,I$ volts.

"    "    " $i_1$ " "  "   "   "     "   "  " $c\,i_1$ "

"    "    " $i_2$ " "  "   "   "     "   "  " $c\,i_2$ "

but $I$ will not be the arithmetical sum of $i_1$ and $i_2$, nor will the drop on $I$ be the sum of the drops of $i_1$ and $i_2$, unless the separate time constants, $\dfrac{l_1}{r_1}$ and $\dfrac{l_2}{r_2}$ are equal, when A B will be in line with B C; the reason being that otherwise the currents in $i_1$ and $i_2$ while of equal strength, are out of step.

In Fig. 3, $r_1$ represents to scale, a resistance of 30 $\omega$, $r_2$ 20 $\omega$, $p\,l_1$ an inductance speed of 10, $p\,l_2$ 30. Then

$$i_1 \text{ is } \sqrt{900+100} = 31.63 \text{ ohms,}$$
$$i_2 \text{ is } \sqrt{400+900} = 36.06 \text{ ohms,}$$
$$I = \sqrt{2500+1600} = 64.0 \text{ ohms.}$$

whereas the arithmetical sum of $i_1$ and $i_2$ would be 67.69 ohms.

Kennelly's emphasis is on the vectorial approach to the calculation of impedance. Complex numbers are mentioned very briefly, but they are not used in his illustrative examples. Voltage-current phase relationships in circuits containing energy storage elements are not discussed.

The paper also mentions the Ferranti effect, the phenomenon in which the terminal voltage may be smaller than the internal voltages across the individual circuit elements, an effect that we today describe as resonance. He gives special attention to the placement of two parallel conductors so as to minimize the inductance speed without placing them too close together to cause breakdown of the dielectric between them.

The paper contains a detailed discussion of the impedance factor of standard wires — the factor by which the resistance per unit length of a wire has to be multiplied to get its impedance per unit length $\left(\sqrt{1+(\omega L / R)^2}\right)$ when inductance is taken into account. For those in need of the impedance factor of a pair of parallel copper wires carrying a sinusoidal current, the author provides eight full-page, handbook-style tables that give impedance factors for a wide variety of wire sizes and for several applied frequencies in the 40 hertz to 140 hertz ranges. The tables account for the series inductive reactance of wire pairs but ignore the capacitive reactance between pairs. Evidently, more precise modeling of transmission lines was still in the future.

After the impedance-factor presentation, the paper shifts to inductors containing iron and the nonsinusoidal current response to a sinusoidal voltage. At the end of the paper the author discusses the inductance per unit length of a pair of wires with the goal of arranging their spacing so as to make the impedance factor as small as possible. His presentation of this topic is testimony to the understanding of field theory in the electrical engineering community of the day.

That the mathematical analysis of a–c circuitry was in a state of flux at the time of Kennelly's paper is evident in his closing paragraph. He states:

> [This] paper has been written with the endeavor to point out that the difficulties which at present shroud the use and working theory of alternating currents are largely fictitious. An alternating current is a very complex thing, but so is the dynamo, and we can predetermine dynamos with a degree of accuracy sufficient for all practical purposes. We know when a machine is designed, within reasonable limits, what voltages will be at its terminals, when driven at a certain speed with a certain excitation and load, although the exact calculation would transcend all capabilities we possess today. Similarly, working theories which are sufficiently good for most practical purposes run through kindred sciences, whereas the exact theories are beyond present human capabilities; and though alternating currents are so difficult when studied accurately and absolutely, the working theory of alternating currents can be made as simple as the working theories of direct currents. I am firmly impressed with the belief—a belief which I trust I may be able to communicate—that the most convincing way of proving this difficulty which has hitherto surrounded the alternating current and its distribution, can be eliminated and removed, ... by the development of the notion of impedance.

The appendix to the paper contains a Fourier decomposition of a nonsinusoidal waveform of arbitrary shape and defines the impedance factor in terms of the square root of the sums of the squared impedance factors, a definition of questionable rigor and usefulness.

The discussion after the talk was recorded, following the model of the meetings of the Royal Society. Noteworthy among the discussants were Pupin, of Pupin-coil fame, who elaborated on the Ferranti effect, and Charles P. Steinmetz, who sent in his comments later since he did not attend the meeting. Steinmetz pointed out that complex-number notation provides a simple framework for Kennelly's vectorial approach. He writes as follows:

*I have read Mr. Kennelly's valuable paper on "Impedance" with the greatest interest, and am only sorry that I was not able to be present at its presentation.*

*One statement, however, I would like to emphasize somewhat more strongly, since in the paper, it is enclosed between so many remarks of the highest practical value as to be liable to escape due notice, viz.: that,*

*"Any circuit whatever, consisting of a combination of resistances, non-ferric inductances and capacities, carrying harmonically alternating currents, may be treated by the rules of unvarying currents, if the impedances are expressed by complex numbers:*

$$a + b\,j = r(\cos\varphi + j\sin\varphi),$$

*the algebraic operations being then performed according to the laws controlling complex quantities."*

*It is well known that the points of a plane can be represented by complex quantities in their rectangular representation*

$$a + b\,j\,(\star),$$

$$(\star) \text{ Where j denotes } \sqrt{-1}$$

*or their polar representation*

$$r(\cos\varphi + j\sin\varphi),$$

*and use has been made hereof repeatedly in the mathematical treatment of vector quantities. It is, however, the first instance here, so far as I know, that attention is drawn by Mr. Kennelly to the correspondence between the electrical term "impedance" and the complex numbers.*

*The importance hereof lies in the following:—The analysis of the complex plane is very well worked out, hence by reducing the electrical problems to the analysis of complex quantities they are brought within the scope of a known and well understood science.*

During the discussion, two interesting comments were made. One concerned the term *impedance* itself. According to one discussant, "Impedance is an extremely modern term, it having been devised and given to us by Mr. Oliver Heaviside within the past seven years." The same discussant later stated, "Hereafter, when we want to know anything about impedance, so far at least as it has up to the present time been investigated, we shall come to Mr. Kennelly's paper."

What a fine paper and what a fine career, especially for a man who left school at the age of fourteen.

**EECS Buildings**

*from top to bottom:*

EE's earliest home, the Walker Building in Boston, housed the first large electrical laboratories. c. 1890.

For many years, EE's teaching laboratories were located in the basement of Building 10, below the MIT dome.

Building 20, built in 1943 as a temporary structure, was home to the Radiation Laboratory during World War II. After fifty-five years of service to various MIT activities, it was demolished in 1998 to make way for the Ray and Maria Stata Center for Computer, Information and Intelligence Sciences.

## EECS Buildings

*from top to bottom:*

NE43 in Technology Square, home for forty years for AI, Project MAC (1963–74) and LCS

The Sherman Fairchild Complex—Buildings 36 and 38—has been home to RLE, MTL, the EECS teaching labs, and the EECS administrative offices since 1973. Upon its completion in 1983, the Edgerton, Germeshausen and Grier Educational Center (EG&G or Building 34) tied together Buildings 36 and 38 and provided additional space for EECS educational activities.

Unveiling the plaque in Building 34 in October 1983, from left to right, are donors Esther and Harold Edgerton, Pauline and Kenneth Germeshausen, Dorothy and Herbert E. Grier, D. Saxon, chairman of the MIT Corporation (to the right of the plaque), President Paul Gray, Dean G. Wilson, and Department Head Joel Moses.

The view from the observation deck of the Stata Center construction site on Saturday, 24 May 2003

# 3 Electrical Engineering Comes of Age

*by Paul L. Penfield, Jr.*

In its hundred-year history, the department has had two leaders who exerted extraordinary influence on its educational mission: Dugald C. Jackson and Gordon S. Brown.

Jackson was recruited from the University of Wisconsin, where he had led the department of electrical engineering since 1891. He came to MIT in 1907 and served twenty-eight years as department head, surely a record that will never be broken.

Jackson had a clear vision of what an electrical engineer should be and understood that the way to make that vision a reality was through an educational program. He respected both scientists and technicians, but thought engineers should be different. Technicians apply known techniques; engineers do that and also develop new techniques when needed. Scientists develop new science; engineers use known science. His philosophy was consistent with that already in place at MIT when he arrived.

In 1903, while still at Wisconsin, Jackson set forth his goals in a paper in *Science*: "…*principles, principles, principles*, and rational methods of reasoning … must be taught."

*Endnotes appear on page 71.

He wanted his graduates to assume positions of leadership in industry by virtue of their good communication skills, scientific knowledge (mathematics, chemistry, physics, and applied mechanics), appreciation of how society works, and acquaintance with business practices. He was interested in educating practical industrial engineers, rather than scientists or academicians. He admired "rational methods of reasoning" and had little patience for purely descriptive and superficial material or the "beauties of nature" or skills that helped students get immediate jobs or "empirical methods of practice that change almost before they can be put to useful account." Jackson definitely believed it was not his responsibility to produce "finished engineers," only graduates "with a great capacity for becoming engineers ... after years of development in the school of life." His was a no-nonsense approach intended to equip the students for forty years, the full duration of an engineering career.

Two major educational milestones mark Jackson's years as department head.

First, the VI-A cooperative program (now called the Internship Program) was launched in 1917. Jackson wanted students to get work experience with educational value. VI-A was not a summer job program or a work-study program designed to help students pay their tuition, but a bona fide educational program. His philosophy has distinguished VI-A from other programs around the nation ever since. Over the decades, about 18 percent of the department's undergraduates have participated in the VI-A program.

Second, in the early 1930s, Jackson started a major curriculum revision, motivated in part by developments in radio and electronics. He ordered the writing of a new series of textbooks, which would come to be known as the "blue books" because of the color of the covers. The series was not actually finished for over a decade (World War II intervened) and two planned volumes were abandoned because of advances in technology. Jackson decreed the books to be team efforts, and individual authors were not to be identified.

Jackson's vision can be interpreted today as having been based on three assumptions. First, the underlying science, as developed by scientists, was in a form engineers could use. Second, science would not change much during a graduate's forty-year career. Third, society itself would not change much during that same time span. His vision guided the department until, in the late 1940s, it became apparent that two of these assumptions were no longer valid. It was the other great department head, Gordon Brown, who would recognize the problem and provide the remedy.

# DUGALD CALEB JACKSON
### 13 FEBRUARY 1865 –
### 1 JULY 1951

*by Abigail Mieko Vargus, '97*

The eldest of three boys, Dugald Jackson grew up in Kennett Square, Pennsylvania, where his father was a math professor at Pennsylvania State University. It is not surprising that education became central to Jackson's life. At the age of twenty, Jackson left Pennsylvania, after obtaining a B.S. in the civil engineering course from Pennsylvania State University, for Cornell University in Ithaca, New York. Jackson taught physics there, while doing postgraduate work in electrical engineering.

After two years at Cornell, Jackson ventured into the business world. In just a few years he made contacts, particularly at what became the General Electric Company, that were invaluable to his innovations in education. His work in industry earned him an impressive reputation as an engineer for the electric and railroad utilities. During this period, Jackson married Mabel Augusta Foss; their children were born in 1890 and 1895.

In 1891, Jackson joined the faculty of the University of Wisconsin at Madison as professor and head of the new electrical engineering department. He did not, however, really leave the business world at any point during his career; he and his youngest brother, William, had a consulting partnership until 1917, when Jackson left to serve in World War I. After the war and until 1930, Jackson ran a consulting firm with colleague Edward L. Moreland. Throughout his career, he earned respect for his abilities as an engineer as well as an educator, and he was assigned more than twenty-five patents for his inventions.

MIT lured Jackson away from the Midwest to become the head of the electrical engineering department in 1907, a position he held for twenty-eight years. These were his most prolific years as an innovative educator. He left an indelible mark on the Institute.

Jackson came to MIT with change in mind. He wrote to MIT President Henry S. Pritchett in an early letter about the position, "There are a number of modifications in the electrical engineering course as laid down in the Institute catalog that I would wish to make as quickly as the conditions allow — the changes tending toward giving the students a broader outlook on engineering. Observations and experience have taught me that many

Professor Dugald C. Jackson

college courses in electrical engineering tend too much toward making mere specially trained electricians instead of (what electrical engineering ought to be), broadly thinking, competent young men each of whom possesses a well balanced outlook on the expanse of engineering and is trained to embrace all proper opportunities."[1]

To implement his vision, Jackson brought many impressive names to the faculty, including Vannevar Bush '16, all of whom believed in his vision of the engineer as a leader in industry and of the educator as a leader in his field. His curriculum changes laid the basis for what most MIT students and alumni encounter, although they probably do not know to credit Jackson.

One of his earliest changes was the creation of VI-A, a cooperative academic program with industry. In partnership with Jackson's former colleagues at GE, students began mixing industry experience with their academic careers, rather than delaying hands-on apprenticeships until after graduation. The academic world initially doubted the worth of such a program, but Course VI-A has thrived and has been copied by numerous institutions.

Another key change under Jackson's leadership was the creation of tutorials for advanced students. He believed that "a voluntary choice in the ordering of his own education is usually an indication of good intellectual fiber in a student, but a slavish following after fashion or habit in education usually indicates the opposite."[2] The new setup allowed honors students to form their own educational framework when possible.

Jackson also founded the research division of the electrical engineering department. This was another educational initiative close to his heart. "Fifteen years of observation and experience at the University of Wisconsin convinced me that making research an integral part of electrical engineering education is of primary value," he wrote. "I therefore took this tenet as a primary one upon going to the electrical engineering department at MIT in 1907, and it has been there maintained with increasing emphasis to the present time."[3]

Engineering education was always foremost in Jackson's mind. In 1930, he retired from consulting to focus his energies on curriculum changes in the Department of Electrical Engineering. He appointed Edward L. Bowles, Ernst A. Guillemin, Carlton Tucker, and Julius A. Stratton to head up this effort — a move that has helped to establish the legacies of those men as well.

Jackson's many honors emphasize the general admiration for his work as an educator. President Herbert Hoover appointed him chairman of the American delegation to the 1929

World Engineering Congress in Tokyo. Jackson took this opportunity to tour much of the East and Middle East, and in turn gained international recognition for his work. His impressive list of offices in professional associations also stands as evidence of well-earned respect: president of the Society for the Promotion of Engineering Education, founder of the Joint Committee on Engineering Education (pulled from several professional societies), president of the American Institute of Electrical Engineers (AIEE), president of the American Academy of Arts and Sciences, and president of the American Institute of Consulting Engineers.

Although he retired from the department in 1935, becoming professor emeritus and honorary lecturer, Jackson did not leave the scene of academia for many years to come. Through the 1930s and 1940s, he delivered countless presentations, including a series of lectures for the Japanese Institute of Electrical Engineering, and published extensively, including *Engineering's Part in the Development of Civilization*.[4] In 1939, he was also awarded the AIEE Edison Medal "for outstanding and innovative leadership in engineering education" — the first time it had been awarded for educational efforts.[5]

While you might have to look closely to find the Dugald C. Jackson Room at MIT (34-466), and you'd have to look even harder to find an undergraduate who would recognize the name, Jackson's contributions to the department are very much in evidence today. His innovations in many ways are the hallmarks of our department.

# The Typical College Courses Dealing with the Professional and Theoretical Phases of Electrical Engineering

DUGALD C. JACKSON

SCIENCE, NEW SERIES 18, NO. 466

(DECEMBER 1903): 710–716.

*Introduced by Paul L. Penfield, Jr.*

Professor Paul Penfield, Jr., in charge of coordinating very large scale integration (VLSI) research at MIT from 1979 to 1989, explains how the circuits in the drawings on the wall ended up in chips on the silicon wafer in his hand.

Dugald C. Jackson served as department head from 1907 until his retirement in 1935. He had a special interest in electrical engineering education, having been called to lead the new electrical engineering department at the University of Wisconsin in 1891, at the age of twenty-six.

Then, as now, industry sought new graduates who could function as engineers immediately. Jackson resisted that pressure. The 1903 paper reproduced here is his personal manifesto, calling on colleges to remember the true role of education — not to produce "finished engineers" but rather those "with a great capacity for becoming engineers…after years of development in the school of life." This philosophy was consistent with what had been MIT's mission from the start.

This role was thus different from educating technicians, who apply known techniques. Engineers, by contrast, would not only apply known techniques but also develop new techniques based on known science when known techniques were insufficient. Jackson's vision guided this department for fifty years, until Gordon Brown observed that engineers should also be able to develop new science when both known techniques and known science are insufficient.

Jackson presented his views with remarkable clarity. They are as relevant in 2004 as they were in 1903. Of course the details have changed — how could he have known that biology and quantum physics would ever be important in electrical engineering? But his focus on timeless principles is refreshing. How thrilling it is to see, at the top of his list of curricular needs, the phrase "that fuller training in the construction of the English language which is requisite to clear thinking and clear writing" and then to realize, one hundred years later, that MIT is implementing a new, stronger communication requirement. Surely, Jackson would be pleased.

### THE TYPICAL COLLEGE COURSES DEALING WITH THE PROFESSIONAL AND THEORETICAL PHASES OF ELECTRICAL ENGINEERING.

AT the Chicago meeting of the American Institute of Electrical Engineers held eleven years ago, I presented a paper relating to the subject now under discussion. The proposed subject then apparently created some consternation amongst the members of the committee on papers, who seemed to fear that it was not of sufficient interest to the society. The old prejudice still held against 'college men' in the minds of so-called 'practical men' who had grown influential in engineering practice without having had experience of college life and training. Happily the foundation for this prejudice has ere this been destroyed through the influence of the industrial results achieved by college men. The old prejudice, so far as it now exists, has more particularly drifted into the way of criticism of the engineering schools rather than their graduates, and the character of the schools and the training they afford are subjects of eager discussion in engineering circles.

This extended interest now manifested in the work of the engineering schools produces a situation which may be of great usefulness to the schools. The character of a college may be that which its alumni determine, and any engineering school may be improved by thoughtful suggestions and broadly considered criticisms emanating from its alumni and others who have its best interests at heart.

Two fundamental propositions must be held clearly in view in all such criticisms, if they are to be of service to the educational administration of the engineering colleges:

1. That it is the business of these colleges to train young men into fertile and exact thinkers guided by common sense, who have a profound knowledge of natural laws and the means for utilizing natural forces for the advantage of man. In other words, it is the business of the engineering colleges to produce, not finished engineers, but young men with *a great capacity for becoming engineers,* the goal being obtained by the graduate only after years of development in the school of life.

2. The problem to be met by the engineering colleges is more particularly a problem in *how to properly train* to the stated purpose. The names attached to the subjects taught are not so important as the results produced by the teaching — namely, the effect impressed

Professor Jackson in his office in 1935

on the students' powers. This is a teacher's problem — a question of pedagogy, rather than of the engineering profession. It must be met with all the directness and power of the engineer's best efforts, but it can not be solved as solely relating to the engineering profession. Much error on this point lies in the minds of many who assume the part of critics of the curricula of the engineering schools.

In this connection I may be permitted to point out that proposals set up as apparently new in the presidential address one year ago, by President Steinmetz of the American Institute of Electrical Engineers, have for many years been largely included within the ideals of numerous American colleges of engineering. It must be admitted that only a few of the engineering schools are living up to their better ideals. This is partially due, on the one hand, to personal or institutional ambitions which foster the sensational or spectacular, and thereby inevitably ruin good teaching, and, on the other hand, to the meager support in both encouragement and funds which I have noticed is the lot of the engineering schools attached to many universities. The latter, like the former, is often the result of personal prejudices or ambitions.

Most of the faults which are so trenchantly and indiscriminately charged to engineering colleges by many engineers should, so far as they are real, be laid to the pedagogical inexperience and faulty ambitions of the authorities of the many colleges; and exception should be made of the few of the first rank, in which, it is safe to say, the ideals are high and well centered and the administrative organizations hold the ideals continuously in view.

The query here naturally arises: Of what do these ideals properly consist and how fairly should they be met by the college before its course in electrical engineering may be approved as of first rank?

Electrical engineering demands industrial engineers—men with an industrial training of the highest type, competent to conceive, organize and direct extended industrial enterprises of broadly varied character. For the highest success, these men must be keen, straightforward thinkers who see things as they are, and are not to be misled by fancies; they must have an extended, and even profound, knowledge of natural laws (more particularly of those relating to energy which rest on the law of conservation of energy), an extended knowledge of the useful applications of these laws, and an instinctive capacity for reasoning straight, from cause to effect. Moreover, they must know men and the affairs of men—which is sociology; and they must be acquainted with business methods and the affairs of the business world. Briefly, to reach his highest influence, each man must combine in one a man in the physical sciences, a man in sociology and a man of business. All engineers can not reach this high mark, but the engineering college course should start each of its students toward that degree of attainment which his individual powers will permit.

Michael Faraday (whose conservatism and intellectual clearness are proverbial) said that it requires twenty years to 'make a man' in the physical sciences. The engineering school must put each student in the way of becoming, so far as his mental and physical powers warrant, not only a man in the physical sciences, but a man in sociology and a man in business as well; and this must be done within the narrow limits of four years. It is clear that only the foundations of 'the man' may be laid in the prescribed time, and the engineering college must, therefore, rigorously hold itself to the fundamentals. The engineering college faculty which is contented to deal out so-called 'information courses' on the narrowly empirical side of engineering practice, deals a wrong to its students which they may not recognize at the moment, but which will ultimately tell heavily against their success.

The students that enter the engineering schools of the west, and I presume likewise of the east, are from amongst the most vigorous minds of the high schools and preparatory schools; and yet it must be admitted that they ordinarily possess little power of clear thinking, power of initiative, regard for accuracy, or understanding of continuous and severe intellectual effort, as these important attributes are understood in industrial circles. They are not yet mature in body and are less mature in mind (the latter being, I think, in accord with the natural order of development). But they are well equipped with physical vigor and latent mental strength. Their preparatory schooling has given them a defective acquaintance with the construction of the English language and the spelling of English words, a still more defective acquaintance with French or German or a fairly good grounding in elementary Latin, a smattering of civics and history, a training in the elementary principles of arithmetic, geometry and algebra from which the factor of accuracy in application has often been omitted, and perhaps an enthusiastic interest in the physical sciences.

This enumeration of the attainments of the students entering the engineering colleges may perhaps be interpreted as reflecting on the secondary school teachers, but I wish vigorously to deny the validity of any such interpretation. I can truthfully say that, considering all of the conditions, there is no more painstaking and right wishing body of people than these teachers.

Many of the faults in the preparatory training of our engineering college students are caused by a doubt which is now apparently agitating educational circles on account of the question whether the high schools shall be the 'people's colleges' or remain in the station of secondary or 'preparatory' schools. This doubt is apparently not yet resolved in the minds of the molders of educational thought: but the traditional old-time secondary school training which produced men who could spell and cipher and who had received a thorough and accurate drill in the details of one language, is certainly to be preferred as a preparation for an engineering college course. In my own estimation, when accompanied with history and a year spent in civics and natural science, it is not only to be preferred as a school course for preparing the student for college, but also a course for those numerous students who can not go through college.

Taking the students as they come and may be expected to come for the present, the electrical engineering course must include the following branches of learning which are preparatory to the more strictly professional studies:

1. That fuller training in the construction of the English language which is requisite to clear thinking and clear writing, preferably accompanied by an additional language for added strength.

2. The collateral art of expression in drawing.

3. Mathematics through an appropriate amount of calculus, including the integration and solution of equations involving derivatives and instruction in the use of coplanar vectors, and perhaps quaternion quantities, all of which should be taught as applied logic, with special emphasis laid on interpreting the meaning of equations.

4. The science of chemistry, soundly taught.

5. The science of physics, soundly taught, with particular emphasis laid on the elementary mechanics.

6. Applied mechanics. Mechanics—the philosophy of matter, force and energy—is the backbone of the electrical engineer's college training.

Instruction in the science branches should be accompanied by well-conceived and properly conducted laboratory work, mostly of quantitative character, accompanying and illustrating the class-room instruction; and all instruction whether in natural science, mathematics or languages, should be under the direction of men who are engineers or in full sympathy with the aims and ideals of engineering.

A limited amount of manual training may well accompany these studies, and likewise, if time can be found for it without over-burdening the reasonable physical powers of the student, a limited amount of proper instruction in surveying (including the use of the compass, transit and level) will always prove a force for quickening the student's perceptions and at the same time put him into possession of processes of probable future value.

In a few of our engineering colleges which rigidly demand the best preparatory work from the high schools, and which are, at the same time, best manned in their faculties, not less than two years are required to cover the ground above described, if the work is done in a reasonably satisfactory manner. But the above ground can not be covered with anything like reasonable success in much or any less than three years in the larger number of engineering schools that are usually accorded high rank. After covering these branches, it seems to be the tendency in many colleges to fly off into superficial or descriptive courses, relating to engineering practice, during the remaining time of the allotted four years. This is especially apparent in those colleges where the faculties are ambitious to see their graduates take an *immediate* place of considerable responsibility in the world. This is a fault that destroys much of the ultimate advantage which the students may derive from their engineering course. It is a fault, also, which casts just suspicion on engineering education alike in conservative academic circles and in well-informed industrial circles.

A resort to mainly descriptive courses of instruction during the latter portion of the students' life in college largely neutralizes the advantage flowing from the instruction in the fundamentals heretofore described. The students are yet to be taught many things relating to engineering life. They must learn something regarding the forms and formalities relating to the affairs of business life. They must learn the characteristics and uses of materials, their correct application to the building of actual structures, the meaning of kinematics and the processes of designing and using real machinery. They must also learn to reason regarding the special principles of hydraulics and thermodynamics, and the way in which they enter into the design, construction and operation of machines, and the manner in which they modify the usefulness of machines and the efficiencies of numerous industrial operations. Again, they must learn to reason clearly and rationally in regard to the specific principles relating to applied electricity, including its widely diverse factors, and the way in which these principles enter into every-day practise. And they should learn something of the history of the development of engineering and of the lives of its great men, for the stirring of proper ambitions.

The electrical engineering department should be divided into not less than four subdivisions, comprising respectively: Applied electromagnetism, which includes the principles relating to electromagnetic machinery and apparatus; the theory and practice of alternating and variable currents, which include the principles relating to all those numerous phenomena which accompany variable current flow; applied electrochemistry and electrometallurgy; and electrical installations, which includes the applications in engineering practice of the numerous principles to the design, construction, operation and testing of complete installations and the component parts thereof.

The teaching force of the department should afford a competent expert engineer for the head of each of these subdivisions, and such additional well-trained force as may be necessary to adequately carry on class-room and laboratory instruction for the particular numbers of undergraduate and advanced students which attend the college. The head of such a department should spend much of his time in supervising the teaching in class-room and laboratory which is performed by his various subordinates.

But through all of this professional instruction of the latter part of the course, it is still *principles, principles, principles,* and rational methods of reasoning which must be taught, if full justice is done the students, until each student becomes a man of open mind, keen observation, analytical thinking and accurate powers of inference. This instruction should be kept close to the tenets of good practise, and the senses of the student should be constantly stimulated by illustrations and problems drawn from practice. The drill in reasoning can undoubtedly be best gained through rational instruction in the useful applications of scientific principles and laws; and no criticism can be justly passed even by the most conservative educational circles because the graduate is enabled to earn his living as a result of this training; but the purely descriptive should ordinarily be avoided except in a few cases where it has a specific function in improving the understanding of an application of principles or is adopted as a desirable auxiliary to stimulate the sustained interest of the students and thus add vitality to the teaching. Indeed, except for the purposes here defined, the introduction of the purely descriptive into the electrical engineering course wastes the students' time and injures their training, thus abridging their prospects of ultimate breadth and power.

The typical courses in electrical engineering which are to-day advertised in college catalogues belong to three classes or combinations thereof. Only the third of these may be acknowledged to fairly meet the proper ideals in such a course. It is to be remembered that I speak of professional engineering. No one possesses a fuller sympathy with the ideals of schools for training men for the mechanical trades short of engineering and bordering thereon, but these schools are not considered in my present discussion.

First, are courses in which predominate the old time instruction in physics with far more to do with the illustration of the beauties of nature than with the great underlying natural laws. The teaching of mathematics, mechanics and like ground-work studies is not ordinarily well supervised in colleges that maintain such courses in electrical engineering, because the administrative authorities are out of touch with the industrial world and mistakenly put the superficial and spectacular in science into the place of that sound instruction only through which an engineering course may be rightly maintained. It is needless to add that the average graduate from courses of this type is ordinarily of less value in engineering than the average graduate from an old-time classical course where at least thoroughness is a requirement; and electrical engineering courses of this type are rapidly disappearing through a merging into one of the following types.

Second, are courses in which the ground-work studies (English, mathematics, chemistry, physics, mechanics) are perhaps reasonably well taught through the earlier years, but in which the latter part of the course is diverted to the training of inexperienced students for immediate 'jobs' where the students may find some responsibility and proportionate pay immediately after graduation. These courses do not teach engineering in the sound sense. They are likely to injure the future of promising students by occupying time in teaching them handicrafts in college which they could better learn in the factory or field, or in teaching empirical methods of practise which change almost before they can be put to useful account by the graduates.

The students in these courses frequently gain the impression that the highest type of engineering practise is no more than an advanced artisanship, and that a graduate from the electrical engineering course is the equivalent of a journeyman. The most serious injury flows from this, through the undesirable narrowing of ideals and ambitions. This unfortunate result occurs the more readily because the popular usage of the word engineer makes it denote either an engine driver (a man of purely manual calling) or a man skilled in the principles and professional practice of engineering.

Third, are courses following the ideals which I have herein earlier described. Incompetent students who enter these courses are soon discouraged and drop out. Those whose calling is to artisanship go elsewhere either to a different school or directly to an apprenticeship. Those who complete the course, as a rule, are competent men; but they are not likely to enter immediately into positions of much responsibility, but rather to go into the so-called 'cadet' positions or 'student' positions of great industrial enterprises, for the purpose of gaining that experience in the crafts which may enable them to make the most extended use of their training in principles. Here they gradually 'find themselves' and ultimately reach the influence in the industrial world for which their caliber and training fit them. These men, if properly taught, have clean-cut ambitions and high ideals as well as the ability to think well and do wisely. Their earnings and perhaps their usefulness to their employers, may be not so great for a short interval as those of the men who are taught more of empiricism and artisanship and less of rational science during their college courses, but the advantage soon flows in a strong current towards the scientifically trained.

The men who are responsible for this third type of electrical engineering courses may reasonably cry to be delivered from judgment upon the success of their work, which is based on the average earnings of the graduates during their first year out of college. The medical schools and law schools are judged by the attainments of their graduates reached in a decade or even in a quarter of a century, and this also should be the basis upon which to judge the work of the electrical engineering courses of this third and highest type.

Do not believe for a moment, however, that I would teach all theory and no practise. The earlier parts of this paper prove the contrary. In truth, right theory and the best practise are one, and practise which is out of accord with right theory is mere rule of thumb and can be bettered. The best college course in electrical engineering is the one which so teaches the fundamentals that right theory may be fully grasped, and which constantly illustrates the bearing of theory by examples derived from good practise. The administration of such a course requires thoughtful, clear-headed men, who are acquainted with the principles and right practise of pedagogy as well as trained in the principles and experienced in the practise of engineering.

My discussion of the subject makes it clear that there is a wide variance between the methods of the colleges which support electrical engineering courses. Complete unity is not only impossible but would undoubtedly be undesirable, since scope for individuality is as essential here as in the control of industrial enterprises; but the cause of sound college training for electrical engineers would be advanced by any action which clearly places the true aims of the college courses in electrical engineering before the authorities of all of our colleges which support such courses. And I may add that many of the greatest weaknesses of electrical engineering courses are due to the fact that the executive heads of the colleges or universities do not always understand what engineering truly stands for, and they equally often have no fair conception of the soundness of training that is required for its practise.

DUGALD C. JACKSON.

UNIVERSITY OF WISCONSIN

# VANNEVAR BUSH
## 11 MARCH 1890 – 30 JUNE 1974

*by Abigail Mieko Vargus '97*

Vannevar Bush

Vannevar Bush, born to a minister and his wife in Everett, Massachusetts, in 1890, did not venture far from home for school. He obtained his B.S. and M.S. from nearby Tufts College and worked briefly in industry and as a mathematics instructor before entering MIT in 1915. Never one to settle for a slow pace, Bush completed his doctorate in engineering (jointly awarded by MIT and Harvard University) in 1916 and married shortly thereafter.

Bush's subsequent appointment as an assistant professor of electrical engineering at Tufts College was short-lived. In 1917, with the dawn of American involvement in World War I, Bush oversaw research on submarine detection. After the war's end, Bush was lured to MIT by Dugald C. Jackson, the head of the electrical engineering department. In 1923, Bush was made a full professor of electrical power transmission.

Over the next decade, Bush developed his first differential analyzer—essentially an analog computer that solved differential equations. Although made obsolete by digital computers, the differential analyzer was a significant contribution to the field. Bush's student Claude Shannon, while working on the analyzer, showed how Boolean algebra could be used to design switching circuits, later used in digital computers.

Bush applied his vision and leadership to more than analog computers in the years before World War II. He was acting department head in 1929–30 and later served six years as dean of the School of Engineering. In 1938, he left MIT to serve as president of the Carnegie Institution. His influence here, however, was far from finished.

Bush's position at the Carnegie Institution allowed him access to some of the most powerful people in the United States at that time—including President Franklin D. Roosevelt. President Roosevelt, following Bush's recommendations, created the National Defense Research Council (NDRC) and appointed Bush director in 1940. In 1941, the NDRC became the Office of Scientific Research and Development (OSRD), which Bush headed until 1947. It was here, during World War II, that Bush changed the face of scientific research and governmental policy by bringing government and university minds together.

Bush addressed the symbiosis between the government, the military, and academia in his landmark report "Science: The Endless Frontier"[6] (1945). President Roosevelt had asked Bush to provide recommendations of how to apply what had been learned from the war effort to peacetime, civilian activities, and this report was Bush's response. In "Science: The Endless Frontier," Bush called for publicly funded basic research at universities; international cooperation and the exchange of ideas across international borders, aided by governmental resources; access to higher education (especially in the sciences) for all citizens, based on ability not money; and the improvement of science education, in particular at the high school level.

Bush stated his recommendations in no uncertain terms, emphasizing the need for separation between government funding and direction. "Support of basic research in the public and private colleges, universities, and research institutes must leave the internal control of policy, personnel, and the method and scope of the research to the institutions themselves," he wrote. "This is of the utmost importance."[7]

This paper became the impetus for the creation of the National Science Foundation in 1950. More importantly, it established (along with Bush's wartime efforts in the OSRD) a completely new relationship between the government, the military, and university research centers. The resulting environment made possible countless future technological advancements.

Yet "Science: The Endless Frontier" does not hold an uncontested place as Bush's most important publication. That same year, Bush wrote an article for *The Atlantic Monthly* entitled, "As We May Think," in which he presaged advancements that most considered science fiction—but that nearly sixty years later are commonplace. (Perhaps this should be expected from a man who was fond of saying, "It's earlier than we think.") The most cited of these is the concept of the *memex*, a machine that would record associations by topic of any publication the user read. His concept of tagged associations became the basis for hypertext—an incontrovertible contribution to the creation of the World Wide Web.

Bush also took the opportunity to stress the importance of scientific advancement to modern life. He wrote, "The applications of science have built man a well-supplied house, and are teaching him to live healthily therein. They have enabled him to throw masses of people against one another with cruel weapons. They may yet allow him truly to encompass the great record and to grow in the wisdom of race experience. He may perish in conflict before he learns to wield that record for his true good. Yet, in the application of science to

The December 1945 issue of *Technology Review* ran this picture with the following caption: "The Institute's new differential analyzer, whose operation on war research projects during the past three years was publicly announced last month, is inspected by (left to right): Professor Henry B. Phillis, Head of the Department of Mathematics; Vannevar Bush, '16, inventor of the original differential analyzer, who, while at M.I.T., initiated the work that led to the new machine; Professor Harold L. Hazen, '24, Head of the Department of Electrical Engineering; and Professor Samuel H. Caldwell, '25, director of the Center of Analysis in the Department of Electrical Engineering."

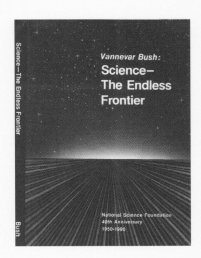

"Science-The Endless Frontier," by Vannevar Bush, as reprinted by the National Science Foundation

the needs and desires of man, it would seem to be a singularly unfortunate stage at which to terminate the process, or to lose hope as to the outcome."[8]

Bush continued to make his imprint on the world of science policy as Carnegie Institution president until 1955, when he returned to teach at MIT. In that time, he had been awarded the Research Corporation award from Columbia University; the Ballou Medal from Tufts College; the Holley Medal of the American Society of Mechanical Engineers (ASME); the Gold Medal of the National Institute of Social Sciences for distinguished service to humanity; the Roosevelt Memorial Association's Distinguished Service Medal; the Marcellus Hartley Public Welfare Medal of the National Academy of Sciences; the Washington Award from the Western Society of Engineers; the Distinguished Service Medal of Tufts University; the Hoover Medal for 1946 by the American Institute of Engineers, American Society of Civil Engineers, American Institute of Mining and Metallurgical Engineers, and ASME; the Medal of Merit with bronze oak leaf cluster and the Medal of the Industrial Research Institute, Inc., presented by President Truman at the White House; as well as being dubbed a knight commander of the civilian division of the Most Excellent Order of the British Empire. He had served on and chaired numerous government committees and several industry boards.

His service to MIT and the world at large was not over, however. He served as president of the MIT Corporation from 1957 to 1959, and as honorary chairman from 1959 to 1971. In 1964, he again went to Lyndon B. Johnson's White House to receive the National Medal of Science. Ten years later, on June 30, 1974, Bush passed away.

# The Differential Analyzer: A New Machine for Solving Differential Equations

VANNEVAR BUSH

JOURNAL OF THE FRANKLIN INSTITUTE

212, NO. 4 (OCTOBER 1931): 447–488.

*Introduced and excerpted by J. Francis Reintjes*

Vannevar Bush (1890–1974) was a faculty member in our department from 1916 to 1932. He also served the Institute as vice president and dean of engineering, and as a life member and honorary chairman of MIT's corporation. (See Vannevar Bush profile, pages 32–34.) Bush's pioneering research in machine computation turned out to be an early milestone in the evolution of mechanical analog, electronic analog, and digital computers. His interest in machine computation was sparked by problems he encountered in his study of operational calculus and electric-power systems. His first machine, the Product Integraph, employed only a single integrator and could, therefore, solve only first-order differential equations, but the Product Integraph was followed by several more complex machines that were capable of handling high-order differential equations with constant or variable coefficients. Collectively, these machines were known as *differential analyzers*.

In 1931, Dr. Bush published "The Differential Analyzer: A New Machine for Solving Differential Equations," which described his most advanced mechanical compu-

J. Francis Reintjes

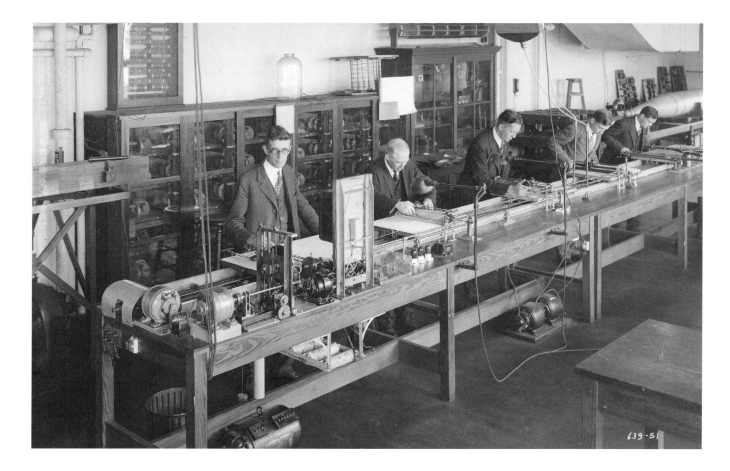

An early computing integraph; left to right:

V. Bush, W. Kershaw, F. Kear, H. Hazen, and

M. Gardner

tational system. Excerpts from this important paper, along with interpretive comments, are presented below.

This paper will describe a new machine for the solution of ordinary differential equations recently placed in service at the Massachusetts Institute of Technology. First, there will be outlined some of the objectives in view, and the general philosophy underlying the development of this type of analyzing device. Various serious mechanical problems have of necessity been met in the effort to produce a machine which is versatile and accurate, and the means by which these have been attacked will be treated. The general method of placing an equation on the machine will be presented and illustrated. Finally, a brief discussion will be given of a method of successive approximations for obtaining solutions of high accuracy, a method for avoiding difficulties due to singularities in coefficients, and a treatment of the problem of obtaining critical values of a parameter in an equation.

The handling of the processes of arithmetic by mechanical computation has recently revolutionized business accounting methods. The use in mechanical analysis of more advanced mathematical processes will ultimately be of comparable importance in scientific research and its applications in engineering. This idea is far from original, for Leibnitz envisaged it comprehensively over two hundred years ago. The far-reaching project of utilizing complex mechanical interrelationships as substitutes for intricate processes of reasoning owes its inception to an inventor of the calculus itself. Leibnitz lived in an age when any comprehensive realization of his plan was prevented by lack of the devices and technique by which we are now surrounded. However, the status of physics and engineering at the present time is peculiarly favorable to a development of this sort.

In the Department of Electrical Engineering of the Massachusetts Institute of Technology the development has followed three lines. First is the process of solving complicated simultaneous algebraic equations as they occur for example in the treatment of modern power networks, by means of alternating-current measurements made on an electrical replica of the power system. The flexible congeries of coils, resistances, and condensers by which this is accomplished is called a network analyzer. Second is the attack on the integral with a variable parameter by an optical method first suggested by Wiener. This gives an approach to the integral equation and to certain processes of statistical analysis. The device itself is called a photoelectric integraph. The third deals with the ordinary differential equation, and provides solutions in the form of plotted curves for specified boundary conditions. The machine treated in this present paper is the latest step along this third line. It is called a differential analyzer.

The present device incorporates the same basic idea of interconnection of integrating units. Use of torque amplifiers has rendered the integrating units capable of carrying a considerable load. A very flexible system of "bus" shafts has been provided by means of which these units can be interconnected or "back coupled" at will. Large size has been preserved in order to obtain accuracy of plotting of the variable coefficients and of the result. Various auxiliary units, such as multipliers, have been provided. The aim has been to produce extreme flexibility, sufficient ruggedness, and reasonable precision. A precision of one part in one thousand under ordinary conditions of use has been arrived at in individual units, with the intention of achieving a somewhat less overall precision except in extraordinary circumstances. The arrangement is still based on the use of integrators because of their inherent average precision.

The machine as constructed is intended for the solution of ordinary differential equations of any order up to the sixth, and with any amount of complexity within reason. The frequency with which problems are encountered involving two or three simultaneous second-order equations made this range desirable, although it could readily be extended. It is readily possible, when plots have been made and a schematic diagram giving scales and connections prepared, to set up the machine for a given problem in a few hours. The time necessary for solutions varies with the complexity of the problem and the precision desired, and in representative cases is about ten minutes for each solution corresponding to a given set of boundary conditions. Experience is necessary, of course, in order to use the device effectively. This is actually one of the most attractive aspects of the machine; one acquires an entirely new appreciation of the innate nature of a differential equation as that experience is gained.

A photograph of the machine is shown in Fig. 1, and a schematic diagram of the layout in Fig. 2. It will be noted that there are provided eighteen longitudinal or bus shafts, and that these can be readily uncoupled at many points. Along the sides of the device are ranged the main units: the integrators, input tables, multipliers and output table, each connected to cross shafts.

FIG. 1

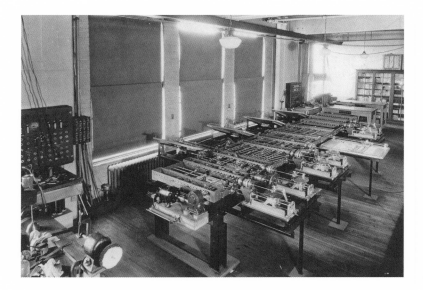

The differential analyzer.

FIG. 2

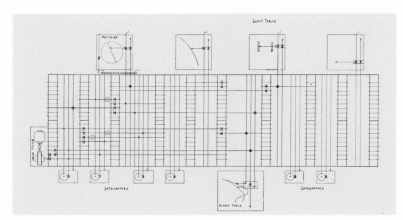

Schematic diagram of the analyzer.

An integrator, Fig. 3, may be considered as a unit with three shafts, the angular movements of which are u, v, and w, so connected that at all instants $u = K\ wdv$. There are six integrating units in the present machine, which form the central feature of the device. Their design constituted a major problem in the development. The task of making a satisfactory integrating unit is that of building a variable-speed drive capable of substantial mechanical power output, accurate in ratio at all speeds and loads, and with this ratio accurately adjustable. Meeting these requirements resulted in a compact rigid mechanical construction, with the backlash in the drives carefully removed, and with a high-ratio torque amplifier added to relieve the friction drive from the necessity of supplying more than a minute torque.

A complete integrating unit is shown in Fig. 3. A massive carriage is moved horizontally on ways by means of an accurate lead screw. This carries a disc in a horizontal plane which can be revolved, independently of the carriage position, by means of splined shafts. Resting on this disc, and pivoted in accurate bearings, is a wheel or roller with its axis parallel to the ways and lying in a vertical plane through the center of the disc. Disc and roller are of hardened steel, ground and lapped. The edge of the roller is given a radius of about 0.002 inch. The outer bearing of the roller shaft is carried by a hinged carriage from the base. This bearing is jewelled and is located directly over the point of contact. End play in roller-shaft and carriage pivots is removable by fine screw adjustment. There are also provided adjustments by which the roller shaft can be brought accurately to its correct position.

Fig. 3

An integrator.

Backlash in the lead-screw drive is almost completely removed by using two nuts on the screw, with spring-backed wedges between them forcing the nuts apart, the wedge supports being rigidly fastened to the carriage. By proper choice of the wedge angle this scheme gives a positive drive in either direction, while allowing the slight irregularities of the screw to be taken up without binding. This device, called a "lashlock," was developed by Mr. C. W. Nieman of the Bethlehem Steel Corporation, and as it has been described elsewhere, will not be discussed in detail here.

As one might expect, minimizing backlash posed a serious challenge in the design of the differential analyzer. Dr. Bush returns to the subject in a later section of the paper to describe a special unit called a "frontlash" that was developed to compensate for backlash. The frontlash unit can be inserted, as needed, to reduce backlash at the point of insertion to a second-order effect.

An input table, Fig. 4, has two shafts with revolutions $p$ and $q$, one of which moves a pointer horizontally in the direction of abscissas and the other vertically in the direction of ordinates across a plot of a function. One shaft is controlled manually to keep the pointer on the plot, thus giving at all times $p = f(q)$. A multiplier is obtained by using an attachment on an input table. There are then three shafts, and the revolutions or total angle turned through by one is, at any instant, equal to the product of the revolutions of the other two.

FIG. 4

An input table.

An output table, Fig. 5, has three shafts, one of which moves a carriage horizontally, and the other two of which move recording pencils carried by this carriage vertically over the recording paper. Thus two quantities may be simultaneously recorded as a function of any chosen variable. Any cross shaft can be readily connected to any bus shaft by inserting a spiral gear box between them, and one will then drive the other. Right- and left-hand boxes are supplied in order to secure correctly related directions of rotation. One bus shaft, assigned permanently to the independent variable, is driven by a variable-speed motor. There are provided also sets of spur gears which can be connected between adjacent shafts so that one will drive the other with a chosen ratio of speed, and differential gears or "adders" which can be connected to three shafts so that the revolutions of one will be the sum of the revolutions of the other two. These last units are inserted as needed in the body of the table.

FIG. 5

An output table.

Thus far, Dr. Bush has described the general features of his differential analyzer. In the next section of his paper he discusses procedures for setting up a problem on the machine. He begins with a simple second-order differential equation with constant coefficients, and then explains how the procedure is modified when the zero-order term is a function of the independent variable. Next he points out that it is prudent to express problems in a form that best suits the capabilities of the machine, and uses the Legendre equation

$$(x^2 - 1)\frac{d^2y}{dx^2} + 2x\frac{dy}{dx} - \lambda x = 0$$

to illustrate his point. His paper concludes as follows:

As a final topic there will be treated a method of successive approximations which is applicable when an accuracy is necessary which is beyond the direct precision of the machine. It is expected that this will be especially expedient when using the machine to tabulate functions which can be defined by means of linear differential equations. The efficacy of the procedure depends upon the fact that complication of the formal expressions which appear as coefficients in an equation does not then render the machine solution appreciably more laborious or less precise. The tactics employed are as follows: A first set of solutions is made as accurately as the precision of the machine will allow. Each of these graphical solutions is closely fitted by use of a formal expression which can be easily computed, and with a sufficient number of readily computed derivatives. Then a new equation is set up and solved to give the difference between the functions sought and the formal expressions which were adopted. Finally a numerical combination is made of the exact values obtainable from the formal expressions and the graphically determined differences from the second machine solution. The percentage accuracy in evaluating the differences in the second solution will be limited by machine precision in the usual way, but a small error in these small differences will make only a second-order error in the final result.

Thus suppose we have made a first solution which is accurate within a few tenths of a per cent, and that we have fitted formally so that the maximum departure between these solutions and the formal expressions is about one per cent. The values attained by the dependent variable in the second solution will be only about one per cent of those appearing in the first solution; but by proper choice of scales approximately the full range of plots and units will be utilized in this second equation as well as in the first. We can then expect to evaluate the differences from the second solution to within a few tenths of a per cent. While the situation will be altered in accordance with the nature of the problem it may be then expected that about four-figure accuracy can be obtained from the double solution. Of course the process may be continued another step if necessary.

The machine is not yet completed; in fact it is questionable whether it will ever be complete, for it can always be extended by the addition of units to cover greater order or complexity of equations. It is capable at the present time, however, of handling a wide range of problems of extreme interest.

It has been thoroughly tested for precision. Its speed has been investigated in connection with a problem in which about 100 solutions of a moderately complex second-order equation were evaluated in five days' work. The procedure in locating critical values of a parameter has been somewhat explored. No great experience has as yet been had in work involving successive approximations. This machine forms part of a departmental program of development. It is a pleasure to recall the effective and enthusiastic support of many of the staff. Prof. H. L. Hazen, who has been associated with me practically throughout the entire development, has consistently contributed in this latest work. Professor M. F. Gardner, and later Mr. S. H. Caldwell have been in direct charge of the laboratory where the work has been in progress, and have greatly helped. I also appreciate the able work of Mr. L. E. Frost, designing draftsman, and Mr. Maurice Forbes, expert machinist.

# Theory of Servo-Mechanisms

HAROLD L. HAZEN

8 AUGUST 1901–2 FEBRUARY 1980

JOURNAL OF THE FRANKLIN

INSTITUTE 218, NO. 3 (SEPTEMBER

1934)

*Introduced and excerpted by Paul E. Gray*

Harold Locke Hazen was born in Philo, Illinois, in 1901 and grew up in Three Rivers, Michigan. He entered MIT in 1920 and earned an S.B. in electrical engineering in 1924. His thesis, completed under the supervision of Vannevar Bush, developed a model of an electric power system and employed static phase-shifting transformers, which Hazen and his classmate Hugh Spencer hand-wound on 0.5-horsepower induction motor frames obtained at the General Electric plant in Lynn, Massachusetts, where they were working on the Course VI-A cooperative program. This work yielded a paper, "Artificial Representation of Power Systems," by Hazen and Spencer in the transactions of the AIEE.[9]

President Paul Gray in Killian Court

Following graduation, Hazen went to work for GE in Schenectady, New York, on the "Test Program," which was intended to give new engineers wide experience in the company. In Hazen's case this objective was not achieved. Hazen and Spencer were assigned to work with Dr. Robert E. Doherty, chief consulting engineer for General Electric, who was concerned at the time about interconnected electric power network stability because the company was planning to bid on a 500-mile transmission line to bring hydroelectric power from Canada to New England and the New York area. Interested in the relevance of Hazen's thesis work, Dr. Doherty sent him back to Cambridge to resurrect the experimental equipment he and Spencer had used in their thesis work, and Dr. Doherty arranged to have Vannevar Bush consult on the problem.

Hazen's experiences with Dr. Doherty stimulated him to pursue further education. In 1925 he became a graduate student and research assistant to Dr. Bush. This marked the beginning of his lifetime association with the Institute, which continued through his 1929 S.M. degree, the award of a Sc.D. and his appointment as assistant professor in 1931, his years as head of the electrical engineering department (1938–52), dean of the Graduate School (1952–67), and foreign study advisor (1967 until his retirement in 1972).

Harold Hazen (right) with "Doc" Edgerton and Katherine Hazen

Hazen greatly admired Bush, and their close collaboration continued for many years. He designed and supervised the construction of the Bush-Hazen Integraph, the first analog computer, which could solve second-order nonlinear differential equations. This machine was a critical component of the six-integrator differential analyzer, and the MIT electric power network analyzer, both of which he designed and built with Bush. When I arrived at the Institute in 1950, the network analyzer occupied nearly all the space around Huntington Hall (10-250) on the second floor of the Maclaurin building.

Hazen's work with these simulators, particularly with output devices capable of following a rapidly changing electrical signal, led him to study the properties of servomechanisms. One of his students and research assistants in this work was Gordon S. Brown, who arrived in 1929 as a transfer student from Australia. At Hazen's memorial service on February 25, 1980, Brown described their relationship:

*I was admitted to a group of selected second-term students for whom Harold was counselor, tutor, big brother, and friend. Here, by his example, he led me to see MIT as it really is. Namely, a place where good companionship and good conversation abound, and where professors will meet every student more than halfway in developing bonds of mutual understanding and support.... [H]e passed to me the opportunity to exploit all that he had created in the field of servomechanisms and control.*

Not only did Brown become the founding director of the MIT Servomechanisms Laboratory in 1940, which made great contributions to the national defense in World War II, but in 1952 he became Hazen's successor as head of the department.

By 1934, servomechanisms—which today are called *feedback control systems*—were employed in several applications: ship steering, stabilization of ships by gyroscopes, and gyro-compass repeaters. Hazen's paper on the theory of servomechanisms was the first general analysis of a feedback control system. It is interesting to me that in the paper, Hazen never refers to the concept of negative feedback per se. A few years were to pass before the term *negative feedback control systems* was commonly used; they were to become extraordinarily important in World War II in gun-direction control and in aircraft automatic pilots. Annotated excerpts are presented below.

Hazen provides a tutorial in his introduction to the paper:

A light-sensitive servomechanism, developed by Harold Hazen at MIT; photographed in September, 1933

As stated before, a servo-mechanism is a power-amplifying device. However, its action differs in one essential particular from that of a simple vacuum-tube amplifier or mechanical power amplifier. Such an amplifier preserves approximately a given functional relation, usually linear, between input and output quantities, due to the properties of the amplifier itself. Thus in a good vacuum-tube amplifier, the current output is very closely proportional to the voltage applied to the grid of the first tube. This linearity of response is due to the constancy of the parameters within the amplifier. Any departure from constancy of these parameters affects the relation between the input and output directly.

The servo-mechanism differs from the simple amplifier in that the responsibility for the functional relation is not placed directly on the amplifying element of the servo. Here it will be necessary to distinguish between the input to the servo-mechanism, which is the indication of the measuring instrument, and the input to the amplifier element in the servo which is something different. The output of the servo amplifier element can be considered as the output of the servo, however. In a servo-mechanism the input to the servo amplifier element is connected to the *difference* between the servo input and output. When this difference is finite the servo output is driven in such manner as to tend to make this difference zero. Thus the only function of the servo amplifier element is to apply sufficient force to the servo output to bring it rapidly to correspondence with the servo input. Such an amplifier element can be a relatively crude affair. In fact it may consist merely of a suitable relay or switch controlling an electric motor. An illustration of this action is furnished by a servo-mechanism used on an early model of a machine used for solving differential equations. The servo input was the angle of a rotating shaft, the output was the angle of another rotating shaft. When the two angles differed, a contact started the electric servo-motor which drove the output shaft in the direction to restore coincidence of the angles.

A servo-mechanism *may thus be defined as a power-amplifying device in which the amplifier element driving the output is actuated by the difference between the input to the servo and its output.*

In the introduction to this paper, Hazen observes that little theory supports the applications of servomechanisms:

Although the subject of servo-mechanisms has been treated in a qualitative or semi-quantitative way...to the writer's knowledge no systematic quantitative treatment of even the simple common types has previously been given. It seems worth while, therefore, in view of the rapidly expanding field of application of servo-mechanisms, to present the beginnings of such a treatment, outlining quantitatively at least a few of the important properties of the familiar types.

Hazen describes the input to the amplifying element that produces the output as "the difference between the servo input and output," and observes that "when this difference is finite the servo output is driven in such a manner as to tend to make this difference zero."

The paper goes on to define three types of servomechanisms.

The first type of servo-mechanism and one that is widely used because of its simplicity, may be called a relay servo, because of the essentially "off" and "on" nature of the forces acting on the output element. Several forms of the gyro-compass repeaters, automatic pilots and gyro-stabilizers for ships use this type of servo. In this type the restoring force applied to the output element is usually substantially constant in magnitude, while operative. Ideally, this force would be brought into operation by an infinitesimal deviation of the output from the input but practically it is usually necessary to have a small range of deviation over which the restoring force is inactive. If the inactive deviation range were infinitesimal, and if there were no time lag in the application of the restoring force, this servo could be made to operate with an infinitesimal amplitude of oscillation, an infinite frequency of oscillation, and an infinitesimal lag error. It is quite evident that such operation represents a limiting case which at best can only be roughly approached with actual physical apparatus. Practically the amplitude and frequency of oscillation are finite, and in most cases lag error is present. The limiting case is of interest however from the point of view of analysis and from its significance as an ideal.

This type of servo has certain disadvantages. The rather sudden application of the entire available driving torque, first in one direction and then in the other is conducive to large wear and tear of the entire mechanism. In practice the restoring force is usually initiated by electric contacts which may be somewhat troublesome especially when only very small forces are available for their operation. This type of servo has the asset of simplicity, however, and may be useful where static friction in the mechanism is troublesome, and a relatively crude type of control suffices.

The second type of servo-mechanism is one in which the correction of the output is made in finite steps at definite time intervals. This type is extensively used in recording instruments and controllers for quantities that vary relatively slowly. It is well illustrated by a temperature recorder in which the position of the pen is periodically tested to ascertain whether or not it corresponds to the indicated temperature. If in error, the pen position is given a small finite change in the correct direction and a short time later its position is again tested, and so on. In this scheme, the magnitude of the step correction is usually made approximately proportional to the deviation between output and input. When properly designed and adjusted this type of servo is non-oscillatory. The necessary conditions for non-oscillation are: first, that any correction and the indication of it shall be substantially completed before a new test is made; second, that the correction applied shall not be greater than that required to reduce the deviation approximately to zero; and third, that the inactive range over which the output can vary without causing a correction to be made shall be at least as large as the smallest possible correction step.

A modification of this type is used in an automatic steering gear suitable for small craft. The rudder, which is the output of the servo, is periodically displaced from mid position an amount approximately proportional to the error in the ship's heading, and then allowed to trail back to mid position before the heading is again tested and another temporary displacement is given to the rudder.

Evidently the finite-step or impulse type of servo-mechanism can be non-oscillatory. However it does have a persistent lag error when the input is so varying that corrections must be applied continually in one direction. It is also inherently somewhat slower than the other types of servos, since in order to be non-oscillatory, the driving force can be effective during only a fraction of the cycle of operation.

The third type of servo considered here is one in which the restoring force, acting continuously on the output element, is approximately proportional to the deviation of the output.

This type is rapidly coming into use and is now employed in a number of devices such as certain gyro-compass followers, and various automatic recorders. By the use of suitable damping, its action can be rendered aperiodic or oscillatory to any desired degree. Where a high speed of response, high sensitivity, and freedom from hunting are desired this type undoubtedly has the greatest possibilities of the three. Small deviations call into play only small restoring forces, hence its operation lacks the somewhat violent nature characteristic of relay servos. Moreover, these small forces can be called into play promptly and large deviations are thereby avoided. This type can be built to have very rapid response.

Hazen goes on to analyze the behavior of "the relay servos"—one in which the output element operates in a bidirectional on–off manner. He addresses this nonlinear problem by calculating the behavior of the output under conditions of both viscous and Coulomb friction, and with and without lag in the response by ingeniously piecing together the response in the linear regions of the operation. The analysis considers both constant-value inputs and constant-rate inputs.

Following a careful discussion of the behavior of the "definite-connection servomechanism," he takes up the important case of the "continuous control servomechanism." In this case he analyzes a linear model of the system using Heaviside operational calculus, under conditions in which the error signal is dependent on the output and on its first and second time derivatives for a constant velocity input.

This analysis yields results that display the time behavior of the error signal for criti-

cally damped and underdamped conditions. Hazen notes that too much use of the

second derivative of the error signal causes unstable behavior of the system.

Hazen summarizes his paper in this manner:

> In this paper the performance of three important types of servo-mechanisms has been analyzed. These types include the relay servo, the definite-correction servo, and the continuous-control servo.
>
> The first or relay servo type is always oscillatory in response to a varying input but under certain conditions the amplitude of oscillation and lag error can be made small. If unidirectional motion occurs, the presence of Coulomb friction alone will not damp out an initial amplitude of oscillation. Time lag in the application of the restoring forces tends to increase the amplitude of oscillation.
>
> The second or definite-correction type is aperiodic in operation when properly adjusted and is quite suitable for use with slowly varying quantities. There is a slight lag error.
>
> The third or continuous-control type is probably the best type where high-speed response and smoothness of control are required. This type can be made to have a response which is aperiodic or oscillatory with any given decrement, by suitable design and adjustment. By using the first and second derivatives of the deviation of the output from the input, as well as the deviation itself, to control the restoring force applied to the output, a very high rate of response and a very small steady-state deviation should be attainable. This type of servo has the advantage of being susceptible to rather easy and complete analysis. Tests on a high-speed or response servo of this type with deviation control alone show an excellent check with the theory. The design and test of this unusually fast servo are given in a companion paper.

The companion paper, "Design and Test of a High-Performance Servo-Mechanism,"

was published in the *Journal of the Franklin Institute* 218, no. 5 (November 1934).

For this work, Hazen was awarded the 1935 Levy Gold Medal of the Franklin Insti-

tute, an award that I suspect was based on consideration of both papers.

# Transmission of Electromagnetic Waves in Hollow Tubes of Metal

WILMER L. BARROW

25 OCTOBER 1903–29 AUGUST 1975

PROCEEDINGS OF THE INSTITUTE OF RADIO ENGINEERS **24** (OCTOBER 1936): 1298–1328

*By Paul E. Gray*

Wilmer Barrow was born in Baton Rouge, Louisiana, in 1903 and earned his B.S.E.E. degree at Louisiana State University in 1926. In 1927 he enrolled in this department and in 1929 he was awarded an S.M. Following study under J. Zenneck and A. Sommerfeld at the Eidgenossische Technische Hochschule in Zurich, and there as holder of the prestigious Redfield Proctor Fellowship, he earned his Sc.D. in 1931.

Barrow returned to MIT as an instructor in electrical engineering in 1931 and commenced work in the Communications Division on high-frequency antennas under the supervision of Professors Edward L. Bowles and Julius A. Stratton. Much of his research was performed at the MIT field station at Round Hill, South Dartmouth, Massachusetts.

President Paul Gray directs traffic as the staff returns to MIT after the blizzard of 1978.

"A simple and efficient apparatus for producing a beam of ultra-high frequency radio waves has been developed by Dr. Wilmer L. Barrow. This electro-magnetic horn 'antenna' is expected to be useful in micro-ray communication over a narrow pencil-like beam at wavelengths only a few inches long. Other applications may be in airplane and ship navigation. Dr. Barrow is shown adjusting the transmitter by which the waves are started from the square hollow tube into the throat of the horn." (News Service, MIT, c. 1941)

His interest in high-frequency radio led to the work reported in this paper, in which he extended the theoretical work of Lord Rayleigh and showed that ultra-high frequency waves could be transmitted through conducting tubes without a central conductor if the wavelength was below a critical value determined by the diameter of the tube. His first experimental verification of the theory employed an abandoned galvanized-iron hot air duct 18 inches in diameter and about 16 feet long. His paper was presented at a meeting of the Institute of Radio Engineers in May 1936. At that meeting he learned that Southworth, Carson, Mead, and Schelkunoff at the Bell Telephone Laboratories had worked along these same lines and had published two papers on hyperfrequency wave guides in the *Bell System Technical Journal* in April of the same year.

In 1936 Barrow was promoted to assistant professor. He supervised the Sc.D. thesis of Lan Jen Chu '38 and numerous S.M. theses. In 1943 he was awarded the Institute of Radio Engineers' Morris Liebmann Memorial Prize "for his theoretical and experimental investigations of ultra-high frequency propagation in waveguides and radiation from horns, and for the application of these principles to engineering practice."

In 1941 Barrow became the first director of the MIT Radar School, which taught the principles of radar to more than 8,800 military officers, enlisted men, and civilians before it closed in early 1946 [see the Radford paper *Technology's Radar School*]. At its peak in late 1944, the Radar School employed a staff of 170, many of whom were from this department. In 1943 Barrow took a leave of absence from MIT and resigned two years later to become chief engineer at the Sperry Gyroscope Company. He retired from Sperry as vice president for research and development in 1970.

In 1966 Barrow was awarded the Edison Medal of the Institute of Electrical and Electronic Engineers—one of the premier honors of the Institute—"for a career of meritorious achievement: innovating, teaching and developing means for transmission of electromagnetic energy at microwave frequencies."

Reproduced below are the summary and introduction of this thirty-page paper.

*Summary* — Electromagnetic energy may be transmitted through the inside of hollow tubes of metal, provided the frequency is greater than a certain critical value; this value is inversely proportional to the tube radius and to the dielectric coefficient for the tube interior. Calculations and measurements of the more important characteristics of this new kind of transmission system have been made, and the conditions for minimum attenuation obtained. Terminal devices for connecting a hollow pipe system to a biconductor system and others, in the form of horns, for directly radiating radio waves, have been *developed; these electromagnetic horns may also be fed with ordinary coaxial lines. Certain types of terminals act as sharply resonant hollow tube elements. Several independent communication channels may be established within a single pipe line by utilizing distinct types of waves for each channel in a unique kind of multiplex operation. A section of a hollow tube may be used as a high-pass filter. Although presupposing adequate technique for the generation and utilization of the shortest radio waves, this new system possesses several features, among which are a minimum dielectric loss, substantially perfect shielding, and a simplicity of structure.*

### INTRODUCTION

THIS paper deals with the transmission of electromagnetic energy at high frequency through the inside of hollow tubes of metal. Although single conductor and multiple conductor transmission circuits of wire, cable, and concentric tube form have been employed for guiding radio-frequency energy from one point to another, the interior of a hollow conducting cylinder does not appear to have been previously suggested or used in this capacity.

The literature is singularly sparse on the subject of waves within conducting cylinders. Heaviside, Thompson, and Rayleigh gave brief discussion of limited aspects of the problem. Indeed, Heaviside indicated at one point that waves could not be sent through a uniform tube without a second center conductor. Rayleigh's paper (1897), although confined to perfectly conducting tubes, differentiates between the various possible types of waves and obtains the critical frequencies below which they cannot exist. Although somewhat related, the work of Hondros and Debye, of Zahn, and of Schriever on waves on dielectric wires applies to a different physical situation. The recent paper by Schelkunoff is confined to problems associated with coaxial conductors. The hollow conducting cylinder, apparently lost sight of since Rayleigh's original paper, reappeared in the literature in a paper by Bergmann and Kruegel (1934), who measured both the field inside a short hollow metal cylinder and the radiation from its open end when a half-wave coaxial antenna was properly excited; the use of hollow pipes for the conduction of ultra-high-frequency energy was not suggested. The transmission characteristics and the attenuation in finitely conducting pipes as well as means for exciting and for receiving the waves at the ends have not been previously discussed.

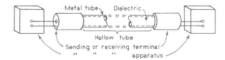

Fig. 1—Elements of a hollow tube transmission system.

A hollow tube transmission system (see Fig. 1) would comprise

(1) A single metal conductor in the form of a tube or pipe having appropriate dimensions relative to the frequency of the excitation and having its interior filled with dielectric material in gaseous, liquid, or solid form, or evacuated, connecting the sending and the receiving points:

(2) A terminal device at each end of the tube for connecting the uniconductor hollow tube proper to the biconductor sending and receiving apparatus for supplying modulated high-frequency energy at one or both ends and for receiving and demodulating the energy transmitted to the opposite end: or

(3) One terminal device as in (2) at one end and a device at the other end for radiating the transmitted energy into the atmosphere directly.

The transmission circuit is formed by the dielectric material or vacuum filling the tube interior and the inner surface of the conducting tube. The tube acts not only as the conductor for the transmission system but also as a highly effective shield against interference, because, at the high frequencies to be used, the skin effect confines the circuit substantially to the interior of the tube. Operation with currents whose free-space wave length is much less than one meter is necessary if the tube size is to remain reasonably small. Hence, the commercial use of hollow tube systems, which presumes adequate technique for generation, amplification, etc., of the shortest radio waves, will probably not be an immediate development. Nevertheless, this type of high-frequency circuit possesses several desirable features, such as the following: a minimum of dielectric loss, substantially perfect shielding, presumable low cost of construction and installation, and possibility of rugged mechanical design. It would seem that a hollow tube might be the ideal "conductor" for waves of several centimeters length and less, as naturally suited to this region of the spectrum as a pair of copper wires is to the lower frequency region. In view of the rapid development at this time of ultra-high-frequency technique for telephone, telegraph, and television purposes, an investigation of the possibilities and limitations of the hollow tube transmission system is of immediate interest. This paper presents some of the results of a theoretical and experimental study carried on by the author for some years. The electromagnetic and the circuit characteristics of the hollow tube proper are first presented; this part of the system may be analyzed rigorously because of its simple geometrical configuration. Terminal devices are then discussed qualitatively; this part of the system has not yielded to mathematical analysis. Finally, the results of an experimental investigation are presented in which the major aspects of the theory are substantiated.

# ERNST A. GUILLEMIN
## 8 MAY 1898 – 6 APRIL 1970

*by Robert M. Fano*

*Ernst A. Guillemin is dead. He died on Monday, April 6 [1970]. Though grown men are not supposed to cry, many will. "After all," I was told emotionally by a circuit theorist who was born and educated in Europe and who had never met Professor Guillemin, "he was the father of us all."*[10]

Professor Robert M. Fano, 1971

So began the eulogy written by Louis Weinberg, one of Ernst Guillemin's many students. Ernie, as he was called by his friends and colleagues, was born on May 8, 1898, in Milwaukee, Wisconsin. He received his B.S. in electrical engineering from the University of Wisconsin in 1922, and he came to MIT as a teaching assistant and graduate student the same fall. After receiving his S.M. in 1924, he went to the University of Munich, Germany, on a Saltonstall Traveling Fellowship; there he became a student of the famous theoretical physicist Arnold Sommerfeld.

On receiving his doctorate in physics in 1926, Ernie returned to MIT as an instructor and member of the faculty. Edward L. Bowles, in his eulogy,[11] remarked that Dugald Jackson, who was the department head at the time, received a letter from Professor Sommerfeld, thanking him for having sent to Munich a man of Ernie's caliber. It is clear to me that Arnold Sommerfeld had a great influence on Ernie; as one of Ernie's students, I feel very much at home reading Sommerfeld's textbooks on theoretical physics.

Ernie was promoted to assistant professor in 1928, but his teaching assignments remained in the electric power area. In the spring of 1929, Bowles, who was in charge of the program on communications engineering, asked Ernie to teach a course on electric filters, which were becoming important components of telephone systems. It was just the right time to enter the fast-developing field of network theory; Ernie saw the opportunity and dove into it with his legendary energy. His first textbook, *Communication Networks, Vol. 1: Classical Theory of Lumped Constant Networks*, was published just two years later, in 1931. It was followed in 1935 by *Communication Networks, Vol. 2: Classical Theory of Long Lines, Filters, and Related Networks*. These two textbooks constitute the first attempt to integrate and present in a coherent manner the contributions of pioneers such as Hendrik Bode, George Campbell, Ronald Foster, Wilhelm Cauer, and Otto Brune.

Ernie was also a major contributor to the curriculum revision of the late 1930s, documented in the "blue books" (see The "Blue Books" Series); he was probably the primary, if unacknowledged, author of *Electric Circuits*,[12] published in 1940, the only book in the series published before World War II. The preparation by Ernie of the reference book *Mathematics of Circuit Analysis*, first announced in 1943, was delayed by the war; the manuscript was completed after the war and published in 1949. Ernie was promoted to associate professor in 1936, a tenured appointment at that time.

Ernie taught throughout World War II and served as a consultant to the MIT Radiation Laboratory. As a consultant, he designed the Guillemin line, a network intended to pulse magnetrons in a way that would produce the rectangular pulses required by radar applications. This was an important development because it provided the theoretical basis for designing networks that could produce pulses of arbitrary shapes. Ernie's account of his design procedure appears in Report # 43 of the Radiation Laboratory[13] and is discussed in Volume 5 of the Radiation Laboratory series.[14]

I returned to MIT in September 1941 as a teaching assistant and graduate student. I had completed my S.B. in the power option the previous February but by the summer my interests had turned to communications engineering. Ernie, whom I had not met as an undergraduate, was clearly the dominant figure in the communications division of the EE department, in spite of the fact that he was not yet a full professor; he was promoted to that rank three years later, in 1944. I attended his classes on network theory and marveled at his lecturing style. I thoroughly enjoyed his classes because they gave me the opportunity to watch a brilliant mind at work. His blackboard technique was superb; his equations were clearly written and his diagrams and curves perfectly drawn.

Ernie was a master of thoughtful approximations that highlighted the important characteristics of expressions by eliminating inconsequential details. While well versed in the mathematics of network theory, he was happily oblivious of mathematical fine points that were irrelevant to the concepts he was trying to convey or the network properties he was describing. It was clear at all times that he was teaching network theory, not mathematics; this was more of Sommerfeld's influence on Ernie. After one class I went to his office to ask about something he'd said that did not seem to be right in certain unusual situations. He replied, "You are correct, of course; I did not point that out in class because most students would not have understood and the others would have asked me later as you did." Lesson from Ernie: do not feed students details that they are not ready to digest.

The communications teaching staff thinned out pretty fast in 1942 as faculty members and teaching assistants left to support the war effort in various capacities. The teaching load, however, did not decrease because drafted students were sent back in Navy and Army uniforms. The result was that the remaining teaching staff had to do double duty, and lowly teaching assistants like me received unusual teaching assignments.

Early in 1942, Ernie called me to his office and said, "How would you like to take responsibility for the two graduate subjects on microwaves and antennas, starting next term?" I replied that I was interested in that subject but I knew hardly anything about it. Ernie continued, "Way back in 1929, Professor Bowles called me to his office and asked me to teach a new subject on filters, starting the very next term. My reply was similar to yours, but he insisted, and that was the beginning of my career in network theory." A more colorful account of the 1929 encounter is given by Professor Weinberg: "When Ed Bowles took me by the scruff of the neck and told me to teach filters, I didn't know the difference between a filter and a hole in the ground. Well…I learned the difference between a filter and a hole in the ground." Similarly, I learned about microwaves and antennas…a couple of weeks ahead of my students. While I did not make a career in that field, I am still grateful to Ernie for giving me the opportunity and the courage to find out that I, too, could do it.

Professor Ernst A. Guillemin

Ernie supervised my doctoral research, completed in 1947. I dedicated my thesis to him using Dante's tribute to Virgil: "You are my teacher and my model, you are the one from whom I acquired the fine style…." Indeed, I owed the successful completion of my research not only to the network theory I had learned in his classes but to the research style that I had acquired from him.

The decade of the 1950s was the golden era of network theory and Ernie was the undisputed leader in both undergraduate and graduate education. His role in undergraduate education began in spring 1948 when his MIT colleague, who had been in charge of the undergraduate two-term sequence on circuit theory, asked to be relieved of that assignment. I heard that news first and immediately went to see Ernie. I told him that, in my view, it was very important he be given charge of the two-term sequence. He thought about it briefly, then jumped up from his chair and started walking in high gear toward the office of the head of the EE department, with me in tow. When he got there, he just demanded the assignment. Harold Hazen, who had been department head since 1938, did not say no but did not say yes either. He knew very well that Ernie would revamp the teaching of circuit theory and was concerned about the effects on the rest of the curriculum. It took several weeks before Hazen officially gave Ernie charge of the two-term sequence on circuit theory.

And exactly as Hazen had anticipated, Ernie changed the teaching of circuit theory. Sophomores learned about zeros, poles, and impulses—sometimes called *kerplunk* functions—all "advanced" concepts that sophomores were not supposed to understand. But they did! According to Ernie, "We refer to things as being 'advanced' only so long as we understand them insufficiently well ourselves to be able to make them clear in simple terms."[15]

Ernie could make things clear in simple terms. He dedicated the textbook *Introductory Circuit Theory*, published in 1953, "To my sophomores, whose enthusiastic cooperation has been the inspiration for this work." One of Ernie's colleagues dubbed the textbook "Guillementary Circuit Theory." It turned out to be a perfect prelude to the five volumes of the "green book" series, published at the end of the decade, which documented the radical revision—often referred to as the "Gordon Brown revolution"—of the rest of the electrical engineering curriculum.

In the aftermath of World War II, the unprecedented support of university research by the federal government enabled many students to continue on to earn advanced degrees. So many of them became interested in network theory that often Ernie had to teach two sections of his two-term graduate sequence. Quite a few students became so enchanted by network theory and Ernie's personality that they did their doctoral theses in that field. "Guillemin's School of Network Theory" acquired national stature as its graduates "Guilleminized" electrical engineering departments around the country. Ernie's opus, *Synthesis of Passive Networks*, was published in 1957 and his last textbook, *Theory of Linear Physical Systems*, was published in 1963, the year he retired.

Ernie was appointed to the Edwin Sibley Webster Chair in 1960, just three years before he reached mandatory retirement age. He was awarded the Medal of Honor of the Institute of Radio Engineers in 1961, and the Education Medal of the American Institute of Electrical Engineers in 1962. Both of these medals are now recorded as having been awarded by the Institute of Electrical and Electronics Engineers, which is the organization that resulted from the merger of these two societies.

Ernie's most obvious legacy is the series of textbooks covering the theory of linear, passive, and bilateral networks, extended in the last textbook to the broader class of linear physical systems. However, of equal importance is Ernie's impact on engineering education, as evidenced by his writing and lecturing style, and in his views on education. The latter are clearly and forcefully expressed in the preface to *Synthesis of Passive Networks*:

*In engineering teaching we cannot overemphasize the importance of having our students grasp the significance and the thrill of acquiring some depth of understanding in a few topics, so that they be aware of the process by which we get to the bottom of things and what we mean by that term. It matters little whether the topic in question promises to be of immediate practical value. The educational value lies in the experience of following a line of reasoning to its logical conclusions; and in the thrill of suddenly realizing that our topic has thereby gained a much wider significance than initially seemed possible. Unless our students are given this kind of experience in at least some spots in the curriculum ("rat race" is the more popular term), I feel we have failed to give them an education in the true sense of the word.* [16]

The thrill of understanding and the excitement of the "aha!" when all the pieces of a puzzle fall into place are also the rewards of lecturing, textbook writing, and original research. Ernie enjoyed all these activities, and his enjoyment was shared by the students who flocked to his classes, and to him as a thesis supervisor and mentor. In the end, students were Ernie's most important products, particularly those who chose academic careers and carried his educational legacy to many other electrical engineering departments.

# The "Blue Book" Series

*Overview by J. Francis Reintjes*

Professors Harold Edgerton and J. Francis Reintjes bury the time capsule for the new EG&G Building on 16 September 1982. (The time capsule is a Skippy peanut butter jar).

Dugald C. Jackson, the department head in the 1930s, was a man with a penchant for excellence and an intense desire to maintain his department's leadership in electrical engineering education. He believed an electrical engineering curriculum should be built on a solid base of science, mathematics, and humanities, and reflect interplay between research and pedagogy. It is unsurprising, then, that he wanted his department to undertake an extensive revision of the Course VI undergraduate curriculum. (See Dugald C. Jackson profile.)

Jackson's precise motivation in calling for the curriculum review is not clear. However, his strong principles and commitment to excellence were a matter of record, and he evidently concluded that the time was ripe for change. A curriculum revision, in his mind, was not merely a rearrangement of existing subject matter. New material would be developed, and to the extent possible, it would incorporate recent advances achieved by electrical engineering research.

In his 1933 report to MIT's president, Jackson wrote, "Our complete review of the undergraduate electrical engineering curriculum, which has been underway and drawing to a close, will enable us to improve the arrangement of subject matter and method of exposition. The results should contribute to the continued leadership of the department in electrical engineering education."[17] The following year, he reported, "This revision…will more than ever emphasize the integration of research and pedagogy in electrical engineering education."

The revision was a department-wide coordinated effort, because Jackson felt that the best results would be achieved that way. It culminated in a plan to prepare a set of six textbooks, officially called the *Principles of Electrical Engineering Series*, but popularly known as the "blue book" series because of the characteristic color and distinctive layout of their covers. The first three volumes *Electric Circuits: A First Course Analysis for Electrical Engineers; Magnetic Circuits and Transformers: A First Course for Power and Communications Engineers*; and *Applied Electronics: A First Course in Electronics, Electron Tubes, and Associated Circuits* were undergraduate textbooks. Volumes IV–VI were designated *Reference Volumes for Collateral Study*. They included *The Mathematics of Circuit Analysis, Applications of Lumped-Circuit Theory*, and *The Theory of Transmission Lines, Waveguides, and Antennas*.

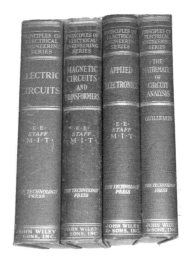

The "blue books"

Professor Jackson did not see this major project through to completion. In 1935, he chose to turn over department leadership to Edward L. Moreland, who, in his first report to the president, clearly showed how the "blue book" series would evolve. A traditional time-tested pattern would be followed. First, notes would be written and tried out in class; the notes would then be refined and perhaps refined again, until they were deemed ready for permanence in the form of textbooks. Thus Professor Moreland wrote, "The introductory subject matter given to sophomores in the second term has been taught two years in revised form. New curriculum notes were also used for the junior students…[and] notes are now in progress [for] the first term of the senior year. This will complete the first draft of the material for the basic course…. It is believed that within two or three years a very significant treatise on electrical engineering will have been developed…."[18]

Actually, more than three years elapsed before the first volume came off the press in 1940; another three years were needed to complete the next two volumes; and still another six years went by before the fourth volume appeared. Although six books had been planned, World War II interrupted the project and the remaining two were never written.

The series was unique in several respects. The decision to create an integrated, seamless treatise on electrical engineering principles eliminated the many duplications and repetitions that so often occurred when authors wrote in isolation. Also, the enormous scope of the material and the rigor with which it was presented were impressive. Extensive use of advanced mathematics was made, starting at the elementary sophomore level; each topic was explained meticulously with the help of illustrative examples, and much more material was included in the series than most students could be expected to master during their undergraduate programs. Hence, the books offered excellent opportunities for additional study and future use as reference texts.

Volume I: *Electric Circuits* was an ambitious work that brought together in one book a breadth of subject matter normally found in two or three separate texts. What set the book apart from others of its kind was its highly mathematical treatment of its content. But once the student mastered the unique set of symbols employed (seven pages were required to list them in the front of the book), the beauty of the presentations became evident. The book began with basic properties of electric charge and fields and ended with a detailed quantitative analysis of transients in nonlinear circuits. In between, the circuit elements of resistance, inductance, and capacitance were introduced, as well as the concepts of direct and alternating voltage, current, power, and energy. There followed, then, analytical methods for dealing with a variety of combinations of these elements under transient and steady-state conditions. The concepts of complex impedance and admittance were presented, along with the theory of complex numbers themselves. Finally, the reader was shown how to analyze circuits that included polyphase voltage sources driving delta- and wye-connected loads. Illustrative examples served to translate the theory into reality, and the reader's mastery of the material was challenged by numerous problems at the end of each chapter.

The subject matter in Volume II: *Magnetic Circuits and Transformers* assumed that the reader had mastered the material in the first volume. In *Magnetic Circuits and Transformers*, mathematics, especially differential equations, were used extensively but not at the expense of explanations of underlying physical phenomena. As the authors explained in the book's preface:

> The text is divided into three parts: Part 1, "Magnetic Circuits," starts with a discussion of the current theory of ferromagnetism, derives the magnetic-circuit concept, and continues with development of the fundamental principles for computation and behavior of magnetic circuits. A chapter is devoted to discussion of iron-core reactors by means of model theory… [and] a brief summary of thermal-circuit problems is also included. Part II, "Transformers," begins with a short discussion pointing out that the theories from which the characteristics of all electric apparatus can be compared are developed through the combination of the fundamental concepts of the electric, dielectric, magnetic, thermal, and mechanical circuits contained in them, and that costs and other practical matters are of paramount importance in their influence on the development of electric apparatus. Part III then continues with a study of the applications of these general principles to transformers. The theory of transformers is developed both from the resolution of their magnetic fields into leakage and resultant mutual components and from the classical theory of coupled circuits, the interrelationships between the two methods of analysis being emphasized.[19]

The publication of Volume III: *Applied Electronics* in 1943 was especially timely; it was in great demand during the war years and by 1946 had gone through eight printings. *Applied Electronics* relied on the preceding two volumes for background material while expanding the foundation of electrical engineering principles into the realm of electronics. Rigor of thought and analysis were the dominating themes. The book began with chapters on the basic phenomena upon which electron tubes were based, namely electron ballistics, electron emission from metals, and electrical conduction through vacuum, gases, and vapors. With this ground work in place, the authors were ready to discuss basic properties of high-vacuum and gas tubes. The rest of the book was devoted to presentations on the performance of circuits that included these tubes: single-phase and polyphase rectifiers; amplifiers in which vacuum tubes operate first as linear devices and then as nonlinear devices; oscillators; and finally modulators and demodulators. Amplitude, frequency, and phase modulation and demodulation (detection) are treated mathematically as processes, and vacuum-tube circuits for implementing these processes are presented.

The first reference volume in the series (Volume IV), Ernst Guillemin's *The Mathematics of Circuit Analysis*, is one of a kind: a comprehensive mathematical text written by an engineer for engineers. Its purpose was to provide a solid mathematical foundation for the analysis and synthesis of electrical networks and for an attack on the theory of fields, transmission lines, waveguides, and antennas. The chapter titles summarize the coverage: Determinants; Matrices; Linear Transformations; Quadratic Forms; Vector Analysis; Functions of a Complex Variable; and Fourier Series and Transforms.

With the exception of Volume IV, the authors remain formally unacknowledged. In the books, authorship is attributed to "The E.E. Staff, M.I.T." Names of individual contributors are conspicuously absent, perhaps to emphasize teamwork rather than individual efforts. Nor can the names be found in the department's files; after an extensive search, only a few clues on authorship have surfaced. Even the department head's annual report in 1939 failed to identify any individuals; it stated only that "a group" of editors was designated to put the class notes into textbook form.

However, principal responsibility for each volume can be inferred. Ernst Guillemin is cited in one well-researched source as "the principal author of the volume called *Electric Circuits*."[20] My own conversations with Professors Richard H. Frazier and Truman S. Gray have led me to believe that Frazier was the editor of, and a major contributor to, Volume II and that Gray served in a similar capacity for Volume III.

Only Volume IV: *Mathematics of Electric Circuits* carries an author's name. Those who knew Professor Guillemin and have read the preface to Volume IV will immediately recognize Ernie's satin-smooth style and will undoubtedly agree that this was his book and his alone.

What a scholar and dedicated man he was! On campus, his students were his major concern. For example, if an unexpected traffic delay looked as though it would cause him to be late for an early morning class, he thought it should be his privilege to leave his car with the parking lot attendant so that he could hurry off to beat the five-after-the-hour class bell; after all, his students deserved their full measure of his time. Alas, valet parking at MIT is an idea whose time still has not come.

After the war, it made no sense to start preparation of the remaining two volumes that had been planned. A huge expansion in electronic technology had occurred during the war and electrical engineers played only a marginal role in the innovative parts of that expansion. If the department was to maintain its educational leadership, much more than a simple continuation of a fifteen-year-old project was needed. Accordingly, shortly after the war, a new critical assessment of the curriculum began. Once again, subjects were revised, new material was created, notes were prepared and tested in the classroom, and a new set of texts was written. This time they were dubbed the "green books." (See the "Green Books" Series, pages 131–138.)

Appreciation given to Professor Ernst A. Guillemin by his students in 1960

# HAROLD E. EDGERTON
## 6 APRIL 1903 –
## 4 JANUARY 1990

*by Gerald L. Wilson*

Professor Harold E. Edgerton transformed the strobe light from a laboratory curiosity into an important tool for science, industry, and the military. He invented the field of high-speed photography.

At MIT, where he was a faculty member in the Department of Electrical Engineering from 1932 until his death in 1990, his official rank was Institute Professor, an honor bestowed on only a handful of faculty. His unofficial title—one he bore as proudly as the loftier one—was simply "Doc." He was called that by nearly everyone, from first-year undergraduates to MIT presidents, one of whom was a student of Doc's in the early 1950s.

An internationally eminent electrical engineer, Dr. Edgerton also was known for developments in sonar technology, which he applied to geology, archaeology, and undersea explorations.

It was as a photographer of the "unseen" that Dr. Edgerton was best known to the general public. Millions of people have seen his stop-action photos—the frozen wings of a hummingbird, the bullet shattering a light bulb, photos that revealed the power and grace that underlie athletic competition or the beauty of a milk drop falling into a red liquid.

Dr. Edgerton lived by a credo that is easy to state but difficult to follow. A Boston newspaper, published the morning of the day he died, quoted this credo in reporting yet another honor for him from a professional organization: "Work like hell, tell everyone everything you know, close a deal with a handshake, and have fun."

Doc was very easy to talk with, and he loved to meet new people. "Hi. My name is Harold Edgerton," he would say as he handed you a postcard with the milk-drop picture in full color. For example, for many years the department held an annual steak fry in the basement of Building 10. Brown paper wrapping was spread over lab benches as tablecloths. The walls were alive with 230 volts bare busbars (no OSHA here), and faculty and students would enjoy the meal as they gingerly began to converse. A key icebreaker was Doc walk-

Professor Gerald Wilson

"Doc" Edgerton in the classroom, 1977

This 1959 self-portrait provides a whimsical demonstration of Edgerton's ultra-high-speed flash. At an exposure of one microsecond, the bullet, balloon, and the inventor guarding his ear are simultaneously frozen.

"Doc" playing his guitar during the faculty/student steak fry in 1967

ing around, playing his guitar and urging, cajoling, and embarrassing students and faculty into crooning off-tune with him.

Doc was a wonderful friendly man, always willing to share his experiences and his equipment, as long as you brought it back! According to one story, Doc and two of his MIT colleagues went winter camping in the woods of New Hampshire. Back in those days sleeping bags left a lot to be desired. Three to a bag, with Doc in the middle, they huddled together as a winter storm blew over their little tent. Noticing that his friend was shivering violently, Doc insisted on moving from the middle to the outside so his friend would be warmer.

Doc was born in Fremont, Nebraska, 6 April 1903, and grew up in Aurora, Nebraska. While in high school, Doc worked as a janitor, meter reader, coal handler, and lineman for the local power company, and he planned to make a career in the power industry. After graduating from the University of Nebraska with a degree in electrical engineering in 1925, he joined General Electric in Schenectady, New York.

But after a year there and at the urging of his father, a lawyer and newsman who was well traveled and had a high regard for the Northeast and its academic institutions, Doc went to MIT to do his graduate work. He received an S.M. in 1927 and became a research assistant in what then was called the Department of Electrical Engineering. Doc earned his Sc.D. in 1931 and was appointed to the faculty the next year.

It was while working on his doctoral thesis that Doc first became interested in stroboscopic photography. Needing to determine the exact position of the rotor of the synchronous motor he was studying, Doc rigged a mercury vapor lamp so that it would flash at the same speed as the rotor. He succeeded in taking excellent pictures of less than ten microseconds' duration.

The first flash picture—using a spark—had been made in 1851, very early in the history of photography, but the technique had been treated as a curiosity until Doc came along. Captivated by the success of the armature picture, Doc and one of his students, Kenneth J. Germeshausen—both enthusiastic amateur photographers—began making still and motion pictures of all kinds of objects in rapid motion.

Doc also made many advances in high-speed motion picture techniques. He devised a system by which action is photographed at a rate of many flashes per second with an open shutter. The exposures are made on a continuously moving film, capturing multiple images of the event illuminated by pulsating strobe flashes. For many years the halls of MIT were enlivened with strobe pictures of various MIT activities taken using his techniques.

During World War II, Doc was asked to devise a strobe system for nighttime aerial photography of ground targets and operations. He developed the necessary apparatus and traveled to Italy and England to supervise its installation and testing. It was used effectively in the Normandy invasion in 1944. After the war, Doc, Germeshausen, and Herbert E. Grier, another former student of Doc's, were asked to photograph the first peacetime test of an atomic bomb. From that project the three got involved in developing the high-speed circuits that triggered such explosions, and the company Edgerton, Germeshausen, and Grier (EG&G) was formed. It exists to this day.

In 1952, the National Geographic Society asked Doc to develop an underwater camera for Jacques Cousteau. This began a collaboration with the famous French explorer that continued for many years. Cousteau's crew called Doc "Papa Flash." Doc's pioneering work with side-scan sonar included development of equipment that could reveal not only the existence of objects on the ocean bottom, but also their shapes. With such apparatus, Doc and Cousteau explored parts of the Mediterranean. They located the *Britannic*, a hospital ship sunk by a mine in the Aegean Sea during World War I, and various ancient wrecks. With the same group, Doc made a successful archaeological survey in Lake Titicaca, near the Inca Temple of the Sun. In 1973 Doc helped find the remains of the Civil War ironclad *Monitor*, which sank in a storm off Cape Hatteras on 31 December 1862.

Harold Edgerton with French underwater explorer Jacques-Yves Cousteau (Edgerton's "Milk Drop Coronet" can be seen in the background)

In 1968 Doc was inducted into the National Inventors Hall of Fame for his invention of ultra high-speed photography. (The patent for the specific invention cited, the stroboscope, had been issued 16 August 1949.) Other awards and honors included the Certificate of Appreciation from the War Department and the National Medal of Science, 1973.

For a man who won many honors, Doc was often self-deprecating, and gave the career advice not to "do anything that somebody else is doing, because they are probably better at it than you are." His memberships included the Academy of Applied Science, Academy of Underwater Arts and Sciences, American Academy of Arts and Sciences, American Philosophical Society, and Boston Camera Club (honorary), and he was elected to the National Academy of Engineering in 1966. Doc was also a fellow of the Institute of Electrical and Electronic Engineers, Photographic Society of America, Royal Photographic Society of Great Britain, and the Society of Motion Picture and Television Engineers.

During his entire, long career, accessibility to students was Doc's hallmark. His office door was always open, and although he might tell a visitor he had "just five microseconds," he would spend hours with students, especially freshmen, sharing the excitement of a new experiment. Professor and Mrs. Edgerton often entertained students at their Cambridge apartment, where a strobe light was used to flash a welcome at the door.

Not long after Doc's death, the MIT student newspaper published a letter from a student who had graduated in 1989. She wanted to relate an incident that had involved her and Professor Edgerton, "one of the most warm-hearted people I have ever met." Her letter captured the essence of MIT's beloved Doc. The student wrote that she encountered Professor Edgerton one day in 1988 when she was walking along the campus in tears over a personal incident. They had not met before. He invited her to his home, introduced her to his wife, and they shared their dinner with her. At this point in her letter there is a memorable passage, more touching perhaps because the writer is not a native speaker of English:

*After the dinner, he went under the dining table and asked me to come under as well. I wondered if he liked to rest under the table after meals, but I soon found out why. There were a lot of writings on the reverse of the table. Many of them were the signatures of people who had visited, some with greetings. He gave me a pen and I wrote my name in Japanese.... After that day they invited me over several times. Some times they would give me take-home food so I could have it for breakfast. Dr. Edgerton told me that I was his first Japanese granddaughter.... In our lives we seldom meet people who really touch our heart.... I greatly miss my beloved Grandpa Edgerton, like those who were also touched by his warmth during his life.*

# Technology's Radar School

WILLIAM H. RADFORD

20 MAY, 1909–9 MAY 1966

TECHNOLOGY REVIEW

(FEBRUARY 1946)

*Introduced and excerpted by David H. Staelin*

Born in Philadelphia in 1909, William H. Radford received his bachelor's degree in electrical engineering in 1931 from Drexel Institute and his master's degree in 1932 from MIT. He was appointed instructor at MIT in 1939 and assistant professor of electrical engineering in 1941, which was the position he held when he helped establish the wartime MIT Radar School. He became the school's associate director in 1944 and published "Technology's Radar School" in *Technology Review* in 1946. The school trained about 8,800 students in modern radar and electronics, and had a strong impact even after its closure in 1946, particularly through Radar School texts such as *Principles of Radar*, which sold nearly 100,000 copies in three editions over a ten-year period.

Professor David Staelin in the lab

Radford became a professor in 1951 and the first head of the Communications and Components Division of the newly established MIT Lincoln Laboratory. There he was responsible for the development of tropospheric and ionospheric radio communications for the DEW Line and Sage air defense system, and led the planning of the Millstone Hill radar complex and the West Ford experiments with a belt of dipoles in space. He became associate director of Lincoln Laboratory in 1964 and in the same year, he became its director, a position he held until he was felled by an

Professor William H. Radford '32

Aerial view of the Rad Lab and environs

untimely heart attack in 1966. His leadership of the Radar School and of Lincoln Laboratory made important contributions to the success and reputation of MIT.

The following has been adapted from the article that appeared in *Technology Review*, "Technology's Radar School."

ESTABLISHED at Technology [MIT] almost six months before Pearl Harbor, the Radar School composed the Institute's largest specialized war training activity. Unique in many respects and noted for the variety and high standards of its courses during the war period, the school served as one of the principal centers for training Army and Navy officers in the theory and applications of radar. At the completion of the war phase of its operations in December [1945], the school had trained approximately 8,800 officers, enlisted men, and civilians, including practically all of the Naval Reserve "electronic specialist" officers who were responsible for procurement, installation, and maintenance of the air-borne and shipboard radar and related electronic equipment of the fleet.

The need for war training of the kind offered at the Radar School was first recognized early in 1941. In November of the preceding year the Radiation Laboratory had been established at the Institute under the sponsorship of the National Defense Research Committee.[1] In the spring of 1941, Professor Edward L. Bowles, '22, of the Department of Electrical Engineering, who was then secretary of the N.D.R.C. microwave committee, discussed this need with Dr. Compton, who agreed that the Institute should offer to provide the special radar training which the Army and Navy would require.

Accordingly, in May, 1941, Edward L. Moreland, '07, Dean of Engineering at the Institute, and Professor Bowles conferred with representatives of the Army and Navy. It was agreed that a selected group of officers should be given thorough training in the fundamentals of radar. These officers would be prepared to master future microwave radar equipment and to instruct other personnel in the principles and techniques of the art. This conference led to establishment of the training activity which later became known as the MIT Radar School.

The first course began on June 23, 1941, and was attended by 44 Army officers and 14 Navy officers. This full-time course was of 12 weeks' duration and included a brief review of radio fundamentals followed by intensive instruction in the principles of radar and their specific applications. The radar instruction, which was classified "secret," was given within a heavily guarded area in Building 32, a temporary building on Vassar Street.

A special full-time, pre-radar course, dealing with nonclassified applications of electronics and radio, was established in the Harvard Graduate School of Engineering. The first class entered on July 17, 1941. Originally of 10 weeks' duration, this course was soon lengthened to three months and later to four and five months for some groups.

Subsequently the Navy set up additional pre-radar training programs at Bowdoin College in August, 1941, and at Princeton University in June, 1943. There was a close liaison between the Institute Radar School and the pre-radar schools. The uniformity and effectiveness of the preparation given by the pre-radar schools greatly eased the task of the Radar School and was an important factor in the success of the entire training program.

[1]See L. A. duBridge and L. N. Ridenour, "Expanded Horizons," *The Review* (November, 1945):23.

Highlights in the history of the Radar School and a Summary of personnel trained in the school are given in the accompanying tables.

## HIGHLIGHTS IN HISTORY OF RADAR SCHOOL
### Period I—June, 1941, to April, 1942

6-23-41    First class of 58 officers started special full-time 12-week course.

7-17-41    Pre-radar training inaugurated at Harvard University.

10-1-41    Improved 12-week course started for second class of 97 officers. Repeated for third class of 115 officers who entered 12-29-41. Operation in MIT Building 32 (9,000 sq. ft.). Laboratory equipped with microwave prototype equipment borrowed from Radiation Laboratory.

### Period II—May, 1942, to January, 1944

5-4-42    School moved to larger quarters (36,000 sq. ft.) on roof, 14th, 13th, and 12th floors of Harbor Building at 470 Atlantic Avenue, Boston. New three-month course including interval of basic instruction for all students followed by separate programs for Army and Navy officers. Some specialization for Sig. C., A.A.F., C.A.C., and Navy engineering and aviation officers. Classes entered monthly. Marked trend toward increased emphasis on production models of Army and Navy radar sets.

Spring, 1943    Annex established at Briggs Field for instruction on Army ground radars. Additional space occupied on 12th floor of Harbor Building.

### Period III—February, 1944, to December, 1945

2-1-44    Separate courses established for Army and Navy with increased specialization for various branches. Prototype radars wholly replaced by service models.

3-1-44    Additional space occupied on 10th and 11th floors of Harbor Building.

4-1-44    Courses for all Navy officers lengthened to four months. Annex established at 19 Deerfield Street, Boston, for instruction in radar countermeasures. Instruction on Navy aviation radio begun at Harbor Building.

5-1-44    Sonar instruction for Navy engineering officers established in new annex at M.I.T. Building 18, increasing total school floor area to approximately 120,000 sq. ft.

10-1-44    Course for Navy engineering officers lengthened to 4 1/2 months. Numerous special courses offered including 3-month course for A.A.F. Weather Wing officers, 2-month refresher courses for Navy officers, and 1-month maintenance course for Navy destroyer officers.

1-1-45    Course for Navy aviation officers lengthened to 4 1/2 months. Navy sonar training barge located in Charles River Basin.

6-29-45    Army war training program completed.

12-15-45    Navy war training program completed.

### Period IV—January 1946

1-1-46    New electrical engineering curriculum established for Navy officers specializing in electronics.

## SUMMARY OF PERSONNEL TRAINED
### June, 1941, to December, 1945

| Course | Officers | Enlisted Men | Civilians | Total |
|---|---|---|---|---|
| Army, regular............. | 2,549* | 24 | 3 | 2,576 |
| Army, special............. | 56 | 3 | | 59 |
| Navy, regular............. | 4,951† | | 7 | 4,958 |
| Navy, special............. | 695 | 227 | 82 | 1,004 |
| Radiation Laboratory ‡...... | | | 265 | 265 |
| Total.................. | 8,251 | 254 | 357 | 8,862 |

\* Includes 6 Royal Air Force and 17 Royal Canadian Air Force officers.

† Includes United States Coast Guard Reserve, United States Marine Corps Reserve, and 4 Allied officers.

‡ Radiation Laboratory staff members who completed the basic course between May, 1942, and December, 1943.

The primary objectives were always to give the student thorough instruction in the basic principles and techniques of radar and to teach him the applications of these principles and techniques in representative ultrahigh-frequency and microwave radar sets and related devices currently used in the field. The courses for engineering and aviation officers were eventually lengthened to four and one-half months, and the two primary training objectives discussed above were supplemented by a third objective, namely, to give each student practice in the maintenance of equipment representative of that which he would normally encounter in the fleet.

Instructional methods at the Radar School were similar to those regularly employed in undergraduate courses at the Institute, although there was greater emphasis on laboratory work and more extensive utilization of charts, films, lantern slides, and other training aids. There were lectures, supervised study and problem periods, laboratory conferences, and examinations.

A student's daily schedule included several hours of lecture and supervised study and a three- or four-hour laboratory period. From 40 to 50 hours of instruction were scheduled each week. For reasons of military security students and instructors were required to do all of their work within the guarded areas of the school.

One of the more important training aids used at the school was the text-book *Principles of Radar*, written by members of the teaching staff.[3] This book covers the fundamental principles on which all modern radar systems operate and was used extensively from the time the first preliminary copies became available in the fall of 1943. Other important training aids were the sets of instructional drawings which the staff prepared for every important radar system used at the school. These drawings were much more suitable for training purposes than the usual manufacturers' wiring diagrams.

Laboratory instruction at the school emphasized the proper use of standard measuring instruments and practical procedures for checking circuit operation. Taking data on prepared setups was avoided, and students were often required to select and arrange apparatus for particular measurements. During the third period of operation many experiments in the Navy courses stressed procedures for obtaining peak performance of a radar system, faultfinding, and preventive maintenance. Whenever possible, schedules were arranged so that no more than two men were assigned to a setup at one time.

The full-time three-, four-, and four-and-one-half-month courses for Army and Navy officers were by far the most important activities of the Radar School. Considerable staff effort, however, was devoted to various short, special programs which were offered from time to time to fill specific needs of the services. Many of these special courses were arranged on very short notice.

The teaching staff of the Radar School included civilians and Army and Navy officers. The civilian instructors included members of the Department of Electrical Engineering,[4] staff members on leave from other colleges, engineers and physicists recruited from industry, and a number of recent Institute graduates. Almost all of the Army and Navy officers were Radar School graduates whose services had been requested by the Institute. Many of the officers had radar field experience before the responsibilities for organizing and conducting the courses of instruction and for general operation of the school rested with a civilian director who was appointed by Dean Moreland. The senior naval officer at the Institute was in charge of all naval personnel and property assigned to the school.

W.L. Barrow, '29, Associate Professor of Electrical Communications, was director of the Radar School from June, 1941, until September, 1943. Professor C.E. Tucker, '18, has been director since that time. Others who served in the school administration are: W.H. Radford, '32, Associate Professor of Electrical Communications, as director in charge of instruction; H.J. Zimmermann, '42, as assistant director in charge of Army courses; J.A. Wood, Jr., Assistant Professor of Electrical Engineering, as assistant director in charge of Navy laboratories; S.K. Haynes as assistant director in charge of Navy lectures; M.S. McIlroy, '41, Assistant Professor of Electrical Engineering, as assistant director in charge of power and student records; and P.D. Appel, '22, as assistant director in charge of security and personnel. Commander J.L. Hornung has been officer in charge for the Navy since May, 1944.

The Radar School was required to operate as a self-contained unit and therefore needed its own guard force, secretarial staff, print shop, photographic service, schedules and records office, maintenance shops, purchasing department, and first-aid facilities. At the peak of activity, in the early summer of 1945, the service staff numbered 152 and included 36 guards, 25 janitors, 10 technicians, 32 secretaries, 20 print-shop clerks, 7 draftsmen, 1 lithographer, 1 nurse, and 20 enlisted personnel, including technicians, yeomen, storekeepers, and pharmacist's mates.

While there was no official connection between the Radiation Laboratory and the Radar School, the laboratory assisted the school greatly, especially during the early years of operation, by lending prototype components of microwave radar systems and other apparatus and by furnishing essential technical information.

[3]Originally confidential, this book is now unclassified. The second edition will soon be published by McGraw-Hill in collaboration with the Technology Press.

[4]Present members of the Department of Electrical Engineering who served were Professor C.E. Tucker, '18; W.L. Barrow, '29, Associate Professor of Electrical Communications; W.H. Radford, '32, Associate Professor of Electrical Communications; M.S. McIlroy, '41, Assistant Professor of Electrical Engineering; G.T. Coate, '42, Assistant Professor of Engineering Electronics; H.J. Zimmermann, '42, assistant; L.W. Evans, '43, instructor; J.P. Chisholm, 2-44, assistant; L.D. Wilson, 2-44, research assistant; P.C. Grosse, 10-44, assistant; E.W. Keller, 10-44, assistant; B.H. Ciscel, research assistant; M.W. Essigmann, instructor; M. Loewenthal, research assistant; J.A. Wood, Jr., Assistant Professor of Electrical Engineering; and Patrick Youtz, research associate.

The school is now being converted for postwar use and, starting with the 1946 spring term, will operate as a facility of the Department of Electrical Engineering. Subjects will be classified and will be open only to officers and civilians designated by the Bureau of Naval Personnel. Most of these subjects are included in a new five-term curriculum in naval electronics which the Department of Electrical Engineering has arranged at the request of the Navy. This course leads to the degree of bachelor of science in electrical engineering and will be taken by selected graduates of the various Naval R.O.T.C. units. Some of the subjects offered at the Radar School will also be taken by officer graduate students from the Navy Postgraduate School and the Army Air Forces.

ENDNOTES TO PART 3

[1] Dugald C. Jackson to Henry S. Pritchett, 14 August 1906, MIT Archives and Special Collections, MIT Libraries, Cambridge, Massachusetts, MC 5, Folder 4.

[2] Dugald C. Jackson, "The Evolution of Electrical Engineering," *Electrical Engineering, Fiftieth Anniversary AIEE*, 1884-1934, American Institute of Electrical Engineers, Vol. 53, No. 5, May 1934, p. 776.

[3] Ibid., p.775.

[4] D.C. Jackson, Six lectures delivered at the University of North Carolina State College of Agriculture and Engineering, Raleigh, N.C., 21–29 January 1938, The American Society of Mechanical Engineers, New York, 1939.

[5] Quoted in IEEE History Center: http://www.ieee.org/organizations/history_center/legacies/jackson.html.

[6] Vannevar Bush, "Science: The Endless Frontier," Report to the President (Washington, D.C.: United States Government Printing Office, 1945).

[7] Ibid.

[8] Vannevar Bush, "As We May Think," *The Atlantic Monthly* 176 (1945): 108.

[9] Harold L. Hazen and Hugh Spencer, "Artificial Representation of Power Systems," *Transactions of the AIEE* (1925): 72.

[10] Louis Weinberg , "Ernst A. Guillemin: An Appreciative Reminiscence," *IEEE Spectrum* (June 1970): 116.

[11] Edward L. Bowles, remarks delivered at memorial services for Professor Ernst A. Guillemin, MIT Chapel, 8 April 1970 (unpublished).

[12] Karl L. Wildes and Nilo A. Lindgren, *A Century of Electrical Engineering and Computer Science at MIT, 1882–1982* (Cambridge, Mass.: MIT Press, 1985), 158–9.

[13] Ernst A. Guillemin, "A Historical Account of the Development of a Design Procedure for Pulse-forming Networks," *RL Report* No. 43, 16 October 1944.

[14] G.N. Glasoe and J.V. Lebacqz, eds., *Pulse Generators*, Radiation Laboratory Series, Vol. 5 (New York: McGraw-Hill, 1948), 189 ff, "Sec. 6-3: Guillemin's Theory and the Voltage-fed Network."

[15] Ernst A. Guillemin, *Introductory Circuit Theory*, (New York: John Wiley & Sons 1953), viii.

[16] Ernst A. Guillemin, *Synthesis of Passive Network* (New York: John Wiley & Sons, 1957), viii.

[17] M.I.T. Publications, President's Report Issue, Vol. 69, No. 3 (October 1933): 77–78. Cambridge, Mass.: The Technology Press.

[18] M.I.T. Publications, President's Report Issue, Vol. 70, No. 1 (October 1934): 79. Cambridge, Mass.: The Technology Press.

[19] EE Staff, MIT, *Magnetic Circuits and Transformers* (Cambridge, Mass.: The Technology Press, Massachusetts Institute of Technology; New York: John Wiley & Sons, 1943), pp. vii-viii.

[20] Wildes and Lindgren, *A Century of Electrical Engineering and Computer Science at MIT*, pp. 158–9.

# Engineering Science

*by Paul L. Penfield, Jr.*

4

During World War II, MIT hosted the Radiation Laboratory, part of which was housed in the legendary Building 20. Its major objective was to transform radar into a practical wartime technology. This work required advances in microwave technology, propagation, antenna design, vacuum-tube amplifiers, and a whole host of electronic components. The personnel included eminent engineers and scientists, some from MIT and Harvard. When the war ended in 1945, most of these people went back to a more normal life. A few came to the MIT Department of Electrical Engineering. And when they did, they had a strange tale to tell.

It seems that the major breakthroughs in radar system engineering had been made not by engineers, but by scientists, mostly physicists. Engineers had played a valuable role, to be sure, but it was a supporting rather than a leading role—one of implementation, not innovation. Dugald Jackson would not have expected this. He had believed he was training leaders. According to his vision, engineers would, as needed, develop new techniques based on known science.

*Endnotes appear on page 167.

Gordon Brown, among others, realized what was wrong. The problem was that the necessary science was not known, or at least was not in a form accessible to engineers. He agreed with Dugald Jackson that engineers must be able to apply known techniques and develop new techniques using known science. But he went further, saying that at least some of them should also be able to extend the relevant sciences in ways required by engineering. Brown called such activities "engineering science." He concluded that changes in the educational programs were needed.

In Brown's view, the science should be taught in the first years, followed by contemporary technology based on the science. Specialization and theses would come in the senior year. The best students would be encouraged to enter an expanded doctoral program, which would produce engineers able to extend engineering science. Brown served on a department curriculum committee and rallied support for these views. When he became department head in 1952, he immediately instituted a curriculum review to identify the underlying sciences in all areas and relate them to engineering techniques. Six undergraduate textbooks, called the "Green Books" for the color of their covers, were written during the late 1950s (see pages 131–138).

Brown kept colleagues at other universities informed, giving them free access to MIT's most recent thoughts. Doctoral graduates from this era took teaching positions here and elsewhere and spread the word. This policy of freely sharing curricular material continues today with the MIT OpenCourseWare program, announced in 2002. In 1959 Brown became Dean of Engineering and started to promote similar ideas for other engineering disciplines.

In short, Brown's update to Jackson's vision was recognizing that science changes rapidly, and if engineers participate in the process, the changes will be in a form usable by engineers. The first major test of this engineering–science approach was provided by semiconductor circuits. The transistor was invented in 1947; circuit applications began in the 1950s; the integrated circuit came along in 1960. Universities had to include transistors and integrated circuits in their undergraduate programs. But how? Should devices be taught in terms of terminal characteristics or the internal physics? What if fields of science not previously thought relevant were needed? Could nonlinear circuits be covered? How much solid-state physics would be required?

MIT led the way in answering these questions. In the fall of 1960 Richard B. Adler and Campbell L. Searle organized the Semiconductor Electronics Education Committee (SEEC). By 1966, thirty-one people from nine universities and six companies produced seven coordinated textbooks and related curricular material, aimed at third-year and fourth-year electrical engineering students. The books featured more solid-state physics than had ever before been used to teach electronics. In the books, semiconductor-device models were derived from the solid-state physics, and the models in turn were used in transistor circuits.

SEEC was a triumph of engineering science, with a substantial, lasting impact. The basic ideas influenced many textbooks written in subsequent years. The approaches are still used in electrical engineering education throughout the world, even though the SEEC books themselves can no longer claim contemporary relevance because they were never updated to cover integrated circuits, MOS devices, or much on digital circuits.

Engineering science, as a paradigm for engineering education, survived its first major test. The next test, posed by the rising importance of computer science, would prove more challenging.

Pedestrians compete for space with a microwave dish on a cart in Building 20's busy corridor during Rad Lab days.

# CLAUDE E. SHANNON: HIS LIFE, WORK, AND IMPACT
## 30 APRIL 1916 – 24 FEBRUARY 2001

*by Robert G. Gallager*[1]

Professor Emeritus Robert Gallager

### INTRODUCTION

Claude Elwood Shannon invented information theory and provided the concepts, insights, and mathematical formulations that form the basis for modern communication technology. In a surprising number of ways, he enabled the information age. Shannon was both a department alumnus and much later, from 1958 to 1981, a department faculty member. A major part of this influence comes from his monumental two-part paper, "A Mathematical Theory of Communication,"[2] published in 1948. This work was viewed initially as a beautiful mathematical theory with philosophical implications to both the physical and life sciences. Years later it came to be recognized as the central set of principles guiding digital communication technology.

### CLAUDE SHANNON'S LIFE

Claude Shannon, born 30 April 1916, grew up in the small town of Gaylord, Michigan. His mother was a language teacher and principal of the Gaylord high school, and his father was a businessman and probate judge.

Shannon went through the public school system, graduating from Gaylord High School at the age of sixteen. The young Shannon led a normal, happy childhood with little indication of his budding genius. As in later life, he was friendly when approached but not outgoing. He was interested in such things as erector sets and model planes, and was curious about how various devices worked.

After high school, Shannon enrolled in the University of Michigan where, in 1936, he received bachelor's degrees in both electrical engineering and mathematics. His dual interests in these fields continued throughout his professional career. While trying to decide what to do next, he saw a help wanted ad for a research assistant to operate Vannevar Bush's differential analyzer (an early analog computer; see Bush profile, pages 32–34). Shannon applied and was accepted as a research assistant and graduate student in the electrical engineering department.

At MIT Shannon became interested in the analog aspects of the computer and in the complex switching circuit controlling it. Along with his academic subjects, he started to explore the possibility that Boolean algebra could be used to understand these switching circuits.

After his first academic year, Shannon spent the summer of 1937 at Bell Telephone Laboratories working on the relationship between Boolean algebra and switching. Back at MIT in the fall, he fleshed out these ideas and showed how to use Boolean algebra both for the analysis and synthesis of relay circuits. He used these ideas for his MIT master's thesis and his first published paper, "A Symbolic Analysis of Relay and Switching Circuits."[3]

The importance of this work was quickly recognized as providing a scientific approach for the rapidly growing field of switching. Switching circuits were of great importance in the telephone industry, and subsequently in the development of computers. The paper won the 1940 Alfred Nobel prize for the best paper in engineering published by an author under 30 and is widely recognized today as the foundation of the switching field.

Claude E. Shannon

Partly on the advice of Vannevar Bush, Shannon started to look for a Ph.D. topic in the area of genetics. He switched from electrical engineering to mathematics and aimed to establish a mathematical basis for genetics. He completed his Ph.D. thesis, "An Algebra for Theoretical Genetics," in 1940. The thesis was never published (Shannon was never interested in recognition) and remained largely unknown until recently. Its results were important, but have been mostly rediscovered independently over the intervening years.

While Shannon was doing his Ph.D. research, he became interested in the fundamental problems of communication and started to nibble around the edges of what would later become "A Mathematical Theory of Communication." He also continued to work on switching theory.

In the summer of 1940 Shannon returned to Bell Labs to further explore topics in switching. He then accepted a National Research Fellowship at the Institute for Advanced Study at Princeton. There, during the academic year 1940–41, he started to work seriously on his nascent mathematical theory of communication.

By the summer of 1941, war was imminent and Shannon joined an elite group at Bell Labs working on fire control for antiaircraft batteries. In his spare time, Shannon continued to work on switching and on his rapidly developing theory of communication.

During the war, Shannon also became interested in cryptography. He realized that the fundamental issues in cryptography were closely related to the ideas he was developing about communication theory. He was not cleared for the major cryptographic projects at Bell Labs, so he explained his ideas to the cryptographers, but they could not tell him about their applications. It appears, however, that his results were used in the speech-scrambling device used by Roosevelt and Churchill during the war.

Shannon wrote up his cryptography results in 1945 in the classified paper, "A Mathematical Theory of Cryptography," which became available in the open literature in 1949 as "Communication Theory of Secrecy Systems."[4] This paper established a mathematical theory for secrecy systems and can be viewed as changing cryptography from an art to a science.

Some of the entropy concepts that Shannon had worked out for his evolving theory of communication first appeared in the cryptography report. Some people supposed that he first developed these concepts there, but in fact he was simply not yet ready to write up his communication work.

By 1948, all the pieces of "A Mathematical Theory of Communication" had come together in Shannon's head. He had been working on this project, on and off, for eight years. There were no drafts or partial manuscripts. Remarkably, he was able to keep the entire creation in his head. In a sense, this was necessary, because his theory was about the entire process of telecommunication, from source to data compression, then channel coding and modulation, then channel disturbances, and finally demodulation, detection, and error correction. The theory concerned the performance of the very best system possible and how to approach that performance. An understanding of each piece of the system was necessary to achieve this objective.

The publication of this monumental work caused a great stir in the technological world and in the broader intellectual world. Shannon employed the provocative term *information* to describe what was being communicated. Moreover, he was able to quantify *information* for sources and for channels. This new conception of information reopened many age-old debates about the differences between knowledge, information, data, and so forth. Furthermore, the idea that something called *information* could be quantified stimulated much excitement and speculation throughout the intellectual community.

Shannon remained in the mathematical research group at Bell Labs until 1956, and created a constant stream of new and stimulating results. He had a remarkable group of brilliant people to interact with, and he tended to quickly absorb what they were working on and to suggest totally new approaches. His style was not that of the expert who knows all the relevant literature in a field and suggests appropriate references. Rather, he would strip away all the complexity from the problem and suggest some extremely simple and fundamental new insight.

For the most part, Shannon tended to work alone. He would concentrate on whatever problem fascinated him at the time, regardless of whether it appeared to have practical or conceptual importance. He felt no obligation to focus on topics of value to the Bell System, and the laboratory administration was happy to have him work on whatever he chose.

Professor C. E. Shannon

In the years immediately after publishing his magnum opus in 1948, Shannon had an amazingly diverse output of papers on switching, computing, artificial intelligence, and games. It is almost as if all these topics had been on the back burner until he had worked out the conceptual issues in his theory of communication. Many of these papers were later important for the Bell system.

One of the wonderful aspects of Shannon is how his work and play came together. For example, the problem of programming a computer to play chess fascinated him. A similar, semiserious project was Theseus, a mechanical mouse, designed to solve mazes. Once Theseus had found the reward, it would remember the path it had taken to get there. If the walls of the maze were changed, or the position of the reward changed, the mouse would recognize the change and find the new solution. Along with being amusing, this was an early and instructive example of machine learning. A short but very popular film was made about Shannon and Theseus.

Shannon had been interested in questions of computability and Turing machines since before the war, and he actually discussed these issues with Alan Turing while working on cryptography during the war. In a 1956 Bell Labs memorandum, he described how a universal Turing machine could be constructed with only two internal states. This is a beautifully written paper, which provides an excellent tutorial introduction to Turing machine theory.

Shannon met his wife, Mary Elizabeth (Betty) Moore, at Bell Labs, where she worked as a numerical analyst. They shared a good-natured, intellectual sense of humor and a no-nonsense but easy-going style of life. They brought up three children, and although Shannon was always thinking about some currently fascinating idea, he was also always available for his family. The family shared a love of toys, many of which Shannon built himself. They had collections of unicycles, looms, chess sets, erector sets, and musical instruments, as well as a gasoline-powered pogo stick and the mechanical mouse Theseus. Shannon was well known for riding a unicycle through the halls of Bell Labs while juggling.

Betty often helped Claude in his work, sometimes checking his numerical calculations, and sometimes writing his papers as he dictated them. It seems astonishing that anyone could dictate a paper and have it come out right without many editing revisions, but Shannon disliked writing, and thus kept thinking about a subject until everything was clear.

In 1956, Shannon spent a year visiting MIT and the following year at the Center for the Study of Behavioral Sciences in Palo Alto, California. In 1958, he accepted a permanent appointment at MIT as Donner Professor of Science, with appointments in electrical engineering and in mathematics.

There was a very active group of graduate students and young faculty studying information theory at MIT around 1958. For them, Claude Shannon was an idol. Many of these students are now leaders in the digital communication field and have made their mark in research and practice.

Shannon's role as a faculty member at MIT was atypical. He did not teach regular courses and did not really like to talk about the same subject again and again. His mind was always focused on new topics he was trying to understand. He was happy to talk about these new topics, especially when he obtained some new insights about them. Thus, he gave relatively frequent seminars. He once gave an entire seminar course with new research results at each lecture.

It was relatively rare for him to be the actual supervisor of a student's thesis, yet he had an enormous influence on the students' lives. He was friendly and helpful when approached. Many students summoned up the courage to approach him, and he usually found interesting and novel ways for them to look at their problems. These interactions were important in two ways. First, they helped the students directly in their research, and second, the students started to understand how to formulate and approach problems in a more fundamental way. Students learned to look at carefully constructed toy problems before getting lost in technical detail.

In his research at MIT, Shannon turned back to information theory and extended the theory in a number of ways. He also continued to work or play with his many mechanical gadgets. For example, he developed an elaborate strategy for winning at roulette by taking advantage of small imbalances in the roulette wheel.

By the 1980s, it became increasingly clear that Shannon was having memory problems, and he was eventually diagnosed with Alzheimer's disease. He spent the final years of his life in a private hospital, but was good-natured as usual and enjoyed Betty's daily visits. He died on 24 February 2001.

## A MATHEMATICAL THEORY OF COMMUNICATION

Shannon's deepest and most influential work established a conceptual basis for both the individual parts and the whole of modern communication systems. It provided an architectural view of the whole as well as the quantitative information measures needed to describe the individual pieces.

Before 1948, engineers had only the fuzziest idea of what a message was. They had some rudimentary understanding of how to transmit a waveform and process a received waveform, but essentially no understanding of how to turn a *message* into a transmitted *waveform*. They grasped various modulation techniques, such as amplitude modulation, frequency modulation, and pulse code modulation, but had little means for comparing them.

Shannon starts by explaining that messages should be thought of as probabilistic choices between alternatives. He gives a beautiful description of how to model the statistical dependencies in English text, and then goes on to analyze the simplest possible model, that of an independent identically distributed (*iid*) sequence of letters in which each letter $i$ of the alphabet has some given probability $p(i)$.

For such an *iid* sequence, the probability of a sequence $x = x_1 x_2 \ldots x_n$ is then $\Pr\{x\} = p(x_1)p(x_2)\ldots p(x_n)$. The familiar law of large numbers asserts that for large $n$, a typical sequence has about $np(i)$ appearances of each letter $i$. This means that

$$\Pr\{x\} \approx \Pi p(i)^{np(i)} = 2^{n \sum_i p(i) \log_2 p(i)} = 2^{-nH}$$

where the entropy $H$ of the source is defined by

$$H = \sum_i -p(i) \log_2 p(i)$$

This simple argument shows that each typical sequence of length $n$ has about the same probability, $2^{-nH}$. Since the aggregate probability of all typical sequences is close to 1, we see that there must be about $2^{nH}$ typical sequences.

Thus each typical sequence can be represented by about $nH$ bits, which means that an *iid* letter source of entropy $H$ can be encoded into about $H$ bits per letter.

The above argument leaves out all the details about the various approximations, but these can be filled in once the general idea is understood. Even more important, Shannon extended the idea to Markov sources, which are probabilistic models that can take into account the statistical dependencies between successive source letters. The definition of entropy then takes on a more complex form reflecting these dependencies.

Shannon viewed the entropy of a source as the fundamental definition of the information in the source, and thus he viewed information not as a property of a single sequence of letters but as a property of a random ensemble of choices from which that particular sequence arose. He also viewed entropy as a measure of uncertainty, which becomes resolved as the particular sequence within the ensemble is chosen.

This random ensemble point of view is particularly appropriate for communication engineers and database engineers, who must deal with information after it is generated and who are primarily concerned with compressing the information in a way that allows later reconstruction.

The word *information* in information theory means something closer to *data* than to *information* in the usual senses of those words. The use of the word *information*, however, is partly justified by the fact that communication and data processing are ultimately concerned with information.

After developing the notions of typical sequences, entropy, and compression for data sources, Shannon went on to use these basics in studying noisy communication channels. He showed that a channel is characterized by a capacity $C$ in bits per second. He showed that for any $R < C$, $R$ binary digits per second can be transmitted over the channel with arbitrarily small probability of bit error. Furthermore, for any discrete source with an entropy of $R$ bits per second, the source output, after appropriate coding, can be transmitted over the channel with arbitrarily small error probability if $R < C$ but not if $R > C$.

Shannon proved these results by an existence argument that gave few clues about the construction of the required error-correcting codes. Another fifty years of research were required as practical techniques gradually approached capacity with vanishing error probability.

A partially hidden consequence of Shannon's coding theorem is the source-channel separation principle. This says that the general problem of encoding a given source for transmission over a general channel can be replaced, without cost in data rate, by first encoding the source into binary digits essentially at the entropy rate, and then by encoding the binary digits for channel transmission. Today, networks and channels typically are designed only to transmit bits, and source compression typically produces only bits, thus making bits the universal interface between sources and channels.

Shannon's entire theory was built on the law of large numbers behavior of both sources and channels. The results thus emphasize data rates and ignore the required coding delays and the need for statistical regularity. Later research has made extensions for finite delay, feedback, and lack of statistical regularity, but the success of the theory required that the central results be developed in a simpler context based on the law of large numbers.

Professor Claude Shannon

## SHANNON'S OTHER CONTRIBUTIONS TO COMMUNICATION THEORY

Although the seeds for the modern age of digital communication were all present in his magnum opus, Shannon made many other important contributions. Two of these appeared in 1948 and 1949 and probably had more impact on the communication engineers of the day than the invention of information theory. The first, "The Philosophy of PCM," coauthored by B.R. Oliver and J.R. Pierce, showed that digital communication has a fundamental advantage over analog communication in that digital data can be regenerated with negligible error at each node, whereas analog data accumulates noise. The second paper, "Communication in the Presence of Noise," applies information theory to a conventional additive Gaussian noise channel. These papers had a significant impact on developments in digital communication.

Aside from a delightful paper on the entropy of printed English in 1951, Shannon spent most of his time from 1949 to 1955 on his many interests outside of information theory. In 1956, when he visited MIT for a year, Shannon's interest in information theory was rekindled. In the following ten years, he wrote a number of seminal papers, some filling the gaps in his original work and some expanding information theory into new areas.

One of the gaps in the original theory was the lack of understanding about the tradeoff between error probability and code constraint length. This delayed the development of coding techniques and led some to question whether the theory would ever produce practical results. Shannon wrote a number of papers in this area, first demonstrating that error probability can be made to decrease *exponentially* in block length for any source rate less than capacity. A later paper refined this by determining tight upper and lower bounds to error probability for the white Gaussian noise channel. A final pair of papers then derived tight lower bounds to error probability for arbitrary, discrete, memoryless channels.

Another gap in the original theory concerned the compression of analog sources subject to a fidelity criterion. Typically, analog sources cannot be digitized without distortion, so the question is how much distortion is necessary at a given digital bit rate. Shannon's solution to this problem was, as usual, elegant, using a novel variation on the random-coding arguments in the noisy channel–coding theorem.

"The Zero-Error Capacity of a Noisy Channel," written in 1956, is a delightful example of a new type of combinatoric problem. When no errors at all are permitted over a noisy channel, the probabilistic aspects of channel coding disappear and only graph-theoretic aspects remain. Surprisingly, the zero-error capacity seems to be harder to determine than the ordinary capacity.

Another new area opened up by Shannon in this period was two-way communication channels in which communication in one direction interferes with that in the other. This was the first example of a network-type information theoretic problem.

## SHANNON'S RESEARCH STYLE

The great mathematician Kolmogorov summed up Claude Shannon's brilliance as a researcher very well when he wrote, "In our age, when human knowledge is becoming more and more specialized, Claude Shannon is an exceptional example of a scientist who combines deep abstract mathematical thought with a broad and at the same time very concrete understanding of vital problems of technology. He can be considered equally well as one of the greatest mathematicians and as one of the greatest engineers of the last few decades."

While recognizing his genius, however, many mathematicians of the day were frustrated by Shannon's style of omitting both precise conditions on theorems and details of proofs. Part of the problem is that modern axiomatic mathematics emphasizes the rigorous establishment of the consequences of given axiomatic systems, as opposed to intuitive understanding of different classes of mathematical models.

It appears that Shannon's engineering side took the dominant role in his theorem/proof style. It was clear that his theorems are valid for simple models of sources and channels without memory. It was also clear that his theorems are valid in the much greater generality needed to understand practical sources and channels. However, his theorems require some additional minor restrictions not explicitly stated.

Was this occasional lack of precise conditions a stroke of genius or a failing? Bear in mind that his seminal paper contained the blueprint of communication systems for at least the subsequent fifty years. It also explained clearly why all of these major results are true, under at least a broad range of conditions. Finally, the ideas form a beautiful symphony, with a repetition of themes and growing power that still provide an inspiration to all of us. This is mathematics at its very best, as Kolmogorov recognized. If these theorems had been stated and proven under the broadest possible conditions, the paper would have been delayed and would probably have been impenetrable to even the theoretically inclined engineers who most needed its unifying ideas.

What was it that made Shannon's research so great? Was he simply such a towering genius that everything he touched turned to gold? He was certainly a genius, but he had several advantages that other researchers could emulate (and that many of the early researchers in information theory have emulated).

First, he took his problems from everyday life and from engineering issues rather than from the literature. Thus he focused on truly new ideas and avoided the minutiae of the scholarly pursuit of who did what and when in an ever-expanding body of research literature. Shannon's papers have remarkably few references, since the problems he looked at were virtually virgin.

Second, Shannon was never interested in programmatic or project-oriented research. He did not like to work in a team to achieve incremental improvements on some product. It was not that he was impatient, or felt himself to be above the details of engineering. He was interested in the theory and structure behind things rather than the thing itself. For example, he built a chess-playing machine and dealt admirably with all the details to make it work. However, his objective was not to manufacture chess machines, but rather to understand how it could be done.

Third, Shannon was not a mathematical specialist in some branch of mathematics or engineering mathematics to whom others would turn for help with some specialized problem. His genius lay in finding appropriate mathematical models for viewing real problems, rather than in intricate knowledge of how to solve the most difficult problems within that category.

Fourth, Shannon disliked complexity and delighted in uncluttered arguments. Since he did his research in his head, long complex calculations were never central to his work, allowing him to focus even more on the creative and novel.

In summary, Shannon focused on simple ideas, theories, and conceptual structures. He avoided scholasticism, project orientation, specialization, and complexity.

SHANNON'S IMPACT ON TELECOMMUNICATION

For the first quarter century after the publication of "A Mathematical Theory of Communication," most informed people viewed information theory as an elegant and deep mathematical theory, but a theory that had relatively little to do with communication practice. At the same time, it was quickly recognized as the right theoretical way to view communication systems. In fact, when "A Mathematical Theory of Communication" was republished in book form in 1949, "A mathematical theory" had been replaced by "*The* mathematical theory."

More recently it has been generally recognized that information theory provides the guiding set of principles behind the practice of modern digital communication. In particular, the source-channel separation principle, with its universal bit interface, is so ingrained that sources and channels are described in terms of bits per second even when the raw source and raw channel are both analog. In addition, the modeling assumptions by engineers in the field now closely follow those developed by Shannon.

The birth of information theory in 1948 led to intense intellectual excitement in the early 1950s. Engineers tried to understand the communication system aspects, mathematicians tried to put a formal axiomatic touch on the central theorems, physicists tried to understand the connection between information theoretic entropy and statistical mechanical entropy, and humanists tried to sort out what Shannon's information had to do with more traditional notions of information.

As time went on, information theorists learned to merge the engineering and mathematical aspects of the theory. In particular, the more engineering-oriented people learned to appreciate the need to be precise about simple models, and mathematicians learned about which models are important.

The physicists learned that, although there are great similarities between the mathematics of statistical mechanics and information theory, statistical mechanics is not particularly helpful to understand the basic ideas of information theory. More recently there have been many cooperative efforts between the two fields, profitably using insights and tools from one on the problems of the other.

The humanists learned that information theory was centrally oriented toward communication engineering, and that it was not going to provide an immediate scientific basis for the human notions of information. Later, the underlying notion of information as a choice between alternatives has provided insight into biological areas.

After the intellectual ferment of the introduction of information theory died down, there was a realization that if information theory was to have an impact, effective coding techniques had to be developed both for data compression and for channel error correction. Research was needed on major new theoretical ideas, fundamental new algorithms, and simple but realistic source and channel models. Many engineering researchers, having studied Shannon's work, used his basic research style over the next fifty years to develop increasingly effective and practical coding techniques.

The development of major improvements in communication systems is very rapid today, but these new developments and inventions rely heavily on the rich background and understanding coming from the previous fifty years of research. It is vital for governments and universities to continue to support basic Shannon-style research in engineering, since without it, the infrastructure needed for rapid development will not be present when needed.

# Physical Limitations of Omni-Directional Antennas

LAN JEN CHU

24 AUGUST 1913–25 JULY 1973

JOURNAL OF APPLIED PHYSICS **19**
(DECEMBER 1948): 1163–75

*Introduced by David H. Staelin*

S. Mason and L. Chu of the Research Laboratory of Electronics discuss the theory behind a new radar antenna, c. 1944.

Lan Jen Chu was born in China in 1913. He received his bachelor's degree at Chiao Tung University, Shanghai, in 1934 and his S.M. and Sc.D. degrees in electrical engineering from MIT in 1935 and 1938. It was at the wartime MIT Radiation Laboratory that his incisive knowledge of electromagnetic theory was first translated into classic designs for UHF and microwave antennas, a tradition he later continued as an MIT professor from 1947 until his death in 1973. He also made important contributions as a private consultant and at Chu Associates, a leading antenna consulting firm he established. Representative of his other contributions was his conception of a missile guidance system based on interferometric radar, which led to establishment of the classified Project Meteor that energized several MIT departments and laboratories on campus for roughly seven years during the 1950s and helped further develop and consolidate MIT expertise in related areas.

His postwar paper "Physical Limitations of Omni-Directional Antennas" was typical of Chu's direct and thorough approach to electromagnetic problems, where he insightfully reduced complex questions to their simple elements before proceeding to the final answer. This emphasis on fundamentals also typified his two coauthored textbooks, which comprised much of the core education for MIT electrical engineering students from the 1950s to the 1980s.

The critical issue treated in "Physical Limitations of Omni-Directional Antennas" involved the fundamental limits to antenna directivity posed by its reactance, bandwidth, and size relative to wavelength. By treating only the simple case of a line antenna, Chu revealed the important physical issues that limit antenna performance and made them accessible to the greater technical community. This ability to reduce obscure problems to their fundamentals was also central to his significant career contributions to the Department of Electrical Engineering and to MIT at large.

The abstract and most of the introduction appear below.

## ABSTRACT

The physical limitations of omni-directional antennas are considered. With the use of the spherical wave functions to describe the field, the directivity gain $G$ and the $Q$ of an unspecified antenna are calculated under idealized conditions. To obtain the optimum performance, three criteria are used: (1) maximum gain for a given complexity of the antenna structure, (2) minimum $Q$, (3) maximum ratio of $G/Q$. It is found that an antenna of which the maximum dimension is $2a$ has the potentiality of a broad band width, provided that the gain is equal to or less than $4a/l$. To obtain a gain higher than this value, the $Q$ of the antenna increases at an astronomical rate. The antenna which has potentially the broadest bandwidth of all omni-directional antennas is one which has a radiation pattern corresponding to that of an infinitesimally small dipole.

## I. INTRODUCTION

AN antenna system, functioning as a transmitter, provides a practical means of transmitting, to a distant point or points in space, a signal which appears in the form of r-f energy at the input terminals of the transmitter. The performance of such an antenna system is judged by the quality of transmission, which is measured by both the efficiency of transmission and the signal distortion. At a single frequency, transmission efficiency is determined by the power gain of the antenna system in a desired direction or directions. The distortion depends not only on the frequency characteristics of the antenna input impedance, but also on variations of phase and of power gain with frequency. It is common practice to describe the performance of an antenna system in terms of its power gain and the band width of its input impedance.

Designers of antennas at *VLF* range have always been faced with the problems of excessive conduction losses in the antenna structure and a narrow band width. At this frequency range, the physical size of the antenna is necessarily small in terms of the operating wave-length. For a broadcasting antenna, with a specified distribution of radiated power in space, it was found that the antenna towers must be spaced at a sufficient distance apart so as not to have excessive currents on the towers. At microwave frequencies, where a high gain has been made possible with a physically small antenna, there seems to be a close relationship between the maximum gain thus far obtainable and the size of the antenna expressed in terms of the operating wave-length. At optical frequencies where a different language is used, the resolving power of a lens or a reflector is proportional to the ratio of the linear dimension to wave-length. Thus, over the entire frequency range, there seems to be a practical limit to the gain or the directivity of a radiating or focusing system.

From time to time, there arises the question of achieving a higher gain from an antenna of given size than has been obtained conventionally.

This paper presents an attempt to determine the optimum performance of an antenna in free space and the corresponding relation between its gain and the band width of the input impedance under various criteria. Let the largest linear dimension of the antenna structure be $2a$, such that the complete antenna structure including transmission lines and the oscillator can be enclosed inside a geometrical spherical surface of radius $a$. The field outside the sphere as a result of an arbitrary current or source distribution inside the sphere can be expressed in terms of a complete set of spherical vector waves. Each of these waves represents a spherical wave propagating radially outward. However, the current or source distribution *inside* the sphere is not uniquely determined by the field distribution *outside* the sphere. It is mathematically possible to create a given field distribution outside the sphere with an infinite number of different source distributions. We shall confine our interest to the most favorable source distribution and the corresponding antenna structure. To circumvent the difficult task of determining the latter, the most favorable conditions will be assumed to exist inside the sphere. The current or source distribution inside the sphere necessary to produce the desired field distribution outside will be assumed to require the minimum amount of energy stored inside the sphere so that one has a pure resistive input impedance at a single frequency. Also, to simplify the problem, the conduction loss will be neglected.

Under these conditions it is not possible to calculate the behavior of this antenna over a finite frequency range since the exact nature of the antenna structure is not known. At one frequency we can determine the radiation characteristics of the system from the expressions for the field, including the directivity gain of the antenna in a given direction. The directivity gain is equal to the power gain in the absence of conduction loss in the antenna structure. We shall utilize the conventional concept of $Q$, computed from the energy and power at a single frequency, to obtain the frequency characteristics of the input impedance by extrapolation. It is understood that the physical interpretation of $Q$ as so computed becomes rather vague whenever the value of $Q$ is low.

After obtaining the gain and $Q$ of the antenna corresponding to an arbitrary field distribution outside the sphere, we then proceed to determine the optimum distribution of the field outside the sphere under different criteria and the corresponding gains and $Q$ through the process of maximization and minimization.

# Coding for Noisy Channels

PETER ELIAS

26 NOVEMBER 1923–7 DECEMBER 2001

IRE CONVENTION RECORD, PART 4

(1955): 37–46

*Introduced by Robert G. Gallager*

In the 1950s and 1960s, the MIT Department of Electrical Engineering made a major transition from a department centered around engineering practice to a department centered around fundamental engineering science. In the same period, computer science became a major part of the department. Peter Elias, through his research and administrative skills, played a central role in both these transitions.

To understand what happened, recall that the international community's foremost mathematicians, physicists, and engineers were working furiously during World War II to develop military systems, and in so doing developed a remarkable fusion between basic science and new engineering systems. By the end of the war, there was a general belief among scientific and intellectual leaders that fundamental engineering research should play a central role in the leading universities, and that engineering education should stress basic research ideas combined with engineering.

In the communication area, these beliefs were particularly strongly held, in part because of the example of AT&T Bell Laboratories, where the beneficial effects of basic research could be clearly seen. In particular, the creation of information theory by Claude Shannon at Bell Labs in 1948 was regarded as a major intellectual breakthrough, one that had the potential to revolutionize communication practice.

Professor Peter Elias, Electrical Engineering Department Head

The electrical engineering department at MIT led this shift toward fundamental research and education, and attracted the very best students and faculty in the world in the 1950s and 1960s, particularly in communication.

After receiving a bachelor's degree from MIT, Peter Elias spent the last two years of the war as a radio technician in the Navy. He then went to Harvard for his graduate work. While looking for a Ph.D. topic, he spotted Shannon's 1948 paper very shortly after its publication—and, like many information theorists, he was hooked for life. Elias rapidly completed a Ph.D. thesis in information theory in 1950, then spent the next three years as a junior fellow in the Harvard Society of Fellows.

In 1953, Elias came to MIT as an assistant professor in the electrical engineering department. He was only twenty-nine years old, but was already highly respected for his wisdom and for his research brilliance.

His 1955 paper "Coding for Noisy Channels," reprinted below, was perhaps the most influential early paper in information theory after Shannon's. This paper takes several major steps toward realizing the promise held out by Shannon's paper.

Shannon's work showed that a noisy communication channel is primarily characterized by a capacity $C$, measured in bits per second. He showed that it is possible, by using sufficient delay and complexity at encoder and decoder, to transmit data over the channel at any rate $R$ less than $C$ with arbitrarily small error probability; it is not possible to transmit at $R > C$ with small error probability. However, Shannon's proof was an existence proof in which the individual code words were randomly chosen. This gave no hint how to design particular encoders and decoders that could approach this performance.

It has taken fifty years to find a satisfactory engineering solution to this design problem. The first three giant steps were provided by Elias's paper.

Elias considered only a particularly simple channel model called the binary symmetric channel (BSC). This model actually embodies all of the significant conceptual problems of coding and decoding, but its simple structure aids both intuition and analysis.

The first major result of the paper is a derivation of upper and lower bounds on the smallest achievable error probability on a BSC using codes of a given block length $n$. These bounds decrease exponentially with $n$ for any data rate $R$ less than the capacity $C$. Moreover, the upper and lower bounds are substantially the same over a significant range of rates up to capacity. This result shows that:

(a) achieving a small error probability at any rate near capacity necessarily requires a code with a long block length; and

(b) almost all randomly chosen codes perform essentially as well as the best codes; that is, most codes are good codes.

Consequently, Elias turned his attention to finding classes of codes that have some special structure, so as to simplify implementation, without sacrificing average performance over the class.

His second major result is that the special class of linear (or "parity check") codes has the same average performance as the class of completely random codes. Encoding of linear codes is fairly simple, and the symmetry and special structure of these codes led to a promise of simplified decoding strategies. R.W. Hamming and others had looked earlier at very simple linear codes, but their approach did not generalize well. Later research led to numerous classes of linear codes with simple decoding, and in practice practically all codes are linear.

Elias's third major result was the invention of convolutional codes. These are linear codes in which a block structure is replaced by a convolutional structure. These codes are even simpler to encode than general linear codes, and they have many other useful qualities. Elias showed that convolutional codes also have the same average performance as randomly chosen codes.

Shortly after Elias's paper was published, Jack Wozencraft discovered that the tree structure of convolutional codes permits decoding by a sequential search algorithm. Somewhat later, it was shown that the trellis structure of convolutional codes could be used for efficient maximum likelihood decoding via the Viterbi algorithm. Convolutional codes have in fact been the workhorses of practical coding from then until now. They are also essential components of turbo codes, a computationally attractive, capacity-approaching technique used today.

In 1998, Elias received an IEEE Information Theory Society Golden Jubilee Award for Technological Innovation for this invention.

Elias's paper is remarkable in several other ways. First, for a paper that had such a profound effect on the evolution of information and coding theory, it is remarkably short and easy to read. Second, it appeared only in an IEEE Convention Record and was never expanded into a journal article (or, as is common today for much lesser works, republished repeatedly in multiple variations of conference and journal papers).

On the occasion of the twenty-fifth anniversary of information theory, the IEEE produced two collections of key papers: "Key Papers in the Development of Information Theory" (D. Slepian, ed.) and "Key Papers in the Development of Coding Theory" (E.R. Berlekamp, ed.). "Coding for Noisy Channels" was the only paper reprinted in both of these volumes, attesting to its major influence over the entire field.

Elias produced a number of other major papers on information theory between 1953 and 1960. Then in 1960, at the age of 36, he was promoted to full professor and also, remarkably, appointed as department head. This appointment turned out to be brilliant, but unfortunately Elias had to put his research career on hold.

Elias was department head from 1960 to 1966, years of great change in the department. Computer science was rapidly growing as a new field and the digital revolution was in full swing. Physics-based work on materials, electromagnetic, and optical systems was growing rapidly. It was obvious even then that the collection of areas within the department would form the foundation of the coming information age. Elias's technical background put him at the center of all of these growth areas. At the same time, his obvious selflessness and his growing wisdom led to his being trusted by all parts of the department. This was a golden age for the department, which established many of the standards and expectations that continue to make it great today.

Kenneth H. Olsen (left) discusses with Charles Townes and Peter Elias Digital Equipment Corporation's donation of a PDP-1 computer to MIT, in Building 26, September 1961.

# CODING FOR NOISY CHANNELS[*]

Peter Elias
Department of Electrical Engineering and Research Laboratory of Electronics
Massachusetts Institute of Technology
Cambridge, Massachusetts

Summary: Shannon's and Feinstein's versions of the channel capacity theorem, specialized to the binary symmetric channel, are presented. A much stronger version is proved for this channel. It is shown that the error probability as a function of delay is bounded above and below by exponentials, whose exponents agree for a considerable range of values of the channel and the code parameters. In this range the average behavior of all codes is essentially optimum, but for small transmission rates this is not true. The results of this analysis are shown to apply to check-symbol codes of four kinds which have progressively simpler coding procedures. The last of these is error-free, and makes it possible to transmit information at a rate equal to the channel capacity with a probability one that no decoded symbol will be in error.

## Introduction

Since Shannon[1,2] showed that information could be transmitted over a noisy channel at a positive rate with an arbitrarily low probability of error at the receiver, there has been considerable interest in constructing specific transmission schemes that exhibit such behavior.

For a signal transmitted over a channel perturbed by Gaussian noise, Golay[3] and Fano[4] found schemes which in the limit had the desired behavior, but it was a limit of infinite bandwidth or vanishing transmission rate. Rice[5] investigated the characteristics of transmission using randomly selected noise waveforms, and got an indication of exponential decrease in error probability with increasing time delay. Feinstein[6] showed that the same sort of behavior, at least as an upper bound, held true for more general channels.

For the binary channel, Hamming[7], Gilbert[8], Plotkin[9], and Golay[10] investigated a variety of codes, and found some basic properties of the binary symmetric channel. Laemmel[11], Muller[12], and Reed[13] also constructed specific codes and classes of codes. The first constructive code for transmission at a nonzero rate over a noisy binary channel was discovered recently by the author[14]. The investigation reported in the present paper started as a continuation of that work, and an investigation of the rate at which the error probability decreased with delay originally developed from a comparison of check-symbol codes with codes of less restricted types. It seems more

sensible to present the results in reverse order. After a definition of the channel and general coding procedures, Shannon's and Feinstein's channel capacity theorems are stated, and a stronger theorem is given for the binary symmetric channel, which shows in considerable detail the behavior of error probability at the receiver as a function of the parameters of the channel and the code, and the delay time. It is then shown that most of these results carry over to a variety of kinds of check-symbol codes. One of these, of primarily academic interest, is error-free[14], and permits the transmission of an infinite sequence of message symbols at an average rate equal to the channel capacity with a probablity one that no decoded digit is in error.

## The Channel

The coding problem we will discuss is illustrated in Fig. 1. The problem is to match the output of an ideal binary message source to a binary symmetric noisy channel.

The message source generates a sequence of binary symbols, say the binary digits zero and one. Zeros and ones are selected with equal probability, and successive selections are statistically independent.

The channel accepts binary symbols as an input and produces binary symbols as an output. Each input symbol has a probability $p_o < 1/2$ of being received in error, and a probability $q_o = 1 - p_o$ of being received as transmitted. The transmission error probability $p_o$ is a constant, independent of the value of the symbol being transmitted: the channel is as likely to turn a one into a zero as to turn a zero into a one. The channel, in effect, adds a noise sequence to the input sequence to produce the output sequence; the noise is a random sequence of zeros and ones, synchronous with the signal sequence, in which the ones have probability $p_o$, and the addition is addition modulo two of each signal digit to the corresponding noise digit $(1+1 = 0+0 = 0, \ 0+1 = 1+0 = 1)$.

If the message source were connected directly to the channel, a fraction $p_o$ of the received symbols would be in error. A coding procedure for reducing the effect of the errors is shown in Figs. 1 and 2. The output of the message source is segmented into consecutive blocks of length M. There are $2^M$ such blocks, and they are selected by the source with equal probability. To each input block of M binary symbols is assigned an output block of N binary symbols, $N > M$.

The input sequences of length M are the messages to be sent; the output sequences of length N are the transmitted signals, and the correspondence between input and output blocks is the code used. The use of the word "code" is justified

[*]This work was supported in part by the Signal Corps; the Office of Scientific Research, Air Research and Development Command; and the Office of Naval Research.

37

by Fig. 2, where the correspondence between input and output blocks is given in the form of a code-book. On the left is a column of the $2^M$ possible messages, listed as M-digit binary numbers in numerical order. Following each message is the N-digit binary number which is the corresponding signal, so that the codebook has $2^M$ entries, each of which lists a message and the corresponding signal.

The system in operation is shown in Fig. 1. The source selects a message that is coded into a transmitted signal and sent over the noisy channel. The received block of N -- the received, or noisy, signal -- differs from the transmitted signal in about $p_o N$ of its N symbol values. The decoder receives this noisy signal and reproduces one of the $2^M$ possible messages, with an average probability $P_e$ of making an incorrect choice.

The most general type of decoder is shown in Fig. 3. It is a codebook with $2^N$ entries, one for each of the possible received signals. The left column is the received sequence, arranged as an N-digit binary number in numerical order. This is followed by the M-symbol message block that will be reproduced when that sequence is received as a noisy signal.

In order to minimize $P_e$, the codebook must be so constructed that the message that is selected when a given noisy signal is received is the one corresponding to the signal most likely to have been transmitted. For the binary symmetric channel, the signal most likely to have been transmitted is the one that differs from the received signal in the smallest number of symbol positions. This follows from the fact that a particular group of k errors has probability $p_o^k q_o^{N-k}$ of being introduced by the channel; this probability decreases as k increases, for $p_o < 1/2$.

For this channel, the codebook may be simplified. In fact, the transmitter codebook may be used in reverse order. The noisy signal is compared with each of the possible transmitted signals, and the number of positions in which they differ is counted. The signal with the lowest count is assumed to have been transmitted, and the corresponding message block is reproduced as the best guess at the transmitted message. This guess may, of course, be incorrect, and will be if the noise has altered more than half of the positions in which the transmitted signal differs from some other listed signal.

This decoding procedure may be described in a geometrical language introduced by Hamming[7]. Each signal is taken as a point or a vector in an N-dimensional space, with coordinates equal to the values (zero or one) of its N binary symbols. The distance between two points is defined as the number of coordinates in which they differ. In this language, the noisy signal is decoded as the nearest of the signal points, and the corresponding message is chosen.

For given M and N, the error probability $P_e$ depends on the set of points that are used as signals. If these are clustered in a small part of

the space, $P_e$ will be large; if they are far from one another, $P_e$ will be small. As specialized to this channel, Shannon's second coding theorem states an asymptotic relationship between M, N, and $P_e$ for a suitable selection of signal points.

Channel Capacity and Error Probability

First, some definitions are required. Given a binary symmetric channel with transmission error probability $p_o$ and $q_o = 1 - p_o$, the equivocation $E_o = E(p_o)$ and the capacity $C_o = C(p_o)$ of the channel, both measured in bits per symbol, are given by

$$E_o = -p_o \log p_o - q_o \log q_o$$
$$C_o = 1 - E_o \tag{1}$$

(Here and later, all logarithms are to the base two.)

Given a coding procedure like that illustrated by Figs. 1, 2, and 3, the redundancy $E_1$ and the transmission rate $C_1$, also in bits per symbol, are given by

$$E_1 = \frac{N - M}{N}$$
$$C_1 = 1 - E_1 = \frac{M}{N} \tag{2}$$

It is convenient to introduce the probability $p_1$ which is the upper bound of the transmission error probabilities for which this particular code can be expected to work, and $q_1 = 1 - p_1$. These are uniquely defined by

$$p_1 < \frac{1}{2}$$
$$E_1 = E(p_1) = -p_1 \log p_1 - q_1 \log q_1 \tag{3}$$

since a plot of $E(p)$ or $C(p)$ is monotonic for $0 \le p \le 1/2$.

Finally, the average probability of an error in decoding, which was written as $P_e$ above, will in general be a function of the block length N, the channel capacity $C_o$ or error probability $p_o$, and the transmission rate $C_1$ or the probability $p_1$. It will be written as $P_e(N; p_o, p_1)$.

Shannon's second coding theorem[1], as applied to this channel, follows.

Theorem 1. Given any fixed $C_1 < C_o$ and any fixed $\epsilon > 0$, for all sufficiently large N there are codes which will transmit information at the rate $C_1$ bits per symbol and will decode it with an error probability per block of N, $P_e(N, p_o, p_1) < \epsilon$. This cannot be done for $C_1 > C_o$.

Shannon's proof of the theorem proves more than the theorem states. A code is a selection of

38

$2^{NC_1}$ signal sequences from among $2^N$ possibilities. Including those codes that select the same signal two or more times to represent several different messages, there are $2^{N \cdot 2^{NC_1}}$ different codes. Each of these will have an average decoding error probability (averaged over the different messages, with equal weights). Shannon shows that the average of all of these (averaged over the different codes, with equal weights) is less than $\epsilon$. Since the error probability for each code is positive, it follows that at least one code has an average error probability less than $\epsilon$; and it also follows, as Shannon remarks, that, at most, a fraction f of the codes can have an average error probability as great as $\epsilon/f$, so that almost all of the codes have arbitrarily small error probability; that is, almost all codes are "good" codes, although some "bad" codes do exist. By the same argument, in any one good code the error probability for most of the individual messages is less than $\epsilon/f$, so that by discarding a few of the signal sequences and transmitting at a very slightly slower rate, any good code can be made into a uniformly good code. This result has considerable practical importance, since a uniformly good code will transmit with the specified small error probability, regardless of the probabilities with which message sequences are selected, and there are many information sources whose statistics are not known in detail.

The major question left open by this theorem is how large N must be for given $p_0$, $p_1$, and $\epsilon$. Feinstein[6] has proved a stronger version which provides an upper bound for $P_e(N, p_0, p_1)$. As specialized to the binary symmetric channel it may be written as:

Theorem 2. Given any $C_1 < C_0$, an $\epsilon(p_0, p_1) > 0$ can be found. For any sufficiently large N, a code may be constructed which will transmit information at the rate $C_1$ bits per symbol which can be decoded with $P_e(N, p_0, p_1) < 2^{-\epsilon N}$.

Feinstein's proof consists of the construction of a code that satisfies the requirements of the theorem and is uniform in the sense that all signals are good signals. Some indication of the relation of $\epsilon$ to the channel and code parameters is also given.

The next theorem is much stronger than this, but unlike Shannon's and Feinstein's it does not apply to the general discrete noisy channel without memory, but only to the binary symmetric case. Some more definitions are needed. It turns out that the error probability $P_e$ is bounded not only above but below by exponentials in N, and that for a considerable range of channel and code parameters the exponents of the two bounds agree. The error exponent for the best possible code is defined as

$$\alpha_{opt}(N, p_0, p_1) = \frac{-\log P_e(N, p_0, p_1)}{N} \qquad (4)$$

and $\alpha_{avg}(N, p_0, p_1)$ is defined as the same function of the average of the error probabilities of all codes.

An additional probability value is also needed, along with the values of $\alpha$, C, and E which go with it:

$$p_{crit} = \frac{p_0^{1/2}}{p_0^{1/2} + q_0^{1/2}}, \qquad q_{crit} = 1 - p_{crit}$$

$$E_{crit} = E(p_{crit}), \qquad C_{crit} = 1 - E_{crit} \qquad (5)$$

$$\alpha_{crit} = \lim_{N \to \infty} \alpha_{opt}(N, p_0, p_{crit})$$

Finally, the margin in error probability and the margin in channel capacity need labeling:

$$\delta = p_1 - p_0 \qquad (6)$$

$$\Delta = C_0 - C_1$$

For a binary symmetric channel with capacity $C_0$ and transmission rate $C_1$, the following statements hold.

Theorem 3. (a) For $p_0 < p_1 < p_{crit}$, $C_0 > C_1 > C_{crit}$, the average code is essentially as good as the best code:

$$\alpha(p_0, p_1) = \lim_{N \to \infty} \alpha_{opt}(N, p_0, p_1) = \lim_{N \to \infty} \alpha_{avg}(N, p_0, p_1)$$

$$= -\Delta - \delta \log \frac{p_0}{q_0} \qquad (7)$$

(b) For $p_{crit} < p_1 < 1/2$, the average code is not necessarily optimum; for $p_1$ near 1/2 it is certainly not. Specifically,

$$\alpha_{avg}(p_0, p_1) = \lim_{N \to \infty} \alpha_{avg}(N, p_0, p_1)$$

$$= \alpha_{crit} + C_{crit} - C_1 \qquad (8)$$

where $\alpha_{crit}$ is the $\alpha(p_0, p_1)$ of Eq. (5) with $p_1 = p_{crit}$, while for $\alpha_{opt}$ there are two upper and two lower bounds:

$$\liminf \alpha_{opt}(N, p_0, p_1) \geq \begin{cases} \alpha_{crit} + C_{crit} - C_1 \\[2ex] \dfrac{p_1}{2} \log \dfrac{1}{4pq} - C_1 \end{cases} \qquad (9)$$

$$\limsup \alpha_{opt}(N, p_0, p_1) \leq \begin{cases} -\Delta - \delta \log \dfrac{p_0}{q_0} \\[2ex] \dfrac{E_1}{4} \log \dfrac{1}{4pq} \end{cases} \qquad (10)$$

As $p_1 \to 1/2$, the second bound in (9) approaches the second bound in (10);

$$\lim_{N \to \infty} \lim_{p_1 \to 1/2} \alpha_{opt}(N, p_0, p_1) = \frac{1}{4} \log \frac{1}{4pq} \qquad (11)$$

which is always greater than

$$\alpha_{avg}\left(p_0, \frac{1}{2}\right) = \alpha_{crit} + C_{crit} \qquad (12)$$

The content of this theorem is illustrated by Fig. 4. This is a plot of the channel capacity $C(p)$ vs. transmission error probability $p$ for a binary symmetric channel. A dashed line is drawn tangent to the curve at the point given by the channel parameters $p_0$, $C_0$. This tangent line has the slope $\log (p_0/q_0)$. The critical point $p_{crit}$, $C_{crit}$ is the point at which the slope of the curve is $(1/2) \log (p_0/q_0)$. For $p_0 < p_1 < p_{crit}$, the $\alpha(p_0, p_1)$ of (7), which is both the average and the optimum error exponent, is the length of a vertical dropped from the channel capacity curve to the tangent line at the ordinate $p_1$.

At $p_1 = p_{crit}$, the dotted line that determines $\alpha_{avg}(p_0, p_1)$ diverges from the tangent line. For $p_{crit} < p_1 < 1/2$ the exact value of $\alpha_{opt}(N, p_0, p_1)$ is not known, but is given by the length of a vertical at ordinate $p_1$, dropped from the channel capacity curve and terminating in the shaded region. `The upper and lower bounds of this region provide lower and upper bounds, respectively, on the value of $\alpha_{opt}$. These bounds converge to $(1/4) \log (1/4pq)$ at $p_1 = 1/2$, and near this point $\alpha_{opt}$ is definitely $> \alpha_{avg}$.

The value of $\alpha$ given by the tangent line at $p_1 = 1/2$, although not approached for the transmission of information at any nonzero rate, is the correct value of $\alpha_{opt}$ for transmission of one bit per block of $N$ symbols.

An outline of the proof of Theorem 3 appears in the Appendix. A more detailed presentation, giving bounds on $P_e(N, p_0, p_1)$, as well as on $\alpha$, will appear elsewhere.

### Check-Symbol Codes

The preceding three theorems are interesting in theory but discouraging in practice. They imply that a good code will require a transmitting codebook containing $N \cdot 2^{NC_1}$ binary digits in all, and either a receiver codebook containing $N \cdot 2^N$ binary digits or another copy of the transmitter codebook and $2^{NC_1}$ comparisons of the received signal with the possible transmitted signals. Since in interesting cases $NC_1$ may be of the order of 100, the requirements in time and space are unmanageable. Furthermore, it would be quite consistent with these theorems if no code with any simplicity or symmetry properties were a good code.

The theorems that follow show that this is fortunately not the case. Four kinds of codes of increasing simplicity and convenience from the point of view of realization are demonstrated to have essentially the same behavior, from both a channel capacity and an error probability point of view, as the optimum code. The last of the four is of theoretical interest as well, since it permits the receiver to set the decoding error probability arbitrarily low without consulting the transmitter.

A check-symbol code of block length $N$ is a code in which the $2^{NC_1}$ signal sequences have in their initial $NC_1$ positions all $2^{NC_1}$ possible combinations of symbol values. The first $NC_1$ positions will be called information positions and the last $NE_1$ will be called check positions. The signal corresponding to a message sequence is that one of the signal sequences whose initial symbols are the message.

A parity check-symbol (pcs) code is a check-symbol code in which the check positions are filled in with digits each of which completes a parity check of some of the information positions. Such codes were discussed in detail first by Hamming[1], who calls them systematic codes. A pcs code is specified by an $NC_1 \times NE_1$ matrix of zeros and ones, the ones in a row giving the locations of the information symbols whose sum modulo two is the check digit corresponding to that row. The process is illustrated in Fig. 5. Such a code requires $NC_1 \times NE_1 = N^2 C_1 E_1 \le \frac{1}{4} N^2$ binary digits in its codebook, these being the digits in the check-sum matrix.

A sliding pcs code is defined as a pcs code in which the check-sum matrix is constructed from a sequence of $N$ binary symbols by using the first $NC_1$ of them for the first row, the second to $(NC_1 + 1)$st for the second row ..., the $NE_1$th to the $N$th for the $NE_1$th row. This code requires only an $N$-binary-digit codebook.

Finally a convolutional pcs code is defined as one in which check symbols are interspersed with information symbols, and the check symbols check a fixed pattern of the preceding $NC_1$ information positions if $C_1 \ge 1/2$; if $E_1 > 1/2$, the information symbols add a fixed pattern of zeros and ones to the succeeding $NE_1$ check positions. Such a code requires $\max(NC_1, NE_1) \le N$ binary digits in its codebook. It is illustrated by Fig. 6.

Theorem 4. All the results of Theorem 3 apply to check-symbol codes and to pcs codes. The results of part (a) of that theorem apply to sliding pcs codes.

In reading Theorem 3 into Theorem 4, the average involved in $\alpha_{avg}$ is the average of all codes of the appropriate type; that is, all combinations of check symbols for the check-symbol codes, all check-sum matrices for the pcs codes, all sequences of $N$ binary digits for the sliding pcs code.

Theorem 5. The results of part (a) of

40

Theorem 3 apply to convolutional pcs codes, if $P_e(N, p_o, p_1)$ is interpreted as the error probability per decoded symbol. For infinite memory (each check symbol checking a set of prior information symbols extending back to the start of transmission over the channel) the N in $P_e(N, p_o, p_1)$ for a particular decoded information symbol is the number of symbols which have been received since it was received.

This theorem shows that error-free coding can be attained at no loss either in channel capacity or in error probability, a question raised by the author when the first error-free code was introduced[14]. By waiting long enough, the receiver can obtain as low a probability of error per digit as is desired, without a change of code being necessary. By gradually reducing the ratio of check to information symbols toward $E_o/C_o$, using the law of the iterated logarithm for binary sequences, it can be shown that in an infinite sequence of message digits transmission is obtained at average rate $C_o$ with probability one of no errors in the decoded message.

## Conclusion

An appreciable gain in simplicity has been achieved in going from an arbitrary average code to a convolutional or sliding pcs code. It is possible to encode and decode either of these codes with a codebook of only N or fewer binary digits. However, the decoding operation will require $2^{NC_1}$ or $2^{NE_1}$ (whichever is smaller) comparisons, which will take a great deal of time in interesting cases. No decoding procedure that replaces this operation by a small amount of computing has yet been discovered, although the iterated Hamming code, which is error-free[14], gives hope that it may be possible to manage this while still keeping optimum behavior in terms of channel capacity and error probability -- a feature which the iterated Hamming code lacks.

## Acknowledgments

After the analytical work reported in this paper was done, but before it had been organized for presentation, I discovered that Dr. Shannon was also working on the problem of error probability, and was to present his results at the same meeting. In discussing the results with Dr. Shannon, he mentioned the geometric relationship between the tangent line and the capacity curve, illustrated in Fig. 4, in the region $p_1 < p_{crit}$. I do not know whether this would have occurred to me in organizing my results, but I do know that it is vital; the information to the right of $p_{crit}$ is my own, but is impossible to present in any other fashion without getting lost in numbers of families of curves.

It is a pleasure to acknowledge my indebtedness to the atmosphere at the Research Laboratory of Electronics, without which this work would not have gotten started; and to my colleagues, Professors Fano, Huffman, and Yngve, who provided that part of the atmosphere most relevent

to this specific project.

## Appendix

### 1. Outline Proof of Theorem 3

Using the symbols and definitions of Eqs. (1), (3), (5), and (6), let $k_1 = Np_1$ be an integer. Define $V_N(k)$, the volume of an N-dimensional sphere of radius k, by

$$V_N(k) = \sum_{j=0}^{k} \binom{N}{j} = \sum_{j=0}^{k} \frac{N!}{j!\,(N-j)!} \qquad (A.1)$$

Select $2^N/V_N(k_1)$ sequences as signaling sequences. Then the signaling rate is

$$\frac{1}{N} \log \left\{ 2^N/V_N(k_1) \right\} = 1 - \frac{1}{N} \log V_N(k_1) \qquad (A.2)$$

If the selection of signal sequences can be made so that every possible received sequence differs from one (and only one) signal sequence in $k_1$ or fewer positions, then the probability of a detection error will be just the probability $P_I(N, p_o, p_1)$ that more than $k_1$ out of N errors are made in transmission. This is the tail of the binomial distribution:

$$P_I(N, p_o, p_1) = \sum_{j=k_1+1}^{N} p_o^j q_o^{N-j} \binom{N}{j} \qquad (A.3)$$

Such a selection is not, in general, possible. However, $P_I(N, p_o, p_1)$ of (A.3) is a lower bound to the average decoding error probability $P_e(N, p_o, p_1)$ for any actual selection of signal points: this follows directly from the fact that $p_o^j q_o^{N-j}$ is a monotonically decreasing function of j.

The average of all possible codes is used to provide an upper bound to the decoding error probability of the best code. The average probability of a detection error, $P_{III}(N, p_o, p_1)$, is the probability $P_{II}(N, j, k_1)$ of a decoding error when just j transmission errors have occurred, averaged over the binomial distribution of j. With Eq. (A.3) this gives

$$P_{III}(N, p_o, p_1) = \sum_{j=0}^{N} P_{II}(N, j, k_1)\, p_o^j q_o^{N-j} \binom{N}{j}$$

$$\leq \sum_{j=0}^{k_1} P_{II}(N, j, k_1)\, p_o^j q_o^{N-j} \binom{N}{j}$$

$$+ P_I(N, p_o, p_1) \qquad (A.4)$$

41

The probability $P_{II}(N, j, k_1)$ of a decoding error when just $j$ transmission errors have occurred is the probability that one of the $\{2^N/V_N(k_1)\} - 1$ incorrect signal sequences differs in $j$ or fewer places from the received sequence. There are a total of $V_N(j)$ sequences which differ from the received sequence in as few as $j$ positions, and the probability of missing all of them in $\{2^N/V_N(k_1)\} - 1$ tries is, for $j < k_1$, bounded by

$$\left(1 - \frac{V_N(j)}{2^N}\right)^{\{2^N/V_N(k_1)\}-1} \geq 1 - \frac{V_N(j)}{V_N(k_1)} \qquad (A.5)$$

Equation (A.5) gives the probability of no decoding error: $P_{II}$ is the probability of a decoding error, so

$$P_{II}(N, j, k_1) \leq \frac{V_N(j)}{V_N(k_1)} \leq \frac{\binom{N}{j}}{\binom{N}{k_1}} \qquad (A.6)$$

Equations (A.4) and (A.6) give

$$P_{III}(N, p_o, p_1) \leq \sum_{j=0}^{k_1} p_o^j q_o^{N-j} \frac{\binom{N}{j}^2}{\binom{N}{k_1}} + P_I(N, p_o, p_1) \qquad (A.7)$$

Now the sums in Eqs. (A.1) and (A.3) are bounded below by the value of their largest term and above by a geometric series multiplied by that term -- the last term in Eq. (A.1), the first in Eq. (A.3). (See Feller[15], p. 126 for the bounds for Eq. (A.3).) The sum in Eq. (A.7) is similarly bounded above and below, if $p_1$ is less than $p_{crit}$, which is the condition guaranteeing that the last term in the sum is the largest. Using these results, taking logarithms, and using Stirling's approximation for the binomial coefficients gives, from (A.2),

$$\lim_{N\to\infty} \left\{1 - \frac{1}{N} \log V_N(k_1)\right\} = 1 - E_1 = C_1 \qquad (A.8)$$

from (A.3), for $p_o < p_1 < \frac{1}{2}$,

$$\lim\sup_N a_{opt}(N, p_o, p_1) \leq \lim_{N\to\infty} \frac{-\log P_{II}(N, p_o, p_1)}{N}$$

$$= -\Delta - \delta \log \frac{p_o}{q_o} \qquad (A.9)$$

and from (A.7), for $p_o < p_1 < p_{crit}$,

$$\lim\inf_N a_{opt}(N, p_o, p_1) \geq \lim_{N\to\infty} \frac{-\log P_{III}(N, p_o, p_1)}{N}$$

$$= -\Delta - \delta \log \frac{p_o}{q_o} \qquad (A.10)$$

Together, Eqs. (A.9) and (A.10) prove the first part of the theorem, and cover the region in which the dashed-line and the dotted curves of Fig. 4 coincide.

Since the length represented by $a_{opt}$ in this region is the difference between the curve and its tangent, it is second-order in $\delta$ or $\Delta$. In fact, for small $\delta$ and $\Delta$,

$$a_{opt}(p_o, p_1) \approx \frac{\delta^2}{2pq} \log e \approx \frac{\Delta^2}{2pq\left(\log \frac{p}{q}\right)^2} \log e$$

For $p_1 > p_{crit}$, the largest term in the sum in Eq. (A.7) is not the last, but is that term for which $j^2/(N-j)^2$ is most nearly equal to $p_o/q_o$. This term is larger than $P_I(N, p_o, p_1)$ for large $N$, and the sum is bounded above by $k_1$, the number of terms, times the largest term. Taking the limit of $(1/N)$ multiplied by the logarithm and using Stirling's approximation gives upper and lower bounds for $a_{avg}(N, p_o, p_1)$ which coincide, giving for $p_{crit} < p_1 < \frac{1}{2}$,

$$\lim\inf_N a_{opt}(N, p_o, p_1) \geq \lim_{N\to\infty} a_{avg}(N, p_o, q_o)$$

$$= \lim_{N\to\infty} \frac{-\log P_{III}(N, p_o, p_1)}{N}$$

$$= C_{crit} + a_{crit} - C \qquad (A.11)$$

This gives the remainder of the dotted curve in Fig. 4.

For $p_1$ less than $p_{crit}$, the probability of a detection error as computed above is essentially the probability of escaping from a sphere of radius $k_1 = Np_1$. For $p_1$ near $1/2$, a different point of view is possible and leads to the two solid curves in Fig. 4.

The probability that transmission errors will cause one transmitted signal to be decoded as another is the probability that the noise will alter half or more of the positions in which they differ. If they differ in $Np_1 = k_1$ positions, this probability is just the upper half of the binomial, $P_I\left(Np_1, p_o, \frac{1}{2}\right)$ as given in Eq. (A.3). This is the probability of a particular transition; the total error probability is certainly less than this multiplied by the number of signal sequences. Gilbert[8] has shown that it is always possible to find $2^N/V_N(k_1 - 1)$ signal sequences each of which differs in at least $k_1$

42

positions from every other. For large N, by Eq. (A.8), this corresponds to a signaling rate of $C_1$ bits per symbol, or $2^{NC_1}$ signal points. Thus

$$P_e(N, p_o, p_1) \leq \frac{2^N}{V_N(k_1 - 1)} P_I(Np_1, p_o, \tfrac{1}{2}) \quad (A.12)$$

and asymptotically, from Eqs. (A.8) and (A.3),

$$\lim_{N \to \infty} \frac{-\log P_e(N, p_o, p_1)}{N} = -p_1 \left\{ C - 0 + \left(\tfrac{1}{2} - p_o\right) \log \frac{p_o}{q_o} \right\}$$

$$= p_1 \cdot \tfrac{1}{2} \left\{ \log \frac{1}{2p_o} + \log \frac{1}{2q_o} \right\}$$

$$= \frac{p_1}{2} \log \frac{1}{4pq} \quad (A.13)$$

and

$$\lim \inf_N \alpha_{opt}(N, p_o, p_1) \geq -C_1 + \frac{p_1}{2} \log \frac{1}{4pq} \quad (A.14)$$

This is the upper solid curve in Fig. 4. For an upper bound to $\alpha_{opt}$ we use a result of Plotkin[9] which shows that there are at most 2N signal points whose mutual minimum distance is as great as N/2. This means that the transmission rate for signal points at this distance is $(1 + \log N)/N$ and approaches zero for large N. This result sets a limit to the number of signal points at smaller distances as well. As Plotkin pointed out, if $B(N,k)$ is the number of signal points at mutual distance $\geq k$, then at least half of these agree in their first coordinate. Eliminating the n first coordinates gives

$$B(N-n, k) \geq 2^{-n} B(N, k) \quad (A.15)$$

Using Eqs. (A.14) and (A.15), let $n = N - 2k$. Then

$$B(N, k) \leq 2^{N-2k} B(2k, k) = 4k \cdot 2^{N-2k} \quad (A.16)$$

For a transmission rate $C_1$ this determines k:

$$C_1 = 1 - E_1 = \lim_{N \to \infty} \frac{\log B(N,k)}{N} \leq 1 - 2\frac{k}{N} \ ,$$

$$\text{or} \quad k \leq \frac{N}{2} E_1 \quad (A.17)$$

Now the error probability for such a set of signal points is certainly greater than the probability of a single transition, which is, in turn, at least as great as the upper half of the binomial

$$P_I\left(\frac{NE_1}{2}, p_o, \tfrac{1}{2}\right)$$

Thus

$$\lim \sup_N \alpha_{opt}(N, p_o, p_1) \leq \lim_{N \to \infty} \frac{-\log P_I\left(\frac{NE_1}{2}, p_o, \tfrac{1}{2}\right)}{N}$$

$$= \frac{E_1}{4} \log \frac{1}{4pq} \quad (A.18)$$

which gives the lower solid curve in Fig. 4. At $p_1 = 1/2$, Eqs. (A.18) and (A.14) give the same value, so that

$$\lim_{N \to \infty} \lim_{p_1 \to 1/2} \alpha_{opt}(N, p_o, p_1) = \frac{1}{4} \log \frac{1}{4pq} \quad (A.19)$$

These results prove the remainder of the theorem. It should be noted that Eq. (A.19) does not imply that it is impossible to transmit any information with an error probability less than approximately $2^{-\frac{N}{4}\log \frac{1}{4pq}}$ for finite N. It is only impossible to do so while transmitting at a positive rate in the limit of large N. The transmission of one bit per block of N symbols can be accomplished by picking two signal sequences that differ in every position, with an error probability equal to $P_I(N, p_o, 1/2)$ for which, from Eq. (A.3),

$$\lim_{N \to \infty} \frac{-\log P_I\left(N, p_o, \tfrac{1}{2}\right)}{N} = \frac{1}{2} \log \frac{1}{4pq} \quad (A.20)$$

This error exponent is twice as great as that for the limit (as $p_1 \to 1/2$) of $\alpha_{opt}$ for positive transmission rates. Other points for the transmission of 2, 3, ... log N bits per block of N symbols fall between the value of Eq. (A.20) and that of Eq. (A.19).

## 2. Outline Proof of Theorems 4 and 5

A large part of the proof of Theorem 3 carries over directly for Theorems 4 and 5. Any upper bound on $\alpha_{opt}$ for the best possible code is automatically an upper bound for the more restricted class of check-symbol codes. Thus Eqs. (A.9) and (A.18), the tangent line and the lower solid curve in Fig. 4, still apply. To get the upper solid curve, Eq. (A.14), it is necessary to show that Gilbert's result, and thus Eq. (A.12), holds for the kind of code considered. This is obvious for pcs codes; Gilbert's proof requires only trivial modifications in this case. Since the pcs codes are a special case of check-symbol codes, the result follows for these as well. For sliding and convolutional pcs codes Gilbert's result is not obvious, although probably still true; that is why only the first part of Theorem 3 is extended to these cases.

The difficult point in Theorems 4 and 5 is the demonstration that the average of all possible codes, of each of the four types considered, is still given by Eqs. (A.10) and (A.11) and the dotted curve in Fig. 4. This requires a demonstration that the inequality of Eq. (A.6) still

43

applies; that is, that the probability of a decoding error when j transmission errors have occurred is essentially the same, on the average, for the different types of check-symbol codes as for the average of all codes. The remainder of the derivation then follows as before.

This will be done for the pcs codes. When a noisy signal is received, the parity-check sums are recomputed at the receiver and added modulo two per position to the received check symbols, as in the Hamming code[7]. The resulting check-symbol pattern is the pattern caused by the transmission errors alone. The probability that this check-symbol pattern will be misinterpreted when j transmission errors have occurred is the probability that some other collection of j or fewer errors has the same check-symbol pattern. There are $V_N(j) - 1$ other patterns of j or fewer errors, and the probability that one of these has the same check-sum pattern is the probability that one of the $V_N(j) - 1$ differences has a check-sum pattern of all zeros. Now, if the check-sum matrix is filled in at random, any error pattern may produce any check-symbol pattern with equal probability. Therefore the probability of any one error pattern having a check-symbol pattern that vanishes is the reciprocal of the total number of possible check-symbol patterns. This number is $V_N(k_1)$, since $2^N/V_N(k_1)$ messages are being sent, and the total probability of a decoding error when j transmission errors have been made is less than this multiplied by the number of difference patterns:

$$P_{II}(N, j, k_1) \leqslant \frac{V_N(j) - 1}{V_N(k_1)} \leqslant \frac{V_N(j)}{V_N(k_1)} \leqslant \frac{\binom{N}{j}}{\binom{N}{k_1}} \quad (A.21)$$

which is the inequality of (A.6) obtained by a different route.

The essential point in this argument is that every transmission error pattern, in the ensemble of possible codes, may cause every check-symbol pattern, with equal probability. Given this, the rest of the argument presented above follows. This is easy, but tedious, to show for sliding and convolutional pcs coding; the proofs will be omitted here.

## References

1. C. E. Shannon, "A mathematical theory of communication," Bell System Tech. J. 27, 379-423, 623-656 (1948).

2. C. E. Shannon, "Communication in the presence of noise," Proc. I.R.E. 37, 10-21 (1949).

3. M. J. E. Golay, "Note on the theoretical efficiency of information reception with PPM," Proc. I.R.E. 37, 1031 (1949).

4. R. M. Fano, "Communication in the presence of additive Gaussian noise," "Communication Theory," Willis Jackson Ed. (Butterworths, London, 1953) 169-182.

5. S. O. Rice, "Communication in the presence of noise -- probability of error of two encoding schemes," Bell System Tech. J. 29, 60-93 (1950).

6. A. Feinstein, "A new basic theorem of information theory," Trans. I.R.E. (PGIT) 4, 2-22 (1954).

7. R. W. Hamming, "Error detecting and error correcting codes," Bell System Tech. J. 29, 147-160 (1950).

8. E. N. Gilbert, "A comparison of signalling alphabets," Bell System Tech. J. 31, 504-522 (1952).

9. M. Plotkin, "Binary codes with specified minimum distance," Univ. of Penna., Moore School Research Division Report 51-20 (1951).

10. M. J. E. Golay, "Binary coding," Trans. I.R.E. (PGIT) 4, 23-28 (1954).

11. A. E. Laemmel, "Efficiency of noise-reducing codes," pp. 111-118 in "Communication Theory," reference 4 above.

12. D. E. Muller, "Metric properties of Boolean algebra and their application to switching circuits," University of Illinois, Digital Computer Laboratory Report No. 46.

13. I. S. Reed, "A class of multiple error-correcting codes and the decoding scheme," Trans. I.R.E. (PGIT) 4, 38-49 (1954).

14. P. Elias, "Error-free coding," Trans. I.R.E. (PGIT) 4, 30-37 (1954).

15. W. Feller, "An Introduction to Probability Theory and Its Applications" (John Wiley and Sons, Inc., New York, 1950).

44

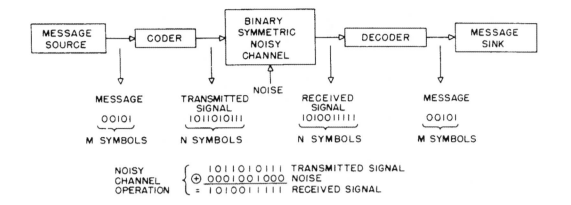

Fig. 1
Noisy communication system

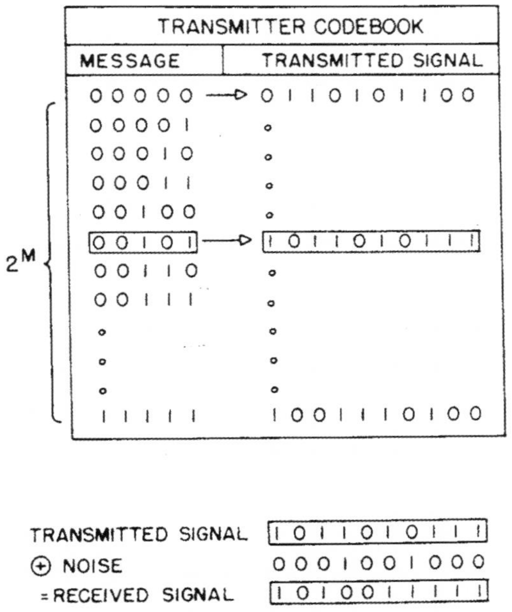

| TRANSMITTER CODEBOOK | |
|---|---|
| MESSAGE | TRANSMITTED SIGNAL |
| 0 0 0 0 0 → | 0 1 1 0 1 0 1 1 0 0 |
| 0 0 0 0 1 | ° |
| 0 0 0 1 0 | ° |
| 0 0 0 1 1 | ° |
| 0 0 1 0 0 | ° |
| 0 0 1 0 1 → | 1 0 1 1 0 1 0 1 1 1 |
| 0 0 1 1 0 | ° |
| 0 0 1 1 1 | ° |
| ° | ° |
| ° | ° |
| ° | ° |
| 1 1 1 1 1 | 1 0 0 1 1 1 0 1 0 0 |

$2^M$

TRANSMITTED SIGNAL　1 0 1 1 0 1 0 1 1 1
⊕ NOISE　　　　　　　0 0 0 1 0 0 1 0 0 0
= RECEIVED SIGNAL　1 0 1 0 0 1 1 1 1 1

Fig. 2
Codebook coding

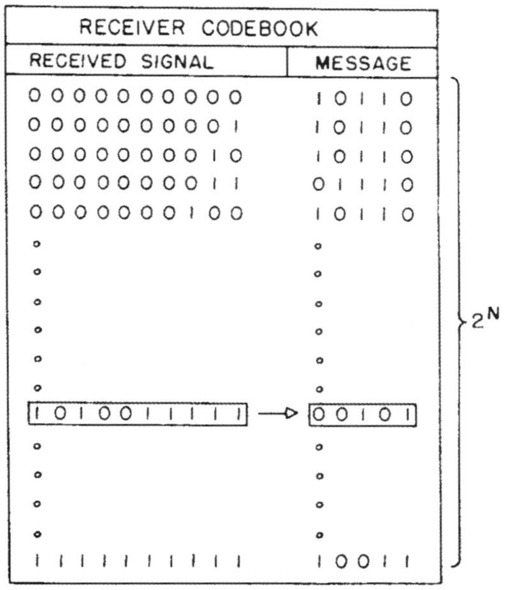

| RECEIVER CODEBOOK | |
|---|---|
| RECEIVED SIGNAL | MESSAGE |
| 0 0 0 0 0 0 0 0 0 0 | 1 0 1 1 0 |
| 0 0 0 0 0 0 0 0 0 1 | 1 0 1 1 0 |
| 0 0 0 0 0 0 0 0 1 0 | 1 0 1 1 0 |
| 0 0 0 0 0 0 0 0 1 1 | 0 1 1 1 0 |
| 0 0 0 0 0 0 0 1 0 0 | 1 0 1 1 0 |
| ° | ° |
| ° | ° |
| ° | ° |
| ° | ° |
| ° | ° |
| ° | ° |
| 1 0 1 0 0 1 1 1 1 1 → | 0 0 1 0 1 |
| ° | ° |
| ° | ° |
| ° | ° |
| ° | ° |
| 1 1 1 1 1 1 1 1 1 1 | 1 0 0 1 1 |

$2^N$

Fig. 3
Codebook decoding

45

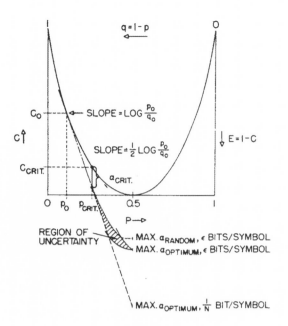

Fig. 4

The error exponent $\alpha$ optimum

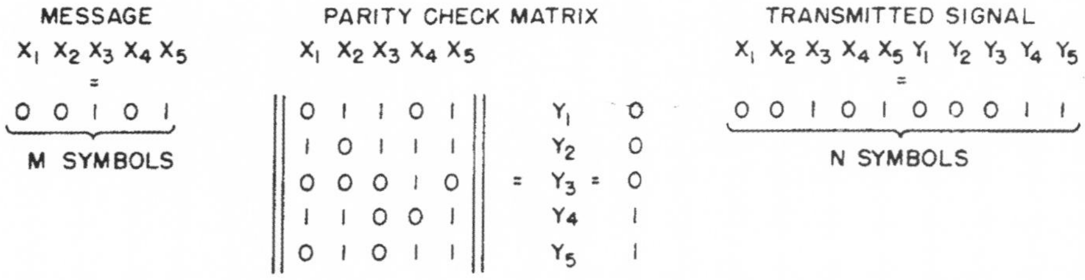

MESSAGE
$X_1\ X_2\ X_3\ X_4\ X_5$
=
O O I O I
M SYMBOLS

PARITY CHECK MATRIX
$X_1\ X_2\ X_3\ X_4\ X_5$

$$\begin{Vmatrix} 0 & 1 & 1 & 0 & 1 \\ 1 & 0 & 1 & 1 & 1 \\ 0 & 0 & 0 & 1 & 0 \\ 1 & 1 & 0 & 0 & 1 \\ 0 & 1 & 0 & 1 & 1 \end{Vmatrix} = \begin{matrix} Y_1 \\ Y_2 \\ Y_3 \\ Y_4 \\ Y_5 \end{matrix} = \begin{matrix} O \\ O \\ O \\ I \\ I \end{matrix}$$

TRANSMITTED SIGNAL
$X_1\ X_2\ X_3\ X_4\ X_5\ Y_1\ Y_2\ Y_3\ Y_4\ Y_5$
=
O O I O I O O O I I
N SYMBOLS

Fig. 5

Parity check coding

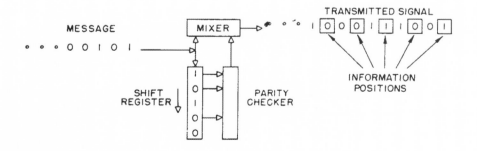

Fig. 6

Convolutional parity check coding

46

# GORDON STANLEY BROWN
## 30 AUGUST 1907 –
## 23 AUGUST 1996

*by Abigail Mieko Vargus '97*

Gordon Stanley Brown was not yet twenty-two years old when he left his native Australia for MIT. He enrolled as a junior, with civil, electrical, and mechanical engineering degrees already in hand from Workingman's College (now known as the Royal Melbourne Technical School). MIT became his home—and the home of many of his impressive accomplishments—for the next forty-four years.

At MIT Brown studied electrical engineering, earning his S.B., S.M., and Sc.D. before joining the faculty as an assistant professor in 1939. (During this time, Brown also married Jean Alfred, a marriage that lasted sixty-one years and created a loving family with daughter Sydney and son Stanley '65.) His undergraduate thesis advisor was Harold "Doc" Edgerton, who later remarked that Brown was a quiet and meek man. It wasn't long, however, before Brown's enthusiasm and energy were the traits most associated with him—by Doc Edgerton and the rest of the campus.[5] After all, this was the man whose oft-quoted statement is, "The only steady state is the steady state of change."[6,7]

Brown's doctoral research focused on the cinema integraph, a precursor to the analog computer, through which he became intimately versed in feedback control. He applied that knowledge by founding MIT's Servomechanisms Laboratory in 1940. While Brown was director, the lab was home to World War II efforts for automatic gun control and to peacetime research on nuclear reactor controls, digital machine tool control, and digital computers. In fact, it was under Brown's leadership of the Servomechanisms Laboratory that Jay Forrester began the development of the Whirlwind Computer.

In all these cases, Brown was renowned for his ability to encourage and motivate the lab's talented staff. Jay Forrester later remarked at a Computer Museum symposium, "Gordon Brown, my mentor at MIT, … was a person who threw a great deal of responsibility onto young staff members, even as research assistants in the electrical engineering department. He provided an environment in which people developed very rapidly, and in which they could attach themselves to some important and overriding goal."[8]

Institute Professor Gordon S. Brown

105

Brown quickly rose through the Institute's ranks; becoming a full professor in 1946, and in 1952, he was appointed head of the electrical engineering department. A core curriculum change was already planned that year, and Brown attacked it with vigor and innovation. He believed that undergraduate engineering education should build knowledge of engineering principles by creating a strong foundation of science and mathematics. "Engineering science, rather than state-of-the-art engineering practice, was his model."[9]

Again, Brown's leadership was invaluable. As Professor Frank Reintjes recalled at Brown's retirement dinner, "He rallied around him a group of young faculty and inspired them to revise old subjects, write class notes, publish new textbooks, design new lab experiments and equipment, and in general form the new base upon which modern electrical engineering is built."[10] His educational efforts as department head were recognized by the American Society for Engineering Education, which gave him the Lamme Medal of American Education, and the American Institute of Electrical Engineers, which awarded him the Medal in Electrical Engineering Education.

Brown's skills, however, took him beyond the department and into the campus at large as dean of the School of Engineering in 1959. This position allowed Brown to champion the creation of interdepartmental, interdisciplinary research. New research centers were established to bridge the previous gap between disciplines, creating a model now common in universities. He also led MIT's participation in international relationships in the educational world. Faculty exchange programs were created with institutions in Berlin, India, and Singapore.

In 1968, Brown stepped down as dean to become the first holder of the Dugald C. Jackson Professorship in Electrical Engineering. He was appointed Institute Professor, one of the highest honors bestowed on MIT faculty, in 1973. He retired one year later, continuing as an active Institute Professor Emeritus.

Over the course of his career, Brown authored or coauthored more than fifty publications. His textbook *Principles of Servomechanisms* (coauthored with Donald P. Campbell) was a long-standing reference in the field. He received multiple honorary degrees and a long list of awards for both his engineering and educational innovations. His work stretched from MIT to professional societies to government committees to industrial organizations.

In the words of the current Dugald C. Jackson Professor of Electrical Engineering, Paul Penfield, "Gordon Brown influenced the directions of engineering education in the past fifty years more than any other single person."[11] Those who knew Brown were not surprised that his educational innovations did not stop when he retired.

Brown and his wife, Jean, moved to Tucson, Arizona, where he became active in the public schools. He called himself a "citizen champion,"[12] and he spurred a revolution in elementary education. His theory was that applying system dynamics techniques to the classroom by introducing computers would spur significant, positive changes. He worked with a local school district to make this happen, and the benefits were quickly apparent.

To share this innovation with more children, Brown began fundraising. His first major effort was to negotiate with Apple for a gift of $100,000 worth of computers for the classroom he was working in. This kind of work, however, was more than one man—even one with the energy and dedication of Gordon Brown—could handle. The Gordon Stanley Brown Fund was established to promote system dynamics teaching in the schools and to pay K–12 teachers for summer and released-time work to document their experiences.

On 23 August 1996, after nearly sixty years of changing the face of education, Gordon Brown passed away. His legacy, however, lives on. At MIT, it is evident not just in the nameplate on Building 39 (the Gordon Stanley Brown Building), but also in interdepartmental research, the engineering-science curriculum, and international relationships. In education at large, his influence can be found in universities that mimic MIT's successful engineering-education programs as well as in elementary and middle school computer labs. In industry, it can be found in myriad applications of feedback control.

# Educating Electrical Engineers to Exploit Science

**GORDON S. BROWN**

**30 AUGUST 1907–23 AUGUST 1996**

**ELECTRICAL ENGINEERING**

**(FEBRUARY 1955): 110–115**

*Introduced and excerpted by Paul L. Penfield, Jr.*

Gordon S. Brown

In our department's pursuit of excellence in undergraduate education, two of its leaders stand out. One is Gordon Brown, who served as department head from 1952 to 1959, and then as dean of engineering for nine years.

During World War II it seemed that engineers played a secondary role in projects requiring the most extreme advances in technology (especially radar, in the MIT Radiation Laboratory, and the atomic bomb). Scientists were the leaders. Although in previous decades engineers had been able to make industrial use of science, they were less effective in the war effort.

Brown figured out why. Normally scientists are motivated by curiosity, wanting to know how nature works. They care less about applications. On the other hand, engineers were motivated by satisfying human needs, but could use only scientific results that were already available. In cases where there was a need but no science, neither group combined motivation and ability to contribute. The urgency of the war effort was enough to make scientists pay attention to applications (radar and atomic energy). Engineers, however, lacked the training and attitude to do the necessary scientific research. It was no wonder which group ended up on top.

The solution was to educate engineers to make advances in science when an engineering project called for them. Engineers needed to learn more science, including areas that were not yet ready for exploitation. They needed to learn how to do research, as opposed to engineering. And their employers needed to value their scientific advances. As department head, Brown presided over the curricular changes needed for electrical engineering. As dean of engineering he did the same for other disciplines. And he made sure that other universities were fully informed of MIT's efforts, so they could do likewise.

The paper reprinted here was written while these reforms were still being implemented, but it is the best description available. There was a core curriculum based on underlying science rather than contemporary practice. There were only two major stems for specialization (energy and information), and Brown predicted (correctly) that the nature of the associated industry would make the energy stem appear less scientific and therefore less appealing to students.

This curriculum was developed in the 1950s and was in use during the 1960s and 1970s. It influenced the programs of many other universities, who were eager to adopt the "engineering science" philosophy. It produced graduates who were excellent at the most challenging engineering projects, projects that required the synthesis of existing and new scientific results from many fields along with advanced mathematics. Research was emphasized, and many graduates went on to earn doctorates and become faculty at other universities, thereby spreading the approach far and wide. A set of coordinated undergraduate textbooks was written. All in all, the 1950s was an exciting decade; the results of the activity served the department, its students, and the nation very well.

**Are the future electrical engineers being trained broadly enough in the sciences? This question has been given serious study at the Massachusetts Institute of Technology, with the result that major changes have been made in the undergraduate electrical curriculum, so as to better equip the students with technical substance and professional vision.**

THE insatiable urge of man for greater command over his environment continues to expand the industrial system. Industry is being called upon to increase both quantity and quality of its product. As science opens up new frontiers, industry is also being called upon to establish wholly new products.

The pace at which technology is asked to achieve these events continues to quicken. The time interval between the birth of a new discovery in science and its exploitation in industry and commerce continues to diminish. Of the various contributory factors, among the most dominant are, first, the expanding nature of science and, second, the versatility and flexibility of scientists and engineers whose roots are deep in the realm of science. Throughout all industry the boundaries between the traditional categories of engineering, such as electrical, mechanical, metallurgical, and so forth, are crumbling as machines and machine systems of greater capability and complexity must be created and kept running.

The engineer who is resourceful in science, who can upgrade the implements of his trade as science advances, and especially the engineer who can couple sound judgment and keen intuition with his exploitation of science, is a precious member of society. But the supply of such men is inadequate in spite of the best efforts of engineering educators. It becomes pertinent, therefore, to pose the question:

Should the future electrical engineers be educated first as electrical scientists and subsequently as electrical engineers?

There are several pedagogical reasons that support the question. One is that science clearly dominates modern engineering. Another is that up to the turn of the century, many electrical engineering departments were formed around a body of science that had split off from physics. Their technical activities were focused mainly at the engineering of electricity and magnetism. A third is that there has been a veering away from a training that would make engineers continually useful as science advances, along with a preoccupation with the training of men to be useful to specific industries immediately upon graduation.

There are many signs that future engineers are not being trained broadly in the sciences. This is an issue in the recent interim report of the Committee on Evaluation of Engineering Education of the American Society of Engineering Education.[1] The question has been given serious study by the faculty of the Department of Electrical Engineering at the Massachusetts Institute of Technology, with the result that major changes have been introduced into the undergraduate curriculum required of all electrical majors. In order to put a discussion of the changes in the proper context, a review of the heritage and growth of engineering is in order.

### THE HERITAGE OF ELECTRICAL ENGINEERING

UP to about the turn of the century, the mission of most electrical engineers was to invent, devise, and manufacture a vast variety of such things as motors, generators, transformers, transmission lines, switchgear, relays; and to integrate them into great energy-processing systems or telephone-telegraph systems. Their tasks called for judgment and intuition coupled with an awareness about economic and social trends. The heritage left by these men is superb, for now the United States has the world's greatest telephone system, and the most efficient, reliable, and extensive electric power system in existence anywhere. Its power systems operate with near-perfect waveform, frequency control, and voltage regulation. However, while the power industry was maturing, science was opening up new areas of technology that attracted the interest of electrical engineers. By the late twenties or early thirties, the era of electronics had attained adolescence. As each young group of engineers expanded electronic technology in new directions, the teacher and student interest in the power area became attenuated.

Under the World War II pressures of survival, the tempo of technology was fueled by the advent of many scientist-engineer teams. Wholly new industries came into being around the fields of radar, computation, television, servomechanisms, nucleonics, and many others, and captured the interest of the best graduate engineers. In response to the demands of industry for engineers who could be immediately useful to it in these fields, engineering school curricula tended to split from the two camps—namely, power and communications—that had dominated the period between World War I and World War II, into upwards of six to ten camps by the turn of the mid century. The early option structure of power and electronics was expanded in some institutions to include such categories as industrial electronics, radar, and control. New subjects were added to overcrowd the curriculum just as more lights are often added to an already overlit Christmas tree. Eventually, educators were trapped by the dilemma of unmanageable specialization. (The roster of Scientific and Technical Personnel prepared by the Engineers Joint Council of the National Science Foundation lists 31 categories of specialization under Electrical Engineering.)

The growth of options led students into the habit of typing themselves prematurely under the pretense that a curriculum with a strong vocational flavor, or patterned along the needs of an industry, would provide the motivation or vehicle for a broad basic education in the fundamentals of electrical engineering. Actually, this was a high price to pay for motivation, for it tended merely to hold captive a body of students for a specific industry and was no guarantee that they would agree to work within that industry or that they would be offered employment in it upon graduation.

Options placed undue emphasis on learning the known art of today rather than understanding the science that would dominate the art of tomorrow. They perpetuated an academic plant that was narrow in its educational value and a deterrent to the development of broad creative thought. They were insensitive to the changing nature of science and to the fact that electrical engineers skilled in the engineering exploitation of science are not restricted to careers in those industries normally thought of as electrical. These engineers are in demand throughout all industry.

Educators traditionally say that their job is to train students to think. Equally important is the job of ascertaining clearly what students should think about. To help avoid the pitfall of thinking too narrowly about training men for the immediate job, perhaps the true role of a university needs re-emphasis.

## THE ROLE OF A UNIVERSITY

No institution of higher learning fulfills its mission by merely keeping abreast of today's knowledge and by training men for the immediate practical industrial task.[2,3] On the contrary, it should continually readjust its goals and remould its environment so that both faculty and students are concerned not only with today, but also with the topics, the ideas, and the issues that will dominate the world a decade or more hence.

Every engineering school should foster a creative interdepartmental environment. It should encourage both student and faculty to think creatively outside the categories of engineering and science that have come into existence because schools, and the engineering profession itself, have traditionally organized by departments. It should guide the student toward the creative nonconformist exploitation of science to do useful things in tomorrow's world, rather than merely rework the solved problems of yesterday. It must achieve an on-campus blending of engineering, science, and the humanities. It must attack mature, sophisticated problems, for the blending cannot occur in a vacuum. This will mean that the environment will undergo constant change. The pace of the change will be dictated, first, by the rate at which science advances and, second, by the rate at which these advances are exploited at the frontiers of engineering.

## THE NUCLEUS OF ELECTRICAL SCIENCE

THE mission of electrical engineering education becomes clearer if one can visualize a nucleus or a conceptual model of electrical science. The blend of technical substance that forms this model must be broad enough to serve the expanding systems and nature of electrical engineering. One statement of a conceptual model is that:

All so-called electrical devices are manifestations of how a creative engineer has exploited the interactions between charge carriers, their fields, and materials.

The charge carriers are ions, electrons, and even the newcomer, the hole. The fields are static and dynamic. The materials interact with the fields by virtue of their physical properties, or magnetic domain structure. The engineer's goal in the exploitation of this conceptual model is to bring into existence an array of engineering systems to perform useful functions.

This model touches every facet of an engineer's life, whether in research, in development, in manufacture, or in business. All devices patterned after this model, when welded into systems, support two great missions of the electrical engineer: the first being to process and transmit information; and the second being to exploit energy. Fulfillment of the former mission has created such industries as radar, radio and wire telephony, television, instrumentation and measurement, electronics, computation, and controls. The lusty newcomer, automation, is its latest offspring. Fulfillment of the latter mission furnishes the means which turn the wheels of American industry and provide the basis of modern civilization. Here the dominant issue is to exploit energy for energy's sake. The fulfillment of either mission is dependent on the same hard core of science. The hardware and the systems that come into being for each mission, and their functions, undergo rapid change as science advances.

## THE PRESENT STATE OF AFFAIRS

MANY of the best minds in letters, science, and engineering have been challenged by the mission to process and transmit information. In an ever-increasing degree, expertness at it is becoming dependent upon an ability to make quantitative deductions from hypotheses and abstractions and to deal with matters that can be neither seen nor felt. The scope of the mission is increasing. It will play a significant role in the future development of the industrial economy and military strength.

The academic life that supports this mission is virile and creative. It is usually backed up by a well-equipped, modern and flexible educational plant. On-campus research is extensive and easy to cultivate at both student and staff levels. The faculties are able and the students are attracted in large numbers.

In sharp contrast with this situation is the fact that since the early thirties, academic work pointed toward the exploitation of energy in the field of electric power has decreased in vigor and has attracted fewer young men. The explanation for this may stem from the fact that the industry has been preoccupied with the task of expanding its facilities under the restrictions of government regulation as isolated monopolies. Although tremendous progress has been made, instances where sharp changes in engineering practice occurred in response to new developments in science were rare. As unrestricted money for the sponsorship of on-campus research by students and faculty was almost nonexistent, power option faculties decreased in number and the students were drilled almost wholly in the solved art of the past within the power industry. Their bandwidth was from 0 to 60 cycles. Much teaching equipment supporting this field was allowed to become old, and by comparison with electronics and communications, was ponderous, inflexible, and lacking in scope for the cultivation of student resourcefulness.

The academic atrophy that now exists in this field disturbs educators as continued growth of the economy necessitates expanding the base of electric power. Complex processes of energy conversion, control, and utilization requiring engineering skill of the highest order continue to increase. Already there are nuclear fission, solid-state energy converters such as the solar battery, supersonic aviation, high-temperature metallurgy, chemical synthesis, and many others. These, coupled with major advances in magnetic, dielectric, and semiconductor materials, which permit wholly new solid-state devices, will expand the field and create a great need for a new type of engineer. But as power engineering has been presented to students, it has failed to attract sufficient numbers with sufficiently high intellectual ability and creative breadth to meet the needs.[4] On nearly every campus power engineering has become the poor relation, both financially and intellectually, by contrast with the fields that support the mission to process and transmit information. A sharp and decisive reversal of this situation is needed.

## A SUGGESTED BREAK WITH TRADITION

THE faculty of the department of electrical engineering at the Massachusetts Institute of Technology has conducted a harsh review of its own practices relative to these matters. It has drastically revised its undergraduate curriculum: first, to broaden and deepen the science instruction for all students; second, to strengthen its training in electrical engineering by a revision of its laboratory facilities to permit more creative work by students with better integration of the sciences; third, to preserve equal opportunity for every student to choose his subsequent career by subordinating mention of vocational aspects of electrical engineering until a strong science foundation has been established; and fourth, to recognize the wide variety of interest and talent among students by allowing a wide choice of elective study in the senior year.[5] It is now clear that the break with tradition must be so great that it will take several years to learn how to achieve these aims. As initial moves toward these aims, the department has:

1. Abandoned all educational plans based on vocational options and established a core curriculum for all electrical majors.[6]

2. Discontinued instruction in traditional a-c and d-c machinery and disposed of much conventional equipment in its machinery laboratory.

3. Initiated new subjects of instruction for about half of its core curriculum to broaden and deepen the student's understanding of the science of fields, materials, and energy conversion.

4. Initiated the development of new laboratory doctrines and facilities to focus a student's attention on the objectives of laboratory investigation rather than on instruments, methods, or techniques, and to afford him a tangible opportunity to study the fundamental concepts of science and to synthesize devices and engineering systems illustrative of them.

5. Attempted to revitalize the old field of power by initiating graduate student and staff research in the broader field of energy conversion, control, and utilization.

The precise meaning of this approach is best illustrated by reference to some of the subjects that are offered.

## THE REVISED CURRICULUM

THE arrangement of the curriculum is shown in tabular form in Table I. The work of the electrical department begins in the sophomore year with a two-term sequence on circuit theory; including laboratory studies on circuits and circuit elements. The treatment is broad. About 80 per cent of the book, "Introductory Circuit Theory," by E.A. Guillemin, together with supplementary notes, is used as text material. Methods of analyzing nonlinear as well as linear circuits, appropriate to power as well as to communications, are emphasized. Statics is treated as a special case of dynamics. Computational aids, such as analogue computers, are mentioned to encourage students to attack advanced practical problems.

**Table I.  Electrical Engineering at MIT**

**Freshmen**

| | | | | |
|---|---|---|---|---|
| Physics | Chemistry | Mathematics | Elective | Humanities |
| Physics | Chemistry | Mathematics | Elective | Humanities |

**Sophomore**

| | | | | |
|---|---|---|---|---|
| Physics | Electric Circuits, 6.00 | Mathematics | Applied Mechanics | Humanities |
| Physics | Electric Circuits, 6.01 | Mathematics | Applied Mechanics | Humanities |

**Junior**

| | | | | |
|---|---|---|---|---|
| Electronic Circuits 6.02 | Fields, Materials and Components 6.03 | Mathematics | Thermo | Humanities |
| Applied Electronics 6.05 | Elec. Energy Convertors, 6.04 | 2 Electives—both out of department | | Humanities |

**Senior**

| | | | | |
|---|---|---|---|---|
| Energy Transmission and Radiation 6.07 | Power Modulators 6.06 | 2 Electives—inside or outside department | | Humanities |
| Integration of above courses via free electives influenced by student's aptitudes and interests | | Thesis | | Humanities |

Leads to Commencement
Followed by

| | |
|---|---|
| Graduate study and research, S.M., E.E., Sc.D. | On-the-job training in industry, or self-development by the graduate |

**Note:** Subjects 6.00 through 6.07 include both classroom and laboratory. Both Junior and Senior subjects are influenced by research of faculty and graduate students.

While the sophomore students study circuit theory, they also study humanities, applied mechanics, physics with emphasis on fields, and mathematics up through differential equations.

## TWO MAIN STEMS

THE electrical subjects of the junior year comprise two main stems. The stems are not options. They blend with each other as they develop, and as teaching personnel transfer back and forth between subjects. They extend into the first term of the senior year and broadly support the two missions discussed. One stem treats the role of electronic devices and the basic principles of application of such devices to perform electrical engineering functions such as rectification, amplification, modulation, oscillation, and energy radiation and transmission, as related appropriately to both information, and energy processing by electronic systems. The other stem treats fields, materials, devices, and engineering functions such as energy conversion, power modulation, and control, with emphasis on higher power systems. The approach followed in the development of both stems exploits the conceptual model by showing the student that an electrical engineer has unique ability to exploit electric charges and their associated electric and magnetic fields in engineering problems, that all devices are built of materials, and that materials interact with the fields. From this elementary viewpoint, he is led to appreciate that all electric systems are basically the result of a creative engineer's ability to exploit the combination of fields and materials to accomplish specific needs. Accordingly, instead of training students as in the past, merely to understand traditional devices such as transformers, motors, generators, or specific kinds of amplifiers, a broader comprehension of a scientific background is coupled with the basic mission of electrical engineers.

## THE ENERGY-CONVERSION STEM

THE third-year work in the energy stem builds on the second-year work in physics. The content of this stem is treated in some detail because it represents the major change in the curriculum.

The first subject, Fields, Materials, and Components, is a cornerstone in the new program. It is still in the trial stage. As now offered, it treats electromagnetism starting from Maxwell's equations, and emphasizes the relationship between fields and network parameters and the physical bases of the electric and magnetic properties of materials. It aims to introduce the universality of the field theory throughout the entire range of electrical engineering as it relates to the operation of circuit components, energy-transfer devices, and energy converters. The student is brought into first contact with the atomic structure aspects of materials, both as to their known properties and as to why they have these properties. It is hoped to show him at an elementary level something of the scope that lies ahead in the exploitation of new kinds of materials in electrical engineering. In the laboratory the students plot and measure 2- and 3-dimensional fields for diverse boundary conditions, conduct elementary studies on dielectric and magnetic materials with a view to relating microscopic behavior to atomic structure, and investigate quasi-static parameters.

The second subject of this stem, Electrical Energy Converters, compares the various methods of electric energy conversion, and emphasizes the importance of electricity as the transport medium for energy of all levels and functions. It illustrates the importance of electromechanical energy conversion and justifies an emphasis on this process and on its devices. The point is made that the electromechanical energy conversion process manifests itself by its effects on the connected systems in the form of forces, voltages and currents, which are the reactions of the coupling fields on the conducting, dielectric, and magnetic boundaries of the device. The student is shown that the behavior can be determined either by integrating the reactions over the boundary surfaces, or by resorting to the concepts of equilibrium and virtual work, leading to the generalized treatment of energies and the use of Lagrange's equation.

These principles are applied to devices ranging in construction from the simple 1-circuit transducer to the multi-circuit rotating machine and in function from the signal and instrumentation devices to the bulk energy converters. Energy flow in these devices is traced through the fields. Analysis is carried out by linear and nonlinear circuit techniques. System representations are made in terms of appropriate functions. Laboratory experience with typical devices complements the analysis.

The mission of this subject is to set the background for the study of energy-conversion devices in systems and to prepare the student for the apparent trend in this field toward more sensitive transducers, more controllable conversion devices—conversion devices operating at higher speed, frequencies, and temperatures—and the use of new direct solar-, thermal-, chemical-, and nuclear-electric conversion methods to supply the energy needs of tomorrow.

The third subject, Power Modulators, treats the dynamics of energy conversion and control devices with specific emphasis on devices used at higher-power levels. The dynamics of energy-conversion devices always involve nonlinear differential equations, and general solutions to these equations are not obtainable. The study of device dynamics, therefore, requires that complete systems be considered in order to make reasonable approximations and simplifications.

Power modulators and their connected systems are studied using elementary feedback concepts and terminology. This includes the concept of gain and time constant of first-order systems, the relationship between frequency response and time response of linear systems, the ideas of absolute and relative stability, and graphic methods for representing system response.

Two important classes of power modulator are treated. The first embraces electric transfer devices in which the input, the output, and the control are all electrical quantities. The modulation properties of these devices are related to the functional nonlinearities of the electrical parameters. Typical examples of this class of power modulator are the switching-type amplifiers, such as magnetic and thyratron amplifiers.

The second class of power modulator is the electromechanical converter. This modulator is capable of controlling the flow of relatively large quantities of energy between two electric systems by means of mechanical command signals, or it is capable of controlling the conversion of energy from a mechanical system to an electric system by an electric or mechanical command signal. The modulating or controlling characteristics of these modulators are made possible by designing the devices so as to allow mechanical freedom of motion between current-carrying conductors or coils. Examples are the commutator-type a-c and d-c machine, induction machines such as the servo-motor, and synchronous machines under steady-state or quasi-steady-state operation.

The dynamic analysis of power modulators is treated using electric-circuit methods rather than electromagnetic field methods. The equations of motion for the power modulators are obtained from Lagrange's equation, and matrix algebra is used to reduce these equations to forms best suited for each application. Throughout the subject, dynamics and control concepts are stressed and steady-state concepts are minimized.

Laboratory studies with devices and systems are being developed to support the classroom analysis. Most notable is the extent to which electronic techniques have entered the laboratory activity. The task of devising and building laboratory facilities for these energy conversion and power modulation subjects that will yield tangible opportunities for resourcefulness by the student offers one of the big challenges in the whole program. It is proceeding.

### THE INFORMATION-PROCESSING STEM

In the information-processing stem, each student studies a 2-term sequence of electronics, Electronic Circuits and Applied Electronics, to show the role of electronic devices in modern technology. The sequence introduces methods of representing a nonlinear device such as the high-vacuum or gas tube and the transistor, and it leads to a concept of piece-wise linear or linear-incremental circuit models. It treats functions such as amplification, modulation, oscillation, information processing, and limitations on system behavior from such factors as nonlinearity, noise, and the effects of inherent residual circuit parameters. It leads to the synthesis of simple electronic systems for specific objectives. Each student draws on the resources of a well-equipped laboratory.

The third subject of this stem, Energy Transmission and Radiation, also correlates closely with the first subject in the energy stem. It treats wave motion, its behavior in physical structures having dimensions comparable with the wavelength, and its specific application to energy transmission and radiation. It reviews the relations between dynamic fields and lumped circuits, and extends these to the concepts of wave impedance and radiation impedance. The laboratory for this third subject offers the opportunity to investigate quantitatively such topics as the limitations of lumped constant models in electrical and acoustical environments, 1-dimensional wave motion on transmission lines, 2-dimensional wave motion in plane waves, and elementary radiation and diffraction patterns in space.

### LABORATORY INSTRUCTION

Laboratory work is a regular part of each core subject and is directed at the technical and professional growth of the student on a broad plane. In addition to illuminating in a practical way the classroom theory, the laboratories provide an integrated series of organized experiences which develop engineering judgment, ability to plan, confidence in making compromises, teamwork, ability to observe effectively, skill at technical writing, and independent creative thought and initiative. Many of these objectives are served by an organizational pattern whereby the student is required to assume a progressively increased responsibility for the planning and execution of his laboratory work, over and above the mere mastery of experimental facts and techniques. For example, during the sophomore year the student is, among other things, made aware of laboratory equipment and effective experimental method by means of a series of problems which always yield a few challenging surprises. During the junior year the students themselves, with periodic counsel from assigned instructors, plan their attack on problems and select the equipment to be used. The instructor should subtly hold the student's attention on the objectives of the study to offset his tendency to become preoccupied with mere instruments and the taking of data. During the senior year the student is urged to take the additional step toward creative thought and initiative by defining problems at the frontiers of his experience and interests around an idea, by decomposing the idea himself, and by carrying through to a formal engineering paper.

The laboratory instruction and the facilities for about one-half of the revised curriculum are in the first stage of a process, which will converge by means of successive approximations. Laboratory topics are being filtered for adoption or discard at a rapid rate as the staff appraises its total accomplishment. It has been learned that students should not be hurried in the laboratory, and experiments should be physically simple but technically comprehensive, with a view to developing in the student a true sense of scientific inquiry.

### ELECTIVES

Each student must elect at least one humanities subject each term, with the stipulation that the humanities sequence establish some depth in at least one area. In his junior year he must, each term, also carry two elective subjects outside of the electrical department. For many students the faculty suggests that these electives comprise a third year of mathematics and a third year of physics pointed toward modern physics. One-half the load for the first term of the senior year comprises the two remaining subjects of the stem sequence. The rest of the senior year comprises the two subjects in humanities, five professional electives, and a thesis.

Wide latitude is allowed students in the selection of professional electives. Students interested in graduate work, or research and development in a creative technical environment, are advised to elect scientific or abstract subjects—for example, advanced mathematics, solid state physics, molecular phenomena of materials and their technical applications. It is felt that these students will have received broad training in electrical science as well as training in electrical engineering. On the other hand, those students who tend to be form- or thing-conscious, rather than abstract-idea conscious, or who have a high degree of tangible ingenuity in contrast with sharply developed skill at creative scientific reasoning, are advised to choose electives from a wide range of more practical topics, either in or out of the department. These electives may comprise manufacturing, management, engineering design, or such electrical engineering subjects as Feedback Control Principles, Electrical Implementation, Principles of Radar, Machine-Aided Analysis, Electronic Control and Measurement, Communication System Engineering, or Engineering Acoustics, depending upon each student's talents and interests.

## CONCLUSION

IT is hoped that a program will be achieved which will equip students with the technical substance and professional vision needed for sustained creative development and backed up by a deep sense of their social responsibility.

Work on the program has just begun. All the subjects in the energy-conversion stem are new, as is about half of the content of the information-processing stem. The third subjects in each stem were offered to students for the first time in the fall term of 1954. The first class to have studied under the new program will graduate in June of 1955.

The accomplishments to date are pleasing, but they are still considered far from satisfactory. It is expected that the core subject substance and the laboratory facilities will need reworking for 3 or 4 years. The skill and technique for presenting the material to the students need much improvement. New class notes, with related problems, are being prepared for five of the eight core subjects.

It is felt engineering students are unlikely to be motivated by a straight mathematics and science curriculum. Therefore, a virile evolving curriculum, well integrated with real engineering problems and a challenging laboratory program, led by a sincere faculty, are essential.

A research program has yet to be established in the area of energy conversion of a magnitude and at a pace that the program needs. It is felt that without a vigorous faculty research effort, the program will not long endure.

## ACKNOWLEDGMENTS

The cooperation of the students is warmly acknowledged. To put it mildly their response has been good and the going has been difficult. An attempt has been made to keep them fully informed. They sense a partnership in an educational experiment and have shown unusual adaptability and versatility.

The staff of the department is enthusiastic about the program. The burden is heavy for all and especially heavy for the many who are evolving the new core subjects. The creative imagination and heavy personal sacrifice of all are gratefully acknowledged.

## REFERENCES

1. Interim Report of the Committee on Evaluation of Engineering Education, *Journal of Engineering Education*, Lancaster, Pa., vol. 45, no. 1, Sept. 1954, p. 40.

2. Letter to a College President, H.L. Hazen, *Electrical Engineering*, vol. 73, May 1954, pp. 391–5.

3. The Universities and the Engineering World, B.L. Goodlet, *Transactions*, South African Institute of Electrical Engineers, Johannesburg, Transvaal, Union of South Africa, August 1950.

4. The Manpower Shortage in Power Education, J.D. Ryder, *Electrical Engineering*, vol. 72, January 1953, pp. 25–27.

5. The Modern Engineer Should Be Educated as a Scientist, G.S. Brown, *Journal of Engineering Education*, Lancaster. Pa., vol. 43, no. 4, December 1952.

6. Integration versus Options in Electrical Engineering, G.S. Brown, *Engineering*, vol. 72, July 1953, pp. 595–97.

# The Quantification of Neuroelectric Activity

Professor Rosenblith, 1978

WALTER A. ROSENBLITH

21 SEPTEMBER 1913–1 MAY 2002

PROCESSING NEUROELECTRIC DATA, **TECHNICAL REPORT 351, CHAPTER 1, MASSACHUSETTS INSTITUTE OF TECHNOLOGY, RESEARCH LABORATORY OF ELECTRONICS, CAMBRIDGE, MASSACHUSETTS**

PROCESSING NEUROELECTRIC DATA BY THE COMMUNICATIONS BIOPHYSICS GROUP OF THE RESEARCH LABORATORY OF ELECTRONICS AND WILLIAM M. SIEBERT

TECHNOLOGY PRESS RESEARCH MONOGRAPH, 1959

*Introduced by Paul E. Gray*

The contribution of Walter A. Rosenblith to the study of electrical activity of the brain is typified by the introductory chapter to the monograph that his group produced under his leadership.

Rosenblith joined the MIT electrical engineering faculty in 1951. He served as chairman of the faculty from 1967 to 1969, provost from 1971 to 1980, and Institute Professor from 1976 until his death in 2002. Before he died, Rosenblith was working on a book about his long-time friend and colleague Jerry Wiesner.

Born in Vienna, Walter Rosenblith was educated in Vienna, Berlin, Lausanne, Bordeaux, and Paris. He came to the United States in 1939 to investigate what American industry was doing to protect workers from noise, and stayed on as a research associate at New York University and at the Cold Spring Harbor Laboratory, where he first measured electrical signals in living organisms—electric eels. Rosenblith then went to the University of California at Los Angeles on a graduate fellowship. Later he taught in and rebuilt the physics department at South Dakota School of Mines and Technology. His interest in hearing and acoustics led to his appointment as a research fellow at the Psycho-Acoustic Laboratory at Harvard, and from there he moved down Massachusetts Avenue to MIT, where he spent the rest of his life.

Rosenblith's interest in the nervous system began with his work on the physical and psychological effects of noise on hearing, which led to work on the psychophysics and neurophysiology of hearing, and then to the broader study of electrical activity of the brain. On several occasions, he described his evolution of interest as being "sucked into the brain through the ear." During Rosenblith's time at Harvard, primitive computers were becoming available to scientists, so when he came to MIT he founded a group in the Research Laboratory of Electronics to study the brain with computers. His skills in organizing and motivating the work of colleagues, his recognition of the importance of interdisciplinary research, and his ability to bring engineers into biology, significantly advanced what is now called computational neuroscience. The group described brain signals in statistical terms and developed quantitative measures in a field which had been mainly descriptive, as reflected in the chapter Rosenblith wrote in the monograph reproduced below.

Together with Provost (and later President) Jerome Wiesner, Rosenblith was instrumental in creating the joint Harvard-MIT Division of Health Sciences and Technology (HST), in which the EECS department plays a major role.

An intellectually stimulating and charming colleague with remarkably broad knowledge and insights, Walter Rosenblith was a force in extending the scope and reach of MIT in the last half of the twentieth century when its reputation expanded far beyond that of an engineering school.

His 1959 paper is reproduced here in its entirety.

Professor Rosenblith talking with MIT visitors

Chapter 1

THE QUANTIFICATION OF NEUROELECTRIC ACTIVITY

W. A. Rosenblith

Throughout the history of science experimenters from different
fields have dealt with the problem of the quantification of their data
in a variety of ways. Technological necessities and the prevailing
theoretical structure of a given field determine to a high degree the
techniques of measurement that are developed and the choice of
variables that are quantified. Experimenters concerned with problems of "organized complexity" [1] often made little effort to report
their observations in quantitative or even systematic form. They
were too aware of the limited range of experimental facts that they
could ascertain with a sufficient degree of invariance and of the
narrow realm in which they could actually verify predictions from
mathematical models.

The se difficulties and an overly narrow interpretation of Lord
Kelvin's doctrine* may be largely responsible for the fact that
neurophysiologists, for instance, have often been hesitant to go
beyond reporting raw data in a somewhat phenomenological manner.
Such an attitude renders communication with fellow scientists haz-
ardous. If verbal statements alone are made to carry the informational burden of large bodies of data, friendly model-makers from
the physical sciences are tempted to construct theories of "how the
brain works" on the basis of a few isolated and easily mathematized
facts.

But it was just not caprice or lack of farsightedness among the
data-rich and theory-poor scientists that produced this mismatch
between their vast labors and the relatively small amount of
theoretically integrable knowledge that became available. They
were handicapped by a lack of adequate data-processing facilities
and by the fact that the mathematical models of classical physics
(and certainly those of quantum physics) had little to offer to the
student of the nervous system or of human behavior. Hence, many

---

* "I often say that when you can measure what you are speaking
about, and express it in numbers, you know something about it;
but when you cannot express it in numbers, your knowledge is of
a meagre and unsatisfactory kind; it may be the beginning of knowledge, but you have scarcely, in your thoughts, advanced to the
stage of Science, whatever the matter may be." Contrast this view
of Lord Kelvin's with Gödel's contention [2] according to which "it
is purely an historical accident that it [mathematics] developed
along quantitative lines."

1

neuroelectric data

among them were interested by cybernetics, which emerged as the philosophical expression of the communications technology of the postwar period. It was under cybernetics' influence that many problems relating to the behavior of complex living systems were reconsidered. Only too often these reconsiderations turned out to be not only suggestive but also frustrating. At that stage a search for general principles of the behavior of the nervous system could not help but be somewhat superficial. The neuroanatomical, the neurophysiological, and the behavioral data extant were not in a form that made theorizing at a fairly general level meaningful.

### 1.1  Problems of Measurement and Analysis in Electrophysiology

For more than two centuries - thanks to various species of electric fish - men have been aware of the existence of "animal electricity." [3]  More than a century ago Helmholtz measured the conduction velocity of nerve, and throughout the second half of the nineteenth century an appreciable amount of knowledge concerning brain potentials accumulated. A recent review article on the "Rise of Neurophysiology in the 19th Century" [4]  summarized the situation at the end of that century as follows: "It was known that the brain had "spontaneous" electric activity, that potential shifts could be elicited in the appropriate cortical areas by sensory stimulation, that these potentials could be recorded from the skull and that anesthesia abolished them." However, electrophysiology entered its period of rapid growth only after the technology of the vacuum tube gave us amplifiers and oscilloscopes. These two instruments permitted electrophysiologists to increase the sensitivity of their observations and to display even rapid fluctuations in voltages as a function of time.

The characteristic deflections or patterns in voltage-versus-time-displays constitute the electrophysiologist's basic data. But how are these characteristics of a waveform to be assessed? As long as scientists deal with DC potentials or sinusoids, an instrument that yields one or two characteristic numbers is perfectly satisfactory, but when they attempt to assess arbitrary waveforms containing sharp "transients" and "noise," several questions arise. Is the voltmeter (even the vacuum-tube voltmeter) the appropriate instrument of measurement? Is it necessary to display the complete waveform by photographing it from the face of an oscilloscope? Can we find selective transformations upon the data that yield meaningful descriptions while reducing the total amount of information displayed?

A further discussion of appropriate methods for the quantification of electrophysiological data leads us to consider issues that the physical sciences have faced - sometimes quite explicitly and sometimes less so - throughout their history. Before we make measurements reflecting the behavior of complex systems, it may

2

quantification

be wise to ask ourselves two sets of questions. Why do we make
a particular measurement? What conclusions (regarding the phenomena under investigation) shall we be able to draw on the basis
of the measurement?

The first set of questions inquires into the purposes of the experi-
menting electrophysiologist: Is he interested in relating the electrical events that he records from an isolated nerve fiber to the
physico-chemical processes that occur in the transmission of a
nerve impulse? Is he using the electrical events in order to trace
certain pathways in the nervous system? Is he trying to study the
responses of certain neural structures to carefully controlled
sensory stimuli? Is he investigating the behavior of neural structures in relation to a mathematical model that he has formulated?
Is he studying the way in which certain chemical substances affect
synaptic transmission? Is he trying to relate changes in an organism's electrical activity to conditioning or learning? Or is he concerned with the presence or absence of certain patterns in this
activity, with a view towards clinical diagnosis? Neurophysiology
includes all of these experiments. The experimenter's purpose
determines the choice of his variables, the display technique for
his data, and affects the very definition of what constitutes an
experiment: Which parameters are to be held constant, how rep-
licable must a phenomenon be, ... ? Neurophysiology - which has,
compared to the physical sciences, little theoretical structure of
its own - is thus characterized by an aggregate of techniques for
the study of the nervous system or of its component parts. As a
science it stands in close relation to fields such as neuroanatomy,
sensory physiology, biochemistry, psychology, biophysics, and
medicine, and the significance of neurophysiological findings is
often assessed in terms of their relevance to the neighboring fields.

The second set of questions deals with the inferences that can
be drawn from electrophysiological "pointer readings." It is here
that our lack of understanding of the organizational principles and
of the mechanisms of the nervous system is felt most seriously.
The organizational structure of this nonhomogeneous medium that
consists of large numbers of highly specific elements has so far
defied useful description in terms of the over-all physical properties of the medium. Much effort has gone into analyzing the fine
structure of its various components in terms of current biophysical and biochemical knowledge, but up to the present these
efforts have not yielded an approach that is capable of dealing with
the unique properties that characterize the nervous system of
higher animals. Here is a system that is composed of many interacting units (all of which are by no means alike), that is organized
both flexibly and hierarchically, that consists of subsystems
(enjoying various degrees of autonomy) that are capable of fulfilling
specific and/or nonspecific functions. Here is a system that reacts

3

neuroelectric data

more reliably and predictably to informationally rich stimuli than
to "simple" ones.  Here is a system that is capable of learning
and of giving reasonably reliable performance throughout an extended
period of time, with all the safety factors and maintenance and
repair requirements that such performance demands.

If we want to understand the "systems neurophysiology" that
underlies the behavior of information-processing organisms, what
is the type of electrical activity that we should study?  What type
of strategy should we adopt in dealing with the signals that we
record from the nervous system - signals whose code is known so
incompletely?  Should we attempt to isolate a single neuron and
and study its behavior in great detail, hoping that we will pick the
"right" (representative) one out of a not-too-well defined population?  Should we at the other extreme, work only with the muffled
polyneural roar that is able to make itself "heard" through man's
thick skull?  Should we limit ourselves to studying recordings of
"spontaneous" activity of a neuron (or of neuronal populations),
that is, the activity that we can still observe when we have turned
off all the stimulus generators that are under our control?  Or
should we study stimulus-response relations, that is, those
response events whose occurrence is by some criterion (usually
a temporal one) linked to the delivery of a definable stimulus?
Can we assume that these latter stimulus-evoked events will always
simply add to the "spontaneous background activity," or must we
study their interaction in different physiological states of the
organism?

Are the biggest voltages, especially when recorded at the outside of the
skull, the most important ones to study?  If we compare this situation
with the facts of speech communication, we find that it is the vowels (yea,
their first formants) that carry most of the energy among the speech
sounds, although - in English at least - it is the consonants (whose clamor
for attention is much less loud) that carry most of the linguistic information.  There are perhaps other lessons to be drawn from the study of
speech communication.  When a Fourier analysis of speech signals is
carried out, the vowels (whose duration is of the order of 1/10 second)
seem to be represented much more meaningfully by Fourier components
than the consonants.  The latter can be viewed as "transients" or "transi-
tionals," whose spectral composition depends much more upon the vowels
that precede or follow them.  The problem of where the vowels end and
the consonants start (technically known as the segmentation problem) presents a challenge all of its own, comparable perhaps to that of defining the
duration of an evoked response.  An "ah" will exhibit rather different spectral components when pronounced by a man, a woman, or a child; it will
even exhibit appreciable differences when pronounced repeatedly, and in
different context, by the same individual.  And yet there is something
invariant about it that makes it recognizable as an "ah."  This "ah"-ness
is not anything that is easily characterizable by absolute numbers, but
rather by distinctive features or parametrically defined patterns, by certain relations among the components of a sound, especially in relation to

4

quantification

other sounds that might have been emitted. Lest this analogy be carried too far, let us not pretend that we are waiting for somebody to break "the" code of the nervous system. Let us realize that we are trying to discover the units of analysis, the distinctive features of neural signals, that will help us order the innumerable data of the nervous system.

What are the techniques of analysis that are readily available to electrophysiologists when they record data to deal with the range of experimental problems that we have mentioned above? Let us briefly mention some sample techniques that have been used. The mathematics of circuit analysis (at least in its simpler forms) assumes that the circuits and their components are linear, lumped, finite, passive, and bilateral. [5]  It would, of course, be absurd to pretend that the nervous system has these properties, though it may be possible to find, by applying circuit theory, in what manner the behavior of a sensory system, for instance, deviates from this model.

If we restrict ourselves to dealing with whatever waveforms may have been recorded, we must ask whether the specific techniques such as Fourier analysis or correlation analysis are actually appropriate to the particular experimental question. Such techniques imply that the time series analyzed satisfy certain conditions.

Obviously, the assumptions implicit in these analytical techniques are a price that we have to pay for their use. Physical scientists also pay this price. They, however, know so much more about the processes that underlie the phenomena they study than we know about the mechanisms that underlie neuroelectric phenomena. Thus, in physical science there is a better chance of adjusting and correcting models than there is in neurophysiology. And yet the student of the nervous system has little choice until more appropriate techniques of analysis have been developed. He must utilize those that are available in order to find out where they cease to fit. It may, nevertheless, be wise to take the precaution of assembling a sufficient body of apparently consistent data before getting involved in ambitious computations.

Is there a moral that imposes itself on the basis of the preceding tedious and yet incomplete enumerations of problems that one faces in this type of research? We believe that there is, and we believe that it can be stated in a single word: pluralism. Only a pluralistic strategy guarantees, at this stage of our knowledge of the nervous system, that we shall not blind ourselves to useful approaches because we have oversold ourselves on one of them. The very multiplicity of purposes precludes our prescribing experimental design or methods of data processing and analysis too rigidly on intrinsic grounds. We must, rather, be prepared to make our choice on the basis of extrinsic values or influences: Given the biases of interest that we _ as a group _ have, given the physical and intellectual surroundings in which we work, we have developed certain methods of data processing and certain types of mathematical

5

neuroelectric data

models. We believe that these techniques are capable of coming
to grips with the statistical character of neural activity which is
one of the essential features of the nervous system. We have,
furthermore, a preference for packaging our results in a form
that is reasonably quantitative; that is, we try to express as many
of our findings as we can in some mathematical representation
without always trying to fit our data to analytical functions. Since
we are dealing with a multivariate system, we are not surprised
that the patterns and relationships that we find are often statistical. Finally, it is fair to say that, while we feel more secure
when we have the guiding influence of a mathematico-physiological
model in our experiments, we are not so narrow-minded as to
ignore the usefulness and even the beauty of a good classification
scheme that relates to variables whose importance to the organism
is undeniable.

1.2. A Statistical View of Neuroelectric Phenomena

No matter which aspect of the electrical activity of the nervous
system we study, we always face the task of defining "typical
events" among those we observe experimentally. This task confronts the experimenter, whether his concern is with evoked
responses or with the EEG (electroencephalograph). He has to
establish certain criteria of judgment. These criteria will be
different when he records with the aid of gross electrodes than
when he studies the activity of a single cell with the aid of a microelectrode. The electrophysiologist has the further problem of deciding whether two observations are "identical." Here the identity-
defining operation may range from identity in one aspect of the event
only (such as occurrence or nonoccurrence of a spike potential) to
identity in all measurable aspects )average spike latency, distribution of spike latencies, and so on).

In order to decide whether an event is typical or whether two
events differ, we really have to know something about the distribution of possible events. This distribution might be obtained
by observing responses to a large number of identical stimuli or
by repeatedly sampling an EEG (electroencephalographic)trace.
Actually, experimenters rarely have such information available to
them, and yet, if they are well trained, they choose representative
records as illustrations for their papers. It is, nevertheless,
necessary to realize that few, if any, systematic studies have
been made to assess an experimenter's information-handling
capacity as applied to his ability to view oscilloscopic traces or
examine film records. In other words, we do not really know
how safe the current procedures are.

We have tried to present and review elsewhere [6, 7, 8] some
of the available evidence on the statistical character of input-
output relations in either single units or for responses from
populations of neuronal elements. Here we shall try to summarize
the essential arguments only.

6

quantification

We faced this problem first when we tried to find criteria for deciding what constitutes a typical evoked response (a response that is evoked by the presentation of a discrete stimulus, most often a sensory one). There exists, to our knowledge, no generally accepted operational definition of what is meant by an evoked response although the concept has been exceedingly useful in electrophysiological and neuroanatomical studies of the nervous system.

Let us briefly see how evoked responses are recorded. The experimenter usually knows when a stimulus is being presented. He then most often establishes the presence or absence of an evoked response by either of two methods or by the two methods conjointly: (1) In recording with gross electrodes, he detects visually the presence of a characteristic waveform or deflection. (2) In recording with microelectrodes, he detects aurally (and/or visually) a change in the acoustic signals that represent the electrical events "seen" by the microelectrode after these events have been appropriately amplified and transduced.

As should be clear from this description, the experimenter's ability to detect such changes in visual and/or aural displays depends upon how stable these changes are in relation to the patterns of "background activity."* These changes will be most easily detected when they have short latencies (that is, when they occur right after the presentation of the stimuli). The more these changes exceed the experimenter's just-noticeable-difference for the visual or aural displays involved, the more reliable their detection will be.

For responses that are recorded with gross electrodes, there is variability both with respect to amplitude and with respect to time. The evoked responses of the classical afferent pathways exhibit relatively short latencies and little variability in latency. It is this relative stability of the temporal aspects of these responses that makes the use of averaging by computing devices (such as the ERD and the ARC-1) possible and useful. It goes without saying that latencies determined from the average evoked response permit us to say little about the latencies of the individual responses. So far no adequate techniques have been developed to deal with electrical events that have longer and more variable latencies (such as the so-called "blocking of the alpha rhythm").

---

*We have already mentioned the problems of the typicality of a response and of the identity of two responses. These problems include in some sense decisions of how typical the background activity is in which these responses are imbedded. Amassian and his co-workers emphasized only recently[9] how the presence of spontaneous cell discharges complicates the analysis of the effect of stimulus variables.

7

neuroelectric data

For responses that are recorded from single units with the aid of microelectrodes, the variability problem is rather different: Here we are dealing with a set of discrete events that are quite comparable in waveshape and amplitude but that occur at latencies that are governed by both stimulus parameters and the existing sequences of "spontaneous" firings of the cell. The changes in the patterns of "spontaneous" firing that do occur may result in either increases ("excitation") or decreases ("inhibition") in average firing frequency; thus variability may now affect (a) changes in number of firings (how many spikes does a given stimulus elicit or inhibit), (b) "first"-spike latency (latency of the spike whose occurrence is most directly linked to the delivery of the stimulus), (c) interspike intervals, and so on.

An overview of the problem of adequate detection and description of evoked responses leads thus to procedures in which computers are instructed to "look" for changes in patterns of ongoing activity that are somehow linked to the delivery of stimuli. "Looking" for changes in averages, such as means, or for changes in distributions within several time intervals becomes thus a method of search in which the properly instructed computer supplements human capacities.

From all that precedes, it should be clear that we must find ways of dealing with the undeniable fact that repeated presentations of the same stimulus do not yield "identical" neuroelectric responses in many physiological preparations. Instead of abdicating before this fact by declaring that neuroelectric activity is thus not tryly quantifiable, one can take advantage of this difficulty.

The variabilities that one observes seem to have their own regularities, which are in turn related to both stimulus and organismic variables. By constructing a model that had relevant statements to make with respect to both mean and variance of population responses, Frishkopf[10] was able to give a much deeper interpretation of neural events at the periphery of the auditory system than had been possible previously.

If we look for an interpretation of this statistical behavior, we must first of all consider the complexity of the system or subsystem under study, the multiplicity of possible interactions,* and the lack of adequate description of state in which a cell or a neuronal population finds itself at the time when a stimulus is presented.

A recent article of Bullock[12] gives a thoughtful discussion of the present status of the neuron doctrine and suggests several

---

*Sholl,[11] who has discussed the quantification of neuronal connectivity, states, for instance, that "impulses arriving along a single primary visual fiber will be dispersed among the 5000 neurons distributed around its terminal branches."

8

quantification

major revisions. Many of the ideas expressed by Bullock force a reconsideration of what is meant by the state of a neuron and emphasize the necessity for looking beyond the occurrence of the spike potential as the sole indicator of neuronal function.

Although there will undoubtedly become available more adequate descriptions of the state of single neurons or of neuronal populations, there is serious doubt whether we shall, in the foreseeable future, be able to dispense with statistical descriptions of neuroelectric phenomena. Given this prognosis, we shall endeavor to develop and use the most appropriate methods available in order to elucidate the statistical aspects of neuroelectric activity.

## REFERENCES

1. W. Weaver, "Science and Complexity," Am. Scientist, 36, 536-544 (1948).

2. R. Oppenheimer, "Analogy in Science," Am. Psychologist, 11, 127-135 (1956).

3. A. v. Muralt, Neue Ergebnisse der Nervenphysiologie, Springer-Verlag, Berlin, Chapter I, 1958.

4. M. A. B. Brazier, "Rise of Neurophysiology in the 19th Century," J. Neurophysiol., 20, 212-226 (1957).

5. E. A. Guillemin, The Mathematics of Circuit Analysis, John Wiley & Sons, Inc., New York, 1949.

6. W. A. Rosenblith, "Some Electrical Responses from the Auditory Nervous System," Proceedings of the Symposium on Information Networks, Polytechnic Institute of Brooklyn, pp. 223-247, April 12-14, 1954.

7. L. S. Frishkopf and W. A. Rosenblith, "Fluctuations in Neural Thresholds," Symposium on Information Theory in Biology, H. P. Yockey, R. L. Platzman, and H. Quastler, Eds., Pergamon Press, New York, pp. 153-168, 1958.

8. W. A. Rosenblith, "Some Quantifiable Aspects of the Electrical Activity of the Nervous System (with Emphasis upon Responses to Sensory Stimuli)," Revs. Mod. Phys. 31, 532-545 (1959).

9. V. E. Amassian, L. Berlin, J. Macy, Jr., and H. J. Waller, "II. Simultaneous Recording of the Activities of Several Individual Cortical Neurons," Transactions of the New York Academy of Sciences, Ser. II, 21, 395-405 (1959).

10. L. S. Frishkopf, A Probability Approach to Certain Neuroelectric Phenomena, Technical Report 307, Research Laboratory of Electronics, M.I.T., March 1, 1956.

9

neuroelectric data

11. D. A. Sholl, The Organization of the Cerebral Cortex, John
    Wiley & Sons, Inc., New York, 1956.

12. T. H. Bullock, "Neuron Doctrine and Electrophysiology, "
    Science, 129, 997-1002 (1959).

### GENERAL BIBLIOGRAPHY

The following list of books and articles is intended to supplement the references given at the end of the various chapters.
This list should provide enough variety to afford the interested
reader an introduction to current research on the nervous system.
A few general references have also been included.

1. E. D. Adrian, F. Bremer, and H. H. Jasper, A CIOMS
   Symposium: Brain Mechanisms and Consciousness,
   Charles C. Thomas, Springfield, 1954.

2. G. H. Bishop, "Natural History of the Nerve Impulse, "
   Physiol. Revs., 36, 376-399 (1956).

3. M. A. B. Brazier, Ed., The Central Nervous System and
   Behavior, The Josiah Macy, Jr. Foundation, New York, 1959.

4. M. A. B. Brazier, The Electrical Activity of the Nervous
   System, MacMillan, New York, 1953.

5. F. Bremer, "Cerebral and Cerebellar Potentials, " Physiol.
   Revs., 38, 357-388 (1958).

6. B. Delisle Burns, The Mammalian Cerebral Cortex,
   Williams & Wilkins Co., Baltimore, 1958.

7. P. E. K. Donaldson, Electronic Apparatus for Biological
   Research, Academic Press Inc., New York, 1958.

8. J. C. Eccles, The Physiology of Nerve Cells, The Johns
   Hopkins Press, Baltimore, 1957.

9. J. F. Fulton, Ed., A Textbook of Physiology, 17th ed.,
   W. B. Saunders Co., Philadelphia, 1955.

10. R. Granit, Receptors and Sensory Perception, Yale
    University Press, New Haven, 1956.

11. H. F. Harlow and C. N. Woolsey, Eds., Biological and
    Biochemical Bases of Behavior, The University of
    Wisconsin Press, Madison, 1958.

12. B. Katz, "Nature of the Nerve Impulse" in Biophysical Science,
    a Study Program, Revs. Mod. Phys., 31, 466-474 (1959),
    and John Wiley & Sons, New York, 1959.

10

quantification

13. B. Katz, "Mechanisms of Synaptic Transmission" in
    Biophysical Science, a Study Program, Revs. Mod. Phys., 31,
    524-531 (1959), and John Wiley & Sons, New York, 1959.

14. H. W. Magoun, The Waking Brain, Charles C. Thomas,
    Springfield, 1958.

15. D. Nachmansohn and H. H. Merrit, Eds., Nerve Impulse,
    Vols. 1-5, Transactions of the Conferences Sponsored by
    the Josiah Macy, Jr., Foundation, Corlies, Macy & Company, Inc.,
    New York, 1951-1956.

16. J. von Neumann, The Computer and the Brain, Yale Univer-
    sity Press, New Haven, 1958.

17. J. W. Papez, Comparative Neurology, Thomas Y. Crowell
    Company, New York, 1929.

18. C. S. Sherrington, The Integrative Action of the Nervous
    System, Cambridge University Press, 1947.

19. D. A. Sholl, The Organization of the Cerebral Cortex,
    Methuen, London, 1956.

20. S. S. Stevens, Measurement and Man," Science, 127,
    383-389 (1958).

21. S. S. Stevens, Ed., Handbook of Experimental Psychology,
    John Wiley & Sons, New York, 1951.

22. A. E. Walker, C. E. Henry, and J. K. Merlis, Eds.,
    A Symposium: Recent Developments in Electroencephalo-
    graphic Techniques; Third International Congress of
    Electroencephalography and Clinical Neurophysiology,
    Electroencephalog. and Clin. Neurophysiol., Suppl. 4, 1953.

23. G. E. W. Wolstenholme and C. M. O'Connor, Ciba Founda-
    tion Symposium on the Neurological Basis of Behavior,
    Little, Brown and Company, Boston, 1958.

24. J. Z. Young, The Life of Mammals, Oxford University Press,
    Oxford, 1957.

11

# The "Green Book" Series

*Overview by Robert M. Fano*

The traditional goal of undergraduate education in electrical engineering before World War II was to prepare students to hold productive jobs in industry immediately upon graduation, without appreciable further training. To that end, the curriculum was focused on the various electrical artifacts such as motors, generators, transformers, and transmission lines for students intending to work in the electric power industry, and vacuum tubes, amplifiers, modulators, and antennas for students interested in the electronics and communications industry. Indeed, Course VI offered three distinct options, albeit with a common core: electric power, communications, and illumination.

This goal was achievable because the electrical industry was relatively young and its technical scope was fairly narrow. However, the situation changed radically in the aftermath of World War II because of the growth of the electronics industry and the unprecedented support by the federal government of university research, which resulted in a sudden explosion of graduate education.

A great many new technologies came into being during World War II, particularly in conjunction with the development of microwave radar at the MIT Radiation Laboratory. It suffices to say that it took twenty-seven volumes of the Radiation Laboratory Series to document them. They led to the postwar development of a great variety of new products, ranging from microwave ovens to television sets, and to the emergence of many new manufacturers of electronic equipment. Thus, the number of important artifacts within the domain of electrical engineering became so large that the traditional goal of undergraduate education could be achieved only

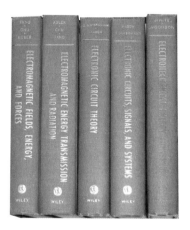

The "green books"

131

by introducing a large number of program options. This is indeed what some electrical engineering departments did. The only alternative seemed to be replacing the focus on the artifacts with a focus on the underlying electrical engineering sciences, with the expectation that students familiar with them would be able to learn the details of any specialty in a relatively short time.

Graduate education was not popular before World War II, because of lack of interest on the part of most employers and very limited availability of research and teaching assistantships. A notable exception was VI-A, the cooperative program with industry leading to an S.M. degree, which included a paid internship. Only about fifty doctorates had been awarded by the Department of Electrical Engineering before the end of the war. The situation changed abruptly after the war, largely because of the obvious critical role that technology had played in the conduct of the war. The military services, anxious to foster peacetime academic research, provided long-term funding for new research laboratories, such as the Research Laboratory of Electronics. The resulting availability of research assistantships, together with the growing demand in industry for people with advanced degrees, made graduate education very popular, particularly among veterans whose education had been interrupted by the war. Thus, graduate education quickly became an additional, major departmental commitment, bound to influence and be influenced by undergraduate education. In particular, the expansion of graduate education called on the undergraduate curriculum to provide an appropriate preparation for graduate studies.

A number of junior faculty members joined the staff of the electrical engineering department in the aftermath of World War II. Most of them had worked during the war at the Radiation Laboratory or at the Radar School that the electrical engineering department had organized and operated to provide postgraduate education for Navy officers in the new technologies of microwave radar. Thus they were quite aware of the technological progress that had taken place during the war and of the inadequacy of the traditional electrical engineering curriculum to prepare students for the postwar world. They were also somewhat embarrassed by the fact that the development of microwave radar at the Radiation Laboratory had been carried out almost entirely by physicists, with electrical engineers playing only a minor role. Clearly, most electrical engineers lacked the necessary scientific preparation.

Some of these junior faculty members began to meet informally with Professor E.A. Guillemin to vent their frustrations and discuss how the curriculum might be improved. Guillemin was a leader in the field of network theory, the only one outside Bell Telephone Laboratories. He had participated in the previous curriculum revision documented by the "blue books" and was, presumably, the primary unnamed author of "Electric Circuits,"[13] in addition to being the author of "The Mathematics of Circuit Analysis." (See profile on the "blue books" series, pages 58–62.) He was an inspiring teacher whose graduate and undergraduate elective subjects displayed the more scientific view of electrical engineering that the younger faculty members were looking for. The first step in the revision of the undergraduate curriculum took place in 1950 when Professor Guillemin was given responsibility for the subjects on electric circuits, the very beginning of the electrical engineering curriculum. The textbook *Introductory Circuit Theory*[14] documenting the material covered in that two-term sequence was published in 1953. It constituted a major innovation in the teaching of electric circuits, in style as well as content, as suggested by the following quotation from the author's preface:

> I feel that circuit theory . . . is the electrical engineer's bread and butter, so to speak. He needs to know this subject well before he can tackle any of the other subjects in his curriculum; and it is of the utmost importance that his first course shall provide him with a set of basic concepts and ways of thinking that will not become obsolete throughout the rest of his undergraduate and graduate years. . . . He will not understand them so well or be able to use them with the same facility as a sophomore, but he should never have to unlearn or discard any of his earlier concepts later on. . . . In other words, his first course should not be a "terminal" first course but the beginning of a career.
>
> I have always held that, where the teaching of basic concepts and procedures are concerned, no distinction should be made between the so-called elementary and the advanced methods. We refer to things as being "advanced" only so long as we understand them insufficiently well ourselves to make them clear in simple terms. Once we understand a subject fully and clearly, it is not difficult to make it clear to the beginner.[15]

*Introductory Circuit Theory* is not part of, but a precursor to the "green books" series of textbooks published at the end of the decade. Intellectually, however, it belongs with the five volumes of the series as the documentation of the major postwar restructuring of the Course VI undergraduate curriculum. That restructuring is often referred to as the "Gordon Brown Revolution," after the head of the Department of Electrical Engineering who conceived it, promoted it, acquired the necessary funding, and led its implementation.

It is easy in retrospect to conclude that a curriculum focused on the sciences underlying electrical engineering was the proper way to meet the postwar educational demands, but way back in the 1950s any such plan was not only controversial but its

Professor E.A. Guillemin

successful implementation could not be taken for granted. It was controversial, of course, just because it was a major departure from past practice. More specifically, it was feared that students with a solid scientific education but unfamiliar with current practice would not be able to carry out, or even accept, practical engineering assignments in industry. The challenge was to develop a curriculum focused on the underlying electrical sciences that would enable students to learn the details of any specialty, as needed. This goal turned out to match the needs of a fast-changing electrical industry. Dr. J.A. Stratton, who was president of MIT at the time the "green books" series was published, stated in their forewords:

> The books have the general form of texts and are being used as such. However, they might be described as reports on a research program aimed at the evolution of an undergraduate core curriculum in Electrical Engineering that will form a basis for a continuing career in a field that is ever-changing.

Professor G.S. Brown

Professor Gordon Brown became head of the electrical engineering department in 1952 but had chaired its curriculum committee. In the fall of 1952 he challenged his audience at a meeting of the American Society of Engineering Education by presenting a paper entitled "The Modern Engineer Should Be Educated as a Scientist." In early 1953 he presented his views and a plan of action to the MIT administration and to the visiting committee of the department, and received their support. The point of no return was reached shortly thereafter, when the electric machinery laboratory in the basement of Building 10, the most visible symbol of the old curriculum, was dismantled to make room for new laboratory facilities.

The new curriculum made its debut in the MIT catalog for the academic year 1954–55, and the first editions of class notes for the fall semester were distributed on schedule. The national debut took place at the 1955 winter meeting of the American Institute of Electrical Engineers, at which Professor Brown presented a paper entitled "Educating Electrical Engineers to Exploit Science."

The character of the new curriculum is succinctly described by Dr. Stratton in the foreword to the "green books" as follows:

The new curriculum subordinates option structures built around areas of industrial practice in favor of a common core that provides a broad base for the engineering applications of the sciences. This core structure includes a newly developed laboratory program which stresses the role of experimentation and its relation to theoretical model building in the solution of engineering problems. Faced with the time limitation of a four-year program for the Bachelor's degree, the entire core curriculum gives priority to basic principles and methods of analysis rather than to the presentation of current technology.

The "green books," published in quick succession at the end of the decade, were the end products of successive yearly editions of class notes distributed to students, as the new curriculum was being evolved and tested. The resulting series includes a pair of volumes on electromagnetism, a pair on electronics, and a final volume on energy conversion.

The first pair consists of *Electromagnetic Fields, Energy and Forces*[16] by R.M. Fano, L.J. Chu, and R.B. Adler, and *Electromagnetic Energy Transmission and Radiation*[17] by R.B. Adler, L.J. Chu, and R.M. Fano. The first book covers the properties of electromagnetic fields and their interactions with matter, with special emphasis on quasi-static phenomena. The second book covers the propagation and reflection of electromagnetic waves in free space and in dissipative media, and the resulting power flow and energy storage, including radiation from antennas.

The authors of the two textbooks undertook their development as a single project but they played different primary roles. The leading authors of the two volumes, R.M. Fano and R.B. Adler, respectively, did the actual preparation of the final manuscripts and of the preceding yearly editions of class notes; they were also responsible for all aspects of the teaching of the corresponding subjects. The middle author, L.J. Chu, being the one most knowledgeable about electromagnetism, provided general guidance in the choice of topics, and deserves full credit for three important innovations.

The first is the unusual problem-solving technique of "analysis by synthesis," which is characteristic of Chu's personal research. Briefly, it starts with the selection of an electromagnetic field with the desired properties by combining free-space solutions of Maxwell's equation. Then, convenient sources and boundary conditions are found that can support the desired field. This is just the opposite of the conventional procedure, and usually leads to approximating the sources and boundary conditions instead of the field.

From left: Dr. R.M. Fano, L.G. Kraft, Jr., and
W.B. Davenport, Jr.

Professor Lan Jen Chu

The second innovation concerns the study of quasi-static electromagnetic fields. It involves representing the individual field vectors in Maxwell's equations as a power series in some appropriate variable such as time, frequency, or velocity. Then, equating equal-power terms in Maxwell's equations yields successive equations that can be solved by static-field methods.

The third innovation concerns the formulation of the field equations in the presence of moving matter, which constitutes a major scientific contribution by L.J. Chu. The four-dimensional, relativistic formulation is presented in Appendix One of the first volume; it was never presented by the author elsewhere. It is a rare case of a major scientific contribution resulting from an undergraduate educational effort. It came about because Chu found previous formulations of the field equations in the presence of moving matter to be either incomplete or internally inconsistent. It turned out that in order to take into account the presence of magnetized matter in a consistent manner, it was convenient, if not necessary, to represent magnetic dipoles in the form of displaced positive and negative magnetic charges, in a manner analogous to the representation of electric dipoles. This, of course, did not imply the existence of isolated magnetic charges, but departed from the usual representation of magnetic dipoles as current loops, which was more consistent with microscopic reality. Shortly after the publication of the first volume, B.D.H. Tellegen of the Philips Laboratories challenged the theory by contending that the force exerted on a current-loop representation of a magnetic dipole differed from that exerted on a magnetic-charge representation. The matter remained unresolved for several years until H.A. Haus and P.L. Penfield, Jr., were able to show that Tellegen's computation had neglected the relativistic effects on the current loop, and that the forces on the two dipole models were actually identical.

Finally, it is important to point out that both volumes are dedicated to "EAG," Ernst A. Guillemin, the inspiring teacher whose pioneering views on undergraduate education guided the preparation of both volumes.

The second pair of textbooks consists of *Electronic Circuit Theory*[18] by H.J. Zimmermann and S.J. Mason and *Electronic Circuits, Signals and Systems*[19] by S.J. Mason and H.J. Zimmermann. Again the two volumes were developed as a single project, although each of them was actually written by the leading author, who was also responsible for the teaching of the corresponding subject.

The first book is devoted to the study of electronic circuits, which, in turn, requires the study of the various available electronic devices and of the functions that may be performed by the circuits embedding them. Each electronic device may be used to perform a variety of functions and each function may be implemented using different electronic devices in different circumstances. Quoting from the preface:

> We have organized our approach to electronics around circuit models and methods of circuit analysis in order to reduce the number of separate ideas and concepts. The many functions performed by electronic systems can be understood in terms of a few fundamental circuits if similarities are sought.[18]

Thus, the first part of the textbook is devoted to the description and modeling of nonlinear devices such as diodes, transistors, and various types of vacuum tubes, with special emphasis on the use of piecewise-linear models. The second part is devoted to the implementation of various operations such as amplification, wave shaping, and the generation of oscillations and other waveforms.

The second book of the pair, *Electronic Circuits, Signals and Systems*,[19] is devoted to the analysis and design of systems including the sort of electronic components studied in the first book. Since most of those components are neither passive nor bilateral, analytical tools are needed in addition to the familiar tools of passive circuit theory. Three methods of analysis are presented: matrix circuit analysis, topological circuit analysis, and flow-graph circuit analysis. Most of the rest of the book is devoted to the analysis of signals and to their transmission through linear systems using the mathematical tools of Fourier transforms and convolution. This is followed by a discussion of the use of nonlinear devices such as multipliers and modulators. The final chapter covers the use of negative feedback for impedance control and for reduction of noise and signal distortion.

The last book of the series is *Electromechanical Energy Conversion*[20] by D.C. White and H.H. Woodson. It presents the theory underlying the conversion of mechanical energy into electric energy and vice versa in various types of rotating machinery, including machines employing feedback. The theory is developed using a generalized rotating machine consisting of a stator and a rotor with coils represented by sinusoidally distributed current sheets, and polar projections in the stator represented, when present, by an angle-dependent magnetic permeability.

The Gordon Brown curriculum revolution ended in 1960 with the publication of the last volume of the "green books" series. What was its long-term influence on undergraduate education? How has the content of the 1960 core curriculum changed since then? The switch from a focus on current practice to a focus on the underlying sciences quickly propagated to other electrical engineering departments, and shortly thereafter to other engineering departments at MIT and elsewhere. The emphasis on applied sciences is now taken for granted throughout the engineering community. As to the content of the core curriculum, circuit theory, which used to be the bread and butter of electrical engineering, has lost most of its importance to digital signal processing. The two terms of linear circuits and one term of electronic circuits required in 1960 are now compressed into a single term required of all Course VI students. The subject on signals and systems is still a core requirement, albeit in an updated form. The two subjects on electromagnetic fields have evolved in the past four decades, but they are still being taught with the original objectives. Only the subject on electromechanical energy conversion appears to have no direct descendant. Thus, approximately half of the 1960 core curriculum is alive and well four decades later. It is still part of the undergraduate program offered by the department whose name was changed to Electrical Engineering and Computer Science fifteen years after the publication of the textbooks of the "green books" series.

# Molecular Designing of Materials

ARTHUR VON HIPPEL

19 NOVEMBER 1898–31 DECEMBER 2003

SCIENCE VOL. 138

(12 OCTOBER 1962): 91–108

*Introduced by Markus Zahn*

Professor Arthur Robert von Hippel, Institute Professor Emeritus since 1962, was widely recognized for his outstanding research in dielectrics, molecular science, and molecular engineering.

Professor Markus Zahn reviewing magnetic fluid experiments

His European schooling and early professional life brought him into contact with major leaders in physics, including Bohr, Sommerfeld, Heisenberg, Wien, Courant, Debye, Born, Franck, Hertz, and Pauli, and in America, Loeb and Oppenheimer. His participation in the scientific revolution of the early twentieth century, together with the upheavals of World Wars I and II, make von Hippel's life an inspiring story.

In 1940 he founded the MIT Laboratory for Insulation Research (LIR), which did pioneering work in materials research, measurements, and instrumentation, and he served as its only head until his first retirement in 1964. His research theme was molecular engineering for the "making of materials to order." His work included ferroelectrics and ferromagnetics; electric breakdown; dielectric polarization; rectifiers and photocells; gas discharges; and solid-state physics. He was distinguished for his pioneering research in the field of molecular science and molecular engineering, which he described as a "broad new discipline ... comprising the structure, formation, and

Professor Arthur von Hippel in his office
with molecular models

properties of atoms, molecules, and ions; of gases, liquids, solids, and their interfaces; the designing of materials and properties on the basis of this molecular understanding; and their imaginative application for devices."[21] The LIR pioneered in materials research, measurements, and instrumentation, evolving into the present-day MIT Center for Materials Science and Engineering (with a von Hippel conference room) and the MIT Laboratory for Electromagnetic and Electronic Systems. The Materials Research Society's highest award, the von Hippel Award, is an international hallmark of excellence in the field of materials research. Von Hippel was the first recipient of this award in 1976, thereafter named for him, for his interdisciplinary and pioneering research in dielectrics, semiconductors, ferromagnetics, and ferroelectrics.

In 1969–70 I was a graduate student in Professor von Hippel's two-term course at MIT, "From Atoms to Living Systems." As part of the coursework, I used to meet weekly with von Hippel to discuss physics. His long-time secretary, Aina Sils, served cookies and tea. His lectures included many slides about materials science. Occasionally a slide of personal history would slip in, such as a picnic scene with Albert Einstein, and Professor von Hippel would entertain us with an anecdote.

Like all of von Hippel's courses, this course attracted students from all science and engineering disciplines who wanted to learn materials science at the frontiers of knowledge as well as to personally experience his reputation as "a great scientist, great lecturer, and a great man."[22] I found, as had all his students, that speaking with "the Prof" (as he was lovingly known ) was never a problem. In my own career, I have tried to model my interactions with students on my experiences with Professor von Hippel —by practicing good teaching, and by mentoring with friendship, accessibility, and commitment to my student's education, welfare, and professional development.

Von Hippel founded and defined modern dielectrics research through his many books and research papers. He surrounded himself with physicists, chemists, electrical engineers, and ceramicists in order to advance the multidisciplinary activities of LIR.

The paper that follows is the lecture that Professor von Hippel delivered on 26 December 1961 at the Denver meeting of the American Association for the Advancement of Science (AAAS) general session, "The Moving Frontiers of Science." I chose this paper as representative of Professor von Hippel's career because it shows his great wisdom and insight, and especially his vision of advances in material science and engineering—using the laws of molecular architecture to design materials with prescribed properties. The article appeared not long before Professor von Hippel's first retirement in 1964 and shows how the achievements of the LIR helped lay the basis for modern materials research that ultimately led to advances that we enjoy today in electronics, lasers, magnetic storage, photovoltaics, piezoelectricity, superconductivity, polymers, and so forth.

The paper is a tour de force in the von Hippel teaching tradition, combining basic and applied research. The rigorous and exhaustive fundamental physics and characterizing measurements in this paper begin with electron clouds, atomic structure, elements and compounds, and molecules and crystals, and extends to the laws of molecular architecture and crystal structure and properties.

The paper demonstrates the quality of research practiced under von Hippel's direction of LIR that justified its worldwide reputation as a research center of excellence. On the occasion of Professor von Hippel's ninety-fourth birthday, the journal *Ferroelectrics* dedicated a special issue to his work on dielectric properties of ferroelectrics [*Ferroelectrics* vol. 135, no. 1–4(1992)]. It noted that "Professor Arthur von Hippel has, through his writings and teachings, been one of a handful of key educators to several generations of scientists and engineers…" and that "he was a pioneer both in setting up an interdisciplinary laboratory and in destroying the barrier between basic and applied research."

The LIR was in existence from 1940 to 1964 and educated about sixty doctoral students, two electrical engineering–degree students, forty-seven master degree students, a large number of bachelor degree students, and many postdoctoral researchers from around the world. At the time of von Hippel's official retirement in 1964, LIR had about seventy members in eight research groups, which formed the new MIT Center for Materials Science and Engineering. Von Hippel continued to teach and do research applying material science to biological systems until about 1979. His last student, Keith W. Karvate, received his Sc.D. in EECS in 1979; his thesis was titled "Electrical Surface Studies on Hexagonal Ice and Their Interpretation." Professor von Hippel died on 31 December 2003.

Professor Emeritus Arthur von Hippel on the occasion of his one-hundredth birthday

# Molecular Designing of Materials

Science, guided by molecular understanding, takes up
the challenge to create materials for the future.

Arthur R. von Hippel

Exploration of the resources of our planet, only a generation ago still left to the individual prospector, geologist, or mining engineer, is now a joint concern of the scientific world community, as the recent International Geophysical Year testifies. Our present knowledge of mineral resources has been summarized with penetrating understanding by Meyerhoff (1). How to sustain an explosively growing world population is the theme of pioneering studies like those of Harrison Brown (2). Catastrophe will be the assured outcome of this situation if political and economic

The author is professor of electrical engineering at the Massachusetts Institute of Technology, Cambridge, and director of the Institute's Laboratory for Insulation Research. This article is the lecture which he delivered on 26 December 1961 at the Denver meeting of the AAAS, at the general session, "The Moving Frontiers of Science."

insight cannot win the race against prejudice and ignorance. It is the unhappy fate of the scientist today that he must play the role of Cassandra in the body politic, sending his fellow men to bed with nightmares in the hope of being heard in time.

Fortunately, an article on the molecular designing of materials need not be gloomy; on the contrary, I want to report on developments bright with promise, starting with the apparently naive question: What shall we most reasonably do with our natural resources? In earlier times the answer was simple: Here are the materials found in nature and transformed by industry; there are their macroscopic properties, defined and tabulated. Add the practical experience of the engineer and the economic incentive of maxi-

mum profit. Into this mold our demands had to fit, rudely deprived of soaring imagination.

Suddenly all this is changing. "Molecular science"—in decades of quiet studies on electrons, atoms, molecules, and their concerted action in gases, liquids, and solids—has made a more powerful approach possible: "molecular engineering," the building of materials and devices to order. We begin to design materials with prescribed properties, to understand the molecular causes of their failings, to build into them safeguards against such failure, and to arrive at true yardsticks of ultimate performance. No longer shackled to presently available materials and characteristics, we are free to dream and find answers to unprecedented challenges. Simultaneously we begin to foresee, in ever-widening perspective, the consequences of our actions. It is about this revolutionary situation, which makes scientists and engineers true allies in a great adventure of the human mind, that I am going to speak (3), though fully aware that most facts here presented are well known to the specialist and that I need your indulgence for trying to unfold a great panorama despite limited insight.

## The Web of Electron Clouds

When an ultimate Power created protons and electrons, the basic building laws for this world were decided. The two particle types, equipped with equal but opposite elementary electric

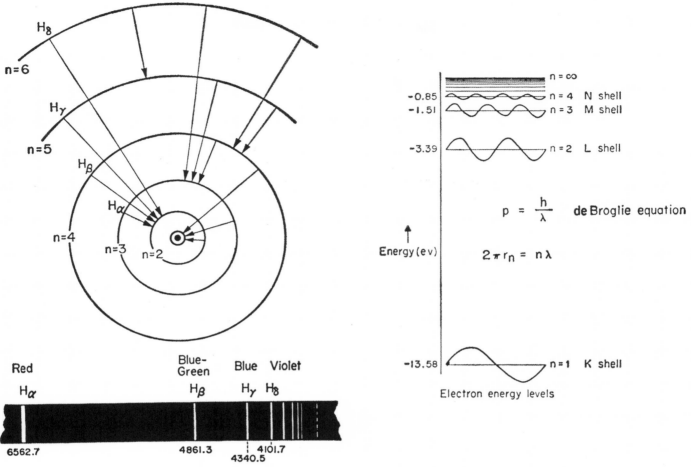

Fig. 1. Standing-wave modes and Bohr orbits of the hydrogen atom.

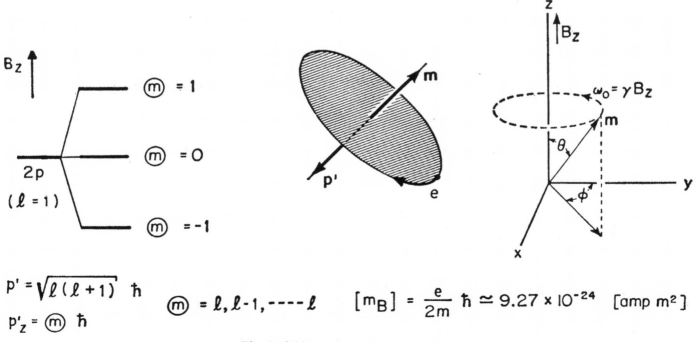

Fig. 2. Orbital electron as a gyroscope.

charges, can hold and neutralize each other electrostatically. However, not only do their masses exercise gravitational action of the same sign, thus offering no shield against gravitational forces, but the proton is heavier by three orders of magnitude ($m_+/m_- \simeq$ 1836). This fact has profound consequences.

The accuracy with which particles can be localized, in our space-time framework, is proportional to their mass (the Heisenberg uncertainty relation). In wave-mechanical language, the wavelength of a particle is inversely proportional to its momentum, hence its mass. The probable whereabouts of particles in stationary states can be described by standing-wave modes of these de Broglie probability waves as solutions of Schrödinger's wave equation (Fig. 1). An electron trapped by the Coulomb field of a proton in its lowest energy state is with greatest probability found in a circular Bohr orbit whose circumference equals one wavelength; hence, its radius is inversely proportional to the electron mass. As for any satellite circling the earth, this orbit must have mechanical stability—that is, the attraction force of the nucleus and the centrifugal force must balance. Thus, its average radius for an electron trapped by a proton in its ground state can be calculated as $r_0 \simeq 5.28 \times 10^{-11} [m]$, while for the proton the corresponding radius would be about 1836 times smaller, or about $3 \times 10^{-14} [m]$. At such small distances, nuclear attraction forces (meson fields) take over and shrink the radius still further. The large gravitational mass ratio of proton to electron thus forces nature to construct atoms from very small positive nuclei surrounded by extended electron clouds.

In addition to charge and mass, electrons and protons have a mechanical angular momentum, a spin; they behave like charged gyroscopes. A rotating charge is akin to a current circling an area; such a ring current produces a magnetic moment (**m**) (Fig. 2). The ratio of this moment to the angular momentum (**p′**) of the spinning particle is inversely proportional to the mass. Since the mechanical spin of the electron and proton prove to be identical ($\frac{1}{2}\hbar$, where $h = 2\pi\hbar$ is Planck's constant), the magnetic moment of the electron, known as the Bohr magneton, is about 1836 times larger than the nuclear magneton of the proton.

By increasing the number of protons in the nucleus (the order number) in steps of 1 and simultaneously adding one electron each to the neutralizing negative atmosphere, the electrostatic sequence of the atoms of the periodic system results. [Actually, the formation of nuclei proceeds by complicated step reactions; hence, the abundance of elements gives a clue to the conditions prevailing at their creation (4).] Intuitively one is inclined to trace back the world, with its glorious variety, to the specific structure of the nucleus, which endows each atom type with a personality of its own. In fact, if we could see with x-ray eyes, the molecular world would appear as an eerie web of electron clouds anchored to positively charged points. These points, examined under much higher magnification, would resolve into spherical potential wells containing, deeply retracted because of their large mass, the nuclei. The actual composition, electric shape, and magnetic moment of these nuclei have only a minor "hyperfine-structure" influence on the electron clouds. The mutual constellation of the nuclear dots in space and the number of positive charges in each dot determine the texture and color of the electron fabric.

Thus, when we understand the electron structure of the atoms and their modes of interaction, we can weave and tear, mend and dye this fabric and thus design materials and devices.

**Atom Structure**

The hydrogen atom—proton and one electron—presents a two-body problem; its possible electron-cloud structures (orbitals) can be calculated accurately, while those of all other atoms —as multibody problems—can only be found by approximation. Thus, the results of the hydrogen atom have served, rightly or wrongly, as the prototype pattern for all atoms and must be briefly recalled (5).

There is a sequence of stationary energy states, characterized in their average distance from the nucleus by a principal quantum number $n$; its integers $n = 1,2,3,4,5, \ldots$ can be visualized as designating circular Bohr orbits, in circumference corresponding to $1,2,3,4,5, \ldots$ electron wavelengths. The ground state $n = 1$ represents the deepest trap in which the proton can bind the electron (13.53 electron volts);

all other modes are a succession of excited states. This sequence of extending orbitals produces the shell structure of the atoms (see Fig. 1).

The ground state of the hydrogen atom binds the electron in a spherical probability pattern ($s$ state); no direction of rotation is preferred, hence the electron has no orbital angular momentum in reference to the nucleus. For the excited states ($n > 1$), an increasing number of eccentric electron-cloud figurations ($l = n - 1$) are also stable solutions of the wave equation; these are characterized by orbital angular momenta $p' = [l(l + 1)]^{\frac{1}{2}}$. The azimuthal quantum number $l = 0,1,$ 2,3,4, . . . designates them as $s,p,d,f,g,$ . . . states, and the integer set ($n, l$) of two quantum numbers prescribes unambiguously the orbital type (standing-wave mode type) in which the electron finds itself.

It becomes apparent, when placing the hydrogen atom in a magnetic field, that each of these orbital types consists of ($2l + 1$) individual orbitals. The orbital angular momentum makes the atom a gyroscope and simultaneously creates an orbital magnetic moment (see Fig. 2). The external field exercises a torque on the gyroscope by coupling to this magnetic moment; the result is a precession around the field axis. Any recurrent motion in the molecular world characterizes a standing-wave mode; the transition from mode to mode requires a discontinuous, quantized energy step. Hence, the orbital angular momentum must assume discrete, quantized orientations with respect to the field axis; its projection on the field axis is $p'_z = m\hbar$, with the magnetic quantum number **m** ranging from $l$ to $-l$. Thus, each orbital can be designated uniquely by a set of three quantum numbers ( $n, l,$ and **m**).

Finally, an electron placed into an orbital can orient its own angular momentum, its spin component $s\hbar$, either parallel or antiparallel to the field ($s = \pm \frac{1}{2}$); an electron in its orbital is therefore characterized by a set of four quantum numbers ($n, l,$ **m**, $s$). Pauli's exclusion principle requires that particles with half-integer spins, like the electron, must be distinguishable each by its own set of four quantum numbers; that is, such particles obey Fermi-Dirac statistics. Each atomic orbital can thus only accept two electrons paired with antiparallel spins.

The periodic system, as presented in

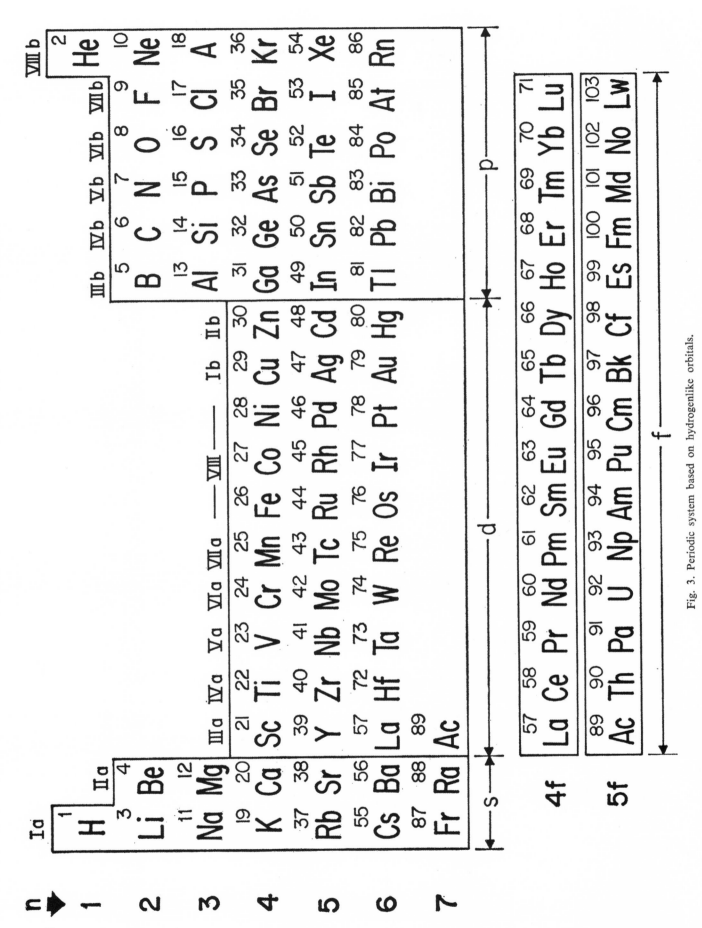

Fig. 3. Periodic system based on hydrogenlike orbitals.

Fig. 3, assumes that the multi-electron systems of the atoms can be described by hydrogen-like orbitals. We have the various shells ($n$) and subshells ($l$) of orbital type $s,p,d,f,g,.$ . . . Since an orbital can accommodate two electrons and each orbital type has $2l+1$ orbitals, the subshells are filled when they contain $2(2l+1)$ or $2,6,10,14,18, . . .$ electrons, respectively. The electron distribution of an atom can be written in shorthand by giving the integer number of the shell and the letter of the subshell, with the number of occupying electrons as superscript; for example, the electron distribution in the Fe atom (order number 26) is represented unambiguously by the symbol $1s^2 2s^2 2p^6 3s^2 3p^6 3d^6 4s^2$.

Here appears our first predicament: only experiment can make it clear that subshell $3d$ takes in six electrons, leaving two in the $4s$ orbitals. The sudden filling of inner $d$ and $f$ subshells shown in Fig. 3 certifies that the mutual energy relations between shells and subshells change with occupation. Furthermore, we can foresee that the energy states, especially those of the outer shells, will be altered by interaction with the surroundings.

Nature designs everything from atoms; hence, we should be able to design any kind of material with foresight if we thoroughly understood the periodic system in all its implications. At this stage—like weather forecasters —we are still members of the gambling profession.

### Elements and Compounds

Atoms are not the inert building stones of fixed size, shape, and connecting links that a model designer has to pretend they are. Isolated, they appear spherical and may be described by some nearest-approach distance: an atomic radius (when neutral) or positive and negative ionic radii (when they shed or trap electrons). However, the distortion of electron clouds by approaching neighbors creates polarity, ranging all the way from a weak van der Waals attraction by fluctuating dipole moments—caused by phase relations between electrons of interacting clouds that try to avoid each other— to the strong permanent dipole moments of polar molecules. Furthermore, atoms are inherently endowed by their eccentric electron clouds with strong

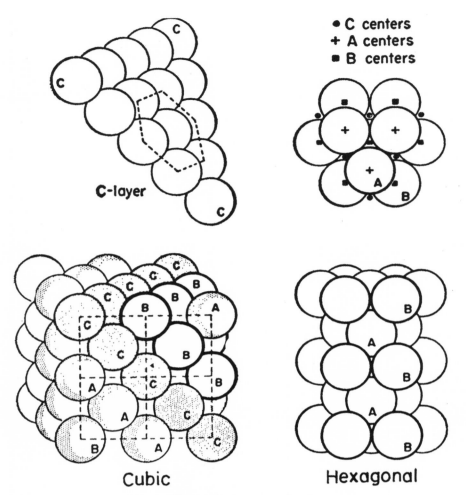

Fig. 4. Close-packed arrays of spheres.

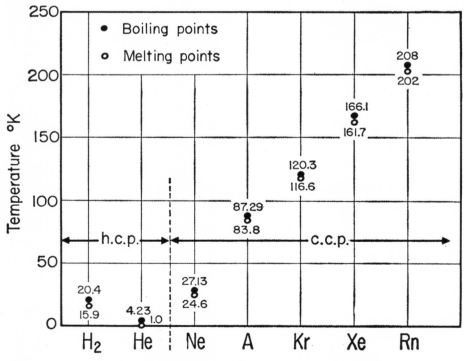

Fig. 5. Melting and boiling points of $H_2$ and the rare gases.

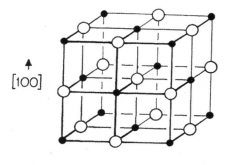

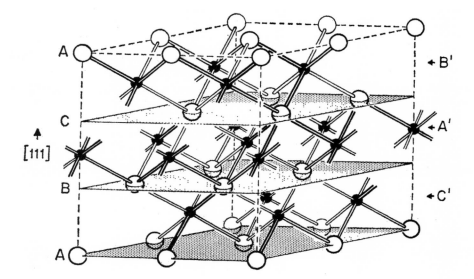

Fig. 6. Rock salt structure as related to close-packed structure.

stereoproperties. Hence, the valence electrons of unfilled outer shells form strong directive links (ligands) with their neighbors.

Gilbert N. Lewis first recognized the electron-pair bond which allows the $1s^1$ electrons of two hydrogen atoms to pair in antiparallel spin orientation, forming molecular hydrogen, $H_2$, or which allows alkali halide molecules to acquire the octet structure $s^2p^6$ of rare-gas atoms. Obviously, the originally spherical electron distribution has been drastically altered by such diatomic molecule formation, to the cylindrical symmetry of dinuclear systems. The overlap of the previously isolated electron clouds becomes a measure of the bond strength. The valence electrons have been saturated, nearly equally strong diatomic molecules $H_2$ or NaCl have been formed (about 103 and 97 kcal/mole, respectively), and one might expect that such molecules will be inert, like rare-gas atoms.

Rare gases cannot form directed bonds as long as their saturated spherical electron-cloud system remains unbroken by excitation. Hence, only the weak van der Waals attraction acts, packing the atoms as equal spheres, like oranges in crates, in one of two densely packed arrays (Fig. 4): in planes with repeat sequence ABAB . . . or ABCABC . . ., yielding hexagonal or face-centered cubic crystals, respectively. In both cases each atom is surrounded by 12 neighbors at equal distances (coordination number $CN = 12$). Very low melting and boiling points result, indicating with their rising trend from helium to radon that the cohesion increases with the number of participating electrons (Fig. 5).

The hydrogen molecules act according to expectation: they pack as densely as possible by van der Waals forces without losing their identity; melting and boiling points are low. The individual alkali halide molecules, in contrast, by condensing lose their identity; they are dissolved, with large energy release, in the ionic rock salt structure. Still, there is a memory left of the rare-gas behavior when this structure is properly drawn: $Na^+$ and $Cl^-$ separately have rare-gas shells and form two interleaving sublattices of the cubic close-packed type (Fig. 6).

Turning to the second row of the periodic system we may predict that lithium and boron, with a lone $2s^1$ and $2p^1$ electron, respectively, will form $Li_2$ and $B_2$ molecules in analogy to $H_2$, and that beryllium, with its $2s^2$ electron pair, will remain monatomic like a rare-gas atom. This is almost true, but instead of condensing into insulating liquids at low temperature, lithium and beryllium become metals and boron becomes a semiconductor. Melting and boiling points (Fig. 7) rise high, and only from nitrogen on is the rare-gas behavior resumed by diatomic molecules (as in the case of $H_2$).

That alkali atoms form metals might have been surmised by their tendency in the alkali halides to regain their rare-gas shell by shedding the lone electron. Thus, the fixed anion sublattice in Fig. 6 can be visualized as being replaced by a mobile electron lattice. The fact that the alkaline-earth atoms share their two electrons in metallic bonding is an extension of this situation. However, the structure of the boron crystal is a complete surprise: its tetragonal unit cell contains four icosahedra of 12 atoms each with ligancy 6 and two interstitial boron atoms of ligancy 4 that knit these regular polyhedra together (Fig. 8) (6). Thus, the boron atom with its three valence electrons can contribute only a fractional electron charge to its six or four bonds, respectively.

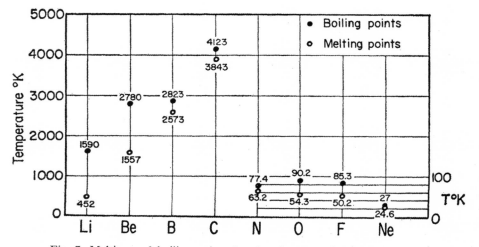

Fig. 7. Melting and boiling points for the elements of the second row.

96

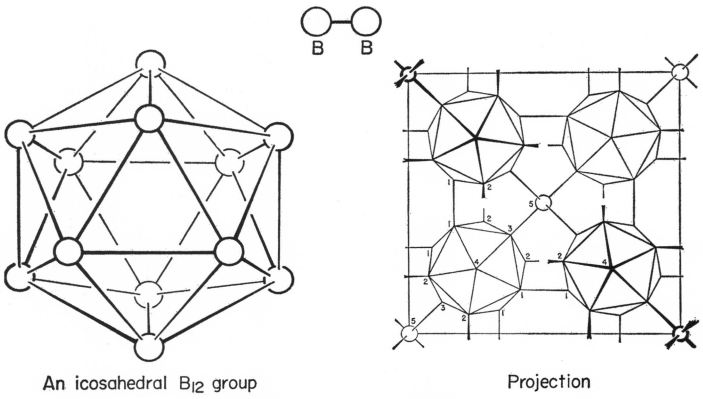

Fig. 8. The structure of boron. [After Pauling (6)]

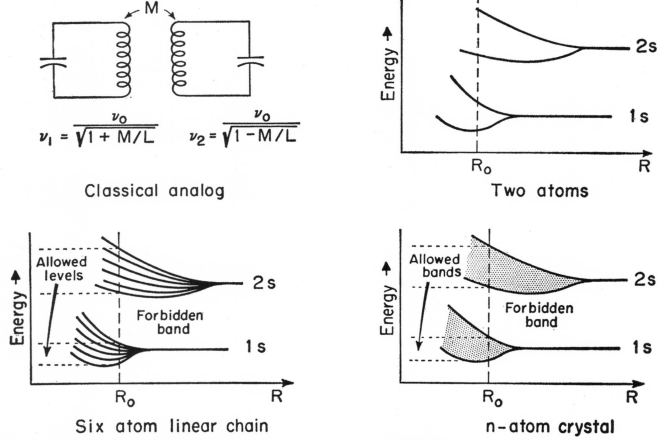

Fig. 9. Coupling of classical oscillators and band structure of crystals.

Obviously, the concept of clamping atoms together with their hydrogen-like $s,p,d, \ldots$ orbitals in pair-bond formation, thereby saturating valencies, and then packing tightly does not suffice. We have neglected the fact that the electron-density patterns assigned to each standing-wave mode actually spread over all space. Hence, coupling must occur between all mutually compatible electron modes inside atoms as well as between neighbors. Such coupling is well known in the case of classical oscillators and splits a resonant mode into a higher and a lower frequency band (Fig. 9). Similarly, the individual energy states of atoms split (i) within the atoms themselves, by magnetic coupling of orbital and spin moments (internal Zeeman effects) and by electrostatic interaction (internal Stark effects), and (ii) through external interactions with neighboring atoms, again by coupling of orbital and spin momenta and by reacting to electrostatic effects (for example, the crystal fields of solids).

One simple outcome of this splitting of energy states is the well-known Bloch-Wilson model classifying crystals as insulators, semiconductors, or metals according to the separation or overlap of the energy bands in which electrons or holes may transfer through a periodic lattice structure. Much ingenious work is at present devoted to the elucidation of the actual stereostructure of such bands, as seen from the standpoint of electrons and their wavelengths (that is, in $k$ space) (7).

A second result of the coupling of wave modes is that combinations of such modes can be excited like the timbre of a musical instrument. In simple cases only two wave-function types may dominantly be involved, as in the celebrated $s$-$p$ hybridization of the carbon atom, which starts organic chem-

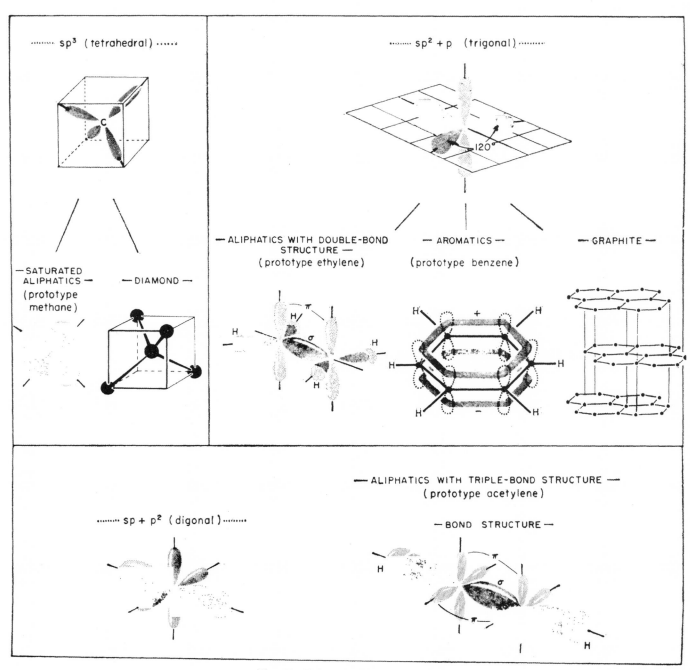

Fig. 10. Hybrid bonds of carbon.

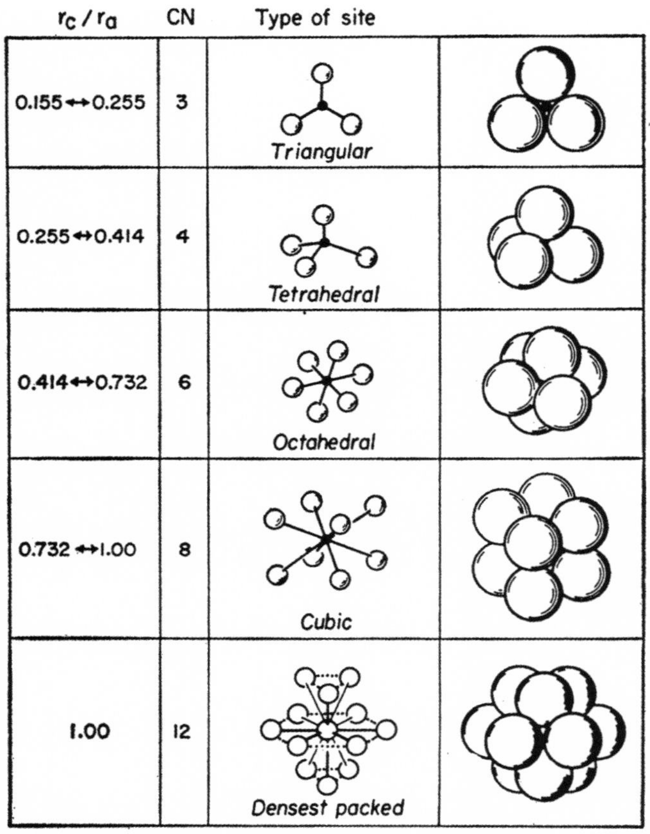

$r_c / r_a$
CN
Type of site
0.155↔0.255
3
Triangular
0.255↔0.414
4
Tetrahedral
0.414↔0.732
6
Octahedral
0.732↔1.00
8
Cubic
1.00
12
Densest packed

Fig. 11. Radius ratio and coordination.

— DIATOMIC —
— RING —
— CHAIN —
Left hand screw
Right hand screw

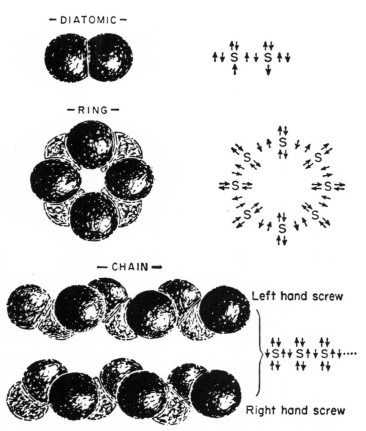

Fig. 12. Various types of sulfur molecules.

Selenium and Tellurium
(hexagonal)
I
II
III
IV
Polonium
(simple cubic)

Se
Semiconductor
Metal
R'
$10^{11}$
$10^9$
$10^7$
$10^5$
$10^3$
10
0.1
0
80
160
240
320
P, Kilobars

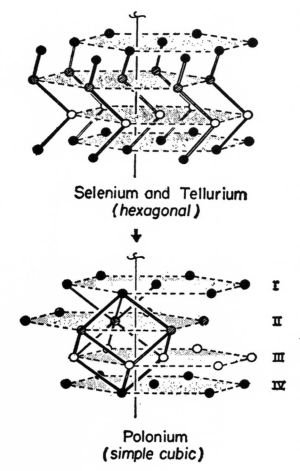

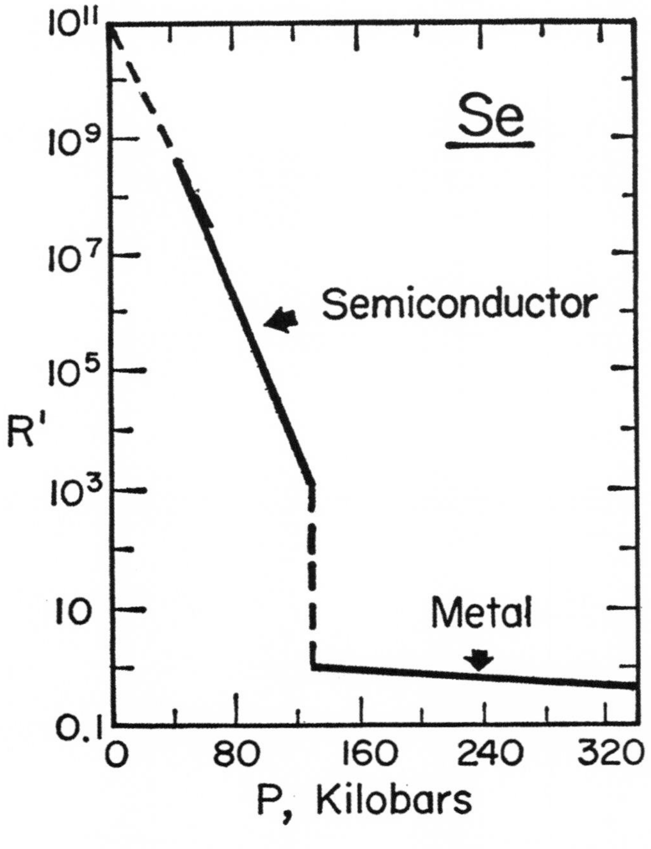

Fig. 13. Selenium- to polonium-type transition. [After Balchan and Drickamer (*9*)]

Polyisoprene $[C_5H_8]_n$

$$\left[\begin{array}{cccc} CH_3 & H & H & H \\ | & | & | & | \\ C & C & C & C = \\ | & | & | & | \\ & H & & H \end{array}\right]_n$$

Fig. 14 (above and right). Stereoisomerism of polyisoprene.

## NATURAL RUBBER
### (elastic <u>cis</u> form)

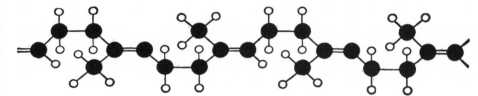

## GUTTA-PERCHA
### (slightly elastic <u>trans</u> form)

istry on its way with aliphatic and aromatic compounds (Fig. 10). Here pair-bonds still suffice, but the structure of boron (see Fig. 8) makes it obvious that individual electrons may spread themselves over various compatible wave modes. Thus, the actual structure can be visualized as containing genes of a variety of individual constellations, each making its contribution to the structure, properties, and cohesive strength of the final array. This is the concept of quantum-mechanical resonance, used so successfully by Pauling (6) in describing the nature of the chemical bond.

### Molecules and Crystals

Such latent properties of electron-cloud formation, called to the fore as the environment dictates, makes designing with atoms an occupation filled with curious anticipation, like gardening in a greenhouse: select the seeds, set the conditions of the surroundings, and things begin to happen.

Three extreme cases became apparent in the preceding discussion:

1) Atoms may stay single in the gaseous phase because they are inert (rare gases), or they may form semi-inert molecules by saturation of primary valence bonds (for example, $H_2$). Weak secondary attraction condenses these entities into close-packed phases without destroying their identity; low melting and boiling points result (see Figs. 5 and 7).

2) Atoms stay single in the gaseous phase (for example, beryllium) because strong primary bonds develop only in multiatomic clusters where common wave functions can bind the array; an electron community arises, usually leading to the metallic state. This is a very common situation, since three quarters of all elements are metals; higher melting or boiling points, or both, and monatomic vapors are the rule.

3) Molecules form in the gaseous state by valence bonding but are torn to pieces by stronger primary bonds of the condensed phases. The cause may be the polarity of the molecule, leading to the far-ranging Coulomb fields of an ionic lattice structure (for example, sodium chloride) (see Fig. 6). It may be the community of metal electrons that dissolves the molecule, as in the case of $Li_2$, or covalent links between nearest neighbors may in continuous sequence build strong three-dimensional networks, as in diamond; two-dimensional planes, as in graphite; or linear chains stretching through space, as in carbon polymers (see Fig. 10).

In their extreme form, metallic and ionic bonds act according to the principle *horror vacui*, compacting and tending to fill space as densely as the radius

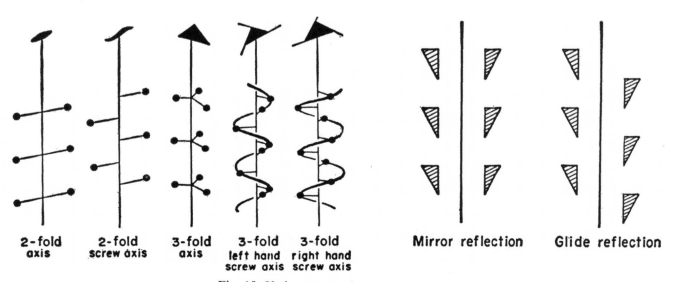

| 2-fold axis | 2-fold screw axis | 3-fold axis | 3-fold left hand screw axis | 3-fold right hand screw axis | Mirror reflection | Glide reflection |

Fig. 15. Various types of symmetry elements.

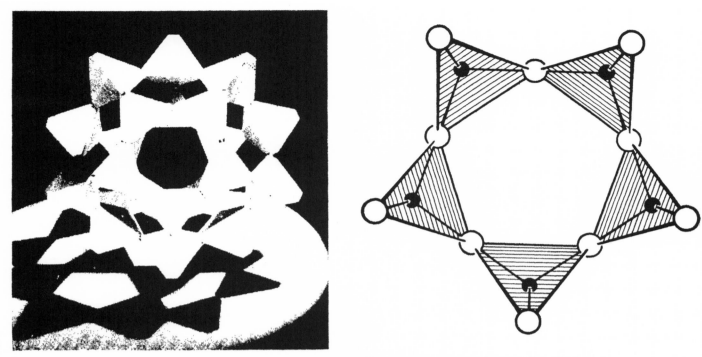

Fig. 16. Pentagonal dodecahedral groups in silicate glass or water. [After Tilton (*12*)]

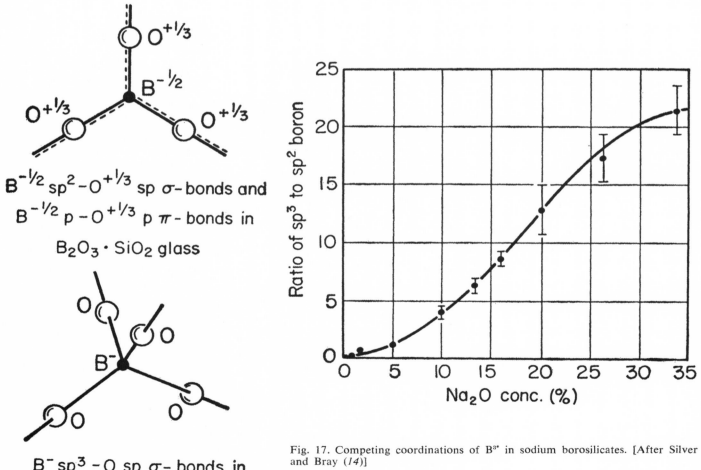

$B^{-1/2}$ sp$^2$–O$^{+1/3}$ sp $\sigma$– bonds and
$B^{-1/2}$ p –O$^{+1/3}$ p $\pi$ – bonds in

B$_2$O$_3$ · SiO$_2$ glass

B$^-$ sp$^3$ –O sp $\sigma$– bonds in
Na$_2$O · B$_2$O$_3$ · SiO$_2$ glass

Fig. 17. Competing coordinations of B$^{3+}$ in sodium borosilicates. [After Silver and Bray (*14*)]

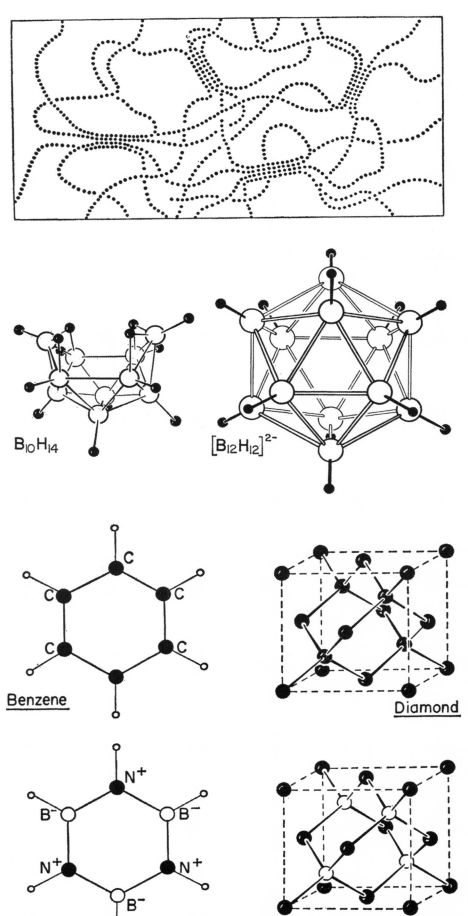

Fig. 18 (top). Combination of amorphous and crystalline regions.

Fig. 19 (middle). Polyhedral molecules of boron hydrides.

Fig. 20 (bottom). Structure preservation by averaging nuclear charges.

$B_{10}H_{14}$

$[B_{12}H_{12}]^{2-}$

Benzene

Diamond

Borazole

Borazon

ratio of the partners permits (Fig. 11). In contrast, the short-ranging, strongly directive covalent bonds are the primary tools of imaginative architecture. Actually, this distinction is blurred in nature, because any bond between unlike atoms imparts polarity; even shared electron clouds can move in cooperative polarity against the residual structure.

The diversity of nature stemming from the various bonding possibilities of more than a hundred atoms would be staggering even if the structure of a material were determined uniquely by temperature and chemical composition. Actually, as everyone knows when ordering his egg boiled, fried, or scrambled, there often are multiple choices in arranging the same elementary constituents. Prehistory enters for samples as for living beings, as a codeterminant of their present state.

In its simplest form, this prehistory dependence becomes apparent in the polymorphism of elements. Oxygen gas, for example, consists normally of $O=O$ molecules, because the double bond is stronger than two single bonds; sulfur and selenium vapor, on the other hand, tend to contain $S_8$ or $Se_8$ ring molecules, because two single bonds are stronger than one double bond (Fig. 12). The double bond, however, is still much stronger than a single bond; hence, the composition of the vapor phase changes with increasing temperature from eight-membered rings to diatomic molecules. When the ring molecules break open, the possibility of chain polymerization arises, as is well known from the formation of plastic sulfur. At room temperature this material reverts to the brittle ring structure, but selenium occurs in stable crystals built from rings or chains and also in amorphous chain-polymer modifications. In the ring form, selenium is an insulator; in the chain form, a semiconductor, since electron defects can be transferred along the chains. When squeezed by very high pressure—as might be expected from the structure relation to tellurium and the metal polonium (8)—selenium becomes a metal (Fig. 13) (9).

Since high temperature breaks down preexisting molecular entities and high

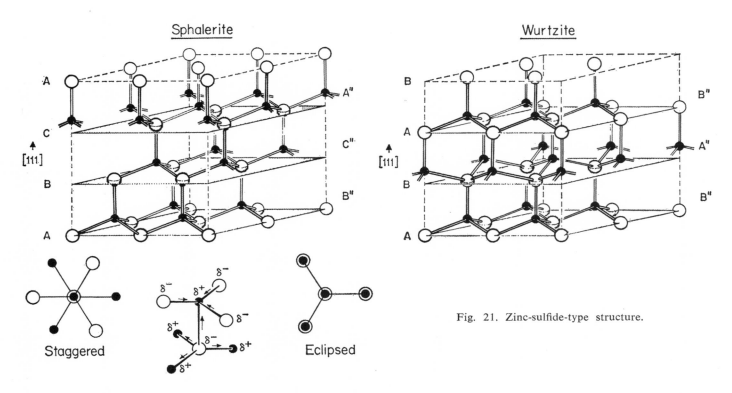

Sphalerite

Wurtzite

Staggered  Eclipsed

Fig. 21. Zinc-sulfide-type structure.

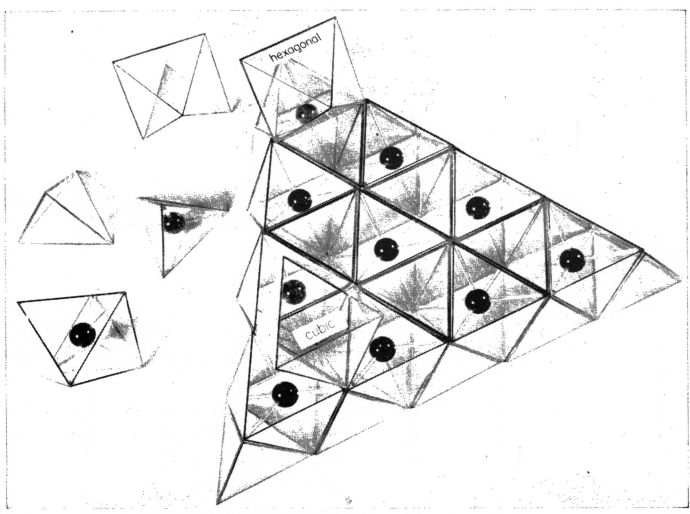

Fig. 22. Close-packed structures built from interstitial tetrahedra and octahedra.

pressure holds the constituents at effective interaction distance, high-pressure, high-temperature techniques are of increasing importance for synthesizing modifications normally precluded by interfering bond formations. The synthesis of diamond, of boron nitride in diamond instead of graphite structure, and of the new silicon dioxide modification coesite—which is proving so useful to the geologist in identifying craters of meteoric origin—are outstanding accomplishments of this approach (10). Synthesizing materials from defined elementary particles by molecular-beam techniques in ultrahigh vacuum is another promising method still in its pioneering stages.

Allotropy and the existence of competing structure types lead automatically to the subject of phase transitions. With falling temperature a material normally contracts, overlap and interaction time between electron clouds increase, and randomizing thermal agitation subsides. Thus, crystals at high temperature tend to be more symmetrical and more tolerant of substitutions, while in cooling the weaker, more specific interaction forces emerge from the sea of thermal noise and enforce special types of order, thereby lowering the crystal symmetry. If this reorganization is incompatible with the preexisting lattice and if the new arrangement can nucleate, the sample will shatter and recrystallize in a first-order transition. On the other hand, a completely continuous transformation may be possible, as is well known from the disorder $\rightleftharpoons$ order transitions of the constituents of alloys, the magnetic moments of electrons forming the spin systems of ferro- and antiferromagnetics, or the electric moments of polar crystals organizing in dipole chains of piezo- and ferroelectrics (5). The time taken by such phase transitions may range all the way from instantaneous explosion or thermal hysteresis of nanosecond duration to the millions of years traceable in geological strata.

Competing types of order are of decisive importance in the organic world. Whether polyisoprene assumes the *cis*- or the *trans*- structure decides whether a useful elastic rubber or an inelastic balata is obtained (Fig. 14). The ordering of water molecules twists protein molecules into spiral structures decisive for life processes (11), and here again the differentiation into right-hand or left-hand screw structures is vital for the activation of such processes.

## Laws of Molecular Architecture

A great variety of individual design concepts have appeared in the preceding discussion: hydrogen-like wave functions of atoms and electron-pair bonding; modifications of simple atomic orbitals by hybridization; combinations described by quantum-mechanical resonance; splitting of energy states by coupling, leading to molecular orbitals and the band structure of crystals; dense packing, as far as radii and their ratio allow; molecular, ionic, covalent, and metallic structures; polarity, polymorphism, and isomers; phase transitions and the importance of prehistory. With the development of magnetic-resonance techniques and devices such as masers and lasers, more and more becomes known about the fine structure of energy states, and the introduction of increasingly powerful computers makes it possible to calculate wave functions with rapidly increasing reliability. We learn—but a nightmarish feeling begins to assail the scientist, of becoming lost in the labyrinth of the Minotaur. Where are the guiding principles that can lead through this maze of phenomena in graphic understanding?

At the outset we stated that the space correlation and charge of the nuclei are the primary determinants for the web of electron clouds; hence, topology should be a guide. Judged from this point of view the structures of molecules and crystals are characterized by the presence (or absence) of certain elements of symmetry: a center of symmetry, planes of reflection or glide reflection, and axes of rotation and screw rotation (Fig. 15). For crystals the stringent requirement of periodic repetition of lattice points limits the admissible periodicity in rotation to 1-, 2-, 3-, 4-, and 6-fold axes and the possible number of space groups to 230. Structure analysis can assign any crystal to one of these 230 compartments.

This type of classification, based on inherent properties of symmetry, is more exact than the Linnaean system, which orders the world of plants, but no more informative. We seek elucidation of the type provided by Darwin's *Origin of Species*: What kinds of structures are chosen for molecular reasons? Which rules guide their design and assure stability—that is, "survival of the fittest"?

Answers to these questions begin to evolve, but they will often not be unique, because a variety of molecular

causes can hide behind the same macroscopic phenomenon. For example, violation of the rule, just stated, that the long-range periodic order of crystalline networks permits only 1-, 2-, 3-, 4-, and 6-fold axes of rotation should allow the forcing of materials into the glassy state of short-range order. This was suggested years ago by Tilton (12), who, in building models of silicates, demonstrated the likely occurrence of groups with 5-fold axes; and a very similar kind of arrangement has been invoked by Pauling for explaining the hydrogen-bonded structure of water (Fig. 16). On the other hand, the symmetry of molecular groups need not transfer to a crystal structure, as is demonstrated by boron, whose icosahedra of 5-fold rotation symmetry are safely tucked away in a unit cell of tetragonal symmetry (see Fig. 8), or by virus particles with 5-fold axes assembled in a close-packed crystal structure.

There are other causes of glass formation: the competition of various molecular constellations on the basis of nearly equal probability—as, for example, in borosilicates, where $B^{3+}$ can enter in either triangular or tetrahedral bonding, as demonstrated by Warren and Bray (Fig. 17) (13, 14); the agglomeration of chain molecules to form glassy polymer structures; or the freezing-in of amorphous structures through suppression of nucleation. By developing crystal nuclei afterwards in glass systems, Stookey (15) pioneered the new pyroceramics, materials that combine the strength of crystalline with the bounce of amorphous regions (Fig. 18) —a trick used by nature in the growing of trees and the formation of muscle fibers.

To return once more to molecular design, the recent spurt in the recognition of polyhedra molecules has made it clear that practically any structure which seems topologically reasonable can be made, and that increased symmetry, *ceteris paribus*, imparts increased stability. A good example is the sequence of boron hydride molecules studied by Lipscomb and his co-workers (16). The regular icosahedral molecule $[B_{12}H_{12}]^{--}$ (Fig. 19) proved so stable that it could be injected into a patient in large doses for cancer treatment by neutron bombardment, while the semi-finished $B_{10}H_{14}$ structure would have been broken down in the body of the victim, causing his speedy demise.

The designing of materials could

Fig. 23. [111] surfaces of indium antimonide etched for 30 minutes at 80°C ($0.2N$ $Fe^{3+}$ in $6N$ hydrogen chloride): (left) indium surface; (right) antimony surface (about $\times$ 495). [After Gatos (*18*)]

start with molecular topology: tentative selection of the space arrangement of nuclei would prescribe the symmetry conditions—formulated by group theory —to which the system of interlinking electron clouds is subjected. Recourse to two types of restrictions, "tolerance conditions" and "property conditions," would then lead systematically to alterations in the proposed array and to specific choices in the selection of nuclei. The procedure is akin to that of an architect who sketchily outlines a building and then, by carefully considering the restrictions imposed by the requirements of mechanical stability and function of the structure, arrives at choices of final design.

Tolerance conditions for a proposed structure are of molecular origin and specify the limits within which alterations in charge distribution and distortions of the space arrangement can be made without causing instability. Property conditions, by contrast, originate as macroscopic specifications for the performance of a material or device and have to be translated into molecular prescriptions.

Figure 20 illustrates the action of

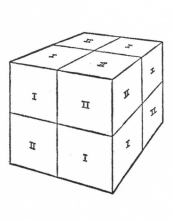

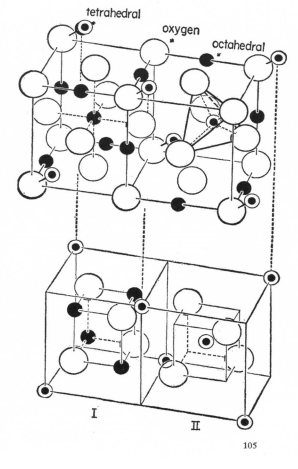

Fig. 24. Magnetite structure formed by cubic close-packed oxygen lattice and iron ions in interstitial sites.

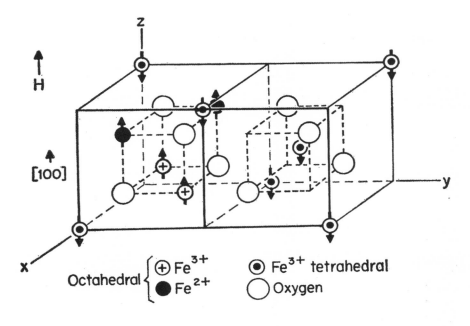

Octahedral $\begin{cases} \oplus Fe^{3+} \\ \bullet Fe^{2+} \end{cases}$  $\odot Fe^{3+}$ tetrahedral  $\bigcirc$ Oxygen

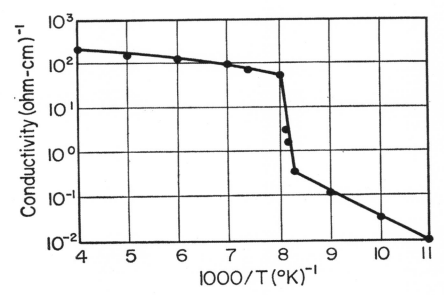

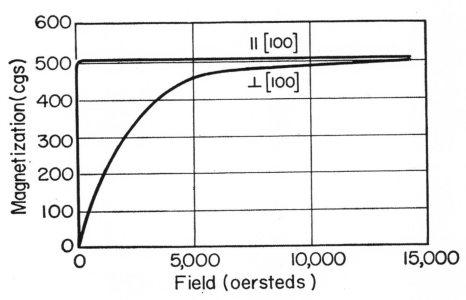

Fig. 25. Freezing-in of order in magnetite.

tolerance conditions: carbon atoms (group IV of the periodic system, Fig. 3) can be replaced by 50 percent each of boron atoms (group III) and of nitrogen atoms (group V) without destroying the structure of the benzene ring or the diamond lattice. Here the electron-cloud structure can average over the nuclear charge distribution. However, if we try to stretch the limits of symmetrical replacement further by introducing the atoms beryllium (group II) and oxygen (group VI) instead of boron and nitrogen, the benzene ring equivalent, beryllium trioxide, does not form and the beryllium oxide crystal does not derive from the diamond structure.

A comparison of the two crystal types boron nitride and beryllium oxide yields more information (Fig. 21): the diamond lattice, when composed of two different types of atoms, is identical with the sphalerite structure (zinc blende); the beryllium oxide lattice, with the wurtzite structure of zinc sulfide. The former can be derived from two interpenetrating cubic close-packed lattices; the latter, from two hexagonal ones. Hence, by increasing the polarity of the array, we have unbalanced the sphalerite in favor of the wurtzite arrangement. In both situations each atom type is tetrahedrally bonded to the other (CN 4), but, viewed in the [111] direction, subsequent tetrahedra in sphalerite are staggered and in wurtzite, eclipsed. The staggered array allows better space accommodation; the eclipsed array, a closer bonding of opposite charges. This explains the transformation observed.

The extreme step in polar substitution is balancing of lithium (group I) against fluorine (group VII). This wipes out the tetrahedral (CN 4) organization of the zinc sulfide lattices in favor of the octahedral (CN 6) coordination of the rock salt structure. The change has been enforced by the increase in radius ratio of cation to anion ($r_c/r_a$ for $Be^{++}/O^{--} = 0.25$; for $Li^+/F^- = 0.52$) as would be expected from Fig. 11. Still, like the sphalerite structure of boron nitride, the rock salt structure of lithium fluoride can be derived from two interpenetrating cubic close-packed sublattices (see Fig. 6).

This switching between crystal types (derived from close-packed arrays) at the command of tolerance conditions concerned with polarity and space accommodation invites clarification of the kinship of such types. Insight is provided by viewing the interstitial space arrangement for the close-packed structures of Fig. 4. This space is partitioned into interlocking tetrahedral and octahedral compartments (Fig. 22); a lattice section of $n$ atoms contains $n$ octahedral and $2n$ tetrahedral sites. The centers of the octahedra lie halfway between the layers of the original lattice; those of the tetrahedra, at ¼ and ¾ of the spacing. [A model design with transparent tetrahedral and octahedral building blocks has recently been perfected by A. Loeb in connection with his imaginative approach to a new crystal algebra (17).]

Starting with a cubic-face-centered array of layer sequence ABCABC . . ., we arrive at the rock salt structure by occupation of all the octahedral interstitial sites (see Fig. 6) or at the sphalerite structure by filling of all tetrahedral sites in either the ¼ or the ¾ location. By choice of the hexagonal close packing with layer sequence ABAB . . . and occupation of one of the two sets of tetrahedral sites, the wurtzite structure is created (see Fig. 21). Since the centers of the octahedra lie midway between the original layers, the spacing between the positive and negative planes of the rock salt structure is uniform and the crystal has a center of symmetry. For the tetrahedrally bonded sphalerite and wurtzite, on the other hand, the occupation of the ¼ or ¾ center positions causes a periodic bunching of the charged planes; the center of symmetry is destroyed.

## Structure and Properties

Such topological differences in competing arrangements should produce profound property changes. Indeed, crystals of the rock salt structure remain electrically neutral under mechanical stress; insulators of the sphalerite type react piezoelectrically (that is, they create potential differences of opposite signs on tension and compression), while those of the wurtzite type are in addition pyroelectric (potential differences of opposite signs develop also on heating and cooling). Thus, both tetrahedrally bonded polar crystal types can serve as electromechanical transducers, and the wurtzite type can serve in addition as a thermosensing device.

For molecular interpretation of these phenomena, the ions of opposite polarity can be visualized as forming a network of permanent dipole moments. In

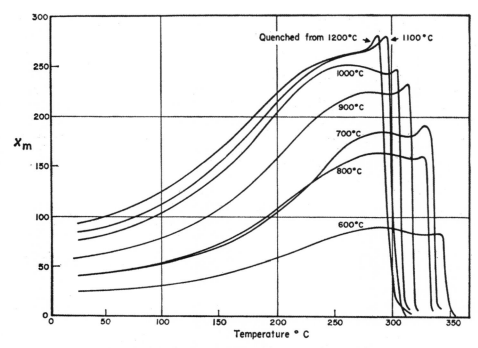

Fig. 26. Freezing-in of disorder in magnesium ferrite.

the rock salt structure the neutralizing balance of these moments cannot be upset by mechanical distortion; in sphalerite it can be, and in wurtzite it does not exist a priori, because the moments do not cancel but create a polar axis.

The polar double-layer structure produces additional differences between the $[111]$ and $[\bar{1}\bar{1}\bar{1}]$ directions in sphalerite, and between the $[001]$ and $[00\bar{1}]$ directions in wurtzite; the x-ray scattering is dissimilar in the two opposite directions, and since the crystals terminate on the one site with a cation and on the other with an anion layer, the electrochemical potentials and etching properties of these end surfaces are quite dissimilar (Fig. 23) (18). By combining sphalerite and wurtzite in twinned arrays, high-voltage photocells can be produced (19).

The structure transformation observed for the sequence of insulators C→BN→BeO→LiF in the second row of the periodic system repeats itself for the $b$ elements of the higher rows (silicon, germanium, and gray tin) in the corresponding group III–V (20), group II–VI, and group I–VII compounds (21). These elements and compounds are the decisive semiconductor materials for transistors and solid-state diodes, for thermoelectric converters, and for solar-energy photocells. Here the band structure, the gap width between valence and conduction band, the mass and mobility of electrons and holes can be adjusted by composition changes, and charge carriers can be mobilized by

cation substitution in minute quantities (doping). An impressive amount of fundamental molecular-science knowledge has been gathered rapidly about these materials under the impact of molecular-engineering applications (21).

The same is true for the ferrites (22), the semiconductors indispensable for magnetic high-frequency applications (memory devices, gyrators, and so on). Again the model of a close-packed array with interstitial sites (Fig. 22) helps to explain basic properties. Magnetite, the prototype ferrite ($Fe_3O_4$) is formed—in ionic description—by a cubic close-packed $O^{--}$ sublattice; one eighth of its interstitial tetrahedral sites are occupied by $Fe^{3+}$; one half of its octahedral sites, by $Fe^{3+}$ and $Fe^{++}$ cations in a 1:1 ratio. The cations in this inverse spinel structure (Fig. 24) are so placed that the electrostatic repulsion is minimized. Since $Fe^{++}$ and $Fe^{3+}$ cations in equal number occupy equivalent octahedral interstices, easy electron exchange between them makes magnetite too conductive for most purposes. The material can be transformed into an insulator by cation substitution that blocks this electron transfer.

The unpaired electrons in the cations of the transition elements are the carriers of the magnetic moments in the ferrites. Electron exchange between $Fe^{++}$ (four Bohr magnetons) and $Fe^{3+}$ (five Bohr magnetons) varies the magnetic arrangement at the same time. This coupling between electric and magnetic properties becomes clearly visible in magnetite by freezing-in an ordered sequence of $Fe^{++}$ and $F^{3+}$ below $-155°C$. The conductivity drops by several orders of magnitude, and if the magnetic spins are ordered by application of an external field during cooling through the transition, a magnetic axis is frozen-in, altering the hysteresis loop completely (5, 23) (Fig. 25). Conversely, since in the ferrites only a fraction of the interstitial sites are occupied, high temperature extends the spread of cations to less favorable positions. In consequence, by quenching-in such disorder, the magnetic properties can be greatly affected (Fig. 26).

These examples must suffice. They show that the connection between structure and properties can be of obvious directness and, in other situations, buried in prehistory effects which challenge the tenacity of a psychoanalyst for their elucidation. The principal reasons for complications are the same as in living systems: a macroscopic phenomenon may be produced by a variety of molecular causes; furthermore, the phenomenon may be related not to the ideal structure of a material but to the faults built into such a structure.

Science in previous times believed that "nature loves simplicity" and that man in his incredible complexity presents a "mighty effort contrary to nature." Dictatorships enslaving man could thus be justified as a return to nature's order. Today, this excuse of tyrants has vanished. Every day we learn with increasing insight that nature is incredibly complex and that man is one incident in its organization. At the outset we raised the question: What shall we most reasonably do with our natural resources? Molecular designing allows us to realize Jules Verne's fantasies. The answer is therefore not any longer what we can do, but what we want to do. Molecular science and molecular engineering must operate as allies of social science and political statesmanship in imaginative planning for the most beneficial transformation of the world's resources.

### References and Notes

1. H. A. Meyerhoff, "Changing concepts of mineral raw materials in the national economy," paper presented at the 128th meeting of the AAAS, Denver, 1961.
2. H. Brown, "Science and government," paper presented at the 128th meeting of the AAAS, Denver, 1961.
3. The work reported in this article was made possible through support extended to the Massachusetts Institute of Technology jointly by the Navy Department (Office of Naval Research), the Army Signal Corps, and the Air Force, under ONR contract Nonr-1841 (10), NR-018-801; also by the Air Force under contract AF 33 (616)-8353. I am greatly indebted to my co-workers C. W. Nelson and J. J. Mara for help in preparing the figures.
4. See, for example, J. L. Greenstein, Am. Scientist 49, 449 (1961).
5. See, for example, A. von Hippel, Molecular Science and Molecular Engineering (Massachusetts Institute of Technology Press and Wiley, New York, 1959).
6. See L. Pauling, The Nature of the Chemical Bond (Cornell Univ. Press, ed. 3, Ithaca, 1960).
7. See, for example, J. C. Slater, in Handbuch der Physik, S. Flügge, Ed. (Springer, Berlin, 1956), p. 1.
8. A. von Hippel, J. Chem. Phys. 16, 372 (1948).
9. A. S. Balchan and H. G. Drickamer, ibid. 34, 1948 (1961).
10. See Progress in Very High Pressure Research, F. P. Bundy, W. R. Hibbard, Jr., H. M. Strong, Eds. (Wiley, New York, 1961).
11. Sci. Am. 205, No. 9 (1961).
12. L. W. Tilton, J. Res. Natl. Bur. Std. 59, 139 (1957).
13. J. Biscoe and B. E. Warren, J. Am. Chem. Soc. 21, 287 (1938).
14. A. H. Silver and P. J. Bray, J. Chem. Phys. 29, 984 (1958).
15. S. D. Stookey, in Ceramic Fabrication Processes, W. D. Kingery, Ed. (Massachusetts Institute of Technology Press and Wiley, New York, 1958), p. 189.
16. W. N. Lipscomb, in Advances in Inorganic Chemistry and Radiochemistry, H. J. Emeleus and A. G. Sharpe, Eds. (Academic Press, New York, 1959), vol. 1, p. 117; ———, A. R. Pitochelli, M. F. Hawthorne, J. Am. Chem. Soc. 81, 5833 (1959); J. A. Wunderlich and W. N. Lipscomb, ibid. 82, 4427 (1960); E. B. More, Jr., L. L. Lohr, Jr., W. N. Lipscomb, J. Chem. Phys. 35, 1329 (1961).
17. A. L. Loeb, Acta Cryst. 11, 469 (1958); I. L. Morris and A. L. Loeb, ibid. 13, 434 (1960).
18. H. C. Gatos, Surface Chemistry of Metals and Semiconductors (Wiley, New York, 1960), p. 399.
19. W. J. Merz, Helv. Phys. Acta 31, 625 (1958).
20. H. Welker and H. Weiss, in Solid State Physics, F. Seitz and D. Turnbull, Eds. (Academic Press, New York, 1956), vol. 3, p. 1.
21. See, for example, "Semiconductors," American Chemical Society Monograph Series (1959); J. Appl. Phys. 32, No. 10 (1961).
22. See, for example, J. Smit and H. P. J. Wijn, Ferrites (Wiley, New York, 1959).
23. B. A. Calhoun, Phys. Rev. 94, 1577 (1954).

# JEROME BERT WIESNER
## 30 MAY 1915 –
## 21 OCTOBER 1994

*Excerpts from the National Academy of Science Biographical Memoirs*

*by Louis D. Smullin*

Professor Louis D. Smullin

Jerome Wiesner—Jerry to almost everybody—led an exciting and productive life and, more than most, he made a difference. As interesting and impressive as is the list of his offices and honors, even more interesting is his transformation from a young engineer just out of college to an "electronic warrior" during World War II, a "cold warrior" during the early days of the "missile gap," and finally to a leading spokesman for the nuclear test ban and a worker for nuclear disarmament.

Wiesner studied electrical engineering and mathematics at the University of Michigan in Ann Arbor. While there, he met Laya Wainger, a fellow student majoring in mathematics. They married in 1940, and developed a deep and abiding lifelong partnership. Besides being the mother of their four children—Steven, Zachary, Lisa, and Joshua—Laya was one of Jerry's primary intellectual companions. Together they explored issues and ideas. She critiqued many of his most important documents (beginning with his Ph.D. thesis).

Throughout his life, Wiesner's glass was always at least half full, as is illustrated by his sister's recollection of his teenage efforts as a radio ham in Michigan. Just after he got his first receiver working and on the air, he burst out of his bedroom to announce that he had picked up a station from a foreign country. Not much later, he came out to amend his announcement. He had, in fact, tuned in to a Polish-language station in Hamtramck, a small city about ten miles from Dearborn.

The story illustrates his abiding optimism about the power and possibilities inherent in technical things, and in his later years about the possibility of saving the world from a nuclear disaster. As noted by MIT's news office, Wiesner was "a leading voice for decades in international efforts to control and limit nuclear arms ... a key figure in the establishment of the Arms Control and Disarmament Agency, in achieving a partial nuclear test ban treaty, and in the successful effort to restrict the deployment of antiballistic missile systems."[23]

Wiesner's life, as for so many engineers and scientists of his generation, was shaped by his World War II experience in the MIT Radiation Lab, where he worked on the development of radar, and by his work at Los Alamos directly after the war.

In the Radiation Lab, he began his weapon systems work on a 3-cm radar for a Navy night fighter. This was followed by his taking over the job of directing the final stages of development of Project Cadillac, an airborne early warning (AEW) radar for the Navy. It was a very big and complex system that brought him into close contact with the highest levels of the Navy command structure. The AEW system played an important role in the Battle of the Pacific.

At the end of the war, Professor Jerrold Zacharias was recruited from the Radiation Lab to set up a new nuclear weapons engineering group at Los Alamos; among those he brought with him was Jerry Wiesner. In his autobiographical notes, Wiesner states, "It was for me an interesting and sometimes exciting period. In later years I realized that the understanding I gained, both about the bomb and the controversy surrounding its use, had provided me with a valuable education on issues that were to occupy a large part of my life."

In 1945, as MIT was moving into its peacetime mode of operation, Professor Harold Hazen, head of the Department of Electrical Engineering, asked that Wiesner be appointed to the faculty. Wiesner accepted the invitation and returned to MIT in 1946 as a faculty member in electrical engineering, conducting his research in the Research Laboratory of Electronics (RLE), the peacetime successor to the Radiation Lab.

After his return to MIT, Wiesner participated in many of the summer studies on military problems (anti-submarine warfare, the distant early warning (DEW) line, etc.). In these studies a select group of scientists and engineers from industry and academia were briefed by appropriate military officers and civilians on the detailed nature of the problems, and various solutions were proposed and discussed. Many important recommendations were made and implemented. In this way Wiesner (and his colleagues) began the move from purely technical matters into the broader domain of policy-making.

The beginnings of the Cold War were symbolized by a number of important technical events. Among these were the race between the United States and the Soviet Union to copy the German ballistic missile technology, the explosion of the first Soviet atomic bomb, and the successful launching of *Sputnik*.

President Jerome Wiesner in a quiet moment in Killian Court

Faced with the threat of the Soviet atomic bomb, the MIT Lincoln Laboratory was established in 1951 to work on the problems of air defense of the continental United States. One of its projects was to set up a distant early warning chain of radar stations to warn of an attack by Soviet bombers coming across the North Pole. To get the maximum warning time, the line would be located along the shore of the Arctic Ocean. However, radio communication in these high latitudes was uncertain and could be blacked out for long periods due to intense electrical activity in the ionosphere. In about 1953 Wiesner and some of his colleagues proposed the use of forward scattering from the troposphere for reliable (but narrow band) communication. For many years, these systems provided secure communication from the DEW line to the North American Air Defense Command in Colorado.

In 1952 Wiesner became the third director of RLE, succeeding professors Jay Stratton and Albert Hill in that role. Under their successive leadership, RLE developed into a multidisciplinary, interdepartmental center. The joint services (Army, Navy, and Air Force) contract under which RLE was organized specified that it should "do research in the field of electronics, physics, and communication, and publish."

Inspired by Professor Norbert Wiener, Wiesner recognized that communication included psychology, language, and sensory physiology. Thus it was that, from its earliest days, the lab brought in linguists, psychologists, and neurophysiologists, as well as information theorists, radio engineers, and physicists. Much later, when he became provost and then president of MIT, he played a similar role in stimulating the growth of the humanities and the arts at MIT.

In 1954 the Office of Defense Management set up the Technical Capabilities Panel (TCP) to study the capabilities of the Air Force. MIT President James Killian was asked to head the study, and he invited Wiesner to join the panel as head of the Overseas Military Communications group. The launching of *Sputnik* produced a scare in Washington that the Soviet Union already had an arsenal of ICBMs when we had almost none. This fear was summarized in one short phrase: *the missile gap*. In 1957 President Eisenhower set up a committee (later known as the Gaither Committee) to study the implications of a nuclear war.

In his own (unpublished) autobiographical notes, Wiesner later commented about the *Gaither Report*:

*As we began to write the report, it became clear that a part of the group regarded its ingredients as recommendations that they felt very strongly about while others of us (cer-*

162

*tainly myself) found it impossible to differentiate between a war that had only 60 million casualties instead of 100 million at a cost of many billions of dollars. I also wondered whether such an increased spending for war preparations might make a war more likely. The Gaither study just made me even more certain than I had been before that nuclear weapons were not useable weapons.*

In 1961 the newly elected President Kennedy chose Wiesner to be his science advisor. During his tenure in that post for the three years of the Kennedy Administration and the first year of Lyndon Johnson's, arms control in various forms was at the center of the agenda. Wiesner had both successes and failures.

Wiesner's outstanding success was his role in the achievement of the 1963 Partial Test Ban Treaty, by which the United States, the United Kingdom, and the Soviet Union agreed to cease nuclear weapons testing in the atmosphere and underwater, and to ban testing in space. The failure to achieve a complete test ban, ending underground tests as well, was a great disappointment to Wiesner and to the administration. The two sides never succeeded in bridging the gap on what quota of on-site inspections in their respective territories was adequate to provide effective verification of a complete test ban.

An equally great, but then not public, disappointment was Wiesner's inability to persuade President Kennedy and the Department of Defense that the rapid buildup of ICBMs and submarine-launched ballistic missiles proposed in the president's first full budget was both unnecessary and undesirable—unnecessary because the new satellite reconnaissance systems showed that the Soviet missile forces were much smaller than the United States had believed, and undesirable because the Soviets would match the U.S. buildup, resulting in greater insecurity for both sides.

Three areas in which Wiesner's arms-control efforts succeeded were in civil defense, the installation of permissive links on nuclear weapons carried by aircraft and ICBMs, and the nondeployment of anti-ballistic missile (ABM) systems.

Wiesner helped to persuade President Kennedy in 1961 to call for a very modest civil defense program of fallout shelters rather than the large program of blast shelters that many in the military and some of Kennedy's political adversaries were calling for. Wiesner also saw the desirability and technical feasibility of installing electronic locks—permissive action links or PALs—on nuclear warheads. These made more certain positive control that prevented launches without presidential authorization. Further, he drove the program through to realization in a remarkably short time, although he never succeeded in over-coming the Navy's resistance to the use of PALs on submarine-launched missiles.

The President's Science Advisory Committee's (PSAC) strong technical criticisms of the ABM systems available in 1961 helped lead to a decision against deployment. Wiesner argued forcefully for the undesirability of deploying even much-improved systems, pointing out that technological improvements would continue to give the advantage to the offense. He continued his advocacy after he returned to MIT, and he made a major contribution to the achievement of the ABM treaty of 1972.

Following the death of President Kennedy, Wiesner served as President Johnson's science advisor for about a year. In 1964, his three-year leave from MIT at an end, Wiesner returned with his family to Cambridge and to their home in Watertown. His reentry into academic life began with his appointment as dean of the School of Science.

(left to right): L. Smullin, J. Wiesner, W. Burke, and H. Johnson at the dedication of the Fairchild Complex, 1973

When Howard W. Johnson became MIT's twelfth president, in July 1966, he appointed Wiesner as provost, beginning a number of years of close teamwork. These were the years of international student unrest and of growing protest against the war in Vietnam. Johnson and Wiesner, by dint of their cool but steady style, were able to keep open communications with the protesting students and faculty. Unlike the experience at many other universities in this period, it was never necessary to call the police onto the campus.

In July of 1971 Wiesner became the thirteenth president of MIT, succeeding Howard Johnson, who became chairman of the MIT Corporation. As president, Wiesner pursued educational reforms and the cultivation of fields not previously represented or represented at less than MIT's potential level of excellence. Professor Paul E. Gray served with Wiesner as the Institute's chancellor during this period, and later succeeded him as president. Reflecting on that era, Gray wrote:

*As dean, provost, and president, Jerry expanded MIT's teaching and research programs in health sciences, humanities, and the arts. And he strengthened the Institute's undergraduate educational programs through creative employment of a fund for educational innovation, which had been provided by his close friend Edwin H. Land, the founder of the Polaroid Corporation.*

*This resource was used in 1970 to enable the late Professor Margaret L.A. MacVicar to start the Undergraduate Research Opportunities Program. This program, now used year after year by approximately three-quarters of the undergraduates at MIT, is widely regarded as the most important educational innovation at the Institute in this half-century.*

*He sought new ways to bring MIT's expertise in science and engineering to bear on social issues, such as health care, urban decay, mass transportation, and housing. He was instrumental in establishing the MIT Program in Science, Technology, and Society, which focuses on ways in which science and technological and social factors interact to shape modern life. This interdisciplinary program has become a highly respected component of the Institute's academic structure.*

*In his later years, Jerry was centrally involved, together with Professor Nicholas Negroponte, in the creation of the Program in Media Arts and Sciences and the Media Laboratory, which are housed at MIT in the Jerome and Laya Wiesner Building.*

*He was deeply committed to the goals of this nation's civil rights movement, and the period of his leadership of MIT produced the greatest progress up to that time in bringing women and minorities to the student body and the faculty.*

President Wiesner (at rear) and Professor Paul Gray (front) march to Gray's installation as MIT president. Between them is Virginia W.G. Army, who gave the invocation at the ceremony. She is also Paul Gray's eldest child.

Wiesner served as president until 30 June 1980, when he retired and resumed the title of Institute Professor, which he had held from 1962 to 1971.

In 1988 Wiesner suffered a heart attack and stroke. The stroke affected his left side and left him with almost no speech. He took his rehabilitation seriously and worked very hard at the various available therapies. Within about a year and a half he had recovered much of his speech and was able to drive a suitably modified car. The recovery was sufficient to allow him to attend meetings, to speak in public, and to travel.

I have tried to capture here some of the ways Jerry Wiesner made a difference in the world, and to trace his transformation from young engineer to a leader of international stature. Sometimes prose just doesn't do it. Wiesner had a long friendship with the poet Archibald MacLeish. They first met when Wiesner came to the Library of Congress in 1940 to work with Alan Lomax on the recording of indigenous American folk music. As Wiesner said in his memoirs, "My title was chief engineer of the Library of Congress. I was also its entire engineering staff." At the time of Wiesner's inauguration as MIT president in 1971, MacLeish wrote a poem in tribute to his old friend. It is a fitting conclusion to this memoir as well:

*A good man! Look at him against the time!*

*He saunters along to his place in the world's weather,*

*Lights his pipe, hitches his pants,*

*Talks back to accepted opinion.*

*Congressional committees hear him say:*

*"Not what you think: what you haven't thought of."*

*He addresses presidents. He says:*

*"Governments even now still have to govern:*

*No one is going to invent a self-governing holocaust."*

*The Pentagon receives his views:*

*"Science," he says, "is no substitute for thought.*

*Miracle drugs perhaps: not miracle wars."*

*Advisor to presidents, the papers call him.*

*Advisor, I say, to the young.*

*It's the young who need competent friends, bold companions,*

*Honest men who won't run out,*

*Won't write off mankind, sell up the country,*

*Quit the venture, jibe the ship.*

*I love this man,*

*I rinse my mouth with his praise in a frightened time.*

*The taste in the cup is mint,*

*Of spring water.*

ENDNOTES FOR PART 4

[1]Abridged from Robert G. Gallager, "Claude E. Shannon: A Retrospective on His Life, Work, and Impact," *IEEE Transactions on Information Theory* 47 (November 2001): 2681–95.

[2]Claude E. Shannon, "A Mathematical Theory of Communication," *Bell System Technical Journal* 27: 379–423, 623–56.

[3]Claude E. Shannon, "A Symbolic Analysis of Relay and Switching Circuits," *Trans. AIEE* 57(1938): 713–23.

[4]Claude E. Shannon, "Communication Theory of Secrecy Systems," *BSTJ* 28(1949): 656–715.

[5]J.F. Reintjes, draft of speech for Gordon S. Brown retirement dinner, Department of Electrical Engineering and Computer Science, Massachusetts Institute of Technology, Cambridge, Mass., 16 May 1973.

[6]J.F. Reintjes, "Gordon S. Brown," *Memorial Tributes: National Academy of Engineering* Vol. 10, National Academy of Engineering, 2002.

[7]"Gordon S. Brown, Pioneer Electrical Engineer and Educator, Is Dead at 88," *Tech Talk* 41(2) (28 August 1996).

[8]Jay Forrester, "Whirlwind's Success," paper presented at Whirlwind's Genesis and Descendants, Boston, Massachusetts, 18 October 1987.

[9]J.F. Reintjes, "Gordon S. Brown," *Memorial Tributes.*

[10]J.F. Reintjes, draft of speech for Gordon S. Brown retirement dinner.

[11]Paul Penfield, memo to EE department and staff, Massachusetts Institute of Technology, 23 August 1996. Available online at http://www.eecs.mit.edu/AY96-97/announcements/1.html.

[12]Jay Forrester, 1992. sysdyn.mit.edu/sdep/papers/D-432.pdf.

[13]Karl L. Wildes and Nilo A. Lindgren, *A Century of Electrical Engineering and Computer Science at MIT, 1882-1982.* Cambridge, Mass.: MIT Press, 1985, pp. 158–9.

[14]Ernst A. Guillemin, *Introductory Circuit Theory.* New York: John Wiley & Sons, 1953.

[15]Ibid., vii-viii.

[16]R.M. Fano, L.J. Chu, R.B. Adler, *Electromagnetic Fields, Energy and Forces.* New York: John Wiley & Sons, 1960, p. vii.

[17]R.B. Adler, L.J. Chu, R.M. Fano, *Electromagnetic Energy Transmission and Radiation.* New York: John Wiley & Sons, 1960, p. vii.

[18]H.J. Zimmermann and S.J Mason, *Electronic Circuit Theory.* New York: John Wiley & Sons, 1959, p. vii.

[19]S.J. Mason and H.J. Zimmermann, *Electronic Circuits, Signals and Systems.* New York: John Wiley & Sons, 1960, p. vii.

[20]D.C. White and H.H. Woodson, *Electromechanical Energy Conversion.* New York: John Wiley & Sons, 1959, p. vii.

[21]Arthur R. von Hippel, "Universities in Transition," *The Technology Review* (April 1959): 293–295, 314.

[22]Maurizio Villauri, "Professor Arthur R. von Hippel and Socrates' Maieutics," *Ferroelectrics* 135 (1992): 9–10.

[23]"President emeritus Jerome Wiesner is dead at 79," *Tech Talk* 39, no. 9 (26 October 1994).

### The Van de Graaf moves

In 1931, a large Van de Graaff generator (2.5 megavolt) was constructed in an unused dirigible dock at Round Hill in South Dartmouth, Massachusetts. It was subsequently moved to MIT, where it was completely modified and used for atom smashing and high-energy X-ray research under the guidance of Electrical Engineering Professor John G. Trump. In 1956 the Van de Graaff was again disassembled and moved from Vassar Street to its current home in the Boston Museum of Science. The moving process was viewed by many residents of Building 20, including Norbert Wiener (in the middle picture on the left).

# 5 Computer Science

*by Paul L. Penfield, Jr.*

The first electronic digital computers were made during World War II. Their importance was recognized in academic circles in the 1950s, and their use became common during the 1960s. Two research groups devoted to computer science were established at MIT—the Artificial Intelligence Group in 1959 and Project MAC in 1963. These gave the department a strong graduate program in computer science.

But to teach computer science at the undergraduate level according to the engineering-science paradigm, an appropriate science base needed to be identified. Here a difficulty was encountered. Unlike the case with electrical engineering topics, there were no natural laws or previously developed science to guide practical techniques in programming, architecture, or artificial intelligence. Mathematical theories of lambda calculus, Turing machines, algorithmic complexity, and Boolean algebra were not enough.

The approach taken was to develop the courses anyway, and not worry about the science base. Some of the early courses were highly theoretical. Some were very practical, tightly coupled to contemporary hardware or mainstream computer

*Endnotes appear on page 210.

languages. These courses were popular, and before long there were enough of them, with enough intellectual coherence, to comprise a degree program in computer science and engineering. In 1969, this program was announced and the first such degrees were awarded in 1975.

But what about the engineering-science paradigm? Was it still relevant? It had given electrical engineering two principal benefits: first, a foundation usable by graduates for their entire careers (forty years), and second, an opportunity for the engineering community to maintain its own intellectual underpinnings. In retrospect it can be seen that those who developed the computer science curriculum obtained these same benefits by other means. They identified fundamental, generic concepts that were commonly encountered in contemporary technologies, and taught them, adding examples from current practice. This body of generic knowledge was meant to last forty years, and was in a form that met the needs of computer scientists. Some day, this body of knowledge may be recognized as a science in its own right, in which case the engineering-science paradigm will have survived in the long run.

The rise of computer science raised fundamental questions about its relation to electrical engineering. Were the two basically inseparable or were they different? How would they evolve? If the two fields were expected to diverge, then computer science should have its own separate department. If not, then establishing a separate department would be a costly mistake. Either way, the wrong departmental structure would seriously jeopardize MIT's position of technical leadership. The discussion of this issue in the early 1970s was surely the most important debate the department has ever had. The future of electrical engineering would be very different without a strong connection to computer science, and vice versa.

There were several arguments in favor of a split. The department was already big — in some minds too big. Because it was technically broad, no single department head could provide leadership in all technical areas. In fact, starting in 1971 there had been associate department heads, one from electrical engineering and one from computer science. The research and teaching styles of the two fields were different, because computer science was new, rapidly evolving, and more empirical. Some computer scientists felt their field should be free to develop in its own way, unencumbered by established engineering traditions. Those making this argument tended to view computer science as a branch of mathematics. Finally, a split would be easy because the computer science people were already housed in a separate building.

But there were powerful arguments in favor of staying as one department. If computer science were not tied to an engineering discipline it could not benefit from proven approaches to engineering. Those making this argument viewed computer science as a type of engineering. Some argued against the extra cost of separate administrations. Others feared that without the excitement of computer science, electrical engineering would stagnate, becoming less interesting to both faculty and students.

Perhaps the strongest argument in favor of a single department was based on the belief that computer hardware and software would eventually be indistinguishable from electrical systems. Of course computers were made of electronic components, but that was not the point. The point was that other electrical systems would, before long, include components that either resembled computers or were computers. Electrical engineering graduates would not be able to design such systems if they did not understand computer science. Electrical engineering and computer science would not diverge, but would remain close together, and in effect act like a single discipline. This argument was repeatedly validated in later years, by advances in digital circuits and digital signal processing in the 1970s, VLSI in the 1980s, networking in the 1990s, and now embedded computing.

In 1974 the decision was made to remain as one department. Soon after, in an informal poll conducted by Joel Moses, the department faculty voted to change the department's name to Electrical Engineering and Computer Science (EECS), in recognition of the permanence and importance of computer science.

With this decision made, the next task was to bring into harmony the two separate curricula, one in electrical engineering and one in computer science. A committee was formed to examine whether the two degree programs should have a common set of beginning courses, and concluded that they should. All EECS graduates needed to know about computer programming, electric and electronic circuits, signal processing, and computer architecture. These four courses already existed and were adapted for this new role. They still serve as the common core of all departmental undergraduate programs.

The retention of computer science in the department's degree programs, however desirable, led to new problems. There was simply too much material in the curricula. And many students wanted to learn both electrical engineering and computer science in more depth than either program permitted. These issues precipitated another curriculum revision during the 1990s.

# JOSEPH CARL ROBNETT LICKLIDER
## 11 MARCH 1915 –
## 26 JUNE 1990

*by Robert M. Fano*

1 July 2003: the fortieth birthday of Project Mac and the inauguration day of the Computer Science and Artificial Intelligence Laboratory (CSAIL). Cutting the cake are R. Fano, first director of Project MAC, and R. Brooks, first director of CSAIL.

J.C.R. Licklider

Joseph Carl Robnett Licklider was called "Lick" by family, friends, colleagues, and almost everybody else. I had the privilege of knowing him as a colleague and friend from the time he first joined the MIT faculty in 1950.

Lick was born on March 11, 1915, in St. Louis, Missouri. He graduated from Washington University, in St. Louis, with majors in psychology, mathematics, and physics in 1937, and was awarded an M.A. degree in psychology the following year. He continued his graduate studies in psychology at the University of Rochester, where he received a Ph.D. degree in 1942.

Lick's Ph.D. research at the University of Rochester was an experimental investigation of the "place" and "frequency-of-neural-impulses" theories about the perception of pitch and loudness. Lick must have completed this research and other degree requirements in 1941, because he accepted a research associate appointment at Swarthmore for the 1941–42 academic year, to work on a related research topic; however, his stay at Swarthmore was cut short by World War II. He never returned to the type of pioneering neuroscience research of his thesis.

Lick's professional career continued at Harvard University in 1942 with his appointment as research associate and, later, as research fellow in the Psycho-Acoustic Laboratory. It was wartime and the laboratory was involved in research for the military services. A major concern was radio communication with aircraft, which was rather poor because of signal distortion and additive noise from various sources. Lick investigated the intelligibility of speech distorted in all sorts of ways and in the presence of various types of additive noise. Of particular importance is his research on infinite peak clipping of speech waves and the resultant discovery that the locations of the "zero crossings" of the wave form (the points where it switches from a negative to a positive value and vice versa) had to contain most of the information necessary to understand speech. This discovery led to significant equipment improvements, for which Lick was granted a patent.

World War II ended in 1945, a year that was a turning point in Lick's personal and professional life. On 20 January 1945, he married Louise Carpenter; their children were born in 1947 and 1949. In the immediate post-war period, he became an active member of the Cambridge research community and the intense interdisciplinary activity centered on Norbert Wiener's notion of cybernetics, or control and communication in the animal and the machine.

In July 1950, Lick joined the MIT faculty as an associate professor. During this stay at MIT (1950–57), he was a group leader at Lincoln Laboratory and a member of the Acoustic Laboratory and the Research Laboratory of Electronics.

Psychoacoustics research was only part of Lick's activities at MIT. Other MIT projects in which he was active included Lincoln Laboratory's development of a new type of air-defense system; this system used digital computers to analyze the information provided by several radars, identify the locations of enemy bombers, and provide control information for the intercepting fighters. It was Lick's first interaction with a powerful digital computer — the Whirlwind, which had a visual display and a capability for real-time man-machine interaction. (See the Bush classic paper, "The Differential Analyzer: A New Machine for Solving Differential Equations," pages 36–42.) Lick had previously been disappointed by analog computers' inability to model brain functions, but he was surely astounded by Whirlwind's capability. The experimental psychologist fell in love with digital computers.

By 1957, Lick's psychology group at MIT was beginning to fall apart. Lick concluded that he could not do what he wanted to do — which now included learning how to use digital computers—while trying to build a psychology department. He joined Bolt Beranek and Newman, Inc. (BBN), at that time a relatively small acoustic consulting firm, as a vice president and head of the departments of psychoacoustics, engineering psychology, and information systems research.

He very quickly became addicted to the first PDP-1 computer, a Digital Equipment Corporation creation made for online use with a light pen, which was delivered to BBN in 1959. But something was still missing: Lick needed a group of bright computer people with whom to interact.

By then, the Research Laboratory of Electronics (RLE) had acquired several computers for use by faculty and students; RLE's computer laboratory, more accessible and informal than the MIT Computation Center, had become a Mecca for faculty and graduate students.

Lick, who was still at home on the MIT campus, found at RLE both a congenial community and a source of talent for his work at BBN.

While Lick was at BBN, his thinking advanced in important ways. First, he published several psychoacoustics papers. One, "On Psychophysiological Models,"[1] is of special interest because it displays Lick's views on the purpose of computer models and the intellectual importance of the modeling process itself. These views foreshadow the origins and rationale of Lick's vision of man-machine symbiosis.

Second, Lick worked on a study of future libraries for the Council on Library Resources. He was selected by the council to lead the project after lengthy consultations with distinguished leaders from a variety of research organizations. The final report on the project—a book published in 1965 called *Libraries of the Future*[2]—presented a vision of future libraries based on Lick's vision of man-computer symbiosis. Lick limited the scope of "libraries" to the body of documents that could be stored in digital form without loss of value, and presented a detailed analysis of the intellectual processes involved in the acquisition, organization, and use of knowledge. This was followed by a description of the structure and usage of the "procognitive systems" he envisioned, capable of searching the body of documents under user control.

Thus, by 1960, Lick had learned a great deal about digital computers and programming with the help of the group of brilliant and knowledgeable people he brought to BBN. This knowledge, together with his experience—and frustration—with the process of model-building using currently available computational tools, led him to envision a future intimate collaboration between man and computer in which each partner would supplement and extend the capabilities of the other. In March, Lick published this vision in his history-making paper "Man-Computer Symbiosis."[3] In the paper, he first postulated his vision of man-computer symbiosis and then presented a detailed and lengthy analysis, similar to an industrial time-and-motion study, of his own research. He found that some 85 percent of his time was devoted to routine clerical or mechanical operations, ranging from calculating and data plotting to collecting information, which in principle could be performed better and faster by a computer. The paper then went on to outline the research program required to develop both the hardware and software needed to implement his vision.

In 1962, Lick got a chance to make his vision a reality. He became the first director of the Information Processing Techniques Office (IPTO) of the Advanced Research Projects Agency (ARPA) of the Department of Defense.

He took the job because he saw it as an opportunity to establish the sort of research program that he had outlined in the 1960 paper, and he accepted the position with the understanding that he would be free to launch his research program mainly in university laboratories, out of the context of any specific military application.

Lick lost no time getting started. He neither mailed out requests for proposals nor waited in his office for proposals to arrive. Rather, he visited many computer research laboratories looking for interesting work and, perhaps even more, for good people. I recall his visiting MIT in mid-October. Whenever he had a chance, he spoke about the virtues of man-computer interaction. His enthusiasm infected me so quickly that by early November we had reached agreement in principle that MIT would organize Project MAC and I would become its first director.

The IPTO program initiated by Lick turned out to be very successful, so much so that it has become by now a model for other government-sponsored research programs. There were various reasons for its quick success—the time was ripe for the blossoming of computer science and the funds were plentiful—but much of the credit must go to Lick for starting the program on the right track. The policies he pioneered were ones from which his successors did not materially depart. The program was structured like no other government research program. It was akin to a single, widely dispersed research laboratory with a clear overall goal; Lick acted as its director and intellectual leader. He fostered close communication and collaboration between all parts of his far-flung laboratory, thereby creating what became known as the "ARPA community." He further instilled in that community the sense of adventure, dedication, and camaraderie that he had learned to value in his research career. Finally, he made sure that the availability of computer resources would not be a limiting factor in the research program, and that plenty of funds would be available for the support of graduate students whom he correctly regarded as a most important and precious resource.

Lick's main point—which at the time was highly controversial—was that computers, while expensive, could be produced on demand, but creative, competent people could not.

Lick completed his two-year tour of duty at ARPA in 1964, spent the next two years at IBM, then returned to MIT in 1966 as a visiting professor. The following year, he accepted a permanent appointment in the electrical engineering department. From 1968 to 1970 he served as the director of Project MAC, the research laboratory he had been instrumental in establishing in 1963, which eventually became the Laboratory for Computer Science. (See LCS profile, pages 254–258.)

Lick was disappointed, on his return to MIT, by the lack of progress in two areas that were crucial to his goal of man-computer symbiosis: visual man-computer interfaces and software systems that would facilitate building computer models and exploring their behaviors without writing elaborate programs from scratch. In order to make progress in those areas, he formed a new research group within Project MAC and quickly attracted to it a large number of students, both graduate and undergraduate. The name chosen for the new group was Dynamic Modeling (later changed to Programming Technology), indicating its intended research objective.

Lick's goal was a self-contained, coherent, interactive computer system that could be used by researchers with moderate computer skills to investigate the behavior of a variety of models with little programming required on their part. The software scheme conceived by Lick was very different from any existing problem-oriented language. Briefly, it was akin to a software Tinkertoy, based on a vast library of software modules that could be readily assembled into specific models and into programs for investigating them. New modules could be constructed and added to the library by users to meet their special requirements, so that the library would eventually become the repository of the work of the community. Both the goal and the implementation scheme were very ambitious, perhaps too ambitious in view of the computers available at the time. Yet they were not unrealistic, given Lick's faith—also visionary for the time—that computer speeds and memory sizes would increase rapidly while their costs would decrease.

In 1974, Lick returned to ARPA to serve again as the director of IPTO at a time when no other suitable person could be found. Unfortunately, that second tour of duty was not as pleasant for him as the first one. He had to contend with budgetary pressures resulting from the war in Vietnam and with new justification requirements for the expenditure of research funds. ARPA had become more bureaucratic and Lick did not feel comfortable in that environment; nevertheless, he did his duty for a year and kept the IPTO program on track.

He returned to MIT in the fall of 1975, reaching mandatory retirement age in 1985.

Lick was an excellent and, at times, very amusing speaker. He was also a gifted and very prolific writer; his bibliography lists more than a hundred formal publications, in addition to laboratory reports. He was in great demand as a keynote and banquet speaker, as a participant in a variety of symposia, and as a member of military and civilian study committees.

Lick was an imaginative experimenter and theoretician, an intellectual leader and a visionary who left major marks in two distinct fields: psychoacoustics and computer science.

At the time of his death, he was a member of the National Academy of Sciences, the American Academy of Arts and Sciences, the New York Academy of Sciences, and the Washington Academy of Sciences. He was also either a fellow or member of a large number of professional societies as well as Professor Emeritus of Computer Science in the Department of Electrical Engineering and Computer Science, and a member of the Laboratory for Computer Science. Among his many honors and awards were the 1950 Biennial Award of the Acoustical Society of America, the 1965 Franklin V. Taylor Award of the Society of Engineering Psychologists, and the 1990 Commonwealth Award for Science and Invention.

Interestingly, upon his election in 1969 to the National Academy of Sciences, Lick chose the Engineering Section as his home even though he had been nominated for membership by the Psychology Section. Yet after I walked through Lick's career in an attempt to understand the evolution of his intellectual interests and motivations, I came to the conclusion that he was first and foremost a psychologist. Psychoacoustics was his primary, long-lasting interest and his source of motivation: his very last research project was still motivated by his interest in modeling psychoacoustics phenomena. More broadly, he was interested in almost any aspect of human cognitive activities. While he became a very knowledgeable and skillful programmer, his focus remained on the cognitive aspects of computer usage. He was fascinated by computers because he understood, in a deep way, their potential to help people in a broad spectrum of activities, by extending and amplifying their intellectual power, by improving the effectiveness of their communication and collaboration, and, last but not least, by freeing them from the drudgery of clerical operations to which he was particularly allergic.

Despite his very significant contributions to psychoacoustics, Lick is most widely remembered as a computer pioneer. Anybody old enough to have been familiar with the state of computers and their usage in 1960, when Lick published his paper on man-computer symbiosis, knows that his vision was considered by many at that time to be science fiction. Yet today, libraries are fast approaching the model he foresaw in *Libraries of the Future*. The U.S. Armed Forces have embraced the views on command and control that he eloquently presented in his 1962 ARPA interview. And the "inter-galactic network" he talked about, gleefully, as far back as 1963, has been realized as the Internet.

Lick's legacy—his visions—are now realities that are so embedded in our lives as to be taken for granted by people around the world.

# An Experimental Time-Sharing System

FERNANDO J. CORBATÓ
1 JULY 1926 –

SPRING JOINT COMPUTER
CONFERENCE, 3 MAY 1962

*Introduced by the author*

The Computation Center's Associate Director, F.J. Corbató beside the IBM 7090 console in the Compton Building c. 1962–63

In the late 1950s, after barely a decade of use, it was clear that modern computers were powerful and exciting tools that could be exploited for research and experimentation. As a consequence, the demand for machine time had already begun to exceed the supply, and vendors and computer center managers, in their quest to make more and more efficient use of the machines, developed a style of computing called batch-processing. In batch-processing, jobs were grouped and recorded on magnetic tape with an auxiliary computer; the tape was then processed by the main computer, which created an output magnetic tape containing, for each individual job, either its output or a massive diagnostic core memory dump if the job had failed. The output tape was then taken back to the auxiliary computer, which printed the results of the sequence of jobs.

Batch-processing quickly caused programmers and computer users to feel extremely frustrated. It was comparable to sending a telegram and waiting many hours for a response. All too often, the job failed because of some trivial or clerical mistake, and the only recourse was to correct the job, resubmit it, and endure another day of frustration. What was really needed was something as interactive as a telephone call.

John McCarthy formulated a vision of time-sharing in 1959 when he wrote an internal memorandum to Philip M. Morse, then director of the MIT Computation Center, in which he argued that key modifications should be made by IBM to the Center's IBM 709 computer (in IBM's jargon, an RPQ—a request for a price quotation). The memo was persuasive and a chain of activities followed.

Herb Teager, with Morse's help, got funding to start a time-sharing implementation project. Teager's goals were extremely ambitious. He wanted to design and build a time-sharing system, using a language he proposed to invent, that could accommodate new input methods, such as handwriting on a tablet that he planned to develop. It soon became apparent that it would take Teager, with only a few individuals in his group, several years to attain his goals.

Because of this probable delay, work was begun informally on what was envisioned as a simple-minded demonstration of time-sharing. The Compatible Time-Sharing System (CTSS) was intended to be a quick implementation for demonstration purposes only. But as everything began to fall in place, the CTSS concept quickly evolved into a usable and effective example of a basic system. And because CTSS had to operate in the context of a working computation center, it needed to coexist with the daily workload of batch-processing; hence the modifier *compatible* in the system's name.

After a demonstration of basic CTSS on the IBM 709 computer at the Computation Center in November 1961, planning began to make it a more practical system by adding new hardware. The Center's tube-based IBM 709 was already scheduled to be replaced by the logically similar but transistorized IBM 7090 in the spring of 1962. Along with that switch would come the implementation of the critical RPQs first suggested by McCarthy, plus an interval timer clock that allowed the supervisor program to seize control of the processor from user programs at suitable intervals. In addition, with funding help from the National Science Foundation, a second bank of 32K of 36-bit words of memory was added to the 7090; the second memory bank was used exclusively by the CTSS supervisor and time-sharing programs. This permitted the batch-processing workload to be handled in the original 32K memory bank without disturbance. IBM was also persuaded to augment the center's machine with two large-scale disk memories (9,000 36-bit words!) capable of storing the programs and data of time-sharing users. Finally, IBM added an IBM 7750 —a telecommunication controller box—to allow a few dozen terminals to simulta-

neously dial up the computer; the 7750 replaced a controller specially built by Teager (and generously shared with the CTSS effort) that allowed a handful of hard-
wired terminals to communicate independently with the central processor.

By the spring of 1962, with all the hardware turmoil just described, work was furiously under way to modify and extend the CTSS supervisor and command software
to match the hardware changes. Not surprisingly the switch from the 709 to the
7090 took longer than expected and did not occur until the summer of 1962. This
led to the embarrassing anomaly where the paper presented in May 1962 (but written several months earlier) refers to operation of the 7090 computer!

Meanwhile the notions of time-sharing had been germinating at many places
around the country. MIT had created the Long-Range Study Committee, which in
the 1961–62 timeframe proposed a time-sharing machine for the Institute's needs,
but the committee's recommendations were too ambitious to be accepted by the
administration. It was in this climate in the fall of 1962 that Professor Robert Fano
was encouraged to form a major time-sharing project, Project MAC, and submit a
proposal to J.C.R. Licklider, a time-sharing visionary and advocate, who was then at
ARPA.[4] A key part of Fano's proposal was a plan to replicate the Computation
Center machine with an IBM 7094 (an improved 7090) and use it to run CTSS as
the initial time-sharing system for the project participants.

Professor Joel Moses and Michael Dertouzos, Project MAC

Fano's creation of Project MAC, using CTSS as a vehicle, had another major effect
in that it unified a large fraction of the computer science work at MIT. Since the
majority of the members of Project MAC were also members of the electrical engineering department, it led directly to the department broadening its leadership by
creating two associate heads. Fano became the first Associate Head for Computer
Science in 1971. (Fano was also active in establishing the initial computer science
option [VI-3] for undergraduates in 1968–69.) Project MAC began to organize in
the spring of 1963; that summer, over a hundred key computer professionals were
invited to a six-week workshop featuring CTSS as a working example of what
time-sharing could be. Participants, by using dial-up access, were also able to compare CTSS and the Q-32 time-sharing system (developed at the System Development Corporation in Santa Monica, California). Since the Project MAC machine
was not to be installed in the Technology Square building until November, the
machine that was actually used for the summer workshop was the CTSS running on
the Computation Center machine a quarter mile away.

Thus there were two versions of CTSS that operated at MIT. The Project MAC machine was not only used by all the project participants, it also served as a staging machine for the development of the Multics[5] system. In 1968 the Computation Center machine was shut down and replaced by the Project MAC machine as Multics usage became imminent. Even after Project MAC began using Multics, the Computation Center continued to operate CTSS, making it available for general MIT research use. The last version of CTSS was shut down in July 1973, after over a decade of life.

The development of the Multics system probably would not have been possible without CTSS. Not only was CTSS an explicit example of what a time-sharing system could be, it also allowed new ideas to be tested and implemented. Most importantly it became the critical development vehicle for planning, designing, programming, and compiling the software for the new system. The efficiency of using then-novel time-sharing was dramatically exhibited as the software for the Multics system had to be engineered from scratch. Even tools such as the assembler and compiler had to be written for the unusual Multics hardware. Furthermore, implementing and testing the many hundred system software modules required intense machine access. On top of all that, the novelty of the Multics design forced the development team to make frequent design iterations and changes to almost all the modules before effective performance was attained. Lastly, by offering dial-up service, CTSS helped alleviate the problems of geographical separation for the codevelopers at Bell Laboratories in New Jersey and the GE computer department in Arizona. Not surprisingly, CTSS has a warm spot in the hearts of all those who participated in the Multics development.

Professor Fernando J. Corbató, c. 1980

# AN EXPERIMENTAL TIME-SHARING SYSTEM

## Fernando J. Corbató, Marjorie Merwin Daggett, Robert C. Daley

Computation Center, Massachusetts Institute of Technology

Cambridge, Massachusetts

[Scanned and transcribed by F. J. Corbató from the original SJCC Paper of May 3, 1962]

## Summary

It is the purpose of this paper to discuss briefly the need for time-sharing, some of the implementation problems, an experimental time-sharing system which has been developed for the contemporary IBM 7090, and finally a scheduling algorithm of one of us (FJC) that illustrates some of the techniques which may be employed to enhance and be analyzed for the performance limits of such a time-sharing system.

## Introduction

The last dozen years of computer usage have seen great strides. In the early 1950's, the problems solved were largely in the construction and maintenance of hardware; in the mid-1950's, the usage languages were greatly improved with the advent of compilers; now in the early 1960's, we are in the midst of a third major modification to computer usage: the improvement of man-machine interaction by a process called time-sharing.

Much of the time-sharing philosophy, expressed in this paper, has been developed in conjunction with the work of an MIT preliminary study committee, chaired by H. Teager, which examined the long range computational needs of the Institute, and a subsequent MIT computer working committee, chaired by J. McCarthy. However, the views and conclusions expressed in this paper should be taken as solely those of the present authors.

Before proceeding further, it is best to give a more precise interpretation to time-sharing. One can mean using different parts of the hardware at the same time for different tasks, or one can mean several persons making use of the computer at the same time. The first meaning, often called multiprogramming, is oriented towards hardware efficiency in the sense of attempting to attain complete utilization of all components (refs.5,6,7,8). The second meaning of time-sharing, which is meant here, is primarily concerned with the efficiency of persons trying to use a computer (refs.1,2,3,4). Computer efficiency should still be considered but only in the perspective of the total system utility.

The motivation for time-shared computer usage arises out of the slow man-computer interaction rate presently possible with the bigger, more advanced computers. This rate has changed little (and has become worse in some cases) in the last decade of widespread computer use (ref.10).

In part, this effect has been due to the fact that as elementary problems become mastered on the computer, more complex problems immediately become of interest. As a result, larger and more complicated programs are written to take advantage of larger and faster computers. This process inevitably leads to more programming errors and a longer period of time required for debugging. Using current batch monitor techniques, as is done on most large computers, each program bug usually requires several hours to eliminate, if not a complete day. The only alternative presently available is for the programmer to attempt to debug directly at the computer, a process which is grossly wasteful of computer time and hampered seriously by the poor console communication usually available. Even if a typewriter is the console, there are usually lacking the sophisticated query and response programs which are vitally necessary to allow effective interaction. Thus, what is desired is to drastically increase the rate of interaction between the programmer and the computer without large economic loss and also to make each interaction more meaningful by extensive and complex system programming to assist in the man-computer communication.

To solve these interaction problems we would like to have a computer made simultaneously available to many users in a manner somewhat like a telephone exchange. Each user would be able to use a console at his own pace and with-out concern for the activity of others using the system. This console could as a minimum be merely a typewriter but more ideally would contain an incrementally modifiable self-sustaining display. In any case, data transmission requirements should be such that it would be no major obstacle to have remote installation from the computer proper.

An Experimental Time-Sharing System

The basic technique for a time-sharing system is to have many persons simultaneously using the computer through typewriter consoles with a time-sharing supervisor program sequentially running each user program in a short burst or quantum of computation. This sequence, which in the most straightforward case is a simple round-robin, should occur often enough so that each user program which is kept in the high-speed memory is run for a quantum at least once during each approximate human reaction time (~.2 seconds). In this way, each user sees a computer fully responsive to even single key strokes each of which may require only trivial computation; in the non-trivial cases, the user sees a gradual reduction of the response time which is proportional to the complexity of the response calculation, the slowness of the computer, and the total number of active users. It should be clear, however, that if there are n users actively requesting service at one time, each user will only see on the average 1/n of the effective computer speed. During the period of high interaction rates while debugging programs, this should not be a hindrance since ordinarily the required amount of computation needed for each debugging computer response is small compared to the ultimate production need.

Not only would such a time-sharing system improve the ability to program in the conventional manner by one or two orders of magnitude, but there would be opened up several new forms of computer usage. There would be a gradual reformulation of many scientific and engineering applications so that programs containing decision trees which currently must be specified in advance would be eliminated and instead the particular decision branches would be specified only as needed. Another important area is that of teaching machines which, although frequently trivial computationally, could naturally exploit the consoles of a time-sharing system with the additional bonus that more elaborate and adaptive teaching programs could be used. Finally, as attested by the many small business computers, there are numerous applications in business and in industry where it would be advantageous to have powerful computing facilities available at isolated locations with only the incremental capital investment of each console. But it is important to realize that even without the above and other new applications, the major advance in programming intimacy available from time-sharing would be of immediate value to computer installations in universities, research laboratories, and engineering firms where program debugging is a major problem.

## Implementation problems

As indicated, a straightforward plan for time-sharing is to execute user programs for small quantums of computation without priority in a simple round-robin; the strategy of time-sharing can be more complex as will be shown later, but the above simple scheme is an adequate solution. There are still many problems, however, some best solved by hardware, others affecting the programming conventions and practices. A few of the more obvious problems are summarized:

Hardware Problems:

1. Different user programs if simultaneously in core memory may interfere with each other or the supervisor program so some form of memory protection mode should be available when operating user programs.

2. The time-sharing supervisor may need at different times to run a particular program from several locations. (Loading relocation bits are no help since the supervisor does not know how to relocate the accumulator, etc.) Dynamic relocation of all memory accesses that pick up instructions or data words is one effective solution.

3. Input-output equipment may be initiated by a user and read words in on another user program. A way to avoid this is to trap all input-output instructions issued by a user's program when operated in the memory protection mode.

4. A large random-access back-up storage is desirable for general program storage files for all users. Present large capacity disc units appear to be adequate.

5. The time-sharing supervisor must be able to interrupt a user's program after a quantum of computation. A program-initiated one-shot multivibrator which generates an interrupt a fixed time later is adequate.

6. Large core memories (e.g. a million words) would ease the system programming complications immensely since the different active user programs as well as the frequently used system programs such as

compilers, query programs, etc. could remain in core memory at all times.

Programming Problems:

1. The supervisor program must do automatic user usage charge accounting. In general, the user should be charged on the basis of a system usage formula or algorithm which should include such factors as computation time, amount of high-speed memory required, rent of secondary memory storage, etc.

2. The supervisor program should coordinate all user input-output since it is not desirable to require a user program to remain constantly in memory during input-output limited operations. In addition, the supervisor must coordinate all usage of the central, shared high-speed input-output units serving all users as well as the clocks, disc units, etc.

3. The system programs available must be potent enough so that the user can think about his problem and not be hampered by coding details or typographical mistakes. Thus, compilers, query programs, post-mortem programs, loaders, and good editing programs are essential.

4. As much as possible, the users should be allowed the maximum programming flexibility both in choices of language and in the absence of restrictions.

Usage Problems

1. Too large a computation or excessive typewriter output may be inadvertently requested so that a special termination signal should be available to the user.

2. Since real-time is not computer usage-time, the supervisor must keep each user informed so that he can use his judgment regarding loops, etc.

3. Computer processor, memory and tape malfunctions must be expected. Basic operational questions such as "Which program is running?" must be answerable and recovery procedures fully anticipated.

## An Experimental Time-sharing system for the IBM 7090

Having briefly stated a desirable time-sharing performance, it is pertinent to ask what level of performance can be achieved with existent equipment. To begin to answer this question and to explore all the programming and operational aspects, an experimental time-sharing system has been developed. This system was originally written for the IBM 709 but has since been converted for use with the 7090 computer.

The 7090 of the MIT Computation Center has, in addition to three channels with 19 tape units, a fourth channel with the standard Direct Data Connection. Attached to the Direct Data Connection is a real-time equipment buffer and control rack designed and built under the direction of H. Teager and his group. [This group is presently using another approach (ref.9) in developing a time-sharing system for the MIT 7090.] This rack has a variety of devices attached but the only ones required by the present systems are three flexowriter typewriters. Also installed on the 7090 are two special modifications (i.e. RPQ's): a standard 60 cycle accounting and interrupt clock, and a special mode which allows memory protection, dynamic relocation and trapping of all user attempts to initiate input-output instructions.

In the present system the time-sharing occurs between four users, three of whom are on-line each at a typewriter in a foreground system, and a fourth passive user of the back-ground Fap-Mad-Madtran-BSS Monitor system similar to the Fortran-Fap-BSS Monitor System (FMS) used by most of the Center programmers and by many other 7090 installations.

Significant design features of the foreground system are:

1. It allows the user to develop programs in languages compatible with the background system,

2. Develop a private file of programs,

An Experimental Time-Sharing System

3. Start debugging sessions at the state of the previous session, and

4. Set his own pace with little waste of computer time.

Core storage is allocated such that all users operate in the upper 27,000 words with the time-sharing supervisor (TSS) permanently in the lower 5,000 words. To avoid memory allocation clashes, protect users from one another, and simplify the initial 709 system organization, only one user was kept in core memory at a time. However, with the special memory protection and relocation feature of the 7090, more sophisticated storage allocation procedures are being implemented. In any case, user swaps are minimized by using 2-channel overlapped magnetic tape reading and writing of the pertinent locations in the two user programs.

The foreground system is organized around commands that each user can give on his typewriter and the user's private program files which presently (for want of a disc unit) are kept on a separate magnetic tape for each user.

For convenience the format of the private tape files is such that they are card images, have title cards with name and class designators and can be written or punched using the off-line equipment. (The latter feature also offers a crude form of large-scale input-output.) The magnetic tape requirements of the system are the seven tapes required for the normal functions of the background system, a system tape for the time-sharing supervisor that contains most of the command programs, and a private file tape and dump tape for each of the three foreground users.

The commands are typed by the user to the time-sharing supervisor (not to his own program) and thus can be initiated at any time regardless of the particular user program in memory. For similar coordination reasons, the supervisor handles all input-output of the foreground system typewriters. Commands are composed of segments separated by vertical strokes; the first segment is the command name and the remaining segments are parameters pertinent to the command. Each segment consists of the last 6 characters typed (starting with an implicit 6 blanks) so that spacing is an easy way to correct a typing mistake. A carriage return is the signal which initiates action on the command. Whenever a command is received by the supervisor, "WAIT", is typed back followed by "READY." when the command is completed. (The computer responses are always in the opposite color from the user's typing.) While typing, an incomplete command line may be ignored by the "quit" sequence of a code delete signal followed by a carriage return. Similarly after a command is initiated, it may be abandoned if a "quit" sequence is given. In addition, during unwanted command typeouts, the command and output may be terminated by pushing a special "stop output" button.

The use of the foreground system is initiated whenever a typewriter user completes a command line and is placed in a waiting command queue. Upon completion of each quantum, the time-sharing supervisor gives top priority to initiating any waiting commands. The system programs corresponding to most of the commands are kept on the special supervisor command system tape so that to avoid waste of computer time, the supervisor continues to operate the last user program until the desired command program on tape is positioned for reading. At this point, the last user is read out on his dump tape, the command program read in, placed in a working status and initiated as a new user program. However, before starting the new user for a quantum of computation, the supervisor again checks for any waiting command of another user and if necessary begins the look-ahead positioning of the command system tape while operating the new user.

Whenever the waiting command queue is empty, the supervisor proceeds to execute a simple round-robin of those foreground user programs in the working status queue. Finally, if both these queues are empty, the background user program is brought in and run a quantum at a time until further foreground system actively develops.

Foreground user programs leave the working status queue by two means. If the program proceeds to completion, it can reenter the supervisor in a way which eliminates itself and places the user in dead status; alternatively, by a different entry the program can be placed in a dormant status (or be manually placed by the user executing a quit sequence). The dormant status differs from the dead status in that the user may still restart or examine his program.

User input-output is through each typewriter, and even though the supervisor has a few lines of buffer space available, it is possible to become input-output limited. Consequently, there is an additional input-output wait status, similar to the dormant, which the user is automatically placed in by the supervisor program whenever input-output delays develop. When buffers become near empty on output or near full on input, the user program is automatically returned to the working status; thus waste of computer time is avoided.

An Experimental Time-Sharing System

## Commands

To clarify the scope of the foreground system and to indicate the basic tools available to the user, a list of the important commands follows along with brief summaries of their operations:

1. | alpha

    alpha = arbitrary text treated as a comment.

2. login | alpha |beta

    alpha = user problem number

    beta = user programmer number

    Should be given at beginning of each user's session. Rewinds user's private file tape; clears time accounting records.

3. logout

    Should be given at end of each user's session. Rewinds user's private file tape; punches on-line time accounting cards.

4. input

    Sets user in input mode and initiates automatic generation of line numbers. The user types a card image per line according to a format appropriate for the programming language. (The supervisor collects these card images at the end of the user's private file tape.) When in the automatic input mode, the manual mode may be entered by giving an initial carriage return and typing the appropriate line number followed by | and line for as many lines as desired. To reenter the automatic mode, an initial carriage return is given.

The manual mode allows the user to overwrite previous lines and to insert lines. (cf. File Command.)

5. edit | alpha | beta

alpha = title of file

beta = class of file

The user is set in the automatic input mode with the designated file treated as initial input lines. The same conventions apply as to the input command.

6. file | alpha | beta

alpha = title to be given to file

beta = class of language used during input

The created file will consist of the numbered input lines (i.e. those at the end of the user's private file tape) in sequence; in the case of duplicate line numbers, the last version will be used. The line numbers will be written as sequence numbers in the corresponding card images of the file.

For convenience the following editing conventions apply to input lines:

a. an underline signifies the deletion of the previous characters of the line.

b. a backspace signifies the deletion of the previous character in the field.

The following formats apply:

a. FAP: symbol, tab, operation, tab, variable field and comment.

b. MAD, MADTRAN, FORTRAN: statement label, tab, statement. To place a character in the continuation column: statement label, tab, backspace, character, statement.

c. DATA: cols. 1-72.

7. fap | alpha

Causes the file designated as alpha,fap to be translated by the FAP translator (assembler). Files alpha,symtb and alpha,bss are added to the user's private file tape giving the symbol table and the relocatable binary BSS form of the file.

8. mad | alpha

Causes file alpha,mad to be translated by the MAD translator (compiler). File alpha,bss is created.

9. madtrn | alpha

Causes file alpha,madtrn (i.e. a pseudo-Fortran language file) to be edited into an equivalent file alpha,mad (added to the user's file) and translation occurs as if the command mad|alpha had been given.

10. load | alpha-1 | alpha-2 | ... | alpha-n

> Causes the consecutive loading of files alpha,bss
> (i=1,2,...,n). An exception occurs if alpha-i = (libe), in
> which case file alpha-i+1,bss is searched as a library
> file for all subprograms still missing. (There can be
> further library files.)

11. use | alpha-1 | alpha-2 | ... | alpha-n

> This command is used whenever a load or previous use
> command notifies the user of an incomplete set of
> subprograms. Same alpha-i conventions as for load.

12. start | alpha | beta

> Starts the program setup by the load and use
> commands (or a dormant program) after first
> positioning the user private file tape in front of the title
> card for file alpha,beta. (If beta is not given, a class of
> data is assumed; if both alpha and beta are not given,
> no tape movement occurs and the program is started.)

13. pm | alpha

> alpha = "lights", "stomap", or the usual format of the
> standard Center post-mortem (F2PM) request:
> subprogram name | loc-1 | loc-2 | mode | direction
> where mode and direction are optional.

> Produces post-mortem of user's dormant program
> according to request specified by alpha. (E.g. matrix | 5
> | 209 | flo | rev will cause to be printed on the user's
> typewriter the contents of subprogram "matrix" from
> relative locations 5 to 209 in floating point form and in
> reverse sequence.)

14. skippm

> Used if a pm command is "quit" during output and the previous program interruption is to be restarted.

15. listf

> Types out list of all file titles on user's private file tape.

16. printf | alpha | beta | gamma

> Types out file alpha,beta starting at line number gamma. If gamma is omitted, the initial line is assumed. Whenever the user's output buffer fills, the command program goes into an I/O wait status allowing other users to time-share until the buffer needs refilling.

17. xdump | alpha |beta

> Creates file alpha,beta (if beta omitted, xdump assumed) on user's private file tape consisting of the complete state of the user's last dormant program.

18. xundump | alpha | beta

> Inverse of xdump command in that it resets file alpha,beta as the user's program, starting it where it last left off.

Although experience with the system to date is quite limited, first indications are that programmers would readily use such a system if it were generally available, It is useful to ask, now that there is some operating experience with the system, what observations can be made. [Note: Operating experience was initially gained using the system on the 709 computer; due to equipment conversion difficulties, it was not possible to use the system on the logically equivalent 7090 computer by May 3.] An immediate comment is that once a user gets accustomed to computer

An Experimental Time-Sharing System

response, delays of even a fraction of a minute are exasperatingly long, an effect analogous to conversing with a slow-speaking person. Similarly, the requirement that a complete typewritten line rather than each character be the minimum unit of man-computer communication is an inhibiting factor in the sense that a press-to-talk radio-telephone conversation is more stilted than that of an ordinary telephone. Since maintaining a rapid computer response on a character by character basis requires at least a vestigial response program in core memory at all times, the straight-forward solution within the present system is to have more core memory available. At the very least, an extra bank of memory for the time-sharing supervisor would ease compatibility problems with programs already written for 32,000 word 7090's.

For reasons of expediency, the weakest portions of the present system are the conventions for input, editing of user files, and the degree of rapid interaction and intimacy possible while debugging. Since to a large extent these areas involve the taste, habits, and psychology of the users, it is felt that proper solutions will require considerable experimentation and pragmatic evaluation; it is also clear that these areas cannot be treated in the abstract for the programming languages used will influence greatly the appropriate techniques. A greater use of symbolic referencing for locations, program names and variables is certainly desired; symbolic post-mortem programs, trace programs, and before-and-after differential dump programs should play useful roles in the debugging procedures.

In the design of the present system, great care went into making each user independent of the other users. However, it would be a useful extension of the system if this were not always the case. In particular, when several consoles are used in a computer controlled group such as in management or war games, in group behavior studies, or possibly in teaching machines, it would be desirable to have all the consoles communicating with a single program.

Another area for further improvement within the present system is that of file maintenance, since the presently used tape units are a hindrance to the easy deletion of user program files. Disc units will be of help in this area as well as with the problem of consolidating and scheduling large-scale central input-output generated by the many console users.

Finally, it is felt that it would be desirable to have the distinction between the foreground and background systems eliminated. The present-day computer operator would assume the role of a stand-in for the background users, using an operator console much like the other user consoles in the system, mounting and demounting magnetic tapes as requested by the supervisor, receiving instructions to read card decks into the central disc unit, etc. Similarly the foreground user, when satisfied with his program, would by means of his console and the supervisor program enter his program into the queue of production background work to be performed. With these procedures implemented the distinction of whether one is time-sharing or not would vanish and the computer user would be free to choose in an interchangeable way that mode of operation which he found more suitable at a particular time.

## A Multi-Level Scheduling Algorithm

Regardless of whether one has a million word core memory or a 32,000 word memory as currently exists on the 7090, one is inevitably faced with the problem of system saturation where the total size of active user programs exceeds that of the high-speed memory or there are too many active user programs to maintain an adequate response at each user console. These conditions can easily arise with even a few users if some of the user programs are excessive in size or in time requirements. The predicament can be alleviated if it is assumed that a good design for the system is to have a saturation procedure which gives graceful degradation of the response time and effective real-time computation speed of the large and long-running users.

To show the general problem, Figure 1 qualitatively gives the user service as a function of n, the number of active users. This service parameter might be either of the two key factors: computer response time or n times the real-time computation speed. In either case there is some critical number of active users, N, representing the effective user capacity, which causes saturation. If the strategy near saturation is to execute the simple round-robin of all users, then there is an abrupt collapse of service due to the sudden onset of the large amount of time required to swap programs in-and-out of the secondary memory such as a disc or drum unit. Of course, Figure 1 is quite qualitative since it depends critically on the spectrum of user program sizes as well as the spectrum of user operating times.

An Experimental Time-Sharing System

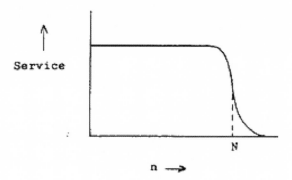

↑
Service

n ⟶

**Figure 1. Service vs. Number of
Active Users**

To illustrate the strategy that can be employed to improve the saturation
performance of a time-sharing system, a multi-level scheduling algorithm is
presented. This algorithm also can be analyzed to give broad bounds on the system
performance.

The basis of the multi-level scheduling algorithm is to assign each user program as
it enters the system to be run (or completes a response to a user) to an ell-th level
priority queue. Programs are initially entered into a level ell-sub-0, corresponding
to their size such that

$$ \ell_0 = \left[ \log_2 \left( \left[ \frac{w_p}{w_q} \right] + 1 \right) \right] \tag{1} $$

where w-sub-p is the number of words in the program, w-sub-q is the number of
words which can be transmitted in and out of the high-speed memory from the
secondary memory in the time of one quantum, q, and the bracket indicates "the
integral part of". Ordinarily the time of a quantum, being the basic time unit, should
be as small as possible without excessive overhead losses when the supervisor
switches from one program in high-speed memory to another. The process starts
with the time-sharing supervisor operating the program at the head of the lowest
level occupied queue, ell, for up to 2**ell quanta of time and then if the program is
not completed (i.e. has not made a response to the user) placing it at the end of the

ell+1 level queue. If there are no programs entering the system at levels lower than ell, this process proceeds until the queue at level ell is exhausted; the process is then iteratively begun again at level ell+1, where now each program is run for 2**(ell+1) quanta of time. If during the execution of the 2**ell quanta of a program at level ell, a lower level, ell-prime, becomes occupied, the current user is replaced at the head of the ell-th queue and the process is reinitiated at level ell-prime.

Similarly, if a program of size w-sub-p at level ell, during operation requests a change in memory size from the time-sharing supervisor, then the enlarged (or reduced) version of the program should be placed at the end of the ell-double-prime queue where

$$\ell'' = \ell + \left[ \log_2 \left( \frac{w_p''}{w_p} \right) \right] . \tag{2}$$

[Note: corrected from the original]

Again the process is re-initiated with the head-of-the-queue user at the lowest occupied level of ell-prime.

Several important conclusions can be drawn from the above algorithm which allow the performance of the system to be bounded.

Computational Efficiency

1. Because a program is always operated for a time greater than or equal to the swap time (i.e. the time required to move the program in and out of secondary memory), it follows that the computational efficiency never falls below one-half. (Clearly, this fraction is adjustable in the formula for the initial level, ell-0.) An alternative way of viewing this bound is to say that the real-time computing speed available to one out of n active users is no worse than if there were 2n active users all of whose programs were in the high-speed memory.

## Response Time

2. If the maximum number of active users is N, then an individual user of a given program size can be guaranteed a response time,

$$t_r \leq 2Nq\left(\left[\frac{w_p}{w_q}\right] + 1\right) \tag{3}$$

since the worst case occurs when all competing user programs are at the same level. Conversely, if t-sub-r is a guaranteed response of arbitrary value and the largest size of program is assumed, then the maximum permissible number of active users is bounded.

## Long Runs

3. The relative swap time on long runs can be made vanishingly small. This conclusion follows since the longer a program is run, the higher the level number it cascades to with a correspondingly smaller relative swap time. It is an important feature of the algorithm that long runs must in effect prove they are long so that programs which have an unexpected demise are detected quickly. In order that there be a finite number of levels, a maximum level number, L, can be established such that the asymptotic swap overhead is some arbitrarily small percentage, p:

$$L = \left[\log_2\left(\left[\frac{w_{pmax}}{pw_q}\right] + 1\right)\right] \tag{4}$$

where w-sub-pmax is the size of the largest possible program.

## Multi-level vs. Single-level Response Times

4. The response time for programs of equal size, entering the system at the same time, and being run for multiple quanta, is no worse than approximately twice the response-time occurring in a single quanta round-robin procedure. If there are n equal sized programs started in a queue at level 1, then the worst case is that of the end-of-the-queue program which is ready to respond at the very first quantum run at

the ell+j level. Using the multi-level algorithm, the total delay for the end-of-the-queue program is by virtue of the geometric series of quanta:

$$T_m \sim q2^{\ell} \left\{ n(2^j-1) + (n-1) \, 2^j. \right\} \qquad (5)$$

Since the end-of-the-queue user has computed for a time of $(2^{**}\text{ell})^*((2^{**}j)-1)$ quanta, the equivalent single-level round-robin delay before a response is:

$$T_s \sim q2^{\ell} \left\{ n(2^j-1) \right\}. \qquad (6)$$

Hence

$$\frac{T_m}{T_s} \sim 1 + \left( \frac{n-1}{n} \right) \left( \frac{2^j}{2^j-1} \right) \sim 2 \qquad (7)$$

and the assertion is shown. It should be noted that the above conditions, where program swap times are omitted, which are pertinent when all programs remain in high-speed memory, are the least favorable for the multi-level algorithm; if swap times are included in the above analysis, the ratio of (T-sub-m / T-sub-s) can only become smaller and may become much less than unity. By a similar analysis it is easy to show that even in the unfavorable case where there are no program swaps, head-of-the-queue programs that terminate just as the quanta are completed receive under the multi-level algorithm a response which is twice as fast as that under the single-level round-robin (i.e. (T-sub-m / T-sub-s) = 1/2).

Highest Serviced Level

5. In the multi-level algorithm the level classification procedure for programs is entirely automatic, depending on performance and program size rather than on the declarations (or hopes) of each user.

As a user taxes the system, the degradation of service occurs progressively starting with the higher level users of either large or long-running programs; however, at some level no user programs may be run because of too many active users at lower levels. To determine a bound on this cut-off point we consider N active users at level ell each running 2**ell quanta, terminating, and reentering the system again at level ell at a user response time, t-sub-u, later. If there is to be no service at level ell+1, then the computing time, Nq(2**ell), must be greater than or equal to t-sub-u. Thus the guaranteed active levels, are given by the relation:

$$\ell_a \le \left[ \log_2 \left( \frac{t_u}{Nq} \right) \right] \qquad (8)$$

In the limit, t-sub-u could be as small as a minimum user reaction time (~.2 sec.), but the expected value would be several orders of magnitude greater as a result of the statistics of a large number of users.

The multi-level algorithm as formulated above makes no explicit consideration of the seek or latency time required before transmission of programs to and from disc or drum units when they are used as the secondary memory, (although formally the factor w-sub-q could contain an average figure for these times). One simple modification to the algorithm which usually avoids wasting the seek or latency time is to continue to operate the last user program for as many quanta as are required to ready the swap of the new user with the least priority user; since ordinarily only the higher level number programs would be forced out into the secondary memory, the extended quanta of operation of the old user while seeking the new user should be but a minor distortion of the basic algorithm.

Further complexities are possible when the hardware is appropriate. In computers with input-output channels and low transmission rates to and from secondary memory, it is possible to overlap the reading and writing of the new and old users in and out of high-speed memory while operating the current user. The effect is equivalent to using a drum giving 100 % multiplexor usage but there are two liabilities, namely, no individual user can utilize all the available user memory space and the look-ahead procedure breaks down whenever am unanticipated scheduling change occurs (e.g. a program terminates or a higher-priority user program is initiated).

Complexity is also possible in storage allocation but certainly an elementary procedure and a desirable one with a low-transmission rate secondary memory is to consolidate in a single block all high-priority user programs whenever sufficient fragmentary unused memory space is available to read in a new user program. Such a procedure is indicated in the flow diagram of the multi-level scheduling algorithm which is given as Figure 2.

It should also be noted that Figure 2 only accounts for the scheduling of programs in a working status and still does not take into account the storage allocation of programs which are in a dormant (or input-output wait status). One systematic method of handling this case is to modify the scheduling algorithm so that programs which become dormant at level ell are entered into the queue at level ell+1. The scheduling algorithm proceeds as before with the dormant programs continuing to cascade but not operating when they reached the head of a queue. Whenever a program must be removed from high-speed memory, a program is selected from the end-of-the-queue of the highest occupied level number.

Finally, it is illuminating to apply the multi-level scheduling algorithm bounds to the contemporary IBM 7090. The following approximate values are obtained:

$$q = 16 \text{ m.s. (based on 1\% switching overhead)}$$

$$w_q = 120 \text{ words (based on one IBM 1301 model 2 disc unit without seek or latency times included)}$$

$$t_r \leq 8Nf_{sec.} \text{ (based on programs of (32k)f words)}$$

$$\ell_a \leq \log_2 (1000/N) \text{ (based on } t_u = 16 \text{ sec.)}$$

$$\ell_0 \leq 8 \text{ (based on a maximum program size of 32K words)}$$

Using the arbitrary criteria that programs up to the maximum size of 32,000 words should always get some service, which is to say that max ell-sub-a = max ell-sub-0, we deduce as a conservative estimate that N can be 4 and that at worst the response time for a trivial reply will be 32 seconds.

The small value of N arrived at is a direct consequence of the small value of w-sub-q that results from the slow disc word transmission rate. This rate is only 3.3% of the maximum core memory multiplexor rate. It is of interest that using high-capacity high-speed drums of current design such as in the Sage System or in the IBM Sabre System it would be possible to attain nearly 100% multiplexor utilization and thus multiply w-sub-q by a factor of 30. It immediately follows that user response times equivalent to those given above with the disc unit would be given to 30 tines as many persons or to 120 users; the total computational capacity, however, would not change.

In any case, considerable caution should be used with capacity and computer response time estimates since they are critically dependent upon the distribution functions for the user response time, t-sub-u, and the user program size, and the computational capacity requested by each user. Past experience using conventional programming systems is of little assistance because these distribution functions will depend very strongly upon the programming systems made available to the time-sharing users as well as upon the user habit patterns which will gradually evolve.

## Conclusions

In conclusion, it is clear that contemporary computers and hardware are sufficient to allow moderate performance time-sharing for a limited number of users. There are several problems which can be solved by careful hardware design, but there are also a large number of intricate system programs which must be written before one has an adequate time-sharing system. An import-ant aspect of any future time-shared computer is that until the system programming is completed, especially the critical time-sharing supervisor, the computer is completely worthless. Thus, it is essential for future system design and imple-mentation that all aspects of time-sharing system problems be explored and understood in prototype form on present computers so that major advances in computer organization and usage can be made.

## Acknowledgements

The authors wish to thank Bernard Galler, Robert Graham and Bruce Arden, of the University of Michigan, for making the MAD compiler available and for their advice with regard to its adaptation into the present time-sharing system. The version of the Madtran Fortran-to-Mad editor program was generously supplied by Robert Rosin of the University of Michigan. Of the MIT Computation Center staff, Robert Creasy was of assistance in the evaluation of time-sharing performance, Lynda Korn is to be credited for her contributions to the pm and madtran commands, and Evelyn Dow for her work on the fap command.

## References

1. Strachey, C., "Time Sharing in Large Fast Computers," *Proceedings of the International Conference on Information processing*, UNESCO (June, 1959), paper B.2.19.

2. Licklider, J. C. R., "Man-Computer Symbiosis," *IRE Transactions on Human Factors in Electronics, HFE-l*, No. 1 (March, 1960), 4-11.

3. Brown, G., Licklider, J. C. R., McCarthy, J., and Perlis, A., lectures given Spring, 1961, *Management and the Computer of the Future*, (to be published by the M.I.T. press, March, 1962).

4. Corbató, F. J., "An Experimental Time-Sharing System," *Proceedings of the IBM University Director's Conference*, July, 1961 (to be published).

5. Schmitt, W. F., Tonik, A. B., "Sympathetically Programmed Computers," *Proceedings of the International Conference on Information Processing*, UNESCO, (June, 1959) paper 8.2.18.

6. Codd, E. F., "Multiprogram Scheduling, *Communications of the ACM, 3*, 6 (June, 1960), 347-350.

7. Heller, J., "Sequencing Aspects of Multiprogramming," *Journal of the ACM, 8*, 3 (July, 1961), 426-439.

8. Leeds, H. D., Weinberg, G. M., "Multiprogramming," *Computer Programming Fundamentals*, 356-359, McGraw-Hill (1961).

9. Teager, H. M., "Real-Time Time-Shared Computer Project," *Communications of the ACM, 5*, 1 (January, 1962) Research Summaries, 62.

10. Teager, H. M., McCarthy, J., "Time-Shared Program Testing," paper delivered at the *14th National Meeting of the ACM* (not published).

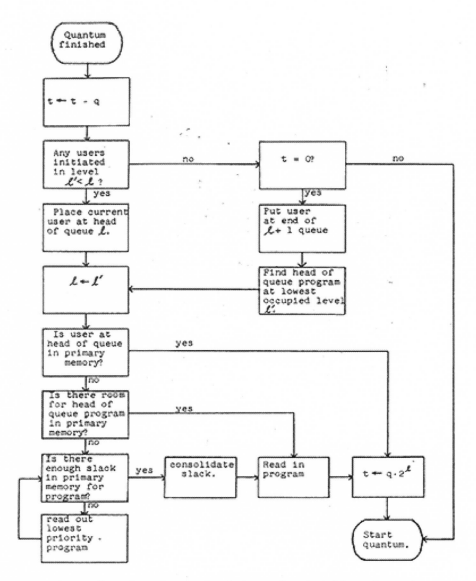

Figure 2. Flow Chart of Multi-Level Scheduling Algorithm

# The "Bit Books"

*Overview by Duane Boning*

Professor Duane S. Boning

In the early 1980s, a massive restructuring of the undergraduate curriculum in electrical engineering and computer science was undertaken to emphasize the principles of engineering design, particularly the means for managing the complexity of systems, whether those systems were to be constructed of circuits, digital hardware, or programs in software. An impressive array of new subjects—notably the core subjects 6.001, 6.002, 6.003, and 6.004—and new textbooks evolved out of this restructuring, built on earlier subjects but also new and fresh in their emphasis and broad in their impact. Some of these texts focused on understanding, abstracting, and modeling physical systems—notable among these are William Siebert's *Circuits, Signals, and Systems*. And some of these texts—which we will call the "bit books"—focused on engineering systems related to "bits" rather than physical systems. Developed throughout the decade of the 1980s, these texts defined not only the core subjects, but also much of the undergraduate computer science curriculum at MIT and elsewhere.

Perhaps the most famous of the "bit books" is *Structure and Interpretation of Computer Programs*, affectionately known as SICP, used in 6.001. The book has its own entry in *The New Hacker's Dictionary*[6]:

**Wizard Book**, *n. Hal Abelson's, Jerry Sussman's and Julie Sussman's* Structure and Interpretation of Computer Programs[7], *an excellent computer science text used in introductory courses at MIT. So called because of the wizard on the jacket. One of the bibles of the LISP/Scheme world. Also, less commonly, known as the Purple Book.*

Rather than focus on the hardware of computers, or even on the mechanics of computer programming, Hal Abelson, Jerry Sussman, and Julie Sussman developed the fundamental *engineering* principles behind any computer language and every

207

computer program. The theme that was to recur throughout many of the "bit books" was made clear: computer systems and programs are complex; we need abstractions to deal with this complexity; and we need ways (engineering "languages") to express and manipulate our abstractions.

In this book, the reader is transported through the basic notions of primitives, means of combination, and means of abstraction that enable the creation of languages to attack any problem. All these ideas are illustrated with a wide range of program styles. The result is a breathtaking *tour de computer science* that develops and demonstrates the themes of procedural and data abstraction, notions of modularity and state, means for creating entirely new languages (or "metalinguistic abstraction"), and abstractions of underlying hardware in the form of register machines. The book is almost mystical in its ambition. The preface states:

*The computer revolution is a revolution in the way we think and in the way we express what we think. The essence of this change is the emergence of what might best be called* procedural epistemology*—the study of the structure of knowledge from an imperative point of view, as opposed to the more declarative point of view taken by classical mathematical subjects.*

The book aims at nothing less than considering computer programs as ways to express "how to" knowledge, as compared to "what is" knowledge.

As an undergraduate at MIT beginning in 1980, I was fortunate to experience the excitement that these new subjects created. SICP and 6.001 introduced me to the wonders of programming—it was like being initiated into a magical realm, where the power of language was bestowed to command computation and control the machine, even if the machine itself was just another abstraction.

Steve Ward and Roger Halstead's *Computation Structures* came out of the development of 6.004 in the early 1980s. This text explains the principle of using layered abstractions to deal with complexity and to build computational systems while avoiding narrow focus on any one of these abstractions. Ward and Halstead taught us that to be truly educated and innovative electrical engineers and computer scientists, we need to see and understand the full spectrum of these abstractions and the interfaces between them. The book and the course seek to instill confidence in students by exploring and building, from the ground up, a computer with all its complexities, from basic gates to logic circuits to finite state machines to register machines to stacks and onward to memory, processor, and other architectural abstractions. There is no "ghost in the machine"—we are taught that we really can understand any of the abstractions within the machine.

The "bit books"

The grand themes of "abstraction" and "managing complexity" continued in the more advanced subjects. *Abstraction and Specification in Program Development*, by Barbara Liskov and John Guttag, developed with the 6.170 laboratory subject. While 6.004 focuses on the hardware abstractions, 6.170 deals with complexity in software engineering. Concrete tools for expressing our procedural and data abstractions, and for construction of modular systems, are developed. The central tenet is that goals, expectations, constraints, and invariants underlying the design and implementation of our software components should all be rendered explicit and not left behind or lost in the mind of the programmer. The power of this "bit book" is that it explains how to define and express the multiple dimensions of our engineered software abstractions, and thus make these abstractions clear, robust, and usable.

While the core subjects and books like *SICP, Computation Structures*, and *Abstraction and Specification in Program Development* emphasize universal principles of engineering design, they also illustrate these with computer hardware and software problems. In the 1980s, two additional "bit books" and related subjects were developed to serve as portals to particular disciplines within computer science.

*Artificial Intelligence* by Patrick Winston is a seminal work in the principles and practice of this large and diverse field. The book, used in subject 6.034 is a wonderful exploration of the things that computers can do and the interesting ways to make computers more useful to people through a variety of "intelligent" capabilities. As described in the introductory chapter, the book focuses on the "study of the computations that make it possible to perceive, reason, and act." More than a bag of magic tricks, the text develops a concrete set of ideas and techniques, ranging from knowledge representation and reasoning methods to learning systems and visual perception and language understanding, that enable broad arrays of computer applications.

A final text also serves as a monumental gateway to a huge area of computer science: *Introduction to Algorithms* by Thomas Cormen, Charles Leiserson, and Ron Rivest (joined by Clifford Stein for the second edition). The book, amazing in its depth and coverage, revels in the mechanics and analysis of algorithms, defined in the text as "any well-defined computational procedure that takes some value, or set of values, as input and produces some value, or set of values, as output." The abstract expression of how-to knowledge, first encountered in 6.001 and *SICP*, is crafted into razor-sharp, steel-hard tools.

Together, these "bit books" embody the discovery of a new curriculum, which continues to broadly influence computer science education. They serve as a foundation covering not only computer hardware and software systems that are pervasive in our modern world, but also the fundamental principles and tools of engineering systems that will shape our world in the future.

ENDNOTES FOR PART 5

[1] In W.A. Rosenblith, ed., *Sensory Communication* (New York-London: MIT Press and John Wiley & Sons, 1961), pp. 49–72.

[2] *Libraries of the Future* (Cambridge: MIT Press, 1965).

[3] In *IRE Transactions on Human Factors in Electronics* HFE-1 (March 1960): 4-11.

[4] A very readable account of the evolution of time-sharing and computer networking can be found in M. Mitchell Waldrop, *The Dream Machine: J. C. R. Licklider and the Revolution That Made Computing Personal*. (New York: Viking, 2001).

[5] A wonderful history of Multics by Tom Van Vleck can be found online at www.multicians.org. This site also includes a section on the role that CTSS played, at www.multicians.org/thvv/7094.html.

[6] Eric S. Raymond, ed., *New Hacker's Dictionary*, 2nd ed. (Cambridge, Mass.: MIT Press, 1993). As quoted on http://mitpress.mit.edu/sicp/.

[7] Harold Abelson and Gerald Jay Sussman, with Julie Sussman, *Structure and Interpretation of Computer Programs* (Cambridge, Mass.: MIT Press, 1984).

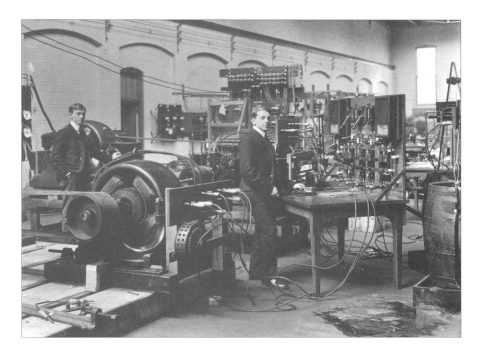

**Scenes from EECS Laboratories**

*Clockwise from top left::*

Edward Whitman (left) and Kenneth Stevens perform adjustments of parameters on the dynamic analog of the vocal tract, 1962.

An enlarged version of this picture of the dynamo room in the Lowell building, c. 1902, hangs in the lobby of Building 34.

Professor Jesús del Alamo (left) converses with EE junior James Hardison in front of the WebLab system, an online lab that can be accessed twenty-four hours a day. The lab's focus is the study of microelectronic devices.

Computer laboratory for 6.001 and 6.004, on the fifth floor of Building 38

# 6 Master of Engineering

*by Paul L. Penfield, Jr.*

The design of electronic circuits changed quickly in the 1970s and 1980s as digital circuits supplanted analog circuits. This revolution reinforced the growing computer field, and computer science gained importance at MIT and elsewhere. Soon it was hard to imagine electronic systems without digital computation or signal processing. So many technologies were essential that a growing number of students studied for a master's degree, either right after earning a bachelor's degree or a few years later. Their employers usually agreed and paid the bill.

MIT had correctly foreseen these developments and had decided to keep electrical engineering and computer science in the same department. This decision had many benefits, but one disadvantage: the technical scope made it difficult to design a single curriculum of adequate breadth without being too shallow. MIT's approach was a compromise: two curricula—one in electrical engineering and one in computer science—with a common core.

During the 1980s some faculty, especially William M. Siebert, concluded that the department was not doing students a favor by restricting either depth or breadth. Both were needed. So in 1989, a curriculum committee was formed to consider how to combine technical depth and breadth. The conclusion was to retain both by extending the program to five years. After five years of study, students would deserve an additional degree, but it would not be the typical research-oriented master of science degree. Thus was born the MIT Master of Engineering degree.

The committee recommended that students who were capable of writing a master's thesis should have that opportunity. Although bachelor's degrees would still be available, the Master of Engineering degree would be considered the department's flagship program, open only to department undergraduates. The S.M. program would be retained for students from outside.

The result, then, was this model for the three degree levels:

**S.B. degree**

> Classroom-oriented, structured program
>
> Appropriate for entry-level engineering positions
>
> Appropriate for graduate work elsewhere
>
> Appropriate for other career goals

**M.Eng. degree**

> Classroom-oriented, structured program with thesis
>
> Appropriate for a career in engineering

**Doctoral degree**

> Research-oriented program
>
> Appropriate for academic and research careers

Curricula based on this model were approved in 1993, and the first M.Eng. degree was awarded in 1994. The M.Eng. program is consistent with Dugald Jackson's 1903 vision, with added research-oriented activities. It is consistent with the engineering–science model of Gordon Brown, with greater technical breadth than he envisioned. It is consistent with the students' demonstrated demand for education beyond the bachelor's degree. It satisfies the desire of many students for more breadth than either the electrical engineering or computer science programs.

The new degree has been popular with students; typically over half of the EECS undergraduates continue for the fifth year. This five-year model has not yet been widely adopted elsewhere. Other MIT engineering departments define their M.Eng. degrees as professional one-year programs open to graduates of other universities. Some let the better undergraduates pursue a five-year combined program, but only on an individually arranged basis. Only a few other universities have been able to put similar programs in place.

In 1998 when the M.Eng. program was evaluated, the principal disadvantage identified was that first-year graduate courses had to be modified to accommodate the large number of M.Eng. students, who were on average less scholarly than the doctoral students.

The curriculum committee also reorganized the two bachelor's degree programs, VI-1 for EE and VI-3 for CS, and gave them the same structure, making it easy for students to design programs that combined EE and CS in novel ways. A new undergraduate program, VI-2, with greater breadth across EE and CS at the expense of some specialization proved very popular. Apparently students want to keep their options open and prepare for a world in which the boundary between things electrical and things computational is at best fuzzy, and perhaps even nonexistent.

The MIT EECS M.Eng. and VI-2 programs are successful, but they are certainly not the final word in the evolution of the department's programs. What will motivate the next curricular changes? Perhaps more biological material will be needed. Perhaps cognitive science will merge with artificial intelligence. Perhaps quantum mechanics will become critical. Perhaps students will need a better appreciation of the social, economic, and political context of engineering. Perhaps our programs can be made more accessible and attractive, particularly to women and underrepresented minorities.

In 1982 the department considered expanding its mission to include life-long education. A report was written by, left to right, Professors James D. Bruce, Louis D. Smullin, Robert M. Fano (chair of the committee), and William M. Siebert. Although the department did not follow through at that time, the study was useful because its results informed the development of the Master of Engineeering program a decade later.

# MIT EECS Master of Engineering: A Status Report

PAUL L. PENFIELD, JR.,

WILLIAM M. SIEBERT,

JOHN V. GUTTAG,

CAMPBELL L. SEARLE

PROCEEDINGS, 1994 FRONTIERS IN
EDUCATION CONFERENCE, SAN JOSE,
CALIFORNIA, 2–6 NOVEMBER 1994,
228–232

*Introduced by Paul L. Penfield, Jr.*

The undergraduate curriculum based on engineering science served the department well for thirty years following its development in the late 1950s. This was a golden age for research, during which the entire field of computer science, as we know it today, matured. The department developed an undergraduate computer science program and awarded the first degrees in 1975. The previous year a decision had been made not to spin off the computer science activities into a new department. Instead, the department acknowledged the importance of the new field by changing its name from the Department of Electrical Engineering to the Department of Electrical Engineering and Computer Science, and by developing a "common core" of four courses that were part of both the EE and the CS programs.

These developments put stress on the faculty and the students. No longer could most faculty members teach all of the core courses. No longer could students study a range of material that spanned the entire department. The technologies were changing and graduates needed to know both sides of the EE/CS boundary to be capable engineers. Yet they also needed enough detailed knowledge to be effective. And they had to learn all that in four years. In other words, the needs for technical breadth, intellectual depth, and program length were in conflict.

By the late 1980s it was clear that something had to give. MIT was not the only university affected. Some, especially those without unified departments of electrical engineering and computer science, neglected either EE or CS. Some decided not to maintain the same depth. MIT, following Professor William M. Siebert's vision, decided on a third approach: the technical breadth and depth would be retained, but the undergraduate programs would be extended to five years. The students would get a newly defined Master of Engineering degree in recognition of their additional effort.

These ideas were consistent with the reality of engineering at the time, as our students, had we listened to them, could have told us. In large numbers they had been going on for master's degrees, either at MIT or elsewhere, supported by their employers. What the M.Eng. program did was make it convenient for them to do so here.

In the early 1990s the program was developed and put in place. The common core was retained. Both undergraduate curricula were put into the same structural form, and as a result it was possible to define a "greater-breadth, less-depth" program, which proved quite popular, for those who did not want to choose between EE and CS. The fifth year retained the structure typical of an undergraduate program. The bachelor's programs were kept.

The underlying technical assumption was that electrical engineering and computer science constituted a single discipline, with EE and CS as possible specialties. The bachelor's degrees were seen as suitable for either entry-level engineering positions, or for further study leading to other professions such as medicine, law, or management. The M.Eng. degrees were designed to serve those seeking a career in engineering. The doctoral program was for those interested in teaching and/or research careers.

The department positioned the M.Eng. as its flagship degree program. It was hoped that other departments at MIT would develop similar programs. (That has not hap-

At the 2004 6.270 Contest, Starbucks 14 (Team Five) tied for third place. Team Five, all EECS juniors, are (left to right) R. Kwok, W. Chang, M. Lee.

pened; other MIT M.Eng. programs retain the traditional distinction between undergraduate and graduate programs.) It was also hoped that other universities would adopt this new model. So far that has happened only in isolated cases.

Nevertheless this model has served our department well. Over half the students have stayed on for the M.Eng. degree each year, even though financial aid is not promised. A 1998 assessment of the program carried out by Professor Jesús del Alamo recommended only a few changes.

Two years ago at this conference[1] we reported our plans for a five-year program in electrical engineering and computer science, leading to the simultaneous award of bachelor's and master's degrees. An update on our plans[2] was presented one year ago. The program has now started and we can describe the implementation and some preliminary results.

**WHY IS CHANGE REALLY NEEDED?**

The new program was motivated by three distinct changes that have occurred since the last major changes in engineering education:

**Changes in technology**

The technology we teach has changed in at least two major ways in recent decades. First, there is a higher digital, as opposed to analog, content in most systems that electrical engineers deal with. Coverage of analog circuits, electromagnetism, and classical control theory must be accompanied by more exposure to digital systems and computation. Second, advances in microelectronics have made it possible to design and fabricate very complex systems, with superior performance, very cheaply. Today the disciplines of computer science and electrical engineering, once considered separate or diverging, are closer than ever.

**Changes in career needs**

Today's engineers, more than ever before, need an appreciation of the societal, business, technical, and human context in which the process or product being designed will work. Gone are the days (if indeed they were ever here) when an engineer designed, to a specification generated by someone else, a product to be manufactured by others. Engineers are now expected to participate in marketing, product definition, manufacturing, cost control, and many nontechnological aspects of the job.

**Changes in society**

Finally, society has benefited greatly from new electrical and computer technology and from such products as global wideband communications, personal computers, and other products with embedded computation. We are just beginning to feel the effects of this information revolution. Yet society is still led, by and large, by people without a deep understanding of science and technology, who cannot appreciate either the technical advances nor their significance and potential. Society needs leaders who are technology-literate. General universities are not filling the need. Maybe it is up to

---

[1]P. Penfield, Jr., J.V. Guttag, C.L. Searle, and W.M. Siebert, "Shifting the Boundary: A Professional Master's Program for 2000 and Beyond," *Proceedings,* 1992 Frontiers in Education Conference, Nashville, TN, November 11–14, 1992, 645–649.

[2]P. Penfield, Jr., J.V. Guttag, C.L. Searle, and W.M. Siebert, "Master of Engineering: A New MIT Degree," *Proceedings,* 1993 ASEE Annual Conference, Urbana-Champaign, IL, June 20–23, 1993, 58–61.

us engineers. If so, we should provide science- and engineering-based general education.

These three external changes call for changes in engineering education. Our new Master of Engineering (M.Eng.) program is designed to meet this need. It has more technical material and a seamless merging of electrical engineering and computer science. It has room for contextual material. The bachelor's degree portion provides an excellent general education grounded in science and technology.

## EDUCATIONAL GOALS

In our zeal to make our graduates fit the needs of society, we must not forget that our primary mission is to educate young people for a successful life, not merely a successful career. Another way of saying this is to note that our customers are not society or prospective employers, but rather the students themselves. They have all the usual problems of young people growing up. They cannot be successful in either career or life without understanding themselves, understanding society, and appreciating the diversity of thought, method, and style they will encounter.

However, engineering education is more than general education. Our students need enough preparation for immediate and, if they wish, lifelong employment as an engineer. They need the necessary mathematical tools, the scientific basics, and a knowledge of their particular engineering discipline, and they also should know (or quickly learn on the job) the way engineers work.

Beyond this, we need to ensure that our education prepares students to do things besides act as engineers. Many if not most of our students will experience career changes more than once after they graduate. We want their engineering education to be an enabling foundation, not a confining one.

With all this in mind, we believe that a modern engineering graduate requires at least the following:

(1) Foundations: understanding of fundamental science and engineering of permanent value;
(2) Breadth: familiarity with many important areas, including for our students both EE and CS;
(3) Depth: ability to deal with specialists, or become one if necessary;
(4) Leadership: judgment and appreciation of the "bigger picture;"
(5) Design: experience with creative, synthetic, integrative activities;
(6) Curiosity: desire and ability to keep learning throughout life;
(7) Communications skills: ability to express ideas persuasively, in written and oral form;
(8) Social skills: ability to interact with others, in professional and social settings;
(9) Global view: appreciation of diversity in the world and in intellectual areas;
(10) Personal strength: ability to cope with life's various difficulties.

The department may not be responsible for satisfying all these needs, but it certainly is for the first six or seven. There are specific features in our new curricula that address these, and there are other programs at our university for the remainder.

## THE MASTER OF ENGINEERING PROGRAM

We will describe our new program from three different points of view. First, we describe the structure we have selected. Next we discuss the content of the curriculum. Finally, we report how the resources needed for the program have been estimated and secured.

Generations of students remember three long-serving EECS staff members: (left to right) John Tucker, VIA Director; Lydia Wereminski, VI-A Assistant; and Marilyn Pierce, Graduate Administrator. 1994.

## Structure

We concluded that it is no longer possible to cover the needs outlined above in four years, without seriously compromising the technical content. The fact that four years is not enough has not escaped the attention of our graduates, since most of them continue for a master's degree, at MIT or elsewhere, either immediately or after some work experience. Their employers agree, and usually support them in their further schooling.

Our new M.Eng. program enables our students to have this experience here at MIT, with a minimum of fuss and a great deal of flexibility. Previously most of our own students could not pursue a master's degree here, because we thought of the master's program as a prelude to the doctoral program, and only admitted those few whom we deemed capable of writing a doctoral thesis. This high standard, not relevant for a program like the M.Eng. which is intended to prepare people for an engineering career, is now only used for those seeking the Ph.D. Admission to the M.Eng. program is based on whether a student is capable of taking graduate-level courses and handling a short thesis project.

In four years it is still possible to provide an excellent general education based on science and technology, even if not one that will be a suitable preparation for the practice of engineering. We have retained four-year S.B. degrees for those who want to do things other than engineering, or who want to attend graduate school elsewhere, or who may want an entry-level engineering position. These are honorable degrees that serve a valid purpose.

The M.Eng. degree is awarded after five years of study. Its requirements include the requirements of our bachelor's degree as a subset, and normally the two degrees are awarded simultaneously. The program is designed to be seamless with respect to the traditional boundary between undergraduate and graduate education. That is, continuation to the fifth year resembles the transition between the third and fourth years, more than the traditional steps of graduation followed by entrance to graduate school. Students know at the end of their third year if they have this opportunity, and can plan accordingly. They can optimize their schedule, for example by postponing some of the undergraduate requirements until the fifth year, or by taking early a specialized graduate course that is not offered every year.

The new curriculum is also seamless in another dimension. For twenty years we have had two S.B. degree programs, in EE and in CS, with different requirements and structures. For the S.B. part of the new program we designed a single structure into which both curricula fit naturally, with overlapping courses. This had a major benefit. A student can now follow a personalized curriculum that is neither EE nor CS but is sort of in-between, yet just as rigorous. We are calling this new, more flexible, curriculum EECS (electrical engineering and computer science). For the benefit of students who (we presume) will want either EE or CS to appear on their diplomas, we have designed the ESE (electrical science and engineering) and CSE (computer science and engineering) curricula. It was easy—we simply replaced a few restricted electives with required courses to force some specialization. A student does not need to declare which of the three S.B. degrees is expected until the last semester. The ESE and CSE curricula are accredited, and we expect the new, more flexible EECS curriculum to be accredited soon.

## Content

We listed above ten things that our graduates need. We now explain the features of the new M.Eng. and S.B. curricula that help provide each.

Let us start at the bottom of the list. The last four items are important for all students, not only those in engineering. They are part of any good general education, and courses to provide them are prescribed by the university and

taught outside the department. There is an extensive humanities requirement (twice as much as ABET requires) and a writing requirement. Because
these needs apply to all our students, they are part of both the M.Eng. and
the S.B. curricula.

Now at the top of the list, the cornerstone of any engineering education is the
technical content. Some have advocated that departments reduce the engineering-science content of curricula to make room for also-needed material
devoted to context, practice, ethics, and other nontechnical topics. On the
other hand, the ability of engineers to keep up with rapid advances depends
on their understanding of fundamental technical material of permanent value
and relevance. For the past forty years engineering education has been served
well by its emphasis on engineering science. Our new curricula have a
stronger, not weaker, technical content. The freshman core (physics, math,
chemistry, and now also biology) is common for students in all departments.
The curricula continue with laboratory experience and technical courses in
EECS. All department students take four courses in the basics of electrical
engineering and computer science, plus some advanced mathematics.

Facility with mathematics is essential for engineers. Our curricula include
two courses in calculus, one in differential equations, and for most students
one in probability and one in discrete mathematics.

The need for breadth and depth is satisfied by a requirement that students
select nine EECS courses (5 for the S.B.) from seven lists grouped by topic:
• artificial intelligence;
• bioelectrical engineering;
• communication, control, and signal processing;
• computer systems and architecture;
• devices, circuits, and systems;
• electrodynamics and energy systems;
• theoretical computer science.
Each list contains a "header" course that is a prerequisite for most of the rest
of the list.

Some of these courses are in the EE side of the department and some are
from CS. Depth is assured by the requirement that three of the nine courses
come from any one of the seven lists; breadth is assured by a requirement
that four of the courses come two each from two other lists. The final two
courses may come from any list. The student has a great deal of flexibility in
the choice of what to specialize in, but must specialize in something. There is
similar flexibility in the choice of breadth. Students who wish their S.B.
degree to be in either ESE or CSE simply make their selections accordingly.

Design experience is distributed throughout the department courses. Each
course carries with it a certain number of "design points" and students must
accumulate a substantial number of points. Again there is great flexibility in
the way individual students can satisfy this requirement.

One of the goals listed above is the desire for continued learning throughout
life. There may not be a single best way to accomplish this goal, but several
things help. First, if the quality of instruction is high, then classroom learning can be fun. Second, learning done under strong immediate motivation is
effective, and hands-on projects can provide such a setting. Finally, learning
done with minimal detailed guidance is usually ultimately satisfying, and the
required thesis includes such an experience.

Lastly, one of the items listed above remains to be discussed, the need of
engineers to appreciate the context of their work. Many students already
have the right attitude, but we have not figured out yet how to best help those
who do not. This area is perhaps the weakest part of the new curricula.

**Resources**

We expect to offer 80% of our undergraduates the opportunity to continue through the fifth year to the M.Eng. degree, and we expect about 80% of those to accept our offer. During the authorization process for the new program we wrote a business plan. We estimated the additional number of course takings per year, and the increases in thesis-supervision, classroom teaching, and advising loads. We estimated classroom teaching to rise by 8%, thesis supervision by 3%, and advising by 3%. We examined in detail the particular courses that would be taken and judged whether additional faculty or teaching assistants would be needed.

We then estimated the increased resources needed. This amounted to a 3% increase in faculty, a 10% increase in the number of TAs, and one support staff, for a total budget increase of 5%. We then estimated the tuition from the additional students, and demonstrated that the added revenue represented about 10% of our budget. Thus the program pays its portion of central costs. It has a 50% "gross margin," or, looked at another way, contributes at an effective overhead rate of 100%.

We actually did this exercise not only for the eventual steady state, but for each of three transition years, and the Provost is approving the increases on a year-by-year basis.

An important question is how the students will pay for the fifth year of study. They are only eligible for university-administered financial aid for their first eight semesters on campus. We have estimated that a combination of additional TA openings, some external fellowships (the students will qualify for most fellowship competitions), and an increase in our industrially supported internship program will cover over half the need. The rest would be covered by a combination of family funds and loans. Other professional education, e.g. legal and medical, is routinely financed by loans which are then paid back with the added earning power conferred by the advanced degree. The same idea should work for engineering education. To encourage this approach, the department has established a program under which it will pay the interest on loans taken out by fifth-year students, thereby making the loans interest-free until the student is done with the program. At the time of writing, this program has just started and it is too early to tell whether it will be effective.

**STATUS**

The Master of Engineering degree was approved by the MIT faculty in December, 1992. About 25 seniors were immediately admitted to the program. They were selected from a larger number who applied. Also, some of the students in our five-year internship program elected to follow the new curriculum. As a result, 35 students were in the first wave of M.Eng. graduates in 1994.

About 75 students from the class of '94 were admitted to the program in June 1993. Members of this class were permitted to follow the new S.B. curriculum. As of this writing we do not know how many of these will register as graduate students in Fall 1994, but we have in our business plan a target of 62 over and above historical levels.

In the summer of 1994, about 130 juniors from the class of '95 were admitted. Our target first-year graduate population of these people, in Fall 1996, is 100. This is the planned steady-state population in later years. Most of the people in this class are following the new S.B. curriculum, even if they are not planning to stay for the M.Eng. Students in later classes are all expected to follow the new curriculum.

Two new courses are currently under development because the act of defining the new curricula exposed a need for them. One is a course in discrete mathematics at the sophomore level, and the other a junior course in signals, control, and communications. These courses were offered during the past year to small groups of students, and from now on will be taught to a much larger group.

To encourage M.Eng. students to develop oral-presentation skills, we held a mini-conference called "EECS Master Works," where students gave talks on their theses. The submissions were refereed, and prizes were awarded for the best presentations.

During the past year or so, as the program has been implemented, many decisions had to be made. The department administration paid great attention to details, under the theory that if we did not, then the details would somehow pay attention to us and we might not be pleased. We have attempted to make the program consistent with all other programs of the department.

## RESULTS

Although it is still too early for many lessons to have been learned from the program, there are some things we can report.

Among the faculty and the students in the program there is high morale and enthusiasm. Most of them sense that they are helping establish a new mode of engineering education that eventually will, for good reasons, be adopted widely. We hope this degree of excitement will continue in future years.

One result of interest involves the percentage of students who declare an undergraduate major in electrical engineering vs. computer science. Traditionally students have preferred ESE to CSE by a ratio of almost two to one. Members of the class of 1997, who selected a major in the summer of 1994 before their sophomore year, had the opportunity to choose ESE, CSE, or the new, more flexible EECS undergraduate major. The students apparently want the flexibility of the new degree. Registration in the three majors was almost equally split, with each drawing between 30% and 35% of the total.

We were initially concerned about the impact of the M.Eng. program on our highly popular internship program. In many ways the structure of the new program is based on that program. In particular, the internship program is a five-year one, with three summers and one fall spent at an industrial plant, and with relatively easy admission to the fifth year. The concern was that students might have been interested in the internship program not because of its industrial experience, but because it led to a master's degree. Now that the M.Eng. program has the same easy admission, the fear was that a much smaller number of students would apply to the internship program. We were pleased to find in Spring 1994 that there was as much interest in the internship program as ever, so apparently our students have been applying to it for the right reason.

Another concern had been that there would not be enough master's-level thesis topics available, or that faculty members would only supervise doctor's theses, because of their higher likelihood of leading to published papers. So far, M.Eng. students have not had difficulty finding thesis topics and supervisors. The real test, however, will come in future years when there will be more M.Eng. students requiring theses.

Our new program violates the customary paradigm that the break between classroom-intensive, structured education and research-oriented, apprenticeship education occurs between undergraduate and graduate years. This paradigm was deeply imbedded in administrative procedures throughout the department and the university, and our new programs required a variety of changes. We have been pleased at how cooperative all parts of the university have been, and how eager people have been to help make the new program a success.

## ACKNOWLEDGMENTS

We wish to gratefully acknowledge the faculty members of the department for the enthusiasm with which these curricular changes have been embraced. We also wish to acknowledge the contributions of countless members of the MIT community, both faculty and administration, for their help in securing the necessary approvals and for thoughtful committee deliberations.

# PIONEERING WOMEN IN EECS

*Introduction by John V. Guttag*

Looking back at the preceding hundred years, we find the only real constant has been surprise. Yet today, looking forward, there is indeed one certainty visible on the horizon: in the century to come, the gifts and intellects of women, in unprecedented numbers, will further enrich electrical engineering and computer science.

This long-overdue transformation is inevitable. In this section, we honor the brilliant and distinguished careers of two women in the vanguard. What both have in common is their love of academia and the pivotal contributions they have made to their respective fields. Young engineers and scientists of both genders look to them as role models, and admire their trailblazing technical contributions.

Yet as they pursued their careers as researchers and educators—*because* they pursued these careers—they simultaneously blazed a parallel trail as well. Each was always, inevitably, the first woman this or the only woman that. These unsought appositives came unavoidably with the territory. Each woman has distilled a finely nuanced appreciation of the role that gender plays in the careers of researchers. What follows is a necessarily brief review of their pioneering activities, and a glimpse of how they strive—each in her own distinctive way— to make the path smoother for the women researchers who are following them.

EECS women faculty, February 2003 (left to right): A. Ozdaglar, B. Liskov, L. Kaelbling, M. Dresselhaus, N. Lynch, M. Médard, L. Kolodziejski, J. Hoyt; not pictured: S. Goldwasser, M. Gray, D. Katabi

# MILDRED S. DRESSELHAUS
## 11 NOVEMBER 1930–

*by Ellen Williams '67*

The appreciation below is based on a series of interviews with Millie Dresselhaus by Ellen Williams in early 2003. The italicized quotes were all part of these interviews.

Professor Millie Dresselhaus working in the lab with graduate student Bob Silverstein, c., 1975

*I try to do a good job on my web page because a lot of kids—junior high and high school students—are asked to do homework assignments about me for their classes. The message I'm trying to give them is that you can come from a very humble background and still succeed. Never feel that you're out of it because of situations out of your control.*

In EECS, the history of women begins—literally—with Mildred Dresselhaus, known as Millie to just about the entire campus. Her childhood was quintessentially American: Millie and her elder brother were prodigies, musically as well as academically, raised by doting parents who themselves were unskilled, impoverished refugees from Eastern Europe.

When Millie entered New York City's Hunter College, she had set her sights on becoming an elementary school teacher. But in her sophomore year, she was "adopted" by physics professor Rosalyn Yalow, who remained a life-long friend, advisor, and mentor. With Yalow's encouragement, Millie became a physicist.

After Hunter, her path was clear. In 1951, she earned an A.B. from Hunter and a Fulbright Fellowship, followed by an A.M. from Radcliffe in 1953. In 1958, she acquired a Ph.D. in superconductivity from the University of Chicago, a husband, and a postdoctoral fellowship at Cornell.

Of her graduate school days, Millie reports:

*[A]t the University of Chicago at that time the students worked very independently. They found their own topics and figured out how to work them out and they basically did everything.... But I was a special case, so I did it even more independently.... I had an advisor who believed that women should not be graduate students, and that women students were a big waste of resources; there were very very few of us at that time, about*

Among the performers of a clarinet quintet are M. Dresselhaus, second violinist, S. Umans clarinetist, and A. Grodzinsky violist..

*two percent of the graduate student body nationwide in these fields was female. So, because I got so much harassment from my advisor, I stayed away from him.*

In 1960, the postdoc appointment ended, and the Dresselhaus's first child, a daughter, was born in 1959. Millie and husband Gene, both at Cornell then, moved to Lincoln Laboratory, where Millie had a lot of freedom to work on "anything other than superconductivity." Gene explains, in his informal biography of Millie (available from Millie's web site: http://eecs-pc-05.mit.edu/index.html), that the bias against superconductivity came from her division leader, who felt that everything about superconductivity had been explained and the field was dead. Millie was disappointed that she would not be allowed to continue working in superconductivity, but, Gene notes, "changing fields turned out to be the best thing that could have happened at this early time in her career." She became involved with Lincoln Laboratory's solid state group, studying magneto-optical effects in semiconductors, and then went on to direct her own program. She soon became interested in studying the electronic structure of graphite using magneto-optics. Gene notes, "Because this magneto-optics experiment was considered very difficult and the graphite electronic structure was at that time considered to be very complex, she had little competition in this field. This situation was fortunate because these were the years when our three sons were born."

*Discover Magazine* also took note of her strategy when it named Millie, in November 2002, one of the fifty most important women in science:

*Before her fourth child hit kindergarten, Dresselhaus deciphered the electronic structure of graphite, the lowest-energy solid-state form of carbon.... The daunting problem had long scared off other researchers, which is why she chose it: "I wanted to be able to move more slowly, without so much competition."*

With the advent of lasers in the 1960s, she was among the first to use the devices for magneto-optics experiments, and in 1968, Millie published a short paper that represented the first use of lasers in magnetoreflection experiments. The findings reported in this paper also turned the band structure of graphite upside down, demonstrating conclusively that the theory of electrons and holes that had been accepted for the previous twenty years was exactly reversed regarding the identification of electrons and holes.[1]

Nineteen sixty-eight was also Millie's first year as an MIT faculty member. Gender figured prominently in the change of venue. As Millie explains it,

Professor Millie Dresselhaus in her office when she was CMSE director, c. 1980

*There must have been about a thousand staff members [at Lincoln] and there were two women out of the thousand. What happened to the two of us is they expected us to start work at eight o'clock in the morning. We found that really difficult to arrange—organize a babysitter, organize the house, drive out [to the lab]—it was just virtually impossible to do this before 8 am. So we were both always late and we got reprimanded very strongly for bad performance. It got to her—it got to me too but it got to her first—so she got another job and left. Then...I was the only one. It got so bad, I really was very very discouraged because, my goodness, I was doing my best, and I was publishing so many papers, I was doing so much work. Nobody complained at all about my work—or hers—because we were, from a performance standpoint, way up there. But we couldn't arrive on time. For young mothers trying to have a career, the expectations were totally unrealistic. I'm not a complainer, nor was [she] a complainer, but it was kind of unbearable. One day, I had lunch with a staff member [George Pratt] who knew me very well and had left Lincoln to go to MIT, and we were talking about how tough life was for women at Lincoln Lab. He said, "You know they have this chair at MIT for women that was just established. Maybe we could appoint you to that. I'll look into it." So he applied on my behalf for the Abby Rockefeller Mauzé Chair. And I got it. I became a visiting faculty member, and I never left [MIT]. From the time I came...I was made to feel very comfortable and welcome.*

Though Millie's formal academic training was in physics, her first departmental appointment at MIT was in electrical engineering rather than physics. In 1983, she received a joint appointment to the physics and EECS departments. She continues to describe her transition:

*As soon as I came to EECS, I was teaching, because they needed somebody to teach physics to engineering students. The curriculum had changed and they were teaching semiconductor physics to the engineering students. The physicists at MIT didn't want to teach physics to engineering students. They wanted the engineering students to come and take the physics courses exactly as they were; they made no effort to have the physics have any relevance to what [the engineers] were doing. And most of the people in the physics department were not willing to bridge the gaps in their training. I was quite willing to do that because it wasn't very hard to put together a different kind of curriculum that would be appropriate to the engineering school. Gordon Brown was dean of engineering and he had the idea that the engineers missed out on World War II because they didn't know enough physics; he wanted people teaching engineers who were trained in physics, in addition to having experience with the engineering side, which I did. That's why I was attractive to them: because I had this dual background and didn't have a prejudice against engineers.*

Within a few months of her arrival as a visiting faculty member, Millie was appointed to a permanent, tenured faculty position. She continued her solid state work, and has throughout her career been active in the study of a wide range of problems in the physics of solids. Much of her early research career at MIT was devoted to studying graphite intercalation compounds, materials consisting of graphite sheets interlaced with layers of other molecules. She has played an important role in the development of several other fields, including magnetic semiconductors in the 1970s, and in the 1990s she played a large role with Erich Ippen in the first observation of coherent phonon generation in a solid and in the development of the research areas of low-dimensional thermoelectricity and bismuth nanowires. Her recent interests have been directed toward the study of the structure and properties of carbon fibers, fullerenes, carbon nanotubes, bismuth nanowires, and low-dimensional thermoelectric materials.

Professor Dresselhaus in Killian Court, 1994

During this long and productive career, Millie has also held a number of administrative positions. Within MIT, she was the associate head of the Electrical Engineering department from 1972–74, and director of the Center for Materials Science and Engineering from 1977–83. In 1985, she was appointed Institute Professor.

Outside MIT, Millie was elected president of the American Physical Society in 1984. She relates the tale with some amusement: "MIT made no provisions whatsoever for me winning this election because they had only had, in a hundred years of [the] American Physical Society—more than a hundred years—they only had one woman president and I was running against a very famous Nobel laureate who was the age of my father." So for the duration of her term as president, she continued to carry a full administrative and teaching load. How did she manage? "I developed a pretty handy-dandy system of running the American Physical Society. I used to do it at night from home on a computer. And it worked out very well. I must say looking back on this period, that it went amazingly well."

In the late 1990s, Millie served first as president and then as chairman of the board of the American Association for the Advancement of Science, and in 2000 toward the end of the Clinton Administration, she became director of the Office of Science in the U.S. Department of Energy.

Millie's interest in mentoring women students started when she first came to MIT in 1967. Emily Wick, who was a professor of food chemistry (half-time) and a dean of women students (half-time), asked Millie to help out in mentoring women MIT students. In this way,

Millie became aware of the academic problems of women students, who at that time constituted only 4 percent of the undergraduate population at MIT.

Through this experience, she became aware of higher admissions requirements for women undergraduates, as compared with the requirement for men. Historically, the different admission requirements reflected the limited dormitory space available for women and the poorer academic performance of women at MIT. From her mentoring experience, Millie concluded that women's lesser academic performance was, to some extent, connected with issues of social acceptance, isolation, harassment, and discrimination. This led Millie to present a motion, at a meeting of the MIT faculty in the late 1960s, to adopt an equal and joint admission process for men and women students. The acceptance of the equal admission process resulted in a rapid doubling of the number of women undergraduates.

Today, Millie looks back with pride on her achievements and her development of a leadership style that not only worked for her, but helped both women and men, and therefore MIT.

*When I came to MIT and EECS I was 37 and a full professor. When I took over the Center for Materials Science and Engineering as director, I was 47. That was pretty young. I was much younger than the other directors had been. Many of the lab's faculty members were much older, much more senior than I was, adult men. The other thing is we had about forty faculty members, and I was the only female. And I was the director.*

*I didn't know about transparency. We didn't have that word then, but I played the leadership role instinctively. That was one of the lessons I learned from MIT President Jerry Wiesner. A long time ago, before any of my administrative jobs, I was doing things for women at MIT. My idea was that we could best do things for women by benefiting men as well. That way it wasn't us against them. I tried some of the same principle when I was running the Center.*

*It's very important for people to feel happy. I felt that one of the [Center's] problems— why people were so unhappy—was because they didn't understand why things were happening, why one project was funded and another wasn't. We couldn't fund everybody, we didn't have that much money. Grants were competitive. So I thought that democracy would be a good thing. I mean I had age and I had sex going against me, and I thought the relationship would work better by being open with people. We needed fairness and we needed a process, and I tried to put in a process for everything, so that there was some rationalization, so that people knew that the decisions that were made reflected a group consensus. I developed a democratic process where all the people at the Center felt that they had some voice, and it made the whole greater than the sum of its parts.*

Millie's numerous honors and awards, more than can possibly be mentioned here, reflect the impact that she has had on the scientific community as a whole. Among the most noteworthy: she has been elected to both the National Academy of Engineering and the National Academy of Sciences, and elected a fellow of the American Academy of Arts and Sciences. She has been awarded the Karl T. Compton Medal for Leadership in Physics from the American Institute of Physics, and received the Hall of Fame Award from Women in Technology International. Recently she was awarded her nineteenth honorary doctoral degree.

Millie Dresselhaus, Institute Professor, c. 2002

Even more noteworthy, the National Medal of Science was awarded to Millie Dresselhaus by then President George H. W. Bush in 1990. This was followed in late 2003 with the IEEE Founders Medal with the citation, "For leadership across many fields of science and engineering through research and education, and for exceptional and unique contributions to the profession." Millie was the first female to win this award, the oldest of IEEE's awards.

In Millie's words, "…most of my career has been focused on research which had impact." Besides her own research, however, she (modestly but proudly) points to the sixty-five Ph.D. students whom she trained and who have already made their own contributions to science and engineering.

[1]P.R. Schroeder, M.S. Dresselhaus, and A. Javan, Phys. Rev. Lett. 20, 1292 (1968).

# BARBARA LISKOV
## 7 NOVEMBER 1939 –

*by John V. Guttag*

Professor Barbara Liskov

*I'm a researcher at heart and the thing I like best about being at MIT has been the opportunity to find interesting problems to work on, [to] create things. Research is my real love.*

—*Barbara Liskov*

Like her mother and her mother's mother, Barbara Liskov (née Huberman) was born and raised in California. She was the eldest of four children in a family that greatly valued education. While Barbara's parents did not particularly encourage Barbara to pursue her interests in science and mathematics, neither did they discourage her. In contrast, her high school peers made it clear that these were not normal interests for a girl, which provoked her to keep a low profile in her classes.

It was always clear that Barbara would go to college. It was less clear that she was expected to pursue a career. A career (for example, secretary or teacher) was viewed as something to have in reserve in case she didn't marry or ended up having to support a family.

Barbara enrolled at U.C.–Berkeley, where she started off as a physics major. Later she switched to mathematics, but continued to minor in physics. She recalls being the only one of two women in all of her classes. As in high school, she kept a low profile, rarely saying anything in class.

When Barbara finished her undergraduate work at Berkeley in 1961, she applied to graduate mathematics programs at Berkeley and Princeton. She was admitted at Berkeley. Princeton returned her application with a form letter informing her that women were not considered for admission at either the undergraduate or graduate level. That Barbara was oblivious to Princeton's policy is indicative of her approach to her career: she has a quiet confidence in herself and doesn't anticipate that there will be obstacles that she cannot overcome.

On reflection, Barbara decided that she was tired of classes, and rather than enroll in graduate school she began looking for a job. She also decided that it was time to try living somewhere other than California. Her father came from Boston, so Barbara decided that she would like to satisfy her curiosity about that area of the country. She has spent most of her life since then in the Boston area.

Barbara looked for a job as a mathematician, but found nothing of interest. As she reports, "All I was offered was a job drawing graphs or something like that." Instead, she took a job as a computer programmer at the Mitre Corporation. She had no programming experience at all, but neither did almost anyone else in those days. At Mitre, Barbara discovered that she had a real aptitude for computers and programming, and she became a nascent computer scientist.

Professors Jack Dennis and Barbara Liskov discussing the programming language CLU, developed by Professor Liskov. 1970s

Throughout her high school and college years, Barbara experienced a certain awkwardness associated with being a woman in a "man's field." At Mitre she observed overt and blatant discrimination against women. Shortly after Barbara was hired, Mitre hired a young woman and a young man, both with M.S. degrees. Though no better qualified, the man was hired into a better position and at a higher salary than the woman. Barbara "felt that what had happened was unfair. It was not directly relevant to me, since I didn't have an M.S. Or at least I chose not to take it that way, and I think maybe I've often chosen not to take things that way. That's been one way I've coped with it all these years. But lots of women, when something negative happens, take it to heart and the next thing you know they can't stand to be in the major anymore because they aren't welcome."

Barbara stayed at Mitre for only a year before taking a programming job at Harvard. At Harvard, she worked on what was then believed to be a simple project, the translation of natural language. The project proved to be more difficult than anticipated.

While working at Harvard, Barbara decided that she wanted to learn more fundamental material at a faster pace than was possible while working full time as a programmer. She applied again to the mathematics program at Berkeley and also to the computer science programs at Harvard and Stanford. She did not apply to MIT, because she "didn't want to be a nerd."

At the time, computer science was not quite reputable as an academic discipline. Neither Harvard nor Stanford had a computer science department. Nevertheless, Barbara opted to study computer science. She was admitted to both Harvard and Stanford. She chose Stanford, partly because she wanted to return to California.

During her first day at Stanford, Barbara ran into Professor John McCarthy. McCarthy had previously been on the faculty at MIT, where, along with Marvin Minsky, he helped to establish the field of artificial intelligence (AI). Barbara arrived at Stanford without any financial support, so she wasted little time before asking McCarthy if he could provide her with support. Her work on language translation at Harvard qualified her as something of an expert in AI, and McCarthy said yes.

While at Stanford, Barbara discovered that she preferred research in computer systems to AI. However, she was being supported to work in the area of AI. She decided that the prudent thing to do was to finish a thesis in AI, then change fields immediately. Her thesis, on chess endgames, was a landmark in the area and is still cited today. By the time Barbara graduated, in 1968, Stanford had formed a computer science department. This meant that Barbara became the first woman in the country (and perhaps the world) to receive a doctorate from a computer science department.

Once again, when it came time to look for a job Barbara's choice was Boston. She had enjoyed her first sojourn there. Furthermore, by then she had met the man, Nathan Liskov, who eventually became her husband, and he lived in Boston. Nate (an MIT EE graduate) and Barbara married in 1970.

Finding an appropriate job was not straightforward. Barbara describes the experience: "When I finished my Ph.D. I received no support in finding a job. And I was also very naive. Now, when I think back about what happened to the people who finished about my time, there was clearly more going on with them than was going on with me. I was on my own and there was no doubt that an old boy's network was at work and it did not include me. But I didn't really know that at the time."

Barbara explored academic opportunities, but ended up returning to Mitre. This time she was on the research staff. In many ways, this worked out better than an academic job, since it gave her the opportunity to make the switch from AI to computer systems without the risks associated with making a career change as an untenured faculty member.

At Mitre, Barbara designed a computer architecture and implemented it using microcode. She then moved on to design and implement a novel operating system called Venus. At the time, architectures and operating systems were closely intertwined, and it was not unusual to build a new operating system designed to exploit features of a new architecture.

Barbara wrote a paper describing the novel aspects of Venus and submitted it to the Symposium on Operating Systems Principles, the top conference in the field. The paper was

Women faculty speaking to GW-VI (Graduate Women in Course VI; left to right): L. Kolodziejski, N. Lynch, J. Hoyt, L. Kaelbling (standing), B. Liskov

not only accepted, it won a best-paper prize. Jerry Saltzer, an MIT faculty member, was chair of the session at which the paper was presented. Saltzer was tremendously impressed by the paper and its author, and urged Barbara to apply for a faculty position at MIT. The timing was excellent. There were very few women on the MIT faculty, and President Wiesner was strongly encouraging departments to hire women. Barbara beat out some strong male candidates and was hired in 1972.

Barbara was the second woman faculty member (after Millie Dresselhaus) to join the department, and the first in computer science. Women were sufficiently rare on the faculty that when Barbara went to the official welcome reception for new faculty members, one of the senior members of the corporation came up and introduced himself to Barbara's husband, under the assumption that he was the new faculty member. While this was an embarrassing moment for the corporation member, Barbara reports that she found it quite amusing. That she was amused rather than annoyed was good, since this was far from the last time this sort of thing happened.

Barbara found her first year at MIT challenging. Her first teaching assignment was computer architecture. Though she had worked in this area at Mitre, she was unprepared for the amount of electrical engineering material covered by the course. It was a struggle, but she managed to stay far enough ahead of the students to survive. And she loved being in an environment that demanded constant and rapid learning.

Before leaving Mitre, Barbara started thinking hard about how best to organize and structure programs, a field that today is called programming methodology. This is what she worked on after arriving at MIT.

By this time, the difficulty of producing high-quality software was widely acknowledged. It was also clear that a large software project could only be managed by dividing it into smaller pieces. The standard approach was to divide a program into subroutines (also called *procedures* or *functions*). Barbara was a leader in developing an alternative mechanism, the abstract data type.

The notion of an abstract data type is quite simple. It is a set of objects and the operations on those objects. The specification of those operations defines an interface between the abstract data type and the rest of the program. The interface defines the behavior of the operations—what they do, but not how they do it. The specification thus defines an abstraction barrier that isolates the rest of the program from the data structures, algo-

Members of the EECS one-hundredth-anniversary panel on healthcare, on 23 May 2003, included (left to right): B. Liskov, moderator; M. Gray, E. Grimson, D. Freeman, and P. Szolovitz.

rithms, and code involved in providing a realization of the type abstraction. Thus one can write code that uses a data abstraction without worrying about how the data abstraction is implemented. If the code that uses the data abstraction depends only on the specification of the data abstraction, one can change the implementation of the data abstraction without affecting the correctness of the code that uses the abstraction. Data abstraction has become one of the major underpinnings of all modern programming methods. Combined with inheritance, it is the essence of object-oriented programming.

Professor Barbara Liskov in her office, c. 1985

Barbara's earliest work on data abstraction was primarily methodological. It involved designing interesting abstractions, devising mechanisms for specifying them, and inventing techniques to implement them and to reason about the correctness of their implementations. She did much of this work in conjunction with Steve Zilles, her first graduate student. By her second year at MIT, Barbara had attracted several other students to her research group, and they began work on a programming language, CLU, designed to support programming with data abstractions.

CLU was a truly audacious language. It tastefully combined the then-novel ideas of (1) data abstraction, (2) iteration abstraction, (3) exception handling, and (4) polymorphic types. CLU was not a "paper" programming language—Barbara and her students produced a high-quality implementation on a variety of platforms. Along the way, they pioneered a number of implementation techniques for raising and catching exceptions, techniques that are still used today. Every important programming language since 1975 has borrowed ideas from CLU. Java, for example, owes its notion of inheritance to Simula and Smalltalk, but almost everything else of interest in it was pioneered in CLU.

For most of the 1970s Barbara's research centered on CLU and data abstraction. In the early 1980s she started working on distributed computing (computing carried out by many computers connected by a network), and that has remained her primary research focus ever since.

Barbara's interest in distributed computing was not new. The work she did in the 1970s focused on sequential programs because it seemed to her that was a way of reducing complexity and concentrating on the main issues of data abstraction. By the late 1970s the Internet was gathering steam. People knew how to get messages from here to there, but they did not know how to build programs that ran well and reliably on distributed computers. So Barbara decided to pick up the piece of the problem that she had put aside. Barbara's work on distributed computing led first to a system called Argus, which was a programming language for distributed applications. Her interests then shifted to fault-tolerant distributed programs, an area in which she continues to work.

Barbara's son Moses was born in 1975. At the time Barbara was an untenured faculty member. There was no parental leave policy in those days, but Barbara did take a term off from teaching following Moses's birth. She comments that, "I was able to manage raising a child while working full time in part because of the flexibility offered by an academic position. Plus I had a lot of help from my husband—we took this on as a joint project." After graduating from Harvard and working for a few years, Moses enrolled as a graduate student in MIT EECS, studying theoretical computer science.

Barbara has always understood that being a successful faculty member involves much more than doing outstanding research. Her research has always been done jointly with students. She has had twenty-one doctoral students complete dissertations under her supervision and many more at the master's and bachelor's levels. Barbara is quick to share credit with her students. As she says, "MIT has been a wonderful place to do research because the students are so good." Many of these students have gone on to have enormously successful careers of their own, most in industry. Other former students are or have been faculty members at Brown, Cornell, CMU, Iowa, Iowa State, MIT, the Naval Postgraduate School, and the University of Massachusetts.

Professor Liskov with her son "Moe" '04, on the day of his Ph.D. hooding at MIT in computer science. They were photographed by Dr. Nathan Liskov, husband and father. June 2004.

For over two decades Barbara has anchored MIT's teaching in the area of software engineering. She has taught an occasional graduate subject, but has thrown her heart and soul into MIT's undergraduate software engineering laboratory course. This course is rather unusual in the way in which it focuses on engineering principles while giving the students an enormous amount of hands-on experience. In survey after survey, many EECS graduates report that this course was the most useful they took at MIT. Barbara has coauthored two well-reviewed and widely cited books based on the course.

Since her arrival at MIT in 1972, Barbara has only taken one break from academia. In January 2000 she signed on as chief architect at a small software company, SightPath. She reports that it was wonderful to have the opportunity to apply ideas developed in her research in a practical setting. The product was successful, and the company was eventually acquired by CISCO.

During the course of her career, Barbara has earned many awards and honors. She is a Fellow of the Association for Computing Machinery, and a member of the National Academy of Engineering and the American Academy of Arts and Science. In 1996, she won the Society of Women Engineers Achievement Award, and by the time this volume appears, she will have been named the recipient of the IEEE's 2004 John von Neumann Medal.

Barbara has contributed to EECS in particular and to MIT in general in many ways. For many years, she ran the computer science graduate admissions committee. In that role, she worked hard and effectively at increasing the number of women in the doctoral program.

She served for three years as associate department head for computer science from September 2001–2004, the first woman to hold that position. This is a position that Barbara was offered several times in the past, but always declined. She was more interested in doing research, working with graduate students, and teaching than she was in career advancement. Now, she says, "it is my turn to do it." There are also some important things she wants to accomplish, in particular increasing the number of women on the faculty. In this she has been strikingly successful. On her watch the department has added five women to its computer science faculty.

The Women's Technology Program, Inaugural class, Summer 2002. The program aims to increase high school girls' interest in pursuing the fields of engineering and computer science. In 2003, forty high school women participated in this four-week residential program.

Barbara has always kept her work in perspective. She says that she tends not to work at night or on weekends, but there is some evidence to the contrary. She does find time to read nontechnical literature, work in her garden, and pursue a variety of other interests. This stands in contrast to some of her colleagues at MIT, both female and male. In this respect, she thinks that being a woman may be advantageous:

*I didn't have to think about a career. I just did what was fun, and I didn't really think about where this was going. On the other hand, when I talk to men, it often turns out they feel desperately pressured to get a job that could support a family. I had my son when I was not yet tenured. I took the position that there were lots of jobs out there and if I didn't get tenure, I would find something else to do that would be interesting. I wasn't going to worry about it.*

Barbara did get tenure at MIT, and the decision has proved to be one of the best ones the department and the Institute has ever made.

**100th Anniversaries: Electrical Engineering and, later, Electrical Engineering and Computer Science at MIT**

*From top to bottom:*

1982 Anniversary dinner in Johnson Athletic Center

Department Head Joel Moses blows out the "candle" on the EECS 100th-birthday cake in 1982. Doc Edgerton, presumably playing "Happy Birthday," is shown with guitar.

A panel discussion during the EECS one-hundredth anniversary in 1982, included, from left to right, Professors Siebert, Bruce, Dresselhaus, Smullin, and Fano.

At the EECS one-hundredth-anniversary symposium 23 May 2003, Rodney Brooks tries to get "robot" John Guttag to pay attention to task.

The EECS one-hundredth-anniversary dinner, Park Plaza Hotel, Boston, 23 May 2003

# 7

## Where Do We Go from Here?

*by Paul L. Penfield, Jr.*

The study of the EECS department over the past century has identified some general trends — in our technology, in our department, and in the global community. These trends suggest what awaits us in the next century. It is natural to ask how the department, especially its educational programs, might evolve. What challenges will our department and our professional field face? Here are this observer's five personal choices.

### TECHNICAL SCOPE AND CULTURE

The technical domain of interest to EECS has steadily expanded. So far, it has been our practice to retain newly developed or emerging technologies. The most prominent example is keeping computer science within the department, but there are many others, including radio, control theory, microwaves, optics, system theory, artificial intelligence, and semiconductor fabrication. Any of these might, under different circumstances, have been considered candidates for specialized degree programs or new departments.

Research carried out by the MIT EE Department in 1911

On 15 March 1944, Dr. Harold Edgerton and his crew made this photo from a modified B-25 bomber outfitted with a standard 9" x 9" roll film aerial camera placed in the bomb bay alongside a specially made electronic flash unit capable of illuminating a square mile at an altitude of approximately 1,500' allowing night-reconnaissance photos to be made safely. Before this invention, for which "Doc" received the U.S. War Department's Medal of Freedom, these photos could be made only by illumination provided by flares, which, unfortunately, illuminated the plane as well, making it a ready target. This picture of the destroyed buildings and bridge was obviously made during the daytime because of the long shadows cast by the buildings and the direct reflection of the sun into the camera from the surface of the water.

In the future, the department will make other such decisions. For example, we might see the development of a discipline — defined by its educational programs — called quantum engineering. The techniques of making physical devices from nanofabrication, photonics, Microelectromechanical Systems (MEMS), or nuclear imaging would be combined with quantum computing, quantum communications, quantum control, quantum cryptography, and quantum information. Quantum systems, we know, can do things classical systems cannot. Who will define what it means to be a quantum engineer? Who will develop the degree programs? Will our department play a leadership role?

Our first challenge in the years ahead, then, will be to embrace new specialties in a way that preserves the intellectual core of the department.

Our increased technical scope has been accompanied by higher and higher levels of abstraction. A hundred years ago the department had a "shop culture" that reflected the electrical industry at that time. Today there is a more abstract, theoretical character to what we expect our students to know. Many arrive at MIT without hands-on experience and never gain much familiarity with the concrete examples from which the abstractions have been drawn.

We cannot stop emphasizing the abstract, because our students need to understand concepts at that level. Our second challenge will be to ensure that the students can intuitively comprehend and appreciate the links between concrete examples and the related abstractions.

## BETTER IDEAS

Some advances in technology are unarguably superior to earlier technology and as a result completely replace it. A new memory chip may be smaller, consume less power, operate faster, and be more reliable than a chip from the previous generation. The older technology is rendered obsolete. Here are a few examples of such technology trends:

- **Smaller.** The trend in devices, from large to small to mini to micro to nano to quantum, will continue as far as the fundamental laws of physics will allow.
- **Faster.** The demand to speed things up shows no sign of slowing down.
- **Stronger.** The public deserves systems that are increasingly robust and secure.
- **Cheaper.** Modern digital systems have the unusual property that every year they cost less, thereby defying inflation.

It is not easy to teach a technology knowing that it could or will be replaced soon. How can we be sure that our graduates are prepared for the long run? Our third challenge is to continue to focus on the fundamentals that will remain valid and relevant during a graduate's forty-year career.

## COMPETING IDEAS

Some trends in technology and its applications do not make older approaches obsolete but merely less dominant. Here are a few examples from the past century:

- **Energy to information.** Our technologies are used for processing energy and information. Lately the emphasis has been on information, but that may or may not continue.

- **Analog to digital.** The noise immunity and universality of digital approaches let them compete in areas once characterized by analog techniques only. However, there will always be some requirements that can only be satisfied by analog techniques.

- **Inorganic to organic.** The incorporation of living systems, or components inspired by the study of living systems, is just starting, so it is too early to judge how their special properties may effectively compete with today's technologies.

These trends may or may not be reversible. The older ideas are not obsolete, or at least not yet. Our graduates should be able to evaluate competing ideas in particular circumstances. The fourth challenge to the department is to teach competing approaches and application areas without letting the new ideas crowd out older ideas that are still of substantial importance.

## MORE RESPONSIBILITY

Gordon Brown's educational vision is fifty years old and Dugald Jackson's twice that. These visions have been expressed here in terms of what engineers should be able to do—apply known techniques, develop new techniques from known science, and develop new engineering science. It falls on us, as heirs to these visions, to decide whether they are still sufficient, or if more should be expected of engineers today. My conclusion is that at least some of our graduates should be prepared to undertake a higher level of social responsibility. A bit of history beyond our department's will help explain this fifth challenge.

In 1893 the University of Wisconsin was small, with only 61 professors. One of them was Dugald Jackson, who had just established Wisconsin's department of electrical engineering. Another was the historian Frederick Jackson Turner, who that

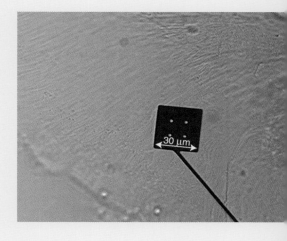

Research in 2002. Microscopic (30 micrometer) mechanical probe using MEMS technology in the research group of Professor Dennis M. Freeman. This photograph shows the probe inserted on the tectorial membrane to study transmission of sound-induced motions to the sensory receptor cells in the inner ear.

year revolutionized the study of American history. In a talk delivered at the Columbian Exposition in Chicago, Turner said that the existence of America's western frontier was "the fundamental, dominating fact" that had shaped the character of the American people and the nature of its institutions. This "Turner thesis" soon became the most important paradigm in the study of American history. (Jackson also attended the Columbian Exposition, and while there he and others founded what is today the American Society for Engineering Education.)

Jackson and Turner had much in common. They were about the same age. Each had worked in Chicago before coming to Wisconsin, had clear vision, could express himself well, and would in time become a leader in his own field. At one point the two men served together on a faculty committee to "consider the condition of athletics in the University"—evidently football rowdiness had led Turner to fear that human values were "put in wrong perspective and the fundamental purpose of the University lost sight of." Three years after Jackson came to MIT, Turner moved to Harvard.

Turner, the historian, understood in 1893 that the western frontier was rapidly vanishing, though its influence would remain. But presumably he did not know what the next dominating influence on America's development would be. It turned out to be a different frontier, one that would be familiar to his colleague Dugald Jackson.

Fifty years after Turner introduced his thesis, World War II was under way. Vannevar Bush, who had left the MIT electrical engineering department, was serving in Washington, D.C. In 1945 Bush wrote a seminal proposal for a system of federal support of scientific and engineering research and called it "Science: The Endless Frontier." Bush had a right to use this title because his own field, electrical engineering, was on that frontier. A young, vibrant, immature discipline, electrical engineering exploited scientific advances rapidly. The intellectual excitement of electrical engineering was a direct consequence of its proximity to the scientific frontier.

Besides being exciting, electrical engineering, and later computer science, have been essential to America's development. Their impact has been enormous. Consider the list of the ten "Greatest Engineering Achievements of the 20th Century," as judged by the National Academy of Engineering (NAE) in 2000. Half are based on EECS-related technologies—electrification, electronics, radio and television, computers, and telephone. (The other five—automobile, airplane, water supply, agriculture mechanization, and refrigeration—are more closely connected to other engineering disciplines.)

Although I am not a historian, it seems to me that the exploitation of this scientific frontier, especially by electrical engineers and computer scientists, has shaped America as much in the twentieth century as the western frontier did in earlier times. The successor to the Turner thesis, then, may be a similar thesis but one involving a different kind of frontier: the frontier of science.

Bush called the scientific frontier "endless." But is it, really? And will electrical engineering and computer science keep their privileged position on this frontier?

It does seem so. Many engineering achievements involving EECS technologies, including Internet, laser, World Wide Web, solar cell, embedded computation, signal processing, artificial intelligence, control systems, and MEMS, were not on the NAE top ten but seem poised to shape the twenty-first century. Or consider Moore's law, the famous observation by Gordon Moore in 1965 that the number of devices on an integrated circuit doubles every year or two. This trend has continued to this day and there is no end in sight, short of the limitations imposed by quantum mechanics (and even those may represent opportunities rather than obstacles). Whenever people try to predict when Moore's law will expire, they forget about the inventiveness of modern engineers and their ability to get around all but the most fundamental limits of nature.

So the coming years will, in my opinion, bring more and more exciting scientific advances to be exploited by our fields of engineering, and these technologies will exert a continuing influence on America and the rest of the world. In other words, in the twenty-first century, as in the twentieth, we will continue to live and work on an important frontier.

Life on the frontier is exciting. Research thrives where there is ambiguity, where much is unknown; overturning a major principle or law is considered a success, an accomplishment worthy of distinction. The disruptive, somewhat chaotic, character of frontier life is one we engineers relish.

But most institutions in a civilized society need stability and predictability. Consider what happened to America's western frontier. Civilization arrived and brought with it law and order. For better or for worse, the frontier became a more predictable and less exciting place.

Is it our turn now? Our scientific and engineering frontier is of critical importance to America. Must our frontier become "civilized"? History suggests that it must. In fact, it is already happening.

We are already confronting, and will continue to confront in the years ahead, tensions between the ambiguity inherent in the scientific frontier and the predictability required by society. Every day newspapers report examples of legal, political, and economic institutions grappling with new technologies that they only vaguely understand and often perceive as a threat. Think of the frictions between technological standardization and product differentiation. Or between intellectual property and information freedom. Think about why regulated monopolies resist new technology. Or why e-mail spam is such a problem.

The issue is not *whether* law and order will be established, but *how*. Will the crude tools available to America's legal, political, and economic systems be used to impose stability in a way that reduces the excitement that nourishes technological development? Will scientific studies of some types be restricted or even forbidden? Will long-established institutions resist the opportunities for improvement afforded by engineering advances? Or can society be persuaded to accept new technologies? Can the engineering community lead the movement for responsive and responsible change?

Dugald Jackson said in 1903 that engineers, besides knowing science, "must know men and the affairs of men ... must be acquainted with business methods and the affairs of the business world." In 1911 he expanded on this point, saying "It is the duty of engineers to do their share in molding their various economic creatures [companies and even sectors] so that the creatures may reach the greatest practicable usefulness to society." But both Jackson and Brown stopped short of saying that engineers should help the nation's institutions change to accommodate new technology.

Today, the need is different. Both science and society are changing rapidly, partly because of advances in technology. Because the institutions of modern society need to adapt to modern technology, they need help from those who fully comprehend that technology. In other words, society will be best served if we engineers take an active role.

The fifth challenge to this department, then, is to educate students so that at least some of them are prepared to help the world understand and embrace rapid changes in technology, and use them wisely. In my judgment, this is our most important challenge of all. If we meet it, society will be better off, and we will have earned the right to continue to work on the scientific frontier with all the excitement that we so cherish.

During the twentieth century, the department has had extraordinary faculty leaders, including department heads, associate department heads, executive officers, VI-A directors, and education officers. Many are pictured below. They have brought us to where we are today. Tomorrow's leaders, facing the challenges outlined here, will take us in new directions for the twenty-first century.

EECS Department leadership, 2003 and earlier. Front row (left to right): Markus Zahn, VI-A Director; Arthur C. Smith, Undergraduate and Graduate Officer; John V. Guttag, Department Head; Barbara H. Liskov, Associate Department Head from Computer Science; Rafael Reif, Associate Department Head from Electrical Engineering; Jeffrey H. Shapiro, former Associate Department Head from Electrical Engineering; J. Francis Reintjes, VI-A Director Emeritus. Back row (left to right): Louis D. Braida, former Executive Officer; Frederick C. Hennie III, Executive Officer Emeritus; Gerald L. Wilson, former Department Head and former Dean of Engineering; W. Eric Grimson, Education Officer; Tomás Lozano-Pérez, former Associate Department Head from Computer Science; Joel Moses, former Department Head, former Dean of Engineering, former Provost, and Institute Professor; Fernando J. Corbató, former Associate Department Head from Computer Science; Paul L. Penfield, Jr., former Department Head; Mildred S. Dresselhaus, former Associate Department Head from Electrical Engineering and Institute Professor.

# Laboratory
# Profiles

# ARTIFICIAL INTELLIGENCE LABORATORY

RODNEY BROOKS, PROFESSOR OF ELECTRICAL ENGINEERING AND COMPUTER SCIENCE, AND DIRECTOR, ARTIFICIAL INTELLIGENCE LABORATORY

Marvin Minsky was one of the original founders of the AI Lab.

The following photos demonstrate the change in robotics over time, culminating with the leg prosthesis developed by Hugh Herr.

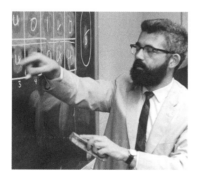

John McCarthy, one of the original founders of the AI Lab, discussing a garbage collection algorithm for Lisp, c. 1960

The MIT Artificial Intelligence Laboratory began as the Artificial Intelligence Project, founded in 1959 by John McCarthy and Marvin Minsky. McCarthy coined the term *artificial intelligence* in 1956 for a summer workshop at Dartmouth College to describe the idea of machines doing things that had previously been thought to require human intelligence. One of the attendees had been Minsky, then a Harvard junior fellow. McCarthy and Minsky had known each other as graduate students at Princeton, where Minsky wrote his thesis on the brand-new field of artificial neural networks. The two men eventually teamed up at MIT as junior faculty in the mathematics department and started the Artificial Intelligence Project as part of the Research Laboratory for Electronics.

The early days of the Artificial Intelligence Laboratory were concerned with producing the first tools for research in the field. McCarthy developed the Lisp programming language and contributed to the design of Algol. He also developed early ideas for time-sharing computers. McCarthy and Minsky consulted with the Digital Equipment Corporation on the design of the PDP-6 (which later became the DEC-10), making the machine code friendlier to recursive search programs and the maintenance of list structures. Minsky also worked on some of the foundational problems in the theory of computation and produced a landmark book in the field, *Computation: Finite and Infinite Machines*.

McCarthy left to found the Stanford Artificial Intelligence Laboratory in 1963, and for the next few years the MIT lab was codirected by Minsky and Seymour Papert as part of Project MAC. Early work was aimed at reproducing human intelligence — a program that could do all the problems in the MIT freshman calculus exam or that could play tournament-level chess. These were the sorts of things that educated, intelligent people could do, and they seemed natural starting points for reproducing human-level intelligence.

Work in the next few years concentrated on symbolic reasoning, including the development of programs that could solve word algebra problems, that could represent and reason about two-dimensional spatial relationships, that could learn from examples, and that could understand simple English text. There were efforts aimed at robotics and vision at different times throughout the 1960s, including the MH1 robot-hand project in 1961, the summer vision project in 1966, and in 1970 the copy-demo, a robot that looked at a stack of white blocks and made a copy. Minsky and Papert also pursued a deep mathematical analysis of the limitations of simple neural networks and published an extraordinarily influential book, *Perceptrons*. Simultaneously, staff members such as Tom Knight and Richard Greenblatt were developing new technologies such as the first bit-mapped displays, early techniques in time-sharing computers, early e-mail systems, and text-setting systems with variable-width fonts.

Tom Knight and Richard Greenblat standing next to Lisp machine, 1975

By 1970 the Artificial Intelligence Project had became a separate laboratory at MIT and its nature was changing. A number of students from the 1960s, including Gerry Sussman, Carl Hewitt, and Ira Goldstein, became faculty members and the lab expanded in size considerably. These researchers created novel approaches to knowledge representation and reasoning. Computer vision and robotics became key areas of research in the lab as one of Minsky's students, Patrick Winston, inherited the mantle of director. Funded largely by a single block grant from DARPA, a wide range of fundamental research was carried out. Reasoning and natural language continued to be of interest, while new ideas in knowledge representations (frames) and computer language design (object-oriented programming) were developed. But the lab also continued to innovate in the area of fundamental tools. This included early work on local area networks and one of the first personal computers— the Lisp Machine. The latter led to two spin-off companies, along with licensing the design to Texas Instruments. Other software efforts were also under way, including the development led by Richard Stallman of Emacs, which eventually spun out as GNU (self-recursively "GNU Is Not UNIX"), which in turn developed core tools for the Linux kernel along with the GNU C Compiler (GCC) and the development of Scheme. Scheme, a version of Lisp with simple, consistent syntax and semantics, which provide enormously powerful capabilities, is used today as a teaching language all over the world.

Tom Knight and his current work in molecular biology

By the late 1970s, computer-vision work had developed along two complementary approaches: physics-based vision (led by Berthold Horn) used fundamental insights into the formation of images to develop methods for recovering information about the world in front of a camera; and David Marr pioneered an approach that used models of human visual capabilities as a foundation for creating machine-vision methods. By the early 1980s, vision and robotics had become the dominant thrust of the AI Lab. These efforts were centered on

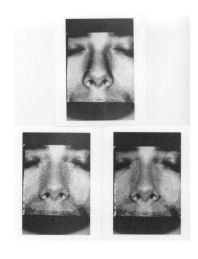

Berthold Horn's early work in shape from shading shows how the structure of a curved surface can be extracted from shading information.

Cog reaching and looking at its hand

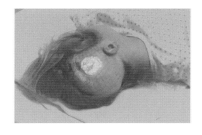

Eric Grimson's current medical-imaging work gives a surgeon "X-ray vision" to see the location of a tumor.

Gil Pratt's Spring Flamingo, a walking robot, was used to explore variable compliance in legs, which led to new work in developing prosthetic legs for amputees.

capabilities that even young children have—the abilities to see and recognize people and objects, to walk and navigate, and to reach for and manipulate objects. Tomás Lozano-Pérez created methods for planning robot motions, Marc Raibert sparked a wave of activity in legged robots, John Hollerbach and Ken Salisbury created dexterous robot hands, and Rod Brooks pioneered the subsumption approach to robot planning. By the early 1980s, the staff members, who in the early days had complemented the faculty by building tools, had largely left to participate in the companies that were spinning off from the laboratory.

As information technology began to have an impact on the world outside the lab, sparking massive investment in computer systems and networks, a place the size of the AI Lab could no longer both pursue first-rate research and produce new tools for computer science. Under Patrick Winston's gentle guidance, the laboratory opted for research. Key ideas developed at this time included Minsky's "society of mind" and the connection machine— Thinking Machines spun off from the lab to turn the latter architecture into reality.

Both the society of mind and the connection machine brought parallelism to AI. The society of mind provided a structure for intelligence as a collection of interacting and competing agents, each one with only limited understanding of the world, but together providing comprehensive context-aware intelligence. On another level, the connection machine, one of the world's largest supercomputers of its day, provided a general-purpose substrate for massively parallel components of intelligence such as vision and information retrieval.

During the late 1980s and into the early 1990s, the laboratory developed new approaches to mobile robotics and started to produce vision systems that were practical in the real world, most notably Eric Grimson's work in systems supporting image-guided surgery.

More companies continued to spin off from the AI Laboratory, such as Ascent Technology, a company that schedules gate allocations at many major airports in the world; Silicon Spice, a successful silicon design company; Imagen, a company that produces machines that visually inspect electronics production processes; and iRobot, a mobile robotics company.

By the turn of the century, artificial intelligence was no longer a weird futuristic technology. Although most people did not know it, AI was firmly in their lives, affecting the way their airline tickets were booked, how their flights were scheduled, how their mutual funds were managed, how their Hollywood entertainment was produced, how much of their personal computer software operated, how they searched the Web, how some of their home appliances worked, and how many of the artifacts in their world were designed.

In a mature field, the challenge for the AI Lab now is to find high leverage points where research can either have a deep impact on science or where ideas are so novel that the research products could penetrate existing markets and infrastructures. For instance, much of our work in vision and in motor control is intimately intertwined with understanding the human vision system and the human cerebellum—papers from lab members are published at both computer conferences and at neuroscience conferences. Recent work at the lab in machine learning has deep connections to mathematics and science in its own right, but is now also being used in the service of other science as tools for understanding aspects of the human genome.

While we continue to develop fundamental technologies within the lab in computer vision, robotics, natural language, and graphics, we are also pushing into new areas. Over the last handful of years we have added a new generation of young faculty such as Leslie Kaelbling and Tommi Jaakkola, who contribute particular strengths in machine learning. We have multiple initiatives at the intersection of computation and biology, some in the service of understanding biological systems better, and some in using biology as a radical new substrate for engineering. A number of newer projects applying AI and robotics to medicine have grown out of this intersection.

We are also working with the Laboratory for Computer Science (LCS) as part of Project Oxygen, an effort to develop human-centered pervasive computing. Over the last twenty years we have all found ourselves drawn into the virtual desktop world of our computers. Within Oxygen, the AI Lab is trying to reverse this process by developing perceptual interfaces in which computers can see and hear people as they work in normal office environments, understanding their gaze direction, their gestures, and their sketches, and then provide appropriate computational resources for what the users really want to do.

The Artificial Intelligence Laboratory is larger than ever, with 70 faculty and staff, 170 graduate students, 40 undergraduates, and another 20 research affiliates and visitors. Our funding is roughly 65 percent from the U.S. government and the rest from private companies. There are plenty of things we do not yet know how to do with computers, and so there will be plenty of new and fresh challenges for the lab in the future.

Hugh Herr with a prosthetic leg that senses how he is walking and responds appropriately, permitting him to climb stairs or walk on soft ground

Randy Davis's sketching tablet, part of Project Oxygen

# LABORATORY FOR COMPUTER SCIENCE

VICTOR ZUE, PROFESSOR,
ELECTRICAL ENGINEERING
AND COMPUTER SCIENCE,
AND DIRECTOR, LABORATORY
FOR COMPUTER SCIENCE

The MIT Laboratory for Computer Science (LCS) grew out of Project MAC, which was established at MIT largely through the efforts of J.C.R. Licklider and Robert Fano. Professor Licklider had long been an advocate of interactive computing, that is, humans working interactively and symbiotically with computers to solve problems. In 1962, after Licklider became director of the newly formed Information Processing Techniques Office within the Department of Defense's Advanced Research Projects Agency (ARPA), he and Fano discussed the central role that MIT could play in establishing this new research direction. Project MAC was launched in the spring of 1963, with a research grant from ARPA and Fano as its founding director. Fano chose the acronym MAC to characterize both the project's means—*multiple access computing*—and its ends—*machine-aided cognition*.

On the multiple-access computing side of the ledger, Project MAC developed the Compatible Time-Sharing System (CTSS), one of the earliest of the time-sharing systems that transformed computing from a batch-mode process to an interactive one. The CTSS development effort was led by Fernando Corbató, who received the 1990 Turing Award for his work. Another ambitious effort during the early days of Project MAC was the development of an operating system called MULTiplexed Information and Computing Service, or MULTICS. The project was also led by Corbató and included a luminous group of researchers including Jack Dennis, Jerry Salzer, and David Clark. Many of MULTICS's pioneering concepts were later captured in the well-known UNIX operating system developed at Bell Laboratories.

The machine-aided cognition thrust, led by Marvin Minsky, explored the workings of the human mind and the nature of intelligence. Professor Minsky's work played a central role in the formation of the field of artificial intelligence, for which he received the Turing Award in 1969. But by 1970, the research agenda for this thrust had diverged substantially from multiple-access computing. Minsky and his AI colleagues split off from Project MAC to form the Artificial Intelligence Laboratory (AI Lab).

From left: Professors Claude Shannon, John McCarthy, Ed Fredkin, and Joseph Wiesenbaum in April 1968

Professor William A. Martin, a graduate student, and Professor J.C.R. Licklider, c. 1975

From left, MIT students in the Computation Center of Building 26, circa 1960; beginnings of multiple users for a computer as demonstrated by students working under Richard Greenblatt in the mid 1960s; MIT students working at computers in one of many Athena Clusters distributed throughout the campus, January, 1990.

Associate Director of the Lab for Computer Science, Joel Moses (standing) and Patrick Winston, Director of the Artificial Intelligence Lab, pictured in the late 1970s

Technology Square, the forty-year home for Project MAC (1963–1974) and LCS

In 1968, Licklider returned to MIT to become the second director of Project MAC. Licklider's vision and influence can still be seen in much of the research being conducted today at LCS and elsewhere.

In 1971, Professor Ed Fredkin took over from Licklider as the third director of Project MAC. He was succeeded in 1974 by Professor Michael Dertouzos, who stayed on as director of LCS for twenty-seven years, until his death in August 2001. Dertouzos was succeeded by Professor Victor Zue.

In 1975, Project MAC was renamed the Laboratory for Computer Science. During his long tenure, Dertouzos helped shape the direction of LCS research. Under his leadership, members of LCS dedicated themselves to the invention, development, and understanding of information technologies, always within the context of their human utility. "We feel extraordinarily privileged to have a hand in shaping the Information Revolution—the third major socioeconomic movement of our world," he said,

*But our quest goes beyond utilitarian increases in human productivity to the broader ways in which information can help people. We find ourselves in the junction of two interrelated challenges: going after the best, most exciting forefront technology; and ensuring that it truly serves human needs. It is this mixture of forefront technology and human utility that is the hallmark of LCS research.*

Indeed, LCS members and alumni have been instrumental in the development of many computer science and information technology innovations, including time-sharing computing, ARPANet, the Internet, the Ethernet, the World Wide Web, RSA public-key encryption, and many more (see http://timeline.lcs.mit.edu/). Many of these technologies have benefited society through companies such as 3Com, Akamai, Open Market, SightPath, RSA Data Security, and SpeechWorks (see http://www.lcs.mit.edu/about/spinoffs.html). LCS has also played an active role in standards setting by hosting the X Consortium and the World Wide Web Consortium (W3C). With nearly five hundred member organizations, the W3C helps set the standards for a continuously evolving World Wide Web.

As an interdepartmental laboratory in the School of Engineering at MIT, LCS brings together faculty, researchers, and students in a broad program of study, research, and experimentation. The laboratory's membership comprises just over 500 people, including 112 faculty and researchers, 287 graduate students, 76 visitors, affiliates, postdoctoral associates, and fellows, and 34 support and administrative staff. In addition, many undergraduate students are affiliated with the laboratory, primarily through MIT's Undergraduate Research Opportunities Program (UROP).

The laboratory's current research falls into four broad categories: theory of computation, computer systems, compilers and machine architecture, and intelligent interfaces.

In the theory of computation area, we study the theoretical underpinnings of computer science and information technology, including work on algorithms, cryptography and information security, complexity theory, and the theoretical bases of systems and programming languages. Fundamental contributions to computer science made by members of the theory group include the work of Ron Rivest on RSA public-key encryption technology; Silvio Micali and Shafi Goldwasser on zero-knowledge proofs; Madhu Sudan on probabilistically correct proofs; David Karger on randomized algorithms; Albert Meyer on programming-language semantics; Nancy Lynch on theory of distributed systems; and Charles Leiserson on theory and practice of parallel computing.

In the area of computer systems, we wish to understand principles and develop technologies for the architecture and use of highly scaleable information infrastructures that interconnect human-operated and autonomous computers. Research in this area encompasses work on networks and systems, as well as on the structure of software. Research on networks and systems increasingly addresses issues of mobile and context-aware networking, and the development of high-performance, practical software systems for parallel and distributed environments. Our research on software is directed toward improving the performance, reliability, availability, and security of computer software by improving the methods used to create and reason about it. Our recent contributions in the computer systems area include the work of Frans Kaashoek on improving operating system performance and correctness through the use of a very small Exokernel; Robert Morris on the Roofnet technology for ad hoc networking; Barbara Liskov on Byzantine fault-tolerant replication algorithms that perform efficiently and correctly even when machines fail arbitrarily; Hari Balakrishnan on the Cricket location-support system; Daniel Jackson on the Alloy tool for finding bugs in software; Michael Ernst on techniques for deriving specifications from code; John Guttag on capturing and analyzing medical information through sensor nets; and David Gifford on computational biology.

In the area of compilers and machine architecture, we are interested in providing better support for programmers through the use of more sophisticated compiler technology and in developing new machine security. Our work includes creating architectural innovations by

Michael Dertouzos (seated left), Professor Victor Zue (standing on the right), and principal research scientist James Glass (seated to Zue's right) observe former U.S. Vice President Al Gore sample a conversational interface demo in 1996.

Artificial Intelligence Lab Director Rodney Brooks (left) speaking in 1998 at the Nippon Telephone and Telegraph Corporation and MIT (NTT-MIT) Collaboration Launch in Tokyo. Michael Dertouzos, LCS Director, and Victor Zue, Associate Director of LCS, are seated to Brooks's left.

From left, Professors Robert Morris, Hari Balakrishnan, and Frans Kaashoek attach a low-cost beacon for the Cricket indoor location support system, a part of the project known as Oxygen, 2002.

directly compiling applications onto programmable hardware, providing software-controlled architectures for low energy, better cache management, and easier hardware design and verification. Notable achievements include the work of Anant Agarwal on the Reconfigurable Architecture Workstation (RAW) chip; Krste Asanovic on low-power machine architectures; Srini Devadas on secure hardware; Arvind on data-flow computing; Steve Ward on the NU bus; Saman Amarasinghe on new approaches to optimizing compilers; and Martin Rinard on new programming language features that allow more errors to be found at compile time.

In the intelligent interfaces area, our technical goals are to understand and construct programs and machines that have greater and more useful sensory and cognitive capabilities so that they may communicate with people toward useful ends. Our research is focused on spoken dialog systems between people and machines, computer graphics, and use of computers in healthcare. Our accomplishments include the work of Victor Zue and his group on the Jupiter system, through which one can obtain weather information using spoken dialogue; the work of Seth Teller on the city-scanning system, which can produce three-dimensional models of a large geographic area from images captured by autonomous mobile sensors; and the work of Peter Szolovits on the guardian angel project, which facilitates better patient-centered healthcare delivery.

In recent years, LCS has increasingly collaborated with our sister lab, the AI Lab. An example of such collaboration is a project called Oxygen. Launched in 2000 and in partnership with six world-class companies—Acer, Delta Electronics, Hewlett Packard, Nokia, NTT, and Philips—Oxygen strives to evoke revolutionary changes in the ways computers and humans interact. In the future, computers will need to fit into the human world as part of our everyday lives.

LCS Director Michael Dertouzos introduces Tim Berners-Lee at the thirty-fifth anniversary of the Lab for Computer Science, held 12–14 April 1999.

LCS's increased collaboration with the AI Lab has led to greater intellectual energy, expanded research opportunities, and a general lowering of boundaries. This climate, coupled with our impending move into the Stata Center in 2004, has offered us the opportunity to permanently remove the boundaries set up more than three decades ago. By the time you read this, the merge of LCS and AI as the Computer Science and Artificial Intelligence Laboratory (CSAIL) will be complete. We take great pleasure in this generational change as the Department of Electrical Engineering and Computer Science moves into its second century.

More information on the Laboratory for Computer Science can be found at: http://www.lcs.mit.edu. More than 270 abstracts of our research can be found at http://www.lcs.mit.edu/research/abstract/pdf/LCSAbstracts2003.pdf.

# LABORATORY FOR ELECTROMAGNETIC AND ELECTRONIC SYSTEMS

JOHN KASSAKIAN, PROFESSOR OF ELECTRICAL ENGINEERING AND DIRECTOR, LABORATORY FOR ELECTROMAGNETIC AND ELECTRONIC SYSTEMS

The Laboratory for Electromagnetic and Electronic Systems (LEES) is an interdepartmental laboratory in the School of Engineering. Its principal focus is the generation, control, and processing of electrical energy for practical purposes.

LEES is the successor laboratory to several other laboratories, whose collective contribution to electric power technology represents a proud tradition of the application of engineering science to problems of fundamental importance to society.

The oldest of the predecessor laboratories is the High Voltage Research Laboratory (HVRL). HVRL, located in Building N10, was where Professor John G. Trump carried out prestigious research for over four decades between the mid 1940s and mid 1980s. Professor Trump's work in HVRL had its origins in the 1930s, when he worked with Professor Robert J. Van de Graaff to develop electrostatic generators. Van de Graaff generators, still known by that name, are used in specialized applications to this day. Trump applied the ability to generate high voltages to produce beams of high-energy charged particles, and he pioneered the use of these particle and electron beams in many important practical applications. High-energy beams were used in the development of vacuum-insulated and high-pressure gas-insulated power transmission systems, advancing our ability to transmit electric power. These beams elevated radiation cancer therapy from the experimental stage to clinical practice, and powered the sterilization of food and of sewage.

Today, the high-energy electron beam facility and multiple compact sources of controlled high voltage comprise a facility that is useful for modern research and is the only one of its kind at MIT. Dr. Chathan M. Cooke, who worked with Trump for many years, continues the application of high-voltage engineering science to power apparatus.

Gerald Wilson (standing on left), John Kassakian, and James Kirtley at the MIT-EPSEL model power system used to study power-system dynamics and control

Professor John G. Trump, c. 1939, with the electrostatic X-ray generator, which was involved in his ongoing research in high voltage

The second predecessor laboratory to LEES was the Electric Power Systems Engineering Laboratory (EPSEL). EPSEL began in 1967 in Building 3 as the Power Systems Engineering Group (PSEG) under the direction of Herbert Woodson. He and Professor Gerald Wilson established the PSEG to address challenging problems in the electric utility industry, such as audible noise and system stability, as the industry was moving to higher transmission voltages and generator powers. Professors Fred Schweppe and Charles Kingsley joined the group shortly after its establishment. Kingsley contributed his vast knowledge of rotating machinery, and Schweppe brought with him expertise in control, which he applied to power systems. Woodson, Schweppe, and Wilson had excellent connections with American Electric Power (AEP), and the lab did extensive research on the modeling and behavior of AEP's 765 kV network during its development. In 1969 the laboratory began research on a superconducting generator in collaboration with Mechanical Engineering Professor Joseph Smith and the Cryogenic Engineering Laboratory. James L. Kirtley joined the laboratory in 1972, focusing his attention on the superconducting generator. This activity persisted for over a decade, producing seminal results in the area of superconducting rotating machine technology.

Having outgrown its space in Building 3, the laboratory moved to the basement of Building 10 in 1970, with a headquarters office on the first floor of Building 10. At the same time, the name Electric Power Systems Engineering Laboratory (EPSEL) was adopted, because it was now too large to be called a "group."

Graduate student Donald Bosack works on his doctoral thesis on audible noise from high voltage–transmission lines under simulated wet conditions, c. 1971.

By occupying space in the basement of Building 10, EPSEL was reconnecting in an important symbolic way with the proud history of electric power engineering at MIT. In the 1920s, Professors Waldo V. Lyon and Ralph R. Lawrence carried out their research on alternating-current machinery in the basement of Building 10. It was here that Lyon encouraged Professor Harold E. Edgerton to develop the stroboscope as a means for studying machine transients and it was here that Professors A.E. Fitzgerald and Charles Kingsley, Jr. developed their classic text *Electric Machinery*. In the 1950s, it was also here that Professors David C. White and Herbert H. Woodson developed the generalized machine and the text *Electromechanical Energy Conversion*.

In 1971, Wilson replaced Woodson as director of EPSEL. In the subsequent years, Wilson firmly established EPSEL as a laboratory dealing effectively with both traditional and novel problems faced by the utilities. In the process, Wilson encouraged a broadening of the EPSEL purview.

The connection between EPSEL and the history of power engineering at MIT was not solely symbolic. The basement space in Building 10 was selected at least in part because it was already equipped with high-power wiring from the MIT utility grid.

In 1973, when John Kassakian joined the EECS faculty and EPSEL, he introduced power electronics to the department's curriculum and the laboratory's research program. The appointments of George Verghese in 1979 and Martin F. Schlecht in 1983 further strengthened the laboratory's activities in this area. In 1991, Kassakian, Schlecht, and Verghese collaborated to write *Principles of Power Electronics*. Conducting activities that involved both EPSEL and the Microsystems Technology Laboratories, Schlecht brought microfabrication expertise to the laboratory. Verghese contributed, and continues to contribute, expertise in the control of electric power systems.

Professor Martin Schlecht as a graduate student, in 1981, working on his doctoral thesis, a "Harmonic Free Utility DC/DC Power Conditioning Interface," under Professor Kassakian's supervision

The third predecessor laboratory to LEES was the Continuum Electromechanics Laboratory (CEL). This laboratory began as the research group of Professor James R. Melcher (who during the 1960s also worked closely with Woodson, coauthoring the three-volume text *Electromechanical Dynamics* and authoring the monograph *Field Coupled Surface Waves*). With engineering applications that ranged from air-pollution control to biosystems, but with a specific interest in electrohydrodynamics, Melcher's approach was inspired by those used in MHD power generation, fusion research, electron beam engineering, and other specialized areas where mathematical models are formulated, tested, and made not only to help explain phenomena of industrial interest, but also to promote invention. Melcher developed his text *Continuum Electromechanics* to support this interdisciplinary and basic approach, which is the hallmark of LEES today.

CEL first came into existence when Melcher realized that special devotion was necessary to do justice to the continuum electromechanics of physiological systems. In the 1970s and 1980s, Alan J. Grodzinsky, Martha Gray, and Raphael C. Lee worked in this lab applying continuum electromechanics to biological systems.

Joining the CEL in 1980, Professor Jeffrey H. Lang combined research in power electronics and control with research in digital electronics and continuum electromechanics.

Professor Wilson was appointed head of the EECS department in 1978 and later became the dean of Engineering. He continued serving as director of EPSEL until Thomas H. Lee became director in 1982. Under Lee's leadership, the laboratory expanded to include the HVRL and the CEL. This broadened the scope of the laboratory's activities to include the contributions of

Graduate student Barry Culpepper cultivating his master's thesis on a radio frequency dc/dc converter, in 1987

Melcher, Cooke, Lang, Grodzinsky, and Gray. Additionally, Professor Markus Zahn, author of *Electromagnetic Field Theory: A Problem Solving Approach* and researcher in both continuum electromechanics and high voltage effects, became part of the laboratory during this reorganization. In 1983, the name of the laboratory was changed to the Laboratory for Electromagnetic and Electronic Systems to more accurately reflect its breadth of interests.

In 1984 Thomas Lee handed the reins to Melcher. Under Melcher's leadership the laboratory engaged in an aggressive program to apply its work in signal processing, sensors, and power systems to the real-time monitoring of power system apparatus.

Professor Kassakian was appointed director in 1991. At about that time the electric utility industry began a period of restructuring and uncertainty, one of the results of which was reduced support for research. The consequence for LEES was ironic in that the restructuring was largely driven by the work of Schweppe and Richard Tabors, a LEES senior research scientist, on deregulation and spot pricing of electricity and their 1988 book, *Spot Pricing of Electricity*. Since then, the laboratory's activities in the electric utility area have largely been superseded by research on new applications of power electronics, automotive electrical and electronic systems, micro-electromechanical systems (MEMS), and sensor and control systems. Typical of this new direction is Jeffrey Lang's work on silicon micro-mechanical turbine-generator devices, Steven Leeb's work on polymer gel-based sensors, David Perreault's development of a new technology for capacitor fabrication, and Mark Zahn's work on dielectric sensors for land mine detection. A diverse portfolio indeed. The recent addition of Joel Schindall, Bernard T. Gordon Professor of the Practice, to the laboratory's faculty has strengthened the laboratory's activities in product development.

Professors Jeffrey Lang and John Kassakian hosting a visit to LEES by His Majesty, King Mowati II of Swaziland, 1991

In recent years, an important activity has been the MIT/Industry Consortium on Advanced Automotive Electrical/Electronic Components and Systems. This consortium has attracted attention from around the world. Member companies include major automakers and auto parts companies from Europe, Asia, and North America. A proliferation of what were once luxury features in mainstream autos and of the increased use of electronic control systems in automobiles has produced a growth in the need for electric power on autos. The industry is reaching the level at which new techniques and technologies will be required to meet the demand. The laboratory's core skills in power electronics, electromagnetics, continuum electromechanics, and other fundamental electrotechnologies make LEES an excellent place to investigate how to use electricity to make better automobiles in the future. Even this seemingly mundane subject has introduced a vital array of interesting new research directions, ranging from the application of modern photonics and thermophotovoltaic power generation to the application of carbon nanotubes to advanced electric energy storage devices.

Principal Research Scientist Dr. Thomas Keim and graduate students Frank O'Sullivan and Ivan Celanovic discuss the apparatus used in testing at 1500K LEES-designed thermophotovoltaic devices using photonic bandgap filters and selective emitters.

Since its inception as the PSEG, the laboratory's funding has been dominated by private industry. As a consequence, the contexts of its research have varied with time as the needs of industry and society change, while the fundamental physics underlying the laboratory's mission remain constant. The automotive industry is currently the largest source of support. A recent grant from the Tyco Foundation and an allocation from the automotive consortium have made possible the planned renovation of space to provide new resources for MEMS and related automotive research.

LEES exists in an open physical architecture unique among laboratories at MIT. The large laboratory area in the basement of Building 10, as well as most instrumentation and equipment, is shared by all members of the laboratory. Graduate student offices, and some faculty offices, are in this space as well. Consequently the laboratory has always enjoyed a very collegial atmosphere and a close relationship between students and faculty. Of course such "communal living" occasionally presents challenges, but these become part of the educational experience for our students (and often for our faculty). Researchers in LEES cannot wall themselves off with their research. Questions and suggestions from others, some with a vastly different research focus, are unavoidable. Collaborative investigations among LEES faculty members, and between LEES personnel and others, are common.

Graduate students Yihui Qiu and Tushar Parlikar work on a unique design for an electrically actuated internal combustion-engine valve drive.

Over the years the laboratory has fielded intramural teams in baseball, basketball, and soccer—occasionally winning a league championship. Several LEES students are responsible for starting the MIT Rugby Club, which resulted in a year of crutches and canes littering the lab. A twenty-year tradition is the annual Tour de Cape bicycle ride from MIT to Provincetown—a four-day, late spring event, which many participants thought they'd never be able to complete. Several Boston Harbor cruises on MIT's sloop *Aleida*, under the command of Lang and Kassakian, have introduced students to the joy of sailing and the side effects of Dramamine.

LEES alumni are making notable contributions to industry, government, and academia. Many have started companies, one of which, American Power Conversion Corporation, was for a time the fastest-growing member of the NASDAQ. The laboratory presently consists of eight faculty, three principal research engineers, one research specialist, three support staff, approximately thirty-five graduate students, and six undergraduates. The faculty are all engaged in both graduate and undergraduate teaching. With energy an increasingly important international issue, the multidisciplinary talents, experience, and facilities available within LEES are continuing to be called on by industry and government to address the critical needs of the twenty-first century. The laboratory is an exciting place to be in these exciting times.

1983 bike trip to Cape Cod (left to right: Chris Kecae, Dave Otten, Mike Slepian, Dave Torrey, Leo Casey, John G. Kassakian, Tom Warner, Gary Fedder, and Marty Schlecht)

# LABORATORY FOR INFORMATION AND DECISION SYSTEMS

ROBERT G. GALLAGER,
VINCENT W.S. CHAN,
SANJOY K. MITTER,
J. FRANCIS REINTJES,
AND LAUREN J. CLARK

The Laboratory for Information and Decision Systems (LIDS) is among the distinguished research centers at MIT that have their roots in World War II. It is an outgrowth of the Servomechanisms Laboratory, established in 1940 by Professor Gordon S. Brown. During the war, the Servo Lab developed a wide variety of servo-controllers urgently needed for military gun systems. Brown directed the laboratory until 1952, when, as the new electrical engineering department head, he led the effort to modernize the EE curriculum by increasing emphasis on mathematics and physics.

Professor Gordon S. Brown, first director of the Laboratory for Information and Decision Systems

LIDS's mission today has evolved far beyond its pragmatic origins in World War II. The control system area is now but one of several research areas related to the current laboratory's broader focus on systems. The other systems-related areas include optimization, signal processing, communication, and networks.

Each of these research areas covers basic theoretical studies through applications in the communication, computer, control, electronics, and aerospace industries. A major strength of the modern LIDS is the extent to which basic theoretical research and application engineering are intertwined.

The wartime work on gun control helped lay the foundations for feedback control, as exemplified in the 1948 textbook *Principles of Servomechanisms*, by Gordon Brown and Donald Campbell. These principles were central to postwar innovations in areas as diverse as the numerical control of machine tools, chemical process control, and the design of computers. In the same year, the renowned MIT mathematician Norbert Wiener published his book on cybernetics, the study of communication and control systems in animals, machines, and organizations. The book had an enormous effect on the later evolution of feedback control and many aspects of engineering.

The Servo Lab's late wartime project to develop a digital flight simulator for the Navy resulted in Whirlwind I, the first major digital computer. In addition to being a milestone in the history of digital computation, the Whirlwind project demonstrated the crucial role that computation would play in control systems.

Jay Forrester, who would later invent the magnetic core memory and create the field of system dynamics, headed the Whirlwind project. Whirlwind was never used as an aircraft simulator, but it played a key role in the development of the U.S. continental air defense system.

After 1945, the laboratory continued to study advanced servo designs for military systems, but it also branched into other areas. Most notably, it developed the rod control system for the Brookhaven National Laboratory's nuclear reactor, along with the first numerically controlled milling machine. The milling machine project marked the introduction of the digital computer as a control element in feedback-control systems and led to a host of other applications where real-time control is required.

This work led naturally to two other projects with industrial applications: the Automatically Programmed Tool (APT) project of the 1950s and the Computer-Aided Design (CAD) project of the early 1960s. The former produced what was perhaps the first major special-

Jay Forrester, at left, with Project Whirlwind

purpose computer language designed for users without special programming training. The latter project was the root of the CAD/CAM field.

Through the 1950s and 1960s, under the leadership of Professor J. Francis Reintjes, the laboratory worked on a rich mixture of large application-oriented projects, ranging from radar systems to computer displays. It acknowledged this broader system focus by changing its name to the Electronic Systems Laboratory (ESL) in 1959.

Reintjes led perhaps the largest project of the newly named laboratory: Project INTREX (INformation TRansfer EXperiments). Project INTREX applied modern digital-electronic techniques to store and retrieve information on technical journal literature. It was an important step toward the automated library with guaranteed, simultaneous remote access by multiple users.

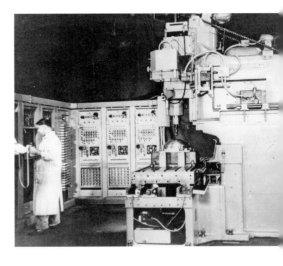

Numerically controlled milling machine, developed at the MIT Servomechanisms Laboratory, c. 1953

To the graduate students and faculty who were pursuing basic research in the control area concurrently with the application-oriented projects in ESL, it was becoming increasingly clear even by 1960 that conventional control theory, with its focus on linear deterministic systems, was no longer adequate. Important problems of the day, such as the control of space vehicles in the U.S. space program, required major fundamental advances.

A dynamic and gifted group of young, mathematically oriented control theorists joined the ESL faculty during the 1960s, including Michael Athans, Roger Brockett, Sanjoy Mitter, Jan Willems, and George Zames. These researchers, plus their students and numerous visitors, created what has been called the Golden Age of Control at MIT. Optimal control, stochastic control, nonlinear control, large-scale systems, stability theory—all were developed during this period, with ESL playing a leadership role. MIT's electrical engineering graduate curriculum in control underwent major development in this period under the leadership of these new faculty members.

Professor J. Francis Reintjes, who lectured in the department in seven different decades

The culture and focus of the laboratory changed during the 1960s as the earlier focus on application-oriented projects shifted. By the mid 1960s, the excitement about fundamental issues led to a search for simple models to explain the new research results. Application-based projects then started to become a test bed for understanding new theoretical advances and for pinpointing important gaps in the new theories.

When Michael Athans became director of the laboratory in 1974 he not only encouraged this cultural shift but also broadened the activities of ESL. Projects during this

Left to right: Professors Leonard Gould, Sanjoy Mitter, Michael Athans, Jan Willems, and Fred Schweppe

period tackled such diverse problems as adaptive control and failure detection systems for the NASA F-8 aircraft, automated detection and control of freeway traffic, and automated manufacturing.

By 1978, it was becoming clear that most large control systems have an important communication component and that communication systems, particularly networks, have important control aspects. Because the research methodologies used in these two fields are based on the same mathematical disciplines, it was natural for the communication and information theory group from the Research Laboratory of Electronics to join with ESL to form the Laboratory for Information and Decision Systems.

The information theory group at MIT had made an illustrious name for itself in the 1950s and 1960s by developing Professor Claude E. Shannon's information theory, converting it from a beautiful theory to its present-day role as the architectural and conceptual guide to modern digital communication. In the 1970s, the work of this group focused increasingly on digital networks as a whole rather than on the individual links of those networks.

The most important problems for the fledgling networks of the 1970s were routing, congestion control, and distributed control algorithms. All of these were ideal research topics for the newly combined control and communication faculty at LIDS. Meanwhile, the LIDS/C3 group explored large-scale system and communication issues in military command, control, and communication (C3) systems. This work, funded by the Office of Naval Research and the Air Force Office of Scientific Research, began in 1977 and continued until 1990.

Professors Robert Gallager (left) and David G. Forney

In the late 1970s and 1980s, LIDS continued to pioneer the fields of systems, control, and data communication. Its research in robust multivariable and adaptive control, random fields and failure detection, and linear and nonlinear filtering theory made it a leader in systems and control theory. Its communication research in networks, as well as wireless communication, optical communication, coding, and multiaccess information theory, has been recognized as unique.

Professor Sanjoy K. Mitter took over directorship of the laboratory in 1981. Under his leadership, with later assistance from Professor Robert G. Gallager (appointed codirector in 1986), LIDS faculty recognized that the laboratory needed to broaden its intellectual horizon to include systems—for example, vision and speech systems integrated with hierarchical control systems—where well-defined models based on differential equations and stochastic processes were not available.

The Center for Intelligent Control Systems (CICS), an interuniversity collaborative involving Brown, Harvard, and MIT, formed in 1986 with its headquarters in LIDS. The intellectual charter of the center was to carry out foundational work on intelligent systems, which required models at different levels of abstraction and uncertainties at different levels of granularity.

As part of this intellectual charter, the center made fundamental contributions in image analysis and vision, hybrid control systems, and multiscale statistical signal processing. It also furthered fundamental understanding of the interaction between information and control.

Today, under the directorship of Professor Vincent W.S. Chan, research at LIDS falls into the following four areas:

**Communication and Networks.** Research in this area includes fundamental work on networks, information theory, and communication theory. The work extends to applications in satellite, wireless and optical communications, and data networks. The objective is to develop the scientific base needed to design data communication networks that are efficient, robust, and architecturally clean. Wide area and local area networks, high-speed networks, and point-to-point and broadcast communication channels are of concern. Current topics include network architectures at all layers; power control; multiple antenna techniques; network coding; media access control protocols; routing in optical, wireless, and satellite networks; quality of service control; failure recovery; topological design; and the use of pricing as a mechanism for efficient resource allocation.

LIDS Director Vincent Chan speaks at the LIDS student conference in 2003.

**Control and System Theory.** The control systems group deals with problems related to complete systems analysis design. These include learning and system identification, controller design and optimization, and basic analysis of distributed systems involving the interaction of information and control. Theoretical research quantifies the fundamental limitations and capabilities of learning and feedback control for various classes of systems in the presence of dynamic uncertainty. Application-oriented work includes control architectures for single and multiple unmanned aerial vehicles and controllers for piloting epitaxy in semiconductor manufacturing. The control group is also involved in a research effort focusing on modeling aspects of the nervous system, conducted in collaboration with other laboratories.

LIDS graduate students (from left to right): Desmond Lun, Siddharth Ray, Todd Coleman, Guy Weichenberg Nathanial Peranginangin, and Minkyu Kim (seated)

**Optimization.** Work in this area looks at analytical and computational methods for solving broad classes of optimization problems arising in engineering and operations research. It

Mohsen Razavi working in the optics lab on a joint LIDS-RLE communications project, c. 2002

has applications in communication networks, control theory, power systems, and computer-aided manufacturing. In addition to traditional subjects in linear, nonlinear, dynamic, convex, and network programming, there is an emphasis on the solution of large-scale problems, including the application of neurodynamic programming methods.

**Statistical Signal Processing.** This group analyzes complex systems, phenomena, and data subject to uncertainty and statistical variability. Research spans the spectrum from broadly applicable basic theory, methodologies, and algorithms to challenging applications in an array of fields. Recent applications for this research include multisensor data assimilation for oceanography, hydrology, and meteorology; biomedical image analysis; object recognition and computer vision; and coordinated sensing and processing of large, distributed arrays of microsensors.

LIDS is home to approximately 130 graduate students and postdoctoral associates primarily from EECS but with major additions from the Department of Aeronautics and Astronautics and the School of Management. Research opportunities are also available for undergraduate students. Recognizing that it is usually more difficult to ask the right question than to answer it, LIDS encourages and helps students to define their own research problems. In addition, the weekly LIDS colloquia and frequent seminars by internal and visiting scholars provide the students with constant stimulation and diversity.

One of the helicopters from the Autonomous Agile Helicopter project on a demonstration flight above MIT, March 2002

The intellectual culture at LIDS encourages students, postdocs, and faculty to develop conceptual structures and to apply these structures to important engineering problems. This is done in a cooperative atmosphere of sharing ideas and questions. This culture is particularly evident each January at the LIDS Student Colloquium, a two-day event at which students present work in a variety of areas. The doctoral students and postdoctoral fellows supported by the laboratory over the past sixty years represent a who's who of industry and academia in the fields of systems, control, communication, and signal processing. In the words of one LIDS alumnus,

*The abilities and perspectives developed through the LIDS experience transcend any specific application, and as such are of lasting value and transportable to different fields. The accomplishments of the lab's alumni in industry and academia in a broad range of fields are evidence of the value of its approach.*

More information on LIDS can be found at http://lids.mit.edu/.

# MICROSYSTEMS TECHNOLOGY LABORATORIES

MARTIN A. SCHMIDT,
DIRECTOR
JUDY L. HOYT,
ASSOCIATE DIRECTOR

Technician at the wafer-cleaning station in the Technology Research Lab of MTL

James M. Carter, research specialist (left), with Eric Anderson working at the X-ray lithography system in 1983

The Microsystems Technology Laboratories (MTL) is an interdisciplinary MIT laboratory consisting of faculty, staff, and students interested in micro- and nanofabrication, microelectronics, and circuits/systems design and testing. MTL houses cleanroom facilities and infrastructure for carrying out research in those areas. The laboratory also features an advisory board called the Microsystems Industrial Group (MIG) that consists of corporations that are interested in guiding MTL's research agenda, interacting with MIT students and their research, and recruiting MIT graduates. The MIG also provides annual contributions that assist in the funding of the laboratory.

Integrated circuits, which form the electronic building blocks of everything associated with the information revolution (e.g., computers), increased in complexity during the 1970s to the point that automated techniques became required to design them. In addition, researchers realized that integrated circuits could form the basis of whole new classes of electronic systems, including systems that sensed the environment and reacted to it, as well as performing computing and communicating functions. In response to this tremendous growth of the integrated circuit industry, MTL was formed in the early 1980s within the EECS department. Research themes included circuit design, silicon fabrication technologies, computer architecture, and microsystems, incorporating novel physical, electrical, mechanical, and chemical structures.

From the beginning the MTL mission was to foster research and provide sophisticated facilities for both circuit design and fabrication technologies that remain key research areas of the laboratory today. Many people contributed to the concept and vision of MTL, including Professors Paul Penfield, Richard Adler, Gerry Wilson, and Joel Moses, and MIT President Paul Gray. The lab was created in 1982 with the formation of the group of corporate sponsors that soon became known as the MIG. Professor Dimitri Antoniadis was the founding director of MTL, and served in that role until 1990 when Professor Rafael Reif became MTL director.

In the early 1980s, the Gordon Stanley Brown Building (MIT Building 39), located at 60 Vassar Street, was retrofitted to house new state-of-the-art cleanroom space and processing equipment that would constitute the experimental facilities of MTL. The renovated building was dedicated and opened in 1985. The project costs associated with rebuilding and retrofitting came to approximately $21 million. Monetary and in-kind contributions from eighteen corporate sponsors provided more than half of the funds. The original corporate sponsors included Analog Devices, AT&T Bell Laboratories, Digital Equipment Corp., GCA Corp., General Electrical Co., GenRad Inc., GTE Laboratories, Harris Semiconductor, Hewlett Packard, Hybrid Systems Corp., IBM, Keithly Instruments, NCR Microelectronics, Polaroid Corp., Raytheon Co., Sanders Associates, Schlumberger/Fairchild, Teradyne Inc., United Technologies Corp., and Eaton Ion Beam Systems Div. When the building was retrofitted, the experimental facilities within MTL were divided into several laboratories in Building 39, including the Integrated Circuits Lab (ICL), which consisted of 6,800 square feet of cleanroom space and equipment for the fabrication of silicon circuits, and the Technology Research Lab (TRL), which occupied 3,600 square feet on the fourth floor and was designed for the investigation of new processing technologies and flexible process flows. The remainder of the renovated building housed individual faculty research group laboratories, computation facilities, and offices for faculty, students, and staff.

Since the inception of MTL, the number of people who entered and used the laboratory cleanroom facilities grew from about fifty per year in the late 1980s to approximately a hundred people per year in 1995. As research on electronic and mechanical devices that could be made out of silicon wafers continued to grow and flourish, MTL became a unique resource for people from many departments throughout MIT. It was thus appropriate that, in 1995, MTL became an interdepartmental lab with the MTL director reporting directly to the dean of engineering.

In 1998, Professor Martin Schmidt became MTL director. In 1999, the microlab equipment from Building 13 was moved to the fifth floor of Building 39 and was incorporated as part of MTL's new Exploratory Materials Laboratory, which enables processing of any type of thin film sample, be it metallic, semiconducting, organic, or biological. This was representative of researchers' growing need to explore novel materials and applications.

In the early days, research included integrated circuit design and fabrication of those chips within the MTL laboratory facilities. An example of a BiCMOS circuit designed and fabricated in MTL was featured on the cover of the MTL annual report in 1989, shown on page 274. As circuit design and fabrication became ever more complex, particularly with the

Researchers working in the Technology Research Lab, c. 1992

Dedication of Building 39 as the Gordon Stanley Brown Building, 6 December 1985 (left to right): Joel Moses, David S. Saxon, Gordon S. Brown, Jean Brown, Paul E. Gray, and Gerald Wilson

EECS graduate student Oluwamuyiwa Olubuyide (left) and Research Specialist Gary Riggott in the new MTL Epi Laboratory

Professor Martin Schmidt (left) with EECS graduate student Javad Shajii in 1991

An MIT BiCMOS Differential Operational Amplifier configured for a multiplied-by-two circuit. The work was carried out by graduate student K.K. O, technical assistance of the ICL staff, and co-principal investigators H.-S. Lee and R. Reif.

advent of multilevel metallization for C integrated circuits, the focus shifted from design and fabrication in the ICL to design at MTL and fabrication in a growing number of commercial foundries. Device research continued in ICL and TRL with the exploration of new processes, materials, and device physics. A novel device structure, fabricated in 1999 (shown on page 275), which consists of a "double-gate MOSFET" that uses two gate electrodes, one on top and one on the bottom. Double-gate MOSFETs may someday form the backbone of commercial silicon technology, near the end of the so-called "CMOS Roadmap."

Research in microelectromechanical systems (MEMS) has become a very strong theme in MTL, with large, multidisciplinary projects dedicated to the design and fabrication of micro-engines, microrockets, and power generators. All of this has been accompanied by a large increase in activity in TRL. In 2000 the equipment in the ICL was upgraded to handle six-inch silicon wafers. The current number of users in the MTL fabrication facilities is roughly three hundred and fifty per year, drawn from twenty-nine departments, labs, and centers within MIT.

MTL's mission today continues to be to provide the intellectual core and physical facilities for education and research in the areas of nanoscale process technology, devices, and circuit and systems design. The lab still supports vigorous interaction with associated industries. MTL also serves as the central provider of fabrication and design infrastructure to the Institute. MTL operates the largest and most complex laboratory facilities on campus, including the building cleanroom infrastructure, the equipment it houses, and a staff of twenty-one people dedicated to semiconductor processing, four computer support staff, and seven administrative staff.

MTL presently has fourteen core faculty and twenty-eight affiliated faculty. Research over the years has spanned areas such as semiconductor devices and processes, manufacturing, CAD, displays, integrated circuits and systems, MEMS, optoelectronics, and compound semiconductors, and new applications in biology and nanotechnology. There is a strong educational component to the mission of MTL, at both the undergraduate and graduate level. MTL runs two popular undergraduate courses, 6.152J and 6.151J, which give undergraduates and young graduate students a chance to learn and apply fabrication principles to research projects.

New research thrust areas and research trends include increased emphasis on nanotechnology, new materials, organics, biology, soft lithography, nanotubes and nanowires, heterogeneous integration of new materials with silicon CMOS (such as copper and silicon

**a**

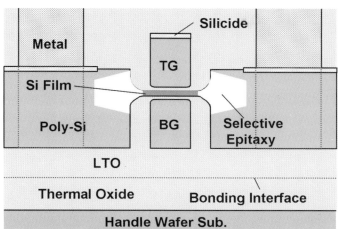

**b**

Concept (a) and scanning electron micrograph (b) of double-gate silicon MOSFET fabricated in MTL in 1999. [TG and BG = top and bottom gates, LTO = low temperature oxide.] From J.-H. Lee, G. Taraschi, A. Wei, T. Langdo, E.A. Fitzgerald, and D.A. Antoniadis.

germanium), sensor arrays and systems, and ultra-low power systems. Synergies among circuit design, fabrication technologies, and systems research have enabled the development of new interdisciplinary research programs. An example of such a program is the work led by Anantha Chandrakasan in MTL involving advanced systems such as ubiquitous sensor networks and associated devices. The intellectual core and fabrication facilities of MTL will continue to reach out and expand as the interest in making things small, so-called tiny technologies, remains a vital part of MIT.

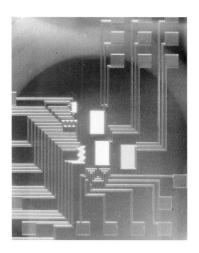

Plated 25, 50, and 75 μm triple-track and interdigitated electrode copper structures, 20 μm high, are used to study effects of process residues on corrosion in copper-polyimide high-density multichip modules. This was the work of Professor Stephen Senturia in the early 1990s.

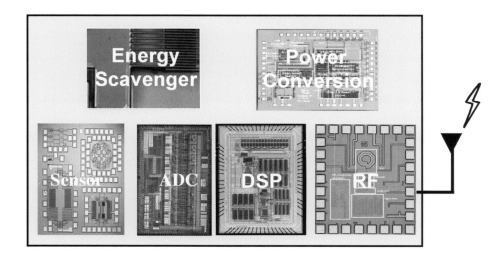

An example of synergies between circuit design, fabrication technologies, and systems research involving advanced systems such as ubiquitous sensor networks and associated devices; this represents work from the labs of Anantha P. Chandrakasan, Jeffrey H. Lang, Harry S. Lee, and Martin A. Schmidt.

Research in Professor Anantha Chandrakasan's group focuses on low-energy computing and communications. This chip photograph shows an ultra-low-power FFT processor that operates from a 0.18V power supply using a standard 0.18mm CMOS technology while consuming less than 100nW. Achieving such low power levels allows operation using energy scavenged from the environment. This work was performed by graduate student Alice Wang in 2002.

A photograph of stress-induced delamination and substrate cracking of a silicon dioxide layer that has been deposited on a silicon substrate is part of a study of stress in deposited films. This appeared on the cover of the May 1999 MTL Annual Report.

Some of the leadership in MTL, including Professors Paul Penfield, Charles Sodini, Rafael Reif, Richard Adler, Dimitri Antoniadis, and Anantha Chandrakasan

Among interdepartmental labs at MIT, MTL is unique in the way it combines an open laboratory facility with a variety of exciting research programs. Since the lab serves a user base made up of students and staff from all over campus, with wide-ranging needs, and because it runs such complex equipment in a cooperative environment, a sense of community spirit and respect for other researchers is naturally fostered. The lab sponsors a number of events ranging from weekly faculty lunches, quarterly meetings of laboratory users (with pizza), and frequent social functions such as afternoon get-togethers for all lab users (with plenty of food!), barbecues, annual picnics, and other fun and games. These events are considered as important to the successful operation and lifestyle of the lab as the more intellectual and formal weekly VLSI seminar series.

# RESEARCH LABORATORY OF ELECTRONICS

JEFFREY H. SHAPIRO
JULIUS A. STRATTON
PROFESSOR OF
ELECTRICAL ENGINEERING
DIRECTOR, RESEARCH
LABORATORY OF
ELECTRONICS

The tide of war in Europe and the Pacific had turned by the summer of 1944, but the conflict was far from over. Federally funded radar research and development by physicists and electrical engineers in MIT's Radiation Laboratory had played a crucial role in turning that tide, and thoughts about the postwar environment for university research were already beginning to emerge. Professor John Slater, head of MIT's Physics Department, was especially concerned that the rapid pace of electronics research in the Radiation Laboratory be maintained after the war. A definite plan for such an electronics laboratory developed from a pivotal meeting that Slater held on August 28, 1944, with MIT's President Karl Compton, Dean of Science George Harrison, Professor Harold Hazen, head of the Electrical Engineering Department, and Professor Julius A. Stratton. The gestation period had begun.

Since 1973, RLE's headquarters have been in the Sherman M. Fairchild Laboratories, Building 36, with research facilities centered there and in the Karl Taylor Compton Laboratories, Building 26 (2002 photo).

On December 31, 1945, the Radiation Laboratory was disbanded. The next day, the Basic Research Division was organized at MIT, under the leadership of Director Julius A. Stratton, to carry on the research of the Radiation Laboratory. On July 1, 1946, the Basic Research Division was incorporated into the newly formed Research Laboratory of Electronics (RLE) with Stratton as its first director.

RLE's charter called for a laboratory "to assure a flow of competent young men trained in electronics, and the steady advance of scientific knowledge in this field" under the joint sponsorship of the Departments of Physics and Electrical Engineering. The charter went on to specify the following program areas for RLE research: microwave electronics; microwave physics; modern electronic techniques applied to problems in physics and engineering; modern communications; and electronic aids to computation. Jointly sponsored by the Army Signal Corps, the Navy, and the Army Air Corps, RLE became the first of the great federally supported interdisciplinary university research laboratories. In the decades since its found-

Professor Jerome Y. Lettvin (left) and research staff member Walter H. Pitts observe a subject from their landmark neurophysiological research published in "What the Frog's Eye Tells the Frog's Brain" (1958 photo).

(Clockwise from top left)

Celebrating RLE's fortieth anniversary: (left to right) Professor Albert Hill (RLE Director 1949–1952), Professor Jerome Wiesner (RLE Director 1952–1961), Professor Jonathan Allen (RLE Director 1989–2000), Professor Julius Stratton (RLE Director 1946–1949), and Professor Henry Zimmerman (RLE Director 1961–1976).

Professors Harold E. Edgerton (left) and Samuel C. Collins (right) examine an electronic flash bulb that made high-speed stroboscopic photography possible (1954 photo).

Professors Erich Ippen (right) and Franz Kärtner (left) with ultrashort laser pulse experiments (2002 photos).

ing, RLE has greatly exceeded the expectations of its charter: it has educated extraordinary cohorts of young men and young women, and it has pioneered research fields that had yet to be imagined in 1946. The gift of this extraordinary history to the RLE of today is a research and learning environment of astonishing intellectual quality and richness.

The fledgling RLE began its life in space vacated by the Radiation Laboratory: the A wing of MIT's Building 20. Buoyed by triservice sponsorship at an annual level of $600,000 and the many key pieces of equipment that had been transferred from the Radiation Laboratory, RLE enjoyed a smooth launch into full operation. From the start, the laboratory's guiding principle was to provide a supportive framework for its faculty, staff, and students. Under the insightful leadership of its first three directors — Professors Julius A. Stratton (1946–1949), Albert Hill (1949–1952), and Jerome Wiesner (1952–1961) — the laboratory's initial concentration on microwaves, communications, and electronics expanded to include other disciplines, such as linguistics and neurophysiology, well outside the bounds of physics and electrical engineering envisaged in RLE's charter. As Professor Jonathan Allen (RLE Director from 1989 to 2000) wrote, on the occasion of the laboratory's forty-fifth anniversary,

*The keys to RLE's success have been an insistence on fundamental understanding, an openness to multiple viewpoints and disciplines, the tight coupling of theory and experiment, motivation through a focus on applications, and an ongoing interaction between the development of probe techniques and the discovery of new phenomena.*

The fruits of this enlightened leadership have been many and rich, and of profound scientific and technological significance. A comprehensive description of these achievements is impossible within the framework of this brief historical summary. Nevertheless, the following highlights will show the remarkable path charted by the laboratory as it progresses through its sixth decade of contribution to Institute life.

RLE inherited from the Radiation Laboratory an abiding interest in electromagnetic radiation. Whether for fundamental studies, like Professor Jerrold Zacharias's microwave spectroscopy of atomic cesium, or for technological advances, like Professor Harold ("Doc") Edgerton's development of electronic flash, this interest, vigorously pursued, led to important practical advances. Thus the atomic cesium studies became the foundation for the cesium atomic clock, without which the Global Positioning System would be impossible, and the electronic flash opened up high-speed stroboscopic photography as a means to probe all manners of mechanical motion. Echoes of this early work still reverberate strongly through today's RLE in its atomic physics and ultrafast optics groups. Professor Wolfgang Ketterle shared the 2001 Nobel Prize in Physics for his work on Bose-Einstein condensates; his atom laser, in which all the atoms "sing in unison," may lead to major advances in precision measurement sensors that employ atom interferometry. Professors Erich Ippen and Franz Kärtner have pushed generation of short optical pules nearly to its limit; their octave-wide optical comb generator produces laser pulses that are only two optical cycles in duration, making them more than one million times shorter than those from an electronic flash. Moreover, they have joined forces with the atomic physics group of Professor Daniel Kleppner (RLE Associate Director) and other RLE investigators to develop an all-optical clock by linking the octave-wide comb generator to the $^1$S–$^2$S transition of atomic hydrogen.

Communications research is part of RLE's charter, and it continues to be an important research theme within the laboratory. The 1948 publication of Claude E. Shannon's "The Mathematical Theory of Communication," with its fundamental theorems on coding for noiseless and noisy channels, instantaneously created a new research field: information theory. During the 1950s, RLE's Processing and Transmission of Information group produced many key results in information theory. Professor David Huffman invented the optimal variable-length source codes that bear his name. Professor Peter Elias invented convolutional codes, which have had extraordinary impact on practical applications. Many information theory luminaries — including Shannon, who joined the MIT faculty and RLE in 1956, Robert Fano, John Wozencraft, Robert Gallager, Frederick Jelinek, James Massey, Jacob Ziv, and David Forney — were members of this group during the 1950s or 1960s, either as faculty members or graduate students. Together, they made landmark contributions to the field.

Professor Claude E. Shannon being filmed for a lecture on information theory (1956 photo).

Professor Alan V. Oppenheim (right) as a graduate student, with graduate student Thomas G. Kincaid (left), violinist George Humphrey of the Boston Symphony Orchestra (center left), and graduate student John F. McDonald (center right) (1963 photo).

Professor Jae S. Lim (standing) and graduate student Mathew Bace with high definition video displays (1989 photo).

Professors Hermann A. Haus (left) and Louis D. Smullin (right) examine measurements of high-frequency noise in microwave vacuum tubes (1954 photo).

Professor Henry I. Smith (right) in clean room facilities for nanoscale science and engineering with graduate student Erik Anderson (standing) and research specialist James M. Carter (1986 photo).

Professor Jacob K. White (left) and graduate students Songmin Kim (center) and Keith S. Nabors (right), who holds a 3-D model of a woven bus interconnect problem solved by FASTCAP (1992 photo).

RLE's deep involvement with communications is also tied to its longstanding concern with manipulating signals. In 1965, James Cooley and John Tukey published their breakthrough paper, "An Algorithm for the Machine Calculation of Complex Fourier Series," whose fast Fourier transform opened the door to real-time digital signal processing. Professor Alan V. Oppenheim, recognizing the importance of this algorithm, created a group within RLE whose dual purposes were (and still are) to perform applications-oriented, as well as speculative, "solutions in search of a problem," research in signal processing. Two of his doctoral students — now faculty colleagues — Jae S. Lim and Gregory W. Wornell, have brought signal processing to bear on communications problems with great success. Professor Lim has pioneered the development of multidimensional signal processing, and, having assumed leadership of the Advanced Television Research Program from Professor William Schreiber, led MIT's participation in the high-definition television "Grand Alliance" during the 1990s. Professor Wornell leads the newly established, industry-sponsored Center for Wireless Networking, which brings together his own work on communication theory and signal processing for modern wireless appliances with the efforts of MIT faculty interested in low-power digital electronics and ad hoc communication networks.

RLE's research hallmarks — the quest for fundamental understanding and the drive to realize new applications — are stamped on many other achievements from the laboratory's fifty-seven years. They appear on career-spanning studies, like those of Professor Kenneth Stevens on acoustic phonetics, Professor David Staelin on microwave remote sensing, Professor Louis Braida on psychoacoustics, and Professor Hermann Haus, whose work on noise in physical systems has run the gamut from microwave tubes to fiber-optic communications using solitons. So too are they found on Professor Henry Smith's efforts, in the Nanostructures Laboratory, to develop and employ the tools needed to meet the insatiable demand for ever smaller and faster electronic and opto-electronic devices. The suite of optical biopsy instruments being developed by Professor James Fujimoto bears their imprint, as does Professor Dennis Freeman's system for micromotion measurements on living and manmade micromechanical systems. You can also find them on the semiconductor lasers being developed by Professors Leslie Kolodziejski and Rajeev Ram for integrated photonics, on Professor Qing Hu's THz lasers, and on Professor Peter Hagelstein's X-ray laser designs.

Integrated circuit (IC) design is another domain in which RLE investigators have brought the laboratory's culture to bear on vital engineering problems. Professors Paul Penfield and John Wyatt used their deep knowledge of circuit theory to develop practical techniques for bounding the signal delays in IC interconnects. Professor Jin Kong's electromagnetic analysis of interconnect structures helped lay the foundation for FASTCAP and FASTHENRY, the freely distributed computer-aided design programs for interconnect analysis that Professor Jacob White (RLE Associate Director) has developed. First-principles metal diffusion models were used by Professors Donald Troxel and Carl Thompson in a collaboration that led to ERNIE, a program for determining interconnect electromigration failure rates. The recent addition of Professor Luca Daniel — whose expertise is the extraction of accurate circuit models from detailed electromagnetic analyses — promises a continuing flow of IC design advances from RLE research.

Like its legendary initial home, Building 20, RLE has been an extraordinary incubator. Professor Robert Fano left RLE in 1963 to become the founding director of Project MAC — MAC stood for Machine-Aided Cognition and Multiple-Access Computer — which has since become the Laboratory for Computer Science. Fano took Professors John McCarthy and Marvin Minsky with him. Their work on artificial intelligence, begun in RLE, later spun off from Project MAC to become the Artificial Intelligence Laboratory. RLE's long involvement with plasma dynamics — starting in 1946, with the microwave gas discharge group of Professors William Allis and Sanborn Brown, through Professor Bruno Coppi's design of the high-field tokomak Alcator A built in 1972 at MIT's Francis Bitter National Magnet Laboratory, and Professor Abraham Bers's continuing theoretical work on wave-plasma interactions and instabilities — made it natural for several RLE investigators to become founding members of the Plasma Fusion Center (now the Plasma Science and Fusion Center) in 1980.

The RLE experience has also nurtured the entrepreneurial spirit. Dr. George Hatsopoulos founded Thermo Electron, drawing upon patents that originated from research he had done in RLE, and turned it into a model for successful technology-based enterprises. Professor Amar Bose built Bose Corporation, starting from his RLE research in electronics and acoustics, into a world leader in sound systems. Dr. Irwin Jacobs cofounded Linkabit and later Qualcomm, leaders in the application of information theory to communication systems. Dr. Robert Shillman founded Cognex Corporation, the world's premier supplier of industrial computer vision systems. Today, RLE continues to provide the rich environment from which future industry leaders will turn their fundamental research into real-world applications.

As RLE moves deeper into its second half-century, what might be said about its future? Predictions are risky but some things are clear. RLE's research in communications and signal processing will become increasingly intertwined with advances in electronics, in photonics, and in computer systems and networks. Likewise RLE's research in materials and devices will delve

Professor Jeffrey H. Shapiro (RLE Director) lecturing on the generation of entangled photon pairs for use in qubit teleportation (2002 photo).

Professor Vladimir Bulovic with a high-vacuum sample transfer line for organic materials (2002 photo).

Professor Rahul Sarpeshkar (center) discusses a novel circuit design for time-based hybrid computing with his graduate students (2002 photo).

deeper into the realm of nanotechnology, taking both top-down and bottom-up routes to this next stage of miniaturized devices and systems. But other trends are emerging. Some of the first tentative steps toward quantum information systems — which exploit nonclassical behaviors such as entanglement — are being taken in RLE. Professor Terry P. Orlando and his collaborators are working on Josephson junction quantum bit (qubit) circuits. Professor Jeffrey H. Shapiro, RLE's current Director, and his collaborators are instantiating their architecture for long-distance qubit teleportation. Other clues to the laboratory's future can be found in the work of its newest faculty. RLE's future will be organic: Professors Vladimir Bulovic and Marc Baldo are pioneering organic electronic and optical devices. It will be bio-inspired: Professor Rahul Sarpeshkar has designed the world's best artificial cochlea. It will also be biological: Professors Jongyoon Han and Joel Voldman are developing bio-MEMS systems for manipulating biomolecules and living cells. The Research Laboratory of Electronics at MIT will be, as it has always been, a laboratory in which interdisciplinary research can flourish, a laboratory in which the Institute's dual missions of research and education reinforce each other to turn future dreams into present reality.

# Abstracts of Favorite Publications by EECS Faculty Members and Senior Research Staff

**Harold Abelson**

*One major theme of my work is to explore how computation can be a valuable language for expressing ideas, rather than just a way to get answers. This paper gives a vision of how computing can support science and engineering in ways that go beyond just number-crunching or shallow qualitative modeling.*

**Paper:** Intelligence in Scientific Computing

**Authors:** H. Abelson, M. Eisenberg, M. Halfant, J. Katzenelson, E. Sacks, G.J. Sussman, J. Wisdom, and K. Yip

**Journal:** *Communications of the ACM* 32, no. 5 (May 1989): 546–562

**Year:** 1989

Combining numerical techniques with ideas from symbolic computation and with methods incorporating knowledge of science and mathematics leads to a new category of intelligent computational tools for scientists and engineers. These tools autonomously prepare simulation experiments from high-level specifications of physical models. For computationally intensive experiments, they automatically design special-purpose numerical engines optimized to perform the necessary computations. They actively monitor numerical and physical experiments. They interpret experimental data and formulate numerical results in qualitative terms. They enable their human users to control computational experiments in terms of high-level behavioral descriptions.

**Anant Agarwal**

*The Alewife machine is a real experimental prototype of a distributed shared-memory multiprocessor (DSM) built at MIT. It pioneered several new mechanisms, including: (1) a multithreaded microprocessor, (2) a scalable shared-memory system, and (3) integrated shared memory and message passing.*

**Paper:** The MIT Alewife Machine

**Authors:** Anant Agarwal, Ricardo Bianchini, David Chaiken, Frederic T. Chong, Kirk L. Johnson, David Kranz, John Kubiatowicz, Beng-Hong Lim, Kenneth Mackenzie, and Donald Yeung

**Journal:** *Proceedings of the IEEE* 87, no. 3 (March 1999): 430–444

**Year:** 1999

A variety of models for parallel architectures such as shared memory, message passing, and dataflow have converged in the recent past to a hybrid architecture form called distributed shared memory (DSM). By using a combination of hardware and software mechanisms, DSM combines the nice features of all the above models and is able to achieve both the scalability of message-passing machines and the programmability of shared memory systems. Alewife, an early prototype of such DSM architectures, uses a hybrid of software and hardware mechanisms to support coherent shared memory, efficient user-level messaging, fine-grain synchronization, and latency tolerance.

Alewife supports up to 512 processing nodes connected over a scalable and cost-effective mesh network at a constant cost per node. Four mechanisms combine to achieve Alewife's goals of scalability and programmability: software-extended coherent shared memory provides a global, linear address space; integrated message-passing allows compiler and operating system designers to provide efficient communication and synchronization; support for fine-grain computation allows many processors to cooperate on small problem sizes; and latency tolerance mechanisms—including block multithreading and prefetching—mask unavoidable delays due to communication.

Extensive results from micro-benchmarks, together with more than a dozen complete applications running on a 32-node prototype, demonstrate that integrating message passing with shared memory enables a cost-efficient solution to the cache coherence problem and provides a rich set of programming primitives. Our results further show that messaging and shared memory operations are both important because each helps the programmer to achieve the best performance for various machine configurations. Block multithreading and prefetching improve performance significantly, and language constructs that allow programmers to express fine-grain synchronization can improve performance by more than a factor of two.

## Akintunde Ibitayo Akinwande

*I chose this paper because this research covers (1) the smallest gate aperture Field Emission Array (70-nm-gate aperture); (2) the highest density (2.5 billion field emitters per square centimeter); and (3) the lowest turn-on voltage (8.5 V) in silicon.*

**Paper:** Field Emitter Arrays for Low Voltage Applications with sub 100 nm Apertures and 200 nm Period

**Authors:** David G. Pflug, Mark Schattenburg, Henry I. Smith, and Akintunde I. Akinwande

**Publisher:** 2001 IEEE International Electron Device Meeting Technical Digest, 179–182. New York: Institute of Electrical and Electronics Engineers

**Year:** 2001

In this work we fabricated 70-nm-gate aperture silicon FEAs with turned-on voltages as low as 10 V. We demonstrated emission currents of 1 μA at $V_g$ of 13 V. Transmission electron microscopy (TEM) of the tips verified that the tip radii have a log-normal distribution with a mean radius of 4.5 nm. The measured tip radii are consistent with the electrical characterization of the devices.

## Saman Amarasinghe

*This work is part of my ongoing research, which I hope will influence both how to build future microprocessors and how to write programs for them.*

**Paper:** A Stream Compiler for Communication-Exposed Architectures

**Authors:** Michael I. Gordon, William Thies, Michal Karczmarek, Jasper Lin, Ali S. Meli, Andrew A. Lamb, Chris Leger, Jeremy Wong, Henry Hoffmann, David Maze, and Saman Amarasinghe

**Publisher:** Proceedings of the Tenth ACM Conference on Architectural Support for Programming Languages and Operating Systems (ASPLOS X), 291–303. New York: ACM Press

**Year:** 2002

With the increasing miniaturization of transistors, wire delays are becoming a dominant factor in microprocessor performance. To address this issue, a number of emerging architectures contain replicated processing units with software-exposed communication between one unit and another (e.g., Raw, SmartMemories, TRIPS). However, for their use to be widespread, it will be necessary to develop compiler technology that enables a portable, high-level language to execute efficiently across a range of wire-exposed architectures.

In this paper, we describe our compiler for StreamIt, a high-level, architecture-independent language for streaming applications. We focus on our back end for the Raw processor. Though StreamIt exposes the parallelism and communication patterns of stream programs, some analysis is needed to adapt a stream program to a software-exposed processor. We describe a partitioning algorithm that employs fission and fusion transformations to adjust the granularity of a stream graph, a layout algorithm that maps a stream graph to a given network topology, and a scheduling strategy that generates a fine-grained static communication pattern for each computational element.

We have implemented a fully functional compiler that parallelizes StreamIt applications for Raw, including several load-balancing transformations. Using the cycle-accurate Raw simulator, we demonstrate that the StreamIt compiler can automatically map a high-level stream abstraction to Raw without losing performance. We consider this work to be a first step toward a portable programming model for communication-exposed architectures.

## Dimitri A. Antoniadis

*This paper received the Paul Rappaport award for best journal paper in the IEEE Transactions on Electron Devices in 1997. While it introduces an interesting and novel device technology, this paper is noteworthy in that it is a rare example of close collaboration of system and circuit designers with process and device designers in implementing and analyzing a system in a novel device technology.*

**Paper:** Back-gated CMOS on SOIAS for Dynamic Threshold Voltage Control

**Authors:** I. Yang, C. Vieri, A.P. Chandrakasan, and D.A. Antoniadis

**Journal:** IEEE Transactions on Electron Devices (May 1997): 831–832

**Year:** 1997

The simultaneous reduction of power supply and threshold voltages for low-power design without suffering performance losses will eventually reach the limit of diminishing returns as static leakage power dissipation becomes a significant portion of the total power consumption. This is especially acute in systems that are idling most of the time. In order to meet the opposing requirements of high performance at reduced power supply voltage and low-static leakage power during idle periods, a dynamic threshold voltage control scheme is proposed. A novel Silicon-On-Insulator (SOI)-based technology called Silicon-On-Insulator-with-Active-Substrate (SOIAS) was developed whereby a back-gate is used to control the threshold voltage of the front-gate; this concept was demonstrated on a selectively scaled CMOS process implementing discrete devices and ring oscillators. For a 250 mV switch in threshold voltage, a reduction of 3-4 decades in subthreshold leakage current was measured.

## Arvind

*Even by most generous account, no more than three or four of my papers have made a seminal contribution. The internal architecture of commercial high performance processors has continually inched closer to our proposals for dataflow and multithreaded architectures, but the connection is not widely acknowledged because of our direct, instead of evolutionary, approach to the problem. My "Commit, Reconcile, and Fences" paper on memory models, written with Shen and Rudolph, describes what continues to be an intriguing and promising idea, but the area (memory models) is somewhat esoteric. I chose my paper on hardware modeling, verification, and synthesis because I think it is novel and may have direct and more near-term impact on the way people design complex integrated circuits.*

**Paper:** Using Term Rewriting Systems to Design and Verify Processors

**Authors:** Arvind and Xiaowei Shen

**Journal:** IEEE Micro 19, no. 3 (May/June 1999, Special Issue on Modeling and Validation of Microprocessors): 36–46

**Year:** 1999

We present a novel use of Term Rewriting Systems (TRSs) to describe micro-architectures. The state of a system is represented as a TRS term while the state transitions are represented as TRS rules. TRS descriptions are amenable to both verification and synthesis. We illustrate the use of TRSs by giving the operational semantics of a simple RISC instruction set. We then present another TRS that implements the same instruction set on a micro-architecture, which permits register renaming and speculative execution. The correctness of the speculative implementation is discussed in terms of the ability of the two TRSs to simulate each other. Our method facilitates understanding of important micro-architectural differences without delving into low-level implementation details.

**Krste Asanovic**

*I chose this paper because I believe the idea will have lasting impact by finally making fine-grained memory protection practical. Fine-grained memory protection simplifies the design of robust extensible software systems, but previous approaches have suffered from excessive overhead and are not compatible with existing hardware and software. Mondriaan memory protection is an efficient, fine-grained protection scheme that is compatible with existing languages, operating systems, and instruction sets.*

**Chapter:** Mondriaan Memory Protection

**Authors:** Emmett Witchel, Josh Cates, and Krste Asanovic

**Publisher:** *Proceedings of the Tenth International Conference on Architectural Support for Programming Languages and Operating Systems*, 304–316. New York: ACM Press

**Year:** 2002

Mondriaan memory protection (MMP) is a fine-grained protection scheme that allows multiple protection domains to flexibly share memory and export protected services. In contrast to earlier page-based systems, MMP allows arbitrary permissions control at the granularity of individual words. We use a compressed permissions table to reduce space overheads and employ two levels of permissions caching to reduce run-time overheads. The protection tables in our implementation add

less than 9 percent overhead to the memory space used by the application. Accessing the protection tables adds less than 8 percent additional memory references to the accesses made by the application. Although it can be layered on top of demand-paged virtual memory, MMP is also well suited to embedded systems with a single physical address space. We extend MMP to support segment translation, which allows a memory segment to appear at another location in the address space. We use this translation to implement zero-copy networking underneath the standard read system call interface, where packet payload fragments are connected together by the translation system to avoid data copying. This saves 52 percent of the memory references used by a traditional copying network stack.

**Hari Balakrishnan**

*Cricket enables a number of new indoor mobile applications that were previously impossible because no good and inexpensive location-discovery methods were available. It is one of the first systems in the world to provide precise location information to devices indoors, while scaling to large-device densities, preserving user privacy, and being inexpensive to deploy.*

**Chapter:** The Cricket Location-Support System

**Authors:** Nissanka B. Priyantha, Anit Chakraborty, and Hari Balakrishnan

**Publisher:** *Proceedings of the Sixth Annual ACM International Conference on Mobile Computing and Networking (MOBICOM),* August 2000.

**Year:** 2000

This paper presents the design, implementation, and evaluation of Cricket, a location-support system for in-building, mobile, location-dependent applications. It allows applications running on mobile and static nodes to learn their physical location by using listeners that hear and analyze information from beacons spread throughout the building. Cricket is the result of several design goals, including user privacy, decentralized administration, network heterogeneity, and low cost. Rather than explicitly tracking user location, Cricket helps devices learn where they are and lets them decide whom to advertise this information to; it does not rely on any centralized management or control, and there is no explicit

coordination between beacons; it provides information to devices regardless of their type of network connectivity; and each Cricket device is made from off-the-shelf components and costs less than U.S. $10. We describe the randomized algorithm used by beacons to transmit information, the use of concurrent radio and ultrasonic signals to infer distance, the listener inference algorithms to overcome multipath and interference, and practical beacon configuration and positioning techniques that improve accuracy. Our experience with Cricket shows that several location-dependent applications such as in-building active maps and device control can be developed with little effort or manual configuration.

**Marc A. Baldo**

*I have been at MIT for just under a year, and so my selection is from my graduate work at Princeton University. Here, we introduced a new type of molecule to organic light-emitting devices, freeing light emission from a restriction to excited states of a particular spin. This work and its later refinements significantly improved the efficiency of organic light-emitting devices and have been applied to video displays.*

**Paper:** Highly Efficient Phosphorescent Emission from Organic Electroluminescent Devices

**Authors:** M.A. Baldo, D.F. O'Brien, Y. You, A. Shoustikov, S. Sibley, M.E. Thompson, and S.R. Forrest

**Journal:** *Nature* 395, no. 6698 (10 September 1998): 151–154

**Year:** 1998

The efficiency of electroluminescent organic light-emitting devices can be improved by the introduction of a fluorescent dye. Energy transfer from the host to the dye occurs via excitons, but only the singlet spin states induce fluorescent emission; these represent a small fraction (about 25 percent) of the total excited-state population (the remainder are triplet states). Phosphorescent dyes, however, offer a means of achieving improved light-emission efficiencies, as emission may result from both singlet and triplet states. Here we report high-efficiency (>90 percent) energy transfer from both singlet and triplet states, in a host material doped with the phosphorescent dye 2,3,7,8,12,13,17,18-octaethyl- 21H,23Hporphine platinum(II) (PtOEP). Our doped electroluminescent devices generate saturated red emission with peak external and internal quantum efficiencies of 4 percent and 23 percent respectively. The luminescent efficiencies attainable with phosphorescent dyes may lead to new applications for organic materials. Moreover, our work establishes the utility of PtOEP as a probe of triplet behavior and energy transfer in organic solid-state systems.

### Abraham Bers

*This paper is a unique contribution to the space-time evolution and propagation of linear instabilities in media in general, and in plasma electrodynamics in particular. It entails the generalization of work with my Ph.D. student Richard J. Briggs—work that he and I initiated in 1962.*

**Paper:** Relativistic Analysis of Absolute and Convective Instability Evolutions in Three Dimensions

**Authors:** A. Bers, A.K. Ram, and G. Francis

**Journal:** *Physical Review Letters* 53, no. 15 (8 October 1984): 1457–1460; errata in vol. 54, no. 3 (21 January 1985): 253

**Year:** 1984

Pinch-point stability and unstable-pulse-shape analyses for relativistic-electromagnetic instabilities in three dimensions are presented. The time-asymptotic, unstable pulse shape is determined by $\omega'_{pi}(\vec{V})/\gamma$ as a function of $\vec{V}$, where $\omega'_{pi}(\vec{V})$ is the observer's frame pinch-point growth rate and $\gamma = \left(1 - V^2/c^2\right)^{-1/2}$. The differential equations for the observer's frame pinch points are established. The results are illustrated for instabilities in an anisotropic, relativistic electron plasma.

### Dimitri Bertsekas

*This paper combines some of the major characteristics of my recent work—dynamic programming and optimization-related computational methodology—with a view to solving large-scale problems.*

**Paper:** A New Value Iteration Method for the Average Cost Dynamic Programming Problem

**Author:** D.P. Bertsekas

**Journal:** *SIAM Journal on Control and Optimization* 36, no. 2 (1998): 742–759

**Year:** 1998

We propose a new value iteration method for the classical average cost Markovian decision problem, under the assumption that all stationary policies are unichain and that, furthermore, there exists a state that is recurrent under all stationary policies. This method is motivated by a relation between the average cost problem and an associated stochastic shortest path problem. Contrary to the standard relative value iteration, our method involves a weighted sup-norm contraction and for this reason it admits a Gauss-Seidel implementation. Computational tests indicate that the Gauss-Seidel version of the new method substantially outperforms the standard method for difficult problems.

### Robert Berwick

*This was the seminal attempt to apply modern computational complexity theory to the analysis of human language. After this publication, it became de rigueur to use this modern tool of computer science, rather than the older, automata-based approaches. It has remained so to this day.*

**Book:** *Computational Complexity and Natural Language*

**Authors:** E. Barton, R. Berwick, and E. Ristad

**Publisher:** Cambridge, Massachusetts: MIT Press

**Year:** 1987

The book *Computational Complexity and Natural Language* marked the first systematic attempt to apply the tools of modern computational complexity theory to the analysis of human languages. Previously, computational approaches to language simply used the tools developed half a century ago, which look just at the strings of sentences that can be generated and not at the intrinsic computational machinery needed to parse, produce, or learn language. In this book, we found an algorithm-neutral way to classify the inherent difficulty of solving problems like recognizing words, parsing sentences, and learning language. From a cognitive science viewpoint, algorithm neutrality is desirable because we do not not want algorithms or machinery the brain has at its disposal. From an engineering

point of view, the book reveals the limits, often hidden and surprising, in most proposed linguistic theories—no matter how clever we are at programming. Just like computational complexity theory in computer science, the results in this book give a bound to how much we can expect to do given a certain amount of computational resources.

Often, seemingly simple problems are inherently intractable, as the book demonstrates. Simple grammars that express agreement between the subject and a verb, as in "The guy eats ice cream/The guys eat ice cream," are intractable. Looking up words in a dictionary and figuring out that *ing* is an ending on *eating* is intractable. For the most part, in fact, and to the surprise of many, almost all proposed models for human language are computationally intractable. Our complexity diagnosis gives important clues as to why this is so and how to patch a model to bring it more in line with linguistic reality. The complexity diagnosis advanced in this book is a first step to insight and repair, and, ultimately, a way to pull linguistic theory and computational theory closer together again.

### Duane Boning

*This paper detailed early MIT work undertaken to understand and model the sources of manufacturing variation in integrated circuit fabrication. The paper introduced a series of CMP test masks that became de facto industry standards, and was the first practical chip-scale model for chemical-mechanical polishing (CMP). The work was produced with my faculty colleague Jim Chung, our students, and industry collaborators.*

**Paper:** Rapid Characterization and Modeling of Pattern-Dependent Variation in Chemical-Mechanical Polishing

**Authors:** Brian E. Stine, Dennis O. Ouma, Rajesh R. Divecha, Duane S. Boning, James E. Chung, Dale L. Hetherington, C. Randy Harwood, O. Samuel Nakagawa, and Soo-Young Oh

**Journal:** *IEEE Transactions on Semiconductor Manufacturing* 11, no. 1 (February 1998): 129–140.

**Year:** 1998

Pattern-dependent effects are a key concern in chemical-mechanical polishing (CMP) processes. In oxide CMP, variation in the interlevel dielectric (ILD) thickness across each die and across the wafer can impact circuit performance and reduce yield. In this work, we present new test mask designs and associated measurement and analysis methods to efficiently characterize and model polishing behavior as a function of layout pattern factors —specifically area, pattern density, pitch, and perimeter/area effects. An important goal of this approach is rapid learning which requires rapid data collection. While the masks are applicable to a variety of CMP applications including back-end, shallow-trench, or damascene processes, in this study we focus on a typical interconnect oxide planarization process, and compare the pattern-dependent variation models for two different polishing pads. For the process and pads considered, we find that pattern density is a strongly dominant factor, while structure area, pitch, and perimeter/area (aspect ratio) play only a minor role.

### Louis D. Braida

*I chose this particular piece of work to represent me in the book because it describes a practical application of my group's research on aids for the deaf. The autocuer we developed could potentially assist many of the deaf who do not benefit from cochlear implants.*

**Paper:** Development of Speechreading Supplements Based on Automatic Speech Recognition

**Authors:** P. Duchnowski, D.S. Lum, J.C. Krause, M.G. Sexton, M.S. Bratakos, and L.D. Braida

**Journal:** *IEEE Transactions on Biomedical Engineering* 47, no. 4 (2000): 487–496

**Year:** 2000

In Manual Cued Speech (MCS) a speaker produces hand gestures to resolve ambiguities among speech elements that are often confused by speechreaders. The shape of the hand distinguishes among consonants; the position of the hand relative to the face distinguishes among vowels. Experienced receivers of MCS achieve nearly perfect reception of everyday connected speech. MCS has been taught to very young deaf children and greatly facilitates language learning, communication, and general education.

This manuscript describes a system that can produce a form of cued speech automatically

in real time and reports on its evaluation by trained receivers of MCS. Cues are derived by an HMM-based speaker-dependent phonetic speech recognizer that uses context-dependent phone models and are presented visually by superimposing animated handshapes on the face of the talker. The benefit provided by these cues strongly depends on articulation of hand movements and on precise synchronization of the actions of the hands and the face. Using the system reported here, experienced cue receivers can recognize roughly two thirds of the keywords in cued low-context sentences correctly, compared to roughly one third by speechreading alone. The practical significance of these improvements is to support fairly normal rates of reception of conversational speech, a task that is often difficult via speechreading alone.

### Rodney A. Brooks

*This was the first work I did upon joining the faculty at MIT. It is my most-referenced paper ever; it was a radical departure from the way robot control systems were previously built, and it became what is now known as the "behavior-based" approach to robotics, which most modern robots use at least for their low-level controllers.*

**Paper:** A Robust Layered Control System for a Mobile Robot

**Author:** Rodney A. Brooks

**Journal:** *IEEE Journal of Robotics and Automation* RA-2, no. 1 (April 1986): 14–23

**Year:** 1986

We describe a new architecture for controlling mobile robots. Layers of control system are built to let the robot operate at increasing levels of competence. Layers are made up of asynchronous modules that communicate over low bandwidth channels. Each module is an instance of a fairly simple computational machine. Higher-level layers can subsume the roles of lower levels by suppressing their outputs. However, lower levels continue to function as higher levels are added.

The result is a robust and flexible robot control system. The system has been used to control a mobile robot wandering around unconstrained laboratory areas and computer machine rooms. Eventually it is intended to control a robot that wanders the office areas of our laboratory,

building maps of its surroundings using an onboard arm to perform simple tasks.

### Vladimir Bulovic

*This work demonstrated controlled hybrid integration of organic and inorganic nanostructures into an active light-emitting device. Its findings enable further research in hybrid nanoscale technologies implementable on large-area substrates.*

**Paper:** Electroluminescence from Single Monolayers of Nanocrystals in Molecular Organic Devices

**Authors:** Seth Coe, Wing-Keung Woo, Moungi Bawendi, and Vladimir Bulovic

**Journal:** *Nature* 420, no. 6917 (20 December 2002): 800–803

**Year:** 2002

The integration of organic and inorganic materials at the nanometer scale into hybrid optoelectronic structures enables active devices that combine the diversity of organic materials with the high-performance electronic and optical properties of inorganic nanocrystals. The optimization of such hybrid devices ultimately depends on the precise positioning of the functionally distinct materials. Previous studies have already emphasized that this is a challenge, owing to the lack of well-developed nanometer-scale fabrication techniques. Here we demonstrate a hybrid light-emitting diode (LED) that combines the ease of processability of organic materials with the narrow-band, efficient luminescence of colloidal quantum dots (QDs). To isolate the luminescence processes from charge conduction, we fabricate a quantum-dot LED (QD-LED) that contains only a single monolayer of QDs, sandwiched between two organic thin films. This is achieved by a method that uses material phase segregation between the QD aliphatic capping groups and the aromatic organic materials. In our devices, where QDs function exclusively as lumophores, we observe a twenty-five-fold improvement in luminescence efficiency (1.6 cd/A at 2,000 $cd/m^2$) over the best previous QD-LED results. The reproducibility and precision of our phase-segregation approach suggests that this technique could be widely applicable to the fabrication of other hybrid organic/inorganic devices.

## Vincent W.S. Chan

*The successful design and demonstration of high-speed optical space communications is a key event in space networks. This paper is included because it points to new possibilities for space system architectures based on this invention.*

**Paper:** Optical Satellite Networks

**Author:** V.W.S. Chan

**Journal:** *Journal of Lightwave Technology* 21, no. 11 (November 2003, Invited)

**Year:** 2003

With high-speed space optical crosslink being a reality, the construction of an optical satellite network as part of a larger integrated space-terrestrial network is now feasible. This paper explores the architecture implications of the invention of such a radical technology building block. Not only can the satellite network performance and cost undergo quantum-leap improvements but also such a network can have profound transforming effects on space system architectures and data network user applications.

## Anantha P. Chandrakasan

*This paper was recently recognized as the second most-cited paper in the* Journal of Solid-State Circuits *since the journal's inception.*

**Paper:** Low-power CMOS Digital Design

**Authors:** A.P. Chandrakasan, S. Sheng, and R.W. Brodersen

**Journal:** *IEEE Journal of Solid-State Circuits* 27, no. 4 (April 1992): 473–484

**Year:** 1992

Motivated by emerging battery-operated applications that demand intensive computation in portable environments, techniques are investigated which reduce power consumption in CMOS digital circuits while maintaining computational throughput. Techniques for low-power operation are shown that use the lowest possible supply voltage coupled with architectural, logic style, circuit, and technology optimizations. An architectural-based scaling strategy is presented that indicates that the optimum voltage is much lower than that determined by other scaling considerations. This optimum is achieved by trading increased silicon area for reduced power consumption.

## David Clark

*This paper, written by three authors all then at*

the Laboratory for Computer Science at MIT, spelled out a basic design principle that shaped the structure of the Internet. The end-to-end design principle has entered the vocabulary of network architects and has become a standard by which design decisions are evaluated.

**Paper:** End-to-End Arguments in System Design

**Authors:** J.H. Saltzer, D.P. Reed, and D.D. Clark

**Journal:** *ACM Transactions on Computer Systems* 2, no. 4 (November 1984): 277–288

**Year:** 1984

This paper presents a design principle that helps guide placement of functions among the modules of a distributed computer system. The principle, called the *end-to-end argument*, suggests that functions placed at low levels of a system may be redundant or of little value when compared with the cost of providing them at that low level. Examples discussed in the paper include bit error recovery, security using encryption, duplicate message suppression, recovery from system crashes, and delivery acknowledgement. Low-level mechanisms to support these functions are justified only as performance enhancements.

## Michael Collins

*This paper describes work on natural language parsing. The development of accurate parsing methods for natural languages could have a substantial impact upon many applications in computer speech and language processing. Unfortunately, parsing is a tough problem, mainly due to the extremely high degree of ambiguity (at least when using syntax alone) encountered when processing natural language text. This paper describes a move toward more sophisticated machine learning methods for the problem, giving some of the best results reported on the task.*

**Chapter:** Discriminative Reranking for Natural Language Parsing

**Author:** M. Collins

**Publisher:** *Proceedings of the Seventeenth International Conference on Machine Learning* (ICML 2000), 175–182. San Francisco: Morgan Kaufman

**Year:** 2000

Machine-learning approaches to natural language parsing have recently shown some success in complex domains such as newswire text. Many of these methods fall into the gen-

eral category of history-based models, where a parse tree is represented as a derivation (sequence of decisions) and the probability of the tree is then calculated as a product of decision probabilities. While these approaches have many advantages, it can be awkward to encode some constraints within this framework. It is often easy to think of features that might be useful in discriminating between candidate trees for a sentence, but much more difficult to alter the derivation to take these features into account.

This paper considers approaches that rerank the output of an existing probabilistic parser. The base parser produces a set of candidate parses for each input sentence, with associated probabilities that define an initial ranking of these parses. A second model then attempts to improve upon this initial ranking, using additional features of the tree as evidence. The strength of our approach is that it allows a tree to be represented as an arbitrary set of features, without concerns about how these features interact or overlap, and without the need to define a derivation that takes these features into account.

The problems with history-based models, and the desire to be able to specify features as arbitrary predicates of the entire tree, have been noted before. In particular, previous work has investigated the use of Markov Random Fields (MRFs), or log-linear models, as probabilistic models for parsing and other NLP tasks. The first method we discuss is based on a feature selection method within the MRF framework. The second approach is based on the application of boosting models for ranking problems. Previous work has drawn connections between log-linear models and boosting for classification problems; one contribution of this paper is to draw similar connections between the two approaches to ranking problems. Efficiency is an important issue in our problem—the training data consists of around one million trees, and there are approximately five hundred thousand distinct features. We show that a naive implementation of the boosting method is computationally expensive, but that the sparse nature of the feature space means that a much improved algorithm can be derived. The MRF algorithm also benefits from the sparseness of the feature space, but for reasons we will discuss is still much less efficient than the boosting approach.

We applied our method to parsing the *Wall Street Journal* treebank. The baseline model achieved 88.1/88.3 percent recall/precision on this task. The new model achieves 89.6/89.9 percent recall/precision, a 13 percent relative decrease in error. Although this paper concentrates on parsing, many other problems in natural language processing or speech recognition can also be framed as reranking problems, so the results of this paper should be quite broadly applicable.

### Munther A. Dahleh

*This paper lays the foundation for understanding the interplay between learning and approximation when data is generated from a complex system. This paper led to further work on defining model quality in an uncertain environment. Work in this area has many applications in fields such as communication and control, data-driven economic modeling, hypothesis testing from biological and biomedical data, and mining and modeling large data structures such as genomic data for pharmaceutical applications.*

**Paper:** On System Identification of Complex Systems from Finite Data

**Authors:** M.A. Dahleh and S. Ventakesh

**Journal:** IEEE Transactions on Automatic Control 46, no. 2 (February 2001): 235–257

**Year:** 2001

System identification deals with computation of mathematical models from an a priori chosen model class, for an unknown system from finite noisy data. The popular maximum-likelihood (ML) principle is based on picking a model from a chosen model-parameterization that maximizes the likelihood of the data. Most other principles, including set-membership identification, can be thought of as extensions of this principle insofar as the concept of choosing a model to fit the data is concerned. Although these principles have been extremely successful in addressing several problems in identification and control, they have not been completely effective in addressing the question of identification in the context of uncertainty in the model class/parameterization.

We introduce a new principle for identification in this paper. The principle is based on choosing a model from the model parameterization that best approximates the unknown real system belonging to a more complex space of systems that do not lend themselves to a finite parameterization. The principle is particularly effective for robust control as it leads to a precise notion of parametric and non-parametric error, and the identification problem can be equivalently perceived as that of robust convergence of the parameters in the face of unmodeled errors. The main difficulty in its application stems from the interplay of noise and unmodeled dynamics and requires developing novel two-step algorithms that amount to annihilation of the unmodeled error followed by averaging out the noise. The principle contributions of the paper are in establishing: 1) robust convergence for a large class of systems, topologies, and unmodeled errors; 2) sample path-based, finite-time polynomial rate of convergence; and 3) annihilation-correlation algorithms for linearly parameterized model-structures, thus illustrating significant improvements over prediction-error and set-membership approaches.

### Trevor Darrell

*I selected this paper as it covers recent research that illustrated one of the core missions of my group—tracking human body appearance and pose—and was evidence of the spirit of collaboration that makes the AI Laboratory and LCS a rewarding research environment. This project involved contributions from Professor McMillan's and Professor Grimson's groups and resulted in an impressive real-time demonstration system.*

**Paper:** Integrated Face and Gait Recognition from Multiple Views

**Authors:** G. Shakhnarovich, L. Lee, and T. Darrell

**Publisher:** Proceedings of the IEEE Conference on Computer Vision and Pattern Recognition. Vol. 1, 439–446. Los Alamitos, California: IEEE Computer Society Press

**Year:** 2001

We develop a view-normalization approach to multiview face and gait recognition. An image-based visual hull (IBVH) is computed from a set of monocular views and used to render virtual views for tracking and recognition. We determine canonical viewpoints by examining the 3D structure, appearance (texture), and motion of the moving person. For optimal face recognition, we place virtual cameras to capture frontal face appearance; for gait recognition we place virtual cameras to capture a side view of the person. Multiple cameras can be rendered simultaneously, and camera position is dynamically updated as the person moves through the workspace. Image sequences from each canonical view are passed to an unmodified face or gait recognition algorithm. We show that our approach provides greater recognition accuracy than is obtained using the unnormalized input sequences, and that integrated face and gait recognition provides improved performance over either modality alone. Canonical view estimation, rendering, and recognition have been efficiently implemented and can run at near real-time speeds.

### Randall Davis

*This paper summed up a considerable body of innovative work in model-based reasoning and helped to make explicit how and why that reasoning paradigm worked. It also provided, in the notion of "adjacency," a revealing insight into the nature of knowledge representations.*

**Paper:** Diagnostic Reasoning Based on Structure and Behavior

**Author:** Randall Davis

**Journal:** Artificial Intelligence 24, no. 1–3 (1984): 347–410

**Year:** 1984

We describe a system that reasons from first principles, that is, using knowledge of structure and behavior. The system has been implemented and tested on several examples in the domain of troubleshooting digital electronic circuits. We give an example of the system in operation, illustrating that this approach provides several advantages, including a significant degree of device independence; the ability to constrain the hypotheses it considers at the outset, yet deal with a progressively wider range of problems; and the ability to deal with situations that are novel in the sense that their outward manifestations may not have been encountered previously.

As background we review our basic approach to describing structure and behavior, then explore some of the technologies used previously in troubleshooting. Difficulties encountered there lead us to a number of new contributions, four of which make up the central focus of this paper. (1) We describe a technique we call *constraint suspension* that provides a powerful tool for troubleshooting. (2) We point out the importance of making explicit the assumptions underlying reasoning and describe a technique that helps enumerate assumptions methodically. (3) The result is an overall strategy for troubleshooting based on the progressive relation of underlying assumptions. The system can focus its efforts initially, yet will methodically expand its focus to include a broad range of faults. (4) Finally, abstracting from our examples, we find that the concept of *adjacency* proves to be useful in understanding why some faults are especially difficult to diagnose and why multiple representations are useful.

### Jesús A. del Alamo

*I have selected this paper because it showcases many of the values that we so much cherish at MIT. It celebrates the ability of our students to carry out hands-on research in our labs (in this case by fabricating InP high-electron mobility transistors). It illustrates our passion to be relevant (in this case by working on a very real and hard problem in collaboration with industry). It also exemplifies our commitment to openness (in this case by collaborating with Universitat de Barcelona).*

**Paper:** Hydrogen-Induced Piezoelectric Effects in InP HEMTs

**Authors:** R. Blanchard, J.A. del Alamo, S.B. Adams, P.C. Chao, and A. Cornet

**Journal:** *IEEE Electron Devices Letters* 20, no. 8 (August 1999): 393–395

**Year:** 1999

In this letter, we have investigated hydrogen degradation of InP HEMTs with Ti/Pt/Au gates. We have found that the $V_T$ shifts negative after exposure to hydrogen and exhibits a $L_G$ and orientation dependence. We postulate that $DV_T$ is at least in part due to the piezoelectric effect. Hydrogen exposure leads to the formation of $TiH_x$, producing compressive stress in the gate. This stress induces a piezoelectric

charge distribution in the semiconductor that shifts the threshold voltage. We have independently confirmed $TiH_x$ formation under our experimental conditions through Auger measurements. Separate radius-of-curvature measurements have also independently confirmed that Ti/Pt films become compressively stressed relative to their initial state after $H_2$ exposure.

### Jack B. Dennis

*I have chosen this paper because it presents a summation of the efforts of my MIT research group to solve the problem of implementing parallel computing in a manner that supports programming with software modules and components, at least as effectively as can be done using the best current sequential programming methods.*

**Chapter:** A Parallel Program Execution Model Supporting Modular Software Construction

**Author:** Jack B. Dennis

**Publisher:** *Proceedings of the Third Working Conference on Massively Parallel Programming Models*, 50–60. IEEE Computer Society

**Year:** 1998

A watershed is near in the architecture of computer systems. There is overwhelming demand for systems that support a universal format for computer programs and software components, so users may benefit from their use on a wide variety of computing platforms. At present this demand is being met by commodity microprocessors together with standard operating system interfaces. However, current systems do not offer a standard API (application program interface) for parallel programming, and the popular interfaces for parallel computing violate essential principles of modular or component-based software construction. Moreover, microprocessor architecture is reaching the limit of what can be done usefully within the framework of superscalar and VLIW processor models. The next step is to put several processors (or the equivalent) on a single chip. This paper presents a set of principles for modular software construction and describes a program execution model based on functional programming that satisfies the set of principles. The implications of the principles for computer system architecture are discussed, together with a sketch of the architecture of a multithread-processing chip that promises to provide efficient execution of

parallel computations while providing a sound base for modular software construction.

### Srinivas Devadas

*I selected this paper, even though it is recent, because I believe that it represents a significant new direction in the development of secure hardware circuits and processors. These ideas can be applied to develop unclonable key cards and digital rights management mechanisms.*

**Chapter:** Silicon Physical Random Functions

**Authors:** Blaise Gassend, Dwaine Clarke, Marten van Dijk, and Srinivas Devadas

**Publisher:** *Proceedings of the Computer and Communication Security Conference,* 148–160. New York: ACM Press

**Year:** 2002

We introduce the notion of a Physical Random Function (also termed Physical Unclonable Function, abbreviated as PUF). We argue that a complex integrated circuit can be viewed as a silicon PUF and describe a technique to identify and authenticate individual integrated circuits (ICs).

We describe several possible circuit realizations of different PUFs. These circuits have been implemented in commodity Field Programmable Gate Arrays (FPGAs). We present experiments that indicate that reliable authentication of individual FPGAs can be performed even in the presence of significant environmental variations.

We describe how secure smart cards can be built and also briefly describe how PUFs can be applied to licensing and certification applications.

### Mildred S. Dresselhaus

*I chose this paper because it had a big impact on the field. Also, it was selected for reprinting in Advances in Physics 51 (2002), appearing unchanged twenty-one years after its original publication.*

**Paper:** Intercalation Compounds of Graphite

**Authors:** M.S. Dresselhaus and G. Dresselhaus

**Journal:** *Advances in Physics* 30, no. 2 (March/April 1981): 139–326

**Year:** 1981

A broad review of recent research work on the preparation and the remarkable properties of intercalation compounds of graphite, covering a wide range of topics from the basic chemistry, physics, and materials science to engineering applications.

**Frédo Durand**

*I believe that digital photography can dramatically improve the way we take pictures, using techniques like the "magic filter" presented in this paper. Digital photography provides unprecedented flexibility to enhance pictures by building upon the craft of master photographers. This contribution also shows the ambiguity of the notion of photorealism: a photo is no longer a mechanical recording of photons; it is enhanced to improve legibility and aesthetics.*

**Paper:** Fast Bilateral Filtering for the Display of High-Dynamic-Range Images
**Authors:** Frédo Durand and Julie Dorsey
**Journal:** *ACM Transactions on Graphics* 21, no.3 (2002, Special Issue: Proceedings of SIGGRAPH): 257–266
**Year:** 2002

We present a new technique for the display of high-dynamic-range images, which reduces the contrast while preserving detail. It is based on a two-scale decomposition of the image into a base layer, encoding large-scale variations, and a detail layer. Only the base layer has its contrast reduced, thereby preserving detail. The base layer is obtained using an edge-preserving filter called the *bilateral filter*. This is a nonlinear filter, through which the weight of each pixel is computed using a Gaussian in the spatial domain multiplied by an influence function in the intensity domain that decreases the weight of pixels with large intensity differences. We express bilateral filtering in the framework of robust statistics and show how it relates to anisotropic diffusion. We then accelerate bilateral filtering by using a piecewise-linear approximation in the intensity domain and appropriate subsampling. This results in a speed-up of two orders of magnitude. The method is fast and requires no parameter setting.

**Michael Ernst**

*I've chosen this paper both because it has spawned a subfield and because it has proved applicable in a wide variety of circumstances. In particular, work that builds on this paper has shown how to identify refactoring opportunities, improve test suites, automate theorem-proving, assist humans performing program verification, identify symptoms of program errors, indicate mismatched components, and more.*

**Paper:** Dynamically Discovering Likely Program Invariants to Support Program Evolution
**Authors:** Michael D. Ernst, Jake Cockrell, William G. Griswold, and David Notkin
**Journal:** *IEEE Transactions on Software Engineering* 27, no. 2 (February 2001): 1–25
**Year:** 2001

Explicitly stated program invariants can help programmers by identifying program properties that must be preserved when modifying code. In practice, however, these invariants are usually implicit. An alternative to expecting programmers to fully annotate code with invariants is to automatically infer likely invariants from the program itself. This research focuses on dynamic techniques for discovering invariants from execution traces.

This article reports three results. First, it describes techniques for dynamically discovering invariants, along with an implementation named Daikon, that embodies these techniques. Second, it reports on the application of Daikon to two sets of target programs. In programs from Gries's work on program derivation, the system rediscovered predefined invariants. In a C program lacking explicit invariants, the system discovered invariants that assisted a software evolution task. These experiments demonstrate that, at least for small programs, invariant inference is both accurate and useful. Third, it analyzes scalability issues such as invariant detection runtime and accuracy as functions of test suites and program points instrumented.

**Shaoul Ezekiel**

*This paper was chosen because it was the first to reveal how light (or electromagnetic radiation) really interacts with the simplest of atoms regardless of the intensity of the field. The data disagreed with all the various theories put forth up to that time with the exception of that of Mollow. This contributed greatly to the fields of ultra-high-resolution studies of atoms, molecules, and solids; optical wavelength/frequency standards; and multistep, multifrequency interactions with matter.*

**Paper:** Investigation of the Spectrum of Resonance Fluorescence Induced by a Monochromatic Field
**Authors:** F.Y. Wu, R.E. Grove, and S. Ezekiel
**Journal:** *Physical Review Letters* 35, no. 21 (24 November 1975): 1426–1429
**Year:** 2001

Measurements of the spectrum of resonance fluorescence induced by a monochromatic laser field in an atomic beam of sodium have been made over a wide range of laser intensities for both on- and off-resonance excitation. The spectra are consistent with theoretical calculations first made by Mollow.

**Robert M. Fano**

*This paper covers the bulk of my doctoral research. I identified my thesis problem while working on microwave components at the Radiation Laboratory and started working on it upon the termination of the laboratory in April 1946. I failed to make any progress through fall 1946, but I finally saw the light just before Christmas and was able to obtain a complete solution to the problem in time to graduate in June 1947. My doctoral thesis was my first major research contribution, and arguably my most important one. I did no further work in that area and went looking for greener pastures.*

**Paper:** Theoretical Limitations on the Broadband Matching of Arbitrary Impedances
**Author:** R.M. Fano
**Journal:** *Journal of the Franklin Institute* 249, no. 1/2 (January/February 1950): 57–83, 139–154
**Year:** 1950

This paper deals with the general problem of matching an arbitrary load impedance to a pure resistance by means of a reactive network. It consists primarily of a systematic study of the origin and nature of the theoretical limitations on the tolerance and bandwidth of match and of their dependence on the characteristics of the given load impedance. Necessary and sufficient conditions are derived for the physical realizability of a function of frequency representing the input reflection coefficient of a matching network terminated in a prescribed load impedance. These conditions of physical realizability are then transformed into a set of integral relations involving the logarithm of the magnitude of the reflection coefficient. Such relations are particularly suitable for the study of the limitations on the bandwidth and tolerance of match. Definite expressions for these quantities are obtained in special cases. The practical problem of approaching the optimum theoretical tolerance by means of a network with a finite number of elements is also being considered. Design curves are provided for a particularly simple but very important type of load impedance. In addition, a very convenient method is presented for computing the values of the elements of the resulting matching network.

### Clifton G. Fonstad, Jr.

*I chose one of a number of papers of which I am proud, not because they will win any of their authors a Nobel Prize, but because of the way in which they embody the satisfaction a professor can experience from mentoring MIT graduate students and watching them develop into the experts in their fields. This paper documents the results of what happened when Wai Lee, one such student on the threshold of receiving his Ph.D., and by then able to grow amazing heterostructures, teamed with a new graduate student, Tom Broekaert, to attempt an unusual new device structure I had proposed to them. We ended up making devices that set a world performance record that stood until Tom, four years later and by then ready to get his own Ph.D., taught a new graduate student, Jurgen Smet, how it was done and they together set a performance record (50:1) that still stands.*

**Paper:** Pseudomorphic InGaAs/AlAs/InAs Resonant Tunneling Diodes with Peak-to-valley Current Ratios of 30 at Room Temperature

**Authors:** Tom P.E. Broekaert, Wai Lee, and Clifton G. Fonstad, Jr.

**Journal:** *Applied Physics Letters* 53 (16) (17 October 1988): 1545–1547

**Year:** 1988

Pseudomorphic In0.53Ga0.47As/AlAs/InAs resonant tunneling diodes have been grown on InP substrates by molecular beam epitaxy. Peak-to-valley current ratios as high as 30 at 300 K and 63 at 77 K are obtained on a structure with barriers of ten atomic layers AlAs, and a well consisting of three atomic layers of In0.53Ga0.47As, six atomic layers of InAs, and three atomic layers of In0.53Ga0.47As. For comparison

pseudomorphic In0.53Ga0.47As/AlAs with In0.53Ga0.47As well structures have also been fabricated. For the In0.53Ga0.47As well structures, peak-to-valley current ratios as high as 23 have been obtained at 300 K, and, in other devices with lower current densities, two resonances are observed at room temperature.

### G. David Forney, Jr.

*This was my first paper, produced during my doctoral work at MIT. It launched my research career in information theory and coding.*

**Paper:** On Decoding BCH Codes

**Author:** G. David Forney, Jr.

**Journal:** *IEEE Transactions on Information Theory* IT-11 (October 1965): 549–557

**Year:** 1965

The Gorenstein–Zierler decoding algorithm for BCH codes is extended, modified, and analyzed; in particular, we show how to correct erasures as well as errors, exhibit improved procedures for finding error and erasure values, and consider in some detail the implementation of these procedures in a special-purpose computer.

### Dennis M. Freeman

*This paper demonstrated the use of light microscopy to measure micromechanical motions with nanometer resolution. The method has led to new insights into how sensory cells in the inner ear sense sound-induced motions. It has also become an important commercially available tool for studying MEMS. This work was done here at MIT, and Quentin Davis (Ph.D. 1997) was my student.*

**Paper:** Using Video Microscopy to Characterize Micromechanics of Biological and Man-made Micromachines

**Authors:** Dennis M. Freeman and C. Quentin Davis

**Publisher:** *Technical Digest of the Solid-State Sensor and Actuator Workshop*, 161–167. Hilton Head Island, South Carolina: Transducers Research Foundation, Inc.

**Year:** 1996

Microscopic mechanics at the scale of individual sensory receptor cells play an important signal-processing role in the inner ear. However, there are few direct measurements, in large part because the measurements are technically challenging. The important structures

are small (micrometers), and the motions are even smaller (nanometers) as well as fast (audio frequencies from 20 Hz to 20 kHz). Furthermore, to relate the motions of different structures, simultaneous measurements from many targets are important.

We have developed a new method for visualizing and measuring the sound-induced motions of inner-ear structures. We use 1) a light microscope to magnify the image of the inner ear and to project the image onto a CCD camera, 2) optical sectioning to obtain sequences of images that characterize the entire 3D structure, and 3) stroboscopic illumination to create slow-motion video sequences in response to audio-frequency stimuli. Even after optical magnification, sound-induced displacements of inner-ear structures are small compared to the pixel spacing of modern CCD cameras. Nevertheless, subpixel motions modulate the brightness field. We have modified robot vision algorithms to determine motion from changes in the brightness field.

Although this system was designed to study mechanics of the inner ear, it has broader application. We illustrate possible applications in MEMS with measurements of the three-dimensional motions of the teeth in a micro-fabricated comb drive.

### William T. Freeman

*This is the most original new work that I've done since arriving at MIT last fall, as well as being the MIT work with which I'm most personally involved.*

**Chapter:** Shape Recipes: Scene Representations that Refer to the Image

**Authors:** William T. Freeman and Antonio Torralba

**Publisher:** In *Advances in Neural Information Processing Systems.* Vol. 15. Cambridge, Massachusetts: MIT Press

**Year:** 2003

The goal of low-level vision is to estimate an underlying scene, given an observed image. Real-world scenes (e.g., albedos or shapes) can be very complex, conventionally requiring high-dimensional representations, which are hard to estimate and store. We propose a low-dimensional representation, called a scene recipe, that relies on the image itself to describe the complex scene configurations. Shape recipes are an example: these are the regression coefficients that predict the bandpassed shape from bandpassed image data. We describe the benefits of this representation and show two uses illustrating their properties: (1) We improve stereo shape estimates by learning shape recipes at low resolution and applying them at full resolution; (2) Shape recipes implicitly contain information about lighting and materials, and we use them for material segmentation.

## Lawrence S. Frishkopf

*This work, done collaboratively with Gerard G. Harris and Ake Flock at Bell Telephone Laboratories, reports the first successful intracellular recordings from "hair cells," the receptor cells of all vertebrate lateral line, vestibular, and auditory organs. I think the work was seminal; it was followed over a period of years by intracellular recordings by other workers from hair cells in other vertebrate organs, leading to a new and better understanding of the operation of these sensory cells.*

**Paper:** Receptor Potentials from Hair Cells of the Lateral Line

**Authors:** Gerard G. Harris, Lawrence S. Frishkopf, and Ake Flock

**Journal:** *Science, New Series* 167, no. 3914 (2 January 1970): 76–79

**Year:** 1970

Intracellular recordings from hair cells in the tail lateral line of mudpuppy *Necturus maculosus* show receptor potentials less than 800 microvolts, peak to peak, from stimuli that are considered large compared to natural stimuli. The hair cells are in neuromasts that are sensitive at the time of recording and are identified by both in vivo and in vitro examination of intracellular staining.

## James G. Fujimoto

*This reference describes the development of Optical Coherence Tomography (OCT), which was performed in our group in the EECS department and the Research Laboratory for Electronics in collaboration with investigators at Massachusetts General Hospital and the Massachusetts Eye and Ear Infirmary. OCT is a new biomedical imaging modality that is anal-ogous to ultrasound or radar except that it uses light. Micron-scale cross-sectional images are generated by measuring the echo time delay of light backscattered from within tissue. OCT functions as a type of "optical biopsy" to provide high-resolution images of tissue microstructure, but imaging can be performed in situ and in real time, without the need to excise a specimen. OCT promises to have a wide range of applications, including ophthalmology, cancer detection, and surgical guidance. OCT has become an active area of research, and there are now many groups internationally who are working in this area. There were two MIT start-up companies formed based on this technology. Advanced Ophthalmic Devices was founded to develop OCT for ophthalmic applications. The company was acquired by Zeiss Humphrey, and a commercial OCT imaging device for ophthalmology was introduced in 1996. In 1998, a second start-up, LightLab Imaging, was formed to develop OCT for intravascular and endoscopic applications. This company was recently acquired by Goodman, Ltd. There are also several other commercial organizations developing OCT or OCT-related technology.*

**Paper:** Optical Coherence Tomography

**Authors:** D. Huang, E.A. Swanson, C.P. Lin, J.S. Schuman, W.G. Stinson, W. Chang, M.R. Hee, T. Flotte, K. Gregory, C.A. Puliafito, and J.G. Fujimoto

**Journal:** *Science* 254 (November 1991): 1178–1181

**Year:** 1991

A technique called optical coherence tomography (OCT) has been developed for noninvasive cross-sectional imaging in biological systems. OCT uses low-coherence interferometry to produce a two-dimensional image of optical scattering from internal tissue microstructures in a way that is analogous to ultrasonic pulse–echo imaging. OCT has longitudinal and lateral spatial resolutions of a few micrometers and can detect reflected signals as small as $\sim 10^{-10}$ of the incident optical power. Tomographic imaging is demonstrated in vitro in the peripapillary area of the retina and in the coronary artery, two clinically relevant examples that are representative of transparent and turbid media, respectively.

## Robert G. Gallager

*I have chosen this paper partly because the work was done in my doctoral thesis, partly because I have always been proud of it, but mostly because the topic, after thirty years of relative obscurity, has become a very hot topic of research in the last few years.*

**Paper:** Low-Density Parity Check Codes

**Author:** R.G. Gallager

**Journal:** *Transactions of the IRE Professional Group on Information Theory,* IT-8 (January 1962): 2l–28

**Year:** 1962

A low-density parity-check code is a code specified by a parity-check matrix with the following properties: each column contains a small fixed number $j \leq 3$ of 1s and each row contains a small fixed number $j > k$ of 1s. The typical minimum distance of these codes increases linearly with block length for a fixed rate and fixed $j$. When used with maximum likelihood decoding on a sufficiently quiet binary-input symmetric channel, the typical probability of decoding error decreases exponentially with block length for a fixed rate and fixed $j$.

A simple but nonoptimum decoding scheme operating directly from the channel a posteriori probabilities is described. Both the equipment complexity and the data-handling capacity in bits per second of this decoder increase approximately linearly with block length.

For $j > 3$ and a sufficiently low rate, the probability of error using this decoder on a binary symmetric channel is shown to decrease at least exponentially with a root of the block length. Some experimental results show that the actual probability of decoding error is much smaller than this theoretical bound.

## David K. Gifford

*In 1982 I joined the MIT faculty to pursue my vision of community information systems and started the Boston Community Information System (BCIS) project with the support of Michael Dertouzos, then the director of the MIT Laboratory for Computer Science. Many of the goals of BCIS were further realized by the Internet and the Web, and as I write this in 2003, the availability of an inexpensive terrabyte of storage for a local information library opens up new possi-*

*bilities for digital broadcast and polychannel architectures.*

**Paper:** Polychannel Systems for Mass Digital Communication

**Author:** David K. Gifford

**Journal:** *Communications of the ACM* 23, no. 2 (February 1990): 141–151

**Year:** 1990

We describe a new type of distributed computer system that looks beyond workstation and local area network assumptions toward the time when computers will be used by everyone at both home and the office. This new system is designed to provide sophisticated information services to an entire metropolitan area. We have combined digital broadcast channels and duplex communication channels in a polychannel system that uses predicate-based database content labels to automatically route queries. Our thesis is that a polychannel system produces substantial cost and system scaling advantages while retaining the flexibility of client-server-style duplex communication. Experimental data from a two-year test of the Boston Community Information System (BCIS) with hundreds of users supports this thesis.

## Shafi Goldwasser

*This is the paper that originated the field of showing NP-hardness results for approximation problems based on probabilistic checkable proofs. This theory of probabilistically checkable proofs and its usefulness for classifying the complexity approximation problems is considered the most significant development in complexity theory in the 1990s. Classifying the complexity of approximate versions of hard optimization problems such as clique, three-coloring, etc., has been open since the mid-1970s when Cook and Karp introduced NP-completeness and showed it applied for exact versions of many optimization problems.*

**Paper:** Interactive Proofs and the Hardness of Approximating Cliques

**Authors:** U. Feige, S. Goldwasser, L. Lovász, S. Safra, and M. Szegedy

**Journal:** *Journal of the ACM* 43, no. 2 (March 1996): 268–292

**Year:** 1996

The contribution of this paper is two-fold. First, a connection is established between approximating the size of the largest clique in a graph and multi-prover interactive proofs. Second, an efficient multi-prover interactive proof for NP languages is constructed, where the verifier uses very few random bits and communication bits. Last, the connection between cliques and efficient multi-prover interactive proofs is shown to yield hardness results on the complexity of approximating the size of the largest clique in a graph.

Of independent interest is our proof of correctness for the multilinearity test of functions.

## Martha L. Gray

*This paper describes the clinical application of a method to measure fixed-charge density in cartilage. It brings electrical engineering principles to bear on an important, unmet medical need.*

**Paper:** Nondestructive Imaging of Human Cartilage Glycosaminoglycan Concentration by MRI

**Authors:** A. Bashir, M.L. Gray, J. Hartke, and D. Burstein

**Journal:** *Magnetic Resonance in Medicine* 41, no. 5 (1999): 857–865

**Year:** 1999

Despite the compelling need mandated by the prevalence and morbidity of degenerative cartilage diseases, it is extremely difficult to study disease progression and therapeutic efficacy, either in vitro or in vivo (clinically). This is partly because no techniques have been available for nondestructively visualizing the distribution of functionally important macromolecules in living cartilage. Here we describe and validate a technique to image the glycosaminoglycan concentration ([GAG]) of human cartilage nondestructively by magnetic resonance imaging (MRI). The technique is based on the premise that the negatively charged contrast agent gadolinium diethylene triamine pentaacetic acid ($Gd(DTPA)^{2-}$) will distribute in cartilage in inverse relation to the negatively charged GAG concentration. Nuclear magnetic resonance spectroscopy studies of cartilage explants demonstrated that there was an approximately linear relationship between $T_1$ (in the presence of $Gd(DTPA)^{2-}$) and [GAG] over a large range of [GAG]. Furthermore, there was a strong agreement between the [GAG] calculated from $[Gd(DTPA)^{2-}]$ and the actual [GAG] deter-

mined from the validated methods of calculations from $[Na^+]$ and the biochemical DMMB assay. Spatial distributions of GAG were easily observed in $T_1$- weighted and $T_1$-calculated MRI studies of intact human joints, with good histological correlation. Furthermore, in vivo clinical images of $T_1$ in the presence of $Gd(DTPA)^{2-}$ (i.e., GAG distribution) correlated well with the validated ex vivo results after total knee replacement surgery, showing that it is feasible to monitor GAG distribution in vivo. This approach gives us the opportunity to image directly the concentration of GAG, a major and critically important macromolecule in human cartilage.

## Paul E. Gray
## (Campbell Searle)

*My research career at MIT wound down in the late 1960s when I got seriously involved in the central administration. None of the research papers from earlier years would be appropriate to highlight now, and I doubt that the readers of this book would be interested in the papers or invited lectures (all non-EECS) that I've prepared in the last thirty-one years.*

*But the book described below was a major, consuming activity for both my coauthor, Campbell Searle, and me. It represented, for both of us, the most serious intellectual undertaking we'd been part of, which is why we've chosen to include it here. Cam and I had both been deeply involved in the work of the Semiconductor Electronics Education Committee (SEEC) from 1961 through its windup in the late 1960s. The SEEC effort produced seven volumes of text that revolutionized the teaching of electronics in the United States and abroad. Cam or I or both appear as authors, among others, on all but one of those volumes, and each of us had taught aspects of the material here repeatedly. By the mid-1960s we believed that we understood the material well enough to do a comprehensive electronics text, which would draw on our SEEC experience and "get it right." The following excerpts have been taken from the book's preface.*

**Book:** *Electronic Principles: Physics, Models, and Circuits*

**Authors:** P.E. Gray and C.L. Searle

**Publisher:** New York: John Wiley & Sons, Inc.

**Year:** 1969

This book has been shaped to meet the educational needs implied by the dominance of integrated circuits in electronic technology and by the use of digital computers in engineering design. These needs emerge directly from the use of integrated circuits in electronic systems, which began as a trend in the early 1960s and have by now revolutionized the conceptualization and fabrication of electronic systems. In consequence, the traditional boundaries between the three disciplines of device or component design, circuit design, and system design have been all but obliterated.

Instead, two broadly defined disciplines are emerging from the areas of activity that encompass electronics from devices through systems. The first of these disciplines is concerned with the general area of devices and circuits. The second is concerned with circuits and systems.

The devices-and-circuits area is primarily the province of those who design and manufacture integrated circuits, discrete semiconductor devices, and other "components" of modern electronics. Engineers who work in this area of activity must be knowledgeable in semiconductor fabrication technology, in the physical electronics and circuit modeling of semiconductor components, and in the methods and techniques of circuit analysis and design; their activity is subject to the constraints and opportunities of both device technology and circuit theory. In addition, the device-and-circuits engineer must have a sufficient knowledge of systems engineering to enable him to communicate with the users of his products who work at the systems design level.

Circuits-and-systems engineers, to be competent in the design of electronic systems, must be able to exploit integrated-circuit functional blocks, such as operational amplifiers, logic gates, and memory elements, and to use passive components and discrete transistors in "interfaces" between integrated assemblies. In addition to being thoroughly familiar with both circuit theory and system theory, these engineers should have some knowledge of device structure and behavior to facilitate communication with those who work in the devices-

and-circuits area and to facilitate the intelligent design of circuits that make use of semiconductor components.

During the same time that semiconductor integrated circuits have come to the fore in electronics, there has occurred an explosive growth both in the use of high-speed computational methods in engineering design and in the availability of computational facilities on university campuses and at industrial laboratories. As a result, it is now commonplace to undertake the analysis of circuits and systems that are orders of magnitude more complex than those that could be studied only a few years ago.

To meet the needs of these new generations of engineers, this book begins with the physical principles that are involved in the operation of semiconductor components, proceeds through the physical electronics, modeling, and circuit characteristics of these components, and engages the questions and problems that arise in the computer-aided design of complex multistage amplifiers and functional assemblies of the type found in modern integrated-circuit packages.

The book covers five principal areas: (1) an introduction to electronics; (2) semiconductor physics; (3) device physical electronics, models, and properties; (4) multistage circuits in which transistors are used as linear amplifiers; (5) multistage circuits in which transistors are used as switches.

Chapter 1 serves as an introduction by illustrating the nature and use of an electronic control valve. Chapters 2 through 5 provide a self-contained treatment of those aspects of the electrical properties of semiconductors, the physical electronics of *pn* junctions, and semiconductor-device-fabrication technology that are essential to an understanding, at the quantitative level, of the behavior of semiconductor active devices and integrated circuits.

Chapters 6 through 14 deal with the physical electronics, circuit modeling, and circuit properties of the most important semiconductor components, including junction diodes, bipolar junction transistors, unipolar (field-effect)

junction transistors, and metal-oxide-semiconductor unipolar or field-effect transistors. Chapters 15 through 20 are concerned with multistage applications of transistors, in which the active devices are used as linear control valves. Finally, chapters 21 through 24 deal with application of the transistor as a switch.

The material in this book can be covered in two or three semesters, depending on the amount of classroom time devoted to the many worked-out examples that are included in the text. More of such examples have been included than would normally be used in one particular year, to provide the instructor with more flexibility in his teaching. We have taught essentially all of this material to undergraduates in the Department of Electrical Engineering at MIT at least twice.

**W. Eric L. Grimson**

*This paper was the most widely cited article published in* TMI *in 1996 and set the standard for the medical image analysis field in segmentation of medical imagery. It led to a large number of follow-on efforts by groups internationally and still serves as the basis for segmentation in a wide variety of applications.*

**Paper:** Adaptive Segmentation of MRI Data
**Authors:** W.M. Wells, III, W.E.L. Grimson, R. Kikinis, and F.A. Jolesz
**Journal:** *IEEE Transactions on Medical Imaging* 15, no. 4 (August 1996): 429–442
**Year:** 1996

Intensity-based classification of MR images has proven problematic, even when advanced techniques are used. Intrascan and interscan intensity inhomogeneities are a common source of difficulty. While reported methods have had some success in correcting intrascan inhomogeneities, such methods require supervision for the individual scan. This paper describes a new method called adaptive segmentation that uses knowledge of tissue intensity properties and intensity inhomogeneities to correct and segment MR images. Use of the expectation-maximization (EM) algorithm leads to a method that allows for more accurate segmentation of tissue types as well as better visualization of magnetic resonance imaging (MRI) data, that has proven to be effective in a study that includes more than one hundred brain scans.

Implementation and results are described for segmenting the brain in the following types of images: axial (dual-echo spin-echo), coronal (three-dimensional Fourier transform (3-DFT) gradient-echo T1-weighted)—all using a conventional head coil—and a sagittal section acquired using a surface coil. The accuracy of adaptive segmentation was found to be comparable with manual segmentation, and closer to manual segmentation than supervised multivariant classification while segmenting gray and white matter.

**Alan J. Grodzinsky**

*For the past twenty-five years, our group has been studying the electromechanical and physicochemical properties of biological tissues such as cartilage, as well as the mechanisms by which physical forces affect living cell biological responses in such tissues, measured in organ culture experiments. This paper represents an approach to designing living replacement cartilage for people with debilitating arthritis and other focal diseases and defects in this tissue.*

**Paper:** Self-Assembling Peptide Hydrogel Fosters Chondrocyte Extracellular Matrix Production and Cell Division: Implications for Cartilage Tissue Repair

**Authors:** John Kisiday, Moonsoo Jin, Bodo Kurz, Han-Hwa Hung, Carlos Semino, Shuguang Zhang, and Alan J. Grodzinsky

**Journal:** *Proceedings of the National Academy of Science* 99, no. 15 (23 July 2002): 9996–10001

**Year:** 2002

Emerging medical technologies for effective and lasting repair of articular cartilage include delivery of cells or cell-seeded scaffolds to a defect site to initiate de novo tissue regeneration. Biocompatible scaffolds assist in providing a template for cell distribution and extracellular matrix accumulation in a three-dimensional geometry. A major challenge in choosing an appropriate scaffold for cartilage repair is the identification of a material that can simultaneously stimulate high rates of cell division and high rates of cell synthesis of phenotypically specific extra-cellular matrix (ECM) macromolecules until repair evolves into steady-state tissue maintenance. We have devised a novel self-assembling peptide hydrogel scaffold for cartilage repair and developed a method to

encapsulate chondrocytes within the peptide hydrogel. During four weeks of culture in vitro, chondrocytes seeded within the peptide hydrogel retained their morphology and developed a cartilage-like ECM rich in proteoglycans and type II collagen, indicative of a stable chondrocyte phenotype. Time-dependent accumulation of this ECM was paralleled by increases in material stiffness, indicative of deposition of mechanically functional neo-tissue. Taken together, these results demonstrate the potential of a self-assembling peptide hydrogel as a scaffold for the synthesis and accumulation of a true cartilage-like ECM within a 3D cell culture for cartilage tissue repair.

**John V. Guttag**

*This paper looks back, a quarter century or so later, at work I did early in my career. Including it is a bit of a cheat, since it allows me to include (by reference) more than one piece of my early work. I look back with pride on the work that I and my colleagues (including Jim Horning, Steve Garland, and Barbara Liskov) did to help develop the notion of data abstraction. Today, data abstraction is taken for granted.*

*The advent of data abstraction foreshadowed a shift of emphasis in programming from decomposition, which had dominated people's thinking for many years, to abstraction. A related development was an increased emphasis on interfaces, in particular on interfaces characterized by operations. Data abstraction encouraged program designers to focus on the centrality of data objects rather than procedures. It also encouraged people to think about programming as a process of combining relatively large chunks since data abstractions typically encompass much more functionality than do individual procedures. This, in turn, leads one to think of the essence of programming as a process not of writing individual lines of code, but of composing modules.*

**Paper:** Abstract Data Types, Then and Now

**Author:** J. Guttag

**Publisher:** In *Software Pioneers: Contributions to Software Engineering*, M. Broy and E. Denert, eds. New York: Springer-Verlag

**Year:** 2002

Data abstraction has come to play an important role in software development. This paper

presents one view of what data abstraction is, how it was viewed when it was introduced, and its long-term impact on programming.

**Peter L. Hagelstein**

*The reason for my choice is that the result is a very important one—we observed a factor of eight improvement in the figure of merit of a semiconductor thermoelectric. This may be one of the most important results that I have gotten at MIT that has been published under my name.*

**Paper:** Enhanced Figure of Merit in Thermal to Electrical Energy Conversion Using Diode Structures

**Authors:** P.L. Hagelstein and Y. Kucherov

**Journal:** *Applied Physics Letters* 81, no. 3 (15 July 2002): 559–561

**Year:** 2002

A characterization of the electrical and thermal properties of thermoelectric diode structures indicates that the figure of merit for thermal to electrical energy conversion is significantly enhanced in our devices over thermoelectric values. Enhancements are due to current injection and blockage of the ohmic return current within the devices. The resulting device takes advantage of both thermoelectric and thermionic effects, and can be considered to be a hybrid. Experiments indicate an enhancement as high as a factor of eight in the effective figure of merit. The best results are consistent with a conversion efficiency on the order of 35 percent of the Carnot limit. Enhancements have been observed in InSb and in HgCdTe, and we believe that the approach applies generally to all thermoelectric semiconductors.

**Jongyoon Han**

*This paper is one of the first to demonstrate an application of micro/nanofabrication technology to a real-world biology problem. Instead of random, polymeric gel, regular nanofluidic channels were used as a molecular sieve for DNA separation, allowing much higher separation efficiency and possibility of mathematical modeling, optimization, and rigorous engineering.*

**Paper:** Separation of Long DNA Molecules in a Microfabricated Entropic Trap Array

**Authors:** J. Han and H.G. Craighead

**Journal:** *Science* 288, no. 5468 (12 May 2000): 1026–1029

**Year:** 2000

A nanofluidic channel device, consisting of many entropic traps, was designed and fabricated for the separation of long DNA molecules. The channel comprises narrow constrictions and wider regions that cause size-dependent trapping of DNA at the onset of a constriction. This process creates electrophoretic mobility differences, thus enabling efficient separation without the use of a gel matrix or pulsed electric fields. Samples of long DNA molecules (5,000 to ~160,000 base pairs) were efficiently separated into bands in 15-millimeter-long channels. Multiple-channel devices operating in parallel were demonstrated. The efficiency, compactness, and ease of fabrication of the device suggest the possibility of more practical integrated DNA analysis systems.

### Hermann A. Haus

*My doctoral thesis was on classical noise, specifically noise in microwave traveling wave tubes. My thesis work showed that there is no fundamental limit imposed by classical physics on the noise level in an electronic amplifier of specified gain; classical noise could be made as small as desired with sufficient effort and sophistication. The following paper was my entry into quantum noise. Quantum physics does impose a lower limit, and quantum amplifier noise became a* leitmotiv *in my later work on noise. It is noteworthy that optical fiber amplifiers today operate within about 1dB of the fundamental limit.*

**Paper:** Quantum Noise in Linear Amplifiers

**Authors:** H.A. Haus and J.A. Mullen

**Journal:** *Physical Review* 128, no. 5 (1 December 1962): 2407–2413

**Year:** 1962

The classical definition of noise figure, based on signal-to-noise ratio, is adapted to the case when quantum noise is predominant. The noise figure is normalized to "uncertainty noise." General quantum mechanical equations for linear amplifiers are set up using the condition of linearity and the requirement that the commutator brackets of the pertinent operators are conserved in the amplification. These equations include as special cases the maser, the parametric amplifier, and the parametric up-converter. Using these equations, the noise figure of a general amplifier is derived. The minimum value of this noise figure is equal to 2. The significance of the result with regard to simultaneous phase and amplitude measurements is explored.

### Berthold K.P. Horn

*This paper introduced the optimization-based approach to machine vision—using the calculus of variation—and furthered the so-called physics-based view of machine vision. Aside from uses in machine vision and photogrammetry, this forms the basis of methods used in optical mice, hand-held cameras for motion compensation, video compression, as well as nanometer motion measurements of tectonic membranes and MEMS devices.*

*This paper is also one of the most referenced papers in the artificial intelligence literature. According to the American Association of Artificial Intelligence, my papers "Determining Optical Flow" and "Numerical Shape from Shading and Occluding Boundaries" were among the fifty articles that received the greatest number of citations in the five years following publication. This led to my election as a fellow of the AAAI in 1990 for significant contributions to the field of AI. Also, www.citeseer.com lists more than a thousand references. The optical flow work was done while I visited Professor Hans-Helmut Nagel at the University of Hamburg in the summer of 1978 and was first published as "AI Memo 572."*

**Paper:** Determining Optical Flow

**Authors:** Berthold K.P. Horn and Brian G. Schunck

**Journal:** *Artificial Intelligence* 16, no. 1–3 (August 1981): 185–203

**Year:** 1981

Optical flow cannot be computed locally, since only one independent measurement is available from the image sequence at a point while the flow velocity has two components. A second constraint is needed. A method for finding the optical flow pattern is presented which assumes that the apparent velocity of the brightness pattern varies smoothly almost everywhere in the image. An iterative implementation is shown which successfully computes the optical flow for a number of synthetic image sequences. The algorithm is robust in that it can handle image sequences that are quantized rather coarsely in space and time. It is also insensitive to quantization of brightness levels and additive noise. Examples are included where the assumption of smoothness is violated at singular points or along lines in the image.

### Judy L. Hoyt

*This piece reviews the current state of the art for a field that I helped to pioneer, along with the other MIT faculty listed on the paper, over the last ten years. With so many Institute contributors, this paper is representative of a strong area of research in electronic devices at MIT. This was an invited paper at a recent IEEE International Electron Devices Meeting: Relativistic Analysis of Absolute and Convective Instability Evolutions in Three Dimensions.*

**Paper:** Strained Si MOSFET Technology

**Authors:** J.L. Hoyt, H.M. Nayfeh, S. Eguchi, I. Aberg, G. Xia, T. Drake, E.A. Fitzgerald, and D.A. Antoniadis

**Journal:** *IEEE International Electron Devices Meeting Technical Digest* (December 2002): 23–26

**Year:** 2002

Mobility and current drive improvements associated with biaxial tensile stress in Si $n$- and $p$-MOSFETs are briefly reviewed. Electron mobility enhancements at high channel doping (up to 6 x $10^{18}$ cm$^{-3}$) are characterized in strained Si $n$-MOSFETs. For low inversion layer carrier concentrations, channel-dopant ionized impurity scattering does reduce the strain-induced mobility enhancement, but the enhancement is recovered at higher inversion charge concentrations, where screening is efficient. Mobility enhancement in strained Si $p$-MOSFETs is also discussed. There are process integration challenges and opportunities associated with this technology. Dopant diffusion, and its impact on profiled engineering in strained Si CMOS structures, is one example. While the slower diffusion of B in Si$_{1-x}$Ge$_x$ enables improved doping profile control, the diffusivity of the n-type dopants is dramatically enhanced in Si$_{0.8}$Ge$_{0.2}$.

### Qing Hu

*This paper describes our recent breakthrough in developing the longest wavelength quantum*

cascade lasers based on resonant phonon scattering for depopulation. This work could lead to solid-state lasers operating in the frequency range where transistors dominate, opening new opportunities in remote sensing and imaging, communications, and ultra-high-speed signal processing.

**Paper:** 3.4-THz Quantum Cascade Laser Based on Longitudinal-optical-phonon Scattering for Depopulation

**Authors:** Benjamin S. Williams, Hans Callebaut, Sushil Kumar, and Qing Hu

**Journal:** *Applied Physics Letters* 82, no. 7 (17 February 2003): 1015–1017

**Year:** 2003

We report the development of the longest wavelength quantum cascade laser to date, at $\lambda = 87.2$ μm corresponding to 3.44 THz or 1.42 meV photon energy. The GaAs/AlGaAs laser structure utilizes longitudinal-optical (LO) phonon scattering for electron depopulation. Laser action is obtained in pulsed mode at temperatures up to 65 K, and at 50 percent duty cycle up to 29 K. Operating at 5 K in pulsed mode, the threshold current density is 840 A/cm², and the peak power is approximately 2.5 mW. Based on the relatively high operating temperatures and duty cycles, we propose that direct LO-phonon-based depopulation is a robust method for achieving quantum cascade lasers at long-wavelength THz frequencies.

### Piotr Indyk

*This paper continues the rich MIT tradition of research in coding theory. In particular, it unifies (in a sense) the results of the doctoral theses of Dan Spielman (on linear time codes) and Venkat Guruswami (on list decoding from an arbitrary fraction of errors).*

**Paper:** Linear Time Encodable and List Decodable Codes

**Authors:** P. Indyk and V. Guruswami

**Publisher:** *Proceedings of the 35th Annual ACM Symposium on Theory of Computing (STOC)*, ACM Press

**Year:** 2003

We present the first construction of error-correcting codes that can be (list) decoded from a noise fraction arbitrarily close to 1 in linear time. Specifically, we present an explicit construction of codes that can be encoded in linear time as well as list decoded in linear time

from a fraction $(1 - \varepsilon)$ of errors for arbitrary $\varepsilon > 0$. The rate and alphabet size of the construction are constants that depend only on $\varepsilon$. Our construction involves devising a new combinatorial approach to list decoding, in contrast to all previous approaches which relied on the power of decoding algorithms for algebraic codes like Reed-Solomon codes.

### Erich P. Ippen

*I chose this particular paper because it represents the success of my transition from industry (Bell Labs) to MIT. My career has been associated with advancing optical technology into the femtosecond time domain. This paper reported a new record in ultrashort pulse duration and put MIT on the map in this context. Jim Fujimoto (MIT) and Andy Weiner (Purdue) are now both highly distinguished senior researchers in ultrafast optics.*

**Paper:** Generation and Measurement of Optical Pulses as Short as 16fs

**Authors:** J.G. Fujimoto, A.M. Weiner, and E.P. Ippen

**Journal:** *Appl. Phys. Lett.* 44 (1 May 1984): 832–834

**Year:** 1984

We describe measurements of pulses consisting of only eight optical periods. The pulses were produced by compression with a short optical fiber and a grating pair. Measurement was by autocorrelation using noncollinear second harmonic generation in a thin crystal of potassium dihydrogen phosphate.

### Tommi Jaakkola

*I chose this paper because it represents a line of research (approximate inference) that I have pursued for years and because the paper won the best paper award at the conference.*

**Chapter:** A New Class of Upper Bounds on the Log Partition Function

**Authors:** Martin Wainwright, Tommi Jaakkola, and Alan Willsky

**Publisher:** *Proceedings of the Eighteenth Annual Conference on Uncertainty in Artificial Intelligence*, 536–543. New York: Morgan Kaufmann Publishers

**Year:** 2002

Bounds on the log partition function are important in a variety of contexts, including approximate inference, model fitting, decision

theory, and large deviation analysis. We introduce a new class of upper bounds on the log partition function, based on convex combinations of distributions in the exponential domain, which is applicable to an arbitrary undirected graphical model. In the special case of convex combinations of tree-structured distributions, we obtain a family of variational problems, similar to the Bethe free energy, but distinguished by the following desirable properties: (1) they are convex and have a unique global minimum, and (2) the global minimum gives an upper bound on the log partition function. The global minimum is defined by stationary conditions very similar to those defining fixed points of belief propagation (BP) or tree-based reparameterization. As with BP fixed points, the elements of the minimizing argument can be used as approximations to the marginals of the original model. The analysis described here can be extended to more structured approximations (e.g., region graph and variants).

### Daniel Jackson

*I chose this paper because it describes a simple idea that has major practical ramifications. In short, it's that a small and subtle change to how structure is encoded can make software models analyzable automatically, with hardly any loss in expressiveness. The Alloy language based on this idea has turned out to be quite effective. Since publishing the paper, we've used Alloy to represent and analyze a variety of software designs, and it has been adopted as a language for teaching software modeling in over a dozen universities.*

**Paper:** A Micromodularity Mechanism

**Authors:** Daniel Jackson, Ilya Shlyakhter, and Manu Sridharan

**Publisher:** *Proceedings of the 8th Annual European Software Engineering Conference Held Jointly with 9th ACM SIGSOFT International Symposium on Foundations of Software Engineering (ESEC/FSE '01, Vienna)*, 62–73. New York: ACM Press

**Year:** 2001

A simple mechanism for structuring specifications is described. By modeling structures as atoms, it remains entirely first-order and thus amenable to automatic analysis. And by interpreting fields of structures as relations, it allows the same relational operators used in the formula language to be used for dereferencing. An extension feature allows structures to be developed incrementally but requires no textual inclusion nor any notion of subtyping. The paper demonstrates the flexibility of the mechanism by application in a variety of common idioms.

## M. Frans Kaashoek

*This paper represents the cumulation of research on a new operating system architecture, called exokernels. The research started out with a paper, "Exokernel: An Operating System Architecture for Application-Level Resource Management," by D.R. Engler, M.F. Kaashoek, and J.W. O'Toole, Jr., in Proceedings of the 15th ACM Symposium on Operating Systems Principles, 1995. The 1995 paper presented the then radical proposal for exokernels, and the 1997 paper demonstrated that one can construct real systems using exokernels. This research had both considerable intellectual and pragmatic impact: it made people think differently about operating systems, it inspired other research, and it led to a practical system.*

**Paper:** Application Performance and Flexibility on Exokernel Systems
**Authors:** M.F. Kaashoek, D.R. Engler, G. Ganger, H. Briceno, R. Hunt, D. Mazieres, T. Pinckney, R. Grimm, and K. MacKenzie
**Journal:** *ACM Operating Systems Review* 31, no. 5 (1997): 52–65
**Year:** 1997

Traditional operating systems limit the performance, flexibility, and functionality of applications by fixing the interface and implementation of operating system abstractions such as interprocess communication and virtual memory. The *exokernel* operating system architecture addresses this problem by providing application-level management of physical resources. In the exokernel architecture, a small kernel securely exports all hardware resources through a low-level interface to untrusted library operating systems. Library operating systems use this interface to implement system objects and policies. This separation of resource protection from management allows application-specific customization of traditional operating system abstractions by extending, specializing, or even replacing libraries.

An exokernel system allows specialized applications to achieve high performance without sacrificing the performance of unmodified UNIX programs. An evaluation of the exokernel architecture measures end-to-end application performance on Xok, an exokernel for Intel x86-based computers, and compares Xok's performance to the performance of two widely used 4.4BSD UNIX systems (FreeBSD and OpenBSD). The results show that common unmodified UNIX applications can enjoy the benefits of exokernels: applications either perform comparably on Xok/ExOS and the BSD UNIXes, or perform significantly better. In addition, the results show that customized applications can benefit substantially from control over their resources (e.g., a factor of eight for a Web server). The work also reports on insights about the exokernel approach gained through building three different exokernel systems and presents novel approaches to resource multiplexing.

## Leslie Pack Kaelbling

*I was originally motivated to work on machine learning by the idea that it would be useful in making autonomous robots behave more robustly. However, most of the techniques developed by myself and others for the problem of learning behavior from experience (reinforcement learning) are much too inefficient for use on actual robots. In this paper, we show how to take advantage of a small amount of human guidance to make reinforcement learning begin to be useful on a mobile robot.*

**Paper:** Practical Reinforcement Learning in Continuous Spaces
**Authors:** William D. Smart and Leslie Pack Kaelbling
**Publisher:** *Proceedings of the Seventeenth International Conference on Machine Learning*, San Francisco: Morgan Kaufmann
**Year:** 2000

Dynamic control tasks are good candidates for the application of reinforcement learning techniques. However, many of these tasks inherently have continuous state or action variables. This can cause problems for traditional reinforcement learning algorithms, which assume discrete states and actions. In this paper, we introduce an algorithm that safely approximates the value function for continuous state control tasks and that learns quickly from a small amount of data. We give experimental results using this algorithm to learn policies for both a simulated task and also for a real robot, operating in an unaltered environment. The algorithm works well in a traditional learning setting and demonstrates extremely good learning when bootstrapped with a small amount of human-provided data.

## Franz X. Kaertner

*This paper shows for the first time the connection between the drift instability observed in actively mode-locked lasers and other synchronized systems, as well as the onset of turbulence in hydrodynamics based on non-normal behavior of the steady-state solution.*

**Paper:** Turbulence in Mode-locked Lasers
**Authors:** F.X. Kaertner, D.M. Zumbühl, and N. Matuschek
**Journal:** *Physical Review Letters* 82 (1999): 4428–4431
**Year:** 1999

We show that the well-known instability in actively mode-locked lasers with detuning between the resonator round-trip time and the modulator period exhibits a transition to turbulence analogous to fluid flow. We derive a universal normalized detuning of the laser that plays the same role as Reynolds number in fluid flow. This is the first time that the recently proposed theory for the onset of turbulence in hydrodynamics is verified in a system outside of hydrodynamics.

## David R. Karger

*This paper reflects some of the first work I did entirely at MIT. Using a simple randomized insight, it solved the problem that had held my attention since I first entered theoretical computer science.*

**Paper:** Minimum Cuts in Near-Linear Time
**Author:** D.R. Karger
**Journal:** *Journal of the ACM* 47(1) (January 2000): 46–76. [A preliminary version appeared in *Proceedings of the 28th ACM Symposium on Theory of Computing*.]
**Year:** 2000

We significantly improve known time bounds for solving the minimum cut problem on undirected graphs. We use a "semi-duality" between minimum cuts and maximum spanning tree packings combined with our previously developed random sampling techniques. We give a randomized (Monte Carlo) algorithm that finds a minimum cut in an $m$-edge, $n$-vertex graph with high probability in $O(m\backslash\log^3 n)$ time. We also give a simpler randomized algorithm that finds *all* minimum cuts with high probability in $O(n^2 \log n)$ time. This variant has an optimal *RNC* parallelization. Both variants improve on the previous best time bound of $O(n^2 \log^3 n)$. Other applications of the tree-packing approach are new, nearly tight bounds on the number of *near-minimum* cuts a graph may have and a new data structure for representing them in a space-efficient manner.

### John G. Kassakian

*This paper represented the first explanation of the high failure rates of power MOSFETs used in parallel configurations. The small chip size of early devices and their negative TC of drain-source resistance encouraged manufacturers to parallel chips in a single package to achieve high device current ratings. The results reported in this paper caused the rapid introduction of methods, such as the two described in the abstract, to damp the oscillations. Current power MOSFET technology employs polysilicon gate electrodes, which have essentially eliminated this problem.*

**Paper:** An Analysis and Experimental Verification of Parasitic Oscillations in Paralleled Power MOSFETs
**Authors:** John G. Kassakian and David Lau
**Journal:** *IEEE Transactions on Electron Devices* ED-31, no. 7 (July 1984): 959–963
**Year:** 1984

An analysis of the small signal dynamic model of the power MOSFET is presented which predicts the existence of high-frequency parasitic oscillations when these devices are electrically paralleled. It is shown that the existence of these oscillations is a strong function of the small signal transfer admittance $g_m$ and the differential mode drain, gate, and source resistances. The sensitivity of the oscillations to these parameters is determined. Experimental data verifying the qualitative aspects of the analytical results is presented. It is concluded that the problem is potentially most severe for devices that are paralleled by the manufacturer at the chip level. A practical

solution to the problem is the introduction of differential mode gate resistance, either as lumped components or by the use of polysilicon overlays.

### Dina Katabi

*I have chosen this paper for the EECS one-hundredth-anniversary book for a number of reasons. First, it addresses an important problem whose relevance will continue to increase over time as link capacity increases. Second, the paper is representative of my style of work, which combines practical easy-to-implement solutions with sound theoretical analysis. Third, XCP, the protocol we propose in this paper, has received much interest from both academic and industrial networking communities: The Information Science Institute (ISI) has implemented XCP and is working on deployment issues; CISCO has assembled a team of engineers to build a prototype; and many researchers have published papers analyzing XCP or comparing it with other congestion control protocols.*

**Paper:** Congestion Control for High Bandwidth-Delay Product Networks
**Authors:** D. Katabi, M. Handley, and C. Rohrs
**Journal:** ACM Sigcomm August 2002, Pittsburgh: http://nms.lcs.mit.edu/%7Edina/xcp.ps
**Year:** 2002

Theory and experiments show that as the per-flow product of bandwidth and latency increases, TCP becomes inefficient and prone to instability, regardless of the queuing scheme. This failing becomes increasingly important as the Internet evolves to incorporate very high-bandwidth optical links and more large-delay satellite links.

To address this problem, we develop a novel approach to Internet congestion control that outperforms TCP in conventional environments, and remains efficient, fair, scalable, and stable as the bandwidth-delay product increases. This new eXplicit Control Protocol, XCP, generalizes the Explicit Congestion Notification proposal (ECN). In addition, XCP introduces the new concept of decoupling utilization control from fairness control. This allows a more flexible and analytically tractable protocol design and opens new avenues for service differentiation.

Using a control theory framework, we model XCP and demonstrate it is stable and efficient regardless of the link capacity, the round trip delay, and the number of sources. Extensive packet-level simulations show that XCP outperforms TCP in both conventional and high bandwidth-delay environments. Further, XCP achieves fair bandwidth allocation, high utilization, small standing queue size, and near-zero packet drops, with both steady and highly varying traffic. Additionally, the new protocol does not maintain any per-flow state in routers and requires few CPU cycles per packet, which makes it implementable in high-speed routers.

### James L. Kirtley, Jr.

*At the time I was interested in problems such as deriving the equivalent circuit coefficients of electric machines and losses in the rotors of machines. The work described in this paper led me into understanding the interactions of fields in electromechanical systems, the relationship between Poynting's theorem and the Maxwell Stress Tensor, surface impedance and the fundamentals of energy flow in induction motor operation. (None of these concepts actually appeared in this paper, by the way, but the technique led directly to them). It was a practical method that led to an abstract theoretical understanding of electromechanical systems.*

**Paper:** Surface Coefficient for Multipole Magnetic Field Boundary Condition Problems
**Author:** J.L. Kirtley, Jr.
**Journal:** *IEEE Transactions on Power Apparatus and Systems* PAS-94, no. 3 (May/June 1975): 934–938
**Year:** 1975

A method for handling boundary conditions in multipolar magnetic field systems is described. This method allows quite complex boundaries (including those with loss) to be handled quite simply. A prototype field problem is worked, and a few boundary conditions are derived.

### Leslie A. Kolodziejski

*I selected this paper for a number of reasons. One is that the paper represents a wonderful long-lived collaboration between the groups of Kolodziejski, Ippen, Smith, and Joannopoulos. Furthermore, the achievements of the paper could not be realized without the technologies offered by several MIT laboratories: the Nano-*

*structures Lab, the Chemical Beam Epitaxy Lab, and the Scanning Electron Beam Lithography Lab. From a research point of view, the science that was discovered and presented in the paper represented a new mechanism for coupling light into or out of a high refractive index slab; the new coupling mechanism can be engineered such that light of any wavelength can be coupled out/in, and such an approach can be utilized in any number of optical devices. I also selected this paper because of the enjoyment we all experienced during the collaboration. We started with great ideas, but our initial expectations never materialized. After gathering a number of unexplained results with a great deal of perplexity surrounding the data, we found the answer, and finally theory and experiment were matched! For me, the paper represents what science is all about: questioning, exploring, bewilderment, and then the joy of knowledge.*

**Paper:** Enhanced Coupling to Vertical Radiation Using a Two-dimensional Photonic Crystal in a Semiconductor Light-emitting Diode

**Authors:** A.A. Erchak, D.J. Ripin, S. Fan, P. Rakich, J.D. Joannopoulos, E.P. Ippen, G.S. Petrich, and L.A. Kolodziejski

**Journal:** *App. Phys. Ltrs.* 78 (5): 563–565

**Year:** 2001

Enhanced coupling to vertical radiation is obtained from a light-emitting diode using a two-dimensional photonic crystal that lies entirely inside the upper cladding layer of an asymmetric quantum well structure. A sixfold enhancement in light extraction in the vertical direction is obtained without the photonic crystal penetrating the active material. The photonic crystal is also used to couple pump light at normal incidence into the structure, providing strong optical excitation.

## J.A. Kong

*The following is the preface of a recent undergraduate text.*

**Book:** *Maxwell Equations*

**Author:** J.A. Kong

**Publisher:** Cambridge, Massachusetts: EMW Publishing

**Year:** 2002

My original book *Electromagnetic Wave Theory* was published in 1975 by Wiley Interscience, New York, entitled *Theory of Electromagnetic Waves*, which was based on my 1968 Ph.D. thesis, where the concept of bianisotropic media, and later the kDB system to study their dispersion relations were introduced. The book was expanded and published by the same publisher in 1986 with the title *Electromagnetic Wave Theory*, and its second edition appeared in 1990. It was subsequently expanded and published by EMW Publishing Company, Massachusetts. This textbook on *Maxwell Equations* is distilled from the introductory part of *Electromagnetic Wave Theory*.

Starting with James Clerk Maxwell's life and his theory, the Maxwell Equations and their implications and applications are studied in detail. Chapter 1 presents Maxwell Equations in the familiar mathematical form. Chapter 2 studies the various fundamental concepts of Maxwell Equations. A fundamental unit $K_0 = 2\pi$ meter$^{-1}$ or spatial frequency is introduced. Chapter 3 illustrates the fundamental importance of the wave vector $\bar{K}$. Chapter 4 examines transmission lines and circuit theory in time domain. Chapter 5 introduces complex notation for continuous waves and employs the transmission line theory to demonstrate some useful concepts. At the end of each section, exercises and problems are designed to provide useful examples for practice and applications.

During the writing and preparation of this and the previous books, many of my teaching and research assistants provided useful suggestions and proofreading, notably Leung Tsang, Michael Zuniga, Weng Cho Chew, Tarek Habashy, Robert Shin, Shun-Lien Chuang, Jay Kyoon Lee, Apo Sezginer, Soon Yun Poh, Eric Yang, Michael Tsuk, Hsiu Chi Han, Yan Zhang, Henning Braunisch, Chi On Ao, and Bae-Ian Wu. I would like to express my gratitude to them and to the many students whose enthusiastic response and feedback continuously give me joy and satisfaction in teaching.

## Jeffrey H. Lang

*I chose this paper because it is the first of many that I have written on the subject of microscale electromagnetic motors and generators. It also appeared in the first conference on micro electromechanical systems. Finally it made many predictions, most of which have finally come true almost twenty years later.*

**Paper:** Electric Micromotors: Electromechanical Characteristics

**Authors:** J.H. Lang, M.F. Schlecht, R.T. Howe

**Journal:** *Proc. IEEE Micro Robots and Teleoperators Workshop*

**Year:** 1987

Planar rotary and linear motors can now be fabricated using silicon micromachining. These motors, referred to here as micromotors, have a gap separation on the order of 1 $\mu$m, and lateral dimensions on the order of 100 $\mu$m or more. This paper examines the electromechanical characteristics of these micromotors. To begin, an analysis of electromagnetic to mechanical energy conversion is presented to demonstrate that electric drive is preferable to magnetic drive in micromotors. This is followed by a discussion of the geometry, design and operation of electric micromotors which emphasizes the duality of electric and magnetic motors. Next, a prototype design for the rotary variable-capacitance micromotor is considered as an example. Rotor speeds over $10^5$ rad$\cdot$s$^{-1}$ and accelerations over $10^9$ rad$\cdot$s$^{-2}$ appear possible for this micromotor. Finally, some of the research problems posed by the development of micromotors are identified.

## Richard C. Larson

*The Queue Inference Engine is an early example of an analytical "data mining" technique, a field that exploded in the 1990s. Queues and congestion are important to systems engineers and operations researchers, and this inference engine combines large transactional data sets, statistics, and recursive computation, which is also important to computer scientists.*

**Paper:** The Queue Inference Engine: Deducing Queue Statistics from Transactional Data

**Author:** Richard C. Larson

**Journal:** *Management Science* 36, no. 5 (May 1990): 586–601

**Year:** 1990

The transactional data of a queueing system are the recorded times of service commencement and service completion for each customer served. With increasing use of computers to aid or even perform service, one often has machine-readable transactional data, but virtually no information about the queue itself. In this paper we propose a way to deduce the queueing behavior of Poisson arrival queueing systems from only the transactional data and the Poisson assumption. For each congestion period in which queues may form (in front of single or multiple servers), the key quantities obtained are mean wait in queue, time-dependent mean number in queue, and probability distribution of the number in queue observed by a randomly arriving customer. The methodology builds on arguments of order statistics and usually requires a computer to evaluate a recursive function. The results are exact for a homogenous Poisson arrival process (with unknown parameter) and approximately correct for a slowly time-varying Poisson process.

### Hae-Seung Lee

*The research covered in this paper resulted in the highest performance bandpass A/D converter ever reported in any technology. This converter is also the first RSFQ circuit of high complexity tested at full speed of over 40 GHz. The paper won the 2002 Jack Kilby Award for Outstanding Student Paper at the 2002 International Solid-State Circuits Conference—the highest honor for student work in integrated circuits.*

**Paper:** Superconducting Bandpass $\Delta\Sigma$ Modulator with 2.23-GHz Center Frequency and 42.6-GHz Sampling Rate

**Authors:** John F. Bulzacchelli, Hae-Seung Lee, James A. Misewich, and Mark B. Ketchen

**Journal:** *IEEE Journal of Solid-State Circuits* 37, no. 12 (December 2002): 1695–1702

**Year:** 2002

This paper presents a superconducting bandpass $\Delta\Sigma$ modulator for direct analog-to-digital conversion of radio frequency signals in the gigahertz range. The design, based on a 2.23-GHz microstrip resonator and a single flux quantum comparator, exploits several advantages of superconducting electronics: the high quality factor of resonators, the fast switching speed of the Josephson junction, natural quantization of voltage pulses, and high circuit sensitivity. The modulator test chip includes an integrated acquisition memory for capturing output data at sampling rates up to 45 GHz. The small size (256 b) of the acquisition memory limits the frequency resolution of spectra based on standard fast Fourier transforms.

Output spectra with enhanced resolution are obtained with a segmented correlation method. At a 42.6-GHz sampling rate, the measured SNR is 49 dB over a 20.8-MHz bandwidth, and a full-scale (FS) input is −17.4 dBm. At a 40.2-GHz sampling rate, the measured in-band noise is −57 dBFS over a 19.6-MHz bandwidth. The modulator test chip contains 4065 Josephson junctions and dissipates 1.9 mW at $T = 4.2$ K.

### Steven B. Leeb

*It's hard to select a single paper to represent my research team. This one might be the best compromise. It represents very interdisciplinary work that we conducted to support the development of a medical drug delivery system. It involved materials research, circuit design, field theory, and careful laboratory work. The authors included students ranging from two doctoral candidates to a UROP (Undergraduate Research Opportunities Program) student commuting from Wellesley. Counting those in the acknowledgements of the paper, almost my entire research group helped with this work. They were one of the finest teams of engineers I have known. They produced incredible results in a remarkably short time, and I am very proud of them. Looking back at this paper reminds me why I love working at MIT.*

**Paper:** Power Electronic Drives for Magnetically Triggered Gels

**Authors:** Deron K. Jackson, Steven B. Leeb, Ahmed H. Mitwalli, Paolo Narvaez Dahlene Fusco, and Elmer C. Lupton, Jr.

**Journal:** *IEEE Transactions on Industrial Electronics* 44, no. 2 (April 1997)

**Year:** 1997

Properly fabricated polymer gels exhibit an abrupt change in volume in response to a small change in an environmental parameter such as temperature. We have developed gels that change volume in response to an applied alternating magnetic field, and we are working to apply these gels as actuators. This paper describes power electronic circuits suitable for electromagnetic activation of these polymer gels.

Issues in the selection of circuit topologies for this application are discussed. Experimental results are presented, which demonstrate magnetic activation of gels using prototype power electronic drives.

### Charles E. Leiserson

*This work is my best example of combining theory and practice, a synthesis I have espoused for my entire research career. The Cilk-5 multithreaded programming language encompasses deep probabilistic analysis in its provably good work-stealing scheduler, clever software design in its two-clone compilation strategy, and an elegant user interface in its notion of being a "faithful" extension of the C programming language.*

**Paper:** The Implementation of the Cilk-5 Multithreaded Language

**Authors:** Matteo Frigo, Charles E. Leiserson, and Keith Randall

**Publisher:** *Proceedings of the ACM SIGPLAN '98 Conference on Programming Language Design and Implementation*, 212–223. New York: ACM Press

**Year:** 1998

The fifth release of the multithreaded language Cilk uses a provably good "work-stealing" scheduling algorithm similar to the first system, but the language has been completely redesigned and the run-time system completely reengineered. The efficiency of the new system was aided by a clear strategy that arose from a theoretical analysis of the scheduling algorithm: concentrate on minimizing overheads that contribute to the work, even at the expense of overheads that contribute to the critical path. Although it may seem counterintuitive to move overheads onto the critical path, this "work-first" principle has led to a portable Cilk-5 implementation in which the typical cost of spawning a parallel thread is only between two and six times the cost of a C function call on a variety of contemporary machines. Many Cilk programs run on one processor with virtually no degradation compared to equivalent C programs. This paper describes how the work-first principle was exploited in the design of Cilk-5's compiler and its run-time system. In particular, we present Cilk-5's novel "two-clone" compilation strategy and its Dijkstra-like mutual-exclusion protocol for implementing the ready deque (double-ended queue) in the work-stealing scheduler.

## Jae S. Lim

*This paper reports the work of a doctoral thesis research I supervised. The work had a significant impact on modern communication systems including cell phone, satellite phone, airphone, land-mobile radio, satellite radio, public safety, and air-traffic control communication systems.*

**Paper:** Multiband Excitation Vocoder

**Authors:** D.W. Griffith, J.S. Lim

**Journal:** *IEEE Transactions on Acoustics, Speech, and Signal Processing* 36 (8): 1223–1235

**Year:** 1988

In this paper, we present a new speech model which we refer to as the Multiband Excitation Model. In this model, the short-time spectrum of speech is modeled as the product of an excitation spectrum and a spectral envelope. The spectral envelope is some smoothed version of the speech spectrum and the excitation spectrum is represented by a fundamental frequency, a voiced/unvoiced (V/UV) decision for each harmonic of the fundamental, and the phase of each harmonic declared voiced. In speech analysis, the model parameters are estimated by explicit comparison between the original speech spectrum and the synthetic speech spectrum. In speech synthesis, we synthesize the voiced portion of speech in the time domain and the unvoiced portion of speech in the frequency domain. To illustrate one potential application of this new model, we develop an 8 kbit/s Multiband Excitation Vocoder. Informal listening clearly indicates that this noisy speech without the "buzziness" and severe degradation in noise typically associated with vocoder speech. Diagnotist Rhyme Tests (DRT's) were performed as a measure of the intelligibility of this 8 kbit/s vocoder. For clean speech with an average DRT score of 97.8 when uncoded, the coded speech has an average DRT score of 96.2. For speech with wide-band random noise with an average DRT score of 63.1 when uncoded, the coded speech has an average DRT score of 58.0. When the V/UV decision for each harmonic of the fundamental is replaced by one V/UV decision for each frame with all other parameters identical to the 8 kbit/s Multiband Excitation Vocoder, the DRT scores obtained are 96.0 for clean speech and 46.0 for the noisy speech case.

## Barbara Liskov

*This paper provides the best description of my early work on data abstraction. It also describes a number of other important ideas in programming languages, including iteration abstraction and parameterized types.*

**Paper:** Abstraction Mechanisms in CLU

**Authors:** Barbara Liskov, Alan Snyder, Russell Atkinson, and Craig Schaffert

**Journal:** *Communications of the ACM* 20, no. 8 (August 1977): 564–576

**Year:** 1977

CLU is a new programming language designed to support the use of abstractions in program construction. Work in programming methodology has led to the realization that three kinds of abstractions—procedural, control, and especially data abstractions—are useful in the programming process. Of these, only the procedural abstraction is supported well by conventional languages, through the procedure or subroutine. CLU provides, in addition to procedures, novel linguistic mechanisms that support the use of data and control abstractions. This paper provides an introduction to the abstraction mechanisms in CLU. By means of programming examples, the utility of the three kinds of abstractions in program construction is illustrated, and it is shown how CLU programs may be written to use and implement abstractions. The CLU library, which permits incremental program development with complete type checking performed at compile time, is also discussed.

## Tomás Lozano-Pérez

*This paper marks the beginning of a new direction in my research; prior to this point my work focused on robotics. This paper grew out of an attempt to predict "in silico" the activity of candidate drug molecules. While working on this problem, we identified a class of machine-learning problems that we have since found to occur in a variety of contexts, for example, in retrieval from image databases.*

**Paper:** Solving the Multiple Instance Problem with Axis-parallel Rectangles

**Authors:** Thomas G. Dietterich, Richard H. Lathrop, and Tomas Lozano-Pérez

**Journal:** *Artificial Intelligence* 89, no. 1–2 (1997): 31–71

**Year:** 1997

The multiple instance problem arises in tasks where the training examples are ambiguous: a single example object may have many alternative feature vectors (instances) that describe it, and yet only one of those feature vectors may be responsible for the observed classification of the object. This paper describes and compares three kinds of algorithms that learn axis-parallel rectangles to solve the multiple-instance problem. Algorithms that ignore the multiple instance problem perform very poorly. An algorithm that directly confronts the multiple instance problem (by attempting to identify which feature vectors are responsible for the observed classifications) performs best, giving 89 percent correct predictions on a musk-odor prediction task. The paper also illustrates the use of artificial data to debug and compare these algorithms.

## Nancy A. Lynch

*This book contains a foundation for many of the basic results of the field of distributed algorithms. I have contributed to many of the research results described in the book, including, notably, the impossibility results involving distributed consensus and mutual exclusion.*

**Book:** Distributed Algorithms

**Author:** Nancy A. Lynch

**Publisher:** San Mateo, California: Morgan Kaufmann Publishers, Inc.

**Year:** 1996

*Distributed Algorithms* provides a blueprint for designing, implementing, and analyzing distributed algorithms. The book is directed at a wide audience, including students, programmers, system designers, and researchers. *Distributed Algorithms* contains the most significant algorithms and impossibility results in the area, all in a simple automata-theoretic setting. The algorithms are proved correct, and their complexity is analyzed according to precisely defined complexity measures. The problems covered include resource allocation, communication, consensus among distributed processes, data consistency, deadlock detection, leader election, global snapshots, and many others. The material is organized according to the system model—first by the timing model and then by the interprocess communication mechanism. The material on system models is isolated in separate chapters for easy reference.

The presentation is completely rigorous, yet is intuitive enough for immediate comprehension. This book familiarizes readers with important problems, algorithms, and impossibility results in the area; readers can then recognize the problems when they arise in practice, apply the algorithms to solve them, and use the impossibility results to determine whether problems are unsolvable. The book also provides readers with the basic mathematical tools for designing new algorithms and proving new impossibility results. In addition, it teaches readers how to reason carefully about distributed algorithms—to model them formally, devise precise specifications for their required behavior, prove their correctness, and evaluate their performance with realistic measures.

### Roger G. Mark

*This is a good summary of one research project that combines engineering modeling with cardiovascular physiology. The project typifies our current research interests: physiologic signal processing and modeling with applications to intensive care.*

**Paper:** Computational Modeling of Cardiovascular Response to Orthostatic Stress

**Authors:** T. Heldt, E.B. Shim, R.D. Kamm, and R.G. Mark

**Journal:** *J. Appl. Physiol.* 92: 1239–1254

**Year:** 2002

The objective of this study is to develop a model of the cardiovascular system capable of simulating the short-term (5 min) transient and steady-state hemodynamic responses to head-up tilt and lower body negative pressure. The model consists of a closed-loop lumped-parameter representation of the circulation connected to set-point models of the arterial and cardiopulmonary baroreflexes. Model parameters are largely based on literature values. Model verification was performed by comparing the simulation output under baseline conditions and at different levels of orthostatic stress to sets of population-averaged hemodynamic data reported in the literature. On the basis of experimental evidence, we adjusted some model parameters to simulate experimental data. Orthostatic stress simulations are not statistically different from experimental data (two-sided test of significance with Bonferroni adjustment for multiple

comparisons). Transient response characteristics of heart rate to tilt also compare well with reported data. A case study is presented on how the model is intended to be used in the future to investigate the effects of postspaceflight orthostatic intolerance.

### Steve G. Massaquoi

**Paper:** A Model of Cerebellum Stabilized and Scheduled Hybrid Long-loop Control of Upright Balance

**Authors:** J. Sungho, S.G. Massaquoi

**Journal:** *Biological Cybernetics* 91 (3): 182–202

**Year:** 2004

A recurrent integrator proportional integral derivative (PID) model that has been used to account for cerebrocerebellar stabilization and scaling of transcortical proprioceptive feedback in the control of horizontal planar arm movements has been augmented with long-loop force~feedback and gainscheduling to describe the control of human upright balance. The cerebellar component of the controller is represented by two sets of gains that each provide linear scaling of same-joint and interjoint long-loop stretch responses between ankle, knee, and hip. The cerebral component of the model includes a single set of same-joint linear force feedback gains. Responses to platform translations of a three-segment body model operating under this hybrid proprioception and force-based long-loop control were simulated. With low-velocity platform disturbances, ankle-strategy-type postural recovery kinematics and electromyogram (EMG) patterns were generated using the first set of cerebellar control gains. With faster disturbances, balance was maintained by including the second set of gains cerebellar control gains that yielded mixed ankle-hip strategy-type kinematics and EMG patterns. The addition of small amounts of simulated muscular coactivation improved the fit to certain human datasets. It is proposed that the cerebellum switches control gainsets as a function of sensed body kinematic state. Reduction of cerebellar gains with a compensatory increase in muscular stiffness yielded posture recovery with abnormal motions consistent with those found in cerebellar disease. The model demonstrates that stabilized hybrid long-loop feedback with scheduling of linear gains may

afford realistic balance control in the absence of explicit internal dynamics models and suggests that the cerebellum and cerebral cortex may contribute to balance control by such a mechanism.

### Muriel Médard

*I chose this paper because it is a mixture of networking and information theory, and I believe information theory will bring to networking the dramatic improvements it has brought to link communications.*

**Paper:** An Algebraic Approach to Network Coding

**Authors:** Ralf Koetter and Muriel Médard

**Journal:** *IEEE/ACM Transactions on Networking*

**Year:** 2003

We take a new look at the issue of network capacity. It is shown that network coding is an essential ingredient in achieving the capacity of a network. Building on recent work by Li et al., who examined the network capacity of multicast networks, we extend the network coding framework to arbitrary networks and robust networking. For networks that are restricted to using linear network codes, we find necessary and sufficient conditions for the feasibility of any given set of connections over a given network. We also consider the problem of network recovery for nonergodic link failures. For the multicast setup we prove the surprising result— there exist coding strategies that provide maximally robust networks, which do not require adaptation of the network interior to the failure pattern in question. The results are derived for both delay-free networks and networks with delays. We give a number of theorems characterizing the existence of network coding strategies for various networks scenarios.

### Alexandre Megretski

*The paper contains an important technical result that greatly improves the quality of a system analysis technique (called "IQC analysis," which I helped to develop and popularize), in the case of systems with saturation-type nonlinear effects. The paper enables the user to discriminate between the "saturation" and "deadzone" types of nonlinearities within the classical absolute stability analysis framework.*

**Paper:** New IQC for Quasi-Concave Nonlinearities

**Author:** A. Megretski

**Journal:** *International Journal of Nonlinear and Robust Control* 11, no. 7 (June 2001): 603–620

**Year:** 2001

A new set of Integral Quadratic Constraints (IQC) is derived for a class of "rate limiters," modeled as a series of connections of saturation-like memoryless nonlinearities followed by integrators. The result, when used within the standard IQC framework (in particular, with finite gain/passivity-based arguments, Lyapunov theory, structured singular values, etc.), is expected to be widely useful in nonlinear system analysis. For example, it enables "discrimination" between "saturation-like" and "deadzone-like" nonlinearities and can be used to prove stability of systems with saturation in cases when replacing the saturation block by another memoryless nonlinearity with equivalent slope restrictions makes the whole system unstable. In particular, it is shown that the $L_2$ gain of a unity feedback system with a rate limiter in the forward loop cannot exceed $\sqrt{2}$.

In addition, a new, more flexible version of the general IQC analysis framework is presented, which relaxes the homotopy and boundedness conditions and is more aligned with the language of the emerging IQC software.

## Albert R. Meyer

*This is the seminal paper that first identified uncontrived computational problems of inherently exponential or greater complexity. It also first formulates the Polynomial-Time Hierarchy —a central concept in Computational Complexity Theory.*

**Paper:** The Equivalence Problem for Regular Expressions with Squaring Requires Exponential Space

**Authors:** A.R. Meyer and L. Stockmeyer

**Journal:** *Proceedings of the 13th IEEE Symposium on Switching and Automata Theory*, 125–129

**Year:** 1972

The equivalence problems for Kleene regular expressions extended with a "squaring" abbreviation ($S^2 = S \cdot S$) is shown to be polynomial-time complete for nondeterministic exponential space. This is the first example of an uncontrived (not constructed by diagonalization) decidable problem that is provably not decidable in polynomial time. The inequivalence problem for ordinary regular expressions is shown to be a polynomial-time complete context-sensitive language. A Polynomial-Time Hierarchy is defined and shown to allow classification of problems of complexity between NP and PSpace.

## Silvio Micali

*My CS Proofs distill what efficient proofs should mean in a simple and compelling way, achieving desiderata not attained by all previous notions (including some of mine). This is only proper: everything fundamental should be powerful and simple. They reflect the yearning for truth and complexity crucial to the twentieth century. Yet, new goals and new notions will soon arise. Nothing so human can remain the same, as long as making Science and lovingly handing it down to future generations remain honored values. Long live proofs!*

**Paper:** Computationally Sound Proofs

**Author:** S. Micali

**Journal:** *SIAM J. COMPUT* (© 2000 Society for Industrial and Applied Mathematics), 30 (4): 1253–1298

**Year:** 2000

This paper puts forward a new notion of a proof based on computational complexity and explores its implications for computation at large. Computationally sound proofs provide, in a novel and meaningful framework, answers to old and new questions in complexity theory. In particular, given a random oracle or a new complexity assumption, they enable us to 1. prove that verifying is easier than deciding for all theorems; 2. provide a quite effective way to prove membership in computationally hard languages (such as Co-NP-complete ones); and 3. show that every computation possesses a short certificate vouching its correctness. Finally, if a special type of computationally sound proof exists, we show that Blum's notion of program checking can be meaningfully broadened so as to prove that NP-complete languages are checkable.

## Robert C. Miller

*This paper highlights one of the key contributions of the LAPIS project, an ongoing effort that combines human-computer interaction, machine learning, and software engineering to build an intelligent user interface for text editing.*

**Chapter:** Multiple Selections in Smart Text Editing

**Authors:** Robert C. Miller and Brad A. Myers

**Publisher:** *Proceedings of the 6th International Conference on Intelligent User Interfaces*, 103–110. San Francisco: IUI2002

**Year:** 2002

Multiple selections, though heavily used in file managers and drawing editors, are virtually nonexistent in text editing. This paper describes how multiple selections can automate repetitive text editing. Selection guessing infers a multiple selection from positive and negative examples provided by the user. The multiple selections can then be used for inserting, deleting, copying, pasting, or other editing commands. *Simultaneous editing* uses two levels of inference, first inferring a group of records to be edited, then inferring multiple selections with exactly one selection in each record. Both techniques have been evaluated by user studies and shown to be fast and usable for novices. Simultaneous editing required only 1.26 examples per selection in the user study, approaching the ideal of one-example programming by demonstration. Multiple selections bring many benefits, including better user feedback; fast, accurate inference; novel forms of intelligent assistance; and the ability to override system inferences with manual corrections.

## Sanjoy K. Mitter

*This paper was influential and literally gave rise to an industry to work out the program outlined in this paper. These ideas have new relevance in view of the current interest in quantum control and quantum information processing.*

**Paper:** On the Analogy Between Mathematical Problems of Nonlinear Filtering and Quantum Physics

**Author:** S.K. Mitter

**Journal:** *Ricerche di Automatica* 10, no. 2 (December 1979, Special Issue on System Theory and Physics, edited by R.W. Brockett): 163–216

**Year:** 1979

The main thesis of this paper is that there are striking similarities between the mathematical problems of stochastic system theory, notably linear and nonlinear filtering theory, and mathematical developments underlying quantum mechanics and quantum field theory—thus the mathematical developments of the past thirty years in functional analysis. Lie groups and Lie algebras, group representations, and probabilistic methods of quantum theory can serve as a guide and indicator to search for an appropriate theory of stochastic systems. In the current state of development of linear and nonlinear filtering theory, it is best to proceed by analogy and with care, since "unitarity," which plays such an important part in quantum mechanics and quantum field theory, is not necessarily relevant to linear and nonlinear filtering theory. The partial differential equations that arise in quantum theory are generally wave equations, whereas the partial differential equations arising in filtering theory are stochastic parabolic equations. Nevertheless the possibility of passing to a wave equation by appropriate analytic continuation from the parabolic equation, reminiscent of the current program in Euclidean field theory, should not be overlooked.

In this paper we outline such a development and also obtain new results in nonlinear filtering using methods of functional integration and representation theory of Lie algebras.

### Frederic R. Morgenthaler

*In October 1956, the IEEE (then IRE) published their first ferrite issue, which served as a primary resource to the emerging technical literature of the field of nonreciprocal microwave ferrite devices. During my tour of active duty in the United States Air Force, I commenced my own research in that field, which continued after I returned to MIT for doctoral studies under the direction of Lan Jen Chu in the late 1950s. Later, I directed related research within the Microwave and Quantum Magnetics Group. Thirty years later, another ferrite issue was planned as an anniversary celebration. I was pleased to be invited to contribute this overview of the theory of wave propagation in such media that my own doctoral students and I had helped to develop. The issue appeared in*

*1988; by then, the field was mature, and so the circle was closed. However, I continued my research on the electrodynamics of polarizable and magnetizable materials and was able to develop new representations of power, energy, stress, and momentum that are exact and connect directly with quasistatics and circuit theory.*

*I have been writing a textbook, with the working title* The Power and Beauty of Electromagnetic Fields, *based on a graduate seminar that I taught near the end of my active MIT career. This comprehensive overview of the subject has provided me a technical focus and much satisfaction during six years of retirement.*

**Paper:** An Overview of Electromagnetic and Spin Angular Momentum Mechanical Waves in Ferrite Media

**Author:** Frederic R. Morgenthaler

**Journal:** *Proceedings of the IEEE* 76, no. 2 (February 1988): 138–150

**Year:** 1988

We review the principal characteristics of gyromagnetic materials that are useful for microwave applications and give both the large and small signal models that govern wave propagation at microwave frequencies. Uniform and nonuniform plane waves in an unbounded ferrite medium are considered from the complementary viewpoints of electromagnetics and mechanics.

Both electromagnetic $\bar{E} \times \bar{H}$ and quantum-mechanical exchange channels of power exist in such materials which can be ascribed to either waves or quasi-particles.

Regimes of wave propagation that are magnetostatic in character are shown to exist, as well as the relationships between the Walker modes of a small spheroid and the magnetostatic waves propagating in thin films. When the power densities within these waves, or modes, exceed certain thresholds, the linear model breaks down and parametric instabilities can create a form of "magnetic turbulence." We review the thresholds of such for both first- and second-order processes that involve the uniform precession mode and "parallel pumping" processes that do not.

### Robert T. Morris

*This paper presents the expected transmission count metric (ETX), which finds high-throughput paths on multi-hop wireless networks. ETX minimizes the expected total number of packet transmissions (including retransmissions) required to successfully deliver a packet to the ultimate destination. The ETX metric incorporates the effects of link loss ratios, asymmetry in the loss ratios between the two directions of each link, and interference among the successive links of a path. In contrast, the minimum hop-count metric chooses arbitrarily among the different paths of the same minimum length, regardless of the often large differences in throughput among those paths, and ignoring the possibility that a longer path might offer higher throughput.*

**Paper:** A High Throughput Path Metric for MultiHop Wireless Routing

**Authors:** D.S. J. De Couto, D. Aguayo, J. Bicket, and R. Morris

**Conference:** Ninth Annual International Conference on Mobile Computing and Networking (ACM MobiCom) 14–19 September 2003, San Diego

**Year:** 2003

This paper describes the design and implementation of ETX as a metric for the DSDV and DSR routing protocols, as well as modifications to DSDV and DSR which allow them to use ETX. Measurements taken from a 29-node 802.11b test-bed demonstrate the poor performance of minimum hop-count, illustrate the causes of that poor performance, and confirm that ETX improves performance. For long paths the throughput improvement is often a factor of two or more, suggesting that ETX will become more useful as networks grow larger and paths become longer.

### Joel Moses

*This is the abstract to my Ph.D. thesis, which was published by Project MAC as MAC-TR-47 in 1967. I like it because the thesis was my biggest contribution to artificial intelligence (AI), as well as a contribution to algebraic formula manipulation. The AI contribution led to the knowledge-based system approach. The SIN program described in the thesis later became a part of the MACSYMA algebraic manipulation system.*

**Chapter:** Symbolic Integration

**Author:** J. Moses
**Publisher:** MAC-TR-47 in *The MIT Project MAC Series*, 262–266. Cambridge, Massachusetts: MIT
**Year:** 1967

SIN and SOLDIER are heuristic programs written in LISP that solve symbolic integration problems. SIN (Symbolic INtegrator) solves indefinite integration problems at the difficulty approaching those in the larger integral tables. SIN contains several more methods than are used in the previous symbolic integration program SAINT and solves most of the problems in less than one second. SOLDIER (SOLution of ordinary DIfferential Equations Routine) solves first-order, first-degree ordinary differential equations at the level of a good college sophomore and at an average of about five seconds per problem attempted. The difference in philosophy and operation between SAINT and SIN are described, and suggestions for extending the work are made.

## Alan V. Oppenheim

*This article is based on my Ph.D. thesis and subsequent work by my first doctoral student, Ron Schafer, our colleague Tom Stockham, and myself. Tom had been an EECS faculty member and at the time of this article was on the research staff at MIT Lincoln Laboratory. He subsequently joined the faculty at the University of Utah and is widely acknowledged as the father of digital audio. Ron, with whom I have co-authored two widely used textbooks, is currently Institute Professor at Georgia Institute of Technology. Ron, Tom, and I have maintained close personal and professional ties. This article has been very widely cited, and its content has had a major impact on the field of signal processing.*
**Paper:** Nonlinear Filtering of Multiplied and Convolved Signals
**Authors:** Alan V. Oppenheim, Ronald W. Schafer, and Thomas G. Stockham
**Journal:** *Proceedings of the IEEE* 56, no. 8 (August 1968): 1264–1291
**Year:** 1968

An approach to some nonlinear filtering problems through a generalized notion of superposition has proven useful. In this paper this approach is investigated for the nonlinear filtering of signals that can be expressed as products or as convolutions of components. The

applications of this approach in audio dynamic range compression and expansion, image enhancement with applications to bandwidth reduction, echo removal, and speech waveform processing are presented.

## Terry P. Orlando

*This work on quantum computing is representative of my style of research: it is at the border of electrical engineering and physics, and it involves long-standing and new collaborators.*
**Paper:** Superconducting Persistent-current Qubit
**Authors:** Terry P. Orlando, Johan E. Mooij, Lian Tian, Caspar H. van der Wal, Leonid S. Levitov, Seth Lloyd, and Juan J. Mazo
**Journal:** *Physical Review* B 60, no. 22 (1 December 1999): 15398–15413
**Year:** 1999

We present the design of a superconducting qubit that has circulating currents of opposite sign as its two states. The circuit consists of three nanoscale aluminum Josephson junctions connected in a superconducting loop and controlled by magnetic fields. The advantages of this qubit are that it can be made insensitive to background charges in the substrate, the flux in the two states can be detected with a superconducting quantum interference device, and the states can be manipulated with magnetic fields. Coupled systems of qubits are also discussed, as well as sources of decoherence.

## Asuman Ozdaglar

*This paper represents an application of mathematical tools provided by optimization theory to an important engineering problem.*
**Paper:** Routing and Wavelength Assignment in Optical Networks
**Authors:** Asuman E. Ozdaglar and Dimitri Bertsekas
**Journal:** *IEEE/ACM Transactions on Networking* 11, no. 2 (April 2003): 1–14
**Year:** 2003

The problem of routing and wavelength assignment (RWA) is critically important for increasing the efficiency of wavelength-routed all-optical networks. Given the physical network structure and the required connections, the RWA problem is to select a suitable path and wavelength among the many possible choices for each connection, so that no two

paths sharing a link are assigned the same wavelength. In work to date, this problem has been formulated as a difficult integer-programming problem that does not lend itself to efficient solution or insightful analysis. In this work, we propose several novel optimization problem formulations that offer the promise of radical improvements over the existing methods. We adopt a (quasi-)static view of the problem and propose new integer-linear programming formulations, which can be addressed with highly efficient linear (not integer) programming methods and yield optimal or near-optimal RWA policies. The fact that this is possible is surprising and is the starting point for new and greatly improved methods for RWA. Aside from its intrinsic value, the quasi-static solution method can form the basis for suboptimal solution methods for the stochastic/dynamic settings.

## William T. Peake

*I chose this paper to represent me because it integrates knowledge of different types (theoretical and experimental acoustics, ear anatomy and physiology, ecology and ethology) to support the idea in the title with quantitative measurements and analysis. My electrical engineering training in description of the physical world was essential to aspects of the analysis, and training in critical thinking carried over to other aspects of the work.*
**Paper:** Mammalian Ear Specializations in Arid Habitats: Structural and Functional Evidence from Sand Cat (*Felis margarita*)
**Authors:** G.T. Huang, J.J. Rosowski, M.E. Ravicz, and W.T. Peake
**Journal:** *Journal of Comparative Physiology A* 188 (2002): 663–681
**Year:** 2002

To test whether structural specializations of sand-cat ears are adaptations to their desert habitats, we measured structural and acoustic features of their ears. The area of the external ear's pinna flange is similar to that of the domestic cat. The dimensions of the ear canal are about twice the domestic cat's, as is the volume of the middle-ear air space. The magnitude of the acoustic input-admittance at the tympanic membrane is about five times larger than that of domestic cat; both the middle-ear cavities and the ossicular chain contribute to the increase. Structure-based models suggest that the acoustic admittance looking outward through the external ear is generally larger for the sand cat than for the domestic cat; the radiation power-efficiency is also larger in sand cats for frequencies below 2 kHz. Hearing sensitivity (estimated from measurements and model calculations) in sand cats is predicted to be about 8 dB greater than in domestic cats for frequencies below 2 kHz. Analysis of the attenuation of sound in deserts implies that this increased sensitivity extends a sand cat's hearing range beyond a domestic cat's by 0.4 km at 0.5 kHz. Thus, the structural specializations can provide habitat-specific survival value.

### Paul Penfield, Jr.

*The Manley-Rowe equations, which relate power at different frequencies in frequency converters, were the subject of my 1960 doctoral thesis. In it, I tried to answer the question, "What characterizes physical systems that obey the Manley-Rowe equations?" Six years later I realized the answer was very simple: such systems are thermodynamically reversible, that is, they conserve entropy. This 1966 paper is my favorite because it gives a simple but surprising answer to a simple question. Most advances in science and engineering make the relevant discipline more complicated. What is harder is to simplify things by showing that concepts from different, previously unrelated areas are actually the same.*

**Paper:** Thermodynamics and the Manley-Rowe Equations

**Author:** Paul Penfield, Jr.

**Journal:** *Journal of Applied Physics* 37, no. 13 (December 1966): 4629–4630

**Year:** 1966

The Manley-Rowe equations describe the flow of power in certain frequency converters, such as nonlinear capacitors and inductors. Systems of many kinds, including all systems that have an energy state function, and those distributed systems that obey Hamilton's principle, are known to obey the Manley-Rowe equations, as are certain quantum systems. Scovil, Schulz-DuBois, and Geusic have investigated three-level masers from a thermodynamic viewpoint.

Here we propose a hypothesis that is not yet proved, although preliminary results suggest its truth. The hypothesis is that a physical system obeys the Manley-Rowe equations if, and only if, it is reversible in the thermodynamic sense. This hypothesis is demonstrated for a three-frequency upconverter pumped sinusoidally and exchanging noise at the other two frequencies.

### David J. Perreault

*I selected this paper because passive components are becoming a dominant consideration in the design of improved power electronic systems. Technologies that improve the size and performance of passive components are thus of increasing importance.*

**Chapter:** Filters and Components with Inductance Cancellation

**Authors:** Timothy C. Neugebauer, Joshua W. Phinney, and David J. Perreault

**Publisher:** *Proceedings of the 2002 IEEE Industry Applications Society Annual Meeting*

**Year:** 2002

Electrical filters are important for attenuating electrical ripple, eliminating electromagnetic interference (EMI) and susceptibility, improving power quality, and minimizing electromagnetic signature. Capacitors are critical elements in such filters, and filter performance is strongly influenced by the capacitor parasitics. This paper introduces a new design technique that overcomes the capacitor parasitic inductance that limits filter performance at high frequencies. Coupled magnetic windings are employed to effectively cancel the parasitic inductance of capacitors, and to add inductance in filter branches where it is desired. The underlying basis of the new technique is treated in detail, and its application to the design of both discrete filters and integrated LC filter components is described. Numerous experimental results demonstrating the high performance of the approach in both discrete filters and integrated filter elements are provided.

### Michael H. Perrott

*Phase-locked loops have been around since at least 1932 and have been critical to the development of nearly all modern communication systems. Despite their widespread use, however, there has been little attention paid to modeling their behavior in a manner that allows joint dynamic and noise estimation of their perfor-mance. This paper attempts to present such a modeling approach and applies it to the more advanced problem of estimating the performance of recently popular phase-locked loop structures whose divide value is dynamically varied in time.*

**Paper:** A Modeling Approach for $\Sigma-\Delta$ Fractional-N Frequency Synthesizers Allowing Straightforward Noise Analysis

**Authors:** Michael H. Perrott, Mitchell D. Trott, and Charles G. Sodini

**Journal:** *Journal of Solid-State Circuits* 37, no. 8 (August 2002): 1028–1038

**Year:** 2002

A general model of phase-locked loops (PLL) is derived that incorporates the influence of divide value variations. The proposed model allows straightforward noise and dynamic analyses of $\Sigma-\Delta$ fractional-N frequency synthesizers and other PLL applications in which the divide value is varied in time. Based on the derived model, a general parameterization is presented that further simplifies noise calculations. The framework is used to analyze the noise performance of a custom $\Sigma-\Delta$ synthesizer implemented in a 0.6 micron CMOS process and accurately predicts the measured phase noise to within 3 dB over the entire frequency offset range spanning 25 kHz to 10 MHz.

### Jovan Popović

*These techniques simplify generation of artistic, highly stylized animations. Future work along these lines will enable kids, high-school teachers, and others who may not have the expertise and training of professional animators to produce high-quality animations quickly and inexpensively. Ultimately, these activities will enable broader use of visual explanations in education and everyday communication.*

**Paper:** Deformation Transfer for Triangle Meshes

**Authors:** R.W. Sumner and J. Popović

**Journal:** *ACM Transactions on Graphics* 23, no. 3: 399–405

**Year:** 2004

Deformation transfer applies the deformation exhibited by a source triangle mesh onto a different target triangle mesh. Our approach is general and does not require the source and target to share the same number of vertices or triangles, or to have identical connectivity. The user builds a correspondence map between the triangles of the source and those of the target by specifying a small set of vertex markers. Deformation transfer computes the set of transformations induced by the deformation of the source mesh, maps the transformations through the correspondence from the source to the target, and solves an optimization problem to consistently apply the transformations to the target shape. The resulting system of linear equations can be factored once, after which transferring a new deformation to the target mesh requires only a backsubstitution step. Global properties such as foot placement can be achieved by constraining vertex positions. We demonstrate our method by retargeting full body key poses, applying scanned facial deformations onto a digital character, and remapping rigid and non-rigid animation sequences from one mesh onto another.

### Rajeev J. Ram

*Kevin Pipe is a Ph.D. student in my group. This particular paper shows that the current that flows in a p-n junction does so because of a large amount of cooling at the diode junction. Since p-n junctions are the basic building block of semiconductor electronics, the ideas in this paper apply to a broad range of devices.*

**Paper:** Bias-dependent Peltier Coefficient and Internal Cooling in Bipolar Devices

**Authors:** Kevin P. Pipe, Rajeev J. Ram, and Ali Shakouri

**Journal:** *Physical Review* B 66, no. 12 (September): article 125316

**Year:** 2002

The work described here is an investigation of thermoelectric phenomena in bipolar semiconductors and p-n junctions. In contrast to majority-carrier semiconductors in which a constant material-dependent Peltier coefficient is defined for a given temperature, bipolar devices can be modeled by introducing a bias-dependent Peltier coefficient at interfaces that takes into account the variation of the carriers' average transport energy. It is shown that this effective Peltier coefficient can vary by orders of magnitude as a function of applied bias, and can give rise to interfacial thermoelectric cooling or heating depending on device parameters. The bias-dependent bipolar Peltier coefficient is modeled analyti-

cally for short-length and long-length diodes, and the different regimes of bias for which cooling is achieved are described, as well as the effects of recombination, length, and doping. Analytical expressions to optimize the thermoelectric effect inside an idealized diode cooler are presented with numerical results for several common semiconductors, a figure of merit for internal diode cooling is introduced, and extensions of the model are given for applications such as the internal cooling of a semiconductor laser diode.

### Rafael Reif

*The first big goal I gave to myself and my research group when I came to MIT was to demonstrate that it was possible to deposit silicon epitaxial layers at low temperatures using a chemical vapor deposition approach. At the time this was viewed as a major challenge. Now the low-temperature deposition of silicon-based epitaxial layers is a well-accepted commercial technology.*

**Paper:** Low-Temperature Silicon Epitaxy Using Low Pressure Chemical Vapor Deposition with and Without Plasma Enhancement

**Authors:** T.J. Donahue, W.R. Burger, and R. Reif

**Journal:** *Applied Physics Letters* 44 (1 February 1984): 346–348

**Year:** 1984

Specular epitaxial silicon films have been deposited at 775°C using a low-pressure chemical vapor deposition process both with and without plasma enhancement. This is the lowest silicon epitaxial deposition temperature reported for thermally driven chemical vapor deposition. It was found that the pre-deposition in situ cleaning of the surface, rather than any plasma effects during the deposition, was essential for achieving epitaxial growth at this low temperature. Surface cleaning in these experiments was done by sputtering the wafer in an argon plasma at 775°C with a dc bias applied to the susceptor. This is the lowest pre-epitaxial cleaning temperature reported for thermally driven chemical vapor deposition.

### J. Francis Reintjes

*This paper reports on early research on the technical and economic feasibility of transferring documents electronically among nodes of a*

library network. The process is now a practical reality, and, through subsequent development of the Internet (unanticipated at the time), the concept has been extended to permit electronic document transfer directly from a library to one's personal computer.

**Paper:** Application of Modern Technologies to Interlibrary Resource-sharing Networks

**Author:** J. Francis Reintjes

**Journal:** *Journal of the American Society for Information Science* 34, no. 1 (1984): 45–52

**Year:** 1984

Examined in this article is the hypothesis that it is now technologically and economically feasible to move the content of documents electronically among nodes of a library network rather than the documents themselves or photocopies thereof. Comparisons are made on the basis of response-to-request time, quality of reproduced copy, and cost factors. The conclusion is reached that electronic interlibrary resource-sharing networks are ideally suited to situations where there are high-frequency occurrences of internode requests for information contained in *serials*, where nodal separation distances do not exceed a few tens of miles, and where copy is in six-point type or larger. A three-node network is examined in detail. Specifications for each element of the network are given, with emphasis placed on a highly critical element, the bound-document scanner. The results of an economic study of interlibrary electronic networks are also presented.

### Martin C. Rinard

*This abstract presents the solution to an old and important problem. The type of each object is an abstraction of its state, and ideally should change to reflect changes in that state. But all previous type systems could not have both full support for object references and types that reflected changing object states. This paper presents the solution to this problem.*

**Chapter:** Role Analysis

**Authors:** Viktor Kuncak, Patrick Lam, and Martin C. Rinard

**Publisher:** *Proceedings of the 29th Annual ACM Symposium on Principles of Programming Languages*, Portland, Oregon: ACM Press

**Year:** 2002

We present a new role system in which the

type (or role) of each object depends on its referencing relationships with other objects, with the role changing as these relationships change. Roles capture important object and data structure properties and provide useful information about how the actions of the program interact with these properties. Our role system enables the programmer to specify the legal aliasing relationships that define the set of roles that objects may play, the roles of procedure parameters and object fields, and the role changes that procedures perform while manipulating objects. We present an interprocedural, compositional, and context-sensitive role analysis algorithm that verifies that a program maintains role constraints.

**Ronald L. Rivest**

*The "RSA paper" seemed like a natural choice for me. . . .*

**Paper:** A Method for Obtaining Digital Signatures and Public Key Cryptosystems

**Authors:** R.L. Rivest, A. Shamir, and L. Adleman

**Journal:** *Communications of the ACM* 21, no. 2 (February 1978): 120–126

**Year:** 1978

An encryption method is presented with the novel property that publicly revealing an encryption key does not thereby reveal the corresponding decryption key. This has two important consequences:

(1) Couriers or other secure means are not needed to transmit keys since a message can be enciphered using an encryption key publicly revealed by the intended recipient. Only he can decipher the message, since only he knows the corresponding decryption key.

(2) A message can be "signed" using a privately held decryption key. Anyone can verify this signature using the corresponding publicly revealed encryption key. Signatures cannot be forged, and a signer cannot later deny the validity of his signature. This has obvious applications in "electronic mail" and "electronic funds transfer" systems.

A message is encrypted by representing it as a number M, raising M to a publicly specified power *e*, and then taking the remainder when the result is divided by the publicly specified

product, *n*, of two large secret prime numbers *p* and *q*. Decryption is similar; only a different, secret, power *d* is used, where $e \cdot d = 1 (\mathrm{mod}(p-1) \cdot (q-1))$. The security of the system rests in part on the difficulty of factoring the published divisor, *n*.

**James K. Roberge**

*A sentence from my book,* Operational Amplifiers: Theory and Practice, *published in 1975, best exemplifies a major conviction of mine. Nearly half of this book is devoted to the study of classical feedback, applied to a wide variety of systems as well as to operational amplifiers. The overview section of the first chapter outlines the material to come and explains my reasons for emphasizing feedback. I conclude this section with the statement: "This in-depth approach is included at least in part because I am convinced that a detailed understanding of feedback is the single most important prerequisite to successful electronic circuit and system design." In the twenty-eight years since this book was published, I have continued to use this material in my research and to teach it to thousands of students, and I am as convinced as ever of its importance. I was pleased to have my position reinforced by Professor William Siebert who quoted a portion of this statement in his book on linear systems.*

**Book:** *Operational Amplifiers: Theory and Practice*

**Author:** J.K. Roberge

**Publisher:** New York: John Wiley & Sons

**Year:** 1975

**Jerome H. Saltzer**

*This paper illustrates best my primary research goal: to discover and explain system design principles. It also illustrates that most work in my field is collaborative. A second paper, "End-to-end Arguments in System Design" (see David Clark, 1984 abstract in this section) similarly illustrates the same two points.*

**Paper:** The Protection of Information in Computer Systems

**Authors:** Jerome H. Saltzer and Michael D. Schroeder

**Journal:** *Proceedings of the IEEE* 63, no. 9 (September 1975): 1278–1308

**Year:** 1975

This tutorial paper explores the mechanics of

protecting computer-stored information from unauthorized use or modification. It concentrates on those architectural structures—whether hardware or software—that are necessary to support information protection. The paper develops in three main sections. Section I describes desired functions, design principles, and examples of elementary protection and authentication mechanisms. Any reader familiar with computers should find the first section to be reasonably accessible. Section II requires some familiarity with descriptor-based computer architecture. It examines in depth the principles of modern protection architectures and the relation between capability systems and access control list systems, and ends with a brief analysis of protected subsystems and protected objects. The reader who is dismayed by either the prerequisites or the level of detail in the second section may wish to skip to Section III, which reviews the state of the art and current research projects and provides suggestions for further reading.

**Rahul Sarpeshkar**

*This work contains the essence of what I do: take inspiration from neurobiological architectures to build low-power analog electronics that are useful for biomedical and other applications and, in turn, use engineering insights to explain why biology may have evolved the solution that it has.*

**Paper:** A Low-Power Wide-Dynamic-Range Analog VLSI Cochlea

**Authors:** Rahul Sarpeshkar, Richard F. Lyon, and Carver Mead

**Journal:** *Analog Integrated Circuits and Signal Processing* 16, no. 3 (August 1998): 245–274

**Year:** 1998

Low-power wide-dynamic-range systems are extremely hard to build. The biological cochlea is one of the most awesome examples of such a system: it can sense sounds over twelve orders of magnitude in intensity, with an estimated power dissipation of only a few tens of microwatts. In this paper, we describe an analog electronic cochlea that processes sounds over six orders of magnitude in intensity, and that dissipates 0.5mW. This 117-stage, 100Hz-to-10Khz cochlea has the widest dynamic range of any artificial cochlea built to date. The wide dynamic range is attained through the use of a wide-linear-range transconductance amplifier, of a low-noise filter topology, of dynamic gain control (AGC) at each cochlear stage, and of an architecture that we refer to as overlapping cochlear cascades. The operation of the cochlea is made robust through the use of automatic offset-compensation circuitry. A BiCMOS circuit approach helps us to attain nearly scale-invariant behavior and good matching at all frequencies. The synthesis and analysis of our artificial cochlea yields insight into why the human cochlea uses an active traveling-wave mechanism to sense sounds instead of using bandpass filters. The low power, wide dynamic range, and biological realism make our cochlea well suited as a front end for cochlear implants.

### Joel Schindall

*Having been with MIT for only one term thus far, I have reached back to the early days of Globalstar, where I was vice president of systems development and later chief engineer. Globalstar was an audacious "bottoms bottoms up" development of a technically successful forty-eight-satellite mobile telephone system, involving thousands of people, about $4 billion of investment capital, and at least thirty MIT graduates working at Globalstar, Space Systems Loral, Qualcomm, and others. Those of us who participated felt that we had been privileged to participate in the development of a new class of worldwide satellite-based telecommunications system.*

**Chapter:** Concept and Implementation of the Globalstar Mobile Satellite System

**Author:** Joel Schindall

**Publisher:** *Proceedings of the Russian Academy of Space and Science Symposium.* Moscow

**Year:** 1994

Globalstar is a satellite-based mobile communications system that provides quality wireless communications anywhere in the world except the polar regions. The Globalstar system uses elements of CDMA and Frequency Division Multiple Access (FDMA), combined with satellite Multiple Beam Antenna (MBA) technology and advanced variable-rate vocoder technology to arrive at one of the most efficient modulation and multiple access systems ever proposed for a satellite communi-

cations system. The technology used in Globalstar includes the following techniques to obtain high spectral efficiency and affordable cost per channel, with minimum coordination required between different portions of the system: (1) CDMA modulation with efficient power control, (2) high efficiency vocoder with voice activity factor, (3) spot beam antenna for increased gain and frequency reuse, (4) weighted satellite antenna gain for broad geographic coverage, (5) simultaneous links through multiple satellites (diversity) to enhance communications reliability, (6) soft handoff between beams and satellites.

The space segment consists of forty-eight low earth orbit satellites that act as "bent pipes" to relay the telephone signal to a local terrestrial gateway. From there, the signal is carried over existing telephony channels. The ground segment can be thought of as a cellular telephone base station that utilizes the satellite relay to greatly extend its coverage area. CDMA technology is used to maximize the system capacity. The ground segment also includes satellite monitoring and control functions. The mobile user segment involves the design and manufacture of portable cellular-telephone-like fixed and mobile user handsets. Although a Globalstar-only handset will be developed, it is anticipated that the largest market will be for dual-mode handsets that combine the local cellular standard with a Globalstar satellite capability.

### Martin A. Schmidt

*This is the first paper in an extensive collaboration with Prof. Klavs Jensen in chemical engineering aimed at exploiting microfabrication technology in the chemical reaction field. This collaboration has led to a substantial research effort that has had a far-reaching impact.*

**Paper:** Micromachined Reactors for Catalytic Partial Oxidation Reactions

**Authors:** R. Srinivasan, I.M. Hsing, P.E. Berger, K.F. Jensen, S.L. Firebaugh, M.A. Schmidt, M.P. Harold, J.J. Lerou, J.F. Ryley

**Journal:** *AICHE Journal* 43 (11): 3059–3069

**Year:** 1997

Silicon-based microfabrication of a novel chemical reactor (microreactor) having submillimeter flow channels with integrated heaters,

and flow and temperature sensors is described. The potential application of this reactor to partial-oxidation reactions is explored by using Pt-catalyzed $NH_3$ oxidation as a model reaction. Investigation of reactor behavior as a function of operating conditions shows that conversion and selectivity behavior of conventional laboratory reactors can be reproduced and demonstrates the feasibility of conducting chemical reactions in microfabricated systems. Ignition-extinction behavior is explored, along with high-temperature microreactor materials degradation. Potential applications and scale-up of microreactors are also discussed.

### Stephen D. Senturia

*Compared with my entire research output, my first textbook is my most important and influential publication. It seems to have had a huge impact. It was developed for 6.071 (originally 6.14), but the educational concept became the basis for the revision of the core curriculum in which a circuits-and-electronics class became the first course, 6.002, and system theory became the second course, 6.003, for the electrical engineering side of the core. This style of teaching spread rapidly. U.C.–Berkeley developed such a course for its majors in the late 1970s (Oldham and Schwartz), after 6.071 but before 6.002, and now this curricular architecture is present virtually everywhere.*

*It would not be proper to say that the Senturia and Wedlock book was the key to making it happen, but it would be correct to say that the book was in the vanguard of curricular revision in the late 1970s and had a long and useful life thereafter. It sold, altogether, more than 45,000 copies and remained in print until 2002, a twenty-seven-year run for a book that had never been revised. The book was widely imitated (one version even paraphrased my jokes). The digital section is now hopelessly obsolete, but I still find many students who refer to it as the best elementary analog electronics and circuits book around.*

**Book:** *Electronic Circuits and Applications*

**Authors:** Stephen D. Senturia and Bruce D. Wedlock

**Publisher:** New York: John Wiley & Sons

**Year:** 1975

This book was one of the first to combine

modern transistor electronics (both analog and digital) with elementary circuit theory and signal and system theory (even including something on modulation and noise) into a single book and course accessible to beginning students.

**Jeffrey H. Shapiro**

*This is the culminating paper of a three-part study of quantum optical communication using what are now called squeezed states of light. Its representation theorem is the most convenient approach to the statistics of quantum photodetection, and it was the first to describe the quantum measurements realized by coherent optical detection. These results have served as foundations for much of my subsequent work, including my current research on entangled light beams.*

**Paper:** Optical Communication with Two-Photon Coherent States—Part III: Quantum Measurements Realizable with Photoemissive Detectors

**Authors:** Horace P. Yuen and Jeffrey H. Shapiro

**Journal:** *IEEE Transactions on Information Theory* IT-26, no. 1 (January 1980): 78–92

**Year:** 1980

In Part I of this three-part study it was shown that the use of two-photon coherent state (TCS) radiation may yield significant performance gains in free-space optical communication if the receiver makes a quantum measurement of a single field quadrature. In Part II it was shown that homodyne detection achieves the same signal-to-noise ratio as the quantum field quadrature measurement, thus providing a receiver that realizes the linear modulation TCS performance gain found in Part I. Furthermore, it was shown in Part II that if homodyne detection does exactly correspond to the field quadrature measurement, then a large binary communication performance gain is afforded by homodyne detection of antipodal TCS signals. The full equivalence of homodyne detection and single-quadrature field measurement, as well as heterodyne detection and two-quadrature field measurement, is established. Furthermore, a heterodyne configuration that uses a TCS image-band oscillator in addition to the usual coherent state local oscillator is studied. This configuration, termed TCS heterodyne detection, is shown to realize all the quantum measurements described by arbitrary

TCS. The foregoing results are obtained by means of a representation theorem that shows that photoemissive detection realizes the photon flux density measurement.

**Henry I. Smith**

*This paper was the first to establish micro/nanofabrication technology as a distinct discipline, with substantial intellectual and engineering content. In writing this paper, I developed a wide range of ideas and inventions that help to guide development of nanofabrication to this day.*

**Paper:** Fabrication Techniques for Surface-Acoustic-Wave and Thin-Film Optical Devices

**Author:** Henry I. Smith

**Journal:** *Proceedings of the IEEE* 62, no. 10 (October 1974): 1361–1387

**Year:** 1974

The techniques of photolithography, electron lithography, x-ray lithography, ion bombardment etching, and liftoff are reviewed, and their advantages and disadvantages assessed from the point of view of fabricating surface-acoustic-wave and thin-film optical devices.

**Louis D. Smullin**

*Soon after the first laser was invented, Professor Smullin and visiting scientist Dr. Giorgio Fiocco were the first researchers to transmit laser pulses to the moon and detect their return. Professor Smullin called this experiment "Luna See" and published it in the* Proceedings of the IRE *50 (July 1962). The feat received a great deal of publicity, including a feature article in* Time *magazine. However, as a serious researcher in the field of microwave tubes and plasmas, he selected the abstract below as a topic at the center of his professional interests.*

—*Hermann Haus*

**Paper:** Beam–Plasma Discharge: Buildup of Oscillations

**Authors:** W.E. Getty and L.D. Smullin

**Journal:** *Journal of Applied Physics* 34, no. 12 (December 1963)

**Year:** 1963

Plasma electron heating was accomplished by exciting plasma oscillations with a pulsed, 10-kV, 1-A electron beam drifting in a longitudinal magnetic field of 100 to 1000 Oe. The oscillatory energy gained by plasma electrons leads to an increase in their density and mean kinetic energy. The resulting plasma, which is

called the "beam-plasma discharge," is an rf discharge in which a beam-plasma interaction generates the rf fields.

At the beginning of a beam pulse, beam electrons generate a plasma by ionization of the background gas. Within a few microseconds excited plasma electrons become the dominant ionization source. This paper describes the transient rf oscillations that appear in the first few microseconds of the beam pulse. From a detailed study of this transient, it was concluded that a convective instability initiates the oscillations, which first appear at the electron cyclotron frequency, and that a convective instability at the plasma frequency generates the oscillations that sustain the discharge.

**Charles G. Sodini**

*This paper was the first to show that higher order Sigma-Delta Conversion is possible. It led to several commercial implementations for high-resolution data conversion in the 1990s. The paper won the 1991 Circuits & System Society Darlington Award for best paper published in 1990.*

**Paper:** A Higher Order Topology for Interpolative Modulators for Oversampling A/D Converters

**Authors:** K.C.-H. Chao, S. Nadeem, W.L. Lee, and C.G. Sodini

**Journal:** *IEEE Transactions on Circuits and Systems* 37, no. 3 (March 1990): 309–318

**Year:** 1990

Oversampling interpolative coding has been demonstrated to be an effective technique for high-resolution analog-to-digital (A/D) conversion that is tolerant of process imperfections. A novel topology for constructing stable interpolative modulators of arbitrary order is described. Analysis of this topology shows that with proper design of the modulator coefficients, stability is not a limitation to higher-order modulators. Furthermore, complete control over placement of the poles and zeros of the quantization noise response allows treatment of the modulation process as a high-pass filter for quantization noise. Higher-order modulators are shown not only to greatly reduce oversampling requirements for high-resolution conversion applications, but also to randomize the quantization noise, avoiding the need for dithering. An experimental fourth-order modulator breadboard demonstrates stability and feasibility, achieving a 90-dB dynamic range over the 20-kHz audio bandwidth with a sampling rate of 2.1 MHz. A generalized simulation software package has been developed to mimic time-domain behavior for oversampling modulators. Circuit design specifications for integrated circuit implementation can be deduced from analysis of simulated data.

### David H. Staelin

*This paper describes our 1975 scientific results that validated the incorporation of imaging passive microwave spectrometers into operational military and civilian weather satellites beginning in 1977 and continuing thereafter with ongoing expansion and improvements. It has recently been said that microwave satellite data has increased numerical weather prediction time horizons approximately ten hours in the northern hemisphere and perhaps two days in the southern hemisphere, relative to other initialization data sets. Our global weather images also graced the cover of this issue of* Science.

**Paper:** Microwave Spectroscopic Imagery of the Earth

**Authors:** D.H. Staelin, P.W. Rosenkranz, F.T. Barath, E.J. Johnston, and J.W. Waters

**Journal:** *Science* 197 (1978): 991–993

**Year:** 1978

The microwave spectrometer on the Nimbus 6 satellite has produced the first microwave spectral images of the earth. It has yielded global maps of (1) atmospheric temperature profiles, (2) the distributions of water vapor and liquid water over ocean, and (3) the coverage and type of ice and snow. The method has potential for operational synoptic monitoring.

### Kenneth N. Stevens

*I chose this abstract because the paper tries to bring together some of my work on basic aspects of human speech production and perception over the past few years, and, based on this work, to formulate a model of how human listeners identify words in running speech. It has application to the technology of automatic speech recognition.*

**Paper:** Toward a Model for Lexical Access Based on Acoustic Landmarks and Distinctive Features

**Author:** Kenneth N. Stevens

**Journal:** *Journal of the Acoustical Society of America* 111, no. 4 (April 2002): 1872–1891

**Year:** 2002

This paper describes a model in which the acoustic speech signal is processed to yield a discrete representation of the speech stream in terms of a sequence of segments, each of which is described by a set (or bundle) of binary distinctive features. These distinctive features specify the phonemic contrasts that are used in the language, such that a change in the value of a feature can potentially generate a new word.

This model is a part of a more general model that derives a word sequence from this feature representation, the words being represented in a lexicon by sequences of feature bundles. The processing of the signal proceeds in three steps: (1) Detection of peaks, valleys, and discontinuities in particular frequency ranges of the signal leads to identification of acoustic landmarks. The type of landmark provides evidence for a subset of distinctive features called articulator-free features (e.g., [vowel], [consonant], [continuant]). (2) Acoustic parameters are derived from the signal near the landmarks to provide evidence for the actions of particular articulators, and acoustic cues are extracted by sampling selected attributes of these parameters in these regions. The selection of cues that are extracted depends on the type of landmark and on the environment in which it occurs. (3) The cues obtained in step (2) are combined, taking context into account, to provide estimates of "articulator-bound" features associated with each landmark (e.g., [lips], [high], [nasal]). These articulator-bound features, combined with the articulator-free features in (1), constitute the sequence of feature bundles that forms the output of the model.

Examples of cues that are used, and justification for this selection, are given, as well as examples of the process of inferring the underlying features for a segment when there is variability in the signal due to enhancement gestures (recruited by a speaker to make a contrast more salient) or due to overlap of gestures from neighboring segments.

### Michael Stonebraker

*I chose this paper because it represents the work I have done at MIT. Most of my other publications predate my relationship with MIT.*

**Chapter:** Aurora: A New Model and Architecture for Data Stream Management

**Authors:** D.J. Abadi, D. Carney, U. Cetintemel, M. Cherniack, C. Convey, S. Lee, M. Stonebraker, N. Tatbul, and S. Zdonik

**Publisher:** *Very Large Database (VLDB) Journal* (12)2: 120–139, August 2003.

**Year:** 2003

This paper describes the basic processing model and architecture of Aurora, a new system to manage data streams for monitoring applications. Monitoring applications differ substantially from conventional business data processing. The fact that a software system must process and react to continual inputs from many sources (e.g., sensors) rather than from human operators requires one to rethink the fundamental architecture of a database management system (DBMS) for this application area. In this paper, we present Aurora, a new DBMS that is currently under construction at Brandeis University, Brown University, and MIT. We first provide an overview of the basic Aurora model and architecture and then describe in detail a stream-oriented set of operators.

### Madhu Sudan

*This paper improves on the ability to correct errors in Reed-Solomon codes—a problem of central engineering and mathematical interest, which had nevertheless seen no progress for almost four decades until this work.*

**Paper:** Improved Decoding of Reed-Solomon and Algebraic-Geometry Codes

**Authors:** Venkatesan Guruswami and Madhu Sudan

**Journal:** *IEEE Transactions on Information Theory* 45, no. 6 (September 1999): 1757–1767

**Year:** 1999

Given an error-correcting code over strings of length $n$ and an arbitrary input string also of length $n$, the list-decoding problem is that of finding all codewords within a specified Hamming distance from the input string. We present an improved list-decoding algorithm for decoding Reed-Solomon codes. The list decoding problem for Reed-Solomon codes reduces to the following "curve-fitting" problem over a field $F$: Given $n$ points $\{(x_i \cdot y_i)\}_{i=1}^{n}$, $x_i$, $y_i \in F$, and a degree parameter $k$ and error parameter $e$, find all univariate polynomials $p$ of degree at most $k$ such that $y_i = p(x_i)$ for all but at most $e$ values of $i \in \{1,\dots,n\}$. We give an algorithm that solves this problem for $e < n - \sqrt{kn}$, which improves over the previous best result, for *every* choice of $k$ and $n$. Of particular interest is the case of $k/n > \frac{1}{3}$, where the result yields the first asymptotic improvement in four decades.

The algorithm generalizes to solve the list-decoding problem for other algebraic codes, specifically alternant codes (a class of codes including BCH codes), and algebraic-geometry codes. In both cases, we obtain a list-decoding algorithm that correct up to $n - \sqrt{n(n-d')}$ errors, where $n$ is the block length and $d'$ is the designed distance of the code. The improvement for the case of algebraic-geometry codes extends the methods of and improves upon their bound for every choice of $n$ and $d$. We also present some other consequences of our algorithm including a solution to a *weighted* curve-fitting problem, which may be of use in soft-decision decoding algorithms for Reed-Solomon codes.

### Gerald Jay Sussman

*In 1988, determining the stability of the solar system was one of the oldest unsolved problems in dynamical astronomy. But we found that the solar system was, in fact, marginally unstable, and our paper provided the first evidence for the solution of this three-hundred-year-old problem. Since publication, our work has been duplicated and confirmed by others.*

*Our work was done using the Digital Orrery, a machine designed to do high-precision integrations for orbital-mechanics experiments; it was designed and built by a few people in a few months, using artificial intelligence-based symbolic simulation and compilation tools. The Digital Orrery was constructed by me, without explicit funding, using parts donated by Hewlett-Packard, and with help from graduate students and post-doctorate researchers in theoretical astrophysics, while I was on sabbatical leave at CalTech in 1983–1984. Richard Feynman helped with some of the numerical algo-*

*rithms. The work with Jack Wisdom, in the design of the experiments, the calibration of the system, and the execution and analysis of the data, was done here at MIT. As a consequence of the importance of this work, the Digital Orrery is now retired in the historical scientific instruments collection of the Smithsonian Institution in Washington, D.C.*

**Paper:** Numerical Evidence that the Motion of Pluto Is Chaotic

**Authors:** Gerald Jay Sussman and Jack Wisdom

**Journal:** *Science* 241 (22 July 1988): 433–437

**Year:** 1988

The Digital Orrery has been used to perform an integration of the motion of the outer planets for 845 million years. This integration indicates that the long-term motion of the planet Pluto is chaotic. Nearby trajectories diverge exponentially with an e-folding time of only about 20 million years.

### Peter Szolovits

*I chose this paper because, after thirty years of research, I have come to the realization that we must overcome social, professional, and political obstacles as well as technical ones in order to see our research impact practice.*

**Paper:** Public Standards and Patients' Control: How to Keep Electronic Medical Records Accessible But Private

**Authors:** K.D. Mandl, P. Szolovits, I.S. Kohane

**Journal:** *British Medical Journal* 322 (3 Feb 2001): 283–287

**Year:** 2001

A patient's medical records are generally fragmented across multiple treatment sites, posing an obstacle to clinical care, research, and public health efforts. Electronic medical records and the internet provide a technical infrastructure on which to build longitudinal medical records that can be integrated across sites of care. Choices about the structure and ownership of these records will have profound impact on the accessibility and privacy of patient information. Already, alarming trends are apparent as proprietary online medical record systems are developed and deployed. The technology promising to unify the currently disparate pieces of a patient's medical record may actually threaten the accessibility of the information and compromise patients' privacy. In this article we propose two doc-

trines and six desirable characteristics to guide the development of online medical record systems. We describe how such systems could be developed and used clinically.

Summary points: Electronic medical record systems should be designed so that they can exchange all their stored data according to public standards. Giving patients control over permissions to view their record—as well as creation, collation, annotation, modification, dissemination, use, and deletion of the record—is key to ensuring patients' access to their own medical information while protecting their privacy. Many existing electronic medical record systems fragment medical records by adopting incompatible means of acquiring, processing, storing, and communicating data. Record systems should be able to accept data (historical, radiological, laboratory, etc.) from multiple sources including physician's offices, hospital computer systems, laboratories, and patients' personal computers. Consumers are managing bank accounts, investments, and purchases on line, and many turn to the web for gathering information about medical conditions; they will expect this level of control to be extended to online medical portfolios.

### Seth Teller

*I have chosen this paper because it showcases the results of several years of effort by a team of students in building a system that can solve a computer vision problem that was previously considered unsolvable by either humans or machines.*

**Paper:** Scalable, Extrinsic Calibration of Omni-Directional Image Networks

**Authors:** Matthew Antone and Seth Teller

**Journal:** *International Journal of Computer Vision* 49, no. 2/3 (September/October 2002): 143–174

**Year:** 2002

We describe a linear-time algorithm that recovers absolute camera orientations and positions, along with uncertainty estimates, for networks of terrestrial image nodes spanning hundreds of meters in outdoor urban scenes. The algorithm produces pose estimates globally consistent to roughly 0.1 degrees (2 milliradians) and 5 centimeters on average, or about four pixels of epipolar alignment.

We assume that adjacent nodes observe overlapping portions of the scene, and that at least two distinct vanishing points are observed by each node. The algorithm decouples registration into pure rotation and translation stages. The rotation stage aligns nodes to commonly observed scene line directions; the translation stage assigns node positions consistent with locally estimated motion directions, then registers the resulting network to absolute (Earth) coordinates.

The paper's principal contributions include: extension of classic registration methods to large scale and dimensional extent; a consistent probabilistic framework for modeling projective uncertainty; and a new hybrid of Hough transform and expectation maximization algorithms.

We assess the algorithm's performance on synthetic and real data, and draw several conclusions. First, by fusing thousands of observations the algorithm achieves accurate registration even in the face of significant lighting variations, low-level feature noise, and error in initial pose estimates. Second, the algorithm's robustness and accuracy increase with image field of view. Third, the algorithm surmounts the usual tradeoff between speed and accuracy; it is both faster and more accurate than manual bundle adjustment.

### Christopher J. Terman

*This particular paper combines many of my long-term interests: VLSI circuit design, computer-aided design tools, and effective educational techniques. Jon Allen shared these interests, and it was great fun working with him to produce this paper and the tools it describes.*

**Paper:** An Interactive Learning Environment for VLSI Design

**Authors:** Jonathan Allen and Christopher J. Terman

**Journal:** *Proceedings of the IEEE* 88, no. 1 (January 2000): 96–106

**Year:** 2000

The interactive learning environment (ILE) is designed to combine the traditional resources of a textbook with the "hands-on" design experiences that are vital to a real understanding of basic engineering principles. The ILE builds on the technology developed for the

World Wide Web to provide a learning environment that can be easily accessed from any browser. In addition to browsable text, Java-based Computer-Aided Design (CAD) tools can be accessed through interactive figures embedded in the text, where students can investigate circuit behavior under the guidance of focused tutorials.

### Bruce Tidor

*This paper represents our first work exploring electrostatic complementarity principles between biological binding partners. The theory derived and the ideas put forward form the basis for what has grown to be a large part of my research effort, full of challenge and reward.*

**Paper:** Optimization of Electrostatic Binding Free Energy

**Authors:** Lee-Peng Lee and Bruce Tidor

**Journal:** *Journal of Chemical Physics* 106, no. 21 (1997): 8681–8690

**Year:** 1997

An analytic result is derived that defines the charge distribution of the tightest-binding ligand given a receptor charge distribution and spherical geometries. Using the framework of continuum electrostatics, the optimal distribution is expressed as a set of multipoles determined by minimizing the electrostatic free energy of binding. Results for two simple receptor systems are presented to illustrate applications of the theory.

### Donald E. Troxel

*This paper describes a system embodying special purpose hardware, software, and integration with commercial devices in order to improve prepress operations. Included were a number of innovative aspects such as imposition, real-time engraving, page composition, tone scale manipulation, and coding of type and images.*

**Paper:** Automated Engraving of Gravure Cylinders

**Authors:** Donald E. Troxel, William F. Schreiber, Samuel M. Goldwasser, Malik M.A. Khan, Len Picard, Michael A. Ide, and Carolyn J. Turcio

**Journal:** *IEEE Transactions on Systems, Man, and Cybernetics* SMC-11, no. 9 (September 1981): 585–596

**Year:** 1981

A computer-based system for automated engraving of gravure cylinders has been developed and

is now used in a normal production environment. Either fully composed pages or individual page components are scanned and stored on a large disk. In the case of fully composed pages, an operator uses a TV display to segment the page image into line and tone areas. The image is then coded by a software process and is ready for subsequent engraving. Prior to the scanning of page components, the operator uses a tablet in order to demark both cropping locations and to specify the location of the components on the final page image. The scanned components are then assembled and coded by a single software process. The encoding process reduces the data storage requirement by a factor of two without any apparent loss of quality. Data are retrieved from disk storage, buffered, decoded, transmitted to a special formatter, and used to drive a Helio Klischograph, which engraves the cylinder in approximately one hour. Completely arbitrary imposition (the arrangement of pages on the gravure cylinder) is accomplished at the time of engraving. Provision is made for the arbitrary intermixture of computer-processed pages and conventional engraving by means of Cronapaques mounted on the companion scanning machine. The motivation for this development was to reduce the cost and time required for the production of gravure cylinders. This has been accomplished by a substantial reduction in the number of photographic steps required in the preparation of input copy and also by the reduction of retouching and makeover due to more precise tone scale control. In addition, the engraving set up time is reduced due to the diminishing use of Cronapaques.

### John N. Tsitsiklis

*This work was chosen because it combines ideas from control theory and computer science to solve a problem in numerical analysis. The resulting algorithm (subsequently named "fast marching") for solving the eikonal equation is used in several application domains, from semiconductor manufacturing to computer vision.*

**Paper:** Efficient Algorithms for Globally Optimal Trajectories

**Author:** John N. Tsitsiklis

**Journal:** *IEEE Transactions on Automatic Control* 40, no. 9 (September 1995): 1528–1538

**Year:** 1995

We present serial and parallel algorithms for solving a system of equations that arises from the discretization of the Hamilton-Jacobi equation associated to a trajectory optimization problem of the following type. A vehicle starts at a prespecified point $x_0$ and follows a unit speed trajectory $x(t)$ inside a region in $\Re^m$, until an unspecified time $T$ that the region is exited. A trajectory minimizing a cost function of the form $\int_0^T r(x(t))dt + q(x(T))$ is sought. The discretized Hamilton-Jacobi equation corresponding to this problem is usually solved using iterative methods. Nevertheless, assuming that the function $r$ is positive, we are able to exploit the problem structure and develop one-pass algorithms for the discretized problem. The first algorithm resembles Dijkstra's shortest path algorithm and runs in time O(nlogn), where $n$ is the number of grid points. The second algorithm uses a somewhat different discretization and borrows some ideas from a variation of Dial's shortest path algorithm that we develop here; it runs in time $O(n)$, which is the best possible, under some fairly mild assumptions. Finally, we show that the latter algorithm can be efficiently parallelized: for two-dimensional problems and with $p$ processors, its running time becomes $O(n/p)$, provided that $p = O(\sqrt{n})/(\log n)$.

### George C. Verghese

*This paper was completed two years after I came to MIT, but much of it is based on my doctoral research at Stanford University. I've chosen it to represent my work because the ideas and results it introduced were quite novel at the time, have endured and worked their way into the now-large literature on differential-algebraic equation (DAE) models, and have turned up in various guises in work I've done—in quite different domains—over my subsequent two decades at MIT.*

**Paper:** A Generalized State-Space for Singular Systems

**Authors:** George C. Verghese, Bernard C. Lévy, and Thomas Kailath

**Journal:** *IEEE Transactions on Automatic Control* AC-26, no. 4 (August 1981): 811–831

**Year:** 1981

Systems of the form $Ex = Ax + Bu$, $y = Cx$, with $E$ singular, are studied. Of particular interest are the impulsive modes that may appear in the free-response of such systems when arbitrary

initial conditions are permitted, modes that are associated with natural system frequencies at infinity. A generalized definition of system order that incorporates these impulsive degrees of freedom is proposed, and concepts of controllability and observability are defined for the impulsive modes. Allowable equivalence transformations of such singular systems are specified. The present framework is shown to overcome several difficulties inherent in other treatments of singular systems, and to extend, in a natural and satisfying way, many results previously known only for regular state-space systems.

### Joel Voldman

*This paper represents the proof-of-concept demonstration of one of the central hubs of my research: using electric fields to manipulate cells, so that we can gather new types of information from them.*

**Paper:** A Microfabrication-Based Dynamic Array Cytometer

**Authors:** J. Voldman, M. Toner, M.L. Gray, and M.A. Schmidt

**Journal:** *Analytical Chemistry* 74, no. 16 (2002): 3984–3990

**Year:** 2002

We have developed a microfabricated device for use in parallel luminescent single-cell assays that can sort populations based upon dynamic functional responses to stimuli. This device is comprised of a regular array of noncontact single-cell traps. These traps use dielectrophoresis to stably confine cells and hold them against disrupting fluid flows. Using quantitative modeling, we have designed traps with a novel asymmetric extruded-quadrupole geometry. This new trap can be physically arrayed and electrically addressed, enabling our cytometer. Situating an array of these traps in a microchannel, we have introduced cells into the array and demonstrated observation of fluorescent dynamic responses followed by sorting. Such a device has potential for use in investigating functional processes—as revealed by temporal behavior—in large numbers of single cells.

### Arthur R. von Hippel

*I am very pleased to select this abstract for Professor Arthur Robert von Hippel, Institute professor emeritus since 1962 in the Department of*

Electrical Engineering at MIT. Professor von Hippel in early 2003 is 104 years old. Throughout his career he has been widely recognized for his outstanding research in dielectrics, molecular science, and molecular engineering.

Von Hippel founded the MIT Laboratory for Insulation Research (LIR) in 1940 and was its sole director until his first retirement in 1964. He has defined modern-day dielectrics research through his many books and research papers. One of his notable discoveries was ferroelectricity and piezoelectricity in barium titanate (BaTiO₃) in 1944. By the late 1950s barium titanate and related ceramics were in wide use as novel electric circuit elements and electromechanical transducers.

I selected this paper to represent von Hippel's career as it demonstrates the research quality practiced by LIR that justified its worldwide reputation as a research center of excellence. The paper summarizes barium titanate research at LIR since 1943, much of it being classified during World War II. In this paper von Hippel acted as a spokesman for his physicist, chemist, electrical engineer, and ceramicist coworkers, and as such demonstrates the multidisciplinary activities of LIR.

The paper is a tour de force in the von Hippel teaching tradition, combining basic and applied research. The rigorous and exhaustive fundamental physics and characterizing measurements of barium titanate ceramics are described, including the Langevin function of dipole orientation; the locally acting electric field on a dipole leading to the "Mosotti catastrophe"; plots of the dielectric constant, spontaneous polarization, specific heat and thermal expansion, X-ray patterns, and piezoelectric coefficient versus temperature; diagrams of crystal structure; hysteresis loops of barium titanate from −175°C to +125°C; field strength dependence of the dielectric constant; and confirmation of the Curie-Weiss law. Realizing that a true understanding could only be obtained from single crystal BaTiO₃, he improved on the crystal growth procedure to produce beautiful crystal patterns viewable with polarized light that depended on applied electric field or mechanical pressure. To describe the beauty of *these patterns he used the phrases "flickering of the transmitted colors resembled Broadway at night" and "patterns which rival in beauty Persian carpet designs."*

*—Markus Zahn*

**Paper:** Ferroelectricity, Domain Structure, and Phase Transitions of Barium Titanate

**Author:** A. von Hippel

**Journal:** *Reviews of Modern Physics* 22, no. 3 (July 1950): 221–237

**Year:** 1950

A summarizing account is given of the research on barium titanate in progress at the Laboratory for Insulation Research at MIT since 1943. The investigations have led to an understanding of the mechanism of ferroelectricity in the titanates and to discoveries such as the piezo-electric effect in the ceramics and the domain structure of the single crystals of $BaTiO_3$. The high dielectric constant, field strength and temperature sensitivity, and piezo-response of the barium titanate dielectrics make them useful for numerous technical applications.

### Stephen A. Ward

*This paper represents the product of several hundred man-years, which overshadows any other paper of mine by orders of magnitude.*

**Paper:** Curl: A Language for Web Content

**Authors:** S. Ward and M. Hostetter

**Journal:** *International Journal of Web Engineering and Technology* 1, no. 1 (April 2003): 41–62

**Year:** 2003

We describe a language designed for the representation of a broad spectrum of Web content, including formatted text, graphics, and programmed application-level function. The approach described maps conventional markup tags to underlying, more general programming constructs, and provides local extensibility of the markup language by addition of programmed objects, procedures, and macros to the underlying object-oriented programming language. An implementation strategy based on a mix of static and dynamic just-in-time compilation techniques is described. The discussion focuses on a number of specific technical challenges raised by the language's breadth and performance goals, and the impact of these issues on Curl's architecture.

### Cardinal Warde

*This paper was chosen because the conventional wisdom at that time was that iron impurities were responsible for the photorefractive effect in barium titanate. In the paper, we were the first to show (via a combination of defect-chemistry and optical experiments) that the presence of iron centers was not a necessary condition for photorefractivity in barium titanate.*

**Paper:** Role of Iron Centers in the Photorefractive Effect in Barium Titanate

**Authors:** P.G. Schunemann, D.A. Temple, R.S. Hathcock, H.L. Tuller, H.P. Jenssen, D.R. Gabbe, and C. Warde

**Journal:** *Journal of the Optical Society of America* B 5, no. 8 (August 1988): 1685–1696

**Year:** 1988

Variably valent iron impurities have been suggested as the source of photorefractive charge carriers in $BaTiO_3$. High-purity $BaTiO_3$ crystals were grown with transition-metal impurity levels below the $10^{16}$ cm$^{-3}$ baseline estimated for photorefractivity. Iron-doped crystals were grown with concentrations of 5, 50, 250, 500, 750, and 1000 parts in $10^6$ of iron. Changes in iron valence monitored by optical absorption in the $P_{O_2}$ range $1-10^{-4}$ atm were found to be consistent with a defect-chemical model indicating $Fe^{3+}$ and $Fe^{4+}$ to be the stable valence states in this range. Photorefractive characterization of high-purity $BaTiO_3$ suggests that variably valent iron ions are not the dominant photorefractive species in these crystals, whereas the role of iron centers in doped crystals is complicated by large absorption losses.

### Thomas F. Weiss

*The idea for this paper came to me quite suddenly, and I recall the pleasure of developing the ideas and of communicating them. The paper was influential in its time and has continued to be cited twenty years after it was written.*

**Paper:** Bidirectional Transduction in Vertebrate Hair Cells: A Mechanism for Coupling Mechanical and Electrical Processes

**Author:** T.F. Weiss

**Journal:** *Hearing Research* 7 (1982): 353–360

**Year:** 1982

It has been proposed that the sharp frequency selectivity exhibited by cochlear hair cells and neurons of alligator lizards results from a mechanical resonance of the stereociliary-tectorial structures of hair cells. In contrast, in the red-eared turtle this selectivity has been attributed to an electrical resonance mechanism located in the hair-cell membrane. In this report a new mechanism is proposed, one which is consistent with observations in the lizard and turtle preparations and in which hair-cell resonances result from coupling of mechanical properties of hair-cell stereociliary-tectorial structures with electrical properties of the hair-cell membrane through a receptor membrane process that has bidirectional, mechanoelectric and electromechanical transduction properties. This same mechanism could also be the physical basis for diverse phenomena observed in mammals, including changes in mechanical properties of the ear in response to electrical stimulation in the cochlea and central nervous system, and the presence of sustained, narrow-band, acoustic emissions in the ear canals of humans.

### Jacob K. White

*Designing complicated three-dimensional structures is a difficult problem common to many engineering disciplines. Where possible, designs are synthesized and optimized using computer simulation to create easily modified "virtual prototypes," thereby avoiding the delay and cost of building physical prototypes. Until recently, insufficiently efficient numerical techniques made it practically impossible to use virtual prototyping for a type of field problem that arises in a variety of applications, including aircraft, micromachined devices, electronic packages, and off-shore structures. The FASTCAP program, developed for analyzing integrated circuit interconnect, demonstrated that multipole-accelerated integral equation methods could provide the needed computational efficiency for the type of field problem mentioned above. Since the publication of the original FASTCAP paper, thousands of designers have used FASTCAP. In addition, the strategies in FASTCAP have been adopted in dozens of commercial simulation programs covering a wide range of applications.*

**Paper:** FASTCAP: A Multipole-Accelerated 3D Capacitance Extraction Program

**Authors:** K. Nabors and J. White

**Journal:** *IEEE Transactions on Computer-Aided Design* 10, no. 10 (November 1991): 1447–1459
**Year:** 1991

In this paper a fast algorithm for computing the capacitance of a complicated 3D geometry of ideal conductors in a uniform dielectric is described, and its performance in the capacitance extractor FASTCAP is examined. The algorithm is an acceleration of the boundary-element technique for solving the integral equation associated with the multiconductor capacitance extraction problem. Boundary-element methods become slow when a large number of elements are used because they lead to dense matrix problems, which are typically solved with some form of Gaussian elimination. This implies that the computation grows as $n$ cubed, where $n$ is the number of panels or tiles needed to accurately discretize the conductor surface charges. In this paper we present a generalized conjugate residual iterative algorithm with a multipole approximation to compute the iterates. This combination reduces the complexity, so that accurate multiconductor capacitance calculations grow nearly as $nm$, where $m$ is the number of conductors. Performance comparisons on integrated circuit bus crossing problems show that for problems with as few as twelve conductors the multipole-accelerated boundary-element method can be nearly five hundred times faster than Gaussian elimination-based algorithms, and five to ten times faster than the iterative method alone, depending on required accuracy.

**Alan S. Willsky**

*I debated whether to submit this paper or one that I wrote in 1978 (also in the* Proceedings of the IEEE*). That earlier paper dealt with the relationships between signal processing and control and estimation theory, and was pivotal in my career as it both launched me into what for me was a new field (signal and image processing) and also highlighted what I feel is one of my strengths, namely bridging between fields and finding areas of intersection that lead to new and important research directions.*

*The paper that I have chosen, which appeared almost a quarter of a century later, represents for me an affirmation of both of those elements.*

*In part this paper outlines a line of inquiry that my group, my collaborators, and I introduced and developed over the past fifteen years. I view this body of work as my most important contribution to the broad field of signal and image analysis because of its intellectual and conceptual significance as well as the exceptionally broad array of disciplines that it has impacted. Indeed, this work has fed my continuing desire to bridge between fields, as our methods have found application in fields ranging from chemical engineering to oceanography and have led to collaborations with MIT colleagues in these and other fields that have greatly enriched the research experience for everyone in my group. Furthermore, this paper also makes a statement that my passion for uncovering and exploring connections between fields is still very much alive, as it includes suggestions of ties to artificial intelligence and computer science that are currently propelling my group into the future.*

**Paper:** Multiresolution Markov Models for Signal and Image Processing
**Author:** Alan S. Willsky
**Journal:** *Proceedings of the IEEE* 90, no. 8 (August 2002): 1396–1458
**Year:** 2002

This paper reviews a significant component of the rich field of statistical multiresolution (MR) modeling and processing. These MR methods have found application and permeated the literature of a widely scattered set of disciplines, and one of our principal objectives is to present a single, coherent picture of this framework. A second goal is to describe how this topic fits into the even larger field of MR methods and concepts—in particular making ties to topics such as wavelets and multigrid methods. A third is to provide several alternate viewpoints for this body of work, as the methods and concepts we describe intersect with a number of other fields.

The principal focus of our presentation is the class of MR Markov processes defined on pyramidally organized trees. The attractiveness of these models stems from both the very efficient algorithms they admit and their expressive power and broad applicability. We show how a variety of methods and models relate to this framework including models for self-simi-lar and 1/f processes. We also illustrate how these methods have been used in practice.

We discuss the construction of MR models on trees and show how questions that arise in this context make contact with wavelets, state space modeling of time series, system and parameter identification, and hidden Markov models. We also discuss the limitations of tree-based models and algorithms and the artifacts that they can introduce. We describe when these are of concern and ways in which they can be overcome. This leads to a discussion of MR models on more general graphs and ties to well-known and emerging methods for inference on graphical models.

**Gerald L. Wilson**

*This article arose out of much of my early work at MIT regarding the design and operation of electric power systems. Because of my knowledge of electric power systems, I was asked to serve as one of three outside experts to review the cause of the 1977 blackout. I chose this article because it involved a critical mix of technology, public policy, politics, and corporate culture that I had not experienced before. The interplay of these disciplines and cultures made the analysis of the blackout and the publishing of an article describing it a most challenging exercise.*

**Paper:** Anatomy of a Blackout: How's and Why's of the Series of Events That Led to the Shutdown of New York's Power in July 1977
**Author:** G.L. Wilson
**Journal:** *IEEE Spectrum* (February 1978): 38–46
**Year:** 1978

On 13 July 1977, at 8:30 p.m., the Consolidated Edison power system was carrying 2860 MW of power from the north into the city of New York over 345- and 138-kV transmission lines. These lines include double circuits—and, in one case, quadruple circuits (neither is indicated for simplicity). By about 9:00 p.m., the system was badly crippled as a result of a series of events triggered by lightning at 8:37 and 8:56. One remaining 345-kV feeder to the north (from Millwood to Pleasant Valley) and the tie to New Jersey (Linden to Goethals) were loaded beyond their short-time-emergency rating. Further escalation led to a complete blackout in New York City by about 9:36 p.m.

## Patrick Henry Winston

*This was the first paper demonstrating how a computer program can learn and reason by retrieving precedents and exploiting analogies. Also, the paper came to be viewed as a prime example of the learning-by-explaining paradigm.*

**Paper:** Learning and Reasoning by Analogy

**Author:** P.H. Winston

**Journal:** *Communications of the ACM Archive* 23, no. 12: 689–703

**Year:** 1980

We use analogy when we say something is a Cinderella story and when we learn about resistors by thinking about water pipes. We also use analogy when we learn subjects like economics, medicine, and law. This paper presents a theory of analogy and describes an implemented system that embodies the theory. The specific competence to be understood is that of using analogies to do certain kinds of learning and reasoning. Learning takes place when analogy is used to generate a constraint description in one domain, given a constraint description in another, as when we learn Ohm's law by way of knowledge about water pipes. Reasoning takes place when analogy is used to answer questions about one situation, given another situation that is supposed to be a precedent, as when we answer questions about Hamlet by way of knowledge about Macbeth.

## Gregory Wornell

*I chose this paper because it is an example of the growing number of research problems with facets in the currently somewhat separate and culturally distinct fields of information theory, communication theory, signal processing, and theoretical computer science. I think we can expect much exciting future work in EECS coming from increasing integration of these fields over the next one hundred years.*

*A full-length version of this work will be published in an upcoming* IEEE Transactions on Information Theory *and an extended version appears in the* Proceedings of the IEEE International Conference on Image Processing 2, 17–20. New York: IEEE, 2002.

**Paper:** Authentication with Distortion Criteria

**Authors:** Emin Martinian, Gregory Wornell, and Brian Chen

**Publisher:** to appear in *IEEE Transactions on Information Theory*, 2004, Washington, D.C.: IEEE

**Year:** 2001

In a variety of applications, there is a need to authenticate a source that may have been degraded, transformed, edited, or otherwise modified, either intentionally or unintentionally. We develop a formulation of this problem, and identify and interpret the associated information-theoretic performance limits. In particular, we develop the inherent trade-off between encoding and reconstruction distortion under a security guarantee, and illustrate the results through some basic binary and Gaussian examples. Useful layered extensions are also developed. The resulting codes can be viewed as natural generalizations of digital signatures, and the associated systems are significantly different from those used for digital watermarking.

## John L. Wyatt

*We are trying to develop a microelectronic retinal-implant device to restore a limited level of vision to patients who are blind with such diseases as retinitis pigmentosa and macular degeneration. While we have worked for years with animals, this paper gives our first results with blind human volunteers.*

**Paper:** Methods and Perceptual Thresholds for Short-Term Electrical Stimulation of Human Retina with Microelectrode Arrays

**Authors:** J.F. Rizzo III, J. Wyatt, J. Loewenstein, S. Kelly, and D. Shire

**Journal:** *Investigative Ophthalmology & Visual Science* 44, no. 12

**Year:** 2003

This paper reports methods for performing epiretinal electrical stimulation with microfabricated electrode arrays and determining perceptual thresholds on awake human volunteers during acute surgical trials. The eventual purpose is the development of a retinal prosthesis for the blind. Five subjects with severe blindness from retinitis pigmentosa and one with normal vision (who underwent removal of the eye because of cancer) were studied. Electrical stimulation of the retina was performed on awake volunteers by placing a single 250-micron (μm) diameter hand-held needle electrode or a 10-μm thick microfabricated array of iridium oxide electrodes (50, 100 or 400-μm diameter) on the retina. Current sources outside the eye delivered charge to the electrodes. No clinically visible damage to the eye or loss of vision occurred. Percepts could not be reliably elicited with the 50-μm diameter electrodes using safe charge densities in one blind patient. With the two larger electrodes, only the normally sighted patient had thresholds at a charge density below 0.25 millicoulombs (mC)/cm$^2$ for 400-μm electrodes or below 1 mC/cm$^2$ for 100-μm diameter electrodes. The latter value is a reasonable estimate of the safe long-term charge-injection limit for this material. The range of charge density thresholds with the 400-μm electrode in blind patients was 0.3 to 2.8 mC/cm$^2$. The normally sighted patient had a threshold of 0.08 mC/cm$^2$, roughly one quarter of the lowest threshold in blind patients. Strength-duration curves obtained in two blind patients revealed the lowest threshold charge at the shortest pulse durations used, 0.25 and 1.0 msec.

## Markus Zahn

*This paper describes three primary experimental research areas that I have contributed to over my thirty years of research. I prepared this paper when I was selected as the 1998 Whitehead Memorial Lecturer of the Conference on Electrical Insulation and Dielectric Phenomena. The conference, for each year since 1955, has invited an international acclaimed authority to deliver a lecture in memory of John Boswell Whitehead (1872–1954), the founder of the conference in 1920 and chairperson of this conference from 1922–1938. Other MIT EECS professors who were Whitehead Memorial Lecturers are Professor A.R. von Hippel in 1960 and Professor J.B. Trump in 1977.*

**Paper:** Optical, Electrical, and Electro-Mechanical Measurement Methodologies of Electric Field, Charge, and Polarization in Dielectrics

**Author:** Markus Zahn

**Journal:** *IEEE Transactions on Dielectrics and Electrical Insulation* 5, no. 5 (October 1998): 627–650

**Year:** 1998

A selective review is presented of the use of optical, electrical, and electro-mechanical measurement methodologies of the electric field, charge, conductivity, and permittivity in dielectrics. Kerr electro-optic measurements are presented to demonstrate how volume charge distributions can significantly distort the electric field distribution and how the field and charge distributions depend on dielectric and electrode materials and geometry and on voltage magnitude, polarity, and time duration. A new class of interdigital dielectrometry sensors is reviewed which from one side can measure profiles in dielectric permittivity and conductivity and related physical properties such as moisture content. Electromechanical devices such as the absolute charge sensor and the couette charger (CC) with a rotating cylindrical electrode are reviewed for their applications in liquid flow electrification measurements.

## Lizhong Zheng

*This following paper covers my research on multiple antenna channels. I think the result and viewpoint of this paper are quite fundamental. It helps to understand the complicated field of space-time coding in a simple and concise way, as well as raising new questions to study wireless communications.*

**Paper:** Diversity and Multiplexing: A Fundamental Tradeoff in Multiple Antenna Channels

**Authors:** Lizhong Zheng and David N.C. Tse

**Journal:** *IEEE Transactions on Information Theory* 49:5 (May 2003) 1073–1096

**Year:** 2003

Multi-antenna communications and space-time coding have been one of the hottest research areas in the communication field in the past few years. There are, however, two distinct points of view on how multiple antennas can be used in a wireless system. First, multiple antennas can be used to provide *diversity* to improve the reliability of the transmission; secondly, multiple antennas allow *spatial multiplexing* by creating parallel spatial channels and therefore allow much higher data rates. These two distinct viewpoints lead to two more or less distinct camps of researchers, using different performance metrics and different tools in their work on space-time codes.

In this paper we propose a new point of view: a multi-antenna system can provide *both* diversity and spatial multiplexing gains simultaneously, but there is a *tradeoff* between how much of each type of gains a system can achieve. The viewpoints of maximizing the diversity gain and of maximizing the spatial multiplexing gains are the two extremes in this tradeoff, but it is the entire tradeoff curve, which provides the unified picture of the capability of multi-antenna systems. The main analytical result is a simple characterization of the optimal tradeoff curve achievable by *any* space-time coding scheme. This fundamental limit provides a common benchmark for evaluating the performance of many proposed schemes, be they diversity-based or multiplexing-based, and also provides insights on the design of new schemes.

## Victor Zue

*Jupiter is our best-known conversational system that allows users to talk to it naturally and receive real information. It is the first of its kind in the literature that illustrates many of the important research topics, such as telephone-based speech recognition, mixed initiative spoken dialogue management, and content processing.*

**Paper:** Jupiter: A Telephone-Based Conversational Interface for Weather Information

**Authors:** Victor Zue, Stephanie Seneff, James R. Glass, Joseph Polifroni, Christine Pao, Timothy J. Hazen, and Lee Hetherington

**Journal:** *IEEE Transactions on Speech and Audio Processing* 8, no. 1 (January 2000): 85–96

**Year:** 2000

In early 1997, our group initiated a project to develop Jupiter, a conversational interface that allows users to obtain worldwide weather information over the telephone using spoken dialogue. It has served as the primary research platform for our group on many issues related to human language technology, including telephone-based speech recognition, robust language understanding, language generation, dialogue modeling, and multilingual interfaces. Since coming online in May 1997, Jupiter has

received, via a toll-free number in North America, more than 30,000 calls (containing more than 180,000 utterances), mostly from naive users. The purpose of this paper is to describe our development effort in terms of the underlying human language technologies as well as other system-related issues, such as utterance rejection and content harvesting. We will also present some evaluation results on the system and its components.

# Ph.D. and Sc.D. Recipients

1 9 1 0 – 2 0 0 2

321

1935

**Hall, William M.** Investigation of the Radiation of Sound from an Intense Source — Sc.D.

**Horton, J. Warren** Electrical Impedance of Living Tissue — Sc.D.

**Sinclair, Donald B.** The Susceptance-variation Method: A New Procedure for Impedance Measurements at High Frequencies — Sc.D.

**Truscott, David N.** Investigation of the Carbon Microphone — Sc.D.

1936

**Neitzert, Carl** Synthesis of a Two-terminal Non-dissipative Network for a Finite Band of Frequencies — Sc.D.

**Buehl, Russell C.** Bulk and Surface Magnetic Studies of Transformations in Iron-chromium-nickel Alloys — Sc.D.

**Fan, Hsu Yun** Transition from Glow Discharge to Arc — Sc.D.

**Fitzgerald, A. Eugene** Steady-state-stability Criteria for Electric Power Systems — Sc.D.

**Hoadley, George B.** Film Studies on a Power Factor Bridge — Sc.D.

**Kimbark, Edward W.** Performance of Protective Relays During Simultaneous Faults — Sc.D.

**Lyon, Dean A.** Electric Strength of Extremely Thin Insulating Films — Sc.D.

1938

**Brown, Gordon S.** The Cinema Integraph: A Machine for Evaluating a Parametric Product Integral — Sc.D.

**Chang, Tsun T.** Short-circuit Analysis of Single-phase Machines — Sc.D.

**Chen, Tsung S.** Effect of External Capacitance on the Operation of Salient-pole Synchronous Machines — Sc.D.

**Chu, Lan Jen** Transmission and Radiation of Electromagnetic Waves in Hollow Pipes and Horns — Sc.D.

**Fussell, Lewis** Cloud Chamber Study of Cosmic Ray Showers in Lead Plates — Sc.D.

**Howell, Alvin H.** Breakdown Studies in Compressed Gases — Sc.D.

**Miller, Arthur** Engineering Aspects of Electrocardiography — Sc.D.

1939

**Hedeman, Walter R., Jr.** The Numerical Solution of Integral Equations on the Cinema Integraph — Sc.D.

1940

**Pollack, Dale** Interference Between Stations in Frequency Modulation Systems — Sc.D.

1941

**Magnusson, Philip C.** Methods of Solving Linear Inhomogeneous Integral Equations — Sc.D.

**Peterson, Arnold P.G.** Measurement of Voltage at Ultrahigh Frequencies — Sc.D.

**White, Walter T.** Integral Equation and Approximate Solutions for Normal Modes of Vibration — Sc.D.

1943

**Hall, Albert C.** Analysis and Synthesis of Linear Servomechanisms — Sc.D.

1944

**Lee, Gordon M.** Development of a High-Speed Cathode Ray Oscillograph — Sc.D.

1946

**Roberts, Shepard** Dielectrics as Nonlinear Circuit Elements — Sc.D.

1947

**Chung, Shih-Mu** Investigation of the Causes of Negative Damping in Synchronous Machines — Sc.D.

**Fano, Robert M.** Theoretical Limitations on the Broadband Matching of Arbitrary Impedances — Sc.D.

**Johnson, Ellis A.** Primary Standard for Measurement of the Earth's Magnetic Vector — Sc.D.

**McIlroy, Malcolm S.** Design of an Electric Analyzer for Fluid Distribution Systems — Sc.D.

**Valdivia, Manuel Cerrillo** Transient Phenomena in Wave Guides — Sc.D.

1948

**Macnee, Alan B.** Electronic Differential Analyzer — Sc.D.

**Tuller, William G.** Theoretical Limitations on the Rate of Transmission of Information — Sc.D.

**Tuttle, David F., Jr.** Network Synthesis for Prescribed Transient Response — Sc.D.

1949

**Adler, Richard B.** Properties of Guided Waves on Inhomogeneous Cylindrical Structures — Sc.D.

**Campbell, Donald P.** Power Studies in Linear Feedback Systems — Sc.D.

**Floyd, George F., Jr.** Design of a Servomechanism Operating in the Presence of Noise and Under Specified Constraints — Sc.D.

**Kochenburger, Ralph J.** Analysis and Synthesis of Contactor Servomechanisms — Sc.D.

**Kretzmer, Ernest R.** Interference Characteristics of Pulse-Time Modulation — Sc.D.

**Linvill, John G.** Amplifiers with Arbitrary Amplification-Bandwidth Product and Controlled Frequency Characteristics — Sc.D.

**Linvill, William K.** Analysis and Design of Sampled-Data Control Systems — Sc.D.

**Moreno, Theodore** On Transmission Techniques Suitable for Millimeter Waves — Sc.D.

1950

**Baruch, Jordan J.** Instrumentation for a Transmission Research Program — Sc.D.

**Davenport, Wilbur B., Jr.** Study of Speech Probability Distributions — Sc.D.

**David, Edward E., Jr.** Some Aspects of R-F Phase Control in Microwave Oscillators — Sc.D.

**Granlund, John** Interference in Frequency Modulation Reception — Sc.D.

**Harris, Lawrence A.** Axially Symmetric Electron Beam and Magnetic Field Systems — Sc.D.

**Moats, Robert R.** Interaction of Modes in Magnetron Oscillators — Sc.D.

**Newton, George C., Jr.** Compensating Network Theory for Feedback-Control Systems Subject to Saturation — Sc.D.

**Russell, John B., Jr.** Sinusoidal Oscillations in Nonlinear Systems — Sc.D.

**Scott, Ronald E.** Analog Device for Solving the Approximation Problem of Network Synthesis — Sc.D.

**Singleton, Henry E.** Theory of Nonlinear Transducers — Sc.D.

**Thurston, James N.** Investigation of Resistance-Bridge Methods as Applied to Dynamic Measurements — Sc.D.

**Truxal, John G.** Servomechanism Synthesis Through Pole-Zero Configurations — Sc.D.

**Tsao, Chien-You** Betatron Characteristics of the MIT Synchrotron — Sc.D.

## 1951

**Costas, John P.** Interference Filtering — Sc.D.

**Hadden, Frederick A.** Precision Magnetic Field Regulation Using Nuclear Magnetic Resonance — Sc.D.

**Hance, Harold V.** Optimization and Analysis of Systems for the Detection of Pulse Signals in Random Noise — Sc.D.

**Johnson, E. Calvin, Jr.** Sinusoidal Analysis of Feedback-Control Systems Containing Nonlinear Elements — Sc.D.

**Kashmiry, Monir A.** Self-Excitation of Induction Motors with Series Capacitors — Sc.D.

**Kusko, Alexander** Study of the Electrical Behavior of Gases at High Pressure — Sc.D.

**Salzer, John M.** Treatment of Digital Control Systems and Numerical Processes in the Frequency Domain — Sc.D.

**Seifert, William W.** Study of Noise in Missile Control Systems — Sc.D.

**Sensiper, Samuel** Electromagnetic Wave Propagation in Helical Conductors — Sc.D.

**Stutt, Charles A.** Experimental Study of Optimum Filters — Sc.D.

**Weinberg, Louis** New Synthesis Procedures for Realizing Transfer Function of RLC- and RC-Networks — Sc.D.

## 1952

**Angell, James B.** Errors in Angle Radar Systems Caused by Complex Target — Sc.D.

**Angelo, Ernest J., Jr.** Electron-Beam Tube for Analog Multiplication — Sc.D.

**Basore, Bennett L.** Noise-like Signals and Their Detection by Correlation — Sc.D.

**Booton, Richard C., Jr.** Nonstationary Statistical Theory Associated with Time-varying Linear Systems — Sc.D.

**Bourne, Henry C.** Study of the Theory of Voltage Breakdown in High Vacuum — Sc.D.

**Cheatham, Thomas P., Jr.** Electronic Correlator and Its Use in Communication Problems — Sc.D.

**Dasher, Benjamin J.** Synthesis of RC Transfer Functions as Unbalanced Two Terminal-Pair Networks — Sc.D.

**Gilleo, M. Alten** Optical Absorption and Photo-Effects in Silver Chloride, Potassium Bromide, and Sodium Chloride — Ph.D.

**Ham, James M.** Solution of a Class of Operational Equations by Methods of Successive Approximations — Sc.D.

**Jones, Thomas F., Jr.** Propagation of Errors in Analog Computers — Sc.D.

**Kautz, William H.** Procedure for the Synthesis of Networks for Specified Transient Response — Sc.D.

**Mason, Samuel J.** On the Logic of Feedback — Sc.D.

**Ruze, John** Physical Limitations of Antennas — Sc.D.

**Siebert, William M.** Design of Amplifiers for Minimum Sensitivity to Drift and Distortion — Sc.D.

**Stevens, Kenneth N.** Perception of Sounds Shaped by Resonant Circuits — Sc.D.

**Verzuh, Frank M.** Solution of Boundary-Value Problems on Automatic Computing Equipment — Sc.D.

**Woods, Cornelius H., Jr.** Homing Missile Guidance Using Body-Fixed Antennas — Sc.D.

## 1953

**Boisvert, Maurice** Band-Pass Amplifiers Using Point-Contact Transistors — Sc.D.

**Chu, Ge Yao** Fundamental Electrical Processes in High-Voltage Acceleration Tubes — Sc.D.

**Cypser, Rudolph J.** Optimum Use of Water Storage in Hydro-Thermal Electric Systems — Sc.D.

**Desoer, Charles A.** Communication Through Channels in Cascade — Sc.D.

**Fricker, Stephen J.** Ionospheric Reflection of Radio Waves — Sc.D.

**Gould, Leonard A.** Dynamic Behavior and Control of Heat Transfer Processes — Sc.D.

**Green, Paul E., Jr.** Correlation Detection Using Stored Signals — Sc.D.

**Harrison, E. Rowe** Shot Noise in Electron Beams at Microwave Frequencies — Sc.D.

**Hli, Freddy Ba** Network Synthesis by Impulse Response for Specified Input and Output in the Time Domain — Sc.D.

**Huffman, David A.** Synthesis of Sequential Switching Circuits — Sc.D.

**Huggins, William H.** Theory of Hearing — Sc.D.

**Lephakis, Achilles J.** Correlation Analysis of VHF Signals — Sc.D.

**Lucal, Harold M.** Synthesis of Three-Terminal RC Networks with Prescribed Short-Circuit Admittances — Sc.D.

**Price, Robert** Statistical Theory Applied to Communication Through Multipath Disturbances — Sc.D.

## 1954

**Berk, Aristid D.** Cavities and Waveguides with Inhomogeneous and Anisotropic Media — Sc.D.

**Chen, Kan** Quasi-linearization Techniques for Transient Study of Nonlinear Feedback-Control Systems — Sc.D.

**Cox, Jerome R., Jr.** Physical Limitations on Free-Field Microphone Calibration — Sc.D.

**Craig, Edward J.** Iteration Procedures for Simultaneous Equations — Sc.D.

**Frost, Harold B.** Transient Changes in Oxide Cathodes — Sc.D.

**Goff, Kenneth W.** Application of Correlation Techniques to Some Acoustic Measurements — Sc.D.

**Haus, Hermann A.** Propagation of Noise and Signals Along Electron Beams at Microwave Frequencies — Sc.D.

**Kerwin, Edward M., Jr.** Study of a Class of Thermoacoustic Oscillations — Sc.D.

**Mathews, Max V.** Technique for the Evaluation of Nonlinear Servomechanisms — Sc.D.

**Sittler, Robert W.** Analysis and Design of Simple Nonlinear Noise Filters — Sc.D.

## 1955

**Armstrong, Douglas B.** Methods of Inferring Aircraft Geometry and Motion from Microwave Radar Reflections — Sc.D.

**Arthurs, Edward** Iterative Procedures for Solving Systems of Inequalities — Sc.D.

**Flanagan, James L.** Speech Analyzer for a Formant-Coding Compression System — Sc.D.

**Hurst, Stanley Reid** New Methods of Transformerless Driving-Point Impedance Synthesis — Sc.D.

**Kosowsky, David I.** Synthesis and Realization of Crystal Filters — Sc.D.

1955 (continued)

**Kotter, F. Ralph** Pulse Voltage Studies on the Conductivity of Electrolytes and Semiconductors — Sc.D.

**McWhorter, Alan L.** 1/f Noise and Related Surface Effects in Germanium — Sc.D.

**Noiseux, Denis U.** Development of a Photo-Electric Function Recorder — Sc.D.

**Pucel, Robert A.** Network Synthesis for a Prescribed Impulse Response — Sc.D.

**Riaz, Mahmoud** Dynamics of D-C Machines in Regulating Systems — Sc.D.

**Rona, Thomas P.** Gas Temperature Measurements by Ultrasonic Pulse Method — Sc.D.

**Selin, Karl I.** Transductors as Modulators — Sc.D.

**Stoft, Paul E.** Compact High-Intensity Source of 14-MEV Neutrons — Sc.D.

**Strieby, Michael** Time Domain Synthesis by Means of Trigonometric Polynomial Approximations — Sc.D.

**Teager, Herbert M.** Analysis of Transients in Mass-Transfer Operations — Sc.D.

**Van Rennes, Albert** Pulse-Amplitude Analysis in Nuclear research — Sc.D.

1956

**Baghdady, Elie J.** Interference Rejection in FM Receivers — Sc.D.

**Bose, Amar G.** Theory of Nonlinear Systems — Sc.D.

**Buckley, Ellery F.** Pulsed Electron Accelerator for Radiation Dose-Time Studies on Biological and Chemical Systems — Sc.D.

**Elkind, Jerome I.** Characteristics of Simple Manual Control Systems — Sc.D.

**Epstein, David J.** Magnetic Lag in Ferrites — Sc.D.

**Garber, H. Newton** A Class of Queueing Problems — Sc.D.

**Haas, Vinton B., Jr.** Evaluation of Feedback Control Systems — Sc.D.

**Hilibrand, Jack** Characterization of Probability Distributions for Excess Physical Noises — Sc.D.

**Lewis, Philip M., II** Synthesis of Voltage Transfer Functions — Sc.D.

**Lorens, Stanley** Theory and Applications of Flow Graphs — Sc.D.

**McCluskey, Edward J., Jr.** Algebraic Minimization and the Design of Two-Terminal Contact Networks — Sc.D.

**Pezaris, Stylianos D.** Analysis of Linear Networks Through Use of the State Concept — Sc.D.

**Powers, Kerns H.** Unified Theory of Information — Sc.D.

**Stern, Thomas E.** Piecewise-Linear Network Theory — Sc.D.

**Turin, George L.** Communication Through Noisy, Random-Multipath Channels — Sc.D.

**Widrow, Bernard** Study of Rough Amplitude Quantization by Means of Nyquist Sampling Theory — Sc.D.

**Woodson, Herbert H.** Magnetic Amplifier Analysis Using a Generalized Model for the Saturable Reactor Core — Sc.D.

1957

**Boffi, Luiz V.** Electrodynamics of Moving Media — Sc.D.

**Goldstein, Moise H., Jr.** Neurophysiological Representation of Complex Auditory Stimuli — Sc.D.

**Meyers, Norman H.** Singly Excited Transducer — Sc.D.

**Nease, Robert F.** Analysis and Design of Nonlinear Sampled-Data Control Systems — Sc.D.

**Pinson, John C.** Transient Correction by Means of All-Pass Networks — Sc.D.

**Shekel, Jacob** Analysis of Linear Networks — Sc.D.

**Thornton, Richard D.** Some Limitations of Linear Amplifiers — Sc.D.

**Unger, Stephen N.** Study of Asynchronous Logical Feedback Networks — Sc.D.

**Wozencraft, John M.** Sequential Decoding for Reliable Communication — Sc.D.

1958

**Brilliant, Martin B.** Theory of the Analysis of Nonlinear Systems — Sc.D.

**Buck, Dudley A.** Superconductive Electronic Components — Sc.D.

**Dennis, Jack B.** Mathematical Programming and Electrical Networks — Sc.D.

**Epstein, Marvin A.** Coding for the Binary Erasure Channel — Sc.D.

**Gruber, Sheldon** Ionospheric Scintillation of Cosmic Radio Noise — Sc.D.

**Gyftopoulos, Elias P.** Fundamental Electric Processes in High Vacuum — Sc.D.

**Harrington, John V.** On the Statics and Dynamics of Magnetic Domain Boundaries — Sc.D.

**Howard, Ronald A.** Studies in Discrete Dynamic Programming — Sc.D.

**Jewell, William S.** Optimal Flow Through Networks — Sc.D.

**Johannessen, Paul R.** Analysis of Magnetic Amplifiers — Sc.D.

**Merriam, Charles W., III** Synthesis of Adaptive Controls — Sc.D.

**Nuttall, Albert H.** Theory and Application of the Separable Class of Random Processes — Sc.D.

**Putman, Thomas H.** Utilization of Traveling Waves for Energy Conversion — Sc.D.

**Wernikoff, Robert E.** Theory of Signals — Sc.D.

**Whitehouse, David R.** Study of Atomic Spectra from Gaseous Discharge Plasmas — Sc.D.

**Youngblood, William A.** Estimation of the Channel Capacity Required for Picture Transmission — Sc.D.

1959

**Bello, Phillip A.** Applications of Linear Transformation Theory to the Synthesis of Linear Active Non-Bilateral Networks — Sc.D.

**Bers, Abraham** Interaction of Electrons with Electromagnetic Fields of Gaps, with Applications to Multicavity Klystrons — Sc.D.

**DeClaris, Nicholas** Synthesis of Linear Active Networks — Sc.D.

**De Russo, Paul M.** Ultimate Performance Limitations of Linear Sampled Data Systems — Sc.D.

**George, Donald A.** Continuous Nonlinear Systems — Sc.D.

**Harris, Lawson P.** Hydromagnetic Channel Flows — Sc.D.

**Hofstetter, Edward M.** Large Sample Sequential Decision Theory — Sc.D.

**Jacobs, Irwin M.** Connectivity in Probabilistic Graphs — Sc.D.

**Kaiser, James F.** Constraints and Performance Indices in the Analytical Design of Linear Controls — Sc.D.

**Kramer, Robert** Effects of Quantization on Feedback Systems with Stochastic Inputs — Sc.D.

**Lees, Robert B.** Grammar of English Nominalizations — Ph.D.

**1959** (continued)

**Leon, Benjamin J.** Frequency-Domain Theory of Parametric Amplification — Sc.D.

**Lerner, Robert M.** Method of Speech Compression — Sc.D.

**Sebestyen, George S.** On Pattern Recognition with Application to Silhouettes — Sc.D.

**Stockham, Thomas G., Jr.** Study of a Class of Nonlinear Systems — Sc.D.

**Subbotin, Boris T.** High-Density Beams in Van de Graaff Accelerators — Sc.D.

**1960**

**Blair, John** An Investigation into the Thermal and Electrical Properties of the Mercury-Telluride Cadmium-Telluride Semiconductor Solid-Solution System — Sc.D.

**Chesler, David Alan** Nonlinear Systems with Gaussian Inputs — Sc.D.

**Gallager, Robert Gray** Low Density Parity Check Codes — Sc.D.

**Gottling, James Goe** Investigation of a Thin-Film Thermal Transducer — Sc.D.

**Gray, Paul Edward** Dynamic Behavior of Thermoelectric Devices — Sc.D.

**Hause, Arthur Dickson** Nonlinear Least-Squares Filtering and Frequency Modulation — Sc.D.

**Horstein, Michael** Sequential Transmission of Digital Information with Feedback — Sc.D.

**Hughes, George Wendell** On the Recognition of Speech by Machine — Sc.D.

**Johnson, Avery Remington** The Servo-analysis of Postural Reflexes — Ph.D.

**Jordan, Kenneth Louis, Jr.** Discrete Representations of Random Signals — Sc.D.

**Manley, Oscar P.** Some Aspects of Copper Transport in Single Crystals of P-type Bismuth Telluride — Ph.D.

**Morgenthaler, Frederic R.** On the General Theory of Microwave Interactions with Ellipsoidal Ferrimagnetic Insulators — Ph.D.

**Peake, William Tower** Analytical Study of Electrical Responses at the Periphery of the Auditory System — Sc.D.

**Penfield, Paul, Jr.** Frequency-Power Formulas — Sc.D.

**Peskoff, Arthur** Waves in a Relativistic Plasma — Ph.D.

**Rafuse, Robert Pendleton** Parametric Applications of Semiconductor Capacitor Diodes — Sc.D.

**Reiffen, Barney** Sequential Encoding and Decoding for the Discrete Memoryless Channel — Ph.D.

**Robinson, Charles Canfield** The Longitudinal Kerr Magneto-optic Effect in Ferromagnetic Thin Films — Sc.D.

**Rosen, George** Dynamic Analog Speech Synthesizer — Sc.D.

**Schissler, Lloyd Robert** Temperature and Thickness Dependence of the Electric Strength of Alkali Halides — Sc.D.

**Schoeffler, James David** Impedance Transformation Using Lossless Networks — Sc.D.

**Tufts, Donald Winston** Design Problems in Pulse Transmission — Sc.D.

**Wells, Walter Irvine** Decoding of Group Codes for Binary Symmetric Channels — Ph.D.

**Zames, George** Nonlinear Operators for System Analysis — Sc.D.

**1961**

**Bliss, James Charles** Communication via the Kinesthetic and Tactile Senses — Ph.D.

**Borrego Larrolde, José Marie** Optimum Impurity Concentration in Semiconductor Thermoelements — Sc.D.

**Chorney, Paul** Power and Energy Relations in Bidirectional Waveguides — Sc.D.

**Davis, Michael Chase** Optimum Systems in Multi-Dimensional Random Processes — Sc.D.

**Dennis, Jane Hodgson** Anisotropy of Thermoelectric Power in Bismuth Telluride — Ph.D.

**Frankenthal, Shimshon** Studies of Plasmas in Unidirectional Magnetic Fields — Sc.D.

**Geisler, Chris Daniel** Average Responses to Clicks in Man Recorded by Scalp Electrodes — Sc.D.

**Hall, Richard Byron** Large Signal Behavior of Plasmas — Sc.D.

**Hennie, Frederick Clair, III** Iterative Arrays of Logical Circuits — Sc.D.

**Kailath, Thomas** Communication via Randomly Varying Channels — Sc.D.

**Kipiniak, Walerian** Variational Approach to Dynamic Optimization and Control System Synthesis — Sc.D.

**MacMillan, Archie J.** Electric and Magnetic Properties of $V_2O_3$ and Related Sesquioxides — Ph.D.

**Massa, Ronald J.** An Investigation of Human Visual Information Transmission — Ph.D.

**Nelson, Robert Erich** Preparation and Electronic Transport Properties of Mercury Telluride — Sc.D.

**Penhume, John P.** Energy Conversion in Laminar Magnetohydrodynamic Channel Flow — Ph.D.

**Rosenfeld, Jack Lee** Adaptive Decision Processes — Sc.D.

**Sakrison, David John** Application of Stochastic Approximation Methods to System Optimization — Sc.D.

**Sarles, Frederick Williams, Jr.** A Magneto-Optic Apparatus for the Dynamic Study of Ferromagnetic Surface Domains — Sc.D.

**Schell, Allan Carter** Multiple Plate Antenna — Sc.D.

**Schetzen, Martin** Some Problems in Nonlinear Theory — Sc.D.

**Scott, Alwyn Charles** Design and Oscillator Applications of High-Current Tunnel Diodes — Sc.D.

**Van Trees, Harry Leslie, Jr.** Synthesis of Optimum Nonlinear Control Systems — Sc.D.

**Vanwormhoudt, Marc C.** Thermal Noise in Linear, Lossy, Electromagnetic Media — Ph.D.

**1962**

**Bahiana, Luiz Carlos** Electromagnetic Induction on an Expanding Conducting Sphere — Sc.D.

**Crawford, Charles Kimball** Electron Ionization Cross Sections for Atoms of Metals — Sc.D.

**Drake, Alvin William** Observation of a Markov Process Through a Noisy Channel — Sc.D.

**Duda, Richard O.** Equivalent and Optimal Equivalent Electrical Networks — Ph.D.

**Ernst, Heinrich Arnold** MH-1, A Computer-Operated Mechanical Hand — Sc.D.

**1962** (continued)

**Getty, Ward Douglas**  Investigation of Electron-Beam Interaction with a Beam-Generated Plasma — Sc.D.

**Haring, Donald Russell**  Some Aspects of the State Assignment Problem for Sequential Circuits — Sc.D.

**Heinz, John Michael**  Reduction of Speech Spectra to Descriptions in Terms of Vocal-Tract Area Functions — Sc.D.

**Helgesson, Alan Lee**  Gain-bandwidth Limitations of Balanced, Three-frequency Parametric Amplifiers — Ph.D.

**Jedynak, Leo**  Investigation of Vacuum Breakdown — Sc.D.

**Jelinek, Frederick**  Coding for Discrete Memoryless Two-way Channels — Ph.D.

**Kain, Richard Yerkes**  Diode Network Synthesis — Sc.D.

**Katzenelson, Jacob**  Design of Nonlinear Filters — Sc.D.

**Kleinrock, Leonard**  Message Delay in Communication Nets with Storage — Ph.D.

**Knowlton, Kenneth C.**  Sentence Parsing with a Self-organizing Heuristic Program — Ph.D.

**Krinitz, Arthur**  Radar Theory Applicable to Dense Scatterer Distributors — Sc.D.

**Lee, Harry B., Jr.**  On the Canonic Realization of Two Element Kind Driving Point Impedances — Ph.D.

**Liu, Chung-Laung**  Some Memory Aspects of Finite Automata — Sc.D.

**Lyden, Henry Albert**  Effective Masses of Free Carriers in Lead Telluride: Their Temperature Dependence and Contribution to Transport Properties — Sc.D.

**Macurdy, William Bradford**  Mathematical Models for Sensory Communication — Ph.D.

**Magid, Leonard M.**  Heat Flow in Crystal Lattices — Ph.D.

**Massey, James L.**  Threshold Decoding — Ph.D.

**Melcher, James Russell**  Electrohydrodynamic and Magnetohydrodynamic Surface Waves and Instabilities — Ph.D.

**More, Trenchard, Jr.**  Relations Between Implicational Calculi — Ph.D.

**Norris, Richard Cromwell**  Studies in Search for a Conscious Evader — Sc.D.

**Pan, John William**  Reduction of Information Redundancy in Pictures — Sc.D.

**Poduska, John William**  Random Theory of Turbulence — Sc.D.

**Schwab, Walter Carlton**  Synthesis of RC Networks by Normal Coordinate Transformations — Ph.D.

**Schwartz, Richard John**  Thermal and Electronic Transport Properties of a $(Bi_2Te_e) - (Sb_2Te_3) - (Bi_2Se_3)$ Semiconducting Alloy — Sc.D.

**Smallwood, Richard Dale**  Automated Instruction Decision Systems — Sc.D.

**Troxel, Donald Eugene**  Tactile Communication — Ph.D.

**Wedlock, Bruce Daniels**  Spectral Response and Conversion Efficiency of P-N Junctions — Sc.D.

**Ziv, Jacob**  Coding and Decoding for Time-Discrete, Amplitude Continuous Memoryless Channels — Sc.D.

**1963**

**Algazi, Vidal R. (Vidal Raphael)**  A Study of the Performance of Linear and Nonlinear Filters — Ph.D.

**Cogdell, John Richard**  Mode Theory of the Active Magnetohydrodynamic Waveguide — Ph.D.

**Cooper, Robert Shanklin**  Traveling Density Variations in Partially Ionized Gases — Sc.D.

**Cox, Henry, Lt.**  Estimation of State Variables for Noisy Dynamic Systems — Sc.D.

**Cummings, John Rodgers**  Limitations on Diagnosis of Radiators and Scatterers from Far-zone Fields — Sc.D.

**Cunningham, James Edward**  Temporal Filtering of Motion Pictures — Sc.D.

**Denker, Stephen Paul**  Electronic Properties of Titanium Monoxide — Ph.D.

**Goblick, Thomas John**  Coding for a Discrete Information Source with a Distortion Measure — Ph.D.

**Grayzel, Alfred I.**  The Bandwidth of the Abrupt Junction Varactor Frequency Doubler — Ph.D.

**Hall, Joseph Lindley, II**  Binaural Interaction in the Accessory Superior Olivary Nucleus of the Cat—an Electrophysiological Study of Single Neurons — Ph.D.

**Huang, Thomas Shi-Tao**  Pictoral Noise — Sc.D.

**Hurwitz, Charles E.**  Growing Helical Density Waves in Semiconductor Plasmas — Ph.D.

**Kellner, Wayne George**  The Measurement of Eye Movements — Sc.D.

**Kennedy, Robert Spayde**  Finite-State Binary Symmetric Channels — Sc.D.

**Kleinrock, Leonard**  Message Delay in Communication Nets with Storage — Ph.D.

**Levine, Richard Carl**  Thermal Sensory Communication — Sc.D.

**Litsios, Socrates**  Class of Sequencing Problems — Sc.D.

**Loomis, Herschel H.**  The Effects of Logic Delay on Computation Rate — Ph.D.

**Pfeiffer, Russell R.**  Electro-physiological Response Characteristics of Single Units in the Cochlear Nucleus of the Cat — Ph.D.

**Pilla, Michael Andrew**  Communication Aids for Complete Paraplegics Using Electro-ocular Signals — Ph.D.

**Roberts, Lawrence G.**  Machine Perception of Three-dimensional Solids — Ph.D.

**Rummler, William David**  Optimum Noise Performance of Multiterminal Amplifiers — Sc.D.

**Schneider, Arthur John**  Alternating-Current Generation from the Interaction of a Moving Conducting Fluid with a Circuit — Ph.D.

**Spinrad, Robert Joseph**  Machine Recognition of Hand-Printed Block Letters — Ph.D.

**Stiglitz, Irvin Gale**  Sequential Decoding with Feedback — Ph.D.

**Sutherland, Ivan Edward**  Sketchpad, a Man-Machine Graphical Communication System — Ph.D.

**Tretiak, Oleh John**  The Picture Sampling Process — Sc.D.

**Weinreb, Sander**  A Digital Spectral Analysis Technique and Its Application to Radio Astronomy — Ph.D.

**Weiss, Thomas Fischer**  A Model for Firing Patterns of Auditory Nerve Fibers — Ph.D.

**Wemple, Stuart H.**  Polarization Effects on Magnetic Resonances in Ferroelectric Potassium Tantalate — Ph.D.

## 1964

**Ballantine, John Harvey, Jr.** Random Phase Errors in Coherent Ground-Mapping Radars — Sc.D.

**Ballantyne, Joseph Merrill** Frequency and Temperature Response of the Polarization of Barium Titanate — Ph.D.

**Belanger, Pierre Rolland** On the Sensitivity of Solutions to Some Optimal Control Problems — Ph.D.

**Berlekamp, Elwyn Ralph** Block Coding with Noiseless Feedback — Ph.D.

**Black, William Lawrence** Acoustic Pattern Presentation — Sc.D.

**Briggs, Richard J.** Instabilities and Amplifying Waves in Beam-plasma Systems — Ph.D.

**Bruce, James Donald** Investigation of Optimum Quantization — Sc.D.

**Canaday, Rudd H.** Two-dimensional Iterative Logic — Ph.D.

**Conklin, James Byron, Jr.** Relativistic Effects in Lead Telluride — Sc.D.

**Dertouzos, Michael L.** Threshold-element Synthesis — Ph.D.

**Ferreira, Luiz Guimarães** Calculation of Electronic Properties of Strained Lead Telluride — Ph.D.

**Gilchrist, Richard Bruce, Lt.** Control of Nonlinear Systems — Sc.D.

**Gronemann, Uri Fritz** Coding Color Pictures — Ph.D.

**Hsieh, Hsien Yuen** Experimental Studies of the Beam-plasma Discharge — Ph.D.

**Hunt, Robert P.** Magnetic Anneal Effects in Some Garnets — Ph.D.

**Janak, James Francis** Theory of Losses in Ferromagnets — Sc.D.

**Kramer, John David Rentschler, Jr.** Partially Observable Markov Processes — Sc.D.

**Levison, William Henry** Nonlinear Analysis of the Pressoreceptor Reflex System — Sc.D.

**Lewis, Arthur Thomas** Large-Signal Behavior of a Parametric Magnetogasdynamic Generator — Sc.D.

**MacDonald, John Spencer** Experimental Studies of Handwriting Signals — Ph.D.

**May, William Gambrill** Plasma Wave Transmission Through Bismuth — Ph.D.

**Mermelstein, Paul** Computer Recognition of Connected Handwritten Words — Sc.D.

**Morse, David Lincoln** Low-Frequency Instability of Magnetized Plasma — Sc.D.

**Oppenheim, Alan Victor** Superposition in a Class of Nonlinear Systems — Sc.D.

**Parker, Don** Effects of Ionospheric Irregularities on Radio Wave Reception — Sc.D.

**Pierson, Edward Samuel** MHD Induction Machine — Sc.D.

**Rook, Charles Wesley, Jr.** Free Surface Waves on Electrically Conducting Fluids — Sc.D.

**Serafim, Philip Evangelos** Analysis of Electron Beam Plasma Systems — Sc.D.

**Shimony, Uri** Mössbauer Studies on Iron in Perovskites — Ph.D.

**Skelton, Grant Bradford** Optimum Fixed Control of an Uncertain Plant — Ph.D.

**Sklar, Jay Robbins** Sequential Measurement of Multidimensional Transducers — Ph.D.

**Van Raalte, John A., Jr.** Conduction Phenomena in Rutile Single Crystals — Ph.D.

**Woodward, Charles Edward** Development of a Quadrupole Mass Spectrometer — Ph.D.

**Zeiger, Howard Paul** Loop-free Synthesis of Finite State Machines — Ph.D.

## 1965

**Allen, Silas James, Jr.** The Quantized Rotational State of HCl Molecules in the Quinol Clathrate Structure — Ph.D.

**Alter, Ralph** Bioelectric Control of Prostheses — Sc.D.

**Andersen, Jonny** Realizability Conditions for New Classes of Three-element-kind Networks — Ph.D.

**Arntz, Floyd Olaf** Properties of Titanium and Rutile ($TiO_2$) Thin Films — Ph.D.

**Bahnsen, Ralph Jacob** An Approach to Synthesis of Bilateral Iterative Systems — Sc.D.

**Bar-David, Israel** Radar Models and Measurements — Sc.D.

**Beusch, John Ulrich** Dynamic Behavior and Control of Communications Networks — Ph.D.

**Bush, Aubrey Marvin** Some Techniques for the Synthesis of Nonlinear Systems — Sc.D.

**Bush, Richard Wright** Performance Limitations of Vibratory Gyroscopes — Sc.D.

**Cahlander, David Allen** Echolocation with Wide-band Waveforms: Bat Sonar Signals — Ph.D.

**Capranica, Robert Rudy** Evoked Vocal Response of the Bullfrog—Study of Communication by Sound — Sc.D.

**Clemens, Jon Kaufmann** Optical Character Recognition for Reading Machine Applications — Ph.D.

**Conley, James Woodworth** Absorption of Photons by Excitons with Assistance from Phonons in a Polar Semiconductor — Sc.D.

**Cook, Gerald** Control Systems Study of the Saccadic Eye-Movement Mechanism — Sc.D.

**Crowley, Joseph M.** Feedback Control of a Convective Instability — Ph.D.

**Donaldson, Robert Wellington** Multimodality Sensory Communication — Ph.D.

**Eastman, Dean Eric** An Ultrasonic Study of Magnetoelastic and Anelastic Properties of Yttrium Iron Garnet — Ph.D.

**Ebert, Paul Michael** Error Bounds for Parallel Communication Channels — Sc.D.

**Fessenden, Thomas J.** A Pulsed Electron-Cyclotron Resonance Discharge Experiment — Sc.D.

**Forney, George D., Jr.** Concatenated Codes — Sc.D.

**Foyt, Arthur G., Jr.** The Gunn Effect in Compound Semiconductors — Sc.D.

**Gray, Peter Russell** A Statistical Analysis of Electrophysiological Data from Auditory Nerve Fibers in Cat — Ph.D.

**Hamann, Donald Robert** The Wavevector-Dependent Spin Susceptibility of an Interacting Electron Gas — Ph.D.

**Holsinger, Jerry Lee** Digital Communication Over Fixed Time-continuous Channels with Memory—with Special Application to Telephone Channels — Ph.D.

**Hui Bon Hoa, Roger** An Electromagnetic Field Analysis in a High-Dielectric Rectangular Resonator in Free Space — Sc.D.

**1965** (continued)

**Katona, Peter Geza**  Computer Simulation of Blood Pressure Control of Heart Period — Sc.D.

**Ketterer, Frederick David**  Electromechanical Streaming Instabilities — Ph.D.

**Kincaid, Thomas Gardiner**  Time Domain Analysis of Trains of Equally Spaced Overlapping Pulses — Ph.D.

**Kliman, Gerald Burt**  Axisymmetric Modes in Nonuniform Hydromagnetic Waveguide — Sc.D.

**Lenoir, William Benjamin**  Remote Sounding of the Upper Atmosphere by Microwave Measurements — Ph.D.

**McMorris, John A., II**  A Comprehensive Analysis of Cryogenic Magnets Suitable for Magnetohydrodynamic Applications — Sc.D.

**Murray Lasso, Marco Antonio**  The Modal Analysis and Synthesis of Linear Distributed Control Systems — Sc.D.

**Niessen, Charles William**  Experimental Facility for Sequential Decoding — Sc.D.

**Plant, John Bertrand**  An Iterative Procedure for the Computation of Optimal Controls — Ph.D.

**Pollon, Gerald E.**  On the Measurement of Randomly Time-Varying Linear Systems — Sc.D.

**Savage, John Edmund**  The Computation Problem with Sequential Decoding — Ph.D.

**Scherr, Allan Lee**  An Analysis of Time-shared Computer Systems — Ph.D.

**Shaver, Paul John**  Thermal and Electronic Transport Properties of Zinc Antimonide — Sc.D.

**Staelin, David Hudson**  Microwave Spectrum of Venus — Sc.D.

**Tchernev, Dimiter Ivanov**  Ferromagnetic Resonance in Silicon and Calcium Doped Garnets — Ph.D.

**Yacoby, Yizhak**  Optical Absorption in Si in Strong Electric Fields — Sc.D.

**Yudkin, Howard Louis**  Channel State Testing in Information Decoding — Ph.D.

**Zeiger, Howard Paul**  Loop-Free Synthesis of Finite State Machines — Ph.D.

**1966**

**Bauer, Ronald Francis**  A Theoretical and Experimental Study of Noise from Magnetic Recording Tape — Ph.D.

**Binsack, Joseph Herbert**  Plasma Studies with the IMP-2 Satellite — Ph.D.

**Broniwitz, Laurence Edward**  Analytical Design of Stable Dynamic Control Policies — Sc.D.

**Chen, Arthur Chih-Mei**  Ferroelectricity in Potassium Nitrate — Ph.D.

**Courtens, Eric Leon Anne**  Contact Properties and Related Conduction Phenomena in Insulating Cadmium Sulfide — Ph.D.

**Crabtree, William Hiter**  Digital Control System Design: A Simulation Approach — Sc.D.

**Crystal, Thomas Herne**  A Model of Laryngeal Activity During Phonation — Sc.D.

**Fitts, Richard Earl**  Linearization of Nonlinear Feedback Systems — Ph.D.

**Gordon-Clark, Matthew Richard**  Dynamic Models for Convective Systems — Ph.D.

**Graham, Donald Norman**  Image Transmission by Two-dimensional Contour Coding — Ph.D.

**Hartwig, Curtis Paul**  Suppression of Spin Wave Instabilities in Ferrimagnets — Ph.D.

**Henke, William L.**  Dynamic Articulatory Model of Speech Production Using Computer Simulation — Ph.D.

**Holland, Richard Walter**  Application of Green's Functions and Eigenmodes in the Design of Piezoelectric Ceramic Devices — Ph.D.

**Ivie, Evan Leon**  Search Procedures Based on Measures of Relatedness Between Documents — Ph.D.

**Landsman, Emanuel**  Mobility-Aid Simulation Studies — Sc.D.

**Lee, Francis Fan**  A Study of Grapheme to Phoneme Translation of English — Ph.D.

**Lieberman, Michael Aaron**  Ion Oscillations Excited by Electron Beam-plasma Interaction — Ph.D.

**Lyon, Ervin F., III**  A Study of the Interplanetary Plasma — Ph.D.

**Mark, Roger Greenwood**  Auditory Evoked Potentials During Conditioning in the Rat — Ph.D.

**Molnar, Charles Edwin**  Model for Convergence of Inputs upon Neurons in the Cochlear Nucleus — Sc.D.

**Nelsen, Donald Edward**  Statistics of Switching-time Jitter for a Tunnel Diode Threshold-crossing Detector — Ph.D.

**Nill, Kenneth Wellman**  Microwave Magnetoacoustic Effects in Indium Antimonide — Ph.D.

**Parente, Robert Bruce**  Functional Analysis of Systems Characterized by Nonlinear Differential Equations — Ph.D.

**Pauwels, Herman Jan E. Hendrik**  Noise Sources Describing Quantum Effects in the Laser Oscillator — Ph.D.

**Portinari, João Candido**  The One-dimensional Inverse Scattering Problem — Ph.D.

**Prabhu, Vasant Krishna**  Narrow-Band Noise Performance of Pumped Nonlinear Systems — Sc.D.

**Pruslin, Dennis Howard**  Automatic Recognition of Sheet Music — Sc.D.

**Rabii, Sohrab**  An Investigation of Energy Band Structure and Electronic Properties of Lead Sulfide and Lead Selenide — Ph.D.

**Roberge, James Kerr**  Gated Amplifiers for Data Processing in Space — Sc.D.

**Sachs, Murray B.**  Auditory Nerve Fiber Responses to Two-tone Stimuli — Ph.D.

**Saltzer, Jerome Howard**  Traffic Control in a Multiplexed Computer System — Sc.D.

**Santoro, Ralph Paul**  Magnetic Properties of the Olivines — Ph.D.

**Schaffer, Michael Joel**  Hydromagnetic Surface Waves with an Alternating Magnetic Field — Sc.D.

**Snyder, Donald Lee**  The State-variable Approach to Continuous Estimation — Ph.D.

**Spann, Richard Nelson**  Generalized Threshold Functions — Ph.D.

**Spiridon, Alexander**  Vibro-Tactile Pattern Perception — Sc.D.

**Steinbrecher, Donald Harley**  Limitations on Parametric Amplifiers and Improved Efficiency Varactor Multipliers — Ph.D.

**Sutherland, William Robert**  The On-line Graphical Specification of Computer Procedures — Ph.D.

**Taylor, Michael Gordon**  Randomly Perturbed Computation Systems — Ph.D.

**Van Horn, Earl Cornelius, Jr.**  Computer Design for Asynchronously Reproducible Multiprocessing — Ph.D.

**1966** (continued)

**Ver Planck, Peter** The Tunnel Diode Superregenerative Mixer — Ph.D.

**Walpole, James Newman** Magnetoplasma Waves in Lead Telluride — Ph.D.

**Wanas, Mahmoud W.A.** Dynamics and Statics of Domain Walls in Pure and Doped Yttrium-Iron Garnets — Sc.D.

**Wilde, Daniel Underwood** Program Analysis by Digital Computer — Ph.D.

**Witsenhausen, Hans Sylvain** Minimax Control of Uncertain Systems — Ph.D.

**1967**

**Almasi, George S.** Photovoltaic Effects in Cadmium Telluride-Mercury Telluride Heterostructures — Ph.D.

**Austin, Michael Edward** Decision-Feedback Equalization for Digital Communication Over Dispersive Channels — Sc.D.

**Burns, Stephen Kent** Methods for the Description of the Temporal Structure of the Human Electroencephalogram — Ph.D.

**Callarotti, Roberto Cesare** The Mixed State in Type II Superconductors — Ph.D.

**Carlson, Alan Walfred** Free Carrier Absorption and Effective Masses in Zinc Antimonide-Cadmium Antimonide Alloys — Ph.D.

**Chandra, Akhileshwari Narain** Computer Simulation of Vagal Control of Heart Rate — Sc.D.

**Chase, David** Communication Over Noisy Channels with no A Priori Synchronization Information — Ph.D.

**Cordover, Ronald Harvey** High Resolution Study of the Structure of Atomic Transitions Using Lasers — Ph.D.

**Cornew, Ronald W.** Error Considerations in Reading Machine Design — Sc.D.

**Edwards, Kent Ralph** Magnetohydrodynamic Wave Propagation in a Partially Ionized Current-carrying Gas — Ph.D.

**Eisenberg, Martin** Multi-queues with Changeover Times — Ph.D.

**Falconer, David Duncan** A Hybrid Sequential and Algebraic Decoding Scheme — Ph.D.

**Gladstone, Robert Jay** Scheduling in Constant Speed Transportation Systems — Ph.D.

**Glaser, Jerome Ira** Low-loss Waves in Hollow Dielectric Tubes — Ph.D.

**Hackett, William Harold, Jr.** Microwave Surface Impedance Measurements of High-[kappa] type-II Superconductors at High Magnetic Fields — Ph.D.

**Heller, Jerrold Allan** Sequential Decoding for Channels with Time Varying Phase — Ph.D.

**Iwasa, Yukikazu** Stability and Spatially Periodic Magnetization of Hard Superconductors — Ph.D.

**Jameson, Paul Walter** Interaction of a Plasma with an RF Magnetic Field — Ph.D.

**Kleinman, David L.** Suboptimal Design of Linear Regulator Systems Subject to Computer Storage Limitations — Ph.D.

**Kocher, David Geiger** On Schlieren Optics and a High-Speed Multiple-spark Camera — Sc.D.

**Martin, Robert Lanham** Studies in Feedback Shift Register Synthesis — Ph.D.

**Martin, William Arthur** Symbolic Mathematical Laboratory — Ph.D.

**Max, Joel** Parallel Channels Without Crosstalk — Ph.D.

**Nahvi, Mahmood Janab** Response of Cerebellar Cells to Acoustic Stimuli — Ph.D.

**Parker, Ronald Richard** Excitation and Propagation of Ion-Cyclotron Waves in a Plasma Column — Sc.D.

**Pilc, Randolph John** Coding Theorems for Discrete Source-channel Pairs — Ph.D.

**Pinkston, John Turner, III** Encoding Independent Sample Information Sources — Ph.D.

**Rabiner, Lawrence Richard** Speech Synthesis by Rule: An Acoustic Domain Approach — Ph.D.

**Richters, John Stephen** Communication over Fading Dispersive Channels — Ph.D.

**Ripper Filho, José Ellis** Effects of Pressure on a Semiconductor Laser Radiation — Ph.D.

**Rogers, Alan Ernest Exel** Emission and Absorption of Microwave Radiation by Interstellar OH — Ph.D.

**Sacks, Barry Howard** Magnetic Field Effects in Semiconductor Lasers — Ph.D.

**Schindall, Joel Elliot** Static and Dynamic Analysis of a Feedback-controlled Two-state Modulation System — Ph.D.

**Smythe, Daniel Lafayette, Jr.** Hole and Electron Mobility in Semiconductors with Large Numbers of Excess Carriers — Ph.D.

**Turnbull, Robert James** Electroconvective Instabilities with a Stabilizing Temperature Gradient — Ph.D.

**Wiederhold, Michael Lewis** A Study of Efferent Inhibition of Auditory Nerve Activity — Ph.D.

**Wilson, Stewart Wade** A Machine as Partner in the Question-answer Process of Learning — Ph.D.

**1968**

**Allen, John Loyd** The Optical Functioning of the Superposition Eye of a Nocturnal Moth — Ph.D.

**Allen, Jonathan** A Study of the Specification of Prosodic Features of Speech from a Grammatical Analysis of Printed Text — Ph.D.

**Baggeroer, Arthur Bernard** State Variables, Fredholm Theory, and Optimal Communication — Sc.D.

**Barrera Rivera, Renato** Structural Stability of Chemical Reactors — Sc.D.

**Bartsch, Robert Richard** Investigation of Non-synchronous Beam-plasma Interaction — Ph.D.

**Bucher, Edward Andrew** Error Mechanisms for Convolutional Codes — Ph.D.

**Burchfiel, Jerry Don** The Design of Transmission Lines and Waveguide Structures Using the Maximum Principle — Sc.D.

**Buss, Dennis Darcy** Characterization of the Lattice Vibration Spectrum in PbTe — Ph.D.

**Canales Ruiz, Roberto de Jesus** A Priori Bounds on the Performance of Optimal Systems — Ph.D.

**Caron, Laurent Gerard** Self-consistent Cluster Treatment of Kinetic and Magnetic Effects in Narrow Energy Bands — Ph.D.

**Collins, Lewis Dye** Asymptotic Approximations to the Error Probability for Detecting Gaussian Signals — Sc.D.

**1969** (continued)

**Ledgard, Henry Francis** A Formal System for Defining the Syntax and Semantics of Computer Languages — Ph.D.

**Lee, Wai-Hon** Computer Generation of Holograms and Spatial Filters — Sc.D.

**Levine, William Silver** Optimal Output-feedback Controllers for Linear Systems — Ph.D.

**McElroy, Alan Joel** Flashover Mechanisms of Insulators with Contaminated Surfaces — Ph.D.

**Medress, Mark Frederick** Computer Recognition of Single-syllable English Words — Ph.D.

**Odoni, Amedeo Rodolfo** An Analytical Investigation of Air-traffic in the Vicinity of Terminal Areas — Ph.D.

**Parada, Nelson de Jésus** Localized Defects in PbTe via a $\vec{K} \cdot \vec{\pi}$ – APW Energy Band Calculation — Ph.D.

**Schneider, Herman Martin** Oscillations of an Inhomogeneous Plasma Slab — Sc.D.

**Sheena, David** A System for Instantaneous Wide Angle Eye Position Measurement — Ph.D.

**Skoog, Ronald Arthur** A Time Dependent Realization Theory with Applications to Electrical Network Synthesis — Ph.D.

**Strahm, Norman Dale** Raman Scattering in Mixed Semiconductors — Ph.D.

**Therrien, Charles William** Tearing of Networks — Ph.D.

**Weinstein, Clifford Joseph** Quantization Effects in Digital Filters — Ph.D.

**White, Ralph Carleton** An Investigation of High Speed Optical Detectors — Ph.D.

**Wolaver, Dan Holden** Fundamental Study of DC to DC Conversion Systems — Ph.D.

**Wolf, Jared John** Acoustic Measurements for Speaker Recognition — Ph.D.

**Young, Ian Theodore** Automated Leukocyte Recognition — Ph.D.

**1970**

**Anderson, Grant Bruce** Frequency-Domain Image Representation — Sc.D.

**Barnwell, Thomas Pinkney, III** An Algorithm for Segment Durations in a Reading Machine Context — Ph.D.

**Carbonell, Jaime Raul** Mixed-initiative Man-computer Instructional Dialogues — Ph.D.

**Chinn, Stephen Robert** Two-magnon Raman Scattering from Magnetic Insulators — Ph.D.

**Cohn, David Leslie** Minimum Mean-Square Error without Coding — Ph.D.

**Cooke, Chathan Mansfield** Insulation of High Voltage in Semi-Vacuum — Ph.D.

**Doane, John Leslie** Reflection and Transmission Coefficients in Multi-wave Inhomogeneous Media — Ph.D.

**Edelberg, Murray** Integral Convex Polyhedra and an Approach to Integralization — Sc.D.

**Fonstad, Clifton Gilbert** Stannic Oxide—Crystal Growth and Electrical Properties — Ph.D.

**Gajda, Walter Joseph, Jr.** X-Ray Scattering from Strained Crystal Lattices — Ph.D.

**Gertz, Jeffrey Lee** Hierarchical Associative Memories for Parallel Computation — Ph.D.

**Goldberg, Aaron Joseph** Visible Speech Displays for the Severely Hard of Hearing — Ph.D.

**Goodman, Lawrence Alan** Defect-related Optical Absorption and Photoconductivity in Cadmium Sulphide — Ph.D.

**Greenwood, Robert Edward** The Visibility of Pictorial Noise — Sc.D.

**Halme, Seppo Juhani** Efficient Optical Communication in a Turbulent Atmosphere — Ph.D.

**Hebalkar, Prakash Gurunth** Deadlock-free Sharing of Resources in Asynchronous Systems — Sc.D.

**Hoff, Paul Walter** Linear and Nonlinear Optical Pulsed Response of $CO_2$ Laser Amplifiers — Ph.D.

**Horn, Berthold Klaus Paul** Shape from Shading: A Method for Obtaining the Shape of a Smooth Opaque Object from One View — Ph.D.

**Jennings, John Baker** Inventory Control in Regional Blood Banking Systems — Ph.D.

**Jones, Thomas Byron** Dynamics of Electromechanical Flow Structures — Ph.D.

**Jones, Thomas Lane** A Computer Model of Simple Forms of Learning — Ph.D.

**Joseph, Keith Millican** On the Design of Optimal and Suboptimal Feedback Systems — Ph.D.

**Krakauer, Lawrence Jay** Computer Analysis of Visual Properties of Curved Objects — Ph.D.

**Laster, Stanley Jerral** Hydromagnetic Stability of the Plasmapause — Ph.D.

**Maidique, Modesto Alex** D.C. and Pulse Voltage Studies on Proton Generation and Transfer through "pure" Ice in Single Crystals — Ph.D.

**Makhoul, John** Speaker-machine Interaction in Automatic Speech Recognition — Ph.D.

**Oliver, Michael Ray** Conductivity Studies in Europium Oxide — Sc.D.

**Papadopoulos, George Demetrios** Ku-Band Interferometry — Ph.D.

**Patil, Suhas** The Coordination of Asynchronous Events — Sc.D.

**Personick, Stewart David** Efficient Analog Communications over Quantum Channels — Sc.D.

**Platzker, Aryeh** Coupling of Photons and Phonons to Electronic and Nuclear Spin Waves in Anti-ferromagnets — Ph.D.

**Prerau, David Stewart** Computer Pattern Recognition of Standard Engraved Music Notation — Ph.D.

**Rahimi, Abdolhossein** Lie Algebraic Methods in Linear System Theory — Ph.D.

**Ramsey, John Loring** Cascaded Tree Codes — Ph.D.

**Robbins, Gregory Manson** The Inversion of Linear Shift-Variant Imaging Systems — Ph.D.

**Saleh, Adel Abdel Moneim Mohamed** Theory of Resistive Mixers — Ph.D.

**Schlaepfer, Felix Martin** Set-theoretic Estimation of Distributed Parameter Systems — Ph.D.

**Shapiro, Jeffrey Howard** Optimal Spatial Modulation for Reciprocal Channels — Ph.D.

**Speck, Carlton Edward** High-Frequency Instability of a Hot-Electron Plasma Generated by Electron-Cyclotron Resonance — Sc.D.

1970 (continued)

**Strong, Robert Michael** An Explorable Electrotactile Display — Ph.D.

**Tse, Edison Tack-Shuen** On the Optimal Control of Linear Systems with Incomplete Information — Ph.D.

**Vanderbilt, Dean Hanawalt** Controlled Information Sharing in a Computer Utility — Ph.D.

**Walpert, Gary Arnold** Image Bandwidth Compression by Detection and Coding of Contours — Ph.D.

**Wang, Kang-Lung** Electron Impact Ionization Cross Sections for Carbon Vapor — Ph.D.

**Wilson, William John** OH Radio Emission Associated with Infrared Stars — Ph.D.

**Winston, Patrick Henry** Learning Structural Descriptions from Examples — Ph.D.

**Woods, John William** Redundancy Reduction by Linear Transformation — Ph.D.

**Yuen, Horace Pak Hong** Communication Theory of Quantum Systems — Ph.D.

**Zahn, Markus** Space Charge Dynamics of Liquids — Sc.D.

1971

**Adler, Michael Stuart** Nuclear Magnetic Resonance in Lead Tin Telluride Alloys — Ph.D.

**Alexander, Peter** Measurement of Dispersive Optical Communication Channels — Ph.D.

**Berninger, Walter Henry** The Preparation and Optical Properties of Aluminum-Gallium-Arsenide — Ph.D.

**Bertsekas, Dimitri Panteli** Control of Uncertain Systems with a Set-Membership Description of the Uncertainty — Ph.D.

**Blankenship, Gilmer Leroy** Stability of Uncertain Systems — Ph.D.

**Brueck, Steven Roy Julien** Spontaneous and Stimulated Spin-flip Raman Scattering in InSb — Ph.D.

**Clark, John Robert** Estimation for Poisson Processes with Applications in Optical Communication — Ph.D.

**Evans, James Everett** Chernoff Bounds on the Error Probability for the Detection of Non-Gaussian Signals — Ph.D.

**Ferreira, Joseph, Jr.** Some Analytical Aspects of Driver Licensing and Insurance Regulation — Ph.D.

**Galiana, Francisco Daniel** An Application of System Identification and State Prediction to Electric Load Modelling and Forecasting — Ph.D.

**Geering, Hans Peter** Optimal Control Theory for Non-scalar-valued Performance Criteria — Ph.D.

**Glover, John Duncan** Control of Systems with Unknown But Bounded Disturbances—Application to Electric Power Systems — Ph.D.

**Goldschmidt, Robert Elliott** File Design for Computer-Resident Library Catalogs — Ph.D.

**Granek, Harold** Cross-Relaxation in the Doppler Profiles of J-levels and Between J-levels of the $00°1$ and $10°0$ Vibrational States in $CO_2$ — Sc.D.

**Guttmann, Endre Gyorgy** Mechanization of the Interpretation of the Vaginal Smear — Ph.D.

**Hartman, Adrian Ralph** Electric Field Effects on the Low Temperature Photoluminescence Spectra of Silicon and Germanium — Ph.D.

**Hatfield, Lansing** Computer Aided Classification of Human Chromosomes — Ph.D.

**Henckels, Lutz Paul** A Parametric Method for Developing and Evaluating Handprinted Character Recognition Algorithms — Sc.D.

**Hewes, Charles Robert** Nuclear Magnetic Resonance in Lead Telluride — Ph.D.

**Houtsma, Adrianus Johannes Maria** Perception of Musical Intervals: The Role of Aural Frequency Resolution in Tracking the Missing Fundamental — Ph.D.

**Hu, Huang-Liang** Studies of Magnetostatic Waves and Magneto-elastic Waves in YIG Using Optical Probing and Microwave Techniques — Ph.D.

**Jenssen, Hans Petter** Phonon Assisted Laser Transitions and Energy Transfer in Rare Earth Laser Crystals — Ph.D.

**Jolly, David Christopher** Physical Processes in the Flashover of Insulators with Contaminated Surfaces — Ph.D.

**Kaliski, Martin Edward** Dynamic Systems: An Automata-motivated Analytic Approach — Ph.D.

**Kirtley, James Logan, Jr.** Design and Construction of an Armature for an Alternator with a Superconducting Field Winding — Ph.D.

**Levitt, Barry Kalman** Variable-rate Optical Communication Through the Turbulent Atmosphere — Ph.D.

**Luck, David Lee** Electromechanical and Thermal Effects of Faults Upon Superconducting Generators — Ph.D.

**Marston, Glendon Peter** Recognition of Characters Transmitted by Picturephone — Sc.D.

**Matison, Gary Gedalyahu** Sonar Detection of Ultrasonic Lesions During and After Production — Ph.D.

**McDowell, George Quincy** Pre-Distortion of Local Oscillator Wavefront for Improved Optical Heterodyne Detection Through a Turbulent Atmosphere — Sc.D.

**McGarty, Terrence Patrick** On the Structure of Random Fields Generated by Multiple Scatter Media — Ph.D.

**Mohajeri, Manouchehr** Seismic Discrimination in the Low Magnitude Range — Sc.D.

**Moore, Robert Lee** Adaptive Estimation and Control for Nuclear Power Plant Load Changes — Ph.D.

**Moxon, Edwin Charles** Neural and Mechanical Responses to Electric Stimulation of the Cat's Inner Ear — Ph.D.

**Murphy, Ralph Allen** Magnetoplasma Excitations in Bismuth — Ph.D.

**Neumann, Bernd** Capacity of Gaussian Feedback Channels with Memory — Ph.D.

**Peterson, Dean Freeman** Small Signal Circuit Models and Performance Limitations of Avalanche Diodes — Ph.D.

**Pindyck, Robert Stephen** Optimal Economic Stabilization Policy — Ph.D.

**Prado, Gervasio** Observability, Estimation and Control of Distributed Parameter Systems — Ph.D.

**Rome, James Alan** The Stability of Sheared Electron Flow — Sc.D.

**Rosenkranz, Philip William** Radiometric Sensing of Atmospheric Water and Temperature — Ph.D.

**Rudzki, John Edward** Remote Sensing of Mesospheric Ozone — Ph.D.

**1971** (continued)

**Schell, Roger Raymond** Dynamic Reconfiguration in a Modular Computer System — Ph.D.

**St. Onge, Hugues** High Electric Field Transport in the Lead Chalcogenides — Ph.D.

**Seitz, Charles Lewis** Graph Representations for Logical Machines — Ph.D.

**Spitzer, Stuart Marshall** The Determination of Semiconductor Band Gap Structure and Surface States Using Tunneling Spectroscopy — Ph.D.

**Stallings, William Walter** Computer Analysis of Printed Chinese Characters — Ph.D.

**Tavernier, Hubert Marie** Mathematical Analysis of Infinite Horizon Planning Models — Ph.D.

**Thomas, Robert Henry** A Model for Process Representation and Synthesis — Ph.D.

**Tocci, Leonard Richard** Ferromagnetic Resonance in Silicon Doped Yttrium-Iron Garnet — Ph.D.

**Waters, Joe William** Ground-based Microwave Spectroscopic Sensing of the Stratosphere and Mesosphere — Ph.D.

**Weinblatt, Herbert** The Scheduling Problem for a Flexibly Routed Subscription Bus Service — Ph.D.

**Welch, Terry Archer** Bounds on Information Retrieval Efficiency in State File Structures — Ph.D.

**Zelazo, Ronald Elliot** Dynamic Interactions of Monomolecular Films with Imposed Electric Fields — Ph.D.

**Zuercher, Joseph Charles** Electromechanics of Fluid Double-Layer Systems — Ph.D.

**1972**

**Bagchi, Amitava** Topics in Complexity Theory & Recursion Theory — Sc.D.

**Baughman, Martin Lynn** Dynamic Energy System Modeling—Interfuel Competition — Ph.D.

**Broderson, Robert William** Optical Properties and Band Structure for the Group V. Semimetals — Ph.D.

**Bullock, David Carl** Magnetic Semiconductor Properties and Applications of Doped Yttrium Iron Garnet and Orthoferrite — Ph.D.

**Charniak, Eugene** Toward a Model of Children's Story Comprehension — Ph.D.

**Dressler, John Lawrence** Video Techniques in the Feedback Control of an Electromechanical Continuum — Sc.D.

**Feldman, Donald Alexander** An Atmospheric Noise Model with Application to Low Frequency Navigation Systems — Sc.D.

**Folk, Joseph Frederick** Models for Investigating the Unreliability of Freight Shipments by Rail — Ph.D.

**Guldi, Richard Lawrence** Diffusion of Selenium and Lead in Lead Selenide — Ph.D.

**Hatch, Kenneth Foster** Semiconductor Gamma Camera — Ph.D.

**Hubelbank, Mark** Computer Enhancement of Ultrasound Images — Sc.D.

**Istefanopulos, Yorgo** Analytic Study of Multiple Runway Operations — Ph.D.

**Jessel, Peter Gabriel** A Theory of Computer-aided Network Analysis — Ph.D.

**Johnson, Timothy Lee** Optimal Control of First-order Distributed Systems — Ph.D.

**Kaplan, Theodore** Electrothermal Mechanisms for Threshold and Memory Switching in Amorphous and Crystalline Semiconductors — Ph.D.

**Kebabian, Paul Logan** Duplicating Filters: A Class of Digital Filters with an Invariance Property — Ph.D.

**Kfoury, Denis Jean** Effective Procedures in Arbitrary Structures — Ph.D.

**Kirkwood, Craig William** Decision Analysis Incorporating Preferences of Groups — Ph.D.

**Kokkas, Achilles George** Analysis and Design of Electrothermal Integrated Circuits — Sc.D.

**Kramer, Leslie Craig** On Stochastic Control and Optimal Measurement Strategies — Ph.D.

**Lee, Stephen Ting-Yee** Transient Stability Equivalents for Power System Planning — Ph.D.

**Lyon, David Lewis** Collisional Relaxation Mechanisms Governing Operation of High-pressure $CO_2$ Lasers — Ph.D.

**Madnick, Stuart Elliot** Storage Hierarchy Systems — Ph.D.

**Marcus, Michael Jay** New Approaches to the Analysis of Connecting and Sorting Networks — Sc.D.

**McMullin, Paul George** Phonon Transfer Effect in Uniaxially Stressed PbSe Lasers — Ph.D.

**Merrill, Hyde McCune** Bad Data Suppression in State Estimation, with Applications to Problems in Power — Ph.D.

**Millner, Alan Roy, Jr.** Nonlinear Feedback Control of Continuum Systems — Sc.D.

**Mitchell, Owen Robert** The Effect of Spatial Frequency on the Visibility of Unstructured Patterns — Ph.D.

**Mower, Herbert William** A Sensitive Calorimeter for the Dosimetry of Low Megavolt Electrons — Sc.D.

**Ross, Arthur Howarth MacNeal** Quantum Electrodynamics of Nonrelativistic Gases — Ph.D.

**Sambur, Marvin Robert** Speaker Recognition and Verification Using Linear Prediction Analysis — Ph.D.

**Sekino, Akira** Performance Evaluation of Multiprogrammed Time-shared Computer Systems — Ph.D.

**Siegel, Joseph** Design of Nonrecursive Approximations to Digital Filters with Discontinuous Frequency Responses — Sc.D.

**Smith, Burton Jordan** An Analysis of Sorting Networks — Sc.D.

**Stark, Eugene Earle, Jr.** Generation and Amplification of Short Laser Pulses — Sc.D.

**Stinger, James Richard** Effective Computing Machines Using Inexact Substructures — Ph.D.

**Stuck, Barton William** Space Satellite Dynamics with Applications to Sunlight Pressure Attitude Control — Sc.D.

**Tien, James M.** Control of a Two Customer Class Interactive-Multi-Facility Queuing System — Ph.D.

**Vandevenne, Herman Felix** Qualitative Properties of a Class of Infinite Dimensional Systems — Ph.D.

**Vilfan, Bostjan Joza** The Complexity of Finite Functions — Ph.D.

**Wallace, Roger Neil** Low-Field Microwave Emission from Indium Antimonide — Sc.D.

**Waltz, David Leigh** Generating Semantic Descriptions from Drawing of Scenes with Shadows — Ph.D.

**1972** (continued)

**Willemain, Thomas Reed** Planning Telemedicine Systems — Ph.D.

**Willems, Yves Didier** The Use of Prosodics in the Automatic Recognition of Spoken English Numbers — Ph.D.

**Womac, James Francis** On the Ohmic Nature of N-N $Al_xGa_{1-x}$ As-GaAs Heterojunctions — Ph.D.

**1973**

**Albuquerque, José Paulo de Almeida** Sensitivity to Structural Errors in Random Process Identification Performance — Ph.D.

**Ayasli, Yalcin** Magnetic Semiconductor Interactions — Sc.D.

**Berliner, Jeffrey Elton** Intensity Discrimination in Audition — Ph.D.

**Bowie, Jack Edward** Syntactic Descriptions of Biological Shape — Sc.D.

**Boxman, Raymond Leon** Interferometric Measurement of Electron and Vapor Densities in a High Current Vacuum Arc — Ph.D.

**Brody, Mitchell David** Engineering Design of a Field Emission Electron Gun — Ph.D.

**Carlo, James Thomas** Magnetoelastic Devices Utilizing a Spatially Varying Magnetization — Ph.D.

**Chong, Chee-Yee** On the Decentralized Control of Large-scale Systems — Ph.D.

**Clark, David Dana** An Input/output Architecture for Virtual Memory Computer Systems — Ph.D.

**Devitt, Edmund Booth** Conduction by Macroscopic Charge Particles in Moving Insulating Fluids — Sc.D.

**Eanes, Robert Sterling** Example Grammars: Techniques for Restricting Context-free Derivation Sets — Ph.D.

**Eckberg, Adrian Emmanuel, Jr.** Algebraic System Theory with Applications to Decentralized Control — Ph.D.

**Fiasconaro, James Gerard** Two-dimensional Nonrecursive Digital Filters — Ph.D.

**Filip, Anthony Edmund** Estimating the Impulse Response of Linear Shift-variant, Image Degrading Systems — Ph.D.

**Glover, Keith** Structural Aspects of System Identification — Ph.D.

**Gruhl, James** Minimizing Cost and Environmental Impact of Electric Power System Operation — Ph.D.

**Hammer, Michael Martin** A New Grammatical Transformation into Deterministic Top-down Form — Ph.D.

**Hartman, Donald Whitesell** Computer Analysis of Photomicrographs of Biological Tissue Sections — Ph.D.

**Hasan, Ziaul** Characterization of Some Nonlinear Properties of Mammalian Muscle Spindles — Ph.D.

**Hawryszkiewycz, Igor Titus** Semantics of Data Base Systems — Ph.D.

**Johnson, Louis Gregory** Optical Properties of Graphite — Ph.D.

**Johnston, Robert deBeauchesne** Linear Systems Over Various Rings — Ph.D.

**Just, James Edward** Impacts of New Energy Technology Using Generalized Input-output Analysis — Ph.D.

**Kassakian, John Gabriel** Effects of Non-transposition and Frequency Dependent Neutral Modeling on the Simulation of Power Transmission Systems — Sc.D.

**Lau, Yue-Ying** Temporal Evolution of a Localized Wavepacket in a Weakly Inhomogenous Plasma — Sc.D.

**Levy, Lucien Maurice** System Identification and Cardiovascular Pathophysiology — Ph.D.

**Linderman, John Parent** Productivity in Parallel Computation Schemata — Ph.D.

**Linford, Rulon Kesler** A Highly Ionized, Steady State, Beam-plasma Source — Ph.D.

**Magnuski, Henry Stanley** Visual System Analysis Through Use of Finite Field Sine Gratings — Ph.D.

**Masiello, Ralph David** Adaptive Modeling and Control of Electric Power Systems — Ph.D.

**Mersereau, Russell Manning** Digital Reconstruction of Multidimensional Signals from Their Projections — Sc.D.

**Miller, Perry Lowell** A Locally-organized Parser for Spoken Input — Ph.D.

**Orr, Richard Sennott** Channel Measurement Receivers for Optical Communication — Ph.D.

**Pippenger, Nicholas** The Complexity Theory of Switching Networks — Ph.D.

**Ramchandani, Chander B.** Analysis of Asynchronous Concurrent Systems by Timed Petri Nets — Ph.D.

**Reinhard, Donnie K.** Electronic Conduction and Switching in Amorphous Chalcogenides — Ph.D.

**Rotenberg, Leo Joseph** Making Computers Keep Secrets — Ph.D.

**Schroeder, Michael David** Cooperation of Mutually Suspicious Subsystems in a Computer Utility — Ph.D.

**Sibru, Marvin Alan, Jr.** Stations, System Performance and Scheduling in Personal Rapid Transit Networks — Sc.D.

**Smith, Arthur Anshel** A Computer Based Test for Evenness of Pulmonary Ventilation — Ph.D.

**Stephenson, Robert Storer** Branching of Regenerated Motoneuron Axons in Axolotl Limbs — Ph.D.

**Stratton, William David** Intonation Feedback for the Deaf through the Tactile Sense — Ph.D.

**Telson, Michael Lawrence** The Economics of Reliability for Electric Generation Systems — Ph.D.

**Tsang, James Chen-Hsiang** Light Scattering in the Europium Chalcogenides — Ph.D.

**Wacks, Kenneth Paul** Design of a Real-time Facsimile Transmission System — Ph.D.

**Willner, Dietner** Observation and Control of Partially Unknown Systems — Ph.D.

**Wood, Jonathan Rotherham** Power Conversion in Electrical Networks — Ph.D.

**1974**

**Boyle, Brian Edward** The Decision to Grant Credit — Ph.D.

**Chan, Vincent Wai-Sum** Characterization of Measurements in Quantum Communications — Ph.D.

**Cheng, T.C.** Mechanisms of Flashover of Contaminated Insulators — Sc.D.

**Crevier, Joseph Francois Daniel** The Simulation of Frequency Transients in Power Systems — Ph.D.

**Crochiere, Ronald Eldon** Digital Network Theory and Its Application to the Analysis and Design of Digital Filters — Ph.D.

**1974** (continued)

**Demko, Paul, Jr.** Dependence of Potassium Conductance on External Potassium Concentration in Lobster Giant Axons — Ph.D.

**Desalu, Adewunmi Aderounmu** Dynamic Air Quality Estimation in a Stochastic Dispersive Atmosphere — Ph.D.

**Dudgeon, Dan Ed** Two-Dimensional Recursive Filtering — Sc.D.

**Grodzinsky, Alan Jay** Electomechanics of Deformable Polyelectrolyte Membranes — Sc.D.

**Henshaw, Philip Dennis** Contributions to Holographic Contour Generation — Ph.D.

**Horowitz, Larry Lowell** Optimal Filtering of Gyroscopic Noise — Ph.D.

**Johnson, Don Herrick** The Response of Single Auditory-nerve Fibers in the Cat to Single Tones: Synchrony and Average Discharge Rate — Ph.D.

**Johnson, Jerry William** Program Restructuring for Virtual Memory Systems — Ph.D.

**Lester, Bruce Paul** The Balance Property of Parallel Computations — Ph.D.

**Li, Eric Kai** Electronic Energy Structure of $FeS_2$ and $NiS_2$ — Sc.D.

**Lopez-Toledo, Alejandro Antonio** Optimal Inputs for Identification of Stochastic Systems — Ph.D.

**Martin, David Newton** Stability Criteria for Systems with Colored Multiplicative Noise — Ph.D.

**Mathur, Bimal Prakash** Switching in Amorphous Chalcogenide Films — Sc.D.

**Nedzelnitsky, Victor** Measurements of Sound Pressure in the Cochleae of Anesthetized Cats — Sc.D.

**Niemeyer, Thomas L.** Permanent-magnet Stepping Motors: Effects of Eddy-currents on Performance — Ph.D.

**Perkell, Joseph Shaile** A Physiologically-oriented Model of Tongue Activity in Speech Production — Ph.D.

**Pfister, Gregory F.** The Computer Control of Changing Pictures — Ph.D.

**Poon, Ronnie Ka Lai** Atmospheric Opacity Near Half Centimeter Wavelength — Sc.D.

**Rackoff, Charles Weill** The Computational Complexity of Some Logical Theories — Ph.D.

**Raines, Jeremy Keith** Application of Integral Equations to Dielectric Waveguides of Rectangular Cross Section — Ph.D.

**Ruth, Gregory Robert** Analysis of Algorithm Implementations — Ph.D.

**Sachar, Kenneth S.** Charged Drop Scrubbing of Submicron Particles — Ph.D.

**Sandell, Nils Richard, Jr.** Control of Finite-state, Finite-memory Stochastic Systems — Ph.D.

**Seiferas, Joel Irvin** Nondeterministic Time and Space Complexity Classes — Ph.D.

**Shillman, Robert Joel** Character Recognition Based on Phenomenological Attributes: Theory and Methods — Ph.D.

**Stockmeyer, Larry Joseph** The Complexity of Decision Problems in Automata Theory and Logic — Ph.D.

**Todd, Lee Trover** Investigation of the Properties of Cathodochromic Sodalite and Cathodochromic CRT Display Devices — Ph.D.

**Tomasetta, Louis Ralph** $Pb_{1-x}Sn_xTe$ Laser Heterostuctures Grown by Liquid Phase Epitaxy — Sc.D.

**Toong, Hoo-min D.** A Study of Time-compressed Speech — Ph.D.

**Venturini, Eugene Leo** Magnetic Properties of Piezoelectric Anti-ferromagnetic $BaMnF_4$ — Sc.D.

**Ward, Stephen Ashley** Functional Domains of Applicative Languages — Ph.D.

**Warren, Michael Edward** On the Decoupling of Linear Multivariable Systems — Ph.D.

**Whitney, Alan Robert** Precision Geodesy and Astrometry via Very-Long-Baseline Interferometry — Ph.D.

**1975**

**Asbeck, Peter Michael** Optical and Minority Carrier Confinement in Lead Selenide Homojunction Lasers — Ph.D.

**Baer, Thomas** Investigation of Phonation Using Excised Larynxes — Ph.D.

**Brown, Allen Leon** Qualitative Knowledge, Causal Reasoning, and the Localization of Failures — Ph.D.

**Cafarella, John Herbert** Surface State Acoustoelectric Memory-Correlator — Sc.D.

**Cammack, David** Interband Recombination Lifetime Studies in Epitaxial Films of $Pb_{1-x}Sn_xTe$ — Sc.D.

**Castleberry, Donald Earl** Energy Transfer in Sensitized Rare Earth Lasers — Ph.D.

**Choo, Duck-soo** SCF Xa Cluster Model Calculations for Crystals and Point Defects — Ph.D.

**Coueignoux, Philippe Jean-Marie** Generation of Roman Printed Fonts — Ph.D.

**Domnitz, Robert Harris** Lateral Position and Loudness in Binaural Experiments — Ph.D.

**Flower, Richard Arthur** An Analysis of Optimal Retrieval Systems with Updates — Ph.D.

**Freuder, Eugene Charles** A Computer System for Visual Recognition Using Active Knowledge — Ph.D.

**Galdos, Jorge Ignacio** Information and Distortion in Filtering Theory — Ph.D.

**Greif, Irene** Semantics of Communicating Parallel Processes — Ph.D.

**Hauser, John R.** A Normative Methodology for Modeling Consumer Response to Design Decisions: Issues, Models, Theory and Use — Sc.D.

**Henderson, Dugald Austin** The Binding Model: A Semantic Base for Modular Programming Systems — Ph.D.

**Himes, John Glenn** The Performance of an Active Optical Imaging Radar in the Turbulent Atmosphere — Ph.D.

**Hoburg, James Frederick** Electrohydrodynamic Mixing — Ph.D.

**Holcomb, Terry L.** Performance Characteristics of a High Pressure Pulsed CO Laser — Sc.D.

**Houpt, Paul K.** Decentralized Stochastic Control of Finite-state Systems with Application to Vehicular Traffic Control — Ph.D.

**Jao, Jen-King** Studies of Coupled Spin/elastic Waves in Antiferromagnetic $RbMnF_3$ Using Microwave and Light Scattering Techniques — Ph.D.

**Jarvis, James Patrick** Optimization in Stochastic Service Systems with Distinguishable Servers — Ph.D.

**Jernigan, Marvin Edward** Eye Movement Analysis in Plotting the Visual Field — Ph.D.

**Kautz, Richard Lloyd** The Surface of a Spin-polarized Electron Gas — Ph.D.

## 1975 (continued)

**Kwong, Raymond Hon-Sing** Structural Properties and Estimation of Delay Systems — Ph.D.

**Leonberger, Frederick John** Lead Sulfide MIS Devices for Charge-coupled Imaging Applications — Ph.D.

**Liu, Jack Sun Heng** Distributed Parameter Systems with Local Memory: A Case Study of Linear Viscoelastic Media — Ph.D.

**Lowney, Jeremiah Ralph** Band-inversion Studies in $Pb_{1-x}Sn_xTe$ — Ph.D.

**Manning, Frank Blase** Automatic Test, Configuration, and Repair of Cellular Arrays — Ph.D.

**Marcus, Steven I.** Estimation and Analysis of Nonlinear Stochastic Systems — Ph.D.

**Maslak, Samuel Harry** An Electronically Steered Ultrasonic Transducer — Sc.D.

**Meldman, Jeffrey Alan** A Preliminary Study in Computer-aided Legal Analysis — Ph.D.

**Millman, Jeffrey Thomas** Error Minimization of Data-converting Systems via Generalized Spectral Analysis — Ph.D.

**Moulton, Peter Franklin** Photoluminescence of Bound Excitons in Tellurium-doped Cadmium Sulfide — Ph.D.

**Moura, Jose** Narrowband Passive Systems Theory with Applications to Positioning and Navigation — Sc.D.

**Parl, Steen Allan** Filtering for Distributed Parameter Systems Using Semigroup Theory — Ph.D.

**Petersen, Kurt Edward** Amorphous/crystalline Heterojunctions, Devices, and Switching Phenomena — Ph.D.

**Peterson, David Walter** Hypothesis, Estimation, and Validation of Dynamic Social Models: Energy Demand Modeling — Ph.D.

**Platts, David Andrew** Far Infrared Studies of Graphite — Ph.D.

**Pusey, Leroy Charles** An Innovations Approach to Spectral Estimation and Wave Propagation — Sc.D.

**Qualitz, Joseph Edward** Equivalence Problems for Monadic Schemas — Ph.D.

**Robinson, Stanley Russell** Spatial Phase Compensation Receivers for Optical Communication — Ph.D.

**Rumbaugh, James Edward** A Parallel Asynchronous Computer Architecture for Data Flow Programs — Ph.D.

**Simonutti, Mario Daniel** Linear Conversion, Absorption, and Finite Source Effects for Lower Hybrid Plasma Waves — Ph.D.

**Solomon, Robert David** Color Coding for a Facsimile System — Ph.D.

**Szajner, Jaime** Local Modal Control of Synchronous Generators — Sc.D.

**Tong, David Woo-Sang** Capillary Absorption as an Audible Noise Reduction Scheme for UHV Transmission Lines — Ph.D.

**Vecchi, Mario Pietro** Electronic Properties of the Group V Semimetals — Ph.D.

**Walker, Laurence Gordon** Tunnel Injection Electroluminescence and Long Term Charge Storage in ZnS MIS Structures — Ph.D.

**Watson, Duncan Charles** Third-order Theory of Pump-driven Plasma Instabilities: Laser-Pellet Interactions — Sc.D.

**Wittels, Norman David** Thin Foils as Correctors of Spherical Aberration in Electron Lenses — Ph.D.

**Woodard, James Body** Electric Load Modeling — Ph.D.

## 1976

**Ausschnitt, Christopher** Transient Evolution of Passive Modelocking— Theory and Experiment — Ph.D.

**Austin, Howard Allen** A Computational Theory of Physical Skill — Ph.D.

**Bosack, Donald James** Acoustic Noise from Corona on Electric Power Transmission Lines — Ph.D.

**Bourk, Terrance Raymond** Electrical Responses of Neural Units in the Anteroventral Cochlear Nucleus of the Cat — Ph.D.

**Brown, William Sumner** A 1/25 Scale Magneplane — Ph.D.

**Cutler, Scott Ellis** Microcomputer Networks in Control Applications — Ph.D.

**Dear, Roger George** The Dynamic Scheduling of Aircraft in the Near Terminal Area — Ph.D.

**Dietz, Peter William** Electrofluidized Bed Mechanics — Sc.D.

**Dolinar, Samuel Joseph** A Class of Optical Receivers Using Optical Feedback — Ph.D.

**Fontana, Robert Edward** Potassium Tantalate Niobate Thin Films for Integrated Optics Applications — Ph.D.

**Furtek, Frederick Curtis** The Logic of Systems — Ph.D.

**Hack, Michel H.T.** Decidability Questions for Petri Nets — Ph.D.

**Hirshman, Steven P.** Transport Theory of a Toroidally Confined Multispecies Plasma — Sc.D.

**Hnyilicza, Esteban** Optimal Economic Growth and Energy Policy — Ph.D.

**Janson, Philippe A.** Using Type Extension to Organize Virtual Memory Mechanisms — Ph.D.

**Maeda, Shinji** A Characterization of American English Intonation — Ph.D.

**Makowski, Lee Chester** An X-ray Diffraction Study of Membrane Gap Junctions — Ph.D.

**Mark, William Scott** The Reformulation Model of Expertise — Ph.D.

**McDermott, Drew V.** Flexibility and Efficiency in a Computer Program for Designing Circuits — Ph.D.

**Metzger, Louis Saul** Nonlinear Estimation of Target Bearing and Signal — Ph.D.

**Miller, John Lawrence** Collisional Processes in the Multi-atmosphere $CO_2$ Laser — Ph.D.

**Morgenstern, Matthew Lawrence** Automated Design and Optimization of Management Information System Software — Ph.D.

**Njoku, Eni Gerald** Microwave Remote Sensing of Near-surface Moisture and Temperature Profiles — Ph.D.

**O'Shaughnessy, Douglas David** Modelling Fundamental Frequency, and Its Relationship to Syntax, Semantics, and Phonetics — Ph.D.

**Paul, Douglas Baker** Estimation of the Vocal Tract Shape from the Acoustic Waveform — Ph.D.

**Rhyne, Theodore L.** Sonar Characterization of Tissue as Applied to the Lung — Sc.D.

**Throop, Alan Larry** The Influence of Four-wave Parametric Interactions on the Nonlinear Evolution of the Beam-plasma Instability — Ph.D.

**Tsang, Leung** Theoretical Models for Subsurface Geophysical Probing with Electromagnetic Waves — Ph.D.

**Umans, Stephen D.** Modeling of Solid Rotor Turbogenerators — Sc.D.

**Veldkamp, Wilfrid Bernard** Quasi-Elastic Light Scattering from Macromolecules and Dense Binary Gases — Ph.D.

1976 (continued)

**Zahedi, Karim** Electrofluidized Bed Filtration: Fundamentals and Applications — Ph.D.

**Zue, Victor W.** Acoustic Characteristics of Stop Consonants: A Controlled Study — Sc.D.

1977

**Akant, Adnan** Segmented Approximation and Analysis of Stochastic Processes — Ph.D.

**Baram, Yoram** Information, Consistent Estimation and Dynamic System Identification — Ph.D.

**Bishop, Peter Boehler** Computer Systems with a Very Large Address Space and Garbage Collection — Ph.D.

**Bloniarz, Peter Anthony** The Complexity of Monotone Boolean Functions and an Algorithm for Finding Shortest Paths in a Graph — Ph.D.

**Capetanakis, John Ippocratis** The Multiple Access Broadcast Channel: Protocol and Capacity Considerations — Ph.D.

**Defenderfer, Joe E.** Comparative Analysis of Routing Algorithms for Computer Networks — Ph.D.

**Ellis, James Riley** An Investigation of Approximate Bit-plane Encoding of Pictorial Information — Sc.D.

**Fahlman, Scott Elliott** A System for Representing and Using Real-world Knowledge — Ph.D.

**Graham, Alan Karl** Principles on the Relationship Between Structure and Behavior of Dynamic Systems — Ph.D.

**Hui, Cha-Mei T.** Numerical Simulation of Fluid Flow in Spherical Geometry and Two-Dimensional Magnetohydrodynamic Turbulence — Ph.D.

**Jackson, Charles L.** Technology for Spectrum Markets — Ph.D.

**Kam, Pooi Y.** Modeling and Estimation of Space-Time Stochastic Processes — Ph.D.

**Kan, Hsin-kuo** A Computerized Template-Driven News-Layout System for Newspapers — Sc.D.

**Karney, Charles Fielding Finch** Stochastic Heating of Ions in a Tokamak by RF Power — Ph.D.

**Kovacs, Zsolt Laszlo** Estimation of the Distribution of Conduction Velocities in Intact Peripheral Nerves — Ph.D.

**Lavin, Mark Alan** Computer Analysis of Scenes from a Moving View Point — Ph.D.

**Lee, Donald L.** An Integral Equation Formulation for Wave Propagation in Spatially-periodic Media — Ph.D.

**Long, William James** A Program Writer — Ph.D.

**McHale, Edward Joseph** A-C Magneto Hydrodynamic Instability — Ph.D.

**Montress, Gary K.** Fabrication and Large-Signal Characterization of BARITT Diodes — Ph.D.

**Okrent, Howard Franklin** Synthesis of Data Structures from their Algebraic Description — Ph.D.

**Platzman, Loren Kerry** Finite Memory Estimation and Control of Finite Probabilistic Systems — Ph.D.

**Rabinowitz, William Mark** Acoustic-reflex Effects on the Input Admittance and Transfer Characteristics of the Human Middle-ear — Ph.D.

**Safonov, Michael George** Robustness and Stability Aspects of Stochastic Multivariable Feedback System Design — Ph.D.

**Sira Ramirez, Hebertt José** Set-Theoretic Control of Large Scale Uncertain Systems — Ph.D.

**Spreen, James Harold** Magnetic Domain Wall Motion Studied Using Optical Diffraction — Ph.D.

**Stern, Richard Martin** Lateralization, Discrimination, and Detection of Binaural Pure Tones — Ph.D.

**Theriault, Kenneth Burton** Accuracy Bounds for Normal-incidence Acoustic Structure Estimation — Ph.D.

**Tribolet, Jose M.** Seismic Applications of Homomorphic Signal Processing — Sc.D.

**Ullman, Shimon** The Interpretation of Visual Motion — Ph.D.

**Woodham, Robert James** Reflectance Map Techniques for Analyzing Surface Defects in Metal Castings — Ph.D.

**Zack, Gregory William** A Computer-based Image Analysis and Pattern Recognition System for Automatically Estimating the Frequency of Sister Chromatic Exchanges in Human Chromosomes — Ph.D.

1978

**Alexander, Jeffrey Carl** Electrofluidized Beds in the Control of Fly Ash — Ph.D.

**Baker, Henry Givens** Actor Systems for Real-time Computation — Ph.D.

**Barta, Steven Michael** On Linear Control of Decentralized Stochastic Systems — Ph.D.

**Birdwell, John Douglas** On Reliable Control System Designs — Ph.D.

**Brown, Donna Jean** Storage and Access Costs for Implementations of Variable-Length Lists — Ph.D.

**Chan, David So Keung** Theory and Implementation of Multidimensional Discrete Systems for Signal Processing — Ph.D.

**DeTreville, John Daniel** An Analytical Approach to Computerized News Layout for Newspapers — Ph.D.

**Ellis, David J.** Formal Specifications for Packet Communication Systems — Ph.D.

**Englander, Irvin Sanford** PIXIE: An Interactive Experimenter for Pictorial Pattern Recognition — Ph.D.

**Fisch, Nathaniel Joseph** Confining and Heating a Toroidal Plasma with RF Power — Ph.D.

**Flanders, Dale Clifton** Orientation of Crystalline Overlayers on Amorphous Substrates by Artificially Produced Surface Relief Structures — Ph.D.

**Greene, Christopher Storm** An Analysis of the Multiple Model Adaptive Control Algorithm — Ph.D.

**Harel, David A.** Logics of Programs: Axiomatics and Descriptive Power — Ph.D.

**Hollerbach, John Matthew** A Study of Human Motor Control through Analysis and Synthesis of Handwriting — Ph.D.

**Horenstein, Mark Nathan** Particle Contamination of High Voltage DC Insulators — Ph.D.

**Humblet, Pierre Amédée** Source Coding for Communication Concentrators — Ph.D.

**Jahns, Thomas Merlin** Improved Reliability in Solid-state Drives for Large Asynchronous AC Machines by Means of Multiple Independent Phase-drive Units — Ph.D.

**Kim, Michael Ern** Electrons, Phonons and Many-body Interaction Effects in Narrow-gap Lead Tin Telluride — Ph.D.

1978 (continued)

**Klinkowstein, Robert Edward** Electron Beam Suppression of Loss-cone Instabilities in a Mirror Confined Plasma — Ph.D.

**Kohn, Wolf** Distributed Hierarchical Automata with Applications to Genetics in Procaryotes — Ph.D.

**Kulp, John Laurence** Toroidal Effects in Lower Hybrid Heating of a Tokamak Plasma — Ph.D.

**Laventhal, Mark Steven** Synthesis of Synchronization Code for Data Abstractions — Ph.D.

**Ledsham, William Henry** Optimum Retrieval Techniques in Remote Sensing of Atmospheric Temperature, Liquid Water, and Water Vapor — Ph.D.

**Lim, Jae S.** Enhancement and Bandwidth Compression of Noisy Speech by Estimation of Speech and Its Model Parameters — Ph.D.

**Lippmann, Richard Paul** The Effect of Amplitude Compression on the Intelligibility of Speech for Persons with Sensorineural Hearing Loss — Ph.D.

**Looze, Douglas P.** Hierarchical Control and Decomposition of Decentralized Linear Stochastic Systems — Ph.D.

**Lynn, Charles W., Jr.** Investigation of Tone Scale Modifications to Improve Digital Pictures — Ph.D.

**Manichaikul, Yongyut** Industrial Electric Load Modeling — Ph.D.

**Marcus, Mitchell Philip** A Theory of Syntactic Recognition for Natural Language — Ph.D.

**Marzetta, Thomas Louis** A Linear Prediction Approach to Two-dimensional Spectral Factorization and Spectral Estimation — Ph.D.

**McLeod, Dennis James** A Semantic Data Base Model and Its Associated Structured User Interface — Ph.D.

**Monauni, Luigi Angelo** Linear Dynamical Systems with Abstract State-spaces — Ph.D.

**Paik, Woo Hyun** Optical Frequency Hopping for High Data Rate Optical Communication through Scattering Channels — Ph.D.

**Portnoff, Michael Rodney** Time-Scale Modification of Speech Based on Short-Time Fourier Analysis — Ph.D.

**Schmutz, Lawrence Edward** Optical Studies of Europium Telluride — Ph.D.

**Shrobe, Howard E.** Logic and Reasoning for Complex Program Understanding — Ph.D.

**Silberstein, Robert Phillip** Raman Scattering and Magnetic Symmetry in EuS and EuSe — Ph.D.

**Tekula, Miloslav Sylvester** Theory of Runaway Electrons in Plasmas — Ph.D.

**Tung, Leslie** A Bi-domain Model for Describing Ischemic Myocardial D-C Potentials — Ph.D.

**Wall, Joseph Edward, Jr.** Control and Estimation for Large-scale Systems Having Spatial Symmetry — Ph.D.

**Wang, Karl Lin** Surface Acoustic Wave Propagation in Grating Structures — Ph.D.

**Waters, Richard C.** A Method for Automatically Analyzing the Logical Structure of Programs — Ph.D.

**Wiegner, Allen Walter** A Laser Scanning System for Isolated Cardiac Muscle: Segment Clamping and Analysis of Muscle Stiffness — Ph.D.

**Withers, Richard S.** Transport of Charged Aerosols — Sc.D.

**Wong, Richard T.** Accelerating Benders Decomposition for Network Design — Ph.D.

**Wunderlich, Eberhard Frank** Buffering and Flow Control in Message Switched Communication Networks — Ph.D.

**Yonezawa, Akinori** Specification and Verification Techniques for Parallel Programs Based on Message Passing Semantics — Ph.D.

1979

**Baden-Kristensen, Keld** Electric Responses to Sound of Cochlear Receptor and Supporting Cells — Sc.D.

**Bayer, Paul Joseph** Average-time Analysis of String-searching Algorithms — Ph.D.

**Berzins, Valdis** Abstract Model Specifications for Data Abstractions — Ph.D.

**Borkin, Sheldon Asher** Equivalence Properties of Semantic Data Models for Database Systems — Ph.D.

**Cox, Charles H.** An Experimental Investigation of the Perceptual Scales of Lightness and Brightness — Sc.D.

**Curlander, Paul Joseph** Quantum Limitations on Communication Systems — Ph.D.

**Davey, Kent Ritter** Flow of Magnetizable Particles in Turbulent Air Streams — Ph.D.

**De Kleer, Johan** Causal and Teleological Reasoning in Circuit Recognition — Ph.D.

**Djaferis, Theodore Euclid** General Pole Assignment by Output Feedback and Solution of Linear Matrix Equations from an Algebraic Viewpoint — Ph.D.

**Dowdle, John Roger** Robust Observer Based Compensators — Ph.D.

**Glasser, Lance Ahern** Modelocking of GaInAsP Diode Lasers — Ph.D.

**Goldwasser, Samuel Marc** A Generalized Segment Display Processor Architecture — Ph.D.

**Halstead, Robert Hunter** Reference Tree Networks: Virtual Machine and Implementation — Ph.D.

**Hsieh, Hung-Hui** Distributed Feedback $Pb_{1-x} Sn_x Te$ Double Heterojunction Laser Diodes Grown by Liquid Phase Epitaxy — Ph.D.

**Isaman, David Lee** Data Structuring Operations in Concurrent Computations — Ph.D.

**Jaffe, Jeffrey Martin** Parallel Computation: Synchronization, Scheduling, and Schemes — Ph.D.

**James, David V.** Real Time Music Synthesis Using High Speed Signal Processing — Ph.D.

**Kahn, Kenneth M.** Creation of Computer Animation from Story Descriptions — Ph.D.

**Kawate, Keith Warren** Electrical Surface Studies on Hexagonal Ice and Their Interpretation — Sc.D.

**Kenyon, Peter Thomas** An Experimental and Theoretical Study of Broadband Rf Fluctuations in a Moderate Gas-pressure, Magnetically Confined Plasma — Ph.D.

**Keshner, Marvin S.** Renewal Process and Diffusion Models of 1/f Noise — Sc.D.

**Kosinski, Paul Roman** Denotational Semantics of Determinate and Non-determinate Data Flow Programs — Ph.D.

**1979** (continued)

**Krasner, Michael Allen** Digital Encoding of Speech and Audio Signals Based on the Perceptual Requirements of the Auditory System — Ph.D.

**Ku, Richard Tse-Min** Adaptive Control of Stochastic Linear Systems with Random Parameters — Ph.D.

**Kuklinski, Theodore Thomas** Graphical Context as an Aid to Character Recognition — Ph.D.

**Lam, Hon Wai** Optical Waveguide Spectroscopy — Ph.D.

**Lawler, Robert Walter** One Child's Learning: A Cybernetic Theory of Learning Based on the Micro-genetic Analysis of an Ecological Study — Ph.D.

**Lyszczarz, Theodore Michael** The Orthogonalized Trimming of Filter Networks — Ph.D.

**Maby, Edward Wilfrid** MeV Ion Implanted Boron Layers in Silicon — Ph.D.

**Mallick, John A.** An Investigation of the Three Dimensional Magnetic and Eddy Current Fields in Superconducting Alternators — Sc.D.

**Miller, Mark Leslie** Planning and Debugging in Elementary Programming — Ph.D.

**Miranker, Glen Seth** The Use of Conflict in the Translation and Optimization of Hardware Description Languages — Ph.D.

**Montgomery, Warren Alan** Robust Synchronization in a Distributed Information System — Ph.D.

**Moore, Robert Carter** Reasoning about Knowledge and Action — Ph.D.

**Moroney, Paul** Issues in the Digital Implementation of Control Compensators — Ph.D.

**Norris, Peter Edward** Heteroepitaxy of Monocrystalline Stannic Oxide for Active Device Applications — Ph.D.

**Ozarow, Lawrence Howard** Coding and Capacity for Additive White Gaussian Noise Multi-user Channels with Feedback — Ph.D.

**Reed, David P.** Naming and Synchronization in a Decentralized Computer System — Ph.D.

**Rhodes, B.R.** Parity Simulation: A New Approach to the Simulation of Power Electronic Energy Conversion Systems — Ph.D.

**Ros Peran, Francisco A.** Routing to Minimize the Maximum Congestion in a Communication Network — Ph.D.

**Sidner, Candace Lee** Towards a Computational Theory of Definite Anaphora Comprehension in English Discourse — Ph.D.

**Snyder, Lawrence Alan** A Machine Architecture to Support an Object-oriented Language — Ph.D.

**Somuah, Clement B.** Emergency State Control of Slow Speed Dynamics — Sc.D.

**Stevens, Kent Allen** Surface Perception from Local Analysis of Texture and Contour — Ph.D.

**Tebyani, Mahmoud** Spatio-temporal Optical Signal Processing — Ph.D.

**Tenney, Robert R.** Distributed Decision Making Using a Distributed Model — Ph.D.

**Wang, Binseng** The Relation Between the Compound Action Potential and Unit Discharges of the Auditory Nerve — Sc.D.

**Weng, Ken Kung-Song** An Abstract Implementation for a Generalized Data Flow Language — Ph.D.

**Yared, Khaled Ibrahim** On Maximum Likelihood Identification of State Space Models — Ph.D.

**Zippel, Richard Eliot** Probabilistic Algorithms for Sparse Polynomials — Ph.D.

**1980**

**Atkinson, Russell Roger** Automatic Verification of Serializers — Ph.D.

**Bishop, Robert P.** Modeling the Charge Transfer Process in Charge Coupled Devices — Sc.D.

**Bosshart, Patrick William** Architectures for Analog LSI Implementations of Speech Processing Systems — Ph.D.

**Brown, Richard Henry** Coherent Behavior from Incoherent Knowledge Sources in the Automatic Synthesis of Numerical Computer Programs — Ph.D.

**Chan, Arvola Yau-Shing** A Methodology for Automating the Physical Design of Integrated Databases — Ph.D.

**Chew, Weng Cho** Mixed Boundary Value Problems in Microstrip and Geophysical Probing Applications — Ph.D.

**Dersin, Pierre** On Steady-state Load Feasibility in an Electrical Power Network — Ph.D.

**Doyle, Jon** A Model for Deliberation, Action, and Introspection — Ph.D.

**Frye, Robert Charles** Transient Effects in Chalcogenide Glasses and Related Materials — Ph.D.

**Goldstein, Ursula Gisela** An Articulatory Model for the Vocal Tracts of Growing Children — Sc.D.

**Golestaani, Seyyed J.** A Unified Theory of Flow Control and Routing in Data Communication Networks — Ph.D.

**Golub, Howard Lawrence** A Physioacoustic Model of the Infant Cry and Its Use for Medical Diagnosis and Prognosis — Ph.D.

**Harris, David Branson** Design and Implementation of 2-D Rational Digital Filters — Ph.D.

**Heflinger, Bruce L.** A Raman Study of Bromine Adsorption on Graphite — Ph.D.

**Kapur, Deepak** Towards a Theory for Abstract Data Types — Ph.D.

**Kopec, Gary Edward** The Representation of Discrete-time Signals and Systems in Programs — Ph.D.

**Lang, Jeffrey Hastings** Computer Control of Stochastic Distributed Systems with Applications to Very Large Electrostatically Figured Satellite Antennas — Ph.D.

**LaPaugh, Andrea Suzanne** Algorithms for Integrated Circuit Layout: An Analytic Approach — Ph.D.

**Lauer, Gregory S.** Stochastic Optimization for Discrete-time Systems — Ph.D.

**Lee, Raphael C.** Cartilage Electromechanics: The Relationship of Physicochemical to Mechanical Properties — Sc.D.

**LeFever, Ronald Stanton** Statistical Analysis of Concurrently Active Human Motor Units — Ph.D.

**Leung, Clement Kin Cho** Fault Tolerance in Packet Communication Computer Architectures — Ph.D.

**Leung, Stephen Y.** Modeling of Graphite Intercalation Compounds — Ph.D.

**Lloyd, Errol Lynn** Scheduling Task Systems with Resources — Ph.D.

1980 (continued)

**Loui, Michael Conrad** Simulations Among Multidimensional Turing Machines — Ph.D.

**Lozano-Pérez, Tomás** Spatial Planning with Polyhedral Models — Ph.D.

**Luniewski, Allen William** The Architecture of an Object Based Personal Computer — Ph.D.

**McDonald, David Daniel** Natural Language Production as a Process of Decision-making Under Constraints — Ph.D.

**Mehta, Rajendra Singh** Studies of Magnetic and Electronic State Dependence of CO Reaction with Nickel Surfaces — Ph.D.

**Quatieri, Thomas F., Jr.** Phase Estimation with Application to Speech Analysis-Synthesis — Sc.D.

**Quint, David W.** Optical Modulation by Induced Absorption in Tellurium — Ph.D.

**Ratzel, John Newland** The Discrete Representation of Spatially Continuous Images — Ph.D.

**Reuveni, Asher** The Event Based Language and Its Multiple Processor Implementations — Ph.D.

**Rich, Charles** Inspection Methods in Programming — Ph.D.

**Ross, Warren Steven** Point Source Optical Propagation in a Multiple Scattering Medium — Ph.D.

**Ruane, Michael F.** Physically Based Load Modeling — Ph.D.

**Short, William R.** Active Noise Attenuation — Sc.D.

**Steele, Guy Lewis** The Definition and Implementation of a Computer Programming Language Based on Constraints — Ph.D.

**Teneketzis, Demosthenis** Communication in Decentralized Control — Ph.D.

**Toldalagi, Paul Michel** Adaptive Filtering Methods Applied to Satellite Remote-sensing of the Atmosphere for Meteorological Purposes — Ph.D.

**Trautman, Edwin DeForest** Multiple-indicator-dilution Measurements of Pulmonary Edema Using Simultaneous Electrical-conductivity and Thermal Sensing in Blood — Ph.D.

**Wicke, Roger William** Human Visual-vestibular Interactions During Postural Responses to Brief Falls — Ph.D.

1981

**Baratz, Alan E.** Algorithms for Integrated Circuit Signal Routing — Ph.D.

**Bello, Martin Glen** Centralized and Decentralized Map-Updating and Terrain Masking Analysis — Ph.D.

**Blaszczynski, George Michael** Principles of Model Determination — Ph.D.

**Bruss, Anna R.** The Image Irradiance Equation: Its Solution and Application — Ph.D.

**Bryant, Randal** A Switch-level Simulation Model for Integrated Logic Circuits — Ph.D.

**Buckley, Robert Roy** Digital Color Image Coding and the Geometry of Color Space — Ph.D.

**Bunza, Geoffrey Joseph** Color Image Coding for Real-Time Transmission — Ph.D.

**Bush, Marcia Ann** Vowel Articulation and Laryngeal Control in the Speech of the Deaf — Ph.D.

**Carney, James K.** Non-Uniform Current Injection in GaAs/GaAlAs Diode Lasers — Ph.D.

**Chan, Sherman Man** Small Signal Control of Multiterminal DC/AC Power Systems — Ph.D.

**Chow, Edward Y.** Failure Detection System Design Methodology — Sc.D.

**Conrad, Chester Harrison** Electrophysiology of Repolarization in Hypoxic Rat Myocardium — Ph.D.

**Davis, James Lawrence** Inertial Rotation Sensing Using a Fiber Sagnac Interferometer — Ph.D.

**Davis, Mark F.** Computer Simulation of Static Localization Cues — Ph.D.

**Delgutte, Bertrand** Representation of Speech-like Sounds in the Discharge Patterns of Auditory-nerve Fibers — Ph.D.

**Fisher, Arthur Douglas** Techniques and Devices for High-Resolution Adaptive Optics — Ph.D.

**Gaudreau, Marcel Pierre Joseph** ICRF Wave Propagation and Damping at High Density in the Alcator Tokamak — Sc.D.

**Hagelstein, Peter Laurence** Physics of Short Wavelength Laser Design — Ph.D.

**Hayes, Monson Henry** Signal Reconstruction from Phase or Magnitude — Sc.D.

**Holford, Stephen K.** Discontinuous Adventitious Lung Sounds: Measurement, Classification, and Modeling — Sc.D.

**Holton, Thomas** Mechanoelectric Transduction by Cochlear Receptor Cells — Ph.D.

**Ibe, Oliver C.** Flow Control and Routing in an Integrated Voice and Data Communication Network — Sc.D.

**Johnson, Leonard Michael** Integrated Optical Devices for Temperature Sensing — Ph.D.

**Kasemset, Dumrong** Single Transverse and Longitudinal Mode Operation of Lead Tin Telluride Heterostructure Lasers — Ph.D.

**Kent, Stephen T.** Protecting Externally Supplied Software in Small Computers — Ph.D.

**Lang, Stephen William** Spectral Estimation for Sensor Arrays — Ph.D.

**Lehtomaki, Norman August** Practical Robustness Measures in Multivariable Control System Analysis — Ph.D.

**Levinstone, Donald Steven** Cell Motion Analysis: Application of an Interactive Computer System to the Study of Sister-fibroblast Differences in Lineages — Ph.D.

**Li, Victor On-Kwok** Performance Models of Distributed Database Systems — Sc.D.

**Lynch, Thomas Joseph, III** Signal Processing by the Cat Middle Ear: Admittance and Transmission, Measurements and Models — Ph.D.

**Moss, John Eliot Blakeslee** Nested Transactions: An Approach to Reliable Distributed Computing — Ph.D.

**Odette, Louis Lawrence** Dynamics of the Photoresponse in Invertebrates: Electrical Cable Model of Transduction and Adaptation — Ph.D.

**O'Leary, Art** Distributed Routing — Ph.D.

**Parker, Kevin J.** The Generation and Analysis of Hyperthermia by Ultrasound — Ph.D.

**Pérez Arriaga, José Ignacio** Selective Modal Analysis with Applications to Electric Power Systems — Ph.D.

**Picheny, Michael Alan** Speaking Clearly for the Hard of Hearing — Sc.D.

**Radun, Arthur Vorwerk** Particle Charging in a Turbulent Air Stream — Ph.D.

**1981** (continued)

**Schluter, Paul Scott** The Design and Evaluation of a Bedside Cardiac Arrhythmia Monitor — Ph.D.

**Shaver, David Carl** Electron Beam Techniques for Testing and Restructuring of Wafer-scale Integrated Circuits — Ph.D.

**Stancil, Daniel D.** Effects of Nonuniform Fields on Magnetostatic Waves in Ferrite Thin Films — Ph.D.

**Streett, Robert Stuart** Propositional Dynamic Logic of Looping and Converse — Ph.D.

**Swartout, William R.** Producing Improved Explanations and Justifications of Expert Consulting Programs Using an Automatic Programming Approach — Ph.D.

**Theilhaber, Kim Stefan** Nonlinear Coupling to Lower Hybrid Waves in a Tokamak Plasma — Ph.D.

**Tom, Victor** Constrained Iterative Signal Reconstruction Algorithms — Sc.D.

**Tsang, Dean Z.** Intracavity Loss Modulation of GaInAsP Diode Lasers — Sc.D.

**White, Barbara Yolan** Designing Computer Games to Facilitate Learning — Ph.D.

**Wright, Peter Vickers** A Coupling-of-Modes Analysis of SAW Grating Structures — Ph.D.

**1982**

**Aeppli, Gabriel Alfred** Neutron Scattering from Random Ferromagnets — Ph.D.

**Barber, Gerald Ramón** Office Semantics — Ph.D.

**Basore, Paul Alan** Self-stabilizing Magnetic Bearings for Flywheels — Ph.D.

**Berwick, Robert Cregar** Locality Principles and the Acquisition of Syntactic Knowledge — Ph.D.

**Chao, Yaoming** An Investigation into the Coding of Halftone Pictures — Sc.D.

**Chizeck, Howard Jay** Fault-Tolerant Optimal Control — Sc.D.

**Clements, Mark A.** A Comparative Evaluation of Different Processing Techniques for the Communication of Speech Through the Tactile Sense — Sc.D.

**Coderch, Marcel** Multiple Time Scale Approach to Heirarchical Aggregation of Linear Systems and Finite State Markov Processes — Ph.D.

**DeGennaro, Steve V.** An Analytic Study of Syllabic Compression for Severely Impaired Listeners — Sc.D.

**Delatizky, Jonathan** Final Position Control in Simulated Planar Horizontal Arm Movements — Ph.D.

**Feigenblatt, Ronald Ira** Bandgap-Resonant High Field Magnetospectroscopy of II-VI Semiconductor Donors — Ph.D.

**Friedman, Daniel Uri** Queuing Analysis of a Shared Voice/Data Link — Ph.D.

**Gafni, Eliezer M.** The Integration of Routing and Flow Control for Voice and Data in a Computer Communication Network — Ph.D.

**Hansell, Gregory Lyn** GaAs Schottky-Barrier Charge-coupled Devices — Ph.D.

**Hawryluk, Andrew M.** Transmission Diffraction Gratings for Soft X-Ray Spectroscopy and Spatial Period Division — Ph.D.

**Hluchyj, Michael Gene** Multiple Access Communication: The Finite User Population Problem — Ph.D.

**Kambe, Nobuyuki** Electron Diffraction from In-plane Multiphases in Alkali Metal-graphite Intercalation Compounds — Ph.D.

**Kanellakis, Paris Christos** The Complexity of Concurrency Control for Distributed Databases — Ph.D.

**Khan, Malik Masaud Anwer** A Type Composition System for Printing of Non-Roman Scripts — Sc.D.

**Kimemia, Joseph Githu** Hierarchical Control of Production in Flexible Manufacturing Systems — Ph.D.

**Kornfeld, William Arthur** Concepts in Parallel Problem Solving — Ph.D.

**Kunin, Jay Stuart** Analysis and Specification of Office Procedures — Ph.D.

**Kurkjian, Andrew Loris** The Estimation of the Cylindrical Wave Reflection Coefficient — Ph.D.

**Malik, Naveed Ahktar** One and Two Dimensional Maximum Entropy Spectrum Estimation — Sc.D.

**Mason, Matthew Thomas** Manipulator Grasping and Pushing Operations — Ph.D.

**Musicus, Bruce Ronald** Iterative Algorithms for Optimal Signal Reconstruction and Parameter Estimation Given Noisy and Incomplete Data — Ph.D.

**Nakai, Jun** Coding and Modulation Analysis for Optical Communication Channels — Ph.D.

**Nawab, Syed Hamid** Signal Estimation from Short-Time Spectral Magnitude — Ph.D.

**Papurt, David Michael** Atmospheric Propagation Effects on Heterodyne-Reception Optical Radars — Ph.D.

**Patil, Ramesh S.** Causal Representation of Patient Illness for Electrolyte and Acid-Base Diagnosis — Ph.D.

**Pearson, Ronald Korin** Optimal Velocity Feedback Control of Flexible Structures — Ph.D.

**Picard, Leonard Lucien** Interactive Picture Segmentation — Ph.D.

**Pinter, Ron Yair** The Impact of Layer Assignment Methods on Layout Algorithms for Integrated Circuits — Ph.D.

**Rohrs, Charles Edward** Adaptive Control in the Presence of Unmodeled Dynamics — Ph.D.

**Rossi, David John** Reconstruction from Projections Based on Detection and Estimation of Objects — Ph.D.

**Roxlo, Charles B.** Optically Pumped Semiconductor Lasers — Ph.D.

**Schaffert, Justin Craig** Specification and Verification of Programs Using Data Abstraction and Sharing — Ph.D.

**Schlecht, Martin Frederick** Harmonic-Free Utility/DC Power Conditioning Interfaces — Sc.D.

**Smith, Brian Cantwell** Procedural Reflection in Programming Languages — Ph.D.

**Srivas, Mandayam Kannappan** Automatic Synthesis of Implementations for Abstract Data Types from Algebraic Specifications — Ph.D.

**Thompson, Peter Murray** Conic Sector Analysis of Hybrid Control Systems — Ph.D.

**Wimpey, David George** Finite-State Control of Discrete-Time Continuous Processes: An Automatic Motivated Approach — Ph.D.

**1983**

**Armiento, Craig Alfred** Impact in (100)-, (110)- and (111)-Oriented InP Avalanche Photodiodes — Ph.D.

**Bloom, Toby** Dynamic Module Replacement in a Distributed Programming System — Ph.D.

**Bogler, Philip Lee** Electromagnetic Wave Propagation in Multiple-scattering Atmospheres with Applications to Adaptive Communication — Ph.D.

**Bondurant, Roy Sidney** Theoretical and Experimental Aspects of Quantum Noise Reduction and Precision Measurement — Ph.D.

**Brock, Jarvis Dean** A Formal Model of Non-Determinate Dataflow Computation — Ph.D.

**Brou, Philippe** Finding the Orientation of Objects in Vector Maps — Ph.D.

**Chieu, Trieu Can** Structural and Electronic Properties of Pristine and Intercalated Highly Ordered Graphite Fibers — Ph.D.

**Chuang, Shun Lien** Electromagnetic and Acoustic Wave Scattering from Periodic and Random Rough Surfaces — Ph.D.

**Church, Kenneth Ward** Phrase-structure Parsing: A Method for Taking Advantage of Allophonic Constraints — Ph.D.

**Constantopoulos, Panos** Computer-Assisted Control of Electricity Usage by Consumers — Ph.D.

**Duckworth, Gregory Lynn** Processing and Inversion of Arctic Ocean Refraction Data — Ph.D.

**Eisenberg, Solomon Rivlin** Non-Equilibrium Electromechanical Interactions in Cartilage: Swelling and Electrokinetics — Ph.D.

**Ekchian, Leon Kevork** Optimal Design of Distributed Detection Networks — Ph.D.

**Ezzeddine, Amin Kama** Modulated Electron Beams in Magnetic Plasmas — Sc.D.

**Fratamico, John Joseph** Millimeter-Wave Propagation Through a Turbid Atmosphere — Ph.D.

**Gabriel, Kaigham Jacob** Binaural Interaction in Hearing Impaired Listeners — Sc.D.

**El-Habashy, Tarek Mohamed** Radiation and Scattering of Electromagnetic Waves in Layered Media — Ph.D.

**Hildreth, Ellen Catherine** The Measurement of Visual Motion — Ph.D.

**Huang, Kuan-Tsae** Query Optimization in Distributed Databases — Ph.D.

**Knight, Thomas Frederic, Jr.** Design of an Integrated Optical Sensor with On-Chip Preprocessing — Ph.D.

**Levin, Beth Carol** On the Nature of Ergativity — Sc.D.

**Mauel, Michael E.** Electron Cyclotron Heating in the Constance 2 Mirror Experiment — Sc.D.

**Mok, Aloysius Ka-Lau** Fundamental Design Problems of Distributed Systems for the Hard-Real-Time Environment — Ph.D.

**Mook, Douglas R.** The Numerical Synthesis and Inversion of Acoustic Fields Using the Hankel Transform with Application to the Estimation of the Plank Wave Reflection Coefficient of the Ocean Bottom — Sc.D.

**Putnam, Roger Scott** Optically Pumped Semiconductor Lasers in the Infrared — Ph.D.

**Roskind, James Anthony** Edge Disjoint Spanning Trees and Failure Recovery in Data Communication Networks — Ph.D.

**Schunck, Brian Gregory** Motion Segmentation and Estimation — Sc.D.

**Shayegan, Mansour** High Magnetic Field Studies of the Graphite Intercalation Compounds — Ph.D.

**Terman, Christopher Jay** Simulation Tools for Digital LSI Design — Ph.D.

**Van Lehn, Kurt Alan** Felicity Conditions for Human Skill Acquisition: Validating an AI-based Theory — Ph.D.

**Wing, Jeannette Marie** A Two-Tiered Approach to Specifying Programs — Ph.D.

**Zdonik, Stanley Benjamin, Jr.** Object Management System Concepts: Supporting Integrated Office Workstation Applications — Ph.D.

**1984**

**Ackerman, William Beekley** Efficient Implementation of Applicative Languages — Ph.D.

**Ali, Ali Daoud S.** Morphological Coding of Images — Ph.D.

**Allen, Barry Ross** Observations of SiO Masers in Multiple Vibration States — Sc.D.

**Anderson, James Clayton** Speech Analysis/Synthesis Based on Perception — Ph.D.

**Batta, Rajan** Facility Location in the Presence of Congestion — Ph.D.

**Bhatt, Sandeep Nautam** The Complexity of Graph Layout and Channel Routing for VLSI — Ph.D.

**Boughton, George Andrew** Routing Networks for Packet Communication Systems — Ph.D.

**Carley, Larry Richard** Characterizing and Comparing the Aftereffects of Activity at Successive Nodes of Ranvier from Frog Sciatic Nerve Fibers — Ph.D.

**Ciccarelli, Eugene Charles** Presentation Based User Interfaces — Ph.D.

**Ehrlich, Richard M.** AC Electrostatic Precipitation — Sc.D.

**Forbus, Kenneth Dale** Qualitative Process Theory — Ph.D.

**Fujimoto, James G.** Generation of High Intensity Femtosecond Laser Pulses and Applications to Studies of Transient Physical Phenomena — Ph.D.

**Gifford, Margaret Lee** The Effects of Selective Stimulation of Medial Olivocochlear Neurons on Auditory Nerve Responses to Sound in the Cat — Ph.D.

**Herlihy, Maurice Peter** Replication Methods for Abstract Data Types — Ph.D.

**Hui, Joseph Yu Ngai** Fundamental Issues of Multiple Accessing — Ph.D.

**Khan, Babar Ali** Studies of Defect States in Chalcogenide Glasses — Ph.D.

**Mangelsdorf, Christopher Wood** A Distributed Bipolar Device for Monolithic Analog-to-Digital Conversion — Ph.D.

**Mitchell, John C.** Lamda Calculus Models of Typed Programming Languages — Ph.D.

**Mosely, Jeannine** Asynchronous Distributed Flow Control Algorithms — Ph.D.

**Paulos, John James** Measurement and Modeling of Small-geometry MOS Transistor Capacitances — Ph.D.

**Ressler, Andrew Lewis** A Circuit Grammar for Operational Amplifier Design — Ph.D.

**Robinson, Andrew Lee** Fabrication and Evaluation of a CMOS Technology with Fully-Self-Aligned Vertically-Stacked Transistors — Ph.D.

1984 (continued)

Sara, Jason J. The Automated Reproduction of Pictures with Non-Reproducible Colors — Ph.D.

Sarin, Sunil Kumar Interactive On-Line Conferences — Ph.D.

Shin, Robert Tong-Ik Theoretical Models for Microwave Remote Sensing of Earth Terrain — Ph.D.

Siegel, R.A. Macromolecular Drug Release from Porous Implants: Sources of Matrix Tortuosity — Sc.D.

Stark, Eugene William Foundation of a Theory of Specification for Distributed Systems — Ph.D.

Sterling, Thomas Lawrence Parallel Control Flow Mechanisms for Dynamic Scheduling of Tightly Coupled Multiprocessors — Ph.D.

Swartz, Mitchell Robert Effect of Methylene Blue and Visible Light on Charge Transfer to Methemoglobin and Oxygen — Sc.D.

Tabatabaie-Alavi, Kamal Ion Implanted InGaAs-In P Heterojunction NPN and InGaAs-InAl as Lateral PNP Transistors — Ph.D.

Tan, Han-Ngee Thermodynamic Relations in Noisy Electrical Networks — Ph.D.

Terzopoulos, Demetri Multiresolution Computation of Visible-Surface Representations — Ph.D.

Timp, Gregory Louis The Structural Lattice Dynamical and Electronic Properties of Graphite Intercalation Compounds — Ph.D.

Trager, Barry Marshall Integration of Algebraic Functions — Ph.D.

Vachon, Guy A Four Color Printing System — Ph.D.

Vlannes, Nickolas Peppino Optical and Induction Probing of Magnetostatic Waves in Thin Films of Yttrium Iron Garnet — Ph.D.

Wang, David Lap Kwan Stochastic Modeling and Parameter Estimation of Residential Electric Loads — Ph.D.

Weihl, William Edward Specification and Implementation of Atomic Data Types — Ph.D.

Weiner, Andrew Marc Femtosecond Optical Pulse Generation and Dephasing Measurements in Condensed Matter — Sc.D.

Williams, Ronald Dean Loosely Coupled Resource Allocation through Barter — Ph.D.

1985

Andreae, Peter Merrett Justified Generalization: Acquiring Procedures from Examples — Ph.D.

Aull, Brian Francis The Impact of Ion-host Interactions on the 5d-to-4f Spectra of Lanthanide Rare Earth Ions — Ph.D.

Avniel, Yehuda Realization and Approximation of Stationary Stochastic Processes — Ph.D.

Bordley, Thomas Edward Improved Paraxial Methods for Modeling Underwater Acoustic Propagation — Sc.D.

Chen, Francine Robina Acoustic-Phonetic Constraints in Continuous Speech Recognition: A Case Study Using the Digit Vocabulary — Ph.D.

Chiu, Sheng-Yang Debugging Distributed Computations in a Nested Atomic Action System — Ph.D.

Chor, Ben-Zion Two Issues in Public Key Cryptography: RSA Bit Security and a New Knapsack Type System — Ph.D.

Christensen, Craig Whittaker Estimation of X-Ray Scatter Component for Improvement of Tomographic Imaging — Sc.D.

Colavita, Michael Mark Atmospheric Limitations of a Two-color Astrometric Interferometer — Ph.D.

Coln, Michael Christian Wohnsen A High Performance Dielectric Measurement System — Ph.D.

Cosmadakis, Stavros Stylianos Equational Theories and Database Constraints — Ph.D.

Curtis, Susan Roberta Reconstruction of Multidimensional Signals from Zero Crossings — Ph.D.

Doerschuk, Peter Charles A Markov Chain Approach to Electrocardiogram Modeling and Analysis — Sc.D.

Donahue, Thomas Joseph The Characterization of Low-Temperature Silicon Epitaxy Deposited by Plasma Enhanced Chemical Vapor Deposition — Ph.D.

Dowla, Farid Ud Bearing Estimation of Wideband Signals by Multidimensional Spectral Analysis — Ph.D.

Estrin, Deborah L. Access to Inter-organization Computer Networks — Ph.D.

Gabriel, Mary Christina Optical Nonlinearities in Group III-V Semiconductor Waveguides — Ph.D.

Garber, Edward Martin Surface Acoustic Wave Single-Phase Unidirectional Transducers and Phase Weighting — Ph.D.

Gasworth, Steven Marc Electrification by Liquid Dielectric Flow — Ph.D.

Goldhor, Richard Scott Representation of Consonants in the Peripheral Auditory System: A Modeling Study of the Correspondence Between Response Properties and Phonetic Features — Ph.D.

Greschak, John Paul Reconstructing Convex Sets — Ph.D.

Islam, Mohammed Nazrul Theory of the Soliton Laser and Picosecond Study of Near-band-gap Nonlinearities in GaInAsP — Sc.D.

Jin, Ya-qiu Strong Fluctuation Theory for a Bounded Layer of Random Discrete Scatterers — Ph.D.

Kim, Sei-Hee Mode-Locking in Monolithic GaAlAs Laser Diode — Ph.D.

Lee, Jay Kyoon Electromagnetic Wave Propagation and Scattering in Layered Anisotropic Random Medium — Ph.D.

Levitt, David A Representation for Musical Dialects — Sc.D.

Marroquin, Jose Luis Probabilistic Solution of Universe Problems — Ph.D.

Matson, Mark Douglas Macromodeling and Optimization of Digital MOS VLSI Circuits — Ph.D.

Minkoff, Alan Seth Real-Time Dispatching of Delivery Vehicles — Ph.D.

Ngugen, Trung Tien Atmospheric Optical Communications for Local Area Networks — Ph.D.

Orlicki, David Mark Model Reference Adaptive Control Systems Using a Dead Zone Non-Linearity — Ph.D.

Propp, Michael Benjamin The Thermodynamic Properties of Markov Processes — Ph.D.

Rose, Christopher Methods of Frequency Selectivity and Synchronization Measurement in Single Auditory Nerve Fibers: Application to the Alligator Lizard — Ph.D.

Rotman, Stanley Richard Defect Structure of Luminescent Garnets — Ph.D.

**1985** (continued)

**Seiler, Larry Dean** A Hardware Assisted Methodology for VLSI Design Rule Checking — Ph.D.

**Seneff, Stephanie** Pitch and Spectral Analysis of Speech Based on an Auditory Synchrony Model — Ph.D.

**Seziginer, Abdurrahman** Forward and Inverse Problems in Transient Electromagnetic Fields — Ph.D.

**Shadle, Christine Helen** The Acoustics of Fricative Consonants — Ph.D.

**Shahjahan, Muhammed** Multivariable Loop Shaping with Frequency Dependant Cost Functionals: A Design Methodology — Ph.D.

**Shih, Shih-Ming** Reduced-Order Model-Reference Adaptive System Identification of Large Scale Systems with Discrete Adaptation Laws — Sc.D.

**Sollins, Karen Rosin** Distributed Name Management — Ph.D.

**Teich, Jonathan Marc** The Theory and Development of a Noninvasive Retinal Fluorescence Scanner with Application to Early Diagnosis of Diabetic Retinopathy — Ph.D.

**Terry, Fred Lewis, Jr.** Electrical Properties of Nitrided Silicon Dioxide as an MOS Gate Insulator — Ph.D.

**Tsitsiklis, John Nikolaos** Problems in Decentralized Decision Making and Computation — Ph.D.

**Vallese, Francesco Joseph** Design and Operation of High-Power Variable Reluctance Motor Drive Systems — Sc.D.

**Vande Vate, John Hagood** The Linear Matroid Parity Problem — Ph.D.

**Wagner, Stuart S.** Multiplexing Methods for Fiber Optic Local Communication Networks — Ph.D.

**Warner, Thomas Hamilton** Modeling and Analysis of Solid-Rotor Alternator Driven Pulsed Rectifiers — Sc.D.

**Wyatt, Karl Wesley** Electron Avalanche Transition in SF6 — Ph.D.

**Yagle, Andrew Emil** Layer Stripping Solutions of Inverse Seismic Problems — Ph.D.

**Zukowski, Charles Albert** Bounding Enhancements for VLSI Circuit Simulation — Ph.D.

**1986**

**An, Chae Hun** Trajectory and Force Control of a Direct Drive Arm — Ph.D.

**Arikan, Erdal** Sequential Decoding for Multiple Access Channels — Ph.D.

**Boettcher, Kevin Lloyd** A Methodology for the Analysis and Design of Human Information Processing Organizations — Ph.D.

**Boppana, Ravi Babu** Lower Bounds for Monotone Circuits and Formulas — Ph.D.

**Briançon, Alain Charles Louis** Estimation and Modeling of Multidimensional Non-Stationary Stochastic Processes: Application to the Remote Sensing of Atmospheric Temperature Fields — Ph.D.

**Bui, Thang Nguyen** Graph Bisection Algorithms — Ph.D.

**Bustamante, Diane Kathleen** Principal Component Amplitude Compression of Speech for the Hearing Impaired — Ph.D.

**Castiñeyra Figueredo, Isidro Marcos** Routing in Unreliable Networks — Ph.D.

**Chapman, Paul Thayer** Decision Models for Multistage Production Planning — Ph.D.

**Cox, Louis Anthony, Jr.** Mathematical Foundations of Risk Measurement — Ph.D.

**Dove, Webster Pope** Knowledge-Based Pitch Detection — Ph.D.

**Esmersoy, Cengiz** The Backpropagated Field Approach to Multidimensional Velocity Inversion — Ph.D.

**Flamm, David Simson** Control of Delay Systems for Minimax Sensitivity — Ph.D.

**Freeman, Dennis Melvin** Hydrodynamic Study of Stereociliary Tuft Motion in Hair Cell Organs — Ph.D.

**Gao, Guang Rong** A Pipelined Code Mapping Scheme for Static Data Flow Computers — Ph.D.

**Garcia, Armando** Efficient Rendering of Synthetic Images — Ph.D.

**Grunberg, Daniel Backer** A Methodology for Designing Robust Multivariable Nonlinear Feedback Control Systems — Ph.D.

**Helman, Daniel Richard** Packet Radio Simulation and Protocols — Ph.D.

**Inkpen, Stuart** Electrical and Mechanical Mechanisms for Color Variation in the Spraying of Metallic Paints — Ph.D.

**Isnardi, Michael Anthony** Modeling the Television Process — Ph.D.

**Izraelevitz, David** Reconstruction of Signals from the Fourier Transform Magnitude — Sc.D.

**Johnson, Bartley Clark** Picosecond Carrier Density and Light Output Dynamics of Modulated Diode Lasers — Ph.D.

**Kuznetsov, Mark** Pulsation and Chaos in Semiconductor Lasers with a Proton-Bombarded Segment — Sc.D.

**Lee, Wing Hong Ricky** On Robust Control Designs for Infinite Dimensional Systems — Ph.D.

**Leung, Janny M.Y.** Polyhedral Structure of Capacitated Fixed Charge Problems and a Problem in Delivery Route Planning — Ph.D.

**Lou, Xi-Cheng** An Algebraic Approach to Time Scale Analysis and Control — Ph.D.

**Malvar, Henrique Sarmento** Optimal Pre- and Post-Filtering in Noisy Sampled-Data Systems — Ph.D.

**Mangano, Joseph Angelo** Microwave Instabilities in a Beam-Plasma Discharge — Ph.D.

**Mark, Martin B.** Multipixel, Multidimensional Laser Radar System Performance — Ph.D.

**Martinez, Dennis Michael** Model-based Motion Estimation and Its Application to Restoration and Interpolation of Motion Pictures — Ph.D.

**McLeod, Kenneth J.** Modulation of Biosynthesis by Physiologically Relevant Electric Fields — Ph.D.

**Milios, Evangelos Eleftherios** Signal Processing and Interpretation Using Multilevel Signal Abstractions — Ph.D.

**Mukherji, Utpal** A Schedule-Based Approach for Flow-Control in Data Communication Networks — Sc.D.

**Myers, Cory Scott** Signal Representation for Symbolic and Numerical Processing — Ph.D.

**Ng, Peng-Teng Peter** Distributed Dynamic Resource Allocation in Multi-Model Situations — Ph.D.

**Ng, Pui** Long Atomic Computations — Ph.D.

**Nussbaum, Jeremy** Electric Field Control of Mechanical and Electrochemical Properties of Polyelectrolyte Gel Membranes — Ph.D.

**Pan, Davis Yen** Adaptive Filtering for Sampled Images — Ph.D.

**1986** (continued)

**Paradis, Albert Raymond** Precision Geodesy Using System Identification and Global Positioning System Signals — Ph.D.

**Pingali, Keshav** Demand-Driven Evaluation on Dataflow Machines — Ph.D.

**Poh, Soon Yun** Transient Electromagnetic Dipole Radiation Over a Stratified Medium — Ph.D.

**Pribyl, Patrick Andrew** Measured MHD Equilibrium in Alcator C — Ph.D.

**Régnier, Jean Michel** Priority Assignment in Integrated Services Networks — Ph.D.

**Schloss, Robert Perry** External Cavity Laser with Coherent Amplifier Array and Multiple Slit Spatial Filter — Ph.D.

**Sheppard, Norman Fred** Dielectric Analysis of the Cure of Thermosetting Epoxy-Amine Systems — Ph.D.

**Stamos, James William** Remote Evaluation — Ph.D.

**Tsai, Wei Kang** Optimal Quasi-Static Routing for Virtual Circuit Networks Subjected to Stochastic Inputs — Ph.D.

**Tseng, Paul** Relaxation Methods for Monotropic Programming Problems — Ph.D.

**Ulichney, Robert A.** Digital Halftoning and the Physical Reconstruction Function — Ph.D.

**Van Hove, Patrick Louis** Silhouette-Slice Theorems — Ph.D.

**Weise, Daniel Wayne** Formal Multilevel Hierarchical Verification of Synchronous MOS VLSI Circuits — Ph.D.

**Weiss, Aryeh Moshe** Real Time Control of the Permeability of Crosslinked Polyelectrolyte Membranes to Fluorescent Solutes — Ph.D.

**Wengrovitz, M.S.** The Hilbert-Hankel Transform and Its Application to Shallow Water Ocean Acoustics — Ph.D.

**Whitaker, Norman Ashton** All-Optical Signal Processing in Semiconductor Waveguides — Ph.D.

**Wiley, R.P.** Performance Analysis of Stochastic Timed Petri Nets — Ph.D.

**Yee, James Ralph** Distributed Routing and Flow Control Algorithms for Communications Networks — Ph.D.

**Zayhowski, John Joseph** Magnetic Polarons in Semimagnetic Semiconductors: A Time-Resolved Photoluminescence Study of Exciton-magnetic Polaron Complexes in $Cd_{1-x}Mn_xSe$ and $Cd_{1-x}MnTe$ — Ph.D.

**1987**

**Abernathy, Jerome Drew** Effects of Optical Nonlinearities on Frequency Multiplexed Single Mode Optical Fiber Systems — Ph.D.

**Atwater, Harry Albert** Ion Beam Enhanced Grain Growth in Thin Films — Ph.D.

**Baldwin, Robert William** Rule Based Analysis of Computer Security — Ph.D.

**Barton, George Edward** The Computational Structure of Natural Language — Ph.D.

**Berger, Ronald David** Analysis of the Cardiovascular Control System Using Broad-Band Stimulation — Ph.D.

**Bickley, Corine Anna** Acoustic Evidence for the Development of Speech — Ph.D.

**Buckley, Stephen John** Planning and Teaching Compliant Motion Strategies — Ph.D.

**Bunks, Carey David** Random Field Modeling for Interpretation and Analysis of Layered Data — Ph.D.

**Burger, Wayne Robert** A Low Temperature (T ≤ 800C) Chemical Vapor Deposition Technique for the Deposition of Device Quality Epitaxial Silicon — Ph.D.

**Canny, John Francis** The Complexity of Robot Motion Planning — Ph.D.

**Chu, Tam-Anh** Synthesis of Self-timed VLSI Circuits from Graph-Theoretic Specifications — Ph.D.

**Coan, Brian Anthony** Achieving Consensus in Fault-Tolerant Distributed Computer Systems: Protocols, Lower Bounds, and Simulations — Ph.D.

**Dagli, Nadir** III-V Waveguides and Couplers for Integrated Optics — Ph.D.

**Denton, Denice Dee** Moisture Transport in Polyimide Films in Integrated Circuits — Ph.D.

**Donald, Bruce R.** Error Detection and Recovery for Robot Motion Planning with Uncertainty — Ph.D.

**Elbuluk, Malik Elsam** Resonant Converters: Topologies, Dynamic Modeling and Control — Ph.D.

**Espy-Wilson, Carol Yvonne** An Acoustic-Phonetic Approach to Speech Recognition: Application to the Semivowels — Ph.D.

**Feder, Meir** Iterative Algorithms for Parameter Estimation from "Incomplete" Data with Applications to Signal Processing — Ph.D.

**Frank, Eliot Henry** Electromechanics of Normal and Degenerated Cartilage: Poroelastic Behavior and Electrokinetic Mechanisms — Ph.D.

**Garverick, Steven Lee** Large Signal Linearity of Scaled MOS Transistors — Ph.D.

**Gelfand, Saul Brian** Analysis of Simulated Annealing Type Algorithms — Ph.D.

**Gennert, Michael A.** A Computational Framework for Understanding Problems in Stereo Vision — Ph.D.

**Goldberg, Andrew Vladislav** Efficient Graph Algorithms for Sequential and Parallel Computers — Ph.D.

**Griffin, Daniel Wayne** Multi-Band Excitation Vocoder — Ph.D.

**Hahne, Ellen Louise** Round Robin Scheduling for Fair Flow Control in Data Communication Networks — Ph.D.

**Harrison, James** Spectral Characteristics of Semiconductor Diode Lasers — Ph.D.

**Hart, George W.** Minimum Information Estimation of Structure — Ph.D.

**Howland, Bradford** An Electronic Aberroscope and a New Type of Eye Chart for Measurement of the Human Eye — Sc.D.

**Iverson, Ralph Benhart** Crystallization in Self-implanted Polycrystalline Silicon-on-Insulator Films — Ph.D.

**Krause, Edward A.** Motion Estimation for Frame-Rate Conversion — Ph.D.

**Kuo, Chung-Chieh** Discretization and Solution of Elliptic PDEs: A Transform Domain Approach — Ph.D.

**LaMaire, Richard Orville** Robust Time and Frequency Domain Estimation Methods in Adaptive Control — Ph.D.

**Lamb, Richard Hubbert, Jr.** Parametric Non-linear Filtering — Sc.D.

**Lucassen, John M.** Types and Effects—Towards the Integration of Functional and Imperative Programming — Ph.D.

**Maley, Franklin Miller** Single-Layer Wire Routing — Ph.D.

**1987** (continued)

**McAllester, David Allen** ONTIC: A Knowledge Representation System for Mathematics — Ph.D.

**Merab, Andre A.** Exact Reconstruction of Ocean Bottom Velocity Profile from Monochromatic Scattering Data — Ph.D.

**Miller, James S.** MultiScheme: A Parallel Processing System Based on MIT Scheme — Ph.D.

**Molter-Orr, Lynne** Integrated Optical Multiple Waveguide Coupler Switches and Lenses — Ph.D.

**Pappas, Thrasyvoulos Nicholaou** Estimation of Coronary Artery Dimensions from Angiograms — Ph.D.

**Rappaport, Carey Milford** Synthesis of Optimum Microwave Antenna Applicators for Use in Treating Deep Localized Tumors — Ph.D.

**Riley, Michael Dennis** Time-Frequency Representations for Speech Signals — Ph.D.

**Rodder, Mark Stephen** Fabrication and Characterization of Hydrogen Passivated Thin Film Polycrystalline-Silicon MOSFETs — Ph.D.

**Rohlicek, Jan Robin** Aggregation and Time Scale Analysis of Perturbed Markov Systems — Ph.D.

**Sherman, Alan T.** Cryptology and VLSI (a two-part dissertation). I, Detecting and Exploiting Algebraic Weaknesses in Cryptosystems. II, Algorithms for Placing Modules on a Custom VLSI Chip — Ph.D.

**Sleefe, Gerard E.** Acoustic Backscatter from Random Media: Signal Modeling, Parameter Estimation, and Application to Ultrasonic Tissue Characterization — Ph.D.

**Tewfik, Ahmed H.** Recursive Estimation and Spectral Estimation for 2-D Isotropic Random Fields — Ph.D.

**Tiedemann, Edward George, Jr.** Queue Arrival Control with Partial Observations — Ph.D.

**Towe, Elias D.** Phase-Locked Semiconductor Quantum Well Laser Arrays — Ph.D.

**Zachary, Joseph L.** A Framework for Incorporating Abstraction Mechanisms into the Logic Programming Paradigm — Ph.D.

**1988**

**Abbas, Gregory L.** Frequency Allocation for Fiber Optic Integrated Services Communication Networks — Ph.D.

**Anderson, Erik Hyde** Fabrication and Electromagnetic Applications of Periodic Nanostructures — Ph.D.

**Borgeaud, Maurice E.** Theoretical Models for Polarimetric Microwave Remote Sensing of Earth Terrain — Ph.D.

**Brewster, Silvano Arturo** Probabilistic Analysis of Soft Errors in VLSI Circuits — Ph.D.

**Chong, Tow C.** (Ga, Al) as Heterostructure Lasers Grown Directly on Si Substrates by Molecular Beam Epitaxy — Ph.D.

**Dhawan, Vivek** VLBI Observations of Extragalactic Radio Sources at 7mm Wavelength — Ph.D.

**Doyle, Richard James** Hypothesizing Device Mechanisms: Opening Up the Black Box — Ph.D.

**Escobar, Julio** Maximum Likelihood Detection for Probabilistic Models of Optical Code Division Multiple Access Channels — Ph.D.

**Fleck, Margaret M.** Boundaries and Topological Algorithms — Ph.D.

**Glass, James R.** Finding Acoustic Regularities in Speech: Applications to Phonetic Recognition — Ph.D.

**Goldberg, Andrew F.** Development of Magnetic Components for 1–10 MHz DC/DC Converters — Ph.D.

**Hamscher, Walter Charles** Model-Based Trouble Shooting of Digital Systems — Ph.D.

**Harton, Austin Vince** Fundamental Lateral Transverse Mode Operation in the Pb-Salt Ion Implanted Ridge Waveguide Laser — Ph.D.

**Hillis, Daniel W.** The Connection Machine — Ph.D.

**Hsu, Stephen C.** Moving-Object Reconstruction from Camera-Blurred Sequences Using Interframe and Interregion Constraints — Ph.D.

**Huttenlocher, Daniel** Three Dimensional Recognition of Solid Objects in a Two-Dimensional Image — Ph.D.

**Iannucci, Robert Alan** A Dataflow/von Neumann Hybrid Architecture — Ph.D.

**Ilderem, Vida** A Very Low Pressure Chemical Vapor Deposition Process for Blanket and Selective Titanium Silicide Films — Ph.D.

**Jayaraman, Rajsekhar** Reliability and 1/f Noise Properties of MOSFETs with Nitride Oxide Gate Dielectrics — Ph.D.

**Jeong, Hong** Mask Extraction from Line Drawings of Optical VLSI Images — Ph.D.

**Kaliski, Burton S.** Elliptic Curves and Cryptography — Ph.D.

**Kapasouris, Petros** Design for Performance Enhancement in Feedback Control Systems with Multiple Saturating Nonlinearities — Ph.D.

**Kesler, Morris P.** Ultrafast Dynamics in GaAlAs Laser Diodes — Ph.D.

**Klein, Philip N.** Efficient Parallel Algorithms for Planar, Chordal, and Interval Graphs — Ph.D.

**Koton, Phyllis Alta** Using Experience in Learning and Problem Solving — Ph.D.

**Kung, Kenneth T.Y.** Polycrystalline Si Thin Films and Devices: I. See Selection through Ion Channeling; II. Thin-Film Transistors — Ph.D.

**Lamel, Lori Faith** Formalizing Knowledge Used in Spectrogram Reading: Acoustic and Perceptual Evidence from Stops — Ph.D.

**LeCoz, Yannick Louis** Simulation of Semiconductor Devices: A Spectral Method for Solution of the Boltzmann Transport Equation — Ph.D.

**Lee, Wai** The Fabrication and Characterization of InGaAs/InAlAs Heterojunction Bipolar Transistors — Ph.D.

**Liew, Soung C.** Capacity Assignment in Non-Switching Multichannel Networks — Ph.D.

**Lim, Willie Y.** Shape Recognition in the Rocks World — Ph.D.

**Linden, Lynette Lois** Functional Representation of Visual Form and Texture: A Model of the Bug Detector — Ph.D.

**MacGinitie, Laura Anne** An Electrical and Thermal Modulation of Protein Synthesis in Cartilage: A Model for Electric Field Effects on Biological Tissues — Ph.D.

**Marujo, Ernesto C.** Dynamic Allocation of Machines to Product Families in the Presence of Setup Delays — Ph.D.

**Oki, Brian M.** Viewstamped Replication for Highly Available Distributed Systems — Ph.D.

**Pang, Xiao-Dong** Effects of Stapedius-Muscle Contractions on Masking of Tone Responses in the Auditory Nerve — Ph.D.

## 1988 (continued)

**Papadopoulos, Gregory Michael** Implementation of a General Purpose Dataflow Multiprocessor — Ph.D.

**Park, Dongwook** High-Resolution Laser Radar Performance Analysis — Ph.D.

**Perlman, Radia J.** Network Layer Protocols with Byzantine Robustness — Ph.D.

**Plotkin, Serge A.** Graph-Theoretic Techniques for Parallel, Distributed and Sequential Computation — Ph.D.

**Prince, Jerry Ladd** Geometric Model-Based Estimation from Projections — Ph.D.

**Sacks, Elisha P.** Automatic Qualitative Analysis of Ordinary Differential Equations Using Piecewise Linear Approximations — Ph.D.

**Saplakoglu, Gurhan** Photodectection Feedback Systems — Ph.D.

**Schmidt, Martin Arnold** Microsensors for the Measurement of Shear Forces in Turbulent Boundary Layers — Ph.D.

**Shapiro, Finley Reuben** Computer Simulation of the Transient Response of Amorphous Silicon Hydride Devices — Ph.D.

**Shepard, Thomas D.** Fast Wave Ion Cyclotron Resonance Heating Experiments on the Alcator C. Tokamak — Ph.D.

**Simmons, Reid Gordon** Combining Associational and Causal Reasoning to Solve Interpretation and Planning Problems — Ph.D.

**Szabo, Bernard I.** Analytical Foundations of Pixel-Based Video Displacement Estimation — Ph.D.

**Thompson, Paul M.** Local Search Algorithms for Vehicle Routing and Other Combinatorial Problems — Ph.D.

**Torrey, David Allan** Optimal-Efficiency Constant-Speed Control of Nonlinear Variable Reluctance Motor Drives — Ph.D.

**Traub, Kenneth R.** Sequential Implementation of Lenient Programming Languages — Ph.D.

**Tung, Thye-Lai** Boundary Element Techniques for Modeling Thermal Oxidation of Silicon — Ph.D.

**Uchanski, Rosalie May** Spectral and Temporal Contributions to Speech Clarity for Hearing Impaired Listeners — Ph.D.

**Vinciguerra, Ralph L.** Color Anti-Aliasing and Transparency in Computer Graphics — Ph.D.

**Wade, Jon Patrick** An Integrated Content Addressable Memory System — Ph.D.

**Welch, Jennifer Lundelius** Topics in Distributed Computing: The Impact of Partial Synchrony, and Modular Decomposition of Algorithms — Ph.D.

**Weld, Daniel S.** Theories of Comparative Analysis — Ph.D.

**Wellman, Michael P.** Formulation of Tradeoffs in Planning Under Uncertainty — Ph.D.

**Wong, Albert K.** Channel Scheduling for Optical Communication Networks with Frequency Concurrency — Ph.D.

**Yap, Daniel** Dry-Etched In GaAs/InP Buried-Heterostructure Lasers and Laser Arrays — Ph.D.

**Zakhor, Avideh** Reconstruction of Multidimensional Signals from Multiple Level Threshold Crossings — Ph.D.

**Zaretsky, Mark C.** Parameter Estimation Using Microdielectrometry with Application to Transformer Monitoring — Ph.D.

## 1989

**Agre, Philip Edward** The Dynamic Structure of Everyday Life — Ph.D.

**Blelloch, Guy E.** Scan Primitives and Parallel Vector Models — Ph.D.

**Bloom, Bard** Ready Simulation, Bisimulation, and the Semantics of CCS-Like Languages — Ph.D.

**Casey, Leo Francis** Circuit Design for 1-10 MHz DC-DC Conversion — Ph.D.

**Chou, Harry** Upconversion Processes and Cr-Sensitization of Er- and Er, Ho-Activated Solid State Laser Materials — Ph.D.

**Connell, Jonathan H.** A Colony Architecture for an Artificial Creature — Ph.D.

**Covell, Michele Mae** An Algorithm Design Environment for Signal Processing — Ph.D.

**Culler, David E.** Managing Parallelism and Resources in Scientific Dataflow Programs — Ph.D.

**de Jong, Stephen Peter** Ubik: A Framework for the Development of Distributed Organizations — Ph.D.

**Drescher, Gary L.** Made-up Minds: A Constructivist Approach to Artificial Intelligence — Ph.D.

**Enders, Robert Hay** Laser Radar Tracking Theory: Track-While-Image Operation — Ph.D.

**Erdmann, Michael Andreas** On Probabilistic Strategies for Robot Tasks — Ph.D.

**Gasiewski, Albin John** Atmospheric Temperature Soundings and Precipitation Cell Parameter Estimation Using Passive 118-GHz $O_2$ Observations — Ph.D.

**Gaylor, Diane Catherine** Physical Mechanisms of Cellular Injury in Electrical Trauma — Ph.D.

**Greenberg, Ronald I.** Efficient Interconnection Schemes for VLSI and Parallel Computation — Ph.D.

**Grimshaw, Paul Edward** Electrical Control of Solute Transport Across Polyelectrolyte Membranes — Ph.D.

**Hall, Leslie Ann** Two Topics in Discrete Optimization: Polyhedral Structure of Capacitated Trees and Approximation Algorithms for Scheduling — Ph.D.

**Heller, Steven K.** Efficient Lazy Data-structures on a Dataflow Machine — Ph.D.

**Ho, Seng-Tiong** Theoretical and Experimental Aspects of Squeezed State Generation in Two-Level Media — Ph.D.

**Huang, Weiping** Modeling and Analysis of Guided-Wave Optoelectronic Devices — Ph.D.

**Ismail, Khaled E.** The Study of Electron Transport in Field-Effect-Induced Quantum Wells on GaAs/GaAlAs — Ph.D.

**Jagannathan, Suresh** A Programming Language Supporting First-Class Parallel Environments — Ph.D.

**Joo, Tae Hong** Detection Statistics for Multichannel Data — Ph.D.

**Kiang, Jean-Fu** On Fields and Propagation Characteristics of Guiding Structures in Stratified Media — Ph.D.

**Ladin, Rivka** A Method for Constructing Highly Available Services and a Technique for Distributed Garbage Collection — Ph.D.

**LaGasse, Michael James** Femtosecond Optical Nonlinearities in AlGaAs — Ph.D.

**1989** (continued)

**Leavens, Gary Todd** Verifying Object-Oriented Programs That Use Subtypes — Ph.D.

**Lee, Chong Uk** Contour Motion Compensation for Image Sequence Coding — Ph.D.

**Lee, Whay Chiou** Channel Reuse Multiple Access in Bidirectional Bus Networks — Ph.D.

**Leung, Hong Chung** The Use of Artificial Neural Networks for Phonetic Recognition — Ph.D.

**Luo, Zhi-Quan** Communication Complexity of Some Problems in Distributed Computation — Ph.D.

**Ma, Moses Hsingwen** Efficient Message-based System for Concurrent Simulation — Ph.D.

**Maggs, Bruce MacDowell** Locality in Parallel Computation — Ph.D.

**McCormick, Steven Paul** Modeling and Simulation of VLSI Interconnections with Moments — Ph.D.

**Nikoukhah, Ramine** A Deterministic and Stochastic Theory for Two-Point Boundary-Value Descriptor Systems — Ph.D.

**Özbek, Ali** Generalized Tomographic Methods for Multidimensional Inverse Scattering — Ph.D.

**Özveren, Cüneyt M.** Analysis and Control of Discrete Event Dynamic Systems: A State Space Approach — Ph.D.

**Palmer, Joyce Ellen** Evolution of Microstructure in Ultra-Thin Films of GaAs and $CaF_2$ on Single Crystal Silicon — Ph.D.

**Peterson, Patrick Mangan** Adaptive Array Processing for Multiple Microphone Hearing Aids — Ph.D.

**Pian, Donald Theodore** Sampling Structure Conversion for Television Pictures — Ph.D.

**Pomeroy, Stephen Dirk Entwistle** High Resolution, High Speed Analog-to-Digital Conversion Techniques — Ph.D.

**Randolph, Mark Anthony** Syllable-based Constraints on Properties of English Sounds — Ph.D.

**Rao, Satish Balusu** Finding Small Balanced Edge Cuts: Theory and Applications — Ph.D.

**Rhoads, Kevin George** An Expert System for Measuring Electric Field Using Electro-optic Imaging — Ph.D.

**Rosenberg, Ronni Lynne** Computer Literacy Education — Ph.D.

**Sanders, Seth Robert** Nonlinear Control of Switching Power Converters — Ph.D.

**Saxberg, Bror Valdemar Haug** A Modern Differential Geometric Approach to Shape from Shading — Ph.D.

**Schoenlein, Robert William** Femtosecond Relaxation Dynamics of Image-Potential States in Metals — Ph.D.

**Schott, Jean-Pierre** Three-Dimensional Motion Estimation Using Shading Information in Multiple Frames — Ph.D.

**Shahidi, Ghavam G.** Non-Stationary Transport Effects in Deep Sub-Micron Channel Si Mosfets — Ph.D.

**Shirley, Mark Harper** Generating Circuit Tests by Exploiting Designed Behavior — Ph.D.

**Sloan, Robert Hal** Computational Learning Theory: New Models and Algorithms — Ph.D.

**Soley, Richard Mark** On the Efficient Exploitation of Speculation Under Dataflow Paradigms of Control — Ph.D.

**Song, William S.** A Fault-Tolerant Multiprocessor Architecture for Digital Signal Processing Applications — Ph.D.

**Spinelli, John Michael** Reliable Data Communication in Faulty Computer Networks — Ph.D.

**Szeto, Yuen Po Simon** A Unified Electrothermal Hot-carrier Transport Model for Silicon Bipolar Transistor Simulations — Ph.D.

**Tuttle, Mark R.** Knowledge and Distributed Computation — Ph.D.

**Van Baalen, Jeffrey** Steps Towards a Theory of Representation Design — Ph.D.

**Wang, John Szeming** Motion-compensated NTSC Demodulation — Ph.D.

**Ware, Kurt Matthew** A High-Frequency Integrated CMOS Phase-Locked Loop — Ph.D.

**Wasem, Ondria Jaffe** Robust Topologies for Passive, Fiber Optic Local Communication Networks — Ph.D.

**Webb, Ian Robert** Period and Phase of Customer Replenishment: A New Approach to Inventory/Routing Problems — Ph.D.

**Williams, Brian Charles** Invention from First Principles via Topologies of Interaction — Ph.D.

**Yang, Ying-Ching Eric** Time Domain Analysis of Electromagnetic Waves in Microelectronic Integrated Circuit Interconnects — Ph.D.

**Yip, Kenneth Man-Kam** KAM: Automatic Planning and Interpretation of Numerical Experiments Using Geometrical Methods — Ph.D.

**Zhang, Lixia** A New Architecture for Packet Switching Network Protocols — Ph.D.

**Zirkind, Naomi Esther** Adaptive Optics for Large Aperture Coherent Laser Radars — Ph.D.

**1990**

**Anderson, Kristin Kay** Disordered Quantum Well Waveguide Fabrication and Ultrafast Optical Characterization — Ph.D.

**Bamji, Cyrus S.** Graph-based Representations and Coupled Verification of VLSI Schematics and Layouts — Ph.D.

**Bart, Stephen F.** Modeling and Design of Electroquasistatic Microactuators — Ph.D.

**Berger, Bonnie Anne** Using Randomness to Design Efficient Deterministic Algorithms — Ph.D.

**Bernstein, Joseph Barry** Electrical Characterization of Polymeric Insulation by Electrically Stimulated Acoustic Wave Measurements — Ph.D.

**Bossi, Donald Elliott** Reduced Confinement GaAlAs Tapered Waveguide Antennas — Ph.D.

**Braunegg, David Jerome** Marvel: A System for Recognizing World Locations with Stereo Vision — Ph.D.

**Brorson, Stuart D.** Femtosecond Thermomodulation Measurements of Transport and Relaxation in Metals and Superconductors — Ph.D.

**Caulkins, Jonathan Paul** The Distribution and Consumption of Illicit Drugs: Some Mathematical Models and Their Policy Implications — Ph.D.

**Chapman, David** Vision, Instruction, and Action — Ph.D.

**Chien, Andrew A.** Concurrent Aggregates: An Object-Oriented Language for Fine-Grained Message-Passing Machines — Sc.D.

**1990** (continued)

**Chow, Chee-Seng** Multigrid Algorithms and Complexity Results for Discrete-time Stochastic Control and Related Fixed-Point Problems — Ph.D.

**Clark, Lloyd D., Jr.** A System for Chronic Neural Signal Transduction, Processing, and Control — Ph.D.

**Cobra, Daniel Távora de Queiroz** Estimation and Correction of Geometric Distortions in Side-Scan Sonar Images — Ph.D.

**Crépeau, Claude** Correct and Private Reductions Among Oblivious Transfers — Ph.D.

**Dorr, Bonnie J.** Lexical Conceptual Structure and Machine Translation — Ph.D.

**Fogg, Dennis C.Y.** Artificial Intelligence and Optimization Solutions to Multi-Criteria Operator Binding — Ph.D.

**Gamble, Edward Bernard** Integration of Early Visual Cues for Recognition — Ph.D.

**Goldman, Kenneth Jerome** Distributed Algorithm Simulation Using Input/output Automata — Ph.D.

**Goldman, Sally Ann** Learning Binary Relations, Total Orders, and Read-Once Formulas — Ph.D.

**Haase, Kenneth W.** Invention and Exploration in Discovery — Ph.D.

**Hajjar, Jean-Jacques J.** Silicon Thin Films Prepared by Plasma Enhanced Chemical Vapor Deposition — Ph.D.

**Hannon, Stephen Michael** Detection Processing for Multidimensional Laser Radars — Ph.D.

**Hosein, Patrick Ahamad** A Class of Dynamic Nonlinear Resource Allocation Problems — Ph.D.

**Hughes, Richard P.** Throughput and Delay Analysis of Frequency Hopped Multiple Access Networks — Ph.D.

**Ito, Yoshiko** Auditory Discrimination of Power Spectra for Roving Two-Tone Stimuli — Ph.D.

**Kathail, Vinod Kumar** Optimal Interpreters for Lambda-Calculus Based Functional Languages — Sc.D.

**Kipnis, Shlomo** Organization of Systems with Bussed Interconnections — Ph.D.

**Kuo, David Da-Ming** Adaptive Spatiotemporal Filtering for Interpolative Image Coding — Ph.D.

**Lathrop, Richard Harold** Efficient Methods for Massively Parallel Symbolic Induction: Algorithms and Implementation — Ph.D.

**Lee, Check Fu** Finite Difference Method for Electromagnetic Scattering Problems — Ph.D.

**Lee, Thomas H.** A Fully Integrated Inductorless FM Receiver — Ph.D.

**Liu, Ling Yi** Additive Pulse Modelocking — Ph.D.

**Mansour, Yishay** On the Complexity of Computing Algebraic Functions — Ph.D.

**Mehregany, Mehran** Microfabricated Silicon Electric Mechanisms — Ph.D.

**Nakazato, Daisuke** Transient Distributional Results in Queues with Applications to Queueing Networks — Ph.D.

**O, Kenneth Kyongyop** BiCMOS Technologies for Analog/Digital Applications Utilizing Selective Silicon Epitaxial Growth — Ph.D.

**Osborne, Randy Brent** Speculative Computation in Multilisp — Ph.D.

**Papastavrou, Jason D.** Decentralized Decision Making in a Hypothesis Testing Environment — Ph.D.

**Phillips, Cynthia A.** Theoretical and Experimental Analyses of Parallel Combinatorial Algorithms — Ph.D.

**Phillips, Mary R.** Near Band-gap Optical Nonlinearities in InGaAs/InAlAs Multiple Quantum Well Structures — Ph.D.

**Piot, Julien** Adaptive Frequency Modulation for Satellite Television Systems — Ph.D.

**Pitrelli, John Ferdinand** Hierarchical Modeling of Phoneme Duration: Application to Speech Recognition — Ph.D.

**Pratt, Gill** Pulse Computation — Ph.D.

**Reubenstein, Howard Bruce** Automated Acquisition of Evolving Informal Descriptions — Ph.D.

**Richardson, Thomas Joseph** Scale Independent Piecewise Smooth Segmentation of Images via Variational Methods — Ph.D.

**Ristad, Eric Sven** Computational Structure of Human Language — Ph.D.

**Rodriguez, Armando A.** Control of Infinite Dimensional Systems Using Finite Dimensional Techniques: A Systematic Approach — Ph.D.

**Rompel, John Taylor** Techniques for Computing with Low-Independence Randomness — Ph.D.

**Roylance, Gerald Rafael** Causality, Constraint, & Mechanism in a Computer Program for Designing Circuits — Ph.D.

**Sepe, Raymond Biaggio** Adaptive Control of the Permanent-Magnet Synchronous Motor — Ph.D.

**Shapiro, Jerome Mark** Algorithms and Systolic Architectures for Real-Time Multidimensional Adaptive Filtering of Frequency Domain Multiplexed Video Signals — Ph.D.

**Smith, Frank William, III** The Device Applications and Characterization of Nonstoichiometric GaAs Grown by Molecular Beam Epitaxy — Ph.D.

**Tom, Adam Sean** Channel Equalization and Interference Reduction Using Scrambling and Adaptive Amplitude Modulation — Ph.D.

**Trumper, David Lippincott** Magnetic Suspension Techniques for Precision Motion Control — Ph.D.

**Tsuk, Michael James** Propagation and Interference in Lossy Microelectronic Integrated Circuits — Ph.D.

**Wills, Donald Scott** Pi: A Parallel Architecture Interface for Multi-Model Execution — Ph.D.

**Yang, Woodward** The Architecture and Design of CCD Processors for Computer Vision — Ph.D.

**Yates, Roy D.** High Speed Round Robin Queueing Networks — Ph.D.

**Yeh, Alexander Sen** Automatic Analysis of Systems at Steady-State: Handling Iterative Dynamic Systems and Parameter Uncertainty — Ph.D.

**Zhang, Hongdao** Cyclic Scheduling in a Stochastic Environment — Ph.D.

**Zissman, Marc Alan** Co-Channel Talker Interference Suppression — Ph.D.

**1991**

**Alkhairy, Ashraf Sharif** Optimal Product and Manufacturing Process Selection: Issues of Formation and Methods for Parameter Design — Ph.D.

**Azizoglu, Murat** Phase Noise in Coherent Optical Communications — Ph.D.

1991 (continued)

**Bagwell, Philip F.** Quantum Mechanical Transport in Submicron Electronic Devices — Ph.D.

**Batali, John Dino** Automatic Acquisition and Use of Some of the Knowledge in Physics Texts — Ph.D.

**Bellare, Mihir** Randomness in Interactive Proofs — Ph.D.

**Binder, Bradley Thomas** Laser Radar Tomography: The Effects of Speckle — Ph.D.

**Blum, Avrim Louis** Algorithms for Approximate Graph Coloring — Ph.D.

**Bonanni, Pierino Gianni** Atmospheric Wave Detection and Parameter Estimation Using Passive Measurements of Thermal Emission Near 118 GHz — Ph.D.

**Boning, Duane S.** Semiconductor Process Design: Representations, Tools, and Methodologies — Ph.D.

**Brent, Michael Richard** Automatic Acquisition of Subcategorization from Unrestricted English — Ph.D.

**Chou, Kenneth Chien-ko** A Stochastic Modelling Approach to Multiscale Signal Processing — Ph.D.

**Clancy, Edward Arthur** Stochastic Modeling of the Relationship Between the Surface Electromyogram and Muscle Torque — Ph.D.

**Clemens, David T.** Region-Based Feature Interpretation for Recognizing 3D Models in 2D Images — Ph.D.

**Early, Kathleen R.** Experimental Characterization and Physical Modeling of Resolution Limits in Proximity Printing X-Ray Lithography — Ph.D.

**Eisenberg, Michael A.** The Kineticist's Workbench: Combining Symbolic and Numerical Methods in the Simulation of Chemical Reaction Mechanisms — Ph.D.

**Fong, Sandiway** Computational Properties of Principle-Based Grammatical Theories — Ph.D.

**Gau, Shiou Heva** Server Management in Queuing Systems — Ph.D.

**Hall, Robert Joseph** Program Improvement by Automatic Redistribution of Intermediate Results — Ph.D.

**Hamdy, Walid M.** Crosstalk in Direct Detection Optical FDMA Networks — Ph.D.

**Heel, Joachim** Temporal Surface Reconstruction — Ph.D.

**Huang, Caroline Bing-yen** An Acoustic and Perceptual Study of Vowel Formant Trajectories in American English — Ph.D.

**Hung, Merit Y.** Double Diffused (DMOS) FETs for Analog Applications — Ph.D.

**Karl, William Clement** Reconstructing Static and Dynamic Shapes from Partial Observations — Ph.D.

**Kashket, Michael Brian** A Parameterized Parser for English and Warlpiri — Ph.D.

**Kottas, James Alan** Limit Cycles in Neural Networks for Information Processing — Ph.D.

**Kulkarni, Sanjeev Ramesh** Problems of Computational and Informational Complexity in Machine Vision and Learning — Ph.D.

**Kuo, Tanni Yen** Delta-Doped Heterojunction Bipolar Transistors — Ph.D.

**Lai, Yinchieh** Quantum Theory of Optical Solitons — Ph.D.

**Leong, Kin Wai** Intensity Quantum Noise Reduction with an Above-Threshold Optical Parametric Oscillator — Ph.D.

**Murguia, James Edward** The Application of Focused Ion Beam Implantation to the Design and Fabrication of MOS Devices — Ph.D.

**Nghiem, Son Van** Electromagnetic Wave Models for Polarimetric Remote Sensing of Geophysical Media — Ph.D.

**Paczuski, Maya** Morphologies and Critical Behavior in Films, Membranes, and Interfaces — Ph.D.

**Park, James Kimbrough** The Monge Array: An Abstraction and Its Applications — Ph.D.

**Picard, Rosalind W.** Texture Modeling: Temperature Effects on Markov/Gibbs Random Fields — Sc.D.

**Prasanna, Gorur Narayana Srinivasa** Structure Driven Multiprocessor Compilation of Numeric Problems — Ph.D.

**Richetta, Octavio** Ground Holding Strategies for Air Traffic Control Under Uncertainty — Ph.D.

**Riecke, Jon Gary** The Logic and Expressibility of Simply-Typed Call-by-Value and Lazy Languages — Ph.D.

**Rogaway, Phillip Walder** The Round Complexity of Secure Protocols — Ph.D.

**Rosenblitt, David Ari** Supporting Collaborative Planning: The Plan Integration Problem — Ph.D.

**Russ, Thomas Anton** Reasoning with Time Dependent Data — Ph.D.

**Schapire, Robert Elias** The Design and Analysis of Efficient Learning Algorithms — Ph.D.

**Sheen, David Mark** Numerical Modeling of Microstrip Circuits and Antennas — Ph.D.

**Siegel, David Mark** Pose Determination of a Grasped Object Using Limited Sensing — Ph.D.

**Stamoulis, George D.** Routing and Performance Evaluation in Interconnection Networks — Ph.D.

**Standley, David L.** Analog VLSI Implementation of Smart Vision Sensors: Stability Theory and Experimental Design — Ph.D.

**Tavrow, Lee Stuart** A LOCOS-based Microfabricated Radial-Gap Variable-Capacitance Electric Motor — Ph.D.

**Tulintseff, Ann N.** A Theoretical Analysis of a Probe-Fed Stacked Circular Microstrip Antenna — Ph.D.

**Van Ryzin, Garrett John** Stochastic and Dynamic Vehicle Routing in Euclidean Service Regions — Ph.D.

**Vlcek, James C.** Molecular Beam Epitaxial Growth and Applications of Graded Bandgap InGaAlAs Semiconducting Alloys — Ph.D.

**Wornell, Gregory W.** Synthesis, Analysis, and Processing of Fractal Signals — Ph.D.

**Yelick, Katherine Anne** Using Abstraction in Explicitly Parallel Programs — Ph.D.

**Yueh, Simon Herngaung** Electromagnetic and Statistical Models for Polarimetric Remote Sensing of Vegetation — Ph.D.

1992

**Alwan, Abeer Abdul-Hussain** Modeling Speech Perception in Noise: The Stop Consonants as a Case Study — Ph.D.

**Armstrong, Robert Clyde** A Formal Approach to Incremental Consistency Maintenance in Multirepresentation VLSI Databases — Ph.D.

**Arnold, David Verl** Electromagnetic Bias in Radar Altimetry at Microwave Frequencies — Ph.D.

**1992** (continued)

**Barth, Paul Savage** Atomic Data Structures for Parallel Computing — Ph.D.

**Bawden, Alan** Linear Graph Reduction: Confronting the Cost of Naming — Ph.D.

**Beckmann, Paul Eric** Fault-Tolerant Computation Using Algebraic Homomorphisms — Ph.D.

**Borchardt, Gary Conrad** Causal Reconstruction: Understanding Causal Descriptions of Physical Systems — Ph.D.

**Bradley, Elizabeth** Taming Chaotic Circuits — Ph.D.

**Braud, John Paul** Whispering-Gallery Mirrors and Laser Cavities for Soft X-Rays and the Extreme Ultraviolet — Sc.D.

**Broekaert, Tom Peter Edward** Characterization of InGaAlAs Resonant Tunneling Transistors — Ph.D.

**Burns, Geoffrey Francis** Monolithic Fabrication of Strain-free (Al,Ga) As Semiconductor Lasers on Silicon Substrates Using Molecular Beam Epitaxy and Epitaxial Separation — Ph.D.

**Chan, Hei-Wai** Numerical Study of Relativistic Multiresonator Cylindrical Magnetrons — Ph.D.

**Chin, Toshio M.** Dynamic Estimation in Computational Vision — Ph.D.

**Colborn, Jeffrey Alan** Current-Drive and Plasma-Formation Experiments on the Versator-II Tokamak Using Lower-hybrid and Electron-cyclotron Waves — Ph.D.

**Delin, Kevin A.** Transport and Magnetic Properties of High-Temperature Superconductors — Ph.D.

**Gajar, Stephanie** An Ionic Liquid-Channel Field-Effect Transistor — Ph.D.

**Green, Thomas Joseph, Jr.** Three-Dimensional Object Recognition Using Laser Radar — Ph.D.

**Gross, Blaine Jeffrey** 1/f Noise in MOSFETs with Ultrathin Gate Dielectrics — Ph.D.

**Hakkarainen, Juha Mikko** A Real-Time Stereo Vision System in CCD/CMOS Technology — Ph.D.

**Hall, Susan Aileen** New Directions in Queue Inference for Management Implementation — Ph.D.

**Han, Hsiu Chi** Electromagnetic Wave Phenomena in Inhomogeneous and Anisotropic Media — Ph.D.

**Hardwick, John Clark** The Dual Excitation Speech Model — Ph.D.

**Heytens, Michael L.** The Design and Implementation of a Parallel Persistent Object System — Ph.D.

**Hicks, James Edward, Jr.** Compiler Directed Storage Reclamation Using Object Lifetime Analysis — Ph.D.

**Huxley, Janice Marie** Ultrashort Pulse Generation and Applications in Optical Fibers — Ph.D.

**Ishii, Alexander Toichi** Timing in Level-Clocked Circuits — Ph.D.

**Iyengar, Arun Kwangil** Dynamic Storage Allocation on a Multiprocessor — Ph.D.

**Jackson, Daniel N.** Aspect: A Formal Specification Language for Detecting Bugs — Ph.D.

**Jacobs, David William** Recognizing 3-D Objects Using 2-D Images — Ph.D.

**Keast, Craig Lewis** An Integrated Image Acquisition, Smoothing and Segmentation Focal Plane Processor — Ph.D.

**Kolodner, Elliot Karl** Atomic Incremental Garbage Collection and Recovery for a Large Stable Heap — Ph.D.

**Kravets, Dina** Combinatorial Geometric Optimization — Ph.D.

**Ku, Yao-Ching** Fabrication of Distortion Free X-Ray Masks Using Low Stress Tungsten — Ph.D.

**Kung, Joseph Tze-Shew** Integrated Capacitive Sensors Using Charge-Redistribution Sense Techniques — Ph.D.

**Lau, Suzanne Dorothy** Optical Phase Difference Measurement and Correction Using AlGaAs Guided-Wave Components — Ph.D.

**Lee, Daniel (Chonghwan)** On Open-Loop Admission Control into a Queuing System — Ph.D.

**Lee, Jintae** A Decision Rationale Management System: Capturing, Reusing, and Managing the Reasons for Decisions — Ph.D.

**Lezec, Henri J.** Tunable-frequency Gunn Diodes Fabricated by Focused Ion-beam Implantation — Ph.D.

**Lumsdaine, Andrew** Theoretical and Practical Aspects of Parallel Numerical Algorithms for Initial Value Problems with Applications — Ph.D.

**Marcus, Jeffrey Neil** Word and Subword Modelling in a Segment-based HMM Word Spotter Using a Data Analytic Approach — Ph.D.

**Miwa, Brett Andrew** Interleaved Conversion Techniques for High Density Power Supplies — Ph.D.

**Mweene, Loveday** The Design of Front-End DC-DC Converters of Distributed Power Supply Systems with Improved Efficiency and Stability — Ph.D.

**Ostrovsky, Rafail** Software Protection and Simulation on Oblivious RAMs — Ph.D.

**Pan, Jeffrey Yen** A Study of Suspended-membrane and Acoustic Techniques for the Determination of the Mechanical Properties of Thin Polymer Films — Ph.D.

**Pankaj, Rajesh Kumar** Architectures for Linear Lightwave Networks — Ph.D.

**Parekh, Abhay Kumar** A Generalized Processor Sharing Approach to Flow Control in Integrated Services Networks — Ph.D.

**Parris, Patrice Michael** Electrical Characterization of GaP on Si Grown by MOCVD after Low Temperature Plasma Cleaning — Ph.D.

**Perl, Sharon Esther** Performance Assertion Checking — Ph.D.

**Polychronopoulos, George Harry** Stochastic and Dynamic Shortest Distance Problems — Ph.D.

**Preisig, James Calvin** Adaptive Matched Field Processing in an Uncertain Propagation Environment — Ph.D.

**Resnick, Mitchel J.** Beyond the Centralized Mindset: Explorations in Massively-Parallel Microworlds — Ph.D.

**Resnick, Paul J.** HyperVoice: Groupware by Telephone — Ph.D.

**Selvidge, Charles William** Compilation-Based Prefetching for Memory Latency Tolerance — Ph.D.

**Shahriar, Selim Mohammad** Fundamental Studies and Applications in Three Level Atoms — Ph.D.

**Siskind, Jeffrey Mark** Naive Physics, Event Perception, Lexical Semantics, and Language Acquisition — Ph.D.

**Stein, Clifford** Approximation Algorithms for Multicommodity Flow and Shop Scheduling Problems — Ph.D.

**1992** (continued)

**Taylor, Darrin** Parallel Estimation on One- and Two-Dimensional Systems — Sc.D.

**Telatar, Emre Ibrahim** Multi-access Communications with Decision Feedback Decoding — Ph.D.

**Tewksbury, Theodore Locke, III** Relaxation Effects in MOS Devices Due to Tunnel Exchange with Near-Interface Oxide Traps — Ph.D.

**Tsai, Curtis** Deposition and Characterization of Very Low Pressure CVD Silicon/Silicon-Germanium Heteroepitaxial Structures — Ph.D.

**Van Aelten, Filip Jozef** Automatic Procedures for the Behavioral Verification of Digital Designs — Ph.D.

**Varvarigos, Emmanouel Andreas** Static and Dynamic Communication in Parallel Computing — Ph.D.

**Velez-Reyes, Miguel** Decomposed Algorithms for Parameter Estimation — Ph.D.

**Waldin, Earl DeWitt, III** Using Multiple Representations for Efficient Communication of Abstract Values — Ph.D.

**White, Steven James** Displacement and Disparity Representations in Early Vision — Ph.D.

**Wills, Linda Mary (Zelinka)** Automated Program Recognition by Graph Parsing — Ph.D.

**Wu, Thomas Dee** A Decompositional Search Algorithm for Efficient Diagnosis of Multiple Disorders — Ph.D.

**Xia, Jake Jiqing** Electromagnetic Inverse Methods and Applications for Inhomogeneous Media Probing and Synthesis — Ph.D.

**Yen, Anthony** Fabrication of Large-area 100 nm-period Gratings Using Achromatic Holographic Lithography — Ph.D.

**Yu, Peter Tuo** A High Data Rate Coherent Optical Costas Receiver — Ph.D.

**Zarinetchi, Farhad** Studies in Optical Resonator Gyroscopes — Ph.D.

**Zhao, Feng** Automatic Analysis and Synthesis of Controllers for Dynamical Systems Based on Phase-Space Knowledge — Ph.D.

**1993**

**Akra, Mohamad A.** Automated Text Recognition — Ph.D.

**Amsterdam, Jonathan Blair** Automated Qualitative Modeling of Dynamic Physical Systems — Ph.D.

**Atkins, Robert George** Microwave Scattering and Synthetic Aperture Radar Imaging of Targets Buried in Random Media — Ph.D.

**Ayers, Andrew Edward** Abstract Analysis and Optimization of Scheme — Ph.D.

**Bahl, Sandeep Raj** Physics and Technology of InAlAs/n+ – InGaAs HFET's — Ph.D.

**Barry, Richard A.** Wavelength Routing for All-Optical Networks — Ph.D.

**Cass, Todd Anthony** Polynomial-Time Geometric Matching for Object Recognition — Ph.D.

**Chaney, Ronald Dean** Feature Extraction Without Edge Detection — Ph.D.

**Christian, Kevin, G.** Generic Compression and Recall of Signals with Application to Dolphin Whistles — Ph.D.

**Chu, William** Inorganic X-Ray Mask Technology for Quantum-Effect Devices — Ph.D.

**Cormen, Thomas H.** Virtual Memory for Data-Parallel Computing — Ph.D.

**Crenshaw, Darius L.** Sidewall Passivation of Submicron Trench Structures in Silicon: Reactive Ion Etching Issues and Novel Passivation Dielectric Evaluation — Ph.D.

**Duchnowski, Paul** A New Structure for Automatic Speech Recognition — Sc.D.

**Eide, Ellen Marie** A Linguistic Feature Representation of the Speech Waveform — Ph.D.

**Eugster, Cristopher Conrad** Electron Waveguide Devices — Ph.D.

**Frost, Daniel Allen** The Dual Jump Diffusion Model for Security Prices — Ph.D.

**Ghanbari, Reza A.** Physics and Fabrication of Quasi-One-Dimensional Conductors — Ph.D.

**Goddeau, David Michael** An LR Parser-Based Probabilistic Language Model for Spoken Language Systems — Ph.D.

**Hall, Katherine Lavin** Femtosecond Nonlinearities in InGaAsP Diode Lasers — Ph.D.

**Hiller, Martha Jean** The Role of Chemical Mechanisms in Neural Computation and Learning — Ph.D.

**Horswill, Ian Douglas** Specialization of Perceptual Processes — Ph.D.

**Huff, Michael Allan** Silicon Micromachined Wafer-Bonded Valves — Ph.D.

**Jang, Yeona** HYDI: A Hybrid System with Feedback for Diagnosing Multiple Disorders — Ph.D.

**Jategaonkar, Lalita A.** Observing "True" Concurrency — Ph.D.

**Kahale, Nabil** Expander Graphs — Ph.D.

**Kim, Young-Jo** Physical Regulation of Cartilage Metabolism: Effects of Compression on Specific Matrix Molecules and Their Spatial Distribution — Ph.D.

**Krisch, Kathleen Susan** Mechanisms of Improved Reliability in Reoxidized Nitrided Oxide MOS Gate Dielectrics — Ph.D.

**Lam, Cheung-Wei** Modelling of Superconductors Transmission Lines and Three-dimensional High Speed Interconnects — Ph.D.

**Leeb, Steven B.** A Conjoint Pattern Recognition Approach to Nonintrusive Load Monitoring — Ph.D.

**Luettgen, Mark Robert** Image Processing with Multiscale Stochastic Models — Ph.D.

**Mahmood, S. Tanveer F.** Attentional Selection in Object Recognition — Ph.D.

**Melcher, Jennifer R.** The Cellular Generators of the Brainstem Auditory Evoked Potential — Ph.D.

**Milanfar, Peyman** Geometric Estimation and Reconstruction from Tomographic Data — Ph.D.

**Moel Modiano, Alberto** An Aligner for X-Ray Nanolithography — Sc.D.

**Mondschein, Susana V.** Optimal Sales Strategies in Stochastic, Dynamic Environments — Ph.D.

**Nabors, Keith Shelton** Efficient Three-Dimensional Capacitance Calculation — Ph.D.

**Nadeem, Shujaat** A 16-Channel Oversampled Analog-to-Digital Converter for Multichannel Applications — Ph.D.

**Nguyen, John** Compiler Analysis to Implement Point-to-Point Synchronization in Parallel Programs — Ph.D.

**Nussbaum, Daniel Seth** Run-time Thread Management for Large-Scale Distributed-Memory Multiprocessors — Ph.D.

**1993** (continued)

**Nuth, Peter Robert** The Named-State Register File — Ph.D.

**Olsen, James Jonathan** Control and Reliability of Optical Networks in Multiprocessors — Ph.D.

**Pang, Lily Yee** Ultrashort Optical Pulse Generation from High Power Diode Arrays — Ph.D.

**Papaefthymiou, Marios Christos** A Timing Analysis and Optimization System for Level-Clocked Circuitry — Ph.D.

**Power, Matthew Hayes** A Physical Measure of Consistency Among Speech Parameter Vectors: Application to Speech Intelligibility Determination — Ph.D.

**Reichelt, Mark William** Accelerated Waveform Relaxation Techniques for the Parallel Transient Simulation of Semiconductor Devices — Ph.D.

**Reinhold, Mark Baldwin** Cache Performance of Garbage-Collected Programming Languages — Ph.D.

**Rittenhouse, George Endicott** Mesoscopic Transport of Cooper Pairs Through Ballistic Superconductor-normal Metal-superconductor Junctions — Ph.D.

**Rozas, Guillermo Juan** Translucent Procedures, Abstraction Without Opacity — Ph.D.

**Sanger, Terence David** Theoretical Elements of Hierarchical Control in Vertebrate Motor Systems — Ph.D.

**Shepard, Scott R.** Phase of the Quantum Harmonic Oscillator — Ph.D.

**Simmons, Jane Marie Zarouni** End-to-End Reliable Communication in Data Networks — Ph.D.

**Simoncelli, Eero Peter** Distributed Representation and Analysis of Visual Motion — Ph.D.

**Srivatsan, Narayanan** Synthesis of Optimal Policies for Stochastic Manufacturing Systems — Ph.D.

**Stankovic, Aleksandar Mihajla** Random Pulse Modulation with Applications to Power Electronic Converters — Ph.D.

**Thompson, Barry Lyn** BiCMOS Phase-Locked Loops for Serial Data Communication — Ph.D.

**Vandevoorde, Mark Thierry** Exploiting Specifications to Improve Program Performance — Ph.D.

**Varghese, George** Self-Stabilization by Local Checking and Correction — Ph.D.

**Von Guggenberg, Philip Antony** Applications of Interdigital Dielectrometry to Moisture and Double Layer Measurements in Transformer Insulation — Ph.D.

**Wells, William Mercer, III** Statistical Object Recognition — Ph.D.

**Williamson, David Paul** On the Design of Approximation Algorithms for a Class of Graph Problems — Ph.D.

**Wu, Peng** A Knowledge Based Program for Selecting Problem Solving Paradigms — Ph.D.

**1994**

**Baltus, Donald George** Efficient Exploration of Affine Space-time Transformations for Optimal Systolic Array Synthesis — Ph.D.

**Bergman, Keren** Quantum Noise Reduction with Pulsed Light in Optical Fibers — Ph.D.

**Berlin, Andrew A.** Towards Intelligent Structures: Active Control of Buckling — Ph.D.

**Blank, Monica** High Efficiency Quasi-Optical Mode Converters for Overmoded Gyrotrons — Ph.D.

**Brewer, Eric A.** Portable High-performance Superconducting: High-level Platform Dependent Optimization — Ph.D.

**Bryant-Moore, Barbara Kirsten** An Analysis of Representations for Protein Structure Prediction — Ph.D.

**Chaiken, David Lars** Mechanisms and Interfaces for Software-Extended Coherent Shared Memory — Ph.D.

**Cheng, Tak Keung** The Excitation and Dynamics of Coherent Lattice Vibrations in Semimetals and Narrow-gap Semiconductors — Ph.D.

**Choi, Woo-Young** MBE-Grown Long Wavelength InGaAlAs/InP Laser Diodes — Ph.D.

**Cuomo, Kevin M.** Analysis and Synthesis of Self-Synchronizing Chaotic Systems — Ph.D.

**Daly, Nancy Ann** Acoustic-phonetic and Linguistic Analyses of Spontaneous Speech: Implications for Speech Understanding — Ph.D.

**Dron, Lisa Glitsch** Computing 3-D Motion in Custom Analog and Digital VLSI — Ph.D.

**Fung, Alex Weng Pui** Localization Transport in Granular and Nanoporous Carbon Systems — Ph.D.

**Haimowitz, Ira J.** Knowledge-based Trend Detection and Diagnosis — Ph.D.

**Hector, Scott D.** Optimization of Image Formation in X-Ray Lithography Using Rigorous Electromagnetic Theory and Experiments — Ph.D.

**Herrmann, Frederick Paul** An Integrated Associative Processing System — Ph.D.

**Hinman, Roderick Thornton** Recovered Energy Logic: A Logic Family and Power Supply Featuring Very High Efficiency — Ph.D.

**Horwat, Waldemar Peter** Active Abstractions — Ph.D.

**Huang, Yen-Chin** Empirical Distribution Function Statistics, Speed of Convergence, and P-Variation — Ph.D.

**Hultgren, Charles Timothy** Femtosecond Nonlinearities in AlGaAs Diode Laser Amplifiers — Ph.D.

**Hutchinson, James M.** A Radial Basis Function Approach to Financial Time Series Analysis — Ph.D.

**Hwang, Deborah Jing-Hwa** Function-Based Indexing for Object-Oriented Databases — Ph.D.

**Ingolfsson, Armann** Earthquake Forecasts: The Life-Saving Potential of Last-Minute Warnings — Ph.D.

**Jachner, Jacek** High-Resolution Direction Finding in Multi-Dimensional Scenarios — Sc.D.

**Karanicolas, Andrew Nicholas** Digital Self-calibration Techniques for High-accuracy, High Speed Analog-to-digital Converters — Ph.D.

**Kaushik, Sumanth** Design and Applications of a Soft X-Ray Detector Using GaAs Multiple Quantum Wells — Ph.D.

**Keen, John Sidney** Logging and Recovery in a Highly Concurrent Database — Ph.D.

**Kumar, Arvind S.** Single Electron Charging Effects in Quantum Dot Nanostructures — Ph.D.

**Kuszmaul, Bradley Clair** Synchronized MIMD Computing — Ph.D.

**Lee, Laurence Hongsing** Modeling and Design of Superconducting Microwave Passive Devices and Interconnects — Ph.D.

**1994** (continued)

**Leong, Tze-Yun** An Integrated Approach to Dynamic Decision Making Under Uncertainty — Ph.D.

**Li, Ying** Probabilistic Interpretations of Fuzzy Sets and Systems — Ph.D.

**Lindblad, Christopher John** A Programming System for the Dynamic Manipulation of Temporally Sensitive Data — Ph.D.

**Lopez, Jose Elias** Structurally Constrained Control Systems Using a Factorization Approach — Ph.D.

**Lucente, Mark** Diffraction-specific Fringe Computation for Electro-Holography — Ph.D.

**Mataric, Maja J.** Interaction and Intelligent Behavior — Ph.D.

**McIlrath, Lisa G.** Computing 3-D Motion in Custom Analog and Digital VLSI — Ph.D.

**McNeil, Vincent Maurice** A Thin-film Silicon Microaccelerometer Fabricated Using Electrochemical Etch-Stop and Wafer Bonding Technology — Ph.D.

**Miller, Eric Lawrence** The Application of Multiscale and Stochastic Techniques to the Solution of Inverse Problems — Ph.D.

**Moore, Barbara B.** An Analysis of Representations for Protein Structure Prediction — Ph.D.

**Moores, John D.** All-Optical Soliton Communications: Devices and Limitations — Ph.D.

**Narasimhan, Sundar** Task Level Strategies for Robots — Ph.D.

**Nicolas, Julien J.** Investigation of Coding and Equalization for the Digital HDTV Terrestrial Broadcast Channel — Sc.D.

**Oates, John H.** Propagation and Scattering of Electromagnetic Waves in Complex Environments — Ph.D.

**Parker, Lynne Edwards** Heterogeneous Multi-Robot Cooperation — Ph.D.

**Paye, Malini** Femtosecond Pulse Generation in Solid-State Lasers — Ph.D.

**Pollard, Nancy S.** Parallel Methods for Synthesizing Whole-Hand Grasps from Generalized Prototypes — Ph.D.

**Richard, Michael D.** Estimation and Detection with Chaotic Systems — Sc.D.

**Sarachik, Karen Beth** An Analysis of the Effect of Gaussian Error in Object Recognition — Ph.D.

**Seidel, Mark N.** Switched-Capacitor Networks for Image Processing: Analysis, Synthesis, Response Bounding, and Implementation — Sc.D.

**Shen, Amelia Huimin** Probabilistic Representation and Manipulation of Boolean Functions Using Free Boolean Diagrams — Ph.D.

**Sherstinsky, Alexander** M-Lattice: A System for Signal Synthesis and Processing Based on Reaction-Diffusion — Sc.D.

**Shinn-Cunningham, Barbara Gail** Adaptation to Supernormal Auditory Localization Cues in an Auditory Virtual Environment — Ph.D.

**Silveira, Luis Miguel** Model Order Reduction Techniques for Circuit Simulation — Ph.D.

**Smith, Stephen Paul** Studies of Stimulated Brillouin Scattering in Optical Fibers and Applications — Sc.D.

**Staats, Richard Charles** Integration of Predictive Routing Information with Dynamic Traffic Signal Control — Ph.D.

**Su, Lisa Tzu-Feng** Extreme-Submicrometer Silicon-on-Insulator (SOI) MOSFETs — Ph.D.

**Subirana-Vilanova, J. Brian** Mid-level Vision and Recognition of Non-rigid Objects — Ph.D.

**Tam, Kimo Y.F.** A Josephson Junction Bridge Track and Hold Circuit — Sc.D.

**Tan, Yang Meng** Formal Specification Techniques for Promoting Software Modularity, Enhancing Documentation, and Testing Specifications — Ph.D.

**Tassoudji, Mohammad Ali** Electromagnetic Interference in Electronic Circuits and Systems — Ph.D.

**Telichevesky, Ricardo** A Numerical Engine for Distributed Sparse Matrices — Ph.D.

**Troxel, Gregory Donald** Time Surveying: Clock Synchronization over Packet Networks — Ph.D.

**Turbak, Franklyn Albin** Slivers, Computational Modularity via Synchronized Lazy Aggregates — Ph.D.

**Veysoglu, Murat E.** Direct and Inverse Scattering Models for Random Media and Rough Surfaces — Ph.D.

**Wilson, Timothy A.** Cochlear Macromechanical Modeling — Sc.D.

**Wissinger, John Weakley** Distributed Nonparametric Training Algorithms for Hypothesis Testing Networks — Ph.D.

**Young, Albert Min-Hsien** Microfabricated Pressure Transducers Based on Anti-Resonant Reflecting Optical Waveguides — Ph.D.

**Younis, Saed G.** Asymptotically Zero Energy Computing Using Split-Level Charge Recovery Logic — Ph.D.

**Zangi, Kambiz Casey** Optimal Feedback Control Formulation of the Active Noise Cancellation Problem: Pointwise and Distributed — Ph.D.

**Zhou, Zen-Hong** Real Time in-situ Monitoring and Control of Silicon Epitaxy by Fourier Transform Infrared Spectroscopy — Ph.D.

**1995**

**Alter, Tao Daniel** The Role of Saliency and Error Propagation in Visual Object Recognition — Ph.D.

**Alvelda, Phillip** VLSI Microdisplays and Optoelectronic Technology — Ph.D.

**Aslam, Javed A.** Noise Tolerant Algorithms for Learning and Searching — Ph.D.

**Bergman, Ruth** Learning Models of Environments with Manifest Causal Structure — Ph.D.

**Betke, Margrit** Learning and Vision Algorithms for Robot Navigation — Ph.D.

**Beymer, David James** Pose-invariant Face Recognition Using Real and Virtual Views — Ph.D.

**Blumofe, Robert David** Executing Multithreaded Programs Efficiently — Ph.D.

**Branicky, Michael S.** Studies in Hybrid Systems: Modeling, Analysis and Control — Sc.D.

**Brennan, James Francis, III** Near Infrared Raman Spectroscopy for Human Artery Histochemistry and Histopathology — Ph.D.

**Burkhardt, Martin** Fabrication Technology and Measurement of Coupled Quantum Dot Devices — Ph.D.

**Burman, Mitchell Henry** New Results in Flow Line Analysis — Ph.D.

**Casadei, Stefano** Robust Detection of Curves in Images — Ph.D.

**1995** (continued)

**Chan, Vei-Han** Hot-Carrier Reliability Evaluation for CMOS Devices and Circuits — Ph.D.

**Chang, Eric I-Chao** Improving Wordspotting Performance with Limited Training Data — Ph.D.

**Clark, Tracy Mark** Position Sensing and Control of a Linear Synchronous Motor — Sc.D.

**Dabby, Diana Stephanie** Musical Variations from a Chaotic Mapping — Ph.D.

**Day, Mark Stuart** Client Cache Management in a Distributed Object Database — Ph.D.

**Doerr, Christopher Richard** Toward a Noise-Free Interferometric Fiber Optic Gyroscope — Ph.D.

**Douglas, Joel Seth** Identification of Parametric Uncertainty for the Control of Flexible Structures — Ph.D.

**Eidson, Donald Brian** State Estimation and Hierarchical Control of Electric Power Systems — Ph.D.

**Fieguth, Paul Werner** Application of Multiscale Estimation to Large Scale Multidimensional Imaging and Remote Sensing Problems — Ph.D.

**Fiske, James Alexander Stuart** Thread Scheduling Mechanisms for Multiple-Context Parallel Processors — Ph.D.

**Flynn, Anita M.** Piezoelectric Ultrasonic Micrometers — Ph.D.

**Gawlick, Rainer** Admission Control and Routing: Theory and Practice — Ph.D.

**Ghemawat, Sanjay** The Modified Object Buffer: A Storage Management Technique for Object-Oriented Databases — Ph.D.

**Greenberg, David Ross** The Physics and Technology of the AlGaAs/n+ – InGaAs/GaAs Heterostructure Field-Effect Transistor — Ph.D.

**Gupta, Shail Aditya** Functional Encapsulation and Type Reconstruction in a Strongly-typed, Polymorphic Language — Ph.D.

**Harris, Robert Michael** Geometric Simulation of Microfabricated Structures — Ph.D.

**Hetherington, Irvine Lee** A Characterization of the Problem of New, Out-of-Vocabulary Words in Continuous-speech Recognition and Understanding — Ph.D.

**Hsieh, Wilson Cheng-Yi** Dynamic Computation Migration in Distributed Shared Memory Systems — Ph.D.

**Irving, William Wood** Multiscale Stochastic Realization and Model Identification with Applications to Large-Scale Estimation Problems — Ph.D.

**Isabelle, Steven Hamilton** A Signal Processing Framework for the Analysis and Application of Chaotic Systems — Ph.D.

**Jacobs, Jarvis Benjamin** Modeling of Electron Transport in Sub-100 nm Channel Length Silicon MOSFETs — Ph.D.

**Kassel, Robert Howard** A Comparison of Approaches to On-Line Handwritten Character Recognition — Ph.D.

**Li, Kevin** Finite Difference-time Domain Analysis of Electromagnetic Interference and Radiation Problems — Ph.D.

**Li, Peter Cheng-Lung** Direct Detection Optical Systems: Intersymbol Interference and Electrical Filter Designs — Ph.D.

**Lim, Beng-Hong** Reactive Synchronization Algorithms for Multiprocessors — Ph.D.

**Lin, Chia-Liang** Theoretical and Experimental Studies of a 17 GHz Photocathode RF Gun — Ph.D.

**Liu, Sharlene Anne** Landmark Detection for Distinctive Feature-based Speech Recognition — Ph.D.

**Livstone, Mitchell M.** Identification, Robust Adaptation and Iterative Schemes — Ph.D.

**Luo, Xiaodong** Continuous Linear Programming: Theory, Algorithms and Applications — Ph.D.

**Maa, Gino Ko** Integrating Compile-time and Runtime Parallelism Management through Revocable Thread Serialization — Ph.D.

**Medard, Muriel** The Capacity of Time Varying Multiple User Channels in Wireless Communications — Sc.D.

**Meng, Helen Mei-Ling** Phonological Parsing for Bi-directional Letter-to-Sound/Sound-to-Letter Generation — Ph.D.

**Menninger, William Libbey** Relativistic Harmonic Gyration Traveling-Wave Tube Amplifier Experiments — Ph.D.

**Niyogi, Partha** The Informational Complexity of Learning from Examples — Ph.D.

**Osterberg, Peter Maynard** Electrostatically Actuated Microelectromechanical Test Structures for Material Property Measurement — Ph.D.

**Patt, Boaz** A Theory of Clock Synchronization — Ph.D.

**Polymenakos, Lazaros C.** $\varepsilon$-Relaxation and Auction Algorithms for the Convex Cost Network Flow Problem — Ph.D.

**Ponzio, Stephen John** Restricted Branching Programs and Hardware Verification — Ph.D.

**Raghavan, S.** Formulations and Algorithms for Network Design Problems with Connectivity Requirements — Ph.D.

**Rahmat, Khalid** Simulation of Hot Carriers in Semiconductor Devices — Ph.D.

**Ramaswamy, Ganesh Nachiappa** Modal Structures and Model Reduction, with Application to Power System Equivalencing — Ph.D.

**Rees, Jonathan A.** A Security Kernel Based on the Lambda-Calculus — Ph.D.

**Rider, Todd Harrison** Fundamental Limitations on Plasma Fusion Systems Not in Thermodynamic Equilibrium — Ph.D.

**Segala, Roberto** Modeling and Verification of Randomized Distributed Real-Time Systems — Ph.D.

**Shenoy, Krishna Vaughn** Monolithic Optoelectronic VLSI Circuit Design and Fabrication for Optical Interconnects — Ph.D.

**Shepard, Timothy Jason** Decentralization Channel Management in Scalable Multihop Spread-spectrum Packet Radio Networks — Ph.D.

**Shumsky, Robert A.** Dynamic Statistical Models for the Prediction of Aircraft Take-off Times — Ph.D.

**Sinha, Pawan** Perceiving and Recognizing Three-Dimensional Forms — Ph.D.

**Skordos, Panayotis Augoustos** Modeling Flue Pipes: Subsonic Flow, Lattice Boltzmann, and Parallel Distributed Computers — Ph.D.

**Smet, Jurgen Hubert** Intrawell and Interwell Intersubband Transitions in Single and Multiple Quantum Well Heterostructures — Ph.D.

**Szajda, Kenneth Stanley** A High Resolution Integrated Circuit Biomedical Temperature Sensing System — Ph.D.

**1995** (continued)

**Tamura, Kohichi Robert** Additive Pulse Mode-locked Erbium-doped Fiber Lasers — Ph.D.

**Theodosopoulos, Theodore** Stochastic Models for Global Optimization — Ph.D.

**Thomke, Stefan H.** The Economics of Experimentation in the Design of New Products and Processes — Ph.D.

**Toledo, Sivan Avraham** Quantitative Performance Modeling of Scientific Computations and Creating Locality in Numerical Algorithms — Ph.D.

**Tolikas, Mary** Dual-Energy Electromagnetic Modeling, with Application to Variable Reluctance Motor Analysis — Ph.D.

**Tse, David N.C.** Variable-rate Lossy Compression and Its Effects on Communication Networks — Ph.D.

**Umminger, Christopher Bruce** Integrated Analog Focal Plane Processing for Automatic Alignment — Ph.D.

**Viola, Paul A.** Alignment by Maximization of Mutual Information — Ph.D.

**Waldspurger, Carl A.** Lottery and Stride Scheduling: Flexible Proportional-Share Resource Management — Ph.D.

**Washabaugh, Andrew Patrick** Flow Induced Electrification of Liquid Insulated Systems — Ph.D.

**Wilde, Lorin Fern** Analysis and Synthesis of Fricative Consonants — Ph.D.

**Wong, Vincent V.** Fabrication of Distributed Feedback Devices Using X-Ray Lithography — Ph.D.

**Wyss, Rolf Andreas** Far-Infrared Radiation Response of Antenna-Coupled Quantum Effect Devices — Ph.D.

**1996**

**Adams, Laura Ellen** All-optical Clock Recovery Using a Mode-locked Fiber Figure-eight Laser with a Semiconductor Nonlinearity — Ph.D.

**Aggarwal, Rajni J.** Design of Resonant-tunneling Diodes for a GaAs Integrated SRAM — Ph.D.

**Bachelder, Ivan Andrew** Visual Map-making and Guided Reinforcement Learning for Mobile Robot Navigation: A Neurocomputational Approach — Ph.D.

**Bloomstein, Theodore M.** Laser Microchemical Etching of Silicon — Sc.D.

**Bolotski, Michael** Abacus: A Reconfigurable Bit-Parallel Architecture for Early Vision — Ph.D.

**Buck, John Richard** Single Mode Excitation in the Shallow Water Acoustic Channel Using Feedback Control — Ph.D.

**Chapman, Jeffrey Wayne** Power System Control for Large-Disturbance Stability: Security, Robustness and Transient Energy — Ph.D.

**Chen, Jerry Chia-yung** Electromagnetic Field Computation and Photonic Band Gap Devices — Ph.D.

**Chen, Yu Ju** A Comprehensive Electromagnetic Analysis of AC Losses in Large Superconducting Cables — Ph.D.

**Cheung, Shiufun** Biorthogonality in Lapped Transforms: A Study in High-quality Audio Compression — Ph.D.

**Damask, Jay N.** Integrated-Optic Grating-Based Filters for Optical Communication Systems — Ph.D.

**Darwish, Ali Mohamed** Wavelength Conversion by Four Wave Mixing in Passive InGaAsP/InP Waveguides — Ph.D.

**DeHon, André** Reconfigurable Architectures for General-Purpose Computing — Ph.D.

**Dellarocas, Chrysanthos N.** A Coordinate Perspective on Software Architecture: Towards a Design Handbook for Integrating Software Components — Ph.D.

**de Marcken, Carl Gustave** Unsupervised Language Acquisition — Ph.D.

**Dennison, Larry Robert** The Reliable Router: An Architecture for Fault Tolerant Interconnect — Ph.D.

**Elia, Nicola** Computational Methods for Multi-Objective Control — Ph.D.

**Ellis, Daniel Patrick Whittlesey** Prediction-Driven Computational Auditory Scene Analysis — Ph.D.

**Galperin, Igal** On Consulting a Set of Experts and Searching — Ph.D.

**Gennaro, Rosario** Theory and Practice of Verifiable Secret Sharing — Ph.D.

**Givan, Robert Lawrence** Automatically Inferring Properties of Computer Programs — Ph.D.

**Goodberlet, James Gregory** An Experimental Investigation of a Table-top, Laser-driven Extreme Ultraviolet Laser — Ph.D.

**Gudbjartsson, Hakon** Magnetic Resonance Imaging of Diffusion in the Presence of Physiological Motion — Ph.D.

**Hasegawa-Johnson, Marik A.** Formant and Burst Spectral Measurements with Quantitative Error Models for Speech Sound Classification — Ph.D.

**Henry, Dana Sue** Hardware Mechanisms for Efficient Interprocessor Communication — Ph.D.

**Ho, Easen** Growth and Doping of Zinc Selenide Using Alternative Gaseous Source Epitaxial Techniques — Ph.D.

**Hsu, Chih-Chien** Theoretical Models for Microwave Remote Sensing of Forests and Vegetation — Ph.D.

**Jankowski, Charles Robert** Fine Structure Features for Speaker Identification — Ph.D.

**Jansen, Eckart Werner** Electric Micromotor with Integrated Rotor Motion Sensors — Ph.D.

**Jim, Trevor** Principal Typings and Type Inference — Ph.D.

**Joerg, Christopher Frank** The Cilk System for Parallel Multithreaded Computing — Ph.D.

**Johnson, Joel Tidmore** Applications of Numerical Models for Rough Surface Scattering — Ph.D.

**Johnson, Kirk Lauritz** High-performance All-software Distributed Shared Memory — Ph.D.

**Johnson, Mark** Formant and Burst Spectral Measurements with Quantitative Error Models for Speech Sound Classification — Ph.D.

**Jones, Lawrence Anthony** Dynamic Electrode Forces in Gas Metal Arc Welding — Ph.D.

**Khatri, Farzana Ibrahim** Optical Soliton Propagation and Control — Ph.D.

**Kleinberg, Jon M.** Approximation Algorithms for Disjoint Paths Problems — Ph.D.

**LaMacchia, Brian Andrew** Internet Fish — Ph.D.

**Lenz, Gadi** Femtosecond Sources at 1.5 Microns and Their Application for Time-Resolved Spectroscopic Studies of Semiconductor Devices — Ph.D.

**Liao, Kenneth Sen-Chun** Vertical Profile Engineering and Reliability Study of Silicon-Germanium Heterojunction Bipolar Transistors — Ph.D.

**Liao, Stan Y.** Code Generation and Optimization for Embedded Digital Signal Processors — Ph.D.

**1996** (continued)

**Lin, Philip Jin-Yi** Wide Area Optical Backbone Networks — Ph.D.

**Lipson, Pamela Robin** Context and Configuration Based Scene Classification — Ph.D.

**Martin, David Andrew** ADAP—A Mixed-signal Array Processor with Early Vision Applications — Ph.D.

**Mattia, John Paul** AC Modeling of Resonant-Tunneling Diodes in the Scattering-Dominated Regime — Ph.D.

**McNamara, Thomas William** Nonvolatile Hologram Storage in $BaTiO_3$ — Ph.D.

**McQuirk, Ignacio Sean** An Analog VLSI Chip for Estimating the Focus of Expansion — Sc.D.

**Monteiro, José Carlos Alves Pereira** A Computer-Aided Design Methodology for Low Power Sequential Logic Circuits — Ph.D.

**O'Toole, James William** Effective Information Sharing Using Update Logs — Ph.D.

**Paschalidis, Ioannis C.** Large Deviations in High Speed Communication Networks — Ph.D.

**Polley, Michael Oliver** Spectrum-Efficient Modulation and Channel Coding for Terrestrial Broadcasting — Ph.D.

**Richmond, Christ David** Adaptive Array Signal Processing and Performance Analysis in Non-Gaussian Environments — Ph.D.

**Savari, Serap Aye** Variable-to-fixed Length Codes for Sources with Known and Unknown Memory — Ph.D.

**Shatz, Lisa Fran** The Effect of Hair Bundle Shape on Hair Bundle Hydrodynamics of Sensory Cells in the Inner Ear — Ph.D.

**Sheldon, Mark Alan** Content Routing: A Scalable Architecture for Network-based Information Discovery — Ph.D.

**Siapas, Athanassios G.** Criticality and Parallelism in Combinatorial Optimization — Ph.D.

**Singer, Andrew Carl** Signal Processing and Communication with Solitons — Ph.D.

**Singh, Mona** Learning Algorithms with Applications to Robot Navigation and Protein Folding — Ph.D.

**Slonim, Donna K.** Learning from Imperfect Data in Theory and Practice — Ph.D.

**Srinivasan, Kamakshi** Integrated Design of High-Speed Permanent-Magnet Synchronous Motor Drives — Ph.D.

**Stata, Raymond P.** Modularity in the Presence of Subclassing — Sc.D.

**Sundaram, Ravi** Interactive Proof System Variants and Approximation Algorithms for Optical Networks — Ph.D.

**Sung, Kah Kay** Learning and Example Selection for Object and Pattern Detection — Ph.D.

**Tan, Hong Zhang** Information Transmission with a Multi-Finger Tactual Display — Ph.D.

**Walrath, Karen Elizabeth** Evanescent Wave Spectroscopy for Detection of Water and Water Treeing in Polymers — Ph.D.

**Wee, Susie Jung-Ah** Scalable Video Coding — Ph.D.

**Wertheimer, Jeremy Michael** Reasoning from Experiments to Causal Models in Molecular Cell Biology — Ph.D.

**Yoo, Chang Dong** Speech Enhancement: Identification and Modeling of Stationary Time-frequency Regions — Ph.D.

**Yu, Paul Chuan-Wei** Low-Power Design Techniques for Pipelined Analog-to-Digital Converters — Ph.D.

**Zobian, Assef A.** A Framework for Cost-Based Pricing of Transmission and Ancillary Services in Competitive Electric Power Markets — Sc.D.

**1997**

**Apostolopoulos, John George** Transform/Subband Representations for Multidimensional Signals with Arbitrary Regions of Support — Ph.D.

**Brothers, Louis Reginald** Terahertz Optical Frequency Comb Generation — Ph.D.

**Cardell, Judith Bernitt** Integrating Small Scale Distributed Generation into a Deregulated Market: Control Strategies and Price Feedback — Ph.D.

**Chaudhari, Upendra Vasant** Probabilistic Pursuit, Classification, and Speech — Ph.D.

**Chiu, Angela Lan** Full Utilization, Fairness, and Access Delay on High Speed Slotted Bus Networks — Ph.D.

**Chong, Frederic Tsyh-An** Parallel Communication Mechanisms for Sparse, Irregular Applications — Ph.D.

**Chou, Andrew** Static Replication of Exotic Options — Ph.D.

**Daniel, Michael M.** Multiresolution Statistical Modeling with Application to Modeling Groundwater Flow — Ph.D.

**Davis, Charles Quentin** Measuring Nanometer, Three-dimensional Motions with Light Microscopy — Ph.D.

**Decker, Steven John** A Wide Dynamic Range CMOS Imager with Parallel On-Chip Analog-to-digital Conversion — Ph.D.

**Deffenbaugh, Max** Optimal Ocean Acoustic Tomography and Navigation with Moving Sources — Sc.D.

**de la Maza, Michael** Together Structures — Ph.D.

**Eggen, Trym H.** Underwater Acoustic Communication over Doppler Spread Channels — Ph.D.

**Ettinger, Gil J.** Hierarchical Three-dimensional Medical Image Registration — Ph.D.

**Fleischer, Siegfried B.** Ultrafast Dynamics of Fullerene Thin Films — Ph.D.

**Gealow, Jeffrey C.** An Integrated Computing Structure for Pixel-Parallel Image Processing — Sc.D.

**Gruber, Robert Edward** Optimism vs. Locking: A Study of Concurrency Control for Client-server Object-Oriented Databases — Ph.D.

**Gupta, Raj Kumra** Electrostatic Pull-in Test Structure Design for in-situ Mechanical Property Measurements of Microelectromechanical Systems (MEMS) — Ph.D.

**Halevi, Shai** Theory and Practice of Secret Commitment — Ph.D.

**Hauskrecht, Milos** Planning and Control in Stochastic Domains with Imperfect Information — Ph.D.

**Hee, Michael Richard** Optical Coherence Tomography of the Eye — Ph.D.

**Hsu, Charles Heng-Yuan** Silicon Microaccelerometer Fabrication Technologies — Ph.D.

**Jaggi, Seema** Multiscale Geometric Feature Extraction and Object Recognition — Ph.D.

**Jones, Michael Jeffrey** Multidimensional Morphable Models: A Framework for Representing and Matching Object Classes — Ph.D.

**Karu, Zoher Z.** Fast Subpixel Registration of 3-D Images — Ph.D.

**Kim, Won-jong** High-precision Planar Magnetic Levitator — Ph.D.

**1997** (continued)

**Knobe, Kathleen Beth** The Subspace Model: Shape-based Compilation for Parallel Systems — Ph.D.

**Krska, Jee-Hoon Yap** SIMOX Buried-Oxide Conduction Mechanisms — Ph.D.

**Lam, Warren Michael** Multiscale Methods for the Analysis and Application of Fractal Point Processes and Queues — Ph.D.

**Learned, Rachel E.** Low Complexity Optimal Joint Detection for Over-Saturated Multiple Access Communications — Ph.D.

**Lethin, Richard Anton** Message-Driven Dynamics — Ph.D.

**Linden, Derek S.** Automated Design and Optimization of Wire Antennas Using Genetic Algorithms — Ph.D.

**Lloyd, Jennifer Anne** An Integrated Circuit Pressure Sensing System with Adaptive Linearity Calibration — Ph.D.

**Ludwig, Jeffrey Thomas** Low Power Digital Filtering Using Adaptive Approximate Processing — Ph.D.

**Lutsky, Joseph Joachim** A Sealed Cavity Thin-film Acoustic Resonator Process for RF Bandpass Filters — Ph.D.

**Maheshwari, Umesh** Garbage Collection in a Large, Distributed Object Store — Ph.D.

**Metcalf, Christopher David** Managing Scheduled Routing with a High-level Communications Language — Ph.D.

**Moghaddam, Baback** Probabilistic Visual Learning for Object Detection and Recognition — Ph.D.

**Narula, Aradhana** Information Theoretic Analysis of Multiple-Antenna Transmission Diversity — Ph.D.

**Nelson, Lynn Elizabeth** Mode-locking of Thulium-doped and Erbium-doped Fiber Lasers — Ph.D.

**Ofori-Tenkorang, John** Permanent-Magnet Synchronous Motors and Associated Power Electronics for Direct-Drive Vehicle Propulsion — Sc.D.

**Parameswaran, Lalitha** Integrated Silicon Pressure Sensors Using Wafer Bonding Technology — Ph.D.

**Patek, Stephen David** Stochastic and Shortest Path Games: Theory and Algorithms — Ph.D.

**Perreault, Brian Michael** A Novel Position-Sensing, Control, and Communication System for Automated Transportation — Ph.D.

**Perreault, David John** Design and Evaluation of Cellular Power Converter Architectures — Ph.D.

**Perrott, Michael Henderson** Techniques for High Data Rate Modulation and Low Power Operation of Fractional-N Frequency Synthesizers — Ph.D.

**Phillips, Joel Reuben** Rapid Solution of Potential Integral Equations in Complicated 3-dimensional Geometries — Ph.D.

**Ringrose, Robert** Self-Stabilizing Running — Ph.D.

**Robles Alegria, Jose L.** Contact Interpretation in Randomized Strategies for Robotic Assembly — Ph.D.

**Rodriguez, Luis Humberto, Jr.** View-based Abstraction: Enhancing Maintainability and Modularity in the Presence of Implementation Dependencies — Ph.D.

**Shen, Eric Bertrand** Alternative Topological Approaches to the Electronic Lamp Ballast — Ph.D.

**Shoemaker, David Robert** An Optimized Hardware Architecture and Communication Protocol for Scheduled Communication — Ph.D.

**Shrauger, Vernon Eugene** Development of a Silicon VLSI Optically Addressed Liquid Crystal Smart Spatial Light Modulator — Ph.D.

**Smith, Mark Anthony Shawn** Formal Verification of TCP and T/TCP — Ph.D.

**Sobalvarro, Patrick G.** Demand-based Coscheduling of Parallel Jobs on Multiprogrammed Multiprocessors — Ph.D.

**Sobek, Daniel** Microfabricated Fused Silica Flow Chambers for Flow Cytometry — Ph.D.

**Stasior, William F.** An Interactive Approach to the Identification and Extraction of Visual Events — Ph.D.

**Sunshine, Lon Eric** HDTV Transmission Format Conversion and Migration Path — Ph.D.

**Tearney, Guillermo J.** Optical Biopsy of In Vivo Tissue Using Optical Coherence Tomography — Ph.D.

**Thompson, Marc Thomas** High Temperature Superconducting Magnetic Suspension for Maglev — Ph.D.

**Velazquez, Scott Richard** Hybrid Filter Banks for Analog/Digital Conversion — Ph.D.

**Wallach, Deborah Anne** High-Performance Application-Specific Networking — Ph.D.

**Wang, John Yu An** Layered Image Representation: Identification of Coherent Components in Image Sequences — Ph.D.

**Yang, Isabel Y.** Study of Sub-0.5 µm SOI-with-Active-Substrate (SOIAS) Technology for Ultra-Low Power Applications — Ph.D.

**1998**

**Abounadi, Jinane** Stochastic Approximation for Non-expansive Maps: Application to Q-Learning Algorithms — Ph.D.

**Afridi, Khurram Khan** A Methodology for the Design and Evaluation of Advanced Automotive Electrical Power Systems — Ph.D.

**Akerson, Jerome Jeffrey** Numerical Techniques for Electromagnetic Applications in Microelectronic and Radar Imaging Systems — Ph.D.

**Allen, Eric Hickcox** Stochastic Unit Commitment in a Deregulated Electric Utility Industry — Ph.D.

**Bailey, Joseph P.** Intermediation and Electronic Markets: Aggregation and Pricing in Internet Commerce — Ph.D.

**Berman, David** The Aluminum Single-Electron Transistor for Ultrasensitive Electrometry of Semiconductor Quantum-Confined Systems — Ph.D.

**Boyd, Mary Jane** Intelligent On-line Transformer Monitoring, Diagnostics, and Decision Making — Ph.D.

**Brungart, Douglas Scott** Near-field Auditory Localization — Ph.D.

**Carter, David John Donat** Sub-50nm X-ray Lithography with Application to a Coupled Quantum Dot Device — Ph.D.

**Catravas, Palmyra Evangeline** Non-perturbative Electron Beam Characterization with a Microwiggler — Ph.D.

**Chalom, Edmond** Statistical Image Sequence Segmentation Using Multidimensional Attributes — Ph.D.

**Chang, Jane Wen** Near-miss Modeling: A Segment-based Approach to Speech Recognition — Ph.D.

**Charny, Anna** Providing QoS Guarantees in Input Buffered Crossbar Switches with Speedup — Ph.D.

1998 (continued)

**Cherkassky, Alexander** Metrology of Very Thin Silicon Epitaxial Films — Sc.D.

**Chou, Mike Chuan** Fast Algorithms for Ill-conditioned Dense Matrix Problems in VLSI Interconnect and Substrate Modeling — Ph.D.

**Coorg, Satyan R.** Pose Imagery and Automated Three-dimensional Modeling of Urban Environments — Ph.D.

**Desloge, Joseph Gilles** The Location-Estimating, Null-Steering (LENS) Algorithm for Adaptive Microphone-Array Processing — Ph.D.

**Ernstmeyer, James** Lightning-excited, Quasi-electrostatic Effects in the Lower Ionosphere — Sc.D.

**Escobar Fernández de la Vega, Marcos** Approximate Solutions for Multi-server Queuing Systems with Erlangian Service Times and an Application to Air Traffic Management — Ph.D.

**Flammia, Giovanni** Discourse Segmentation of Spoken Dialogue: An Empirical Approach — Ph.D.

**Gabbay, Lynn Daniel** Computer Aided Macromodeling for MEMS — Ph.D.

**Golubovic, Boris** Study of Near-infrared Pumped Solid-sate Lasers and Applications — Ph.D.

**Hazen, Timothy James** The Use of Speaker Correlation Information for Automatic Speech Recognition — Ph.D.

**Ho, Terrence Tian-Jian** Multiscale Modeling and Estimation of Large-scale Dynamic Systems — Ph.D.

**Houh, Henry H.** Designing Networks for Tomorrow's Traffic — Ph.D.

**House, Jody** The Growth and Microstructural Characterization of ZnSe/GaAs Quantum Wells and Double Heterostructures — Sc.D.

**Hung, Elmer S.** Positioning, Control, and Dynamics of Electrostatic Actuators for Use in Optical and RF Systems — Ph.D.

**Isbell, Charles Lee** Sparse Multi-level Representations for Text Retrieval — Ph.D.

**Jackson, Deron Keith** Inductively-coupled Power Transfer for Electromechanical Systems — Ph.D.

**Jiang, Wenjie** Hot-carrier Reliability Assessment in CMOS Digital Integrated Circuits — Ph.D.

**Joseph, Anthony Douglas** Mobile Computing with the Rover Toolkit — Ph.D.

**Kamon, Mattan** Fast Parasitic Extraction and Simulation of Three-dimensional Interconnect via Quasistatic Analysis — Ph.D.

**Keckler, Stephen William** Fast Thread Communication and Synchronization Mechanisms for a Scalable Single Chip Multiprocessor — Ph.D.

**Kubiatowicz, John** Integrated Shared-memory and Message-passing Communication in the Alewife Multiprocessor — Ph.D.

**Lau, Raymond** Subword Lexical Modeling for Speech Recognition — Ph.D.

**Levow, Gina-Anne** Characterizing and Recognizing Spoken Corrections in Human–Computer Dialog — Ph.D.

**Lyons, Robert Joseph** Determining Distributed Source Waveforms in Casual, Lossy, Dispersive, Plane-wave (CLDP) Materials — Ph.D.

**Mackenzie, Kenneth Martin** An Efficient Virtual Network Interface in the FUGU Scalable Workstation — Ph.D.

**Maley, Carlo Casebier** The Evolution of Biodiversity: A Simulation Approach — Ph.D.

**Marbach, Peter** Simulation-Based Optimization of Markov Decision Processes — Ph.D.

**Maron, Oded** Learning from Ambiguity — Ph.D.

**Matsuoka, Yoky** Models of Generalization in Motor Control — Ph.D.

**McCandless, Michael Kyle** A Model for Interactive Computation: Applications to Speech Research — Ph.D.

**Micciancio, Daniele** On the Hardness of the Shortest Vector Problem — Ph.D.

**Mitwalli, Ahmed H.** Polymer Gel Actuators and Sensors — Sc.D.

**Ooi, James M.** A Framework for Low-Complexity Communication over Channels with Feedback — Ph.D.

**Papadopoulos, Haralabos Christos** Efficient Digital Encoding and Estimation of Noisy Signals — Ph.D.

**Randall, Keith Harold** Cilk: Efficient Multithreaded Computing — Ph.D.

**Rao, Satyajit** Visual Routines and Attention — Ph.D.

**Royter, Yakov** Monolithic Integration of Etched Facet Lasers with GaAs VLSI Circuits — Ph.D.

**Shaw, Andrew** Compiling for Parallel Multithreaded Computation on Symmetric Multiprocessors — Ph.D.

**Sherony, Melanie Jane** Design, Process, and Reliability Considerations in Silicon-On-Insulator (SOI) MOSFETs — Ph.D.

**Shih, Shih-En** Direct and Inverse Scattering Models for Electromagnetic Remote Sensing of Time-varying Sea Ice and Snow Cover — Ph.D.

**Somerville, Mark Harold** Limiting Physics of mm-Wave InP Power High Electron Mobility Transistors — Ph.D.

**Spertus, Ellen R.** ParaSite: Mining the Structural Information on the World-Wide Web — Ph.D.

**Stein, Gideon P.** Geometric and Photometric Constraints: Motion and Structure from Three Views — Sc.D.

**Steward, Duane Allen** Utility Assessment Based on Individualized Patient Perspectives — Ph.D.

**Stine, Brian Eugene** A General Methodology for Assessing and Characterizing Variation in Semiconductor Manufacturing — Ph.D.

**Van Roy, Benjamin** Learning and Value Function Approximation in Complex Decision Processes — Ph.D.

**Xu, Bin** Development of Intersubband Terahertz Lasers Using Multiple Quantum Well Structures — Ph.D.

**Yeung, Donald** Multigrain Shared Memory — Ph.D.

**Yuret, Deniz** Discovery of Linguistic Relations Using Lexical Attraction — Ph.D.

1999

**Adya, Atul** Weak Consistency: A Generalized Theory and Optimistic Implementations for Distributed Transactions — Ph.D.

**Amirtharajah, Rajeevan** Design of Low Power VLSI Systems Powered by Ambient Mechanical Vibration — Ph.D.

**Ang, Boon Seong** Design and Implementation of a Multi-purpose Cluster System Network Interface Unit — Ph.D.

**Armstrong, Mark Albert** Technology for SiGe Heterostructure-Based CMOS Devices — Ph.D.

**Bala, Kavita** Radiance Interpolants for Interactive Scene Editing and Ray Tracing — Ph.D.

1999 (continued)

**Bashir, Adil** Magnetic Resonance Imaging of Proteoglycans in Cartilage — Ph.D.

**Blanchard, Roxann Russell** Hydrogen Degradation on InP HEMTs — Ph.D.

**Bose, Vanu Gopal** Design and Implementation of Software Radios Using a General Purpose Processor — Ph.D.

**Bounds, Jeffrey K.** Quantum Noise Propagation in Nonlinear Optical Media — Sc.D.

**Cabrera-Mercader, Carlos Rubén** Robust Compression of Multispectrtal Remote Sensing Data — Ph.D.

**Caro, Alejandro** Generating Multithreaded Code from Parallel Haskell for Symmetric Multiprocessors — Ph.D.

**Carter, Nicholas Parks** Processor Mechanisms for Software Shared Memory — Ph.D.

**Choi, Jeung-Yoon** Detection of Consonant Voicing: A Module for a Hierarchical Speech Recognition System — Ph.D.

**Coore, Daniel** Botanical Computing: A Developmental Approach to Generating Interconnect Topologies on an Amorphous Computer — Ph.D.

**Chiou, Derek T.** Extending the Reach of Microprocessors: Column and Curious Caching — Ph.D.

**Denison, Douglas Robert** Gyrotron Mode Converter Mirror Shaping Based on Phase Retrieval from Intensity Measurements — Ph.D.

**Du, Yanqing** Measurements and Modeling of Moisture Diffusion Processes in Transformer Insulation Using Interdigital Dielectrometry Sensors — Ph.D.

**Duwel, Amy E.** Harmonic Resonances in Nonlinear Josephson Junction Circuits: Experimental and Analytical Studies — Ph.D.

**Engler, Dawson R.** The Exokernel Operating System Architecture — Ph.D.

**Fallah, Farzan** Coverage-Directed Validation of Hardware Models — Ph.D.

**Frakt, Austin Berk** Internal Multiscale Autoregressive Processes, Stochastic Realization, and Covariance Extension — Ph.D.

**Frank, Michael Patrick** Reversibility for Efficient Computing — Ph.D.

**Frigo, Matteo** Portable High-Performance Programs — Ph.D.

**Greenspun, Philip G.** Architecture and Implementation of Online Communities — Ph.D.

**Grumet, Andrew Eli** Electric Stimulation Parameters for an Epi-Retinal Prosthesis — Ph.D.

**Gung, Tza-Jing** Kerr Electro-optic Measurements and Nonuniform Electric Field Reconstructions — Ph.D.

**Hadjicostis, Christoforos Nikos** Coding Approaches to Fault Tolerance in Dynamic Systems — Ph.D.

**Halberstadt, Andrew King** Heterogeneous Acoustic Measurements and Multiple Classifiers for Speech Recognition — Ph.D.

**Hanono, Silvina Zimi** AVIV: A Retargetable Code Generator for Embedded Processors — Ph.D.

**Hinds, Raynard Orin** Robust Mode Selection for Block-Motion-Compensated Video Encoding — Ph.D.

**Huang, Gregory Tsan-Kao** Measurement of Middle-Ear Acoustic Function in Intact Ears: Application to Size Variations in the Cat Family — Ph.D.

**Husbands, Parry** Interactive Supercomputing — Ph.D.

**Jones, David John** Generation and Storage of Ultrashort Pulses Using Optical Fiber Devices — Ph.D.

**Kapur, Tina** Model Based Three Dimensional Medical Image Segmentation — Ph.D.

**Kim, Seok-Won Abraham** Hot-Carrier Reliability of MOSFETs at Room and Cryogenic Temperature — Ph.D.

**Lakshmi Ratan, Aparna** Learning Visual Concepts for Image Classification — Ph.D.

**Larson, Bruce Carl** An Optical Telemetry System for Wireless Transmission of Biomedical Signals Across the Skin — Ph.D.

**Le, Huy X.P.** On the Methodology of Assessing Hot-Carrier Reliability of Analog Circuits — Ph.D.

**Lee, Whay Sing** Mechanisms for Efficient, Protected Messaging — Ph.D.

**Lee, Zachary Ka Fai** A New Inverse-Modeling-Based Technique for Sub-100-nm MOSFET Characterization — Ph.D.

**Lemus Rodriguez, Gerardo José** Portfolio Optimization with Quantile-Based Risk Measures — Ph.D.

**Lim, Kuo-Yi** Design and Fabrication of One-Dimensional and Two-Dimensional Photonic Bandgap Devices — Ph.D.

**Lyubomirsky, Ilya** Toward Far Infrared Quantum Well Lasers — Ph.D.

**Mamishev, Alexander V.** Interdigital Dielectrometry Sensor Design and Development of Parameter Estimation Algorithms for Non-Destructive Materials Evaluation — Ph.D.

**Martin, Keith Dana** Sound-Source Recognition: A Theory and Computational Model — Ph.D.

**Massoud, Yehia Mahmoud** Simulation Algorithms for Inductive Effects — Ph.D.

**Massaquoi, Steven G.** Modeling the Function of the Cerebellum in Scheduled Linear Servo Control of Simple Horizontal Planar Arm Movements — Ph.D.

**Meila-Predoviciu, Marina** Learning with Mixtures of Trees — Ph.D.

**Mermelstein, Michael S.** Synthetic Aperture Microscopy — Ph.D.

**Myers, Andrew Clifford** Mostly Static Decentralized Information Flow Control — Ph.D.

**Nastov, Ognen Jovan** Spectral Methods for Circuit Analysis — Ph.D.

**Nee, Phillip Tsefung** Optical Frequency Division via Periodically-Poled-LiNbO$_3$-Based Nonlinear Optics — Ph.D.

**Osgood, Nathaniel David** TACHYON: Customizable Program Analysis via Generic Abstract Interpretation — Ph.D.

**Ouma, Dennis Okumu** Modeling of Chemical Mechanical Polishing for Dielectric Planarization — Ph.D.

**Pan, Janet Lin** Design of Quantum Well Infrared Photodetectors — Ph.D.

**Paul, Susanne A.** Pipelined Oversampling Analog-to-Digital Converters — Ph.D.

**Poletto, Massimiliano Antonio** Language and Compiler Support for Dynamic Code Generation — Ph.D.

**Pollak, Ilya** Nonlinear Scale Space Analysis in Image Processing — Ph.D.

**Simon, Thomas David** A Low Power Video Compression Chip for Portable Applications — Ph.D.

**Starks, Michael James** Measurement of the Conjugate Propagation of VLF Waves by Matched Filter and Application to Ionospheric Diagnosis — Sc.D.

**1999** (continued)

**Surati, Rajeev Jayantilal** Scalable Self-Calibrating Display Technology for Seamless Large-scale Displays — Ph.D.

**Tessier, Russell George** Fast Place and Route Approaches for FPGAs — Ph.D.

**Üstündag, Afsin** Kerr Electro-Optic Tomography for Determination of Nonuniform Electric Field Distributions in Dielectrics — Ph.D.

**Velez-Rivera, Bienvenido** Query Lookahead for Query-based Document Categorization — Ph.D.

**Verbout, Shawn Matthew** A Framework for Non-Gaussian Signal Modeling and Estimation — Ph.D.

**Vieri, Carlin James** Reversible Computer Engineering and Architecture — Ph.D.

**Wang, Junfeng** A New Surface Integral Formation of EMQS Impedance Extraction for 3-D Structures — Ph.D.

**Wetherall, David James** Service Introduction in an Active Network — Ph.D.

**Williamson, Matthew Murray** Robot Arm Control Exploiting Natural Dynamics — Ph.D.

**Wong, William Shung-Kei** Characterization and Nonlinear Cleanup of Noise in Optical Communication Systems — Ph.D.

**Wu, Cynara C.** Dynamic Resource Allocation in CDMA Cellular Communications Systems — Ph.D.

**Xanthopoulos, Thucydides** Low Power Data-Dependent Transform Video and Still Image Coding — Ph.D.

**Yang, Yao-Joe J.** Numerical Analysis and Design Strategy for Field Emission Devices — Ph.D.

**Yeang, Chen-Pang** Target Identification Theory for Synthetic Aperture Radar Images Using Physics-Based Signatures — Sc.D.

**Zamdmer, Noah** The Design and Testing of Integrated Circuits for Submillimeter-Wave Spectroscopy — Ph.D.

**2000**

**Ahadian, Joseph Farzin** Development of a Monolithic Very Large Scale Optoelectronic Integrated Circuit Technology — Ph.D.

**Arkoudas, Konstantinos** Denotational Proof Languages — Ph.D.

**Barua, Rajeev Kumar** Maps: A Compiler-Managed Memory System for Software-Exposed Architectures — Ph.D.

**Barron, Richard John** Systematic Hybrid Analog/Digital Signal Coding — Ph.D.

**Batzoglou, Serafim** Computational Genomics: Mapping, Comparison, and Annotation of Genomes — Ph.D.

**Baylon, David M.** Video Compression with Complete Information for Pre-recorded Sources — Ph.D.

**Becker, Matthew E.** Resonant Transmission Line Drivers — Ph.D.

**Berry, Randall Alexander** Power and Delay Trade-Offs in Fading Channels — Ph.D.

**Boyko, Victor V.** On All-or-Nothing Transforms and Password-Authenticated Key Exchange Protocols — Ph.D.

**Breazeal, Cynthia L.** Sociable Machines: Expressive Social Exchange Between Humans and Robots — Ph.D.

**Caliskan, Vahe** A Dual/High Voltage Automotive Electrical Power System with Superior Transient Performance — Sc.D.

**Chen, Brian** Design and Analysis of Digital Watermarking, Information Embedding, and Data Hiding Systems — Ph.D.

**Coram, Geoffrey John** Thermodynamically Valid Noise Models for Nonlinear Devices — Ph.D.

**Chou, George Tao-Shun** Large-Scale 3D Reconstruction: A Triangulation-Based Approach — Ph.D.

**Chung, Sae-Young** On the Construction of Some Capacity-Approaching Coding Schemes — Ph.D.

**Daly, Peter M.** Stochastic Matched Field processing for Localization and Nulling of Acoustic Sources — Sc.D.

**Denison, Timothy Allman** The Development of a Nanoscale Coulter Counter for Rapid Genetic Sequence Recognition — Ph.D.

**De Prisco, Roberto** On Building Blocks for Distributed Systems — Ph.D.

**Dodis, Yevgeniy** Exposure-Resilient Cryptography — Ph.D.

**Engels, Daniel Wayne** Hardware/Software Partitioning in Embedded System Design — Ph.D.

**Evans, David Elliot** Policy-Directed Code Safety — Ph.D.

**Evgeniou, Theodoros Kostantinos** Learning with Kernel Machine Architectures — Ph.D.

**Ferrera Uranga, Juan** Nanometer-Scale Placement in Electron-Beam Lithography — Ph.D.

**Fiore, Paul David** A Custom Computing Framework for Orientation and Photogrammetry — Ph.D.

**Gonçalves, Jorge Manuel Mendes Silva** Constructive Global Analysis of Hybrid Systems — Ph.D.

**Goodman, James Ross** Energy Scalable Reconfigurable Cryptographic Hardware for Portable Applications — Ph.D.

**Gruhl, Daniel F.** The Search for Meaning in Large Text Databases — Ph.D.

**Gutnik, Vadim** Analysis and Characterization of Random Skew and Jitter in a Novel Clock Network — Ph.D.

**Hadjiyiannis, George Ioannou** An Architecture Synthesis System for Embedded Processors — Ph.D.

**Healey, Jennifer Anne** Wearable and Automotive Systems for Affect Recognition from Physiology — Ph.D.

**Heinzelman, Wendi Beth** Application-Specific Protocol Architectures for Wireless Networks — Ph.D.

**Hockenberry, James Richard** Evaluation of Uncertainty in Dynamic, Reduced-order Power System Models — Ph.D.

**Hoe, James Chu-Yue** Operation-Centric Hardware Description and Synthesis — Ph.D.

**Howitt, Andrew W.** Automatic Syllable Detection for Vowel Landmarks — Sc.D.

**Hu, Jianjuen** Stable Locomotion Control of Bipedal Walking Robots: Synchronization with Neural Oscillators and Switching Control — Ph.D.

**Kam, Anthony Chi-Kong** Efficient Scheduling Algorithms for Quality-of-Service Guarantees in the Internet — Ph.D.

**Karecki, Simon M.** Development of Novel Alternative Chemistry Processes for Dielectric Etch Applications — Ph.D.

**Kassab, Hisham Ibrahim** Low-Energy Mobile Packet Radio Networks: Routing, Scheduling, and Architecture — Ph.D.

2000 (continued)

**Kilfoyle, Daniel Brian** Spatial Modulation in the Underwater Acoustic Communication Channel — Ph.D.

**Kohler, Eddie** The Click Modular Router — Ph.D.

**Koontz, Elisabeth Marley** The Development of Components for Ultrafast All-Optical Communication Networks — Ph.D.

**Lee, Junehee** Blind Noise Estimation and Compensation for Improved Characterization of Multivariable Processes — Ph.D.

**Lee, Li** Distributed Signal Processing — Ph.D.

**Leventon, Michael Emmanuel** Statistical Models in Medical Image Analysis — Ph.D.

**Lim Chin Siong, Desmond Rodney** Device Integration for Silicon Microphotonic Platforms — Ph.D.

**Logan, Cedric Leonard** An Estimation-Theoretic Technique for Motion-Compensated Synthetic-Aperture Array Imaging — Ph.D.

**Lorigo, Liana Michelle** Curve Evolution for Medical Image Segmentation — Ph.D.

**Lovelace, Edward Carl Francis** Optimization of a Magnetically Saturable Interior Permanent-Magnet Synchronous Machine Drive — Ph.D.

**Malkin, Tal Geula** A Study of Secure Database Access and General Two-Party Computation — Ph.D.

**Mazières, David Folkman** Self-certifying File System — Ph.D.

**Mellor, John P.** Automatically Recovering Geometry and Texture from Large Sets of Calibrated Images — Ph.D.

**Millis, Kathryn Ann** Distributed Measures of Solution Existence and Its Optimality in Stationary Electric Power Systems: Scattering Approach — Ph.D.

**Mitra, Robi David** Polony Sequencing: DNA Sequencing Technology and a Computational Analysis Reveals Chromosomal Domains of Gene Expression — Ph.D.

**Mohamed, Jama Awil** Existence and Stability Analysis of Ferroresonance Using the Generalized State-Space Averaging Technique — Ph.D.

**Mohtashemi, Mojdeh** Qualitative Analysis of Transience in Population Dynamics — Ph.D.

**Moyne, William Patrick** Enhancing MEMS Design Using Statistical Process Information — Ph.D.

**Mukkamala, Ramakrishna** A Forward Model-Based Analysis of Cardiovascular System Identification Methods — Ph.D.

**Narváez Guarnieri, Paolo Lucas** Routing Reconfiguration in IP Networks — Ph.D.

**Neveitt, William Tyler** Spatial Knowledge Navigation for the World Wide Web — Ph.D.

**Ng, Kenney** Subword-based Approaches for Spoken Document Retrieval — Ph.D.

**Papageorgiou, Constantine P.** A Trainable System for Object Detection in Images and Video Sequences — Ph.D.

**Patterson, Steven G.** Bipolar Cascade Lasers — Ph.D.

**Pflug, David George** Low Voltage Field Emitter Arrays Through Aperture Scaling — Ph.D.

**Pratt, Jerry E.** Exploiting Inherent Robustness and Natural Dynamics in the Control of Bipedal Walking Robots — Ph.D.

**Sahai, Amit** Frontiers in Zero Knowledge — Ph.D.

**Schwartz, Russell S.** The Local Rules Dynamics Model for Self-Assembly Simulation — Ph.D.

**Shaw, Steven R.** System Identification Techniques and Modeling for Nonintrusive Load Diagnostics — Ph.D.

**Shen, Xiaowei** Design and Verification of Adaptive Cache Coherence Protocols — Ph.D.

**Shu, Li** A Power Interval Perspective on Additive White Gaussian Noise (AWGN) Channels — Ph.D.

**Smith, Taber Hardesty** Device Independent Process Control of Dielectric Chemical Mechanical Polishing — Ph.D.

**Spina, Michelle Suzanne** Analysis and Transcription of General Audio Data — Ph.D.

**Squire, James Conrad** Dynamics of Endovascular Stent Expansion — Ph.D.

**Tatikonda, Sekhar Chandra** Control Under Communication Constraints — Ph.D.

**Thoen, Erik R.** Development of Ultrashort Pulse Fiber Lasers for Optical Communication Utilizing Semiconductor Devices — Ph.D.

**Trias, Enrique** Vortex Motion and Dynamical States in Josephson Arrays — Ph.D.

**Tsien, Christine Liming** TrendFinder: Automated Detection of Alarmable Trends — Ph.D.

**Wage, Kathleen E.** Broadband Modal Coherence and Beamforming at Megameter Ranges — Ph.D.

**Wang, Cheuk-San** Determining Molecular Conformation from Distance or Density Data — Ph.D.

**Welborn, Matthew Lee** Flexible Signal Processing Algorithms for Wireless Communications — Ph.D.

**Wells, Martin David** Estimation of Peripheral Nerve Conduction Velocity Distributions from a Short Segment of Nerve — Ph.D.

**Wilkenfeld, Ari Jacob** Biologically Inspired Autoadaptive Control of a Knee Prosthesis — Ph.D.

**Wren, Christopher Richard** Understanding Expressive Action — Ph.D.

**Yanco, Holly Anne** Shared User-Computer Control of a Robotic Wheelchair System — Ph.D.

**Xiong, Rebecca Wen Fei** Visualizing Information Spaces to Enhance Social Interaction — Ph.D.

**Zhang, Yan** Forward and Inverse Problems in Microwave Remote Sensing of Objects in Complex Media — Ph.D.

2001

**Abou Faycal, Ibrahim Chafik** An Information Theoretic Study of Reduced-Complexity Receivers for Intersymbol Interference Channels — Ph.D.

**Antone, Matthew E.** Robust Camera Pose Recovery Using Stochastic Geometry — Ph.D.

**Asavathiratham, Chalee** The Influence Model: A Tractable Representation for the Dynamics of Networked Markov Chains — Ph.D.

**Babb, Jonathan William** High Level Compilation for Gate Reconfigurable Architectures — Ph.D.

**Braunisch, Henning** Methods in Wave Propagation and Scattering — Ph.D.

**Bryson, Joanna J.** Intelligence by Design: Principles of Modularity and Coordination for Engineering Complex Adaptive Agents — Ph.D.

**2001** (continued)

**Castrillón Candás, Julio Enrique** Spatially Adaptive Multiwavelet Representations on Unstructured Grids with Applications to Multidimensional Computational Modeling — Ph.D.

**Castro, Miguel O.** Practical Byzantine Fault Tolerance — Ph.D.

**Chan, Tung** Artificial Markets and Intelligent Agents — Ph.D.

**Chatterjee, Sandeep** Composable System Resources as an Architecture for Networked Systems — Ph.D.

**Chou, Patrick Chien-pang** Optical Pulse Distortion and Manipulation Through Polarization Effects and Chromatic Dispersion — Ph.D.

**Chung, Grace Yuet-Chee** Towards Multi-domain Speech Understanding with Flexible and Dynamic Vocabulary — Ph.D.

**Cohen, Aaron Seth** Information Theoretic Analysis of Watermarking Systems — Ph.D.

**Dvorson, Leonard** Micromachining and Modeling of Focused Field Emitters for Flat Panel Displays — Ph.D.

**Eng, Tony Liang** De Novo Peptide Sequencing from Matrix-Assisted Laser Desorption/Ionization-time of Flight Post-Source-Decay Spectra — Ph.D.

**Farhoud, Maya Sami** Fabrication and Characterization of Nanostructured Magnetic Particles for Applications in Data Storage — Ph.D.

**Fini, John Michael** Coherent Multi-Photon Interference and Compensation of Polarization Dispersion — Ph.D.

**Firebaugh, Samara L.** Miniaturization and Integration of Photoacoustic Detection — Ph.D.

**Golland, Polina** Statistical Shape Analysis of Anatomical Structures — Ph.D.

**Gower, Aaron Elwood** Integrated Model-based Run-to-Run Uniformity Control for Epitaxial Silicon Deposition — Ph.D.

**Gulati, Kush** A Low-Power Reconfigurable Analog-to-Digital Converter — Ph.D.

**Guruswami, Venkatesan** List Decoding of Error-Correcting Codes — Ph.D.

**Hartemink, Alexander John** Principled Computational Methods for the Validation Discovery of Genetic Regulatory Networks — Ph.D.

**Irie, Robert Eiichi** A Visually-Guided Microphone Array for Automatic Speech Transcription — Ph.D.

**Jackson, Keith Matthew** Optimal MOSFET Design for Low Temperature Operation — Ph.D.

**Jarecki, Stanislaw Michal** Efficient Threshold Cryptosystems — Ph.D.

**Kao, James Ting Yu** Subthreshold Leakage Control Techniques for Low Power Digital Circuits — Ph.D.

**Kim, Andrew J.** Exploring Scatterer Anisotrophy in Synthetic Aperture Radar Via Sub-Aperture Analysis — Ph.D.

**Kim, Dong-Hyun Charles** Design, Development and Characterization of an Integrated Multispectral Polarimetric Sensor System — Ph.D.

**Klein, Thierry Etienne** Capacity of Gaussian Noise Channels with Side Information and Feedback — Ph.D.

**Kohler, Edward William** The Click Modular Router — Ph.D.

**Koile, Kimberle** The Architect's Collaborator: Toward Intelligent Tools for Conceptual Design — Ph.D.

**Krause, Jean Christine** Properties of Naturally Produced Clear Speech at Normal Rates and Implications for Intelligibility Enhancement — Ph.D.

**Lochtefeld, Anthony Joseph** Toward the End of the MOSFET Roadmap: Investigating Fundamental Transport Limits and Device Architecture Alternatives — Ph.D.

**Luchangco, Victor M.** Modeling Memory for Distributed High-Performance Computing — Ph.D.

**Manolatou, Christina** Passive Components for Dense Optical Integration Based on High Index-Contrast — Ph.D.

**McMahill, Daniel R.** Automatic Calibration of Modulated Fractional-N Frequency Synthesizers — Ph.D.

**Mehrotra, Vikas** Modeling the Effects of Systematic Process Variation of Circuit Performance — Ph.D.

**Minka, Thomas Peter** A Family of Algorithms for Approximate Bayesian Inference — Ph.D.

**Murphy, Thomas E.** Design, Fabrication and Measurement of Integrated Bragg Grating Optical Filters — Ph.D.

**Nagle, Steven Francis** Analysis, Design, and Fabrication of an Electric Induction Micromotor for a Micro Gas-turbine Generator — Ph.D.

**Nagpal, Radhika** Programmable Self-Assembly: Constructing Global Shape Using Biologically-Inspired Local Interactions and Origami Mathematics — Ph.D.

**Olfati-Saber, Reza** Nonlinear Control of Underactuated Mechanical Systems with Application to Robotics and Aerospace Vehicles — Ph.D.

**Pruette, Laura Catherine** Oxide Etching with $NF_3$/Hydocarbon Chemistries for Global Warming Emissions Reductions — Ph.D.

**Rahman, Arifur** System-Level Performance Evaluation of Three-Dimensional Integrated Circuits — Ph.D.

**Ramzan, Zulfikar Amin** A Study of Luby-Rackoff Ciphers — Ph.D.

**Reed, Eric Christopher** Multi-Dimensional Bit Rate Control for Video Communication — Ph.D.

**Reyzin, Leonid Natanovich** Zero-Knowledge with Public Keys — Ph.D.

**Richards, John Alfred** Target Model Generation from Multiple Synthetic Aperture Radar Images — Ph.D.

**Rixner, Scott** A Bandwidth-Efficient Architecture for a Streaming Media Processor — Ph.D.

**Sahai, Anant** Anytime Information Theory — Ph.D.

**Sarmenta, Luis Francisco Gumaru** Volunteer Computing — Ph.D.

**Scassellati, Brian M.** Foundations for a Theory of Mind for a Humanoid Robot — Ph.D.

**Schein, Brett Eric** Distributed Coordination in Network Information Theory — Ph.D.

**Schneider, Michael K.** Krylov Subspace Estimation — Ph.D.

**Secor, Matthew Joelson** Geometric Modeling and Analysis of Dynamic Resource Allocation Mechanisms — Ph.D.

**Shabra, Ayman Umar** Oversampled Pipeline A/D Converters with Mismatch Shaping — Ph.D.

**Sheiretov, Yanko Konstantinov** Deep Penetration Magnetoquasistatic Sensors — Ph.D.

**Shelton, Christian Robert** Importance Sampling for Reinforcement Learning with Multiple Objectives — Ph.D.

**Sinha, Amit** Energy Efficient Operating Systems and Software — Ph.D.

**Skantze, Petter L.** A Fundamental Approach to Valuation, Hedging and Speculation in Deregulated Electricity Markets — Ph.D.

**2001** (continued)

**Sweeney, Latanya** Computational Disclosure Control: A Primer on Data Privacy Protection — Ph.D.

**Torres, Wade Patrick** Modulation of Dynamical Systems for Communication — Ph.D.

**Viggh, Herbert E.** Surface Prior Information Reflectance Estimation (SPIRE) Algorithms — Ph.D.

**Voldman, Joel** A Microfabricated Dielectrophoretic Trapping Array for Cell-Based Biological Assays — Ph.D.

**Wang, Chao** Prosodic Modeling for Improved Speech Recognition and Understanding — Ph.D.

**Wang, Ching-Chun** A Study of CMOS Technologies for Image Sensor Applications — Ph.D.

**Wei, Andy Chih-Hung** Device Design and Process Technology for Sub-100 nm SOI MOSFET's — Ph.D.

**Weiss, Ron** Cellular Computation and Communications Using Engineered Genetic Regulatory Networks — Ph.D.

**White, David A.** Multivariate Analysis of Spectral Measurements for the Characterization of Semiconductor Processes — Sc.D.

**Yang, Charles D.** Knowledge and Learning in Natural Language — Ph.D.

**Yeh, Edmund Meng** Multiaccess and Fading in Communication Networks — Ph.D.

**Yoon, Yong T.** Electric Power Network Economics: Designing Principles for a For-profit Independent Transmission Company and Underlying Architecture for Reliability — Ph.D.

**Yu, Charles Xiao** Soliton Squeezing in Optical Fibers — Ph.D.

**2002**

**Basu, Sumit** Conversational Scene Analysis — Ph.D.

**Bazzi, Issam** Modelling Out-of-Vocabulary Words for Robust Speech Recognition — Ph.D.

**Behesti, Soosan** Minimum Description Complexity — Ph.D.

**Blackwell, William Joseph** Retrieval of Cloud-Cleared Atmospheric Temperature Profiles from Hyperspectral Infrared and Microwave Observations — Ph.D.

**Brown, Jeremy Hanford** Sparsely Faceted Arrays: A Mechanism Supporting Parallel Allocation, Communication, and Garbage Collection — Ph.D.

**Buehler, Christopher James** Rendering from Unstructured Collections of Images — Ph.D.

**Cho, Seong Hwan** Energy Efficient RF Communication Systems for Wireless Microsensors — Ph.D.

**Deutsch, Erik Robertson** Achieving Large Stable Vertical Displacement in Surface-Micromachined Microelectromechanical Systems (MEMS) — Ph.D.

**Djomehri, Ihsan J.** Comprehensive Inverse Modeling for the Study of Carrier Transport Models in Sub-50 nm MOSFETs — Ph.D.

**Draper, Stark Christiaan** Successive Structuring of Source Coding Algorithms for Data Fusion, Buffering, and Distribution in Networks — Ph.D.

**Duerr, Erik K.** Distributed Photomixers — Ph.D.

**Eldar, Yonina Chana** Quantum Signal Processing — Ph.D.

**Ezzat, Tony F.** Trainable Videorealistic Facial Animation — Ph.D.

**Fan, Mingxi** Interference Characterization and Suppression for Multiuser Direct-sequence Spread-spectrum System — Ph.D.

**Fiorenza, James G.** Design and Fabrication of an RF Power LDMOSFET on SOI — Ph.D.

**Focia, Ronald J.** Investigation and Characterization of Single Hot Spot Laser-Plasma Interactions — Ph.D.

**Fujimori, Iliana Lucia** CMOS Passive Pixel Imager Design Techniques — Ph.D.

**Gbondo-Tugbawa, Tamba Edward** Chip-scale Modeling of Pattern Dependencies in Copper Chemical Mechanical Polishing Processes — Ph.D.

**Grein, Matthew Edward** Noise and Stability of Actively Modelocked Fiber Lasers — Ph.D.

**Hall, Timothy D.** Radiolocation Using AM Broadcast Signals — Ph.D.

**Hitko, Donald Anthony** Circuit Design and Technological Limitations of Silicon RFICs for Wireless Applications — Ph.D.

**Huang, Andrew Shane** ADAM: A Decentralized Parallel Computer Architecture Featuring Fast Thread and Data Migration and a Uniform Hardware Abstraction — Ph.D.

**Jiang, Leaf Alden** Ultralow-Noise Modelocked Lasers — Ph.D.

**Janotti, John H.** Network Layer Support for Overlay Networks — Ph.D.

**Kanapka, Joseph Daniel** Fast Methods for Extraction and Sparsification of Substrate Coupling — Ph.D.

**Karameh, Fadi Nabih** A Model for Cerebral Cortical Neuronal Group Electric Activity and Its Implications for Cerebral Function — Ph.D.

**Khan, Mohammad Jalal** Integrated Optical Filters Using Bragg Gratings and Resonators — Ph.D.

**Khazan, Roger Igor** A One-Round Algorithm for Virtually Synchronous Group Communication in Wide Area Networks — Ph.D.

**Khodor, Julia** DAN-based String Rewrite Computational Systems — Ph.D.

**Konda, Vijaymohan Gao** Actor-Critic Algorithms — Ph.D.

**Köser, Hür** Development of Magnetic Induction Machines for Micro Turbo Machinery — Ph.D.

**Laneman, J. Nicholas** Cooperative Diversity in Wireless Networks: Algorithms and Architectures — Ph.D.

**Lee, Brian** Modeling of Chemical Mechanical Polishing for Shallow Trench Isolation — Ph.D.

**Lee, Lily** Gait Analysis for Classification — Ph.D.

**Lehman, Eric Allen** Approximation Algorithms for Grammar-Based Data Compression — Ph.D.

**Levine, Matthew Steven** Algorithms for Connectivity Problems in Undirected Graphs: Maximum Flow and Minimum K-way Cut — Ph.D.

**Lim, Michael H.** Development of X-ray Lithography and Nanofabrication Techniques for III-V Optical Devices — Sc.D.

**Lopez, Michael J.** Multiplexing, Scheduling, and Multicasting Strategies for Antenna Arrays in Wireless Networks — Ph.D.

**Lundberg, Kent H.** A High-Speed Low-Power Analog-to-Digital Converter in Fully Depleted Silicon-on-Insulator Technology — Ph.D.

**Lyssyanskaya, Anna A.** Signature Schemes and Applications to Cryptographic Protocol Design — Ph.D.

2002 (continued)

**Maessen, Jan-Willem** Hybrid Eager and Lazy Evaluation for Efficient Compilation of Haskell — Ph.D.

**Mason, Elliot James** Applications of Optical Parametric Downconversion: I. Self-phase Locking, [and] II. Generation of Entangled Photon Pairs in Periodically-Poled Lithium Niobate — Ph.D.

**Miller, Erik Gundersen** Learning from One Example in Machine Vision by Sharing Probability Densities — Ph.D.

**Mou, Xiaolong** Towards a Unified Framework for Sub-lexical and Supra-lexical Linguistic Modeling — Ph.D.

**Narendra, Siva Gurusami** Effect of MOSFET Threshold Voltage Variation on High-Performance Circuits — Ph.D.

**Nedic, Angelina** Subgradient Methods for Convex Minimization — Ph.D.

**Park, Tae Hong** Characterization and Modeling of Pattern Dependencies in Copper Interconnects for Integrated Circuits — Ph.D.

**Raju, Balasundara Iyyavu** High Frequency Ultrasonic Characterization of Human Skin In Vivo — Ph.D.

**Romano, Raquel Andrea** Projective Minimal Analysis of Camera Geometry — Ph.D.

**Russell, Andrew I.** Regular and Irregular Signal Resampling — Ph.D.

**Saengudomlert, Poompat** Architectural Study of High-Speed Networks with Optical Bypassing — Ph.D.

**Salcedo, Ante** Coupled Modes Analysis of SRS Backscattering, with Langmuir Decay and Possible Cascadings — Ph.D.

**Sotiriadis, Paul Peter P.** Interconnect Modeling and Optimization in Deep Sub-micron Technologies — Ph.D.

**Stauffer, Christopher Paul** Perceptual Data Mining: Bootstrapping Visual Intelligence from Tracking Behavior — Ph.D.

**Sun, Yao** Information Exchange Between Medical Databases through Automated Identification of Concept Equivalence — Ph.D.

**Szummer, Marcin O.** Learning from Partially Labeled Data — Ph.D.

**Tucker-Kellogg, Lisa** Systematic Conformational Search with Constraint Satisfaction — Ph.D.

**Varghese, Mathew** Reduced-Order Modeling of MEMS Using Modal Basis Functions — Ph.D.

**Wainwright, Martin James** Stochastic Processes on Graphs with Cycles: Geometric and Variational Approaches — Ph.D.

**Wan, Wade Keith** Adaptive Format Conversion Information as Enhancement Data for Scalable Video Coding — Ph.D.

**Wang, Xin** FastStokes: A Fast 3-D Fluid Simulation Program for Micro-Electro-Mechanical Systems — Ph.D.

**Wessler, Michael Alan** NPL: A Graphical Programming Language for Motor Control and Its Application to Bipedal Walking — Ph.D.

**Wu, Ona** Predictive Models of Tissue Outcome in Acute Human Cerebral Ischemia Using Diffusion and Perfusion Weighted MRI — Ph.D.

**Yang, Changhuei** Harmonic Phase Based Low Coherence Interferometry: A Method for Studying the Dynamics and Structures of Cells — Ph.D.

**Zhao, Ruilin** Functional Analysis of Middle Temporal Visual Area and Its Associated Behavior — Ph.D. (in HST)

# Index